A DICTIONARY

OF

CLASSICAL AND FOREIGN
QUOTATIONS

CLASSICAL AND FOREIGN QUOTATIONS

A POLYGLOT MANUAL OF

HISTORICAL AND LITERARY SAYINGS
NOTED PASSAGES IN POETRY AND PROSE
PHRASES, PROVERBS, AND BONS MOTS

COMPILED, EDITED, AND TOLD,

𝔚𝔦𝔱𝔥 𝔱𝔥𝔢𝔦𝔯 𝔚𝔢𝔣𝔢𝔯𝔢𝔫𝔠𝔢𝔰, 𝔗𝔯𝔞𝔫𝔰𝔩𝔞𝔱𝔦𝔬𝔫𝔰, 𝔞𝔫𝔡 𝔍𝔫𝔡𝔢𝔵𝔢𝔰,

BY

W. FRANCIS H. KING, M.A., Oxford.

THIRD EDITION, REVISED AND REWRITTEN

" A Quotation without a reference is like a geological specimen of unknown locality."
—Prof. SKEAT, *Notes and Queries*, 6th Series, vol. ix. p. 499.
" . . . . l'exactitude de citer.   C'est un talent plus rare que l'on ne pense."
—BAYLE, Dict., art. SANCHEZ, Remarques.
" They have been at a great feast of languages, and have stolen the scraps."
—SHAKESPEARE, " Love's Labour Lost," v. 1.

LONDON
J. WHITAKER & SONS, LIMITED
12 WARWICK LANE, PATERNOSTER ROW
1904

REPUBLISHED BY GALE RESEARCH COMPANY, BOOK TOWER, DETROIT, 1968

Library of Congress Catalog Card Number 68–30647

INSCRIBED TO

FERDINAND HOFFMANN

OF

STOCKBRIDGE, MASSACHUSETTS, U.S.A.,

WHOSE

LEARNING IS ONLY EQUALLED

BY THE

LIBERALITY WITH WHICH IT IS PLACED

AT THE DISPOSAL OF OTHERS.

b

PREFACE TO THE THIRD EDITION.

In preparing a new Edition of this Dictionary for the Press, the work of revision has been guided by two main objects: the one, the relieving the book of a multitude of superfluous trivialities; the other, the addition of references to those entries that were still lacking in that most essential portion of their literary outfit. As both aims tend to raise directly the value of the work as a standard book of reference in such matters, they will, no doubt, be appreciated by all who read or consult the volume.

The original plan included, among other items, the whole of the Mottoes of the British Peerage, and the plan was duly carried out: whether the noble owners of the Mottoes were flattered by this delicate attention, it is impossible to say, but their insertion evoked many protests, and when the late William Lewis Hertslet* complained of the excessive "lordolatry" of the thing, I had nothing to reply. The only answer possible, in the circumstances, was the assurance that the cargo should never be shipped again; and, accordingly, the Mottoes, along with a quantity of equally cumbersome top-hamper, have gone by the board.

The other principle of reconstruction is of greater importance. No more apposite sentiment could have been chosen as the epigraph of any collection of Quotations than the maxim of Professor Skeat, which once more re-appears on the title-page. Yet, considering the number of passages and sayings that had been admitted without any reference whatever, the Professor's aphorism seemed like nothing so much as a perpetual reflection upon the non-performance of the very principle that it enunciated. This reproach has now been removed. With the exception of certain Proverbs, Maxims, and other kindred sayings that are incapable of affiliation, no quotation has been admitted without its proper author, chapter and verse; or, in the more difficult instances, without the authority to which it may be approximately referred. Not, however, to lose altogether for want of exact

---

* Author of *Der Treppenwitz der Weltgeschichte*.

reference some of the world's current sayings of uncertain paternity, a short appendix is added of ADESPOTA, or "ownerless" quotations, in which certain unverified instances of this kind will be found, and with them a few other passages which I have been unable to trace, and which are submitted to the curious in such matters, in the hope that some of them at least may be restored to their respective authors.

Great as are the difficulties and responsibility attaching to the task, in the way of selection or rejection, of correctness of text, translation, and comment, they are slight compared with the labour that the "chapter and verse" principle imposes upon the compiler. It will necessitate not only a long, long haunting of the bookshelves of the British Museum, but perhaps a search through the catalogues and contents of other great collections in the kingdom. It may even involve visits to Continental Libraries, in the hope of finding what is not to be found at home; and, after all, much of the time and toil may be thrown away! In short, the searcher must be content with a moderate success. He is rewarded not so much by putting the finger on some phrase or passage that had evaded all previous investigation, as by discovering the original wording of some commonly misquoted line, and reinstating it in the shape in which the author left it on record.

As revised and rewritten, the Dictionary contains far fewer quotations than its predecessor, a result which may perhaps be a fresh illustration of the old saying, that "the half is often more than the whole." Yet, in spite of this heavy reduction in quantity, the amount of new matter introduced is very considerable. Citations from the French are much more numerous than heretofore, preference being given to instances illustrating the lighter side of that witty nation. The German passages have been more than doubled, and there is now no German author of note that is not represented, and in some cases largely represented, in the contents. Additions have also been made to the Greek selections, from all quarters—tragedy, philosophy, history, lyric poetry, *ana* of many kinds—and, for the first time, the Greek Comics contribute an appreciable proportion to the whole.

Italian, too, figures on a greater scale than before; Dante has been freely drawn upon, and the *Inferno* is here placed in a category of certain world-famous works and writers that are cited so frequently as to necessitate the writing *Passim* after their names in the Index, rather than perplex the reader with a long succession of barren figures, which he would never have the patience to explore.*

A generation or so ago, quotation still maintained its ancient vogue in Parliament, and had even its own unwritten laws. In Lord Beaconsfield's *Endymion*, Sir Fraunceys Scrope tells the hero, " Charles Fox used to say as to quotation: ' No Greek ; as much Latin as you like ; never French, in any circumstances ; and no English poet unless he had completed his century.'" Nowadays, however, the practice has fallen into desuetude: but what has been lost to the oratory of the senate, has proved the gain of literature, and no better instance of a free and felicitous employment of classic authors could be adduced than Mr Morley's recent " Life of Gladstone." It is, therefore, not so much the speaker, as the author, essayist, critic, journalist, and historian, whose needs have been studied in the compilation of this volume and its indexes ; and even the high office of the *vates sacer* has not protected him from suggestions and hints more or less relevant to his special craft.

For the rest, it is to be hoped that the Dictionary may serve something more than the office of a reference-book of either familiar or obscure quotations, and that being taken up for the purposes of consultation, it may be retained in the hand as a piece of reading that is not at times devoid of the elements of humour and amusement. Besides the conciser and more epigrammatic loci and *bon mots* of universal currency, stories and historical sayings, there are included here and there a few passages of somewhat greater length, which belong rather to the " extract " order, sometimes known as " Beauties from the Poets," and which supply a slight " anthologic " element to a collection that does not pretend to the character of an Anthologia proper. Virgil's description of " Night " in the Fourth Æneid, the lines from " Piccolomini " beginning *'Die Fabel ist der Liebe Heimatwelt,'* Byron's translation of Filicaja's famous sonnet on Italy, and the " *La Feuille* " of Arnault, may be mentioned as examples. After all, they are only too few, and too short.

Of the four Indexes—which, with the exception of the Greek Quotations, are for convenience' sake placed at the beginning instead of the end of the volume—the first gives the name, profession, and date of every author cited, with the quotations accredited to him indicated

* The other authors (and works) indicated in Index I. as *Passim*, are the whole of Horace, Juvenal, La Rochefoucauld, Lucan, Martial, Ovid, Publilius Syrus, and Virgil ; the *Fables* of La Fontaine, and the *Epistles* of Seneca.

by the quotation-numbers that follow.   The Subject Index (No. II.) has entailed more labour of thought than all the rest put together, not the least part of it being the task of pointing out the various applications, direct and indirect, of which any particular quotation was capable.   To most of us it has not fallen to our lot to originate these famous " good sayings " of the world, and any " originality " that we may claim in this connection, consists in the ingenuity that wittily applies the old *dicton* in some new and unexpected direction.

Index III. (Quotations Index) * gives all first lines or first words of quotations, and all parts of such quotations, that are not printed in the Dictionary's alphabetical order.   It also includes all parts of quotations, the first words of which follow the alphabetical sequence of the book, and must be sought for in their proper place.   Thus, to give an instance, Alfred de Musset's,

> "C'est imiter quelqu'un que de planter des choux,"

occurs, not in letter C, as might have been expected, but far away (No. 1390) among the L's, and is therefore provided for by the Index. So, also, the familiar *Es wär zu schön gewesen, es hat nicht sollen sein* of the " Trompeter von Säkkingen," is duly indexed, as being part, though the essential part, of a distich beginning with the letter B— " Behüte dich Gott', *es wär zu schön gewesen,*" u.s.w.   On the other hand, *O tempora, O mores!* will be searched for in vain in the Quotation Index, since it stands, in its exact order of " literal " sequence, among the O's—between ῞Οταν τύχῃ κ.τ.λ., on the one side, and " O tenebris," etc., on the other.   The principle of the Dictionary being the alphabetical arrangement of its entries, their *repetition* in the index (with the exceptions just named) would be a mere work of supererogation.

The obligations due to fellow-compilers of similar collections— Edouard Fournier and George Büchmann in the past, and Messieurs Roger Alexandre, Giuseppe Fumagalli, and Harbottle and Dalbiac in the present, have been acknowledged in every case in which recourse has been had to their researches.   In particular, I owe thanks for the endorsement of a number of passages that had been tentatively put in circulation, and that may now be presumably added to the world's common stock of quotable sayings.   In one case, something more than gratitude is owing, in return for a generous and free-handed use of the " Dictionary " that was unattended by any acknowledgment of indebtedness whatsoever.

* *See* page lxviii (Note).

I can never sufficiently thank the various correspondents who have lent their valuable assistance in the compilation of the Dictionary, and in contributing to its correctness both of text and translation. The Rev. George Händler, the Rev. Edward J. Crawley, S.J., Mr P. J. Anderson, Librarian of the University of Aberdeen; Mr C. J. Purnell, Assistant Bodleian Librarian; Mr Walter King; "G. H. J.," gentlest and most forbearing of friends and helpers; M. Georges Barrington, of the Bibliothèque Nationale, Paris; and the officers and assistants of the British Museum, the most complete, and most generous Library in the world, are among the number of those to whom the compilation of the work is, in one way or another, variously indebted. Dr Theodor Lorenz of Erfurt, Ph.D., has also lent much kind assistance in looking over the German quotations; and to Mr Ferdinand Hoffmann, of Stockbridge, Massachusetts, I owe a debt which exceeds all repayment. He it was that primarily urged a new and revised edition of the Dictionary, that pointed out defects and deficiencies, suggested additions and improvements, and, with a generosity beyond all praise, has read and corrected the proofs throughout the whole passage of the work through the press. Nor must I forget the intelligent co-operation of the printers, Messrs M'Farlane & Erskine, in carrying through the book to its final conclusion. I wish also to repeat my indebtedness to the proprietors of the copyright of Conington's *Æneid* and Horace, for the permission granted by his literary executor, the late Mr Alfred Robinson, to make use of his admirable translations under certain fixed conditions.

FRANCIS KING.

Chelsea, Whitsuntide, 1904.

₊ CORRECTION OF INACCURACIES.

With the object of making the collection more perfect as a work of reference, I venture to appeal to all who may make use of the volume to have the kindness to point out any inaccuracies which they may detect, and particularly

1. To call attention to faulty Quotation, or Reference, or both.
2. To supply Author and Reference of the Quotations in the Appendix of ADESPOTA.
3. To point out faulty Translation, or Application and missing of the point generally.
4. To suggest any further quotations which it is desirable to include in the collection, as also the omission of such as seem unsuitable.

CONTENTS.

INDEX I.—AUTHORS, AUTHORITIES, AND EDITIONS.

ABBREVV.: *agricult. writer*, agricultural writer; *art.*, artist; *astron.*, astronomer; *biogr.*, biographer; *chr. writer*, Christian writer; *com.*, comic dramatist; *diplom.*, diplomatist; *dram.*, dramatist; *eccl. hist.*, ecclesiastical historian; *epigramm.*, epigrammatist; *emp.*, emperor; *fab.*, fabulist; *gen.*, general; *geogr.*, geographer; *geol.*, geologist; *gramm.*, grammarian; *hist.*, historian; *journ.*, journalist; *law.*, lawyer; *libr.*, librettist; *lit.*, litterateur; *math.*, mathematician; *med.*, medical; *mil. writer*, military writer; *moral.*, moralist; *mus.*, musician; *natur.*, naturalist; *novel.*, novelist; *orat.*, orator; *philos.*, philosopher; *pol.*, politician; *rhet.*, rhetorician; *sat.*, satirist; *schol.*, scholar; *scld.*, soldier; *statesm.*, statesman; *trag.*, tragic dramatist; *theol.*, theologian.

All dates B.C. are so indicated. Authors too frequently cited for enumeration are marked *passim*. All editions printed in *italics*.

Accius, L., *com.*, (*fl.* B.C. 135)—556, 1857, (*Ribbeck*, vol. 1).

Ælius Donatus, *v.* Donatus.

Æschines, *orator*, (B.C. 389-314)—238. [*dorf.*

Æsch., Æschylus, *trag.*, (B.C. 525-454)—*Din-*
,, Ag., Agamemnon, 511, 2042, 2732, 2970.
,, Fr., Fragmenta, 1984, 2175.
,, Pers., Persæ, 1893.
,, Prom., Prometheus, 2127, 2177.
,, Theb., Septem c. Thebas, 371, 675.

Æsop, *fab.*, (*fl.* B.C. 570)—656, 903 (*ed. Halm*).

Afranius Lucius, *com.*, (*fl.* B.C. 100)—1255, (*Ribb.*, vol. 2).

Aissé, Mlle. de (1693-1733)—1021.

Alanus de Insulis, *chr. writer*, (1114-1203)—777, 2297.

Alberus, Erasmus, *poet*, (1500-53)—1322.

Album Perdu, Paris, 1829—1035, 1962, 2288.

Alciphron, *lit.*, (*fl.* 190)—1881.

Alcuin, *theol.*, (735-804)—2971.

Alex., Alexandre, R., *Musée de la Conversation*, 3rd ed. (1897).

Alfieri, V., *poet*, (1749-1803)—1796.

Ambrose (St), *chr. writer*, (340-97)—967, 1702, 1759, 1810, 2371.

Ammonius, s. of Hermeas, *philos.*, (*fl.* 470)—108.   [vol. iii.).

Anacreon, *poet*, (*fl.* B.C. 540)—2867 (*Bergk*, Anacreontea—2728, (*Bergk*, vol. iii.).

Andrieux, F.G.J.S., *poet*, (1759-1833)—288.

Andronicus. L. Liv., *dram.*, (*fl.* B.C. 250)—1448.

Anseaume, *dram.*, (*ob.* 1784)—1036.

Anth. Pal., *Anthologia Græca ad Palatini Codicis Fidem Ed.*, 3 vols. (Tauchnitz, 1829).

Antiphanes, *com.*, (B.C. 404-380)—2101 (in *Meineke*).

Apost., Mich. Apostolius (*ob.* 1480)—144, 584, 1129, 1440A, 1514, 1665, 2081, 2581 (in *Paroem. Gr.*).

App., L. Appuleius, *philos.*, (*fl.* 160).
,, Apol., Apologia, 745.
,, Flor., Florida, 1821.
,, Met., Metamorphoses, 810, 1919, 2488, 2962.

Aquaviva, Cl., *Jesuit*, (1543-1615)—2642.

Aquilius, *com.*, (? B.C. 200)—2850 (*Ribbeck*).

Archimedes, *math.*, (B.C. 287-212)—1729, 2138.

Aretino, P., *poet*, (1492-1557)—323.

Argenson, Cte. d' (1652-1721)—1184.

Ariosto, Lud., *poet*, (1474-1533)—663, 1543, 1613.

Ar., Aristophanes, *com.*, (B.C. 444-380).
,, Av., Aves, 1109, 1618.
,, Fr., Fragmenta, 302.
,, Plut., Plutus, 826.
,, Vesp., Vespæ, 184, 1290, 2081.

Arist., Aristotle, *philos.*, (B.C. 384-322) *in Didot.*
,, de An., de Anima, 2674.   [1552.
,, Eth. Nic., Nicom. Ethics, 94, 769, 1542,
,, Hist. An., Hist. Animalium, 2267.
,, Œc., Œconomica, 2745.
,, Pol., Politica, 136, 1539, 2002.
,, Rhet., Rhetorica, 358.
,, Sayings of, 498, 1374, 1963.

Arnault, A.V., *poet*, (1766-1838)—491.

Arndt, E.M., *poet*, (1769-1860)—482.

Armin-Boytzenburg, Ct., *pol.*, (1803-68)—524.

Arrian, *hist.*, (100-160)—1521.

Arvers, Félix, *poet*, (1806-50)—1569.

Athenæus, *lit.*, (*fl.* 220)—2030.

Atilius, *com.*, (B.C. ?)—2640.

Auct. Her., Q. Cornificius, *rhet.*, (*fl.* B.C. 80)—2722.

Aug., St Augustine, *chr. writer*, (354-430)—358, 501, 547, 618, 747, 783, 1127, 1312, 1442, 1495, 1982, 2072, 2327, 2418, 2459, 2681, 3141 (*Benedictine Ed.*, Antwerp, 1702, fol., 10 vols.).

Augustus Cæsar (B.C. 63-A.D. 14)—33, 259, 793, 1493, 2310, 2581 (5.).

c

INDEX II.—ENGLISH SUBJECT INDEX.

d

Obvious, *v.* Plain.   [1836, 1837.
Occupation (*v.* Busy, Business, Work), 761, 1812,
' Ocean's many-twinkling smile,' 2127.
Odd numbers, Luck in, 1832.
Ode, The, 319.
Office, 1091; its burden, 1960, 3097.
Officer, A superior officer is always right, 1652.
Old order (The), and the new, 428, 1018, 1292, 1293.
  ,, fashions and things, Praise of, 52, 934, 1933,
     2335, 2671.
  ,, *versus* new, *v.* Modern, etc.
'Old, Be, young, to be old long,' 1500, 2591.
  ,, The, 545, 1654; extol their young days,
     545; should quit youthful things, 873, 2591.
Old Age (*v.* Years), 1434, 1500, 2096, 2531.
  ,, Approach of, 161, 794, 812, 1105, 1148, 1610,
     2711; blessings of, 867; evils of, 1434, 1576
     (xvii.), 1969, 2101, 2197, 2553; not
     necessarily moral, 1702; pays youth's
     debts, 2184.
Old Age, A venerable, 1702; a vicious, 2488;
     a vigorous, 143.
Old men in love, 302.
Oligarchy, 1996.
Oliphant, Lawrence, 1512.
Omelette, No, without eggs, 2287.
  ,, ' What a fuss about an omelette !' 2954.
Omens, 639, 990, 1732, 1890.
Ominous, 3070.
Omniscience (*v.* Knowledge), 90, 855, 3017.
One against two, 1730; one against three, 2234;
     one way or the other, 988, 3086.
Opinion (*v.* Mind, Tastes), 958, 2214, 3032;
     difference of, 1436, 1550, 2363, 2365, 2746;
     identity of, 1804.
Opinionated, *v.* Self-opinionated.
Opportune, 503, 975.
Opportunity (*v.* Moment), 413, 1568, 2250, 2362,
     2800 ; a lost, 29, 456; never returns, 413; seize
     your, 224, 2374, 3008; watch your, 641, 1209, 2767.
Opposition, Useless, 1605.
Optimism, 2751.
Oracles, 69, 355, 2598.   [3053, 3092.
Orat-or, -ory (*v.* Eloquence, Speak, -ing), 276, 1373,
' Order reigns in Warsaw,' 1439.
  ,, ' The old order changeth,' etc., 428.
Organ, Inscription for an, 3052.
Origen, 3109.
Origin, 1977.
Originality, 206, 538, 973, 2819.
  ,, impossible, 1390, 1824.
Ornate (style), 1978, 1979, 2890.
Orpheus, 954.
' Other days, other ways,' 200.
Others, Affairs of, 78; caution in speaking of
     others, 1009, 1010, 2252; 'do unto *o.* as you
     would,' etc., 3 ; judge *o.* by yourself, 3007.
Others' money, 1348; we always admire *o.* things,
     79; we can all bear *o.* misfortunes, 1799.
Outcast, 491, 2050.
Outwitted, 940, 2239.
Ovid and Horace compared, 1192.
Ovid's recollections, 716, 2618, 2713.
Own, 'A poor thing, but my own,' 1573, 2032.
  ,, One's, 1189, 2352.
Oxford University motto, 580.

Padua, the learned, 228.
Paganism, Fall of, 1354.
Pain, 578, 1748A, 1966; and joy, 841, 1218; is
     gain, 1965, 2042; *p.* long, death short, 1233.
  ,, ' The pleasing pain,' 115.
Paint, ' I paint for posterity,' 2105.
Painted (rouged), 586, 616.
  ,, Not so black as he's painted, 955.
Painter, ' I, too, am a painter,' 118.
Paint-ers, -ing (*v.* Pictures), 1489, 1812, 2103.
Palindromes, 2528.
' Palm, Let the deserving bear the,' 2010.
  ,, Winning the, 350.
Pantheism, 687.
Paolo and Francesca, 1496, 2224, 2873.
Papacy, The, 60, 1600, 2418, 2558, 2843.
Paper, A blank sheet of, 2674.
Paradise, 514, 631, 1680; ' Fool's Paradise,' 2532.
Paradoxes, 1442.
Parallel, *v.* Unequalled.
Parasites, 681, 792, 1742, 2850.
Parasols, 14.
Pardon ! 2881.
Parents (*v.* Father, Mother), 1204; a parent's ex-
     ample, 2448, 2520, 2818, 2877.
Paris, 2019, 2090, 2571, 3133; noted for sharp
     tongues, 1013; the one place to live in, 1945.
  ,, ' Paris is well worth a mass,' 2020.
Paris, The judgment of, 149, 1483, 2179.
Part, A leading, 2186.
Parting of friends, 662, 670, 1868, 2362, 2995.
' Partridges every day,' 2749.
Party, Of no, 2212, 2822.
Parvenus, 163, 2166.
Passes, ' Everything *p.*, e. palls, e. perishes,' 2765.
Passion, Slaves to, 2539, 2565, 2639.
Passions (The), 1234, 1373, 2241, 3073; decay of,
     2202; master of one's, 818, 2323, 2539, 3062.
Past, The, 1036, 1889; extolling the *p.*, 545; recol-
     lections of, 441, 815, 1467, 1677, 2487, 2566, 2615.
  ,, present, and future, 2190, 2633.
Path, A dangerous, 3112; without a guide, 3063.
Pathos of life, The, 2655.
Patience, 592, 843, 2043, 2075, 2977; heals
     trouble, 125, 604, 2353; *p.* is genius, 1316;
     p. sorely tried, 2368.
Patient, *v.* Doctor.
Patient man, Beware the fury of the, 375.
Patriot, -ism, 132, 639, 909, 1420, 1576 (ix.), 1582,
     2154, 2222.
Patron, -age, 42, 2559, 2759.
Paul Pry, 150, 411, 873.
Paul, Saint, 2366.
Pavia, 228.
Peace (*v.* War), 1571, 1672, 2054, 2423.
  ,, A false, 565, 1494; disturbers of, 2797; evils of,
     1834; international, 1672; *p.* of mind, 1703,
     2248, 2264; the peace of death, 429, 2977.
Peace, ' Make a solitude, and call it peace,' 2589.
Pedigrees, 846, 1599, 2568, 2624.
Peers, Modern, 858, 1272, 2421.
Penalty, Paying the, 622, 1149, 2313, 2317.
Penance, 484A, 602.
People, The (*v.* Mob, Public), 2231, 2242, 2330,
     2350, 2919.
  ,, Like people, like priest, 2518.

People, The silence of the *p.* is a warning to kings, 1366.
,, The voice of the, the voice of God, 2459, 2971.
Perfection is difficult, 542; *p.* is gradual, 1691.
Perfidy, 1088, 2820.
Perfumes, 1738.
Pericles on culture, 2100.
Period, A new, 1471.
'Perish our colonies,' etc., 2083.
'Perish the world,' etc., 142, 2082.
Perishes, Nothing, 1911.
Perjury, 617, 2084.
Perron, Cardinal du, 1022.
Persecution (*v.* Martyrs), 326, 2068, 2562.
Perseverance, 880, 1222.
Personalities, 2541.
Perverse, 1518, 1806.
Pet, Death of a, 1443.
Petard, 'Hoist with his own petard,' 773, 2996.
Pétaud, 'The Court of King Pétaud,' 1227.
'Peter, The years of,' 2558.
Petition, *v.* Prayer, Request.
Pew-door, A, 2158.
Phaeton, 803, 983, 1140, 2546, 2597.
Pharsalia, 1473.
Philanthropy, 909.
Philip, Philip drunk and *P.* sober, 2170.
,, II. (Spain), 959; Philip V. (Macedon), 141.
,, Philip VI. (France), 2003.
'Philippi, We meet at,' 1967.
Philosophers, 758, 1699, 2100A, 2573.
Philosophy, 1993, 2147; *p.* ignores birth, 2568.
Photography, 2587.
Phrase, 'Without phrase,' 2440.
Phrases, Fine, 466, 2705, 2890.
Physician heal thyself, 1504, 2329.
Physiocratic school, The, 1247.
Pico of Mirandola, 3040.
Picture, 'Hands off the picture!' 1489.
Pictures and poetry compared, 2722, 2855.
Piety, 1204.
Pigs, 473, 2667, 2846.
Pilate, 178.
Piron's epitaph, 327.
'Pitcher, The, goes oft to the well,' etc., 2230.
Pity, 1758, 2457, 2655; children have no *p.*, 308.
Place (*v.* Sites, Spot), 1757, 2564.
,, Out of *p.* (Incongruous), 1756, 2470.
Places (Appointments), 188, 409, 2759.
Plagiarism, 1879, 2144, 2823.
Plague, 569.
Plain (*v.* Simple), 141, 1728.
Plain-speaking, 1170, 2440.
Plank in a shipwreck, A, 2673.
Plans, Disappointed, 164, 211, 2255.
Plato, 'I'd sooner err with *P.* than,' etc., 668.
,, 'is dear, truth dearer,' 108.
,, 'Plato is worth them all,' 2106.
Play (*v.* Fun, Relaxation), 2006; all work and no *p.*, etc., 2336.
Please, Do as you, 782; we can't *p.* all, 1938.
Pleasure (*v.* Enjoy life, Happiness), 1178, 2770.
,, always alloyed, 730, 1689, 2848; and instruction combined, 1901; *p.* and pain, 516, 841; and virtue, 3018; *p.* bought with pain, 516, 1713, 2612; giving *p.* to others, 1336; *p.* in

work, 1221; its perils, 1178, 2666, 2845; making a toil of *p.*, 2629; should be shared, 847; transitoriness of, 479, 1793, 2765, 3024.
Pleasures, curtailed by age, 2553; enjoy *p.* sparingly, 2666, 2956; forbidden *p.*, 1230, 1309,1725, 2192; guilty, 1713, 1892; sensual, 119, 3018.
Pleasures embrace us in order to strangle, 1178.
Poem, An elegant, 2121; a thrilling, 1776.
Poems resemble pictures, 2722, 2855.
,, Old pictures preferred to new, 1063.
Poet, The, and his art, 650, 830, 1284; born, not made, 1076, 2791, 3092; a great, 2305, 2643.
,, inspired by heaven, 680, by indignation, 2547, by love, 113, by night, 1533, and wine, 1813.
Poet (The) gentle, 1745; ideal, 1901, 2475; licentious, 257, 1412; unappreciated, 1777.
Poetasters, 2238, 2342, 2632.
Poetical extracts, 564.
Poetry, 206, 712, 830, 1533, 2553; and verse compared, 1076, 1754, 2123, 2706, 3135; art of, the, 1284; good *p.*, 1776, 1901; immortal *p.*, 264; inferior, 1507, 1638, 1754, 1777, 1818, 1823, 2706; original, 206; ornate, but feeble, 2890, 2898; writing, 172, 195, 252, 1533, 1754.
Poetry, a poor profession, 712, 2059; needs quiet, 252, 2475; springs from thought, 275.
,, Water-drinkers can't write poetry, 1813.
Poet's (The) ambition, 564; childhood, 2618; immortality, 724, 1166, 1659; morals, 257.
Poets, 198, 719, 893, 1507, 2103, 2455, 2547, 2552, 2658, 2680, 2821, 2869, 2997; an irritable class, 1588; *p.* and patrons, 2559; *p.* confer immortality, 494, 1284, 2088, 2951; are greater than kings, 264, 1284.
Poets, The prince of, 1855, 1948.
Point, A particular, 1496; not to the *p.*, 1686; wandering from the *p.*, 2969.
'Poison, One man's meat is another's,' 2860, 2955.
Poland, 804, 1439.
Policy, A timid, 1937.
,, 'The policy of the free-hand,' 522.
Polish, Literary, 880, 1421, 1975, 2244, 2431.
Politeness, 1398, 3134.
'Politics is an art and not a science,' 523.
Pompadour, Madame de, 142.
Pompey, 1865, 2143, 2622.
Poor, but ambitious, 341; *p.* but happy, 248, 834, 1874, 2945, 2946; *p.* but honest, 1298, 2399; *p.* but patient, 2048.
Poor, Made *p.* by plenty, 1100, 1460.
,, 'A poor thing, but my own,' 1573, 2032.
Poor, The, 248, 409, 825, 1103, 1482, 1641, 2007, 2484, 2501; always suspicious, 1898; the *p.* and his rulers, 1104; the *p.* and the rich, 589, 2484; is all schemes, 927.
,, The public-house is the *p.* man's club, 1308.
Popes, can't dispense from death, 1934, 3082; their length of reign, 2558; prophecies of the, 1444; their transitory glory, 2516.
Popularity, 169, 2453.
,, 'Popularity is glory in coppers,' 1274.
Possession, To be in, 43, 209, 1207, 2478.
Possessions (*v.* Possession), 1217, 1767.
Possibilities, 1179.
Posterity, 461, 706, 2497; its verdict, 2670.
Pot-luck, 2820.

INDEX III.—QUOTATIONS INDEX.*

*Note.—The Index includes all quotations, and parts of quotations, not occurring in the Dictionary's alphabetical order. The remainder will be found in their proper place in the literal sequence of the work's numbered entries. See page x, and page lxviii (Note). For all Greek quotations, see Index IV., page 403.

Facile ærumnam ferre possum, etc., 3129.
Facit indignatio versum, 2547.
Faire de la prose sans le savoir, 2021.
Fais ce que dois, advienne que pourra, 3044.
Fallentis semita vitæ, 2264.
Famam extendere factis, hoc virtutis opus, 2623.
Fas est et ab hoste doceri, 1139.
Fatis accede deisque, etc., 1201.
„ nunquam concessa moveri, 1514.
Felicior Augusto, melior Trajano, 2376.
Felicis memoriæ, judicium expectans, 2359.
Félicité passée, qui ne peut revenir, etc.,1677 (vi.).
Fel in corde, fraus in factis, 1516.
Felix opportunitate mortis, 2806.
„ quicunque dolore alterius discit, 786.
Fere totus mundus exercet histrioniam, 2581 (4.).
Festinare nocet, nocet et cunctatio sæpe, 3045.
Festinatio improvida est et cæca, 793.
Fides individua, corpus unum, 967.
Fieri infectum non potest, 769.
Finis coronat opus, 3046.
Fit ex his consuetudo, deinde natura, 358.
Fit scelus indulgens per nubila sæcula virtus, 3047.
Fixa et mutari nescia, 2683.
Flagrante delicto, 1072.
Flectere si nequeo superos, etc., 2350.
Flosculus angustæ miseræq. brevissima vitæ, 794.
Fola di romanzi, 2584.
Fons et origo, 1977.
Fortes adjuvat ipsa Venus, 182.   [2642.
„ in fine consequendo, suaves in modo assequendi,
„ non modo fortuna juvat, sed ratio, 182.
Fortibus est fortuna viris data, 182.
Fortissimus ille qui promtus metuenda pati, 1597.
Fortuna fortes metuit, ignavos premit, 182.
Fortunam citius reperias, quam retineas, 823 (2.).
Fortuna meliores sequitur, 182.
„ multis dat nimis, satis nulli, 823 (3.).
„ non mutat genus, 1418.
„ obesse nulli contenta est semel, 823 (4.).
Fortunatos, O, nimium sua si bona nôrint, 1872.
Fortuna vitrea est, tum quum splendet, frangitur,
  823 (6.).
Frange toros, pete vina, rosas cape, etc., 1521.
Fratres Carmeli navigant in a bothe, etc., 2044.
Frequens meditatio, carnis afflictio, 752.
Frigida bello dextera, 1282.
Fronte capillata est, post est occasio calva, 413.
Fronti nulla fides, 831.
Fruges consumere nati, 1791.
Fugiendo in media fata ruitur, 789.
Fugit hora, hoc quod loquor inde est, 600 (6.),
Fuimus Troes, fuit Ilium, etc., 2884.   [(iv.).
Fuisti Rex, nunc fex; fuisti maximus, etc., 1677
Fuit Ilium et ingens gloria Teucrorum, 2884.
Fumo comburi nihil potest, flamma potest, 805.
Funesta, atroce, orribil notte! 1796.
„ dote d'infiniti guai, 1153.
Fungar inani munere, etc., 918.
Furiosi manibus commissus gladius, 1667.
Furor arma ministrat, 1165.
„ fit læsa sæpius patientia, 375.
Galeatum sero duelli pœnitet, 2702.
Gallinæ filius albæ, 824.
Gaudia discursus nostri est farrago libelli, 2241.
Gefrorne Musik, 1301.

Genus et proavos, et quæ non fecimus ipsi, 1601.
„ irritabile vatum, 1588.
Geteilter Schmerz ist halber Schmerz, 847.
Gladiator in arena capit consiliam, 2702.
Gli irrevocati dì, 2487.
Glissez, mortels, n'appuyez pas, 2666.
Gloriosa et splendida peccata, 2616.
Gourmand, ivrogne et asseuré menteur, 1171.
Gracchi de seditione querentes, 2329.
Græcum est, non potest legi, 3048.
Gram loquitur; Dia verba docet, etc., 3049.
Grano salis, Cum, 403.
Grata superveniet quæ non sperabitur hora, 1125.
Gratia fama valetudo contingat abunde, 2286.
Gratior et pulcro veniens in corpore virtus, 1228.
Gratis pœnitet esse probum, 1627.
Grèce est notre pays, Mémoire est notre mère, 1255.
Guarda, e passa, 1773.
Habemus ad Dominum, 2664.
Habent parvæ commoda magna moræ, 535.
„ sua fata libelli, 2155.
Hac fini ames, tanquam forte fortuna osurus,1152.
Hac ibat Simois, hic est Sigeia tellus, 170.
Hæc est ærugo mera, 902.
„ olim meminisse juvabit, 815.
„ placuit semel, hæc decies repetita, etc., 2855.
„ quicum secum portet tria nomina regum,
  etc., 3058.
„ te victoria perdet, 2285.
Halb Tier, halb Engel, 2983.
Hanc veniam petimusq. damusq. vicissim, 2449.
Hand wird nur von Hand gewaschen u.s.w., 1491.
Haud ignara ac non incauta futuri, 2035.
„ ignara mali miseris succurrere disco, 1758.
Hélas! nos plus beaux jours s'envolent les
  premiers, 1969.
Heureux comme un roi, 2386.
„ les peuples dont l'histoire est ennuyeux, 3050.
„ l'inconnu qui c'est bien sceu connaître, 1576
  (xxii.).
Hic humanæ vitæ mimus, etc., 2581 (3.).
„ labor, hoc opus est, 756.   [3051.
„ liber est in quo quærit sua dogmata quisque,
„ niger est, hunc tu, Romane, caveto, 9.
„ toto tecum consumerer ævo, 897.
„ vivimus ambitiosa paupertate omnes, 341.
Hinc venti dociles resono se carcere solvunt, 3052.
Hippias eloquentia nulli secundus, 1821.
Hi sapiunt aliis, desipiuntque sibi, 390.
„ sunt invidiæ nimirum, Regule, mores, etc.,676.
Hoc est quod unum est pro laboribus tantis,1973.
„ est ut vitale putes, 106.
„ lege, quod possit dicere vita, meum est, 2280.
„ opus, hic labor est, 756.
„ tantum possum dicere, non amo te, 1734.
Hoher Sinn liegt oft im kind'schem Spiel, 2975.
Hominem te memento, 1521.
Homines amplius oculis qu. auribus credunt, 2476.
Homo proponit, sed Deus disponit, 1404.
„ semper aliud, Fortuna aliud cogitat, 1404.
„ sum, humani nihil a me alienum puto, 324.
„ unius libri, 1598.
Honesta quædam scelera successus facit, 2168.
Horæ momento cita mors venit, aut victoria, 349.
Horatii curiosa felicitas, 2643.
Horrendum, informe, ingens, cui lumen, etc.,1572.

Militiæ species amor est, 1549.
Militia est vita hominis super terram, 2940.
Minimæ vires frangere quassa valent, 1056.
Minuit præsentia famam, 1021.   [1576.
Miremur periisse homines? monumenta fatiscunt,
Miror magis, 1749.
Misera beatitudo mortalium rerum, 1579.
Miseræ ludibria chartæ, 2280.
Misera pax vel bello bene mutatur, 217 (5.).
Miserum istuc verbum, Habuisse, 1677 (ii.).
M. l'ambassadeur, j'ai touj. été le maître, 3080.
Mobile vulgus, 1565.
Modus agri non ita magnus, 920.
Moi, aussi je fus pasteur dans l'Arcadie! 3128.
Molliti sunt sermones ejus super oleum, 1516.
Momento cita mors venit aut victoria, 349.
Monsieur, vous avez fait trois fautes, etc., 2963.
Mons parturibat, gemitus immanes ciens, 2030.
Monstror digito prætereuntium, 169.
Monstrum, nulla virtute redemptum, 610.
Morbus signa cibus blasphemia, etc., 3081.
Morem fecerat usus, 358.
Mores multorum vidit et urbes, 2301.
Morituri te salutant, 204.
Mors aut victoria, 349.
„ etiam saxis nominibusque venit, 1576 (vi.).
„ misera non est, aditus est miser, 1576 (xviii.).
„ sola fatetur quantula sint hominum corpuscula,
    1576 (viii.).
„ sua quemque manet, 1576 (iv.).
„ ultima linea rerum est, 1576 (vii.).
Mort Dieu! Bouvard, je souffre, etc., 3037.
Morte magis metuenda senectus, 1576 (xvii.).
Mortem aliquid ultra est? 1576 (xxiii.).
„ optare malum, timere pejus, 1576 (xii.).
Mourir n'est rien, c'est notre dernière heure, 1576.
Mugitusque boum mollesq. sub arbore somni, 175.
Multa cadunt inter calicem, etc., 1124.
„ novit vulpis, sed felis unum magnum, 158.
Multis utile bellum, 916.
Multos castra juvant, etc., 216.
Multum legendum est, non multa, 1598.
Mundus vult decipi, decipiatur, 2210.
„ scena, vita transitus, etc., 2581.
Munus et officium nil scribens ipse docebo, 837.
Musæo contingens cuncta lepore, 206.
Musik, Die Architektur ist die erstarrte, 1301.
Mutato nomine de te fabula narratur, 2274.
Nam scelus intra se tacitum qui cogitat ullum, 879.
„ vitiis nemo sine nascitur, etc., 626.
Nascimur poetæ, fimus oratores, 3092.
Nascitur ridiculus mus, 2030.
Nati natorum et qui nascentur ab illis, 706.
Natura beatis omnibus esse dedit, 2945.
Naturæ dedecus, 819.
Naturam sequi, 909.
Natura non facit saltus, 1614.
„ nusquam magis quam in minimis, 2396.
Natus nemo, 1664.
Nave senza nocchier in gran tempesta, 62.
Navibus atq. quadrigis petimus bene vivere, 2629.
N'ayez pas de zèle, 2665.
Nè anco quand' annotta, il Sol tramonta, 959.
Necessitas rationum inventrix, 1497.   [1576.
Nec forma æternum, aut cuiq. fortuna perennis,
„ sibi, sed toti genitum se credere mundo, 909.

Nec tecum possum vivere, nec sine te, 541.
„ te, tua plurima, Panthu, labentem, etc., 3134.
„ vixit male qui natus moriensque fefellit, 379.
Negat quis? Nego. Ait? Aio, etc., 681.
Neglecta solent incendia sumere vires, 1608.
Ne Hercules quidem contra duos, 1730.
Nemo adeo ferus est ut non mitescere possit, 1128.i
„ impetrare potest a Papa bullam nunquam
    moriendi, 3082,
„ in sese tentat descendere, 2853.
„ omnes, neminem omnes fefellerunt, 1517.
„ repente fuit turpissimus, 808.
Ne moveas Camarinam, 1514.   [1456.
N'en déplaise aux docteurs, Cordéliers, Jacobins,
Ne parler jamais qu'à propos, etc., 1367.
Ne plus ultra, 1637.   [3135.
Neque enim concludere versum, dixeris esse satis,
Ne quid nimis, 961.
Nervis alienis mobile lignum, 2854.
Nescia fallere vita, 175.
„ virtus stare loco, 2469,
Nescio quid meditans nugarum, 2517.
Nescit vox missa reverti, 455.
N'est-on jamais tyran qu'avec un diadême? 488.
Nihil ad Bacchum (rem, versum), 1686.
„ decet invita Minerva, 2791.
„ est nisi mortis imago, 2337.
„ infelicius quam fuisse felicem, 1677 (iv.).
„ interit, 1911.
„ mihi cum mortuis bellum, 1743.
„ perfectum dum aliquid restat agendum, 2074.
„ sic revocat a peccato quam mortis meditatio,
    1576 (xx.).
„ tam inæquale, quam æqualitas, 1485.
„ „ miserabile, quam ex beato miser, 1677.
„ vacuum, neque sine signo, apud Deum, 3136.
„ vident nisi quod lubet, 1518.   [2460.
Nil actum credens, si qd. superesset agendum,
„ agere delectat, 980.
„ conscire sibi, nulla pallescere culpa, 901.
„ cupientium nudus castra peto, 2218.
„ fuit unquam sic impar sibi, 1704.
„ homine terra pejus ingrato creat, 1086.
„ igitur fieri de nilo posse fatendum est, 464.
„ prodest, quod non lædere possit idem, 1784.
„ scribens ipse docebo, 837.
Nimium ne crede colori, 1870.
Nisi inter omnes possibiles mundos optimus, 2751.
„ quod ipse fecit, nil rectum putat, 929.
Ni trop haut ni trop bas, c'est le souverain style,
    1843.
Nobilitas sola est atque unica virtus, 2624.
Nobis obsequi gloria relicta est, 2730.
Nocet empta dolore voluptas, 2612.
Nocte pluit tota, redeunt spectacula mane, 946.
Noctes cœnæque deum, 1947,
Noli turbare circulos meos, 1729.
Nolunt ubi velis, ubi nolis cupiunt ultro, 1806.
Non ætate, verum ingenio adipiscitur sapientia,
    1702.   [3083,
„ aliena putes homini quæ obtingere possunt,
„ annorum canities sed morum, 1702.
„ canimus surdis, 511.
„ cani, non rugæ auctoritatem arripiunt, 1702.
„ deficiente crumena, 2286.
„ di, non homines, non concessere columnæ, 1507.

ERRATA.

No.
66. *For* Regnier *read* Régnier.
209. *For* censertur *read* censentur.
425. *For* comedie *read* comédie.
563. *For* Diseurs de bon mots *read* Diseurs de bons mots.
640. *For* enemy's work *read* enemy's worth.
647. *For* Beranger *read* Béranger.
881. *For* Slow rises worth by poverty oppressed *read* Slow rises worth by poverty depressed.
961. *For* utile, ne quid nimis *read* utile, ut ne quid nimis.
961. *For* μεσ' ἄριστα *read* μέσ' ἄριστα.
975. *For* Çarême *read* Carême.
995. *For* ἀνέμοισιν *read* ἀνεμοῖσιν.
1014. *For* believe *read* understand.
1027. *For* réculant *read* reculant.
1035. *For* receuillis *read* recueillis.
1036. *For* Il sont *read* Ils sont.
1039. *For* Francaise *read* Française.
1044. *For* seinem *read* seinen.
1052. *For* Lyrische *read* Lyrisches.
1055. *For* ultramvis *read* utramvis.
1063. *For* les grand *read* les grands.
1152. *For* ἐς τοσόνδ' *read* ἐς τοσόνδ'.
1172. *For* Regnier *read* Régnier.
1182. *For* je n'ai pas en *read* je n'ai pas eu.
1184. *For* necessité *read* nécessité.
1207. *For* Dites a *read* Dites à.
1209. *For* Ansonius *read* Ausonius.
1305. *For* Raç. *read* Rac.
1342. *For* Henry II. *read* Francis I.
1385. *For* Tout État *read* Tout l'état.
1434. *For* "χεις *read* ἔχεις.
1443. *For* honinum *read* hominum.
1444. *For* Those prophecies *read* These prophecies.
1491. *For* nahmen *read* nehmen.
1542. *For* ποιἐι *read* ποιεῖ.
1576 (vii.). *For* Hors. *read* Hor.
1877. *For* Ich bin es müde über *read* Ich bin es müde, über.
2212. *For* être sui *read* être sur.
2286. *For* matricula *read* nutricula.
2323. *For* Sapiens qui sibi *read* Sapiens sibi qui.
2359. *For* James Dupont *read* James Duport.

ABBREVIATIONS, SIGNS, Etc.

Abbrev., *Abbreviat-ed, -ion.*
Acc., *According to.*
Ad. fin., *Towards the end.*
Ap., or Apud., *In,* or *Quoted by.*
App., *Appendix.*
Attrib., *Attributed to.*
C., *Chapter.*
Cant., *Canto.*
Cap., *Chapter.*
Carm., *Carmen,* or *Carmina.*
Cf., *Compare,* or *See.*
Ch., *Chanson,* or *Chant.*
Conn., *Connected, Connection.*
Cp. *Compare.*
Dict., *Dictionary.*
Ep., Epp., *Epistle, Epistles.*
Epigr., *Epigram.*
Epil., *Epilogue.*
Fin., *At the end.*
Fr., Fragm., *Fragment, Fragments.*
Gen., Generally.
Gk., *Greek.*
Ibid., *The same work.*
Id., *The same author.*
Inc., *or* Incert., *Anonymous,* or *Unknown.*
Init., *At the beginning.*
In l., *In the passage-cited.*

Inscr., *Inscription.*
L. and S., *Liddell and Scott's Lexicon.*
L.c., *In the place cited.*
Lew. and S., *Lewis and Short's Latin Dictionary.*
Lit., *Literal, Literally.*
Med., *Mediæval,* or *In the Middle.*
N., *or* n., *Note.*
Passim, *Frequently, Throughout.*
Pop., *Popular, Popularly.*
Pref., *Preface, Prefixed.*
Prob., *Probably.*
Prol., *Prologue.*
Prov., *Proverb,* or *Proverbially.*
Qu., *Quotation, Quoted,* or *Quotes.*
Q.v., *Which see.*
Sc., *Scilicet.*
St., *Stanza.*
Str., *Strophe.*
Subj., *Subject.*
S.v., *Sub verbo, Under the word.*
Tr., or Transl., *Translated,* or *Translation.*
Trad., *Traditional, -ly.*
Trag., *Tragic.*
Undesign., *Undesignated.*
Usu., *Usually.*
V., *See.*

NOTE.—All quotations, whether in the Dictionary or its Index, are printed in the order of the *letter* of the alphabet, and are so to be looked for: each entry being taken as one word, and following the other *in strict order of literal sequence.* Thus, we get

-159. Arte magistra, etc.
160. Ἄσβεστος γέλως.
161. A soixante ans, etc.

directly following one another; and, to take another instance, the *Olet lucernam, O Liberté,* etc., and *O lieb' so lang,* etc., of Nos. 1884, 1885, 1886, will be found to conform to the same rule. The arrangement may have its drawbacks, but it has one redeeming feature, that it is absolutely infallible.

DICTIONARY

OF

CLASSICAL AND FOREIGN QUOTATIONS.

1. **A aucuns les biens viennent en dormant.** Prov.—*Good fortune comes to some people while they are asleep, i.e.*, without their seeking it.

> Prov. traditionally connected with Louis XI., who, in the church of Notre Dame de Cléry one day, being importuned for a certain vacant benefice, turned from the petitioner and gave the preferment to a poor clerk whom he espied asleep in one of the choir stalls, "in order to verify the prov. which says, *A aucuns les biens*," etc. Thus Fumag. (p. 139), following Du Verdier. Isaac Disraeli, *Curiosities of Literature*, 1858, ii., 10, puts the lucky slumberer in the porch, and Quit. (p. 140) in a confessional, and neither introduce a rival candidate. The saying is an old one, taken from the fisherman's trade and the luck attaching to the "traps" or "lines" set by them at sundown to work during the night, as in the "Rete dormientis trahit," and the εὕδοντι κύρτος αἱρεῖ (*'Tis the sleeper's weel that catches*) of Chil. p. 116. Cic. (Verr. 2, 5, 70, § 180) has a hit at the privileges of the Roman noblesse, "who got all the government appointments *in their sleep*" (quibus omnia P. R. beneficia dormientibus deferuntur); and Ter. (Ad. 4, 5, 59) makes Micio say to the scapegrace Æschinus, "Quid? credebas dormienti hæc tibi confecturos deos?"—*Did you imagine that the gods would do this for you, and you snoring all the time?*

2. **Ab abusu ad usum non valet consequentia.** Law Max.—*The abuse of anything is no argument against its proper use.*

3. **Ab alio expectes, alteri quod feceris.** Syr. 2.—*Expect from others what you have done to them.*

> Prout vultis ut faciant vobis homines, et vos facite illis similiter. Vulg. Luc. vi. 31.—*As you would that men should do to you, do you also to them in like manner.* In connection with this, it may be noted that Lampridius, in his Life of Alex. Severus (222-235 A.D.), says (c. 51) that the Emperor used to repeat "some Jewish or Christian saying" (*quod tibi fieri ne vis, alteri ne feceris*), which so pleased him that he made the crier proclaim it in the streets, and had it inscribed on the public buildings.

4. **Abeunt studia in mores.** Ov. Her. 15, 83.—*Pursuits grow into habits.*

A

5. Abiit, excessit, evasit, erupit.　Cic. Cat. 2, 1, 1.—*He has departed,
retired, escaped, broken away.*　Said of Catiline's flight on the
discovery of his conspiracy.　A good description of any one
absconding.

6. Abnormis sapiens crassaque Minerva.　Hor. Ep. 2, 2, 3.—*Of
strong good sense, untutored in the schools.*　Full of mother-wit.

7. Ab ovo Usque ad mala.　Hor. S. 1, 3, 6.—*From the eggs to the
apples.*　From beginning to end: "eggs and apples" being
respectively the first and last courses at a Roman dinner.

　　The phrase applies to any topic, or speaker, that monopolises the whole
of the conversation.

8. Absentem lædit, cum ebrio qui litigat.　Syr. 12.—*To quarrel
with a drunken man is harming the absent.*

9. Absentem qui rodit amicum,
　Qui non defendit alio culpante, solutos
　Qui captat risus hominum, famamque dicacis;
　Fingere qui non visa potest, commissa tacere
　Qui nequit, hic niger est, hunc tu, Romane, caveto.
　　　　　　　　　　　　　　　　　　Hor. S. 1, 4, 81.

A Blackguard.

The man that will malign an absent friend,
Or when his friend's attacked, does not defend;
Who seeks to raise a laugh, be thought a wit;
Declares "he saw," when he invented it;
Who blabs a secret—Roman, friend, take care!
His heart is black, of such a man beware.—*Ed.*

10. Absit invidia verbo.　Liv. 9, 19, 15.—*I say it without boasting.*

11. Abyssus abyssum invocat.　Vulg. Ps. 42, 7.—*Deep calleth unto deep.*

12. Acceptissima semper Munera sunt, auctor quæ pretiosa facit.
　Ov. H. 17, 71.—*Those presents which derive their value from the
donor are always the most acceptable.*

　　You gave—with words of so sweet breath composed,
　　As made the things more rich.—*Shakesp.* "Hamlet," 3, 1, 98.

13. Accipe nunc Danaum insidias, et crimine ab uno
　Disce omnes.　　　　　　　　　　　　Virg. A. 2, 65.

　　Mark now the enemy's tricks, and take one case
　　To shew the treach'ry that infects the race.—*Ed.*

　　Crimine ab uno d. o., or *Ab (Ex) uno d. o.*, is often used of forming
general conclusions from a single instance produced.

14. Accipe quæ nimios vincant umbracula soles;
　Sit licet et ventus, te tua vela tegent.　　Mart. 14, 28.

Umbrellas.

An umbrella for the sun you'll handy find,
Or it may serve as shelter from the wind.—*Ed.*

15. Acer, et indomitus: quo spes, quoque ira vocasset,
　Ferre manum, et nunquam temerando parcere ferro:

Successus urgere suos: instare favori
Numinis: impellens quicquid sibi summa petenti
Obstaret: gaudensque viam fecisse ruina.   Luc. 1, 146.

Julius Cæsar.

Undaunted, keen: where Hope or Passion called
He'd fight, nor ever sheathe the murderous sword.
Pressing advantage, following up his star,
And sweeping all between him and his prize,
He hailed the ruin that bestrew'd his way.—*Ed.*

16. A chi un segreto? Ad un bugiardo o un muto : questi non parla, e quei non è creduto. Prov.—*To whom may you tell a secret? To a liar, or a dumb man: the one cannot speak, and the other is not believed.*

17. Ach, wie bald
Schwindet Schönheit und Gestalt! W. Hauff, Reiters Morgengesang.—*Ah, how soon form and beauty disappear!*

18. Ach, wie glücklich sind die Todten! Schiller, Das Siegesfest, st. 4.—*Ah! how happy are the dead!*

19. A cœur vaillant rien d'impossible.—*Nothing is impossible to a valiant heart.*   Motto of Jeanne d'Albret of Navarre (1528-72), mother of Henry IV., and adopted by him as his own *devise.*

20. A confesseurs, médecins, avocats, la vérité ne cèle de ton cas. Prov.—*With your confessor, doctor, and lawyer, use no reservation whatsoever.*   Tell the whole truth—the "worst." Yet nothing is said of the "wife."

21. Acribus, ut ferme talia, initiis, incurioso fine. Tac. A. 6, 17.—*As is generally the case with such movements—a spirited beginning and a most perfunctory conclusion.*

22. Actum, aiunt, ne agas. Ter. Phor. 2, 3, 72.—*What's done, they say, don't do again.* You are wasting your time: acting to no purpose. Cf. Stultus es, Rem actam agis. Plaut. Ps. 1, 3, 28.—*You fool, you're doing work twice over.*

23. Ad calamitatem quilibet rumor valet. Syr. 17.—*Every rumour is believed where disaster is concerned.*   Ill news travels apace.

24. Adde quod injustum rigido jus dicitur ense;
Dantur et in medio vulnera sæpe foro.   Ov. T. 5, 10, 43.

Miscarriage of Justice.

The sword of justice cuts in cruel sort,
And wounds are often dealt in open court.—*Ed.*

25. Adeo in teneris consuescere multum est. Virg. G. 2, 272.—*So important is it to grow inured to anything in early youth.*   The value of sound principles early instilled in the mind.

'Tis education forms the common mind;
Just as the twig is bent, the tree's inclined.
                    —*Pope,* "Moral Essays," Ep. 1, 149.

26. Adeon'homines immutarier
 Ex amore, ut non cognoscas eundem esse ? Ter. Eun. 2, 1, 19.—
 *Is it possible a man can be so changed by love, that one would not
 know him for the same person?*

27. Adhibenda est munditia non odiosa, neque exquisita nimis;
 tantum quæ fugiat agrestem ac inhumanam negligentiam.   Cic.
 Off. 1, 36, 130.—*Good taste in dress observes the mean between
 either loud or finikin attire, and the boorish garments of a
 country bumpkin.*

28. Adieu, brave Crillon, je vous aime à tort et à travers.—*Adieu,
 my brave Crillon, I love you to distraction.*

 Apocryphal conclusion, due to Voltaire (*Henriade*, Chant viii., v. 109,
 Note), of a letter of Henry IV. to Louis des Balbes de Berthon de Crillon
 (1541-1615), *le brave des braves* of his time.   The actual letter (pub. in
 Berger de Xivrey's *Recueil des lettres missives de Henri IV.*, vol. 4, pp.
 848 and 899) is dated during the siege of Amiens, Sept. 20, 1597.   It
 begins: "Brave Crillon, pendés-vous de n'avoir esté icy près de moy lundy
 dernier, à la plus belle occasion qui se soit jamais veue," etc.; and ends,
 "Il ne manque rien que le brave Grillon, qui sera toujours le bien venu et
 veu de moy." Fourn. *L.D.L.*, chap. xxxv.

29. Adieu, paniers, vendanges sont faites.   Prov., Rab. 1, 27.—
 Goodbye, baskets! vintage is over!   The opportunity has gone
 by, there is nothing to be done.

30. Adieu, plaisant pays de France!
 O ma patrie, la plus chérie, etc.
 Meusnier de Querlon, *Anthologie* (Monet), 1765, vol. 1, p. 19.—
 *Adieu, pleasant land of France!   Oh! my country, the dearest
 in the world,* etc.

 These lines, supposed to have been sung by Mary Stuart on embarking
 at Calais for Leith (15th August 1561), are now known to have been
 written by the journalist Meusnier de Querlon, as confessed by himself to
 the Abbé Mercier de Saint Léger.   V. *L'esprit des Journaux*, vol. for Sept.
 1781, p. 227 ; and Fourn. *L.D.L.*, chap. xxvii.

31. Ad infinitum.—*To infinity; without end.*

 So, naturalists observe, a flea
 Has smaller fleas that on him prey;
 And these have smaller still to bite 'em,
 And so proceed *ad infinitum.*—*Swift,* "Rhapsody."

32. A diverticulo repetatur fabula.   Juv. 15, 72.--*To return from
 the digression.*   Like the Fr.—*Revenons à nos moutons,* q.v.

33. Ad Kalendas Græcas.   Suet. Aug. 87.—*At the Greek Kalends.*
 The next day after never.

 As the Greeks had no Kalends, the phrase is used for an indefinite
 date.   Quit. (p. 673) produces a parallel illusory date used by the French
 kings of the 13th and 14th centuries, who promised repayment of loans *à
 Pâques ou à la Trinité*—an engagement generally more honoured in the
 breach than in the observance.   The time of Malbrouck's home-coming (in
 the old song) is, it will be remembered, attended with the same vagueness
 of fixture: "Il reviendra *à Pâques, ou à la Trinité.*"

34. Ad majorem Dei gloriam, or A.M.D.G.—*To the greater glory of God.* Motto and maxim of the Society of Jesus.

35. Ad ogni uccello suo nido par bello. Prov.—*Every bird thinks its own nest beautiful.*
> Be it never so humble, there's no place like home.
> —*J. H. Payne, Opera of " Clari, the Maid of Milan."*

36. Ad pœnitendum properat, cito qui judicat. Syr. 32.—*Hasty decisions are on the high road to repentance.*

37. Ad populum phaleras, ego te intus et in cute novi. Pers. 3, 30. —*Keep your finery for the mob, I know your nature to the very bottom.*

38. Ad quæ noscenda iter ingredi, transmittere mare solemus, ea sub oculis posita negligimus: seu quia ita natura comparatum, ut proximorum incuriosi, longinqua sectemur: seu quod omnium rerum cupido languescit quum facilis occasio est; seu quod differimus, tanquam visuri, quod datur videre, quoties velis cernere. Plin. Ep. 8, 20, 1.

Foreign Travel.
> We generally cross the sea in pursuit of sights, neglecting all the while what is under our nose: either because it is only natural to seek distant scenes, and to care little for what is near; or, because the greater the facility there is for gratifying a desire, the less is the advantage taken of it; or else, because we keep putting off what can be done any day, with the intention of seeing it some day.

39. Adsit Regula, peccatis quæ pœnas irroget æquas;
Ne scutica dignum horribili sectere flagello. Hor. S. 1, 3, 117.
> Be just: and mete to crime its condign pain;
> Nor use the murd'rous lash where suits the cane.—*Ed.*

40. Ad summos honores alios scientia juris, alios eloquentia, alios gloria militaris provexit; huic versatile ingenium sic pariter ad omnia fuit, ut natum ad id unum diceres, quodcunque ageret.
Liv. 39, 40.
The Elder Cato.
> Some men attain power by legal science, some by eloquence, some by military achievement; but he was a person of such versatile talents, that let him be doing what he would, you would have said that it was the very thing for which nature had designed him.

41. Ad tristem partem strenua est suspicio. Syr. 7.—*One is keen to suspect a quarter from which one has once received hurt.* " A burnt child dreads the fire."

42. Adulandi gens prudentissima laudat
Sermonem indocti, faciem deformis amici. Juv. 3, 86.
Flatterers.
> The crafty flattering race their patron praise;
> His talk tho' stupid, and tho' plain his face.—*Ed.*

43. Adversus hostem æterna auctoritas. Law of the XII. Tables ap. Cic. Off. 1, 12, 37.—*Against a stranger the right of possession*

is perpetual; i.e., a stranger cannot by prescription obtain right of possession to the property of a Roman. Lew. and S., *s.v.* "Auctoritas."

44. Ægrescitque medendo. Virg. A. 12, 46.—*His disorder only increases with the remedy.* Lew. and S., *s.v.* "Medeor." The life of the valetudinarian. V. *Spectator*, No. 25. Celuy meurt tous les jours, qui languit en vivant. Pierrard Poullet, La Charité, Sc. 5. (Orleans, 1595, p. 69.)—*He is always dying who lives a lingering life.*

45. Ægroto, dum anima est, spes esse dicitur. Prov. ap. Cic. Att. 9, 10, 3.—*While there's life in the sick there's hope, as the saying is.* "While there is life, there is hope, he cried." Gay, Fables (Sick Man and Angel). Cf. ἐλπίδες ἐν ζωοῖσιν· ἀνέλπιστοι δὲ θανόντες. Theocr. Id. 4, 42.—*Hope there is for the living, 'tis only the dead who are hopeless;* and, Omnia homini dum vivit speranda sunt. Telesphorus ap. Sen. Ep. 70, 5.—*While there's life in a man everything may be hoped for him.*

46. Ἀεὶ γὰρ εὖ πίπτουσιν οἱ Διὸς κύβοι. Soph. Frag. 763.—*Jove's throws (dice) are always good.* God's work is no mere accident.

47. A.E.I.O.U.—Initial letters of the following mottos of the Austrian Empire. 1. Austriæ Est Imperare Orbi Universo (*It belongs to Austria to govern the world*). 2. Austria Erit In Orbe Ultima (*Austria will be last in the world*). 3. Aquila Electa Juste Omnia Vincit (*The elect eagle justly conquers everything*). 4. Alles Erdreich Ist Oesterreich Unterthan (*The whole surface of the globe is subject to Austria*). 5. Aller Ehren Ist Oesterreich Voll (*Austria is full of all honours*).

48. Æquâ legé necessitas
Sortitur insignes et imos ;
Omne capax movet urna nomen. Hor. C. 3, 1, 14.

> Even-handed Fate
> Hath but one law for small and great:
> That ample urn holds all men's names.—*Calverley.*

49. Æque pauperibus prodest, locupletibus æque,
Æque neglectum pueris senibusque nocebit. Hor. Ep. 1, 1, 26.
—*It is of service to the poor equally with the rich, and the neglect of it will prove equally injurious to young and old.* The poet refers to the moral counsels which he offers as a panacea for the vices of the age.

50. Æquum est Peccatis veniam poscentem reddere rursus.
Hor. S. 1, 3, 74.

> It is but right that they who claim
> Forgiveness should extend the same.—*Ed.*

51. Ætatem Priami Nestorisque
Longam qui putat esse, Martiane,
Multum decipitur falliturque.
Non est vivere, sed valere, vita. Mart. 6, 70, 12.

Health, not Long Life.
The man to whom old Priam's years
Or Nestor's a long life appears,
Mistaken is and much deceived :
Health, not long life, is life indeed. *—Ed.*

52. Ævo rarissima nostro Simplicitas.   Ov. A. A. 1, 241.

Most rare is now our old simplicity. *—Dryden.*

Motto of Spectator 269, on Sir Roger de Coverly in Gray's Inn Walks.

53. Afflavit Deus et dissipantur.   Addison, Spectator 293, fin.*—He blew with his Wind, and they were scattered.*

The story of this line of Latin, relative to a medal struck in [com-memoration of the Spanish Armada, is a curious one.   Addison, with the above as legend, makes it the work of Q. Elizabeth.   Schiller in a note to his "Die unüberwindliche Flotte" (Thalia, 2, 71), represents the motto as *Afflavit Deus et dissipati sunt;* while the actual medal, which was struck by the Dutch (with Maurice of Nassau's arms on the exergue), bears for superscription *Flavit · Jehovah* (in Hebrew)· *Et · Dissipati · Sunt · 1588 ·*, and on the reverse, *Allidor non Lædor.*   In Exodus (xv. 10) is *Flavit spiritus tuus et operuit eos mare,* from which the idea was probably derived. *V.* Van Loon's *Nederlandsche Historipenningen,* 1, 392, and Büchm. p. 11.

54. A force de peindre le diable sur les murs, il finit par apparaître en personne.   Prov.*—If you go on painting the devil on the walls, it ends by his appearing in person.*   It is one way to hasten disasters to be always talking of them.

55 Age, libertate Decembri,
Quando ita majores voluerunt, utere.   Hor. S. 2, 7, 4.

Christmas comes but once a year.
Well, since our wise forefathers so ordained,
Enjoy December's licence unrestrained.

During the Saturnalia (the Roman Christmas) the slaves were allowed an unwonted freedom, treating their masters as equals, and being at liberty to speak without restraint.   The line is applicable to the relaxation of the Christmas holidays, which come, as it is said, "but once a year"— as if Easter and Whitsuntide were continually recurring.   Cf. Non semper erunt Saturnalia. Sen. Apoc. 12, 2.*—Every day can't be a holiday.*

56. Agere considerate pluris est quam cogitare prudenter. · Cic. Off. 1, 45, 160.*—To act with caution, is better than wise reflection.*

57. Agnoscere solis Permissum est, quos jam tangit vicinia fati,
Victurosque Dei celant, ut vivere durent,
Felix esse mori.   Luc. 4, 517.

'Tis only known to those who stand
Already on death's borderland,
The bliss it is to die :
Where life is vigorous still, to give
Men courage to endure to live,
The gods have sealed the eye.*—Ed.*

58. Agnosco veteris vestigia flammæ.   Virg. A. 4, 23.*—I feel the traces of my ancient flame* (attachment).   Cf. Conosco i segni dell' antica fiamma.   Dante, Purg. 30, 48.

E'en in our ashes live their wonted fires.*—Gray,* "Elegy," st. 23.

59. Ah! frappe-toi le cœur, c'est là qu'est le génie. De Musset,
Œuvres, Paris (Bélin), 1818, p. 127.—*Ah! knock at thine heart,
'tis there that genius dwells.* Cf. Vauvenargues, *Réflex. et Max.*
No. 127, Les grandes pensées viennent du cœur.—*The great
thoughts come from the heart.*

60. Ahi! Constantin, di quanto mal fu matre,
Non la tua conversion, ma quella dote,
Che da te prese il primo ricco patre.   Dante, Inf. 19, 115.

> Ah, Constantine! to how much ill gave birth,
> Not thy conversion, but that plenteous dower,
> Which the first wealthy Father gained from thee.—*Cary.*

61. Ah! il n'y a plus d'enfants. Mol. *Mal. Imagin.* 2, 11 (Argant
loq.).—*Ah! there are no children nowadays!* Regret for the
simplicity of childhood of former ages.

> Une jeune fille de huit ans répondit un jour à sa mère qui voulait lui
> faire accroire que les enfants naissaient sous des choux : Je sais bien qu'ils
> viennent d'ailleurs.—Et d'où viennent ils donc, mademoiselle ?—Du ventre
> des femmes.—Qui vous a dit cette sottise ? Maman, c'est l' *Ave Maria.*
> Quit. p. 341-2.

62. Ahi! serva Italia, di dolor ostello,
Nave senza nocchier in gran tempesta,
Non donna di provincia, ma bordello.   Dante, Purg. 6, 76.

> Ah, slavish Italy! thou inn of grief!
> Vessel without a pilot in wild storm!
> Lady no longer of fair provinces,
> But brothel-house impure !—*Cary.*

63. Ah! le bon billet qu' a La Châtre! Ninon de Lenclos (1616-
1705).—*Ah! what a good letter La Châtre has got!* A billet à
la Châtre = any engagement that is not worth the paper it is
written on.

> Among the changing succession of Ninon's lovers was one Marquis de la
> Châtre (1633-1684), whose amours were rudely interrupted by summons to
> the seat of war. The man had the conceit to demand of her a written
> promise of "fidelity" during his absence! But it was ill kept, and,
> "à chaque fois qu'elle y manquait, s'écrioit-elle, Oh! le bon billet qu'a là
> La Chastre !" Questions and explanations ensued, with the result that
> poor La Châtre never heard the last of it. *Mémoires de St Simon,* ed.
> Boislisle, Paris, 1857, vol. xiii. p. 142 ; and Fumag. 1132.

64. Ah! pour être dévot, je n'en suis pas moins homme. Mol. Tart.
(1664), 3, 3, v. 966 (Tartuffe loq.).—*Ah! I'm religious, but I'm
none the less of a man for that reason.*

> Alex. points out (pp. 248-9) the obvious imitation of Corneille's
> "Sertorius" (1662), 4, 1 (v. 1194), "Ah! pour être Romain, je n'en suis
> pas moins homme," and of Boccaccio (Decam. Giornata iii. Novell. viii.),
> where the priest says to his fair penitent, "Oltre a questo, come che io sia
> Abate, io sono uomo come gli altri" (*Besides, granted that I am an Abbé,
> I am a man like the rest*).

65. Ah! que je fus bien inspiré,
Quand je vous reçus dans ma cour.
Marmontel, *Didon* (1783), (music by Piccini), 2, 3.—*What a
happy inspiration that was that made me invite you to my court!*

These were the verses, so Paul Gallot tells us in his *Un ami de la Reine* (Eng. transl., Lond., 1895, p. 31), in which Marie Antoinette, singing at her harpsichord, avowed her love for Count Fersen.

66. Aide-toi, le ciel t'aidera. La Font. 6, 18, Le Chartier embourbé.—*Help thyself and Heaven will help thee.* Regnier long before had said (Sat. 13), *Aidez-vous seulement et Dieu vous aidera.* Cf. the following—

αὐτός τι νῦν δρᾶ, χοὔτω δαίμονας κάλει,
τῷ γὰρ πονοῦντι χὠ θεός συλλαμβάνει. Eur. Fr. 435.

Bestir yourself and then call on the gods,
For heav'n assists the man that laboureth.

In Plaut. (Cist. 1, 1, 51) Gymnasium exclaims *Dii faxint!* ("The gods grant it!"); on which Lena rejoins, *Sine opera tua nihil Di horum facere possunt*—"'Grant it'! they can't unless you're up and doing yourself!"

67. Aἰὲν ἀριστεύειν καὶ ὑπείροχον ἔμμεναι ἄλλων. Hom. Il. 6, 208.— *Always to be best, and distinguished above the rest.* The charge given by Hippolochus to his son Glaucus when he sent him to Troy. Cic. (ad Quint. Fratrem. 3, 5) quotes it as a favourite line of his youth. Motto of Univ. of St Andrews.

68. Ai nostri monti ritorneremo,
L'antica pace ivi godremo ;
Tu canterai sul tuo liuto
In sonno placido io dormirò. Salvat. Camarano, *Trovatore*, 4, 3 (Azucena sings).—*We will return to our mountains, and there enjoy their ancient peace. You shall sing to your lute, and I will sleep undisturbed.* Music by Verdi.

69. Aio te, Aeacida, Romanos vincere posse. Ennius ap. Cic. Div. 2, 56, 116.—*I say the son of Æacus the Romans can defeat.* Instance of *Amphibolia* (ambiguous speech), from the response said to have been given (281 B.C.) by the Delphic Apollo to Pyrrhus, King of Epirus.

For other examples, cf. the oracle's reply to Crœsus, King of Lydia (545 B.C.), *Crœsus Halym penetrans magnam pervertet opum vim.* Cic. Div. 2, 56, 115.—"Crœsus by crossing the Halys will overthrow a large force," *i.e.*, his own. The "original" reply from Delphi, as preserved in Hdt. 1, 53, is, ἢν στρατεύηται ἐπὶ Πέρσας, μεγάλην ἀρχήν μιν καταλῦσαι.—*If he should go to war with Persia he would overthrow a great power.* Also, *Ibis, redibis, non morieris in bello* (Thou shalt go, thou shalt return never, thou shalt die in battle), which by a different punctuation may be made to give an exactly opposite meaning. When Edward II. was a prisoner at Berkeley Castle, the queen (Isabella) sent the following message (said to be written by Orleton, Bishop of Hereford) to the king's gaolers : *Edwardum occidere nolite timere bonum est.* Read one way, it would mean, "Beware of killing Edward : it is good to fear ;" but it might also signify, "Fear not to kill Edward : the deed is good." At a certain conventual council, one of the monks wrote his vote thus : "*Si omnes consentiant ego non dissentio*" ("If all agree, I do not disagree"); but when his words were claimed by the Ayes, he showed that they had been wrongly read : *Si omnes consentiant, ego non. Dissentio.* ("If all agree, I do not. I disagree.")

70. Αἱ περιστάσεις εἰσὶν αἱ τοὺς ἄνδρας δεικνύουσαι. Epictet. Dissertat. Lib. 1, c. 24.—*Circumstances* (or *a crisis*) *show the man*. The chapter is headed πῶς πρὸς τὰς περιστάσεις ἀγωνιστέον, and begins with the quotation.

Cf. Difficile est, fateor, sed tendit in ardua virtus. Ov. Ep. 2, 2, 113:— *'Tis hard, I own, but difficulties are what courage aims at.* Also, id., T. 4 3, 79.

Quæ latet inque bonis cessat non cognita rebus
Apparet virtus arguiturque malis.

Brave men in peace-time hide and take no heed;
Let trouble come, they'll up and show their breed.—*Ed.*

71. A la cour d'un tyran, injuste ou légitime,
Le plus léger soupçon tint toujours lieu de crime;
Et c'est être proscrit que d'être soupçonné.
Crébillon, Rhadamiste, 5, 2.—*At the court of a tyrant, whether usurped or legitimate, the least suspicion always amounts to crime, and to be suspected is to be proscribed.*

72. A la lanterne!—*To the lamp-post with him!*
Lynch-law cry of the French Revolution, first heard at the summary execution of Foulon (Bureau des Conseillers d'État)—the detested minister, famous for his remark that "the people should be too happy if they had only grass to eat," (*que le peuple était trop heureux de pouvoir brouter l'herbe*)—on July 22. 1789, at the Place de la Grève. The street-lamps then hung from a stout horizontal stanchion in the wall, like a sign-board, thus suggesting a ready-made gibbet (rope and all) for stringing up an offender. "*Pendu,*" the infuriated mob shouted, "*Pendu sur-le-champ!*" and hanged he was, and his head promenaded afterwards on a pike with a symbolical bunch of hay stuffed into the mouth. Next day (July 23) Barnave, defending the assassination in the National Assembly, asked "*Le sang qui vient de se répandre était-il donc si pur?*" ("Was it quite innocent, then, the blood that has just been shed?")—a remark which was remembered against the speaker, and risposted to his face at his own *guillotinement* four years later (Nov. 29, 1793). Hugou, *Mém. Hist. de la Rév.*, vol. 4, pp. 24-40; Fourn. *L.D.L.*, pp. 367-8; Alex., 466-7; and Chamf., vol. 3, pp. 147-9).

73. A l'amour satisfait tout son charme est ôté. T. Corn. Fest. de Pierre, 1, 2.—*All the charm of love vanishes once it is satisfied.*

74. Alea jacta est.—*The die is cast.*
Founded upon the *jacta alea esto* of Suet. Cæs. 32, "Let the die be cast!" Let the game be ventured! the memorable exclamation of Julius Cæsar, 49 B.C.—spoken in Gk., so Plutarch says—when, after long hesitation, he finally decided at the Rubicon (the Pisciatello) to march on Rome. *V.* Lew. and S., *s.v.* "Alea." Plut. Cæs. 32. p. 863, gives the saying as Ἀνερρίφθω κύβος, with which cp. the Δεδογμένον τὸ πρᾶγμ᾿ ἀνερρίφθω κύβος of Men. p. 880. "Judice fortuna cadat alea" is the poetical expression of Cæsar's saying in Petronius, Petr. 122, v. 173.

75. Aleator quanto in arte est (aptior), tanto est nequior. Syr. 33.
—*The more practised the gambler, the worse the man.*

Sic, ne perdiderit, non cessat perdere lusor,
Et revocat cupidas alea sæpe manus. Ov. A. A. 1, 451.

The Gambler.

He loses, loses, still in hope of gain:
"Just one more throw, to try my luck again!"—*Ed.*

Both these passages were cited by Abp. Thomson in his "Sermon on Gambling" at St Mary's, Oxf., Nov. 27, 1881.

76. *Alfana* vient *d'equus* sans doute ;
Mais il faut avouer aussi
Qu'en venant de là jusqu'ici
Il a bien changé sur la route. Jacques de Cailly ("D'Aceilly").
Recueil des . . . poëtes depuis Villon jusqu' a M. de Benserade
par Fs. Barbin. (5 vols.), Paris, 1692, 12°, vol. 1, p. 201.

Absurd Etymologies.

Alfana 's from *Equus*—of course ;
But perhaps you'll allow me to say
That, in coming so far, the poor horse
Has very much changed on the way.—*Ed.*

Epigrammatical skit on the etymological works of Giles Ménage (1613-1692). It is in his *Origini della lingua Italiana* (Paris, 1699, pp. 32-3) that his famous derivation of *Alfana* occurs, which proceeds thus : *equa, eka, aka, haka, faca, facana, fana* ; "et enfin, avec l'article Arabe, *Alfana.*" In the same way he derived *valet, laquais,* and *garçon* from the Latin *verna* —much as school-boys used to "derive" Pigeon from Eel-pie, thus :—*eel-pie, fish-pie, jack-pie, John-pie, pie-John, pigeon* [Alex. p. 78; Fumag. No. 1422 ; Fourn. *L.D.A.*, chap. xxxii.]

77. Aliæ nationes servitutem pati possunt, populi Romani est propria libertas. Cic. Phil. 6, 7, 19.—*While other nations can endure servitude, liberty is the prerogative of the Roman people.*

78. Aliena negotia centum
Per caput, et circa saliunt latus. Hor. S. 2, 6, 33.

For other people's matters in a swarm
Buzz round my head and take my ears by storm.—*Conington.*

79. Aliena nobis, nostra plus aliis placent. Syr. 28.—*Every one prefers other persons' things to his own.*

80. Alieni appetens, sui profusus, ardens in cupiditatibus; satis loquentiæ, sapientiæ parum. Sall. C. 5, 4.

Catiline.

While coveting the wealth of others, he was at the same time lavish with his own. A man of passionate desires, fluent enough in speech, but lacking wisdom.

81. Alieno in loco Haud stabile regnum est. Sen. Herc. Fur. 344.—*Sovereignty over an alienated people is insecure;* as, *e.g.*, the hold of Spain over her American colonies in the nineteenth century.

82. Alieno more vivendum 'st mihi. Ter. And. 1. 1, 125 (Simo loq.).
—*I have to live according to another's humour.*

83. A l'impossible nul n'est tenu. Prov. Quit. p. 463.—*No one can be obliged to do what is impossible.*

84. Alitur vitium vivitque tegendo. Virg. G. 3, 454.—*The evil is fostered and developed by concealment.*

85. Alles schon dagewesen. Karl Gutzkow, "*Uriel Acosta*," (Rabbi Ben Akiba, loq.).—*Everything has been already;* and there is nothing new under the sun. Büchm. p. 259.

86. Alles was ist, ist vernünftig.—*Everything that is, is reasonable.* Abbrev. form of Hegel's words (*Rechtsphilosophie*, 1821, Pref. p. 17), *Was vernünftig ist, das ist wirklich; und was wirklich ist, das ist vernünftig.* Cf. Pope, "Essay on Man," 1, 294 : "Whatever is, is right;" and Arist. N. Eth. 1, 8, 1. Büchm. pp. 228-9.

87. Ἀλλ' ἦ τοι μὲν ταῦτα θεῶν ἐν γούνασι κεῖται. Hom. Il. 17, 514.— *But in truth these things lie on the knees of the gods* The event is unknown.

88. Allons, enfants de la patrie! Rouget de Lisle.—*Come, children of our country!*
First words of *La Marseillaise*, composed, both words and music, by Joseph Rouget de Lisle on the night of April 24, 1792, after dining with Mayor Dietrich of Strasburg, and sung by him to his host next day. Its author called it *Chant de guerre de l'armée du Rhin*, and in the *Almanach des Muses* (Paris, 1793) it is styled "Le Chant des Combats." It was owing to the song having been taken up by the Marseilles volunteer contingent, the "Reds of the Midi," on their march to the capital in July '92, that it received its present name, and by so much identified itself with the spirit of anarchy. *V.* Alfred Leconte's *Rouget de Lisle, Sa Vie*, etc., Paris, 1892; Fourn. *L.D.A.*, chap. lxi., fin.; and Fumag. No. 629.

89. Allons, saute Marquis! Regnard, Joueur, 4, 10.—*Come, Marquis, jump for joy!* The soi-disant Marquis's self-congratulatory soliloquy.
Près du sexe tu vins, tu vis, et tu vainquis :
Que ton sort est heureux ! Allons, saute Marquis !

You come near the sex, see, and conquer—my boy!
You're the luckiest of mortals ! Jump, marquis, for joy !—*Ed.*

90. Allwissend bin ich nicht; doch viel ist mir bewusst. Goethe, *Faust* (Studirzimmer).
Meph. Omniscient am I not, though I know much.—*Ed.*

91. A l'œuvre on connaît l'artisan. La Font. 1, 21 (Les Frelons).— *By the work one knows the workman.*

92. Alta mane; supraque tuos exsurge dolores;
Infragilemque animum, quod potes, usque tene. Ov. ad Liv. 353.
Be brave, and rise superior to your woes,
And keep that spirit that no weakness knows.—*Ed.*

93. Alta sedent civilis vulnera dextræ. Luc. 1, 32.—*Deep-seated are the wounds of civil war.*

94. Alter ego. Cf. the "alterum me" of Cic. Fam. 2, 15, 4.—*A second self.* Said of intimate friends.
Cic. (Am. 21, 80) has *Est enim tanquam alter idem*, "A (true friend) is like a second self"; in Gr. we have the ἕτεροι αὐτοί (second selves) of Arist. N. Eth. 8, 12, 3 ; the saying of Zeno that a friend was "another I," ἄλλος ἐγώ (Diog. Laert. 7, 23) ; and the ὁ ἑταῖρος, ἕτερος ἐγώ of Clem. Alex. Strom. 2, 9. (163, 2).—*A comrade is another I.*

95. Alterius non sit qui suus esse potest. Gualterus Anglus (chaplain to Henry II. of England, and Abp. of Palermo), *Romuleæ fabulæ*, Fab. xxi., fin.(*De ranis regem petentibus*), publ. in Leopold Hervieux' *Les Fabulistes Latins*, Paris, 1884, vol. 2, p. 395 — *Let none be at the beck of another who can be his own master.*
Si quis habet quod habere decet, sit lætus habendo,
Alterius non sit, etc.

One of John Owen's (Audoenus) Epigrams (lib. 1, 13, p. 124), *Ad Henricum Principem* (P. of Wales, + 1612), runs,
Primum est esse suum ; tamen hoc cui fata negarunt,
Alterius non sit, qui Tuus esse potest.

96. Ama nesciri et pro nihilo reputari. A Kempis, 1, 2, 3.—*Love to be unknown, and to be reckoned as nothing.*

97. Amans semper, quod timet, esse putat. Ov. A. A. 3, 720.—*A lover always believes it to be as he fears.*

98. Amantes, amentes. Chil. p. 52.—*Lovers, Lunatics.* In Love, Insane. " Who loves, raves," Byron, *Ch. Har.*, 4, 123.

Taken from the *Inceptio est amentium, haud amantium* of Ter. Andr. 1, 3, 13. Cf. Amare et sapere vix deo conceditur. Syr. 22.— *To love and to be wise is hardly granted to the gods*; and " For to be wise and love exceeds man's might." Shakesp. *T. and Cressida*, 3, 2, 264 (Cressida loq.) ; also, Quum ames non sapias, aut quum sapias non ames. Syr. 117.—*If you are in love throw prudence to the winds, or else put love away if you would be serious.* *See* La Font. (Le Lion Amoureux), 4, 1.
Amour, amour, quand tu nous tiens,
On peut dire—Adieu, prudence!
and Bret, copying directly from P. Charron's *Sagesse*, has in his *École Amoureuse*, sc. 7 (Théatre de Mr Bret, Paris, 1778, i. 21),
Julie loq. : Le premier soupir de l'amour
Est le dernier de la sagesse.

99. Amantium iræ amoris integratio 'st. Ter. And. 3, 3, 23.—*Lovers' quarrels are but a renewal of their love.* Discordia fit carior concordia. Syr. 131.—*Discord makes the return to harmony all the sweeter.* Menand. (Mon. 410) has, ὀργὴ φιλοῦντος σμικρὸν ἰσχύει χρόνον.—*A lover's anger lasts but a little while.*

100. Amare autem nihil aliud est, nisi eum, ipsum diligere, quem ames, nulla indigentia, nulla utilitate quæsita. Cic. Am. 27, 100.—*To love is to esteem anyone for himself, apart from all question of need or of advantage.*

101. Ambitiosa non est fames. Sen. Ep. 119, 14.—*Hunger is not over nice.*

102. Ambo florentes ætatibus, Arcades ambo. Virg. E. 7, 4.—*Both in the flower of youth, Arcadians both.*

103. Amici vitia si feras, facias tua. Syr. 10.—*If you wink at your friend's vices, you make them your own.*

104. Amico d'ognuno, amico di nessuno. Prov.—*Every one's friend is no one's friend.* " A favourite has no friend."—*Gray.*

105. Amicorum esse communia omnia.   Prov. ap. Cic. Off. 1, 16, 51.
     —*Friends' goods are common property.*

> This refers to the saying of Bion—κοινὰ τὰ φίλων, Diog. Laert. 4, 53,
> and perhaps to Menelaus' words in Eur. Androm. 376, Φίλων γὰρ οὐδὲν
> ἴδιον, οἴτινες φίλοι 'Ορθῶς πεφύκασ', ἀλλὰ κοινὰ χρήματα.—"Friends who are
> truly friends, have nought that they may call their own, but all is shared
> alike." Cf. Ter. Ad. 5, 3, 17.—Vetus verbum hoc quidem est; Com-
> munia esse amicorum inter se omnia. (Micio): *'Tis an old saying, that
> friends enjoy all things in common. V.* Chil. p. 42.

106. Amicum Mancipium domino et frugi, quod sit satis, hoc est Ut
     vitale putes.   Hor. S. 2. 7, 2.—*A faithful servant to his master
     and an honest, as honesty goes, but not too good to live.*

107. Amicus certus in re incerta cernitur.   Enn. Incert: XLIII. (i.
     82).—*True friends are known by trouble.*

108. Amicus est Socrates, magister meus, sed magis est amica veritas.
     ap. Rog. Bacon, Opus Maj. 1, cap. vii.—*Dear to me is my
     master Socrates, but truth is dearer still.*   Tr. from Ammonius's
     Aristotelis Vita (ed. Westermann, p. 399), φίλος μὲν Σωκράτης,
     ἀλλὰ φιλτέρα ἡ ἀλήθεια.—"Socrates is a friend, but truth is
     dearer still."

> In Don Quixote, pt. ii. cap. 51, occurs, *Amicus Plato, sed magis amica
> veritas.*—Plato is my friend, but truth is dearer still. Cf. Plato, *Phædo*
> 40, p. 91, where Socrates says of himself, ὑμεῖς δὲ μέντοι, ἄν ἐμοὶ πείθησθε,
> σμικρὸν φροντίσαντες Σωκράτους, τῆς δὲ ἀληθείας πολὺ μᾶλλον.—*If you will
> be guided by me, you will make little account of Socrates, and much more of
> truth.*   Consideration for great names must not be allowed to weigh against
> truth; for, *Magna est veritas et prævalet.* Vulg. Esdras, 3, 4, 41.—Great is
> truth, and mighty above all things. [Büchm. p. 350, and Fumag. No. 1351.]

109. Amis, de mauvais vers ne chargez pas ma tombe.   Jean Passerat,
     Recueil, etc., par F. Barbin, Paris (Cl. Barbin), 5 vols., 1692,
     vol. 2, p. 114.—*Friends, I beg you not to load my tomb with bad
     verses.*   Last line of epitaph written for himself, the first stanza
     of which is as follows:—

> Jean Passerat icy sommeille,
>   Attendant que l'ange l'esveille;
> Et croit qu'il se resveillera
>   Quand la trompette sonnera.
> S'il faut que maintenant en la fosse je tombe,
>   Qui ay tousiours aymé la paix et le repos,
>   Afin que rien ne pèse à ma cendre et mes os,
> *Amis, de mauvais vers ne chargez pas ma tombe.*

> A Latin version is given in Passerat's *Kalendæ Ianuariæ,* etc., Paris
> (Cl. Morel), 1606, p. 248, of which the last lines are—

> Hoc culta officio mea molliter ossa quiescent,
>   Sint modo carminibus non onerata malis.

> Certainly, if his "friends'" verses were no better than this, the poet had
> some reason for the parting deprecation.

110. Amissum non flet, quum sola est Gellia, patrem;
       Si quis adest jussæ prosiliunt lacrymæ.
     Non dolet hic quisquis laudari, Gellia, quærit,
       Ille dolet vere, qui sine teste dolet.   Mart. 1, 34, 1.

Affected Grief.

Jane weeps not for her dad when none is by,
Yet when one enters she begins to cry.
Not by its wish for praise is true grief shown:
He mourns indeed who mourns when he's alone.—*Ed.*

Cf. Plerique enim lacrimas fundunt, ut ostendant; et toties siccos oculos habent, quoties spectator defuit. Sen. Tranq. 15.—*Very many shed tears merely for show; and have perfectly dry eyes when no one is looking on.*

111. Amitié, que les rois, ces illustres ingrats,
Sont assez malheureux pour ne connaître pas.
Volt. Henr., Chant 8.—*Friendship, which kings, as ungrateful as they are exalted, are unhappy enough not to know.*

112. Amittit merito proprium, qui alienum appetit. Phædr. 1, 4, 1.
—*Who covets another's goods. deservedly loses his own.* From the Fable of the Dog and its Shadow.

113. Amor mi mosse, che mi fa parlare. Dante, Inf. 2, 72.—*(Beatrice to Dante)*: "Love brought me thence, who prompts my speech."— *Cary.*

114. Amour, folie aimable; ambition sottise sérieuse. Chamf., vol. ii. 33.—*Love is a pardonable insanity; ambition, downright folly.*

115. Amour, tous les autres plaisirs
Ne valent pas tes peines. Charleval, Faucon de Ris (Sr. de), Chanson LXV. (Poésies de Saint Pavin et de Charleval, Amsterdam, 1739, 12°, p. 72).—*O love, thy pains are worth more than all other pleasures put together.*

The preceding lines are:

Bien que mes espérances vaines
Fassent naître en mon cœur d'inutiles désirs,
Bien que tes lois soient inhumaines,
Amour, tous les autres plaisirs
Ne valent pas tes peines.

The Pleasing Pain.

Though my hopes are but idle and vain,
 Though my fears and desires are at strife,
And though harsh and inhuman thy reign—
 Yet the rest of the pleasures of life
Cannot match, Love, the bliss of thy pain.—*Ed.*

116. Am Rhein, am Rhein, da wachsen uns're Reben! M. Claudius.
—*The Rhine, the Rhine, there grow our vines!* The "Rhine-wine Song," beginning *"Bekränzt mit Laub,"* etc., first published in the Vossischen "Musenalmanach" for 1776. Music by J. André. Büchm. 153.

117. Ἀνάγκᾳ δ᾽ οὐδὲ θεοὶ μάχονται. Pittacus. Diog. Laert. 1, 77.— *Even the gods do not battle against necessity.* Needs must when the d—— drives. Cf. Hom. Il. 4, 300.

118. Anch' io sono pittore!—*I too am a painter!* Exclamation of Correggio before the St Cecilia of Raphael in the Ch. of S. Giovanni del Monte, Bologna.

As an historical saying, the words have been much disputed, and anyone who wishes to sift the merits of the case should consult Pungileoni's *Memorie istoriche di Antonio Allegri detto il Correggio*, Parma, 1817, vol. i. p. 60, and the *Correggio* of Julius Meyer, Leipsic, 1871, p. 23. After all, what does it matter whether Correggio made the exclamation or not? The *mot* remains.

119. Ἀνέχου καὶ ἀπέχου.   Gell. 17, 19.—*Bear and forbear*   (In Lat., Sustine et abstine.)

The two words which summed up Epictetus's Golden Rule of life; meaning that true peace of mind is to be had by "bearing" injuries and by "forbearing" pleasures. In this, its true sense, the maxim is of real moral value: unhappily, the words in common parlance have dropped into a mere jingle, which, if it means anything, implies the recognition of mutual rights—a totally different question.

120. Ἀνὴρ ὁ φεύγων καὶ πάλιν μαχήσεται.   Menand. Mon. 45. (qu. by Demosthenes when reproached for running away at the battle of Chæronea, 338 B.C.   Gell. 17, 21, 9).

He who fights and runs away,
May live to fight another day.—*Goldsmith*, "Art of Poetry," etc., 1761.

Tertullian, de Fuga in Persecutione, cap. 10, quotes "Illum Græcum versiculum, Qui fugiebat, rursus præliabitur."—*He who fled will fight again.*

121. Anglica gens, optima flens, pessima ridens.   *Reliquiæ Hearnianæ*, ed. P. Bliss, 1869, i. 140.—*The English people are best at weeping, worst at laughing.*   Is it possible that this may be an echo, or the source, of the med. saying traditionally ascribed to Froissart, that the English *s'amusent moult tristement?*

122. Animæ dimidium meæ.   Hor. C. 1, 3, 8.—*The half of my life.* Horace thus speaks of Virgil.   In Gr., ἁμισύ μευ ψυχῆς, Meleager, Anthol. Pal. 2, 464.

123. Animula, vagula, blandula,
Hospes, comesque corporis,
Quæ nunc abibis in loca
Pallidula, rigida, nudula;
Nec. ut soles, dabis jocos!   Spart. Hadr. 25.—(Hist. Aug.).

The Dying Emperor to his Soul.
Ah! gentle, fleeting, wavering sprite,
Friend and associate of this clay!
To what unknown region borne,
Wilt thou now wing thy distant flight?
No more with wonted humour gay,
But pallid, cheerless, and forlorn.—*Lord Byron.*

124. Animum pictura pascit inani.   Virg. A. 1, 464.
He feeds his spirit on the pictured scene.—*Ed.*

125. Animus æquus optimum est ærumnæ condimentum.   Plaut. Rud. 2, 3, 71.—Trachalio loq.: *Patience is the best seasoning for trouble.*   What can't be cured must be endured.

126. Animus quod perdidit optat,
Atque in præterita se totus imagine versat.   Petr. Sat. 128.—
The mind longs for what it has lost, and is wholly occupied in conjuring up the past.   Useless regrets.

127. An nescis longas regibus esse manus? Ov. H. 17, 166.—*Don't you know that kings have long arms?* The ramifications of the machinery of State are so widely extended as to be able to track an offender on a distant shore.

128. An nescis, mi fili, quantilla prudentia regitur orbis? Axel Oxenstierna (J. F. af Lundblad, Svensk Plutark, Stockholm, 1826, pt. ii. p. 95, Note).—*Dost thou not know, my son, with how very little wisdom the world is governed?*

> The original is, "Vet du icke, min son, med huru liten wishet verlden regeras," and was addressed by the great Swedish statesman to his son John, on the latter hesitating to accept the post of Plenipotentiary at the Conference of Münster, 1648, which concluded the Treaty of Westphalia and terminated the 30 years' war. Büchm. pp. 466-7, citing from a coll. of Apophthegms published at Lisbon, 1733, makes Julius III. (1550-55) the author of the words, in conversation with a Portuguese friar who commiserated the Pope on the burden of his world-wide responsibilities. Selden seems to be referring to the same story when (Table Talk, *art.* POPE) he tells of a certain Pope who welcomed a friend of former days with, "We will be merry as before, for thou little thinkest what *a little foolery governs the whole world.*"

129. Annuimus pariter vetuli notique columbi. Hor. Ep. 1, 10, 5.— *We bill and coo like two familiar doves.* Conington.

130. Annus mirabilis.—*A year of wonders,* or *the wonderful year.*

> Thus 1797 is called the *annus mirabilis* of Coleridge, being that in which he composed his finest poems. 1871 may be called the *annus mirabilis* of the Papacy, as the year in which the reigning pontiff attained and passed the twenty-five years of St Peter; and 1897, as commemorating the longest reign of any English sovereign. Dryden has a poem of this name, treating of the events of the year 1666, which witnessed the fire of London, and the gallant attack on the Dutch fleet led by Prince Rupert.

131. An quisquam est alius liber, nisi ducere vitam
Cui licet, ut voluit? Pers. 5, 83. (Dama, the enfranchised slave, loq.).—*Can any man be considered free, except he is free to live as he likes?*

132. Ans Vaterland, ans teure, schliess dich an,
Das halte fest mit deinem ganzen Herzen,
Hier sind die starken Wurzeln deiner Kraft. Schiller, W. Tell, 2,1.

> Cling to the land, the dear land of thy sires,
> Grapple to that with all thy heart and soul!
> The power is rooted deep and strongly here.—*Sir T. Martin.*

133. Ante mare, et tellus, et, quod tegit omnia cœlum,
Unus erat toto naturæ vultus in orbe,
Quem dixere Chaos; rudis indigestaque moles. Ov. M. 1, 5.

> Ere sea, and land and heaven's vault were made,
> Nature, throughout the globe, bore one aspect,
> Called chaos—a rude and undigested mass.—*Ed.*

134. Ante oculos errat domus, Urbs, et forma locorum;
Succeduntque suis singula facta locis. Ov. T. 3, 4, 57.—*My home, the town, and each well-known spot comes before me; and*

B

each item of the day follows in its proper place. Realising in absence what is taking place at home.

135. Ἄνθρωπός ἐστι ζῶον δίπουν, ἄπτερον, πλατυώνυχόν. Diog. Laert. 6, 40.—*Man is a two-footed animal, wingless and flat-nailed.* Plato's definition, the addition of "flat-nailed" being Diogenes' suggestion in order to make the description complete.

136. Ἄνθρωπος (ὁ) φύσει πολιτικὸν ζῷον. Arist. Pol. 1, 2, 9.—*Man is by nature a political animal.*

137. Antiquitas sæculi, juventus mundi. Prov. ap. Bacon, De Augm. lib. i. (vol. 7, 81).—*The olden time was the world's youth.*

On this Bacon says: These times are the ancient times, when the world is ancient, and not those which are accounted ancient *ordine retrogrado*, by a computation backward from ourselves.

Cf. Lord Tennyson, *Day Dream.*

We are ancients of the earth
And in the morning of the times.

138. Aperte mala quum est mulier, tum demum est bona. Syr. 20.— *When a woman is openly bad, then at least she is honest.*

139. Apis Matinæ More modoque. Hor. C. 4, 2, 27.—*Like Matinata's busy bee.*

140. Apparent rari nantes in gurgite vasto. Virg. A. 1, 118.—*A few appear, swimming in the vasty deep.* Used of such authors, or passages, as have survived the wreck of time; or where a good work, painting, or line of poetry appears amongst an ocean of rubbish.

141. Apparet id quidem etiam cæco. Liv. 32, 34, 3.—*Even a blind man can see that;* or, as related in Polyb. 17, 4, τοῦτο μέν, ὦ Φαινέα, καὶ τυφλῷ δῆλον—*One can see that with half an eye.* Rejoinder of Philip V. (of Macedon) to the one-eyed Ætolian commander, Phæneas, in the 2nd Maced. War, 198 B.C.

142. Après nous le déluge !—*After us, the deluge!*

Després (J. B. D.) in his *Essai sur la Marquise de Pompadour*, (Biblioth. des Mémoires rél. à l'Hist. de France pendant le XVIIIᵉ Siècle, ed. Fs. Barrière, Paris, 1846, vol. iii. p. 33), says, "Mme. de Pompadour dans l'ivresse de la prospérité, répondait à toutes les menaces de l'avenir par ces trois mots, qu'elle répétait souvent : Après nous, le déluge." Ch. Desmaze in his *Le Reliquaire de M. Q. de La Tour* (Paris, 1874, p. 62, note) confirms this on the authority of de La Tour, who heard the Marquise use the expression himself, and told the story to Mdlle Fel, the singer. The excellent Larousse (*Fleurs Historiques*, Paris, 5th ed., n.d., pp. 46-7) cites Henri Martin, the historian (without any references whatever), for a reported conversation between Louis XV. and his favourite, in which the king expressed his anxiety about the disturbing elements of the time—the clergy, the philosophers, and—above all—the parliaments, which he declared "finiront par perdre l'État. Ce sont des assemblées de républicains! Au reste, les choses comme elles sont, dureront bien autant que moi. Berry (the Dauphin, aft. Louis XVI.) s'en tirera comme il pourra. *Après moi le déluge!*" Martin's own version of the conversation differs from this, and omits the critical words. (*Hist. de la France*, 1853, vol. 18, p. 103.)

The sentiment itself was anticipated by Nero, who on hearing some one repeat the line, Ἐμοῦ θανόντος γαῖα μιχθήτω πυρί ("When I am dead let earth with fire mingle"), rejoined, "Immo, ἐμοῦ δὲ ζῶντος" (*Aye, and while I am alive too!*): and, as Suetonius (Nero 38) goes on to say, "so it came about, for without any attempt at concealment he proceeded to set the city on fire." The passage is from Phrynichus, *Incert. Fab.* 5, 17 (in Wagner's ed., Paris, *Poet. Trag. Gr. Fragmenta,* p. 16), the complete distich being:—

> ἐμοῦ θανόντος γαῖα μιχθήτω πυρί,
> οὐδὲν μέλει μοι· τἀμὰ γὰρ καλῶς ἔχει.

> When I am dead let th' earth be fused with fire !
> I care not, I ; for things go well with me.—*Ed.*

Claudian makes Rufinus exclaim:—

> Everso juvat orbe mori ; solatia letho
> Exitium commune dabit.   Rufin. 2, 19.

> So the world perish, I'll not ask to live ;
> Comfort in death the general doom will give.—*Ed.*

143. Aquilæ senectus. Ter. Heaut. 3, 2, 10.—*The old age of the eagle.   A vigorous old age.*

144. Aquila non captat muscas, or ἀετὸς μυίας οὐ θηρεύει. Apost. 1, 144 (Contemptûs et vilitatis).—*An eagle don't hawk flies:* and ibid. Elephantus non capit murem.—*Elephants don't catch mice.* Great minds should be above resenting petty provocations.

145. A raconter ses maux, souvent on les soulage.   Corn. Polyeucte, 2, 4.—*To tell our troubles is often the way to lighten them.*

146. Araignée le matin, chagrin : midi, souci : le soir, espoir.   Prov.— *If you find a spider in the morning, it betokens trouble : at noon, it means anxiety : in the evening, hope.*

147. Arbeit macht das Leben süss.   G. W. Burmann, Kleinen Liedern für kleine Jünglinge, Berlin, 1777.—*Labour makes life all the sweeter.*

148. Arbeit, Mässigkeit, und Ruh
Schlägt dem Arzt die Thüre zu.   Prov.
> Labour, Temperance, and Repose
> Slam the door on the Doctor's nose.—*Ed.*

149. Arbiter bibendi.—*The toast-master.*   Like the Greek βασιλεὺς τοῦ συμποσίου (king of the feast).   Cf. Quem Venus arbitrum Dicet bibendi ? Hor. C. 2, 7, 25.—*Whom shall the dice appoint as chairman of the carouse ?*   (2.) Arbiter elegantiarum.—*Judge of taste.*   Cf. Elegantiæ arbiter. Tac. A. 16, 18—said of one of Nero's intimates, presumably Petronius "Arbiter."   (3.) Arbiter es formæ. Ov. H. 16, 69.—*You are the* (or *a*) *judge of beauty.*   Mercury to Paris, appointing him to award the prize to the most fair.

150. Arcanum neque tu scrutaberis ullius unquam ;
Commissumque teges, et vino tortus et irâ.   Hor. Ep. 1, 18, 37.

> Avoid all prying : what you're told, keep back,
> Though wine and anger put you on the rack.—*Conington.*

151. Arenæ funis effici non potest.   Col. 10, præf. § 4.—*You can't make a rope of sand.*   (2.) Arena sine calce. Suet. Cal. 53.— *Sand without lime.*   Said by Caligula of the Tragedies of Seneca, from their unconnected character; and applicable to any desultory, disjointed performance.

152. Ἀρετὴ δὲ, κἂν θάνῃ τις, οὐκ ἀπόλλυται,
ζῇ δ᾽ οὐκέτ᾽ ὄντος σώματος· κακοῖσι δὲ
ἅπαντα φροῦδα συνθανόνθ᾽ ὑπὸ χθονός.   Eur. Fr. 722.

> Virtue's not killed at death.   The body dies
> But virtue lives; while all that bad men had
> Dies with them, and is clean gone underground.—*Ed.*

153. Argentum accepi, dote imperium vendidi.   Plaut. As. 1, 1, 74.— *I have received her dowry, and in return have parted with my authority.*   The fate of one who has married for money.

154. Arguit, arguito: quicquid probat illa, probato:
Quod dicet, dicas: quod negat illa, neges.
Riserir, arride: si flebit, flere memento;
Imponat leges vultibus illa tuis.   Ov. A. A. 2, 199.

> *To a Lover.*
>
> Blame, if she blames; but if she praises, praise.
> What she denies, deny; say what she says.
> Laugh, if she smiles; but if she weeps, then weep,
> And let your looks with hers their motions keep.—*Ed.*

155. Ἄριστον μὲν ὕδωρ.   Pind. Ol. 1, 1.—*Water is best.*   Inscription over the Pump-room at Bath.

156. Ars artium omnium conservatrix.—*The art that preserves all other arts*, viz., printing.   Inscription on façade of Laurent Koster's house at Haarlem, 1540.

157. Ars longa, vita brevis.—"*Art is long and time is fleeting.*" Longfellow.

> The orig. (Hippocrates, Ἀφορίσμοι, 1, 1) reverses the order, ὁ βίος βραχὺς, ἡ δὲ τέχνη μακρή, ὁ δὲ καιρὸς ὀξὺς, ἡ δὲ πεῖρα σφαλερὴ, ἡ δὲ κρίσις χαλεπὴ (*Life is short and art long; the occasion brief and the experiment hard, and the issue severe*); which Seneca (Brev. vit. 1, 1) renders, *Vita brevis, longa ars;* and Chaucer (*Assembly of Fools*, 1)—
>
> > The life so short, the craft so long to lerne,
> > Th' assay so hard, so sharpe the conquering.

158. Ars varia vulpi, ast una echino maxima.   Prov.   Tr. from the πόλλ᾽ οἶδ᾽ ἀλώπηξ, ἀλλ᾽ ἐχῖνος ἕν μέγα, of Plut. Mor., p. 1189 (de Sollert. Animal. c. 16).—*The fox has various devices, but the hedgehog only one, though it is the greatest,*—viz., to roll itself up in a ball.   (2.) Multa novit vulpis, sed felis unum magnum. Prov. ap. Bacon, De Augm., vi. 3, Sophisma XII.—*The fox knows many tricks, but the cat one great one,*—viz., to run up a tree.

159. Arte magistra.   Virg. A. 8, 442.—*By the aid of art.*

160. Ἄσβεστος γέλως.   Hom. Il. 1, 599.—*Unquenchable laughter,* or, *Homeric laughter.*

161. A soixante ans il ne faut pas remettre
L'instant heureux qui promet un plaisir.
    Désaugiers, *Dîner de Madelon*, Sc. II.

> At sixty years old 'tis not well to postpone
> E'en a moment that promises joy.—*Ed.*

> Désaugiers' Vaudeville came out at the *Variétés*, Paris, 6th Sept. 1813
> (music by Tourterelle); and the above are the first lines of the song of
> Benoît, "ancien patissier." Alex. 427.

162. Asperitas agrestis et inconcinna gravisque,
Quæ se commendat tonsa cute, dentibus atris
Dum volt libertas dici mera veraque virtus. Hor. Ep. 1, 18, 6.

> A brutal boorishness, which fain would win
> Regard by unbrushed teeth and close-shorn skin,
> Yet all the while is anxious to be thought
> Pure independence, acting as it ought.—*Conington.*

163. Asperius nihil est humili, quum surgit in altum. Claud. Eutr.
1, 181.—*Nothing so odious as a clown that has risen to power.*
"Set a beggar on horseback," etc.

164. Aspettare e non venire,
Stare in letto e non dormire,
Ben servire e non gradire,
Son tre cose da morire. Bruno, *Candelaio*, 4, 1 (S. Vittoria loq.).

> To wait for one who ne'er comes by,
> To be in bed and sleepless lie,
> To serve, and not to satisfy,
> Are reasons three to make one die.—*Ed.*

165. At est bonus ut melior vir
Non alius quisquam; at tibi amicus, at ingenium ingens
Inculto latet hoc sub corpore. Hor. S. 1, 3, 32.

> But he's the soul of virtue: but he's kind;
> But that coarse body hides a mighty mind.—*Conington.*

166. Ἀθανάτους μὲν πρῶτα θεούς, νόμῳ ὡς διάκεινται, Τιμά. Fragment.
Philosoph. Gr., ed. Mullachius, Paris (Didot), 1860, vol. i. p. 193.
One of the "golden sayings" of the Pythagoreans.—*Pay rever-
ence, first of all, to the immortal gods, as is laid down by law.*
The Established Religion. Motto of Spectator, 112 (Sunday
at Sir Roger's).

> First in obedience to thy country's rule,
> Worship the immortal gods.

167. Ἄθλα δὲ τῶν κότινος, μῆλα, σέλινα, πίτυς. Anth. Pal. 9, 357.—
The (victors') crowns are wild olive. apples, parsley, and pine.
The prizes respectively given at the four great national Hellenic
games—Olympian, Pythian, Isthmian, and Nemean. Ausonius
(Eclog. de Lustral. Agonibus) puts the subj. into Latin with:

> Quatuor antiquos celebravit Achaia ludos:
> Cælicolum duo sunt, et duo festa hominum.
> Sacra Jovis, Phœbique, Palæmonis, Archemorique;
> Serta quibus pinus, malus, oliva, apium.

168. At non ingenio quæsitum nomen ab ævo
     Excidet: ingenio stat sine morte decus.   Prop. 3, 2, 23.
> Time cannot wither talents' well-earned fame:
> True genius has secured a deathless name.—*Ed.*

169. At pulchrum est digito monstrari et dicier, Hic est.   Pers. 1, 28.
     —*It's a fine thing to be pointed out with the finger, and for people
     to say, There he is!* Love of notoriety. Cf. Monstror digito
     prætereuntium. Hor. C. 4, 3, 22.—*I am pointed out by the finger
     of passengers.*

170. Atque aliquis posita monstrat fera prælia mensa,
     Pingit et exiguo Pergama tota mero.
     Hac ibat Simois: hic est Sigeïa tellus;
     Hic steterat Priami regia celsa senis.   Ov. H. 1, 31.
> At dinner, some will fight their fights again,
> And with some drops of wine all Troy explain.
> Here Simois runs: this, the Sigeian land:
> Here Priam's lofty palace used to stand.—*Ed.*

Applicable to maps or plans indicated on the table or on paper
by conventional signs. Boswell writes (Croker ed., 1853, p. 240)
—" Dr Johnson said, 'Pray, General (Oglethorpe), give us an
account of the siege of Belgrade.' Upon which the general,
pouring a little wine upon the table, described everything with
a wet finger: 'Here we were: here were the Turks,' etc., etc.
Johnson listened with the closest attention." *See* also Shakesp.
Taming of the Shrew, 3, 1, where the last two lines of the
passage are quoted.

171. Atque in rege tamen pater est.   Ov. M. 13, 187.
> And yet he feels the father in the king.—*Ed.*

Said of Agamemnon, unwilling, even at the beheṣt of Diana, to
sacrifice his daughter Iphigenia.

172. At qui legitimum cupiet fecisse poema,
     Cum tabulis animum censoris sumat honesti:
     Audebit, quæcunque parum splendoris habebunt
     Et sine pondere erunt, et honore indigna ferentur,
     Verba movere loco.   Hor. Ep. 2, 2, 109.
> But he who meditates a work of art,
> Oft as he writes will act the censor's part:
> Is there a word wants nobleness and grace,
> Devoid of weight, nor worthy of high place ?
> He bids it go though stiffly it decline,
> And cling and cling like suppliant to a shrine.—*Conington.*

173. Atqui vultus erat multa et præclara minantis. Hor. S. 2, 3, 9.—
     And yet you had the air of one that promised many fine things.

174. At scio, quo vos soleatis pacto perplexarier;
     Pactum non pactum est; non pactum pactum est, quod vobis
     lubet.   Plaut. Aul. 2, 2, 81.—*I know the way you have of con-
     fusing things; a bargain's no bargain, or no bargain's a bargain*

—just as it pleases you. Euclio to Megadorus when the latter announces that his daughter is to have no portion.

175. At secura quies, et nescia fallere vita,
Dives opum variarum; at latis otia fundis,
Speluncæ, vivique lacus; at frigida Tempe,
Mugitusque boum, mollesque sub arbore somni
Non absunt. Virg. G. 2, 467.

Country Life.
Untroubled peace, a life untaught to cheat,
And rich in varied wealth; a calm retreat
'Mid ample fields; cool grots and running lakes;
Valleys like Tempe's dewy lawns and brakes,
Soft lowing herds, and sleep beneath the plane—
These are the pleasures of the country swain.—*Ed.*

176. At vindicta bonum vitâ jucundius ipsa.
Nempe hoc indocti, quorum præcordia nullis
Interdum aut levibus videas flagrantia causis;
Quantulacunque adeo est occasio, sufficit iræ. Juv. 13, 180.

Revenge is Sweet.
Revenge is sweet, dearer than very life:
At least fools think so; fools so fond of strife
That none or little cause sets them a-fire;
However slight, it serves to rouse their ire.—*Ed.*

177. At vos incertam, mortales, funeris horam
Quæritis, et qua sit mors aditura via;
Quæritis et cœlo Phœnicum inventa sereno,
Quæ sit stella homini commoda, quæque mala. Prop. 2, 27, 1.

Fortune Telling.
Into death's hidden hour ye mortals are prying,
Searching what is the way ye shall come to your end.
To interpret the teaching of planets ye're trying—
Which star is man's enemy, which is his friend.—*Ed.*

178. Auctor nominis ejus Christus, Tiberio imperitante, per procura-
torem Pontium Pilatum, supplicio affectus erat; repressaque in
præsens exitialis superstitio rursum erumpebat, non modo per
Judæam, originem ejus mali, sed per urbem etiam, quo cuncta
undique atrocia aut pudenda confluunt celebranturque. Tac. H.
15, 44.—*Christ, the leader of the sect, had been put to death by the
procurator Pontius Pilate in the reign of Tiberius. The deadly
superstition was for the moment suppressed: but it broke out again;
infecting not only Judæa, the original seat of the evil, but even Rome
—the general sink for all the abominations and infamies of the
world at large to collect together and run riot in.* Celebrated passage
of the Roman historian, in which the death of Our Blessed
Lord and the gradual spread of Christianity are mentioned.

179. Aucun chemin de fleurs ne conduit à la gloire. La Font. 10, 14
(Les Deux Aventuriers).—*No path of flowers leads to glory.*
Cf. Non est ad astra mollis e terris via. Sen. Herc. Fur. 437.
(Megara to Lycus).—*There is no velvet path to reach the stars.*

180. Audacem fecerat ipse timor. Ov. F. 3, 644.—*Fear made her bold.* Cf. Audendo magnus tegitur timor. Luc. 4, 702.—*Under a show of daring great fear is concealed.*

181. Aude aliquid brevibus Gyaris et carcere dignum,
Si vis esse aliquis. Probitas laudatur et alget.　　Juv. 1, 73.

　　Dare a life sentence—prison, or the mines,
　　If you'ld be some one: virtue's praised and—pines.—*Ed.*

182. Audentes Fortuna juvat.　Virg. A. 10, 284.—*Fortune favours the brave.*

　　Cf. Fortes fortuna adjuvat. Ter. Phorm. 1, 4, 26.—*Fortune aids the brave.* Fortibus est fortuna viris data. Ennius ap. Macrob. S. 6, 1, 62.— *Good fortune is given to brave men.* Fortes enim non modo fortuna juvat, ut est in vetere proverbio, sed multo magis ratio. Cic. Tusc. 2, 4, 11.—*It is not only fortune that "favours the brave," as the old prov. says, but much more prudence.* Fortuna fortes metuit, ignavos premit. Sen. Med. 159.—*Fortune fears the brave, and crushes the coward.* Fortuna meliores sequitur. Sall. H. 1, 48, 15.—*Fortune befriends the better man.* Fortuna, ut sæpe alias, virtutem secuta est. Liv. 4, 37.—*Fortune, as is not uncommon, befriended valour.* Οὐ τοῖς ἀθύμοις ἡ τύχη συλλαμβάνει. Soph. Fr. 666.—*Not with the craven does fortune co-operate.* Audentes deus ipse juvat. Ov. M. 10, 586.—*Heaven itself helps the brave.* Of boldness in love:—Audendum est: fortes adjuvat ipsa Venus. Tib. 1, 2, 16.—*We must venture it: Venus herself assists the brave;* and Audentem Forsque Venusque juvant. Ov. A. A. 1, 608.—*Fortune and Venus befriend the daring.*

183. Au diable tant de maîtres, dit le crapaud à la herse.　Prov.— *The devil take so many masters, as the toad said to the harrow!*

184. Audi alteram partem.　Law Max.—*Hear the other side.* No man should be condemned unheard.

　　Cf. Qui statuit aliquid parte inaudita altera,
　　Æquum licet statuerit, haud æquus fuerit. Sen. Med. 198.—*Whoever shall decide a question without hearing the other side, even though he decide justly, will not act with justice.* (2.) ἦ πού σοφὸς ἦν ὅστις ἔφασκεν, πρὶν ἂν ἀμφοῖν μῦθον ἀκούσῃς, οὐκ ἂν δικάσαις. Ar. Vesp. 725.—*Certainly he was wise who declared, Never pronounce until you have heard both sides of the story;* and (3.) Μηδὲ δίκην δικάσῃς πρὶν ἀμφοῖν μῦθον ἀκούσῃς. Pseudophocylidea, p. 93.—*Never adjudge any case till you hear both sides of the question.*

185. Auditis?　An me ludit amabilis Insania?　Hor. C. 3, 4, 5.

　　Did ye hear? Or is some sweet delusion mine?—*Calverley.*

186. Auferimur cultu: gemmis auroque teguntur
Omnia; pars minima est ipsa puella sui.　Ov. R. A. 343.

　　　　　　　　　　Dress.

　　Dress but deceives—all jewels, gold and pelf;
　　A girl is oft the least part of herself.—*Ed.*

187. Augurium ratio est, et conjectura futuri:
Hac divinavi, notitiamque tuli. Ov. T. 1, 9, 51.—*Reason is my augury and forecast of the future; by her aid have I divined events, and got my knowledge of what is to come.*

188. Aurea nunc vere sunt sæcula; plurimus auro
Venit honos: auro conciliatur amor.   Ov. A. A. 2, 277.

The Age of Gold.
Joking apart, this is the age of gold;
Love, place, preferment—all is bought and sold.—*Ed.*

189. Aurea prima sata est ætas, quæ vindice nullo,
Sponte sua, sine lege, fidem rectumque colebat.
Pœna metusque aberant.   Ov. M. 1, 89.

The Golden Age.
First came the Golden Age, that without lord
Or law kept justice of its own accord :
All fear of punishment was still unknown.—*Ed.*

190. Aut amat, aut odit mulier, nihil est tertium.   Syr. 6.—*A woman
either loves or hates; there is no medium.*

191. Autant de langues que l'homme sçait parler, autant de fois est
il homme.   Charles V., qu. in Donaldson's *New Cratylus*, p. 10
(1839): "*For every language that a man learns he multiplies his
individual nature,* and brings himself one step nearer to the
general collective mind of Man" (Donaldson tr.).   Vambéry,
Travels in C. Asia, 1864, p. 219, qu. the prov. "quot linguas
cales (calles ?), tot homines vales."

192. Aut bibat aut abeat.   Cic. Tusc. 5, 41, 118.   In Gr., ἢ πῖθι, ἢ
ἄπιθι.—*Either drink or depart.*
Cicero quotes this old rule of Gk. feasts as the maxim he had ever
observed when Fortune frowned.   By retiring, (he says), "Injurias fortunæ
quas ferre nequeas, diffugiendo relinquas."—*The rude blows of fortune which
you are unable to encounter, you may by flight leave behind you.*

193. Aut Cæsar aut nihil.—*Either Cæsar or nothing.*
Cæsar Borgia, nat. son of Alexander VI., born 1476, killed in a sortie at
Mendavia, Navarre, 1507; the most notorious adventurer of his day.   His
chosen device was the quotation; either alone (Paolo Giovio, *Ragionamento
sopra i motti e disegni d'arme, etc..* Milan, 1863, p. 5), or surmounted by a
Cæsar holding orb in hand (Carlo Yriarte, *Autour des Borgia,* Paris, 1891,
p. 114).   A. M. Graziani, in his *Theatrum Hist. de virtutibus, etc., Ill. Vir-
orum,* Francofurti, 1661, says, "Nominis sui omen secutus, superbum vex-
illis titulum, *Aut Cæsar, aut nihil,* inscribi jussit."   Cæsar Borgia's brief
but extraordinary career, combined with his boastful motto, produced more
than one contemp. epigram.   Fausto Maddalena has (*v. P. Giovio, supra*):

Borgia Cæsar erat ; factis et nomine Cæsar ;
Aut nihil aut Cæsar, dixit, utrumque fuit.

Borgia was Cæsar—name, and deeds : he quoth,
"Cæsar or nothing" ; and the fool was both.—*Ed.*

And Jacopo Sannazaro writes (*Epigr. Del.,* p. 363) :

Aut nihil aut Cæsar, vult dici Borgia : quidni ?
Quum simul et Cæsar posset, et esse nihil ?

"Cæsar *or* nothing!" Borgia would be thought :
Why ? since he can both Cæsar be *and* nought.—*Ed.*

Stanford *s.v.* traces the idea of the quotation to the saying of C. J. Cæsar to his mother on the eve of his candidature for the office of Pontifex Maximus (63 B.C.), that he would "return home as Supreme Pontiff, or not at all." Plut. *Cæs.* 7, 1; Suet. *Julius*, 13; and Fumag. No. 883.

194. Aut disce, aut discede: manet sors tertia cædi.—*Learn, Leave, or be Licked.*

Inscription on a large board in the schoolroom of Winchester College. Over *Disce* are represented the rewards of learning—mitre and crosier; over *Discede* the symbols of the alternative professions of the army and the law; and over *Cædi* the "bibling-rod" of four apple twigs. Leach, *Hist. of Winchester Coll.*, London, 1899, p. 123.

195. Aut insanit homo, aut versus facit. Hor. S. 2, 7, 117.—*The man is either mad, or else he's writing verses.* Davus' (Horace's slave) description of his master's eccentric and irregular habits.

196. Aut non tentaris, aut perfice. Ov. A. A. 1, 389.—*Either carry it through, or don't make the attempt at all.*

197. Auto da fé.—*An act of faith.*

Name popularly given to the execution of those condemned by the tribunals of the Inquisition in Portugal and Spain in the 16th and 17th centuries. The *Auto* itself was an examination conducted by the Inquisitors, the object of which was to reconcile the erring to the Church; those who were willing to abjure their errors making a public recantation, or *Auto da fé* (act of faith): the "relaxed," *i.e.*, those who persisted in their heresy, being delivered to the secular arm, and in many cases burnt.

198. Aut prodesse volunt aut delectare poetæ,
Aut simul et jucunda et idonea dicere vitæ. Hor. A. P. 333.

A bard will wish to profit or to please,
Or, as a *tertium quid*, do both of these.—*Conington.*

199. Aut regem aut fatuum nasci oportere. Sen. Apoc. init.—*One ought to be born either a king or a fool,*—sc. to have unlimited licence allowed one. *V.* Chil. pp. 399-400.

200. Autres temps, autres mœurs. Prov.—*Other days, other ways.*

201. Aux petits des oiseaux il donne leur pâture,
Et sa bonté s'étend sur toute la nature. Rac. Ath. 2, 7.

For the hungry young nestlings His providence fends,
And over all nature His goodness extends.—*Ed.*

The parody of the second line, *Mais sa bonté s'arrête à la littérature*, ("But His bounty draws the line at authors"), is ascribed to Léon Gozlan in Maxime du Camp's *Souvenirs Littéraires*, i. 226. Alex. p. 353.

202. A vaincre sans péril, on triomphe sans gloire. Corn. Le Cid. 2, 6 (1636).—Rodrigue loq.: *To conquer without risk is to triumph without glory.* George de Scudéry's *Arminius*, 1, 3 (1644), has, "Et vaincre sans péril seroit vaincre sans gloire."

203. Avant dix ans toute l'Europe peut être cosaque, ou toute en république. Napoleon, April 18, 1816. Las Cases' "Mémorial de Ste Hélène," 1828, vol. 3, p. 111.—*Before ten years Europe may be all Cossack (Russian), or else a series of republics.*

204. Ave! Imperator, morituri te salutant. Suet. Claud. 21.—
Hail! Emperor, those who are about to die salute you! Greet-
ing of the combatants to the Emperor Claudius at a naval
contest on the Lago Fucino. Claudius, instead of "Valete,"
replied, "*Avete vos,*" as bidding them farewell: but the gladiators
taking it in its usual sense, as, "*Live! Long life to you,*"
refused to proceed with the show.

205. Avenio ventosa: sine vento venenosa; cum vento fastidiosa.
Prov.—*Windy Avignon; unhealthy without wind, and with it*
(the Mistral) *unbearable.*

206. Avia Pieridum peragro loca, nullius ante
Trita solo. Juvat integros accedere fontis
Atque haurire, juvatque novos decerpere flores,
Insignemque meo capiti petere inde coronam,
Unde prius nulli velarint tempora Musæ:
Primum quod magnis doceo de rebus et artis
Religionum animum nodis exsolvere pergo,
Deinde quod obscura de re tam lucida pango
Carmina, musæo contingens cuncta lepore. Lucr. 1, 925.

The New Poetry.
Be it mine t' explore the Muses' devious ground
As yet untrod ; to drink at virgin springs
And cull new flowers to make a special wreath
Was never twined before for mortal brows.
For, first, I seek—upon an arduous theme—
To loose the mind from superstition's bonds ;
Next, to put clearly a question most obscure,
And touch it all with true poetic grace.—*Ed.*

B.

207. Barbarus hic ego sum, quia non intelligor ulli :
Et rident stolidi verba Latina Getæ. Ov. T. 5, 10, 37.

The Traveller in Foreign Parts.
I'm a foreigner here on this shore,
For none understand what I say.
At my Latin the Thracian boor
Only laughs in his thick-headed way.—*Ed.*

208. Beati gli occhi che la vider viva. Petrarch, Son. in Morte di M.
Laura, 268.—*Blessed are the eyes that saw her (Laura) alive!*

209. Beati possidentes.—*Blessed are those that possess* (or *are* "*in possession*"), regarded from the point of view of one debarred
from such enjoyment.

The doctrine that "possession is nine points of the law" has taken the
shape of a "ninth" Beatitude in legal maxims—*Beati in jure censertur
possidentes*—which is apparently derived from Horace's *Non possidentem,*
etc. (*q.v.*), and of which, it will be observed, it is the exact opposite.

210. Beatus ille qui procul negotiis,
　　 Ut prisca gens mortalium,
　　 Paterna rura bobus exercet suis,
　　 Solutus omni fœnore.　　Hor. Epod. 2, 1.

　　　　　The Bliss of Country Life.
　　　　Happy the man who far from town,
　　　　(Like one of earth's primeval nations,)
　　　　Ploughs his own land—with team his own,
　　　　Untroubled by the last quotations.—*Ed.*

211. Behüte dich Gott! es wär' zu schön gewesen,
　　 Behüte dich Gott! es hat nicht sollen seyn. Victor v. Scheffel,
　　 Trompeter von Säkkingen (1854), Pt. 14.

　　　　　Bless you! it would have been too beautiful:
　　　　　Bless you! 'twas fated not to be.—*Ed.*

212. Bei Geldfragen hört die Gemütlichkeit auf.　David Hansemann.
　　 —*Where it's question of money, all good nature ends.*　Often qu.
　　 (*v.* Büchm. p. 537) as "In Geldsachen hört, etc."

213. Bekker schweige in sieben Sprachen.　Friedr. D. E. Schleier-
　　 macher; qu. in Halm's *Nekrolog auf Immanuel Bekker*
　　 ("Sitzungbericht der bayerisch. Akad. d. Wissenschaft," 1872,
　　 p. 221).—*Bekker is silent in seven languages.*

　　　Schleiermacher's witty *mot* upon the celebrated philologist, of whom, in
　　his *Correspondence with Goethe* (vol. 5, p. 413) Zelter wrote (in Letter of
　　March 15, 1830), "Bekker, den sie den stummen in sieben Sprachen
　　nennen."—*Bekker, whom they call the dumb man in seven languages.*
　　Büchm. p. 226.

214. Bélier, mon ami, lui dit le géant en l'interrompant, si tu voulais
　　 commencer par le commencement, tu me ferois plaisir; car
　　 tous ces récits qui commencent par le milieu, ne font que
　　 m'embrouiller l'imgination.　Hamilton (Count Anthony), author
　　 of the Grammont Memoirs—*Le Belier*, Œuvres, Paris, 1812,
　　 vol. 2, p. 153.—"*Bélier, my good friend,*" interrupted the
　　 giant Moulineau, "*if you would begin at the beginning I should
　　 be much obliged; for all stories that begin in the middle only
　　 confuse the mind.*"

215. Bella gerant alii; tu, felix Austria, nube:
　　 Nam quæ Mars aliis, dat tibi regna Venus.—Qu. in Sir W.
　　 Stirling-Maxwell's *Cloister Life of Charles V.*, chap. i. p. 3, note.

　　　　Fight those who will, let well-starred Austria wed;
　　　　And conquer kingdoms in the marriage-bed.—*W. Stirling-Maxwell.*

　　　The first words of this well-known distich are from Ovid's Her. 13, 84.
　　(Laodamia and Protesilaus), *Bella gerant alii: Protesilaus amet.* When
　　and by whom the quot. was composed is unknown (see Büchm. 407);
　　although it probably belongs to the 16th century, and to the sudden rise
　　of the house of Hapsburg by the fortunate marriages of Maximilian I.
　　(1459-1519), his son Philip (†1506), and grandson Ferdinand (1503-1564),
　　which united the Spanish and Austrian succession, and added the Nether-
　　lands, Hungary, and Bohemia to the domain of the Hapsburgs.

216. Bella! horrida bella! Virg. A. 6, 86.—*War! horrible war!*

> Multos castra juvant, et lituo tubæ
> Permixtus sonitus, bellaque matribus
> Detestata. Hor. C. 1, 1, 23.

Some love the camp, the clarion's joyous ring,
And battle, by the mother's soul abhorred.—*Conington.*

217. BELLUM *joined with* PAX.—*War and Peace.*

(1.) Bellum ita suscipiatur, ut nihil aliud nisi pax quæsita videatur. Cic. Off. 1, 23, 80.—*If a war is undertaken, it should be shown that peace is the only object sought to be gained.* (2.) Suscipienda quidem bella sunt ob eam causam, ut sine injuria in pace vivatur. Cic. Off. 1, 11, 35.—*An honourable peace should be the object for engaging in any war.* (3.) Pax paritur bello. Nep. Epam. 5.—*War is the road to peace.* (4.) Qui desiderat pacem, præparet bellum. Veg. Mil. Prol. 3.—*If you want peace, be prepared for war.* Commonly qu. as, "Si vis pacem, para bellum." (5.) Miseram pacem vel bello bene mutari. Tac. A. 3. 44.—*Even war is a preferable alternative to a shameful peace.* (6.) Vel iniquissimam pacem justissimo bello anteferrem. Cic. Fam. 6, 6, 5.—*I should prefer peace even on the most unfavourable terms to the justest war that was ever waged.*

218. Bellum omnium contra omnes. Hobbes, Leviathan, Cap. 18.—*All warring against all.* A general mêlée. Anarchy.

219. Βέλτιόν ἐστιν ἅπαξ ἀποθανεῖν, ἢ ἀεὶ προσδοκᾶν. Plut. Cæs. 57.—*Better die once than always live in apprehension.* Recorded saying of Julius Cæsar, which Shakespeare renders "Cowards die many times before their deaths: The valiant never taste of death but once" (2, 2).

220. BENEFICIUM.—*A favour; kindness.* Service; gift.

(1.) Beneficium non in eo quod fit aut datur, consistit, sed in ipso dantis aut facientis animo. Sen. Ben. 1, 6.—*A favour does not consist in the actual service done or given, but in the feeling that prompted it.* (2.) Tempore quædam magna fiunt, non summa. Sen. Ben. 3, 8.—*The value of gifts depends not so much on the amount, as the time when they are given.* (3.) Bene facta male locata, male facta arbitror. Enn. Incert. 44.—*Favours injudiciously conferred are only so much injury.* Indiscriminate charity. (4.) Sunt quædam nocitura impetrantibus; quæ non dare, sed negare, beneficium est. Sen. Ben. 2, 14.—*Where the gifts would be injurious to those who seek them, to refuse instead of granting, is a real kindness.* (5.) Nullum beneficium esse duco id, quod, quoi facias, non placet. Plaut. Trin. 3, 2, 12.—*I do not consider that a kindness, which gives no pleasure to the person you show it to.* (6.) Un bienfait reproché tient toujours lieu d'offense. Rac. Iphig. 4, 6.—*To reproach a man with favours conferred is tantamount to an affront.* (7.) Un bienfait perd sa grâce à le trop publier. Corn. Théod. 1, 2.—*A favour loses its grace by publishing it too loudly.*

> (8.) Crede mihi, quamvis ingentia, Postume, dona
> Auctoris pereunt garrulitate sua. Mart. 5, 52, 7.

Great are your gifts, but when proclaimed around,
The obligation dies upon the sound.—*Hay.*

(9). Un service au dessus de toute récompense A force d'obliger tient presque lieu d'offense. Corn. Suréna, 3, 1.—*A service which exceeds all possibility of returning it, becomes an obligation so great that it almost amounts to an injury.* (10.) Leve æs alienum debitorem facit, grave inimicum. Sen. Ep. 19.—*A small debt makes a man your debtor, a large one makes him your enemy.* (11.) Qui grate beneficium accepit, primam ejus pensionem solvit. Sen. Ben. 2, 22.—*To accept a kindness with gratitude is to take the first step towards returning it.* (12.) Beneficium accipere libertatem est vendere. Syr. 48.—*To accept a favour is to barter one's liberty.*

221. Bene mones; tute ipse cunctas caute.   Enn., vol. i. p. 323.—*You give good advice, but you take good care not to follow it yourself.*

222. Benigno ai suoi ed a nemici crudo.   Dante, Par. 12, 27. —*"Gentle to his own, and to his enemies terrible."* Cary.   Said of St Dominic, and probably copied from Eur. Med. 809, where Medea describes herself in the same terms—βαρεῖαν ἐχθροῖς, καὶ φίλοισιν εὐμενῆ. Cf. Shakesp. *H. VIII.*, 4, 2.   "Lofty and sour to those that lov'd him not, But to those men that sought him sweet as summer."

223. Ben tetragono ai colpi di ventura.   Dante, Par. 17, 24.—*Firm and four-squared against fortune's blows.*   Cf. Tennyson (*D. of Wellington*), "That tower of strength Which stood four-square to all the winds that blew!"

224. Benutzt den Augenblick.—*Seize the present moment!* Favourite maxim of Goethe.   Cf. Horace's *Carpe diem, etc.*, and·Herrick's "Gather ye roses while ye may, etc."

225. Bernardus valles, colles Benedictus amabat,
     Oppida Franciscus, magnas Ignatius urbes.   Med. Distich.

Religious Orders.

Bernard the vale, Benedict the hill approved;
Francis the town, great cities Ignatius loved.—*Ed.*

Memorial verse, particularising the different situations respectively affected, for their houses, by the Cistercians, Benedictines, Franciscans, and Jesuits.

226. Bis.—*Twice.*   Proverbial sayings depending on:

(1.) Inopi beneficium bis dat qui dat celeriter. Syr. 235.—*He gives a double favour to a poor man, who gives quickly.*   Hence (2.) Bis dat qui cito dat.—*He gives twice, who gives at once.*

Si bene quid facias, facias cito; nam cito factum
   Gratum erit; ingratum gratia tarda facit.   Aus. Epigr. 83.

Your gifts give quickly: gratitude awaits
The ready giver; slowness breeds ingrates.

(3.) Bis peccare in bello non licet.—*It is not allowed to make a mistake in war more than once.*   Cf. δὶς ἐξαμαρτεῖν ταὐτὸν οὐκ ἀνδρὸς σοφοῦ. Menand. Mon. 121.—*No wise man will commit the same fault twice.* (4.) Bis vincit qui se vincit in victoria. Syr. 64.—*He conquers twice who conquers himself in the hour of victory.*

227. Blinder Eifer schadet nur.   Lichtwer, Fabeln, Bk. 1, Fab. 22 (Die Katzen u. der Hausherr), fin.—*Blind zeal only does harm.* Büchm. p. 142.

228. Bologna la grassa, Firenze la bella, Genova la superba, Lucca l'indústriosa, Mantua la gloriosa, Milano la grande, Padova la forte, Pavia la dotta, Venezia la gran mendica, Verona la degna. —*Bologna the rich (or fat), Florence the beautiful, Genoa the superb, Lucca the busy, Mantua the glorious, Milan the grand,*

Padua the strong, Pavia the learned,Venice the great beggar,Verona the worthy. The cities of North Italy, with their distinguishing titles.

229. Bona nemini hora est, ut non alicui sit mala. Syr. 49.—*No hour that brings happiness to one, but brings sorrow to another.*

230. Bon chien chasse de race. Prov.—*A well-bred dog hunts by nature.* Breeding "tells."

231. Bon dieu ! l'aimable siècle où l'homme dit à l'homme,
Soyons frères, ou je t'assomme. Lebrun (Ponce Denis Écouchard), Epigr. 5, 23. Œuvres, Paris, 1811, vol. 3, p. 236.

> *Fraternité, ou la Mort!*
> 1793.
> Heav'ns ! what a sweet age, when one says to another,
> I'll kill you if you don't own me for a brother !—*Ed.*

Chamfort it was, who, disgusted with the sanguinary excesses of '92 and '93, paraphrased this watchword of the Revolution in the mot, "Sois mon frère, ou je te tue " ; with the result that, with other duly reported "malignancies," he was frightened into suicide, April 13, 1794. No one mourned him, and no one deserved to perish more justly than he on the altar of a Revolution the fires of which he had assiduously helped to kindle.

232. Boni pastoris est tondere pecus, non deglubere. Suet. Tib. 32, fin. —*It is the duty of a good shepherd to shear his flock, not flay them.* Reply of Tiberius to Provincial Governors advocating increase of taxation; with which may be compared the Letter of Edward III. to Clement VI. (1343), on the extravagant Papal "Provisions" of that day, in which he reminds the successor of St Peter that his Divine commission extended only *ad pascendum, non ad tondendum oves dominicas* (to the feeding, and not the shearing of the sheep of Christ). Walsingham, Hist. Angl., p. 162.

233. Bonum summum quo tendimus omnes. Lucret. 6, 26.—*That sovereign good at which we all aim.*

234. Briller par son absence.—*To be conspicuous by one's absence.*

Tacitus (A. 3, 76), speaking of the funeral of Junia, wife of Cassius, says: "Sed præfulgebant Cassius atque Brutus, eo ipso quod effigies eorum non videbantur."—*Brutus and Cassius, however, were all the more conspicuous from the fact of the busts of neither being seen in the procession.* Chénier (Joseph), in his *Tibère* (1, 1), translates the historical episode into verse:
> Devant l'urne funèbre on portait ses aieux:
> Entre tous les héros qui, présents à nos yeux,
> Provoquaient la douleur et la reconnaissance,
> *Brutus et Cassius brillaient par leur absence.*

235. Bruta fulmina et vana, ut quæ nulla veniant ratione naturæ. Plin. 2, 43, 113.—*Thunderbolts that strike blindly and harmlessly, being traceable to no natural cause.*

A *brutum fulmen* is used metaphorically of any loud but idle menace An inoperative law. The idea is that of some terrestrial Jupiter whose bolts have lost their potency.

C.*

236. Cædimus, inque vicem præbemus crura sagittis:
Vivitur hoc pacto.   Pers. 4, 42.

> Life consists in kicking others'
> Shins, and letting them kick ours.—*Shaw.*

237. Cælo tegitur qui non habet urnam.   Luc. 7, 819.

> *The Unburied Dead.*
> The vault of heaven
> Doth cover him who hath no funeral urn.—*Ed.*

238. Cælum non animum mutant qui trans mare currunt.
                           Hor. Ep. 1, 11, 27.

> *Change of Scene.*
> Who fly beyond the seas will find
> Their climate changed, but not their mind.—*Ed.*

Ὅστις ἐστὶν οἴκοι φαῦλος, οὐδέποτ᾽ ἦν ἐν Μακεδονία καλὸς κἀγαθός· οὐ γὰρ τὸν τρόπον ἀλλὰ τὸν τόπον μετήλλαξεν. Æschines in Ctes. 78.—*The man who at home is a paltry fellow, was never yet made a gentleman of by going to Macedonia; he changed his country, not his character.*

239. Cæsarem vehis Cæsarisque fortunam.   Suet. Cæs. 58, not., and Plut. Cæs. 38. Καίσαρα φέρεις, καὶ τὴν Καίσαρος τύχην.—*You carry Cæsar and Cæsar's fortunes.*

> The traditional reply of Cæsar to the mariner, Amyclas, when overtaken by tempest as he was secretly crossing from Durazzo to Brindisi (50 B.C.) in an open boat. The man declared he would go no farther. Cæsar, grasping his hand, bade him fear nothing. "Perge audacter, Cæsarem vehis, etc." —*Go on boldly, you carry Cæsar*—as above.
>
> Lucan (5, 577) renders the incident in verse:—
>
> > Fisus cuncta sibi cessura pericula Cæsar
> > Sperne minas, inquit, pelagi, ventoque furenti
> > Trade sinum. Italiam si cælo auctore recusas
> > Me pete. Sola tibi causa hæc est justa timoris
> > Vectorem non nosse tuum.
>
> > *Cæsar and the Mariner.*
> > Reckoning all dangers to surmount
> > Cæsar replied, Make little count
> > Of threatening sea or furious gale,
> > But boldly spread the bellying sail.
> > And if in spite of Heaven's acclaim
> > Thou would'st turn back, then ask my name.
> > There's a just reason for thy fears,
> > Thou know'st not whom thy vessel bears.—*Ed.*

240. Ça ira, ça tiendra!—*It will go, it will catch on!*   'Twill be a success.

* Including the Greek X (Chi).

"Benj. Franklin, when young France importuned him in 1776-7 with inquiries as to the prospects of the American War of Independence, was wont to reply, *Ça ira*. His phrase became a watchword of freedom in Paris, and now the Revolution took it up and marched to its music." Edith Sichel, *Household of the Lafayettes*, Lond., 1897, p. 107. The famous revol. "hymn" (*Ça ira! les aristocrates à la lanterne!*) was composed by Ladré, with Bécourt's music, and was called the "Carillon National." Fourn. *L.D.L.*, p. 406 n.

241. Calomniez! calomniez! il en restera toujours quelque chose. Beaum. Barb. de Sév. 2, 8 (Basile to Bartholo).—*Calumniate away! Some of the slander will always fasten on.*

Bacon, de Augm. 8, 2, 34 (vii. 415), says, Audacter calumniare, semper aliquid hæret.—*Calumniate boldly, some of it is sure to stick.* Identical sayings will be found in Manlius' *Locorum Comm. Collectanea* (Basileæ, 1563), vol. ii. p. 268; and in Caspar Peucer's *Historia Carcerum* (Tiguri, 1605), p. 57; both being referred to one Medius, a flatterer at the court of Alexander the Great, who enforced the use of slanderous accusation with the argument that, κἂν θεραπεύσῃ τὸ ἕλκος ὁ δεδηγμένος, ἡ οὐλὴ μενεῖ τῆς διαβολῆς, Plut. Mor. p. 78 (de Adulatore, c. 24), *Even if the bitten man's wound should heal, the scar of the accusation remained behind.* Büchm. 449-50.

242. Calumniari si quis autem voluerit,
    Quod arbores loquantur, non tantum feræ;
    Fictis jocari nos meminerit fabulis.   Phædr. 1, Prol. 5.

Æsop's Fables.
But if the critics it displease
That brutes should talk, and even trees,
Let them remember I but jest,
And teach the truth in fiction drest.—*Ed.*

243. Candida, perpetuo reside, concordia, lecto,
    Tamque pari semper sit Venus æqua jugo:
    Diligat illa senem quondam; sed et ipsa marito,
    Tunc quoque quum fuerit, non videatur anus.   Mart. 4, 13, 7.

Marriage Wishes.
Sweet concord ever o'er their home preside,
And mutual Love the well-matched couple guide:
May she love him when time hath touched his hair,
And he, when she is old, still think her fair.—*Ed.*

244. Candidus in nauta turpis color: æquoris unda
    Debet et a radiis sideris esse niger.   Ov. A. A. 1, 723.

The Sailor.
I hate a fair-skinned sailor: he should be
Tanned brown with wind and sun and the salt sea.—*Ed.*

245. Cane decane canis: sed ne cane, cane decane,
    De cane: de canis, cane decane, cane.   Sandys' *Specimens of Macaronic Poetry*, Lond., 1831, 8vo, Introd. p. ii.—*You sing, grey-haired dean; but sing not, grey-haired dean, of dogs (sport): rather sing of grey-haired men, grey-haired dean!* Attrib. to Porson. Perhaps prompted by some college dean of the name of Hoare, who was fonder of hunting-songs than became his calling.

C

246. Cane mihi et Musis.   Val. Max. 3, 7, Ext. 2.—*Sing to me and the Muses.*

> Antigenidas, the flute player, having a pupil who in spite of his proficiency did not please the public, said one day to him in the hearing of all the audience, "Mihi cane et Musis."—*Play to me and the Muses!*

247. CANIS.—*A dog.*   Proverbial expressions connected with :

> (1.) Cane pejus et angui. Hor. Ep. 1, 17, 30.—*Worse than a dog or snake.*   (2.) Canina eloquentia. Quint. 12, 9, 9. (Cf. Canina facundia, Appius ap. Sall. H. Fragm. 2, 37 Dietsch.)—*Dog-oratory.* Snarling, abusive. (3.) Cave canem. Petr. 29.—*Beware of the dog.*   Warning inscription to trespassers.   (4.) Ut canis e Nilo.—(*To drink*) *like a Nile dog—i.e.,* quickly, to avoid being snapped up by crocodiles.   Macrobius (Sat. 2, 2, 7) relates how, after Antony's defeat at Mutina (43 B.C.), when it was asked what he was doing, it was answered, *Quod canis in Ægyptu: bibit et fugit.* ("Like the Nile dog: he drank and ran away").
>
> > Canes currentes bibere in Nilo flumine,
> > A corcodilis ne rapiantur, traditum est.—*Phædr.* 1, 25, 3.
> > They say that dogs "drink running" at the Nile,
> > For fear of being snapt up by crocodile.
>
> (5.) Canis a corio nunquam absterrebitur uncto. Hor. S. 2, 5, 83.—*You will never scare a dog away from a greasy hide.*   Bad habits stick closely. (6.) Canis in præsepi.— *The dog in the manger.*   In Gr. ἡ ἐν τῇ φάτνῃ κύων. Lucian, Timon. 14; cf. Anth. Pal. 12, 236; and Æsop, Fab. 228, ed. Halm, (κύων κ. ἵππος).

248. Cantabit vacuus coram latrone viator.   Juv. 10, 22.—*The traveller, whose pockets are empty, will sing in the presence of robbers.*

249. Cantat vinctus quoque compede fossor,
> Indocili numero cum grave mollit opus.
> Cantat et innitens limosæ pronus arenæ,
> Adverso tardam qui trahit amne ratem.   Ov. T. 4, 1, 5.
>
> > The convict shackled by his chains,
> > His labour cheers with artless strains:
> > Or sings as bent by oozy marge,
> > He slowly drags against the stream the barge.—*Ed.*

250. Cantilenam eandem canis. Ter. Phorm. 3, 2, 10.—*You are singing the same (old) song.*   Cf. Citharædus Ridetur chorda qui semper oberrat eadem.   Hor. A. P. 355,

> > The harp-player who for ever wounds the ear
> > With the same discord, makes the audience jeer.—*Conington.*

251. Caput mundi.—*The head of the world.*   Applied anciently to Imperial and, later, to Papal Rome; Ipsa, caput mundi Roma. Luc. 2, 655   Caput imperii. Tac. H. 1, 84 —*Head of the Empire;* and, Caput rerum, id. A. 1, 47.—*Centre of civilisation.*

> The Latin poets vied with one another in adding new titles of honour to the world's capital. Tibullus (2, 5, 23) calls her *Æterna urbs;* Virg. (G. 2, 534) *pulcherrima Roma;* Propertius (3, 13, 60) *Superba.* To Horace, Rome is *ferox* (C. 3, 3, 44), *beata* (C. 3, 29, 11), *princeps urbium* (C. 4, 3, 13), and *Roma domina* (C. 4, 14, 44). Statius (S. 1, 2, 191) styles her *septemgemina,* the city of the seven hills; and Auson. (Urb. 1, 1) *Prima urbes inter, divûm domus, aurea Roma.*

252. Carmina proveniunt animo deducta sereno;
Nubila sunt subitis tempora nostra malis.
Carmina secessum scribentis et otia quærunt;
Me mare, me venti, me fera jactat hiems.
Carminibus metus omnis abest: ego perditus ensem
Hæsurum jugulo jam puto jamque meo.   Ov. T. 1, 1, 39.

> Poems the offspring are of minds serene;
> My days are clouded with ills unforeseen.
> Poems retirement need and easy leisure;
> Sea, winds and winter tease me at their pleasure.
> Poems must have no fears; I, luckless wight,
> Fancy the knife is at my throat each night.—*Ed.*

253. Carmina spreta exolescunt; si irascare, agnita videntur.   Tac.
A. 4, 34.—*Treat a libel with contempt, and it will pass away;
resent it, and you seem to admit its application.*

254. Carmine di superi placantur, carmine Manes.   Hor. Ep. 2, 1, 138.

> The gods above, the shades below, are both appeased by song.—*Ed.*

255. Caseus est nequam quia concoquit omnia sequam.
Caseus ille bonus quem dat avara manus.   Coll. Salern. i. 390 and
387.   *Cheese is injurious, because it digests all other things with
itself. Cheese when given with a sparing hand is wholesome.*   One
of the hygienic precepts of the School of Salerno, from a poem
in leonine verse, called *Regimen* (or *Flos*) *Sanitatis.* Sæc. XI.

256. Castigat ridendo mores—Abbé Jean de Santeul.   Santoliana,
etc., par M. Dinouart, Paris (Nyon), 1764, 12mo, p. 73.—*He
corrects morals by ridicule.*

> Inscription composed (1665) for portrait (? bust) of Domenico Biancolelli,
> then playing Harlequin in the "Troupe Italienne" Paris, by Santeul, the
> celebrated epigrammatist of the day.   The characteristic and original *ruse*
> by which "Arlequin Doménique" drew from the witty and eccentric Abbé
> the desired epigram will be found in the above reference.   The words were
> subsequently adopted by the Comédie Italienne and Opéra Comique of
> Paris, and by the San Carlino of Naples, 1770.   *V.* also Fumag. No. 239.

257. Castum esse decet pium poetam
Ipsum: versiculos nihil necesse est.   Cat. 16, 5.

> A poet should be chaste himself, I know:
> But nought requires his verses should be so.—*Ed.*

258. Casus ubique valet; semper tibi pendeat hamus:
Quo minime credas gurgite, piscis erit.   Ov. A. A. 3, 425.

> *Luck.*
> There's always room for chance, so drop your hook;
> A fish there'll be where least for it you look.—*Ed.*

> *Semper T. P. H.* (above), legend of a James II. (and Queen) medal, struck
> 1687, commemorating W. Phipps' successful recovery of sunken treasure
> (£300,000) off Hispaniola.

259. Cato contra mundum.—*Cato against the world.*

> This saying and the similar one (*Athanasius contra mundum*) is quoted
> of any man who, like Cato in his ineffectual struggle against Cæsar, or

Athanasius in his single-handed defence of the truth, champions an un-
popular and desperate cause in the face of general public opinion. Lucan
(1, 128) expresses the same idea in verse:

Victrix causa diis placuit, sed victa Catoni.

The conquering side had Heaven's applause,
But Cato chose the losing cause.—*Ed.*

Cicero, writing to Atticus (4, 15, 8), says, "Plus unus Cato potuerit quam
omnes quidem judices," (*Cato will single-handed have more influence than all
the judges*); and cf. the common remark of Augustus (Suet. 87), *Contenti
simus cum Catone* ("Let us be content with the maxim of Cato"), on the
duty of resigning oneself to the existing condition of things.

260. Caton se le donna.   Socrate l'attendit. Lemierre, Barnevelt, 4, 7.
   —(Stautembourg) *Cato's death was self-inflicted.* (Barnevelt, his
   father).—*Socrates waited till it came.*

261. Causa latet, vis est notissima.   Ov. M. 4, 287.
   The cause is hidden, its effect most clear.—*Ed.*

262. Caveat emptor, quia ignorare non debuit quod jus alienum emit.
   Law Max.—*Let a purchaser beware, for he ought not to be
   ignorant of the nature of the property which he is buying from
   another party.*
   The maxim *Caveat Emptor* applies in the purchase of land and goods,
   with certain restrictions, both as to the *title* and *quality* of the thing sold.
   Out of the legal sphere, the phrase is used as a caution in the case of any
   articles of doubtful quality offered for sale.

263. Cedant arma togæ, concedat laurea linguæ.   Cic. Off. 1, 22, 77.—
   *Let arms give place to the long robe, and the victor's laurel to the
   tongue of the orator.*   Sometimes said of the diplomatic discus-
   sions which follow upon, and not unfrequently fritter away, the
   successes gained in the field.   *V.* Lew. & S., *s.v.* "Laureus."

264. Cedant carminibus reges, regumque triumphi. Ov. Am. 1, 15, 33.
   To verse must kings, and regal triumphs yield.—*Ed.*

265. Cede repugnanti: cedendo victor abibis. Ov. A. A. 2, 197.—
   Yield to your opponent: by yielding you will come off conqueror.
   A prudent concession is often tantamount to a victory.

266. Cedite Romani scriptores, cedite Graii,
   Nescio quid majus nascitur Iliade.   Prop. 2, 34, 65.

The Æneid.
Your places yield, ye bards of Greece and Rome,
A greater than the Iliad has come!—*Ed.*

267. Cedunt grammatici, vincuntur rhetores.   Omnis
   Turba tacet.   Juv. 6, 438.—*The philologists are dumb, the rheto-
   ricians worsted, and the whole circle silent*, while Messalina
   descants upon the comparative merits of Homer and Virgil.

268. Cela ne va pas: cela s'en va.   Fontenelle, in his last illness, to
   one who asked how he was "going on" (*Comment cela va-t'-il?*).
   Chamf. 1, 95.—*I am not going on: I am going off.*

269. Célébrité! l'avantage d'être connu de ceux qui ne vous connaissent pas. Chamf. Max., vol. 2, 29.—*Celebrity! the honour of being known by those who know you not.*

270. Ce n'est ni le génie, ni la gloire, ni l'amour qui mesurent l'élévation de l'âme: c'est la bonté. Lacordaire, ap. Mrs Bishop's *Life of Mrs Augustus Craven,* vol. 2, p. 280.—*Nobility of soul is not a question of genius, or glory, or love: its real secret is kindness.*

271. Ce n'est plus qu'à demi qu'on se livre aux croyances;
Nul dans notre âge aveugle et vain de ses sciences,
Ne sait plier les deux genoux. V. Hugo, Les deux Archers.

The Decay of Faith.

We believe but by halves in this wise age of ours,
So blind, and so vain of its science and powers;
None will bend both his knees to the ground.—*Ed.*

272. Centum doctum hominum consilia sola hæc devincit dea
Fortuna, atque hoc verum est: proinde ut quisque fortuna utitur
Ita præcellet; atque exinde sapere eum omnes dicimus.
Plaut. Ps. 2, 3, 12.

Fortune.

Dame Fortune will of herself upset the plans
Of a hundred wiseacres—and that's the truth.
As each trades with his chance, so he'll excel;
And then we all say, What a clever man!—*Ed.*

273. Centum solatia curæ
Et rus, et comites et via longa dabunt. Ov. R. A. 241.

A hundred ways you'll find to soothe your care;
Travel, companions, fields and country air.—*Ed.*

274. Ce que je sais le mieux, c'est mon commencement. Rac. Plaid. 3, 3 (Petit Jean, the porter, loq.).—*What I know best is the beginning* (of my speech).

275. Ce que l'on conçoit bien s'énonce clairement
Et les mots pour le dire arrivent aisément. Boil. L'A. P. 1, 153.

A felicitous thought is as clearly exprest,
And the words are not wanting in which it is drest.—*Ed.*

276. Ce qui manque aux orateurs en profondeur, ils vous le donnent en longueur. Montesquieu, Pensées Div. ("Variétés"), Panthéon, p. 626.—*Orators make up in length for what their speeches lack in depth.*

277. Ce qui n'est pas clair, n'est pas Français. Quit. p. 410.—*What is not clear (intelligible) is not French.*

278. Ce qui ne vaut pas la peine d'être dit, on le chante. Beaum. Barb. de Sév. 1, 2; Figaro loq.—*What is not worth saying sounds very well when it is sung.*

279. Ce qu'on donne aux méchants, toujours on le regrette :
     Pour tirer d'eux ce qu'on leur prête,
     Il faut que l'on en vienne aux coups ;
     Il faut plaider, il faut combattre.
     Laissez-leur prendre un pied chez vous,
     Ils en auront bientôt pris quatre.
                 La Font. 2, 7 (La Lice et sa compagne).

> What one lends to the bad, one is sure to deplore.
>   To get from them what one has lent
>   You must sue, come to blows, act the belligerent ;
>   Give them one foot, they'll soon have got four.—*Ed.*

280. Ce qu'on nomme libéralité, n'est, souvent, que la vanité de donner, que nous aimons mieux que ce que nous donnons. La Rochef. Max., § 271, p. 66.—*What is called liberality is often nothing more than the vanity of giving, which we love better than what we actually bestow.*

281. Cereus in vitium flecti, monitoribus asper,
     Utilium tardus provisor, prodigus æris,
     Sublimis cupidusque et amata relinquere pernix. Hor. A. P. 163.

>   *Youth.*
> Pliant as wax to those who lead him wrong,
> But all impatience with a faithful tongue ;
> Imprudent, lavish, hankering for the moon,
> He takes up things and lays them down as soon.—*Conington.*

282. Cernite sim qualis, qui modo qualis eram ! Ov. F. 5, 460.—*See what I am, and think how great I was !* Remus' ghost at the bedside of Romulus.

283. Certa amittimus dum incerta petimus, atque hoc evenit
     In labore atque in dolore, ut mors obrepat interim. Plaut. Ps. 2, 3, 19.—*We throw away certainties for uncertainties, and so it comes about that between labour and sorrow death meanwhile steals upon us.*

> Νήπιος ὅς τά γ' ἔτοιμα λιπών, ἀνέτοιμα διώκει. Hes. Fr. 62, Gaisf. Poet. Minor. Gr.—*Fool, to leave what is at hand to pursue the unattainable !* Also, Sall. C. 17, 6. Incerta pro certis, bellum quam pacem, malebant.—*They preferred uncertainties to certainties, and war to peace.* Said of the sprigs of nobility who joined Catiline's rising.

284. Certe ignoratio futurorum malorum utilior est quam scientia. Cic. Div. 2, 9, 23.—*Certainly our ignorance of impending evils is better than our knowledge of them.*

285. Certum est quia impossibile est. Tert. de Carne Christi, cap. 5.— *It is certain, because it is impossible.*

> One of Tertullian's characteristic paradoxes on the Creed. The Crucifixion is glorious (*non pudet*), *because* it is shameful (*quia pudendum est*). The death of the Son of God is credible beyond doubt, *because* the proposition is absurd ; and His resurrection from the grave is certain, *because* such a thing is impossible (*certum est, quia impossibile est*). The phrase is sometimes quoted as *credo, quia absurdum* (or *quia impossibile*) *est.*

286. Certum voto pete finem.   Hor. Ep. 1, 2, 56.—*Put a fixed limit to your wishes.*

287. Cervi luporum præda rapacium
Sectamur ultro, quos opimus
   Fallere et effugere est triumphus.   Hor. C. 4, 4, 50.

> Weak deer, the wolves' predestin'd prey,
>   Blindly we rush on foes, from whom
> 'Twere triumph won to steal away.—*Conington.*

288. Ces malheureux rois
Dont on dit tant de mal, ont du bon quelquefois.   Andrieux,
Meunier de Sans Souci, (Contes et Opuscules, Paris, 1800, pp.
47-8).—*These wretched kings of whom so much evil is said, have their good points sometimes.*

> Beginning of poem on Frederick the Great and the Miller.   The King, in order to extend the grounds of Sans Souci, offered to buy—if not, to seize— his neighbour's mill.   The miller protested:—

> > Vous! de prendre mon moulin!
> > Oui! si nous n'avions pas de juges à Berlin.

> In the end the mill is spared, and the piece concludes, with reference to Frederick's annexation of Silesia (1745),

> > Il mit l'Europe en feu.   Ce sont là jeux de prince:
> > On respecte un moulin, on vole un province.

> Cf. La Font. 4, 4 (*Le Jardinier et son seigneur*), and the old adage, "*Jeux de prince, qui ne plaisent qu'à ceux qui les font.*"   Quit. p. 478.

289. C'est ainsi qu'en partant je vous fais mes adieux.   Quinault,
Thésée, 5, 6 (1675).   Music by de Lulli.   Œuvres Choisies,
Paris, 1824.—*'Tis thus that in parting I make my adieu.*
Medea from her dragon-car thus announces to Theseus the approaching catastrophe of the house of Jason.

290. C'est double plaisir de tromper le trompeur.   La Font. 2, 15 (Le
Coq et le Renard).—*It is double pleasure to trick the trickster.*
Jockeying the jockey.

291. C'est du Nord aujourd'hui que nous vient la lumière.   Volt. *Épitre
a l'Impératrice de Russie, Catherine II.* (1771) ver. 8.—*It is from the North nowadays that we get our light.*

> On Dec. 22, 1766, Voltaire wrote to the Empress, "Non, vous n'êtes point l'aurore boréale: vous êtes assurément l'astre le plus brillant du Nord."   On Feb. 27, 1767, he added, "Un temps viendra, madame, . . . où toute la lumière nous viendra du Nord."   Alex. p. 289.

292. C'est elle! Dieu que je suis aise!
Oui, c'est la bonne edition;
Voilà bien—pages douze et seize,—
Les deux fautes d'impression
Qui ne sont pas dans la mauvaise.
                    Pons de Verdun, *Contes et poésies*, 1807, p. 9.

The Bibliomaniac.

The very book itself ! Thank Heaven !
Without doubt—the right edition.
Yes ! on pages twelve and seven
Are the two faults of impression
Which in th' others are not given.—*Ed.*

*** The lines were borrowed in 1832 by Scribe for insertion in his Vaudeville of *Le Savant* (2, 3), and sung by "Professor Reynolds."

293. C'est la profonde ignorance qui inspire le ton dogmatique. La Bruyère, Car., chap. v. p. 99.—*Dogmatism is the offspring of profound ignorance.*

294. C'est le bon sens, la raison qui fait tout,
Vertu, génie, esprit, talent, et goût.
Qu'est ce vertu ?   Raison mise en pratique :
Talent ?   Raison produite avec éclat ;
Esprit ?   Raison qui finement s'exprime ;
Le goût n'est rien qu'un bon sens delicat ;
Et le génie est la raison sublime.   M. J. Chénier, *La Raison*, (Panthéon Littér., Paris, 1835, vol. 2, p. 610).

In good sense and reason are all things embraced,
Both virtue and genius, wit, talent, and taste.
What is virtue but reason in practice displayed?
What talent, but reason in brilliant dress?
What is wit but the same that can finely express?
Taste is delicate sense, like a rose at its prime,
And genius itself is but reason sublime.—*Ed.*

295. C'est le commencement de la fin.   Talleyrand, *Album Perdu*, p. 128.
—*'Tis the beginning of the end.*   Saying common in Paris (after the battle of Leipsic), in the autumn and winter of 1813-14, and ascribed to Talleyrand.   *V.* Sainte Beuve's *M. de Talleyrand*, cap. 3, p. 112, ed. 1870.   Shakesp. *Mids. N. Dr.*, 5, 1, has, "*That is the true beginning of our end.*"

296. C'est le lapin qui a commencé, (in German "Der Karnickel hat angefangen ").—*The rabbit began it first.*

A pleasantry which owes its origin to the *Mixpickel und Mengemus* of Heinrich Lami (Magdeburg, 1828, pp. 21-2).   According to the tale, a poodle following his master one day through the market snapped up a rabbit among the live stock of a poulterer's stall.   Although the dog's owner volunteered ten times the price of the animal, nothing would content the good lady of the establishment except taking the offender before the magistrate.   A street urchin, however, that had been watching the dispute, called the gentleman aside, and offered to state, *for a consideration,* that "it was the rabbit that began it first."   Büchm. p. 241 ; Alex. p. 278.

297. C'est le propre de l'érudition populaire de rattacher toutes ses connaissances à quelque nom vulgaire.   Charles Nodier, *Questions de Littérature Légale*, p. 68 n., 2nd ed., Paris (Crapelet), 1828.—*It is the characteristic of the learning of the lower class to couple all its information with some well-known name.*

298. C'est magnifique, mais ce n'est pas la guerre.   Gen. Bosquet.—*It is magnificent, but it is not war.*   Said of the charge of the Light Brigade at Balaçlava (Oct. 25, 1854) to Mr A. H. Layard on the field, and at the time of the charge.   Kinglake's "Crimea," orig. ed., vol. 4, p. 369 n. (Lond., 1863-1887, 8ᵛᵒ).

299. C'est posséder les biens que savoir s'en passer.   Regnard, Joueur, 4, 13.   (Hector, the valet, reading Seneca to his master, Valère).—*To be able to dispense with good things is tantamount to possessing them.*

> Je suis riche du bien dont je sais me passer.   Vigée, Épitre à Ducis sur les Avantages de la Médiocrité (Poésies de L. B. E. Vigée, 5th ed., Paris, 1813, p. 103).—*I am enriched by the goods that I have learnt to do without.*

300. C'est souvent hasarder un bon mot . . que de le donner pour sien. Il tombe avec des gens d'esprit . . qui ne l'ont pas dit, et qui doivent le dire.   C'est, au contraire, le faire valoir que de le rapporter comme d'un autre. Il est dit avec plus d'insinuation, et reçu avec moins de jalousie.   La Bruy. ch. xii. (ii. p. 84). —*It is risking a good saying to report it as your own.   It generally falls flat, especially with the wits of the company who will feel that they ought to have said it themselves.   On the other hand, you set it off by telling it of another, besides making the mot all the more insinuating, and disarming any feeling of jealousy.*

301. C'est un droit qu' à la porte on achète en entrant.   Boil. L'A. P. 3, 150.—*'Tis a right* (sc., to hiss the performance) *that is included in the price of the ticket*

302. C'est une grande difformité dans la nature qu'un vieillard amoureux. La Bruy. ch. xi. (ii. p. 50).—*An old man in love is a monstrous anomaly.*   Amare juveni fructus est, crimen seni: Syr. 29.—*Love is the right of youth, and the reproach of age:* and cf. οὔ τοι σύμφορόν ἐστι γυνὴ νέα ἀνδρὶ γέροντι. Theogn. 457: and, αἰσχρὸν νέᾳ γυναικὶ πρεσβύτης ἀνήρ. Ar. Fr. 497.

303. C'est une grande folie de vouloir être sage tout seul.   La Rochef. Max. § 238, p. 61.—*Nothing so silly as to insist on being the only person who is in the right.*

304. C'est une grande misère que de n'avoir pas assez d'esprit pour bien parler, ni assez de jugement pour se taire. La Bruy. ch. v. (i. p. 84).—*It is a miserable thing that men should not have wit enough to speak well, nor sufficient tact to hold their tongues.*

305. C'est une sphère infinie, dont le centre est partout, la circonférence nulle part. Pasc. Pensées, c. 22.—*The universe is an infinite sphere, the centre of which is everywhere and the circumference nowhere.*

> Blaise Pascal's celebrated definition of the universe.   The context runs, "Tout ce que nous voyons du monde n'est qu'un trait imperceptible dans

42 C'EST UN—CETTE.

l'ample sein de la nature. Nulle idée n'approche de l'estenduë de ses espaces . . *C'est une sphère infinie*, etc." Ernest Havet in his ed. of the *Pensées*, (Paris, 1866, 2 vols. 8vo, 2nd ed.), vol. 1, pp. 17-19 note, traces the saying to earlier sources:—(1.) Mdlle de Gournay's .Pref. to Montaigne's *Essais*, (Paris, 1635), "Trismegiste appelle la Déité cercle, dont le centre est partout, la circonférence nulle part." (2.) Gerson, *Œuvres*, Paris, 1606, vol. i. p. 366. (3.) S. Bonaventure (*Œuvres*, Mayence, 1609, vol. 8, p. 325), *Itinerarium mentis in Deum*, cap. v.: beside other parallels cited *ibid.* Rabelais, Bk. 5, cap. 47, has, "Allez, mes amis, en protection de cette sphère intellectuelle; de laquelle en tous lieux est le centre, et n'a en lieu aucun circonférence, que nous appelons Dieu."

306. C'est un meschant mestier d'estre pauvre soldat. Daniel d'Anchères, *Tyr et Sidon*, (1608), Pt. I. Act 5, sc. 1. (Paris, 1628). La Ruine,(a soldier)loq.—*A poor soldier's a wretched trade enough.*

"Daniel d'Anchères" is the anagram and pseudonym of Jean d'Schelandre. In the same play (Act 5) is, *C'est un faible roseau que la prospérité* ("Prosperity's but a weak reed to lean on").

307. C'est un verre qui luit, Qu'un souffle peut détruire, et qu'un souffle a produit. De Caux, L'Horlöge de Sable, line 11, (comparing the world to his hour-glass).—*It is but a glittering glass that a breath can destroy, as a breath has created it.* Cf. Goldsmith, "Deserted Village," 54:

A breath can make them, as a breath has made.

308. Cet âge est sans pitié. La Font. 9, 2. (Les deux Pigeons.)— *This age* (childhood) *has no pity.* Children have no mercy.

309. Cet animal est très méchant, Quand on l'attaque il se défend. Théodore P. K., (?) *La Ménagerie;* music by Edmond Lhuillier, Paris, (Petit, 18 Rue Vivienne), 1828.—*This animal (the leopard) is so vicious, that if you attack him he will defend himself!*

Music-hall song of the day, burlesquing the recently published *Histoire Générale des Voyages* of C. A. Walckenaer, Paris (Lefèvre), 1826, where an account is given (vol. 1, p. 114) of the adventures of Vasco de Gama and his comrades amongst some "sea-wolves" of an extraordinary size and armed with tremendous teeth. "*Ces animaux*," it proceeds, "*sont si furieux, qu'il se défendent contre ceux qui les attaquent.*" It is difficult to say which is the most ludicrous, the serious prose or the burlesque verse. Alex. pp. 19-20.

310. Cet œuvre n'est pas long, on le voit en une heure, La plus courte folie est tousiours la meilleure. La Giraudière, (Sr de), *Recueil des Joyeux Epigrammes*, 1633, p. 149, last words.

Au Lecteur.
This work is not long, as one sees at a glance,
And shortness does always a folly enhance.—*Ed.*

*** The second line is borrowed by Charles Beys to terminate his five-act comedy of *Les Illustres Fous*, Paris, 1653.

311. Cette maladie qui s'appelle la vie. Mdlle de l'Espinasse à Condorçet, Mai, 1775, (Lettres inédites, Ed. Ch. Henry, Paris, 1887, p. 148).—*This disease which men call life.*

312. Chacun son métier,
    Les vaches seront bien gardées. Florian, Fab. 1, 12, fin.—*Each
    one attend to his own business, and the cows will be properly
    looked after.* Moral of the story in which the Cowherd and
    Gamekeeper exchanged duties for the day with disastrous results.

313. Χαλεπὰ τὰ καλά, τὰ δὲ κακὰ οὐ χαλεπά. Theoctist. ap. Stob.
    Floril. 126, 22.—*Noble deeds are difficult, but vice is easy enough.*
    First part of quot. attrib. to Solon (L. and S., *s.v.* χαλεπός), and
    quoted as "an old proverb" by Socrates (Plato, Cratylus I.
    p. 384A; Didot, p. 283). In Lat., "Difficilia quæ pulchra." George
    Herbert (*Providence*), says, "Hard things are glorious; easy
    things, good cheap." John Owen (Audoenus) has, (Epigr. 1, 140),
        Si sit difficilis quæ pulchra, Marine; puellam
        Accipe tu facilem : da mihi difficilem.

314. Chambre introuvable. Louis XVIII.—*A matchless chamber* (or
    Parliament). Said of the Chamber of Deputies which met after
    the second return of the King, July, 1815. It was too favour-
    able to the monarchy to be possible, and such as the King
    himself scarcely believed could be "found." It was the reaction
    against the Revolution—the "White Terror."

315. Χάρις χάριν γάρ ἐστιν ἡ τίκτουσ' ἀεί. Soph. Aj. 522.—*A favour
    done begets a favour felt.*

316. Chercher à connaître, c'est chercher à douter.—*To seek to know
    is to seek to doubt.* Inquiry which is not guided by faith
    generally ends in scepticism.
        Vous ne prouvez que trop que chercher à connaître,
        N'est souvent qu'apprendre à douter.—*Mme. Deshoulières*, Réflex. Div. (11).
        You prove but too clearly that seeking to know
        Is too frequently learning to doubt.—*Ed.*

317. Cherchez la femme! Alex. Dumas (père), *Mohicans de Paris,*
    1864, A. 3, Tabl. 5, sc. 6.—*Enquire for the woman!*
        In the scene, Jackal, the police officer, is interrogating Mme. Desmarets,
    the lodging-house keeper, about the abduction of Rose de Noel.
        Jackal.—Il y a une femme dans toutes les affaires; aussitôt qu'on me fait
    un rapport, je dis: "Cherchez la femme!" On cherche la femme, et quand
    la femme est trouvée . . .
        Mme. Desmarets.—Eh bien?
        Jackal.—On ne tarde pas à trouver l'homme.
        In the *Revue des Deux-Mondes,* Sept. 1845 (art. "L'Alpuxarra"), p. 822,
    Charles Didier says of Charles III. of Spain that he was so convinced of the
    truth of this principle, "que sa première question en toutes choses était
    celle-ci: Comment s'appelle-t-elle?" George Ebers' *Uarda,* vol. 2, chap. 14
    (1876), has, "Du vergisst, dass hier eine Frau mit im Spiel ist." "Das ist
    sie überall" entgegnete Ameni, etc.—"*You forget that there is a woman in
    the case.*" "*That is so all the world over,*" replied Ameni, etc.; and
    Richardson (*Sir Chas. Grandison,* 1753, vol. 1, Letter XXIV.) says, "Such a
    plot must have a woman in it." The saying has been attributed to Fouché,
    de Sartine, the Abbé Galiani, etc., but a much earlier instance is found in
    Juvenal (6, 242),

Nulla fere caussa est in qua non femina litem
Moverit: accusat Manilia, si rea non est.
Are not women at the bottom of all law suits?
Yes; Manilia plaintiff is, if not defendant. —*Shaw.*

318. Che sarà, sarà.   Prov.—*What will be, will be.*   Motto of the Bedford family.

"The fatalism of the economists (the Whigs)," she remarked, "will never do in a great trial like this"—the Irish Famine of 1847; and she read us a letter from Lord John Russell, complimentary and courteous, but refusing to listen to certain projects of relief. "He is true," she wittily said, "to the motto of his house; but *Che sarà, sarà,* is the faith of the infidel." Anecdote of Miss Edgeworth in W. O'Connor Morris's *Memoirs and Thoughts of a Life,* Lond., 1894, p. 105.

319. Chez elle un beau désordre, est un effet de l'art.   Boil. L'A. P. 2, 72.
—*Her fine disorder is a work of art.*   Said of the "unshackled numbers" of the "Ode."

320. Chi compra terra, compra guerra.   Prov.—*Who buys land, buys war* (trouble).   Buy soil, buy moil.

321. Chi troppo abbraccia nulla stringe.   Prov.—*He who grasps too much, will hold nothing.*   An over ambitious attempt.

322. Chi va piano va sano, e (chi va sano) va lontano.   Prov. qu. in Goldoni's "I Volponi," 1, 2.   Harb. p. 273.—*Who goes quietly goes well, and* (he who goes well) *goes far in a day.*

323. Chi vuol vada, chi non vuol mandi.   Prov. qu. in Pietro Aretino's La Talanta, 1, 13.   Harb. p 275.—*If you want a thing, go yourself: if you don't, send.*

324. Chreme, tantumne ab re tua est otii tibi
Aliena ut cures, eaque nihil quæ ad te attinent?
Homo sum; humani nihil a me alienum puto.   Ter. Heaut. 1, 1, 23.

Menedemus. Have you such leisure, Chremes, from your own affairs,
To attend to those of others, which concern you not?
Chremes. I'm man, and nought that's man's to me's indifferent.—*Ed.*

325. Χρὴ ξεῖνον παρεόντα φιλεῖν, ἐθέλοντα δὲ πέμπειν.   Hom. Od. 15, 74.
"Welcome the coming, speed the parting guest." Pope tr. *ibid.,* v. 83.

326. Christianos ad leonem!   Tert. Apol. 40.—*To the lions with the Christians!*   Cry of the pagans in the early persecutions of the Church, when anything adverse occurred either in the natural or political world.

327. Ci-gît Piron, qui ne fût rien
Pas même Academicien.   Alexis Piron, *Poésie.*   Petits poétes Français, Panthéon Littér., p. 158.—*Here lies Piron, who was nothing; not even a member of the Academy.*

328. Ci Loth, sa femme en sel, sa ville en cendre,
Il but, et fut son gendre.   A. F. B. Deslandes, *Réflexions sur les grands hommes qui se sont morts en plaisantant.*   Nouv. Éd. par M. D., Amsterdam, 1776 (*Épitaphes,* p. 166).

Sur Loth.

Here lies poor Lot, who saw
His wife in salt, his town in flame;
He drank, and then became—
His son-in-law.—*Ed.*

329. Cineri gloria sera venit. Mart. 1, 26, 8.—*Glory comes too late when one is turned to ashes.*

330. Citius venit periclum quum contemnitur. Syr. 92.—*Danger comes all the sooner for being laughed at.*

331. Cito rumpes arcum, semper si tensum habueris,
At si laxaris, quum voles, erit utilis.
Sic ludus animo debet aliquando dari,
Ad cogitandum melior ut redeat tibi.   Phædr. 3, 10.

The bow that's always bent will quickly break;
But if unstrung 'twill serve you at your need.
So, let the mind some relaxation take
To come back to its task with fresher heed.—*Ed.*

Cf. Allzu straff gespannt, zerspringt der Bogen. Schiller, W. Tell, 3, 3.
—*The bow that's bent too tight will break.* Danda est remissio animis; meliores acrioresque requieti surgent. Sen. Tranquil. 15, ad fin.—*The mind should have some relaxation, in order to return to its work with all the greater vigour for the rest.*

332. Cito scribendo non fit ut bene scribatur, bene scribendo fit ut cito. Quint. 10, 3, 10.—*Quick writing does not make good writing; the way to write quickly is to write well.*

333. Clarus ob obscuram linguam magis inter inanes
Quamde graves inter Graios qui vera requirunt:
Omnia enim stolidi magis admirantur amantque
Inversis quæ sub verbis latitantia cernunt.   Lucr. 1, 640.

Heraclitus.

His obscure style took with the shallower pates,
(Not with the serious Greeks who ask for facts):
For nothing captivates your dull man more
Than dark, involved, mysterious verbiage.—*Ed.*

334. Cœpisti melius quam desinis: ultima primis
Cedunt: dissimiles hic vir, et ille puer. Ov. H. 9, 23.—*You began better than you end: your last attempts must yield the palm to your previous achievements. How little does the man correspond to the promise of the boy!* Deianira reproaching Hercules.

335. Cœur content soupire souvent. Prov.—*A satisfied heart will often sigh.* The cross prov. says: *Cœur qui soupire n'a pas ce qu'il désire.* Montluc, Comédie de Proverbes, 3, 5.—The heart that sighs has not got what it wants.

336. Combien de héros, glorieux, magnanimes,
Ont vécu trop d'un jour! J. B. Rousseau, Bk. 2, Ode 10,
p. 111.—*How many illustrious and noble heroes have lived too long by one day!*

337. Comédiens, c'est un mauvais temps,
La tragédie est par les champs.
> Mazarinade (17th cent.): *see* Fourn. *Variétés hist. et littér.*, vol. 5, p. 17 (*Les Triboulets du temps*).—*Comedians! what a wretched time with tragedy abroad!*   Cf. Que me parles-tu, Vallier, de m'occuper à faire des tragédies? La tragédie court les rues! Ducis, (Campenon, Essais, etc., sur la vie de Ducis, Paris, 1824, p. 79).—*Why do you talk to me of working at tragedies, when Tragedy herself is stalking the streets?* Fourn. *L.D.L.*, p. 392.

338. Comes facundus in via pro vehiculo est. Syr. 104.—*A chatty companion on a journey is as good as a coach.* Text of *Spectator* 122, Sir Roger riding to the County Assizes.

339. Come te non voglio: méglio di te non posso.—*Like thee, I will not: better than thou, I cannot.* Traditional apostrophe of M. Angelo, as he turned to gaze on the Duomo of Brunelleschi, when setting out from Florence (1542) to build the dome of St Peter's. Rogers' "Italy" (1836), Notes, p. 269, "Beautiful Florence."

340. Comme la vérité, l'erreur a ses Héros. Volt. Henr. Chant. V., 200 (1st ed., Lond., 1728).—*Like truth, error has also its heroes.*

341. Commune id vitium est: hic vivimus ambitiosa
Paupertate omnes.   Quid te moror? Omnia Romæ
Cum pretio.   Juv. 3, 182.
> *Society in Rome.*
> The vice is universal: we all want,
> As pushing as we're poor, to cut a dash—
> And terms for "life" in Rome are strictly cash.—*Ed.*

342. Comparaison n'est pas raison. Prov. Quit. 251.—*Comparison is not argument.*

343. Compedes, quas ipse fecit, ipsus ut gestet faber. Aus. Id. 6, fin.
—*The smith must wear the fetters he himself has made.* As you have made your bed, so must you lie. Cf. Tute hoc intristi; tibi omne est exedendum. Ter. Phorm. 2, 2, 4.—*You have made this dish, and you must eat it up.*

344. Compendiaria res improbitas, virtusque tarda. Chil. 310. Tr. of the Gr. prov. attrib. to Cleomenes: Σύντομος ἡ πονηρία, βραδεῖα ἡ ἀρετή. Paroem. Gr. ii. p. 647.—*Knavery takes short cuts, and honesty travels slowly.*

345. Componitur orbis
Regis ad exemplum; nec sic inflectere sensus
Humanos edicta valent, ut vita regentis. Claud. IV. Cons. Hon. 299.
> *A Prince's Example.*
> The king's example's copied by the world,
> And his own life does more than all the laws.—*Ed.*

Fredk. II., in his *Épitre à mon frère* (Œuvres, Berlin, 1789, 8°, vol. iv. p. 53), writes:

L'exemple d'un monarque impose et se fait suivre:
Lorsqu' Auguste buvait, la Pologne était ivre.

A monarch's example is bound to be followed:
When Augustus drank, Poland in drink simply wallowed.—*Ed.*

346. Compositum miraculi causa. Tac. A. 11, 27.—*A tale got up to create sensation.*

347. Concordia discors. Luc. 1, 98, and Hor. Ep. 1, 12, 19.—*Discordant harmony.* Ill-assorted union or combination of persons or things.

348. Concordia parvæ res crescunt, discordia maxumæ dilabuntur. Sall. J. 10, 16.—*Unanimity will give success even to small undertakings; but dissension will bring the greatest to the ground.*

349. Concurritur: horæ
Momento cita mors venit, aut victoria læta. Hor. S. 1, 1, 7.

Battle.
One short, sharp shock, and presto! all is done:
Death in an instant comes, or victory's won.—*Conington.*

350. Conditio dulcis sine pulvere palmæ. Hor. Ep. 1, 1, 51.—*The certainty of winning the palm (prize) without effort.*

351. Confiteor, si quid prodest delicta fateri. Ov. Am. 2, 4, 3.—*I confess my fault if the confession be of any avail.*

352. Conjugium vocat, hoc prætexit nomine culpam. Virg. A. 4, 172.

Dido.
She calls it marriage now; such name
She chooses to conceal her shame.—*Conington.*

353. Conscia mens recti famæ mendacia risit,
Sed nos in vitium credula turba sumus. Ov. F. 4, 311.

The innocent smile at scandal's lying tongue,
But, as a race, we're prone t' imagine wrong.—*Ed.*

Si quid Usquam justitia est, et mens sibi conscia recti. Virg. A. 1, 603. —*If justice, and a sense of conscious right yet avail anything:* and, Quænam summa boni? Mens quæ sibi conscia recti. Auson. Sept. Sap. (Bias).— *What is the greatest human blessing? A good conscience.*

354. Conscientia mille testes. Quint. 5, 11, 41.—*A good conscience is worth a thousand witnesses:* and, Bona conscientia turbam advocat, mala etiam in solitudine anxia atque solicita est. Sen. Ep. 43, 5.—*A good conscience invites the inspection of a multitude, a bad one is all anxiety even when alone.*

355. Consilia firmiora sunt de divinis locis. Plaut. Most. 5, 1, 55.— *Counsel is more sure that comes from holy places.*

356. Consuetudinem sermonis vocabo consensum eruditorum ; sicut vivendi consensum bonorum. Quint. 1, 4, 3.—*The practice of educated men is the best standard of language, just as the lives of the good are our pattern in morals.*

357. Consuetudo est altera lex.   Law Max.—*Custom is a second law.* Chil., p. 389.

358. Consuetudo quasi secunda natura dicitur. S. Aug. de Musica, vi. c. 7. (vol. i. 387 f.).—*Custom is called a second nature;* or, altera natura, Cic. Fin. 5, 25, 74.   Cf. Morem fecerat usus. Ov. M. 2, 345.—*Custom had made it a habit.*

> Quint. (1, 2, 8), describing the depraved influences that surrounded even the infancy of a Roman child, says, " Fit ex his consuetudo, deinde natura." —*Hence a familiarity with vice, which in time becomes mere nature.* Cf. Arist. Rhet. 1, 11, 3, (Didot, i. p. 335), τὸ εἰθισμένον ὥσπερ πεφυκὸς ἤδη γίγνεται. —*What we have got accustomed to becomes a sort of nature to us;* and, Consuetudinis magna vis est. Cic. Tusc. 2, 17, 40.—*Great is the force of habit.*

359. Contemnuntur ii, qui *nec sibi, nec alteri,* ut dicitur : in quibus nullus labor, nulla industria, nulla cura est.   Cic. Off. 2, 10, 36.—*Deservedly are they despised who are "no good to themselves or any one else," as the saying is; who make no exertion, show no industry, exercise no thought.*

360. Contemporains de tous les hommes,
Et citoyens de tous les lieux.
   Houdard de Lamotte, Ode à MM. de L'Académie Française.

> Contemporaries of every age,
> And citizens of every land.—*Ed.*

361. Conticuisse nocet nunquam, nocet esse locutum.   Lang., p. 673, Anth. Sacr. Jac. Billii (*In Loquaces*).—*Silence ne'er hurts, but speech does often harm.*

362. Continuo culpam ferro compesce, priusquam
Dira per incautum serpant contagia vulgus.   Virg. G. 3, 468.

> *Prompt Measures.*
> Cut off at once with knife the mischief's head,
> Lest thro' the unthinking crowd the poison spread.—*Ed.*
> Prompt measures must be taken with disorders, either of the natural or the political body: sedition, like any other ulcer, must be at once removed.

363. Con todo el mondo guerra, y paz con Inglaterra.   Prov.—*War with all the world, and peace with England.*

364. Contra verbosos noli contendere verbis ;
Sermo datur cunctis, animi sapientia paucis.   Dion. Cato. Dist. de Mor. 1, 10.—*Avoid disputing with men of many words: speech is given to every man, wisdom to few.*   Qu. by Bridoye in his story of the "Apoincteur de procès," Rab. lib. iii. cap. 41.

365. Contra vim mortis, non est medicamen in hortis.   Coll. Salern., vol. i. p. 469, ver. 718.—*The herb isn't grown that will act as a remedy against death.*

366. Contre les rebelles, c'est cruauté que d'estre humain et humanité d'estre cruel.　Corneille Muis, Bp. of Bitonte.　*Biblioth. choisie de Colomiez,* 1682, p. 179.　*V.* Fourn. *L.D.L.,* cap. 30.—*Against rebels, it is cruelty to be humane, and humanity to be cruel.*　A maxim that Catherine de Medici duly impressed upon her son Charles IX.

367. Contumeliam si dices, audies.　Plaut. Ps. 4, 7, 77.—*If you abuse others, you will have to listen to it yourself.*

368. Conveniens vïtæ mors fuit ista suæ.　Ov. Am. 2, 10, 38.—*His death was in keeping with his life.*

369. Convier quelqu'un, c'est se charger de son bonheur pendant tout le temps qu'il est sous nôtre toit.　Brillat-Savarin, Physiologie du goût, 1826, Aphor. 20.—*To invite any one as a guest is to be responsible for his happiness all the time that he is under your roof.*

370. Corpora magnanimo satis est prostrasse leoni :
Pugna suum finem, quum jacet hostis, habet.—Ov. T. 3, 5, 33.

> The noble lion's content to fell his foe:
> The fight is done, when th' enemy's laid low.—*Ed.*

371. Corrumpunt bonos mores colloquia mala.　Vulg. Cor. 1, 15, 33.—*Evil communications corrupt good manners.*

> Tert. (ad Uxor. 1, 8) turns it into metre—"Bonos mores corrumpunt congressus mali." The original, quoted by S. Paul, is a line from the *Thais* of Menander (vol. ii. p. 908), φθείρουσιν ἤθη χρήσθ' ὁμιλίαι κακαί. Cf. also id. (Monost. 274, p. 1050), κακοῖς ὁμιλῶν καὐτὸς ἐκβήσῃ κακός.—*Who keeps bad company will turn out bad himself;* and, ἐν παντὶ πράγει δ' ἔσθ' ὁμιλίας κακῆς κάκιον οὐδέν. Aesch. Theb. 599.—*In everything, there's nought worse than bad company.*

372. Corruptissima in republica plurimæ leges.　Tac. A. 3, 27.—*The most corrupt governments produce the greatest number of laws.* "Laws!" exclaimed a Frenchman to me in 1895, "Why, we have more than we know what to do with! Nous en avons à vendre."

373. Cosa fatta, capo ha.　Prov.—*When a thing's done, it's done.*

> Old Ital. prov. used in advising instant action in any matter, and notably employed by Mosca de' Lamberti (1215 A.D.) to recommend the prompt punishment of Buondelmonte for breaking his contract of marriage with a lady of the Amidei family. Buondelmonte was accordingly killed, and with this, says Giov. Villani (*Istorie Fiorentine,* 5, 38), began the feud of the Guelphs and Ghibellines. In the *Inferno* (28, 107), Mosca introduces himself to Dante as the man—

> > Che dissi, lasso! Capo ha cosa fatta ;
> > Che fu 'l mal seme per la gente tosca.

> > I who, alas! exclaim'd
> > "The deed once done, there is an end," that prov'd
> > A seed of sorrow to the Tuscan race.—*Cary.*

D

374. Così fan tutti.—*So do they all.* The way of the world. "Così fan tutte" (*All women are alike*) is the title of the opera of Mozart, Vienna, 1790, words by Lorenzo da Ponte.

375. Craignez la colère de la colombe.　　Prov. Quit. p. 248.—*Beware the anger of the dove!* Syrus has (178), Furor fit laesa sæpius patientia.— *Patience provoked often turns to fury;* and Dryden, (*Abs. and Achit.*, ver. 1005),

> "Beware the fury of a patient man."

376. Cras amet, qui nunquam amavit, quique amavit, cras amet.
> Pervigilium Veneris (Lemaire, Poet. Minor., ii. p. 514).

> Let those love now who never loved before,
> Let those who always loved, now love the more.—*T. Parnell,*

"Vigil of Venus," 1717.　(*Brit. Poets,* 1794, vol. vii. 7.)　Byron writing from Clarens (1817) says,

> " He who hath loved not, here would learn that love,
> And make his heart a spirit; he who knows
> That tender mystery will love the more."—Ch. Har. 3, 103.

377. Cras te victurum, cras dicis, Postume, semper.
> Dic mihi cras istud, Postume, quando venit?—Mart. 5, 58, 1.

> To-morrow, you always say, I'll wisely live:
> Say, Posthumus, when does to-morrow arrive?—*Ed.*

378. Credat Judæus Apella,
> Non ego : namque deos didici securum agere œvum ;
> Nec, si quid miri faciat natura, deos id
> Tristes ex alto cœli demittere tecto.　　Hor. S. 1, 5, 100.

> *The Miraculous Liquefaction.*
> Tell the crazed Jews such miracles as these!
> I hold the gods live lives of careless ease,
> And, if a wonder happens, don't assume
> 'Tis sent in anger from the upstairs room.—*Conington.*

Credat Judæus Apella is often used in contemptuous fashion, meaning that the thing is too improbable to obtain general credence; like "Tell that to the marines!"

379. Crede mihi bene qui latuit bene vixit, et intra
> Fortunam debet quisque manere suam.　　Ov. T. 3, 4, 25.

> *Seclusion.*
> He lives the best who from the world retires,
> And, self-contained, to nothing else aspires.—*Ed.*

Nam neque divitibus contingunt gaudia solis,
Nec vixit male qui natus moriensque fefellit!—Hor. Ep. 1, 17, 9.

> Joys do not happen to the rich alone ;
> Nor he liv'd ill, that liv'd and died unknown.—*Ed.*

Cp. also Epicurus' maxim, "Live unobserved" (λάθε βιώσας), Plut. Mor. p. 1379 (de Latent. Vivendo, 1, 2); and Gresset's *Vert-Vert*, Chant ii., 86.

Ah ! qu'un grand nom est un bien dangereux !
Un sort caché fut toujours plus heureux.

> What dangers threaten a great reputation !
> Far happier the man of lowly station.—*Ed.*

380. Crede mihi, res est ingeniosa dare   Ov. Am. 1, 8, 62.—*Believe me, giving is a matter that requires judgment.*

381. Credite, posteri!   Hor. C. 2, 19, 2.—*Believe it, after years!* Conington.

382. Creditur ex medio quia res arcessit habere
Sudoris minimum; sed habet comœdia tanto
Plus oneris, quanto veniæ minus.   Hor. Ep. 2, 1, 168.

> *The Comic Dramatist.*
> 'Tis thought that Comedy, because its source
> Is common life, must be a thing of course;
> Whereas there's nought so difficult, because
> There's nowhere less allowance made for flaws.—*Conington.*

383 Credula res amor est.   Ov. M. 7, 826.—*Love is a credulous thing.*

384. Credula vitam
Spes fovet, et fore cras semper ait melius.   Tib. 2, 6, 19.

> *Hope.*
> Hope fondly cheers our days of aching sorrow,
> And always promises a brighter morrow.—*Ed.*

385. Crescentem sequitur cura pecuniam
Majorumque fames.   Hor. C. 3, 16, 17.

> *Greed.*
> Cares follow on with growth of store,
> And an insatiate thirst for more.—*Ed.*

> Cf. Crescit amor nummi quantum ipsa pecunia crescit,
> Et minus hanc optat, qui non habet.   Juv. 14, 139.
>
> The love of money is with wealth increased,
> And he that has it not, desires it least.—*Ed.*

And

> Creverunt et opes, et opum furiosa cupido:
> Et quum possideant plurima, plura volunt.   Ov. F. 1, 211.
>
> Wealth has increased, and wealth's fierce maddening lust,
> And though men have too much, have more they must.—*Ed.*

And

> Effodiuntur opes irritamenta malorum. Ov. M. 1, 140.—*Men dig the earth for gold, seed of unnumbered ills.* Cf. Radix enim malorum omnium cupiditas. Vulg. Tim. 1, 6, 10.—*The love of money is the root of all evil.*

386. Crescit occulto velut arbor ævo.   Hor. C. 1, 12, 45.—*It grows as trees grow with unnoticed growth.* A line applied by Sainte Beuve to the growth of the Catholic Church.

387. Cressa ne careat pulcra dies nota.   Hor. C. 1, 36, 10.

> Note we in our calendar
> This festal day with whitest mark from Crete.—*Conington.*

388. Creta an carbone notandi?   Hor. S. 2, 3, 246.—*Are they to be marked with chalk or charcoal?* Were they happy days, or no?

389. Cretizandum est cum Crete.—*We must do at Crete as the Cretans do.* Tr. of the Gk. Prov. πρὸς Κρῆτα κρητίζειν. Polyb. 8, 21, 5; and Paroem. Gr., i. p. 297.

390. Crimina qui cernunt aliorum, nec sua cernunt;
Hi sapiunt aliis, desipiuntque sibi. Joh. Owen. Epigr. Lib. 3, 79.—*Those who see the faults of others, and are blind to their own, are wise as regards others, fools as regards themselves.*

391. Croire tout découvert est une erreur profonde,
C'est prendre l'horizon pour les bornes du monde.
Lemierre, Utilité des découvertes, 1.

> To think all discovered's an error profound;
> 'Tis to take the horizon for earth's mighty bound.—*Ed.*

392. Crudelis ubique
Luctus, ubique Pavor, et plurima mortis imago. Virg. A. 2, 368.

> Dire agonies, wild terrors swarm,
> And death glares grim in many a form.—*Conington.*

393. Cui bono?—*Who benefits by it?* Who is the gainer by the transaction?

> Cicero (Rosc. Am. 30, 84), in his defence of Sextus Roscius of Ameria (now Amelia, Umbria) on a charge of parricide (79 B.C.), reminds the court of the practice of a famous judge, L. Cassius Pedanius, who, in trying a case, always inquired, "Who benefited by the action committed?" (*Cui bono fuisset?*): and he adduces the maxim to show that, while his client "got nothing" by his father's death, the two Roscii brothers, Titus Capito and T. Magnus, had secured the murdered man's estates for a mere song—something under £50. Cf. Cui prodest scelus, Is fecit. Sen. Med. 500.—*His is the crime who profits by it most.*

394. Cui dolet, meminit. Prov. ap. Cic. Mur. 20, 42.—*He who suffers, remembers.* A burnt child, etc.

395. Cuilibet in arte sua perito est credendum. Law Max.—*Every man should be given credence on points connected with his own special profession.* Chil., p. 433, has it, "Peritis in sua arte credendum."

> Thus, questions relating to any particular trade must be decided by a jury after examination of witnesses skilled in that particular profession. Surgeons on a point of surgery, pilots on a question of navigation, and so on.

396. Cui licitus est finis, etiam licent media. Hermann Busenbaum, Medulla Theol. Moralis (1650), Lib. 6, Tract. 6, Cap. 2, Dub. 2, Art. 1, § 8.—*Where the end is lawful, the means thereto are lawful also.* Generally cited as "The end justifies the means." *V.* Büchm. p. 439.

397. Cui non conveniat sua res, ut calceus olim,
Si pede major erit, subvertet; si minor, uret. Hor. Ep. 1, 10, 42.

> Means should, like shoes, be neither great nor small;
> Too wide, they trip us up, too strait, they gall.—*Conington.*

398. Cui peccare licet, peccat minus.   Ipsa potestas
Semina nequitiæ languidiora facit.   Ov. Am. 3, 4, 9.

Who's free to sin, sins less: the very power
Robs evildoing of its choicest flower.—*Ed.*

399. Cuique sua annumerabimus.   Col. 12, 3, 4.—*We will put down to the account of each what belongs to him.*

400. Cujus est regio, illius est religio.   Law Max.—*Religion goes with the soil: i.e.,* the sovereign power in any country may prescribe the form of worship of its citizens.   The peace of Westphalia (1648) allowed each German potentate to determine the creed of his principality; and, to this day, the principle is more or less acted upon in every country that has an Established Church.

401. Cujus omne consilium Themistocleum est.   Existimat enim qui mare teneat, eum necesse esse rerum potiri.   Cic. Att. 10, 8, 4. —*Pompey's plan is just that of Themistocles. He considers that whoever has the command of the sea must necessarily be the master of the situation.*

402. Culpam pœna premit comes.   Hor. C. 4, 5, 24.—*Swift vengeance follows sin.*   An ideal state of things supposed to be realised under the government of Augustus.

403. Cum grano salis.—*With a grain of salt.*

Said of the qualification or latitude with which statements of a doubtful nature are to be received.   "Addito grano salis" (*With the addition of a grain of salt*) is found in a medical prescription in Plin. 23, 77, 149.   The tropical use of the phrase is apparently modern.

404. Cum multis aliis, quæ nunc perscribere longum est.   Eton Latin Grammar (Genders of Nouns).—*With many other things which it would now be too long to recount at length:* in other words, *Et cætera.*

405. Cuncta prius tentata: sed immedicabile vulnus
Ense recidendum, ne pars sincera trahatur.   Ov. M. 1, 190.

The Rebellion of the Giants.

All has been tried that could: a gangrened wound
Must be cut deep with knife, before the sound
And unaffected parts contract decay.—*Ed.*

406. Cunctis potest accidere quod cuivis potest.   Syr. 119.—*What may happen to any one may happen to all.*

407. Curæ leves loquuntur, ingentes stupent.   Sen. Hipp. 607.

Light sorrows speak, but deeper ones are dumb.—*Ed.*

408. Curarum maxima nutrix Nox.   Ov. M. 8, 81.—*That best nurse of troubles, Night.*

409. Curia pauperibus clausa est: dat census honores:
Inde gravis judex, inde severus eques.   Ov. Am. 3, 8, 55.

The senate's closed to poor men: gold, gold, gold
Makes peers and judges: every honour's sold!—*Ed.*

410. Cur indecores in limine primo
    Deficimus? Cur, ante tubam tremor occupat artus?
                                        Virg. A. 11, 423.

> Why fail we on the threshold? why,
> Ere sounds the trumpet quake and fly?—*Conington.*

411. Curiosus nemo est, quin idem sit malevolus.   Plaut. Stich. 1, 3,
    54.—*Nobody acts the part of a meddlesome person, unless he
    intends you harm.*

412. Cur opus adfectas, ambitiose, novum? Ov. Am. 1, 1, 14.—*Why,
    ambitious youth, do you undertake a new work?*

413. Cursu volucri, pendens in novacula,
    Calvus, comosa fronte, nudo corpore;
    Quem si occuparis, teneas; elapsum semel
    Non ipse possit Jupiter reprehendere.   Phædr. 5, 8, 1.

Occasio.

> Swiftest of flight, just hanging on a razor,
> Bald-polled, locks on forehead, body nude:
> Seize when you meet him, if he once elude,
> Not Jove himself could catch the run-a-way, sir!—*Ed.*

Greg. Naz. Carm. Lib. ii., Historica, (Migne, vol. 3, p. 1513) has,

> Καιροῖο λαβώμεθα, ὃν προσίοντα
> ἔστιν ἐλεῖν, ζητεῖν δὲ παραθρέξαντα μάταιον.

> Seize we th' occasion now, while it is nigh:
> 'Tis vain to seek it when it's once gone by.—*Ed.*

Imitations will also be found in Auson. Epigr. 12, and Chil. (Tempestiva), p. 687.   Dion. Cato, Dist. de Moribus, 2, 26, has,

> Rem, tibi quam nosces aptam dimittere noli;
> Fronte capillata, post est occasio calva.

> Don't let escape what's suited to your mind;
> Bushy in front, occasion's bald behind.—*Ed.*

> Was man von der Minute ausgeschlagen,
> Giebt keine Ewigkeit zurück.   Schiller, Resignation.

> The opportunity you once let slip,
> Eternity 'll not give you back again.—*Ed.*

414. Cur tua præscriptos evecta est pagina gyros?
    Non est ingenii cymba gravanda tui.   Prop. 3, 3, 21.

The Ambitious Poet.

> Why has your page transgressed th' appointed mark?
> You must not overload your talents' bark.—*Ed.*

415. Cy gist ma femme, ah! qu'elle est bien,
    Pour son repos, et pour le mien.   J. Du Lorens, Satires
    de Du Lorens (or Laurens), ed. Prosper Blanchemain, Geneva,
    1868, p. xvi.

> Here lies my wife: there let her lie!
> She's in peace, and so am I.

D.

416. Dæmon languebat, monachus tunc esse volebat:
Dæmon convaluit, dæmon ut ante fuit. Rab. lib. iv. cap. 24.

> The Devil was sick, the devil a monk would be :
> The Devil got well, the devil a monk was he.

417. Δάκρυ' ἀδάκρυα. Eur. Iph. Taur. 832.—*Tearless tears.*

418. Damnosa quid non imminuit dies?
Ætas parentum, pejor avis, tulit
Nos nequiores, mox daturos
Progeniem vitiosiorem. Hor. C. 3, 6, 45.

> *Degeneracy.*
> Time, weakening Time, corrupts not what?
> Our sires less stout than theirs begat
> A still lower race—ourselves ; and we
> Hand down a worse posterity.—*Ed.*

419. Damnum appellandum est cum mala fama lucrum. Syr. 135.—
Gain made at the expense of character is no better than loss.

420. Da modo lucra mihi, da facto gaudia lucro ;
Et face ut emptori verba dedisse juvet. Ov. F. 5, 689.

> *The Tradesman's Prayer.*
> Put profits in my way, the joy of gain ;
> Nor let my tricks on customers be in vain !—*Ed.*

Prayer to Mercury, the patron of thieves and shopkeepers.

421. Dans l'adversité de nos meilleurs amis, nous trouvons toujours
quelque chose qui ne nous déplaît pas. La Rochef. Max. 26,
p. 109.—*In the troubles of our best friends, there is always some-*
thing which does not altogether displease us.

422. Dans le nombre de Quarante Ne faut-il pas un zéro? Boursault,
Epigrâme. *Lettre à Mgr. Lévesque et duc de Langres* (Lettres
Nouvelles du feu M. Boursault, Paris, 1709, vol. 2, p. 173).—
Among the forty (Academicians) must there not be a zero?

> Said of the French Academy, and still more true of the Society of Painters
> which bears the name in England. The amusing thing is, that it was the
> admission of La Bruyère into an academy of nonentities that prompted the
> lines, La Bruyère being the zero !

423. Dans les premières passions, les femmes aiment l'amant; dans les
autres elles aiment l'amour. La Rochef. Max., § 494, p. 91.

> In her first passion, woman loves her lover,
> In all the others, all she loves is love.—*Byron*, "D. Juan," c. 3, st. 3.

424. Dans le temps des chaleurs extrêmes,
Heureux d'amuser vos loisirs,
Je saurai près de vous appeler les Zéphyrs,
Les Amours y viendront d'eux-mêmes.
Lemierre, Madrigal, Œuvres, Paris, 1810, vol. 3, p. 451.

The Fan.

In summer times' stifling heat
Your amusement shall be my care;
The Zephyrs shall come at my beat,
The Loves of themselves will be there.—*Ed.*

Said to have been written originally on a lady's fan, and a favourite quotation of Louis XVIII., who was flattered for the time by the attribution of the lines to himself, until a newspaper brutally robbed the king of the supposititious authorship.

425. Dans l'opinion du monde, le mariage, comme dans la comedie, finit tout. C'est précisément le contraire qui est vrai: il commence tout. Mme. Swetchine, Pensée lxviii. vol. 2, p. 121.— *In the world's opinion marriage is supposed to wind up everything, as it does on the stage. The fact is, that the precise contrary is the truth. It begins everything.*

426. Da populo, da verba mihi, sine nescius errem;
Et liceat stulte credulitate frui.   Ov. Am. 3, 14, 29.

To a Faithless Mistress.

Pray undeceive me not, nor let me know that I mistaken be,
I would a little longer yet enjoy my fond credulity.—*Ed.*

427. Daran erkenn' ich meine Pappenheimer. Schiller, Wall. Tod, 3, 15. (Wallenstein).—*Therein I recognise my Pappenheimers.* I know my man. I am not taken in.

428. Das Alte stürzt, es ändert sich die Zeit,
Und neues Leben blüht aus den Ruinen. Schiller, W. Tell, 4, 2.

Attinghausen. The old is crumbling down, the times are changing,
And from the ruins blooms a fairer life.—*Sir T. Martin.*

429. Das arme Herz, hinieden
Von manchem Sturm bewegt,
Erlangt den wahren Frieden
Nur, wo es nicht mehr schlägt.   J. G. Count Salis-Seewis.

The Grave.

The poor heart, here o'erdriven,
By many a storm distrest,
Longs for the peaceful haven
Where it from strife may rest.—*Ed.*

430. Das eben ist der Fluch der bösen That,
Dass sie fortzeugend immer Böses muss gebären.
Schiller, Piccol. (1800), 5, 1.

This is the curse of every evil deed,
That, propagating still, it brings forth evil.—*Coleridge.*

431. Das Erste und Letzte, was vom Genie gefordert wird, ist Wahrheitsliebe. Goethe, Sprüche.—*The first and last thing which is demanded of Genius, is love of truth.*

432. Das Ewig-Weibliche
Zieht uns hinan. Goethe. *Second part of Faust,* last lines.
Chorus Mysticus.—*The ever-womanly draws us along.*

433. Das fünfte Rad am Wagen. Prov.—*The fifth wheel of the wagon.*
Said of any superfluity or incumbrance. Büchm. (p. 118) finds
an early use of the phrase in Herbort von Fritzlar's (14th
cent.) *Liet von Troye,* 83.

434. Das ganz Gemeine ist's, das ewig Gestrige,
Was immer war und immer wiederkehrt,
Und morgen gilt, weil's heute hat gegolten!
Denn aus Gemeinem ist der Mensch gemacht,
Und die Gewohnheit nennt er seine Amme.
Schiller, Wall. Tod, 1, 4.

> *Wall.* O no! It is the common, the quite common,
> The thing of an eternal yesterday,
> What ever was, and evermore returns,
> Sterling to-morrow, for to-day 'twas sterling!
> For of the wholly common is man made,
> And custom is his nurse.—*Coleridge.*

435. Das ist das Loos des Schönen auf der Erde. Schiller, Wall. Tod,
4, 12 (Thekla).—*That is the lot of heroes on the earth.*

436. Das Jahrhundert ist meinem Ideal nicht reif. Schiller, D.
Carlos, 3, 10 (Marquis Posa, loq.).—*The world is not yet ripe
for my ideal.*

437. Das Leben ist der Güter höchstes nicht,
Der Uebel grösstes aber ist die Schuld. Schiller, Braut. v. Mess,
fin.—*Life is not the highest blessing, but of evils sin's the worst.*

438. Das Naturell der Frauen
Ist so nah mit Kunst verwandt. Goethe, Faust, Pt. 2, Act 1,
Weitläufiger Saal.—*Nature in women is so nearly allied to art.*

439. Da spatium, tenuemque moram: male cuncta ministrat
Impetus. Statius, Theb. 10, 704.

> Give time and some delay, for passionate haste
> Will ruin all.—*Ed.*

440. Das Publikum, das ist ein Mann,
Der alles weiss und gar nichts kann. Ludw. Robert, *Das
Publikum* (Works, Mannheim, 1838, vol. 1, p. 19).—*The Public,
that means a man who knows everything and can do nothing.*
Büchm. p. 234-5.

441. Das Rechte, das ich viel gethan,
Das ficht mich nun nicht weiter an;
Aber das Falsche, das mir entschlüpft
Wie ein Gespenst mir vor Augen hüpft. Goethe, Sprichwört-
lich.—*All that I have done aright no longer now concerns me; but
the wrong that has slipped from me dances before me like a ghost.*

442. Das schöne Land des Weins und der Gesänge.   Goethe, Faust
(Auerbach's Keller), Meph. loq.—*That beautiful country of
wine and song, i.e.*, Spain.

443. Das Wenige verschwindet leicht dem Blick,
Der vorwärts sieht, wie viel noch übrig bleibt.   Goethe, Iphig.
1, 2.   (Iphig. loq.).—*The little (that is accomplished) is soon lost
sight of by one who sees before him how much still remains (to be
done).*   Mr M. Arnold quotes the words (*Essays in Criticism*)
against self-satisfied people, as "a good line of reflection for
weak humanity."

444. Dat veniam corvis, vexat censura columbas.   Juv. 2, 63.
[*Who will deny that justice has miscarried?*]
The crows escape, the harmless doves are harried.—*Ed.*

445. Davus sum non Œdipus.   Ter. And. 1, 2, 23.—*I am Davus not
Œdipus.*   I am a plain man; not a riddle-solver, like Œdipus.

446. Debilem facito manu,
Debilem pede, coxâ;
Tuber adstrue gibberum,
Lubricos quate dentes;
Vita dum superest, bene est.   Mæcenas ap. Sen. Ep. 101, 11.—
*Make me weak in hand, foot, and hip; add to this a swollen
tumour.   Knock out my loosening teeth; only let life remain, and
I am content.*

447. Decipimur specie recti; brevis esse laboro,
Obscurus fio.   Hor. A. P. 25.
We aim at the ideal, and fail.   I try
To be concise, and end in being obscure.—*Ed.*
Cf. J'évite d'être long, et je deviens obscur. Boil. L'A. P. 1, 66; and, Crede
mihi labor est non levis, esse brevem. Oweni Epigr. i. 168.   The latter part
of the quotation is said to have been humorously repeated by Thomas
Warton on his snuffing *out*, when he would have snuffed, his candle.

448. Dedimus tot pignora fatis.   Luc. 7, 662.—*We have given so many
hostages to fortune.*

449. Dediscit animus serò quod didicit diù.   Sen. Troad. 634.—*The
mind is slow to unlearn anything it has been learning long.*

450. Dedit hanc contagio labem
Et dabit in plures.   Juv. 2, 78.—*Contagion has communicated
the mischief and will spread it much further.*   The contagious
effect of immoral habits.

451. De gustibus non est disputandum.   Prov.—*There is no disputing
about tastes.*   Cf. Diversos diversa juvant; non omnibus annis
Omnia conveniunt.   Maximianus, *Elegies*, 1, 103.—*Different
things delight different people; it is not everything that suits
all ages.*

452. Dein redseliges Buch lehrt mancherlei Neues und Wahres:
Wäre das Wahre nur neu, wäre das Neue nur wahr. J. H. Voss
in *Vossischen Musenalmanach* for 1772 (p. 71). Büchm. p. 186.

> Your gossipy book has what's new and what's true;
> If the new were but true, and the true were but new.—*Ed.*

Mme. Aug. Craven (Mrs Bishop's *Memoir*, 2, 125) gives a French rendering, *àpropos* of "John Inglesant":—

> C'est du bon, c'est du neuf, que je trouve dans votre livre;
> Mais le bon n'est pas neuf, et le neuf n'est pas bon.

453. De l'audace, encore de l'audace, toujours de l'audace!—Danton,
Moniteur, Sept. 4, 1792, p. 1051.—*Audacity, still more audacity,
and always audacity.*

Famous conclusion of Danton's speech delivered before the Legislative
Assembly (Sept. 2, 1792) on the eve of the frightful September massacres,
of which he may be said to have thus fired the first spark. He concluded
with a powerful appeal to the nation to crush the enemies of France and of
the Revolution. *Pour les vaincre, Messieurs, il faut de l'audace, encore de
l'audace, toujours de l'audace, et la France est sauvée!* "Be bold, be bold,
and everywhere be bold." Spenser, *F. Queene*, 3, 11, 54.

454. Delendam esse Carthaginem, et quum de alio consuleretur, pro-
nuntiabat. Florus, 2, 15.—[So virulent was Cato's hatred against
that nation that] *Even when consulted on other matters, he would
deliver his opinion that Carthage ought to be destroyed.*

Cry of M. Porcius Cato, throughout the year 151 B.C., on the political
necessity for crushing a neighbouring power that menaced the peace and
commerce of Rome. His speeches in the senate at that time, no matter
on what subject, are said to have ended with the words, "Ceterum censeo
delendam esse Carthaginem"—*For the rest, I am of opinion that Carthage
must be destroyed.*

455. Delere licebit
Quod non edideris: nescit vox missa reverti. Hor. A. P. 389.
—*You may strike out what you please before publishing; but once
sent into the world the words can never be recalled.*

This applies to the evidential force, not only of published or written
statements, but of those that are made by word of mouth. Once written
or spoken, they cannot be recalled. Cf. Semel emissum volat irrevocabile
verbum. Hor. Ep. 1, 18, 71. "You can't get back a word you once let go"
(*Conington*). On the other hand, the differential value of documentary and
verbal evidence finds its expression in the med. hemistich, *Litera scripta
manet; verbum at inane perit.*—"The writing remains, while the mere
spoken word dies on the sound."

456. Deliberando sæpe perit occasio. Syr. 140.—*Opportunity is often
lost through deliberation.*

Cf. Dum deliberamus quando incipiendum sit, incipere jam serum est.
Quint. 12, 6, 3.—*While we are considering when to begin, it becomes already
too late to do so.*
And

> Eja, age, rumpe moras, quo te spectabimus usque?
> Dum quid sis dubitas, jam potes esse nihil. Mart. 2, 64, 9.
>
> Come, come, look sharp! How long are we to wait?
> While doubting what to be, you'll be too late.—*Ed.*

457. Deliberandum est, quicquid statuendum est semel.   Syr. 132.—
Whatever has to be decided once for all requires careful deliberation.

458. De loin c'est quelque chose, et de près ce n'est rien.   La Font,
4, 10 (Chameau et Bâtons flottants).—*At a distance it looks like
something, but close by it is nothing at all.*

> Like sticks floating on water, things at a distance seem important to those
> watching them, but on nearer inspection they turn out to be insignificant
> enough.   Hence, any such deceptive appearances are said to be *bâtons
> flottants sur l'onde.*

459. De minimis non curat lex.   Law Max.—*The law does not concern
itself about trifles.*   The Court, though strict, is not harsh and
pedantic in its requirements.

460. Demitto auriculas ut iniquæ mentis asellus.   Hor. S. 1, 9, 20.—
Down go my ears, like a surly young ass.   I rebel against the
proposition.

461. Dem Mimen flicht die Nachwelt keine Kränze.   Schiller, Wall.
Lager. Prol.—*Posterity binds no wreaths for the actor.*

> "The actor has always before him the haunting fact, that the art-work
> to which he has devoted his life must die with him: that, unlike the
> poet, painter, and sculptor, he cannot hand down to posterity any visible
> proof of the result of his labours, etc."   Mr G. Alexander, *Lecture before the
> Leeds Amateur Dram. Society*, Oct. 3, 1895.

462. De mortuis nil nisi bonum.   Prov.—*Say nothing of the dead but
what is good.*

> One of Chilo's maxims (Diog. Laert. 1, 69) is τὸν τεθνηκότα μὴ κακολογεῖν.
> —*Speak not evil of the dead.*   Dum vivit hominem noveris: ubi mortuus
> est, quiescas. Plaut. Truc. 1, 2, 62.—*As long as a man is living, you may
> criticise him: but after he is dead, keep silence.*

463. Demosthenem ferunt, ei qui quæsivisset quid primum esset in
dicendo, actionem: quid secundum, idem, et idem tertium re-
spondisse.   Cic. Brut. 38, 142.—*It is said of Demosthenes, that,
whenever he was asked what was the principal thing in public
speaking, he replied, Action; what was the second? Action; the
third? the same.*

464. De nihilo nihilum, in nihilum nil posse reverti.   Pers. 3, 84.—
From nothing nought, and into nought can nought return.

> Matter being eternal, the creation of the world "out of nothing," and
> its ultimate resolution into nothingness, was rejected by Epicureans as
> absurd.   Acc. to Diog. Laert. (10, 38), the first principle of Epicurus'
> cosmogony is οὐδὲν γίνεται ἐκ τοῦ μὴ ὄντος.—*Nothing can be produced from
> that which does not exist.*
>   Nil igitur fieri de nilo posse fatendum est;
>   Semine quando opus est rebus. Lucret. 1, 206.—*The formation
> of matter without material is unimaginable, since things must have a seed to
> start from.*

465. Denique non omnes eadem mirantur amantque. Hor. Ep. 2, 2, 58.—*Men do not, in short, all admire or love the same things.* Diversity of taste.

466. Denn eben wo Begriffe fehlen,
Da stellt ein Wort zur rechten Zeit sich ein.
Goethe, Faust, Schülerscene.

Metaphysics.

Meph. Be thought or no thought in your head,
Fine phrases there will do instead.—*Sir T. Martin.*

467. Denn wer den Besten seiner Zeit genug
Gethan, der hat gelebt für alle Zeiten. Schiller, Wall. Lager.
Prol.—*He who has satisfied the best men of his time, has lived for all time.* Qu. by Tourgénieff (to G. Sand) in acknowledging her praise of his "Récit d'un Chasseur," in the *Temps*, Oct. 30, 1872 (*Tourgénieff and his French Circle*, Lond., 1898, p. 147).

468. Denn wo das Strenge mit dem Zarten,
Wo Starkes sich und Mildes paarten,
Da giebt es einen guten Klang. Schiller, Lied. von d. Glocke.

For where the rough and tender meet;
Where strength and grace each other greet,
The tone produc'd rings true and clear.—*Ed.*

469. De non apparentibus, et non existentibus, eadem est ratio. Law Max.—*That which is not forthcoming must be treated as if it did not exist.* If the Court cannot take judicial notice of a fact, it is the same as if the fact had not existed.

470. Deos fortioribus adesse. Tac. H. 4, 17.—*The gods are on the side of the strongest.*

R. de Rabutin, Comte de Bussy, writing to the Count of Limoges (*Correspondances*, ed. Lalanne, Paris, 1858, vol. 3, p. 393, Letter 1196), Oct. 18, 1677, says: "Dieu est d'ordinaire pour les gros escadrons contre les petits."—*As a rule God is on the side of the big squadrons as against the small ones.* Voltaire in his *Ep. à M. le Riche*, Feb. 6, 1770, writes: "Le nombre des sages sera toujours petit. Il est vrai qu'il est augmenté; mais ce n'est rien en comparaison des sots, et par malheur on dit que Dieu est toujours pour les gros bataillons."—*The number of the wise will be always small. It is true that it has been largely increased; but it is nothing in comparison with the number of fools, and unfortunately they say that God always favours the heaviest battalions.*

471. Deprendi miserum est. Hor. S. 1, 2, 134.—*'Tis awful to be found out.* Caught in the act.

472. De profundis clamavi ad te, Domine. Ps. cxxix. 1.—*Out of the deep have I called unto thee, O Lord.* One of the Penitential Psalms chanted in the Office for the departed.

473. De rabo de puerco nunca buen virote. Prov.—*You will never make a good arrow of a pig's tail.*

474. Der brave Mann denkt an sich selbst zuletzt. Schiller, W. Tell (1804), 1, 1. (Tell to Ruodi, the fisherman):—*A brave man thinks of himself the last.*

475. Der den Augenblick ergreift
Das ist der rechte Mann. Goethe, Faust, Schülerscene.—*He who seizes the (right) moment is the right man.*

476. Der Hahn schliesst die Augen, wann er krähet, weil er es auswendig kann. Prov.— *The cock shuts his eyes when he crows, because he knows it by heart.*

477. Der Historiker ist ein rückwärts gekehrter Prophet. Fried. von Schlegel, "Athenæum," Berlin, 1798-1800, vol. i. pt. 2, p. 20.— *The historian is a prophet who casts backward glances on the past.*

478. Der Lebende hat Recht. Schiller, An die Freunde.—*The living is in the right.*

479. Der Mensch erfährt, er sei auch, wer er mag,
Ein letztes Glück und einen letzten Tag. Goethe, Essex, Epilog.—*Man experiences, be he who he may, a last pleasure and a last day.*

480. Der Mensch ist frei geschaffen, ist frei,
Und würd' er in Ketten geboren.
                    Schiller, Die Worte des Glaubens.

> Man is created free, all free,
> E'en were he born in chains.—*Ed.*

481. Der Mensch ist was er isst. Ludwig Feuerbach. Pref. to Moleschott's " Lehre der Nahrungsmittel für das Volk " (1850). —*Man is what he eats.* Prob. borrowed from Brillat-Savarin's "Physiologie du Goût," Aphor. IV.: Dis-moi ce que tu manges, je te dirais ce que tu es.—*Tell me what you eat, and I will tell you what you are.*

482. Der Rhein, Deutschlands Strom, aber nicht Deutschlands Grenze. Ernst Moritz Arndt, Title of work pub. at Leipzig (W. Rein), 1813.—*The Rhine, Germany's river, but not Germany's boundary.*

483. Der Umgang mit Frauen ist das Element guter Sitten. Goethe, Wahlverwandtschaften.—*The society of women is the school of good manners*

484. Der ungezogene Liebling der Grazien. Goethe, Epilogue to his tr. of the *Birds* of Aristophanes (1787).— *The spoiled darling of the Graces,* sc. Aristophanes : also said of H. Heine. Büchm. p. 163.

484A. Der Wahn ist kurz, die Reu' ist lang. Schiller, Lied v. der Glocke.—*Th' illusion 's-short, the penance long.*

485. Desinant Maledicere, facta ne noscant sua.   Ter. And. Prol. 22.—
*Let them cease to speak ill of others, lest they come to hear of
their own misdoings.*

486. Des Lebens Mai blüht einmal und nicht wieder.   Schiller, Resignation.—*The May of life blooms once, and not again.*   Οὐκ αἰεὶ θέρος
ἐσσεῖται. Hes. Op. 501.—*'Twill not be always summer.*

487. Des Lebens ungemischte Freude
Ward Keinem Irdischen zu Teil. Schiller, Ring des Polycrates, st. 9.

> For never yet has earthly joy
> Been granted man without alloy.—*Ed.*

488. Des lois et non du sang; ne souillez point vos mains:
Romains, vous oseriez égorger des Romains! **M. J.** Chénier.
Caius Gracchus, 2, 2 (Feb. 9, 1792).   Gracchus, calming the
popular fury against the senators, says:

> Laws, and not blood! stain not your hands, I pray:
> Shall Romans dare their brother-Romans slay?—*Ed.*

The sentiment was so little to the popular taste of the hour, that at a
later representation it was challenged by a "gallery" rejoinder of *Du sang et
non des lois!* (Biogr. Michaud).   In his *Timoléon* (Sept. 11, 1795) the passage
(3, 2), where to Timophane's plea that he had never claimed "sovereign"
rank, Démariste retorts with "N'est-on jamais tyran qu' avec un diadême?" (*Need a man be crowned to be a tyrant?*), was considered so ill-
timed that the play never got beyond the first public rehearsal.

489. Des Menschen Engel ist die Zeit.   Schiller, Wall. Tod. 5, 11
(Octavio loq.).—*Time is man's good angel.*

490. Des Menschen Wille, das ist sein Glück.   Schiller, Wall. Lager,
Act 7.—*The will of man, that is his happiness.*   Cf. Sebastian
Franck's *Sprichwörter Sammlung* (1532), No. 16, Des Menschen
Wille ist sein Himmelreich.—*Man's will is his kingdom of heaven.*

491. De ta tige détachée
Pauvre feuille desséchée,
Où vas-tu?
            Je n'en sais rien.
L'orage a frappé le chêne
Qui seul était mon soutien.
De son inconstante haleine
Le zéphyr ou l'aquilon
Depuis ce jour me promène
De la forêt à la plaine,
De la montagne au vallon;
Je vais où le vent me mène,
Sans me plaindre ou m'effrayer,
Je vais où va toute chose,
Où va la feuille de rose
Et la feuille de laurier.   A. V. Arnault, Fab. 5, 16.

1815.

Poor withered leaf, torn from thy bough,
Say, wanderer, whither travellest thou ?

I cannot tell. The tempest broke
And felled to earth the parent oak.
Since then, wild winds from west and north,
This way and that, have driven me forth;
From wood to field, from hill to dale,
The merest plaything of the gale.
I move just as the breeze may steer,
Without complaint and without fear;
I go where all that's earthly goes—
The victor's laurel, and love's rose.—*Ed.*

⁎ The "touchingness" of Arnault's lines will not be denied. Written at the end of 1815, they sound the swan-song and note of despair of the Bonapartists. Arnault's Œuvres (ed. Bossange), Paris, 1826, vol. 2, p. 39. Alex. 196.

492. Détestables flatteurs, présent le plus funeste
Que puisse faire aux rois la colère céleste. Rac. Phèdre, 4, 6.

> *Phèdre loq.:* Detested flatterers ! the most fatal gift
>   That Heaven in its wrath can send to kings!—*Ed.*

(Phèdre's dying words.) Cf. Pessimum genus inimicorum, laudantes. Tac. Agr. 41.—*The worst kind of enemies—flatterers.*

493. Det ille veniam facile, cui venia est opus. Sen. Agam. 267.
—*Who needs forgiveness should readily extend the same.*

494. Detrahat auctori multum fortuna licebit;
     Tu tamen ingenio clara ferere meo.
Dumque legar, mecum pariter tua fama legetur;
     Nec potes in mœstos omnis abire rogos.   Ov. T. 5, 14, 3.

> *To his Wife.*
> Let fortune disparage my verse as she will,
>   Your fame shall shine bright enough thanks to my art.
> As long as I'm read, they'll remember you still,
>   And your mem'ry survive e'en when life shall depart.—*Ed.*

495. Deus hæc fortasse benigna Reducet in sedem vice. Hor. Epod. 13, 7.—*God will, perhaps, by some gracious change, restore matters to their former state.*

496. Deus nobis hæc otia fecit. Virg. E. 1, 6.—*This peace and rest we owe to God.*

497. Deus vult.—*God wills it.*

The Council of Clermont, 1095, held under Urban II. for considering the project of a crusade against the Turks, broke up amid unanimous shouts of *Deus vult* ("It is God's will "), and the words became eventually the battle-cry of the First Crusade.

498. Deux eftions et n'avions qu'ung cuer. Fr. Villon, Rondeau, Grand Testament, 985, p. 62. —*Two were we, with but one heart between us.*

Arist. (ap. Diog. Laert. 5, 20) defines "friends" to mean "two bodies inhabited by one soul,"—μία ψυχὴ δύο σώμασιν ἐνοικοῦσα. Cf. Pope's "Iliad" (16, 267), "Two friends, two bodies with one soul inspired." Friedrich Halm has in his *Der Sohn der Wildniss* (1842), Act 2,

> Zwei Seelen und ein Gedanke,
> Zwei Herzen und ein Schlag.
> Two souls with a single thought,
> Two hearts that beat as one.—*F. Hoffmann.*

499. Deversorium viatoris Hierosolymam profisciscentis. Inscr. on Dean Alford's tomb in St Martin's Churchyard, Canterbury.— *The resting-place of a traveller on his way to Jerusalem.*

500. Devine si tu peux, et choisis si tu l'oses. Corn. Héracl. 4, 5.— *Guess if you can, and choose if you dare.* Léontine to Emp. Phocas, on introducing Heraclius and Martian, one of whom is his unknown son.

501. De vitiis nostris scalam nobis facimus, si vitia ipsa calcamus. St Aug. Serm. 176, 4. Vol. v., Append. p. 213.—*We make to ourselves ladders of our vices when we tread the vices themselves under foot.*

> Saint Augustine! well hast thou said
> That of our vices we can frame
> A ladder, if we will but tread
> Beneath our feet each deed of shame.—*Longfellow.*

502. De votre esprit la force est si puissante
Que vous pourriez vous passer de beauté:
De vos attraits la grâce est si piquante
Que sans esprit vous auriez enchanté. Volt. Poés. Mêlées, xxiii.

> *A Mme. de . . .*
> The sparkle of your wit is such
> You'd charm, were beauty wanting:
> Your looks and air attract so much
> That dumb, you're still enchanting.—*Ed.*

503. Dextro tempore. Hor. S. 2, 1, 18.—*At a lucky moment.*

504. Dicere quæ puduit, scribere jussit amor. Ov. Her. 4, 10.
What shame forbade me speak, Love made me write.—*Ed.*

505. Dices, Habeo hic quos legam non minus disertos. Etiam: sed legendi occasio semper est, audiendi non semper. Præterea multo magis, ut vulgo dicitur, viva vox afficit. Nam licet acriora sint quæ legas, altius tamen in animo sedent quæ pronuntiatio, vultus, habitus, gestus etiam dicentis affigit. Plin. Ep. 2, 3.

> *Lectures v. Books.*
> You will say, "I have just as eloquent authors that I can read at home." Perhaps: but while you can always read, you cannot always hear. Besides, the "living voice," as they say, is much more effective. Your book may be witty enough, and yet its teaching is not so impressive as that which comes with all the force of a speaker's voice, looks, bearing, and action.

E

₊ "There is a great difference in hearing and reading. Hearing a first-rate lecturer makes far more impression. If this is the case even with people accustomed to the use of books, how much more with those not used to them?"—R. H. Quick, *Life and Remains*, Lond., 1899, p. 485.

506. Diceva Carlo Quinto, che parlerebbe in lingua Francese ad un amico, in Tedesco al suo cavallo, in Italiano alla sua signora, in Spagnuolo a Dio, in Inglese agli uccelli.   Ravizzotti, Italian Grammar, 5th ed., Lond., n.d. (p. 402).—*Charles Quint used to say that one should speak to a friend in French, to one's horse in German, one's mistress in Italian, to God in Spanish, and in English to birds.*

507. Dic, hospes, Spartæ nos te hic vidisse jacentes,
Dum sanctis patriæ legibus obsequimur.—Transl. ap. Cic. Tusc. 1, 42, 101, of the following epigr. of Simonides (Bergk, iii. p. 451), on the Three Hundred that fell with Leonidas at Thermopylæ in attempting to resist the Persian invasion, 480 B.C.

> Ὦ ξεῖν' ἀγγέλλειν Λακηδαιμονίοις, ὅτι τῇδε
> Κείμεθα, τοῖς κείνων ῥήμασι πειθόμενοι.
>
> *Thermopylæ.*
>
> Go, tell the Spartans, thou that passest by,
> That here, obedient to their laws, we lie.—*Sterling.*

508. Dicite Iö Pæan, et Iö bis dicite Pæan;
Decidit in casses præda petita meos.   Ov. Art. Am. 2, 1.

> Hurrah! hurrah! and give one cheer more yet!
> The game I chased has fallen into my net.—*Ed.*

509. Dicta fides sequitur.   Ov. M. 3, 527.—*The promise is followed by performance*—like the following.

510. Dictum factum. Ter. And. 2, 3, 7.—*No sooner said than done.* Hdt. (3, 135) has, ἅμα ἔπος τε, καὶ ἔργον ἐποίεε.—*He no sooner said the word than it was done.*   Immediately.

511. Dictum sapienti sat est. Ter. Phorm. 3, 3, 8 (Antipho).—*A word to the wise is enough.*   So also "Verbum sapienti," with same meaning.

> Cf. the following:—Non canimus surdis. Virg. E. 10, 8.—*We sing to those that hear.*   Μαθοῦσιν αὐδῶ, κοὐ μαθοῦσι λήθομαι. Æsch. Ag. 39.—*I speak to those who understand, and pass over those who do not:* φωνάεντα συνετοῖσιν. Pind. O. 2, 152.—*A message to those who comprehend.*   A bon entendeur peu de paroles, Le sage entend à demi mot, etc., etc.

512. Die Botschaft hör' ich wohl, allein mir fehlt der Glaube;
Das Wunder ist des Glaubens liebstes Kind. Goethe, Faust, Nacht.

> *Faust:* I hear the message plain; there only lacks belief:
> Miracle is the dearest child of faith.—*Ed.*

513. Die Bretter, die die Welt bedeuten.   Schiller, *An die Freunde* (1803).—*The "boards" which represent the world.*   The stage.

514. Die Erinnerung ist das einzige Paradies, aus dem wir nicht vertrieben werden können. Jean Paul Richter, Gesammelte Aufsätze u. Dichtungen.—*Memory is the only Paradise from which no one can drive us.*

515. Die Fabel ist der Liebe Heimatwelt,
Gern wohnt sie unter Feen, Talismanen;
Glaubt gern an Götter, weil sie göttlich ist.
Die alten Fabelwesen sind nicht mehr,
Das reizende Geschlecht ist ausgewandert;
Doch eine Sprache braucht das Herz, es bringt
Der alte Trieb die alten Namen wieder.   Schiller, Picc. 3, 4.

> *Max.* For fable is Love's world, his home, his birthplace:
> Delightedly dwells he 'mong fays and talismans
> And spirits; and delightedly believes
> Divinities, being himself divine.
> The intelligible forms of ancient poets,
> The fair humanities of old religion,
> The power, the beauty, and the majesty,
> That had their haunts in dale, or piny mountain,
> Or forest by slow stream, or pebbly spring,
> Or chasms and wat'ry depths; all these have vanished;
> They live no longer in the faith of reason!
> But still the heart doth need a language, still
> Doth the old instinct bring back the old names.—*Coleridge.*

516. Die Freuden, die man übertreibt,
Die Freuden werden Schmerzen.   Fried. Justin Bertuch, Das Lämmchen.—*The pleasures in which men indulge too freely, become pains.*

517. Die Geister platzen aufeinander. Luther, Letter of Aug. 21, 1524, to the Princes of Saxony.—*The spirits explode against each other*, referring to the fanatical excesses of the Prophets of Zwickau, headed by Thos. Münzer. The original is "Man lass die Geister auf einander platzen und treffen." Büchm. p. 122. Applicable to angry recriminations between political, literary, or other opponents.

518. Die Irrthümer des Menschen machen ihn eigentlich liebenswürdig. Goethe, Sprüche.—*It is a man's faults that make him really lovable.*

519. Die jüdische Religion ist gar keine Religion, sondern ein Unglück. Heine, Reisebilder, Bk. 2, cap. 3.—*Judaism is no religion at all, but simply a misfortune.*

520. Die Liebe ist der Liebe Preis. Schiller, Don Carlos, 2, 8 (Princess Eboli loq.).—*Love is love's reward.*

521. Diem perdidi. Suet. Tit. 8.—*I have lost a day!* Reflection of the Emperor Titus, if on finding at night that he had done no good action during the preceding day.

> Count that day lost whose low descending sun
> Views from thy hand no noble action done.
> *Staniford's* "Art of Reading," 3rd ed., p. 27, Boston, 1803.

Chamfort (ii. 20) has, La plus perdue de toutes les journées est celle où l'on n'à pas ri.—*The most wasted of all days is that on which one has not laughed.* To which may be added the paradox of one Claude Mier (source unknown), Le temps le mieux employé est celui que l'on perd.—*The time best employed is that which one wastes, i.e.,* in day dreams, theorising, etc.

522. Die Politik der freien Hand.—*The policy of the free hand.* First employed by von Schleinitz in 1859 àpropos of Prussia's attitude towards the Franco-Austrian war, and repeated by Bismarck in the Lower House of Parliament, Jan. 22, 1864. Büchm. p 548.

523. Die Politik ist keine exakte Wissenschaft. Bismarck in Prussian Upper House, Dec. 18, 1863.—*Politics is not an exact science.* On Mar 15, 1884, he repeated the remark in the Reichstag:— "Politics is not a science, as many of our professors imagine, but an art" (Die Politik ist keine Wissenschaft, wie viele der Herren Professoren sich einbilden, sondern eine Kunst). Fumag. No. 596.

524. Die Regierung muss der Bewegung stets einen Schritt voraus sein.—*The Government must always be in advance of public opinion.* Count Adolf Heinrich Arnim-Boytzenburg, speech on the address to the Throne, April 2, 1848. Büchm. p. 539.

524A. Dies adimit ægritudinem. Ter. Heaut. 3, 1, 13.—*Time effaces grief.*

525. Dieser Monat ist ein Kuss, den der Himmel giebt der Erde,
Dass sie jetzund seine Braut, künftig eine Mutter werde.
                                        Friedr. von Logau.
                    May.
    This month is the kiss Heav'n imprints upon earth:
    The bride who, as mother, shall shortly give birth.—*Ed.*

526. Dies iræ, dies illa
Sæclum solvet in favilla,
Teste David cum Sibylla, etc. Thomas de Celano, disc. of S. Francis.
        Day of wrath! O Day of mourning!
        See fulfilled the prophet's warning,
        Heaven and earth in ashes burning! etc.—*Dr Irons.*
    Sung as the *Prose* in the Mass for the Dead; also used in the Commemoration of the Faithful Departed on All Souls' Day.

527. Dies regnis illa suprema fuit. Ov. F. 2, 852.—*That was the last day of the royal line.* Said of the expulsion of the kings from Latium.

528. Die Stätte, die ein guter Mensch betrat,
Ist eingeweiht; nach hundert Jahren klingt
Sein Wort und seine That dem Enkel wieder. Goethe, Tasso, 1, 1.
        The places trodden by a good man's foot
        Are hallowed ground: after a hundred years
        His words and deeds come back to his posterity.—*Ed.*

529. Die Toten reiten schnell! G. A. Bürger, Lenore, stroph. 20, l. 6.
(Göttinger Musenalmanach, 1774, p. 214).—*The dead travel fast!*

("Les morts vont vite.") The words are the cry of Wilhelm, as the heroine is being carried off on horseback by her phantom lover, and appear to have been taken by Bürger from some simple country ditty upon which he built his famous ballad. They are generally used nowadays to mean that the dead are soon forgotten.

530. Dieu et mon droit.—*God and my right hand.* Motto of the Sovereigns of Great Britain.

> Originally referred to Richard I. and his military successes in 1197-8—"God and my right hand have conquered France"—the words seem to have been first assumed as the royal *devise* by Henry VI.

531. Dieu fit du repentir la vertu des mortels. Volt. Olimpie, 2, 2.—*God made repentance the virtue of mankind.*

532. Die Uhr schlägt keinem Glücklichen. Schiller, Picc. 3, 3.—*The clock does not strike for the happy:* often qu. as *dem Glücklichen schlägt keine Stunde.*

533. Dieu mesure le froid à la brebis tondue. Henri Estienne, Les Prèmices, p. 47 (1594), and Quit. p. 175.—*God tempers the wind to the shorn lamb.* Sterne, *Sent. Journey,* Lond. 1782, 8ᵛᵒ, p. 53, *"Maria."*

534. Die Weltgeschichte ist das Weltgericht. Schiller, Resignation. —*History is the world's judgment.* "The world's own annals are its doom." E. P. Arnold-Forster tr.

535. Differ: habent parvæ commoda magna moræ. Ov. F. 3, 394.—*Wait a while: a short delay often has great advantages.*

> Beware of desp'rate steps: the darkest day,
> Live till to-morrow, will have passed away.
> —*Cowper,* "The Needless Alarm."

536. Difficile est crimen non prodere vultu. Ov. M. 2, 447.—*It is difficult not to betray guilt by one's looks.*

537. Difficile est longum subito deponere amorem:
Difficile est; verum hoc qualubet efficias. Cat. 76, 13.

> 'Tis hard to quit at once long-cherished love;
> 'Tis hard, yet somehow you'll successful prove.—*Ed.*

538. Difficile est proprie communia dicere. Hor. A. P. 128.

> 'Tis hard, I grant, to treat a subject known
> And hackneyed, so that it may look one's own.—*Conington.*

539. Difficile est satiram non scribere. Nam quis iniquæ
Tam patiens urbis, tam ferreus, ut teneat se? Juv. 1, 30.

> Indeed the hard thing's not to satirise.
> For who's so tolerant of the vicious town,
> So cased in iron, as to hold his spleen?—*Ed.*

540. Difficilem habere oportet aurem ad crimina. Syr. 133.—*Our ears ought to be slow in listening to accusations.*

541. Difficilis, facilis, jucundus, acerbus es idem;
Nec tecum possum vivere, nec sine te.   Mart. 12, 47, 1.

Obviously borrowed from the "Sic ego nec sine te, nec tecum,
vivere possum," of Ov. Am. 3, 11, 39.

> You please, provoke, by turns amuse and grieve,
> That not without, nor with thee, can I live.— *Ed.*

or

> In all thy humours, whether grave or mellow,
> Thou'rt such a touchy, testy, pleasant fellow,
> Hast so much wit, and mirth, and spleen about thee,
> That there's no living with thee nor without thee.   Addison, *Spectator,* **68.**

542. Difficilis optimi perfectio atque absolutio.   Cic. Brut. 36, **137.**—
Perfection and finish of the highest kind is very hard to attain.

543. Dignus est operarius mercede sua.   Vulg. S. Luc. 10, 7.—*The
labourer is worthy of his hire.*

544. Dii laneos pedes habent.   Macr. Sat. 1, 8, 5.—*The gods have
feet of wool.*   Though noiseless and unperceived, retribution
certainly overtakes the sinner.   Petr. 44, 789 has, *Dii pedes
lanatos habent.*

545. Dilator, spe longus, iners, avidusque futuri,
Difficilis, querulus, laudator temporis acti
Se puero, censor castigatorque minorum.   Hor. A. P. 172.

The Old Fogey.

> Inert, irresolute, his neck he cranes
> Into the future, grumbles and complains;
> Extols his own young years with peevish praise,
> But rates and censures these degenerate days.—*Conington.*

546. Dilexi justitiam et odi iniquitatem; propterea morior in exilio.
Baron. Annal. 1085, A.D.—*I have loved righteousness and hated
iniquity, and therefore I die in exile.*   Dying words of Hildebrand
(Gregory VII.) at Salerno, 1085 A.D.) whither he had fled from
the wrath of the Emperor Henry IV.   Cf. Ps. xliv 7, *Dilexisti
justitiam,* etc., from which the speech was borrowed.

547. Dilige (*sc.* Deum) et quod vis fac.   Aug. in Ep. S. Ioan. Tractat.
vii. 8 (vol. iii. pt. ii. 637 F).—*If you love God, you may do what
you please.*   Sometimes qu. as *Ama, et fac quod vis.*

548. Diligentia, qua una virtute omnes virtutes reliquæ continentur.
Cic. de Or. 2, 35, 150.—*Diligence, the one virtue that contains in
itself all the rest.*   Cf. "'Diligent!' that includes all virtues in
it a student can have."—Carlyle, *Installation Address,* Edinburgh,
April, 1866.

549. Di, meliora piis, erroremque hostibus illum! Virg. G. 3, 513.—*God
give His servants better fortune, and send that error to His enemies!*

For similar imprecations, cf. Eveniat nostris hostibus ille pudor. Ov. Am. 3, 11, 16.—*May such shame be the portion of my enemy!* Sic pereant omnes inimici tui, Domine: qui autem diligunt te, sicut sol in ortu suo splendet, ita rutilent! Vulg. Jud. 5, 31.—*So let all Thine enemies perish, O Lord, but let them that love Thee shine as the sun shineth in his rising!*

550. Di melius duint! Ter. Phorm. 5, 8, 16. (Di meliora velint! Ov. M. 7, 37).—*God forbid!*

551. Dimidium facti, qui cæpit, habet: sapere aude; Incipe. Hor. Ep. 1, 2, 40.

> Come now, have courage to be wise: begin;
> You're half way over when you once plunge in.'—*Conington.*

and

> Incipe: dimidium facti est cæpisse. Supersit
> Dimidium: rursum hoc incipe, et efficies. Aus. Epigr. 81.

> "Begun's half done"; thus half your task's diminished:
> "Begin" once more, and so the whole is finished.—*Ed.*

Plato (Leges 6, p. 753) has, Ἀρχὴ γὰρ λέγεται μὲν ἥμισυ παντός.—*Acc. to the proverb, "the beginning is half the battle."* Ἀρχὴ δέ τοι ἥμισυ παντός (same meaning), is ascribed to Hesiod by Lucian (*Hermotimus*, 3), but is more prob. a maxim of Pythagoras, as Iamblichus states (Vit. Pythag. 29).

552. Diruit, ædificat, mutat quadrata rotundis. Hor. Ep. 1, 1, 100.

A Flighty Inconsequent Fellow.

> Builds castles up, then pulls them to the ground,
> Keeps changing round for square, and square for round.—*Conington.*

553. Dis aliter visum. Virg. A. 2, 428.—*The gods have judged otherwise.*

554. Disce hinc quid possit fortuna, immota labascunt, Et quæ perpetuo sunt agitata, manent.
> J anus Vitalis, Epigr. Del. p. 366.

The Tiber at Rome.

> See fortune's power: th' immovable decays,
> And what is ever moving, ever stays.—*Ed.*

Spenser ("Ruines of Rome") repeats the idea:—

> No ought save Tyber, hastening to his fall,
> Remains of all: O world's inconstancie!
> That which is firm doth flit and fall away,
> And that is flitting doth abide and stay.

555. Disce mori. Luc. 5, 364.—*Learn to die.* Chamfort (i. 146) makes a girl of twelve ask, "Pourquoi donc cette phrase, *Apprendre à mourir?* Je vois qu'on y réussit très bien dès la première fois."

556. Disce puer virtutem ex me, verumque laborem, Fortunam ex aliis. Virg. A. 12, 435.

Æneas to Ascanius.

> Learn of your father to be great,
> Of others to be fortunate.—*Conington.*

Cf. ὦ παῖ, γένοιο πατρὸς εὐτυχέστερος,
τὰ δ᾽ ἄλλ᾽ ὅμοιος· καὶ γένοι᾽ ἂν οὐ κακός.—Soph. Aj. 550. (Ajax to
Teucer): *My son, resemble thy father in all things except in fortune, and
thou wilt not do amiss.* This is tr. by Accius (vol. i. p. 180), Virtuti sis
par, dispar fortunis patris.—*Be thy father's match in valour, but not in
fortune.*

557. Discere si cupias, gratis quod quæris habebis.—*If you desire to
learn, you shall have what you desire free of cost.* Inscription
on school at Salzburg.—*Times* of October 13, 1885.

558. Discipulus est prioris posterior dies.   Syr. 123.—*Every day is
yesterday's disciple.*   Experience teaches.

559. Discite justitiam moniti, et non temnere divos.   Virg. A. 6, 620.
—*Learn justice by the event, and fear the gods.*

560. Discit enim citius, meminitque libentius illud
Quod quis deridet, quam quod probat et veneratur.

Hor. Ep. 2, 1, 262.

Far easier 'tis to learn and recollect
What moves derision than what claims respect.—*Conington.*

Cf. Dociles imitandis
Turpibus ac pravis omnes sumus.   Juv. 14, 40.

Quick are we all to learn what's vile and base.—*Ed.*

561. Discitur innocuas ut agat facundia causas:
Protegit hæc sontes, immeritosque premit.   Ov. T. 2, 273.

The Bar.

In the cause of truth men study eloquence;
Tho' it screen guilt, and bully innocence.—*Ed.*

562. Δὶς ἢ τρὶς τὰ καλά.—*Give us a fine thing two or three times over!*
Encore!   Cf. Plat. Gorg. cap. 53, 498, fin.

563. Diseur de bons mots, mauvais caractère. Pasc. Pens. 29, 26.—
'Tis a bad sign to be a sayer of good things.

La Bruyère, vol. i. p. 162 (La Cour), echoes the sentiment, and amplifies it.
" 'Diseurs de bon mots, mauvais caractère'—je le dirais s'il n'avait été dit.
Ceux qui nuisent à la réputation ou à la fortune des autres, plutôt que de
perdre un bon mot, méritent une peine infamante: cela n'a pas été dit, et je
l'ose dire."—*That a reputation for telling good stories shows a bad disposition,
is a remark that I should have made myself, if it had not been already said.
Those who would sooner damage another man's character or prospects than
miss a good story deserve the worst punishment possible.   This has not been
said before, and I venture to put the reflection in circulation.*   Quint. (6, 3,
28) has, "potius amicum, quam dictum perdidi."—*I had rather lose a friend
than a bon mot;* and Horace (Sat. 1, 4, 34) speaks of one who

Dummodo risum
Excutiat sibi, non hic cuiquam parcet amico.—*If he can raise a laugh
at his expense, there's not a friend he'll spare.*

On the other hand, Quitard (p. 44) cites the prov., *Il vaut mieux perdre
un bon mot qu'un ami,* "It is better to lose a clever saying than a friend."

564. Disjecti membra poetæ. Hor. S. 1, 4, 62.—*Limbs of the dis-
membered poet.* Lines of a poet divorced from their contëxt,
or absurdly applied, are still good poetry, though they be but
the poet's *mangled remains.*

565. Disjice compositam pacem, sere crimina belli;
Arma velit, poscatque simul, rapiatque juventus. Virg. A. 7,
339. Juno bidding Alecto sow hostilities between Trojans and
Latins.

> Break off this patched-up peace, sow war's alarms!
> Let youth desire, demand, and seize its arms!—*Ed.*

566. Dis proximus ille
Quem ratio, non ira movet, qui facta rependens
Consilio punire potest. Claud. Cons. Mall. 227.
Impartial Justice.

> He most resembles God, whom not blind rage
> But reason moves: who weighs the facts, and thence
> Gives penalties proportionate to th' offence.—*Ed.*

567. Districtus ensis cui super impia
Cervice pendet, non Siculæ dapes
Dulcem elaborabunt saporem ;
Non avium citharæque cantus.
Somnum reducent. Hor. C. 3, 1, 17.

> *Damocles.*
> When o'er his guilty head the sword
> Unsheathéd hangs, not sumptuous board
> Spread with Sicilian cates will please,
> Nor voice of singing-birds give ease,
> Or music charm to sleep.—*Ed.*

568. Distringit animum librorum multitudo. Sen. Ep. 2, 3.—*A multitude of authors only confuses the mind.*

569. Di talem terris avertite pestem ! Virg. A. 3, 620.—*God preserve
the land from such a scourge !*

570. Di tibi dent annos ! a te nam cætera sumes,
Sint modo virtuti tempora longa tuæ. Ov. Ep. 2, 1, 53.

> God grant thee years ! the rest thou canst provide,
> If for thy virtues time be not denied.—*Ed.*

571. Diverse lingue, orribili favelle,
Parole di dolore, accenti d'ira,
Voci alte e fioche, e suon di man con elle. Dante, Inf. 3, 25.

> *The Sounds of Hell.*
> Various tongues,
> Horrible language, outcries of woe,
> Accents of anger, voices deep and hoarse,
> Mix'd up with sounds of smitten hands.—*Cary.*

572. Dives qui fieri vult, Et cito vult fieri. Juv. 14, 176.—*Who would
be rich would be so quickly.*

573. Divide 'et impera. Coke, Inst. (1669), Pt. iv., cap. i. p. 35.—
Divide and conquer.

> Coke, insisting on the invincibleness of unity, stigmatises the qu. as
> "explosum illud diverbium,"—*that exploded adage.* As a policy, how-
> ever, the principle served Louis XI. well enough, who by embroiling one
> great vassal of the crown with another, and setting Parliament against
> Parliament, raised the royal prerogative to a higher place than it had ever
> enjoyed before. A century later, Catherine de Medici made the axiom her
> own: "*Diviser pour régner*, c'était déjà sa maxime, la règle de sa conduite"
> (Philarète Chasles, Hist. de France, Paris, 1847, vol. 2, p. 136). In Vol-
> taire's *Don Pèdre* (4, 2), the hero, speaking of his "ally," Charles V. of
> France, says, "Divisez pour régner ; voilà sa politique."—*Divide to reign ;
> there you have his policy.*

574. Divina natura dedit agros, ars humana ædificavit urbes. **Varr.**
R. R. 3, 1.—"*God made the country and man made the town.*"
                          Cowper, Task (Sofa), 1, 749.

575. Divitiæ grandes homini sunt, vivere parce
Æquo animo; neque enim est unquam penuria parvi. **Lucret.**
5, 1117.—*It is wealth to a man to be able to live contentedly
upon a frugal store: nor can there be want to him who wants
but little.*

576. Dixit, et avertens rosea cervice refulsit,
Ambrosiæque comæ divinum vertice odorem
Spiravere: pedes vestis defluxit ad imos ;
Et vera incessu patuit Dea.   Virg. A. 1, 402.

> *Venus.*
>
> She turned and flashed upon their view
> Her stately neck's purpureal hue;
> Ambrosial tresses round her head
> A more than earthly fragrance shed:
> Her falling robe her footprints swept,
> And show'd the Goddess as she stept.—*Conington.*

577. Doctor.—*A learned divine.* Theological professor.

> *D. Angelicus*, title of Thomas Aquinas; *D. Authenticus*, Gregory of
> Rimini ; *D. Christianissimus*, John Gerson ; *D. Ecstaticus*, John Ruys-
> brock ; *D. Irrefragibilis*, Alexander de Hales; *D. Mirabilis*, Roger Bacon;
> *D. Profundus*, Thomas Bradwardine ; *D. Singularis*, William Occam ;
> *D. Seraphicus*, Bonaventura ; *D. Subtilis*, Duns Scotus, etc., etc. The
> Paris Univ. degree of D.D. (Sanctæ Theologiæ Professor) was so difficult to
> obtain, and so highly esteemed in the 14th century, that Pope John XXII.
> (so Crévier says in *Hist. de l'Université de Paris*, Paris, 1761, vol. ii. p. 321),
> who had it not, feared that the fact might be made use of to lessen his
> authority.

578. Dolendi modus, non est timendi. Plin. Ep. 8, 17, fin.—*Pain has
its limits, apprehension none.*

579. Dolus, an virtus, quis in hoste requirat ?   Virg. A. 2, 390.

> Who questions when with foes we deal,
> If craft or courage guide the steel?—*Conington.*

Cf. Dolo erat pugnandum, quum par non esset armis. Nep. Hann. 10, 4.—*He must fight by stratagem who cannot match his foe in arms.* All's fair in love and war. Si leonina pellis non satis est, vulpina addenda. Chil. p. 350.—*If the lion's skin should not suffice, add the fox's hide.* Employ cunning if force fail.

580. Dominus illuminatio mea.   Vulg. Ps. xxvi. 1.—*The Lord is my Light.*   Motto of University of Oxford.

581. Domus amica, domus optima.   Chil. p. 221, tr. of οἶκος φίλος, οἶκος ἄριστος. Apost. 12, 39.—*One's own house is best.*   There's no place like home.   East, west; Home's best.   The Gk. form of the prov. is told of the tortoise, who was invited with all the other animals to Jove's wedding, and on arriving late, pleaded the qu. as excuse.   Thereupon he was condemned ever after to carry his house on his back (*Testudo domiporta*).

582. Domus tutissimum cuique refugium atque receptaculum.   Dig. lib. 2, tit. 4, 18.—*Every man's house is his castle.*

583. Dona præsentis cape lætus horæ, et
Linque severa.   Hor. C. 3, 8, 27.

> The guerdon of the passing hour
> Seize gladly while 'tis in thy power,
>   And bid dull care begone.—*Ed.*

584. Donec eris felix multos numerabis amicos,
Tempora si fuerint nubila, solus eris.   Ov. T. 1, 9, 5.

Fortune.

While fortune smiles you'll have a host of friends,
But they'll desert you when the storm descends.—*Ed.*

Res amicos invenit. Plaut. Stich. 4, 1, 16.—*Money finds us friends;* and Εὐτυχία πολύφιλος. Apost. Cent. 8, 7.—*Prosperity has many friends.*

585. Donner à quelqu'un le sac.   Prov. Quit. p. 639.—*To give anyone the sack.*

Absurdly modern as this saying appears to us, it has long been domesticated in France in precisely the same sense of "abrupt dismissal." Perhaps the proverbial use extends to other countries; and Quit., *in l.*, points out *à propos* the identity of word-form in a variety of languages; from the Gk. σάκκος to the Spanish *saco* and Turkish *sak*.   This universal circumstance is accounted for by him, or rather by his authority, Jean Goropius Beccanus, from the fact that when the building of Babel was suddenly interrupted, though the workmen forgot their own language, they none of them forgot their own "sack" of tools.

586. Dont elle eut soin de peindre et orner son visage,
Pour réparer des ans l'irréparable outrage.   Rac. Ath. 2, 5.—
She had taken care to make up her face in order to repair the irretrievable ravages of time.   Athalie describes the apparition of her mother, Jezebel, in the dress worn on the day of her death.   The passage is often qu. of ladies who "paint"; the last line being also said *à propos* of any refurbishment of faded things.

587. Dos est magna parentium
　　　Virtus, et metuens alterius viri
　　　Certo fœdere castitas,
　　　　　Et peccare nefas, aut pretium emori.　　Hor. C. 3, 24, 21.

Domestic Chastity.

　　　Theirs are dowries not of gold,
　　　　Their parents' worth, their own pure chastity
　　　True to one, to others cold:
　　　　They dare not sin, or, if they dare, they die.—*Conington.*

　Horace contrasts the strict conjugal fidelity of the wild races of the North with the licentious manners of Roman society.

588. Δόσις δ' ὀλίγη τε, φίλη τε.　Hom. Od. 6, 208.—*A little gift, but a valued one.*

589. Dos linajes solo hay en el mundo, el tener y el no tener. Cervantes, D. Quijote, 2, 20.　Sancho loq.—*There are but two families in the world—the "Haves" and the "Haven'ts."*

590. Do ut des, do ut facias : facio ut des, facio ut facias.　In Karl Marx's *Capital*, Lond., 1896, 8º, p. 551.—*I give that you may give, I give that you may produce. I produce that you may give, I produce that you may produce.*

　A maxim as old as Justinian and Ulpian, and the basis, expressed or implied, of all pecuniary transactions. It may be stated in the *Contractus est ultro citroque obligatio* of Dig. 50, 16, 19 ("Any agreement implies a mutual obligation"), and the fourfold nature of such contract is defined by the R. jurists in the four parts of the quotation. Marx (*l.c.*) says, "The exchange between capital and labour first presents itself to the mind in the same guise as the buying and selling of all other commodities. The buyer gives a certain sum of money, the seller an article of a nature different from money; and the jurists' consciousness recognises in this, at most, a material difference expressed in the juridically equivalent formulæ, *Do ut Des*," etc.　Mr Goschen (speech at Leeds, Feb. 11, 1885) summarised the formula to mean, "The exchange of friendly offices, based on the avowed self-interest of the parties concerned" (*Times*, Feb. 12, 1885).

591. Duce tempus eget.　Luc. 7, 88.—*The times require a leader.* The hour has come, but not the man.

592. Ducimus autem
　　　Hos quoque felices, qui ferre incommoda vitæ,
　　　Nec jactare jugum, vita didicere magistra.　　Juv. 13, 20.

　　　But, they are also to be reckoned blest
　　　Who've learnt as 'prentices in life's stern school
　　　To bear life's ills, nor fret beneath his rule.—*Ed.*

593. Ducunt volentem fata, nolentem trahunt.　Sen. Ep. 107, 11, tr. from the Gk. of the Stoic Cleanthes.

　　　Fate leads th' obedient, drags those that resist.—*Ed.*

594. Dulce domum resonemus.　John Reading, 1690.—*Let us make the sweet song of "Home" to resound !*

Burden of the *Domum*, or well-known school-song, sung on the eve of the holidays. It begins:

> Concinamus, O sodales,
> Eja! quid silemus?
> Nobile canticum, dulce melos domum,
> Dulce domum resonemus, etc.

The source of the words is unknown, and the melody is traditionally ascribed to John Reading (or Redding), or to his harmonising of some old English air. Though now adopted by most public schools, the song is originally of Winchester College. Until 1835 it used to be sung round the "Domum" tree, but now the scene takes place in Meads. "If I wanted a stranger," says Mr Leach (*Hist. of Winch. Coll.*, Lond., 1899, p. 454), "to realise the charm by which Winchester holds its sons . . . beyond and above that felt by the scions of all other schools, I should place him under the clear sky and in the balmy airs that breathe across the scented water-meadows, to see and hear a Domum."

595. Dulcis inexpertis cultura potentis amici;
Expertus metuit.   Hor. Ep. 1, 18, 86.

> A patron's service is a strange career,
> The tiros love it, but the experts fear.—*Conington.*

596. Dummodo sit dives, barbarus ipse placet.   Ov. A. A. 2, 276.—
Provided he be rich, even a foreigner pleases well enough.

597. Du moment qu'on aime, l'on devient si doux.   Marmontel, Zémire et Azór, (Music by Grétry) 3, 5.   Azor sings: *The moment one is in love, one becomes so amiable.*

598. Du musst glauben, du musst wagen,
Denn die Götter leihn kein Pfand;
Nur ein Wunder kann dich tragen
In das schöne Wunderland.   Schiller, Sehnsucht, fin.

> *Aspirations.*
> Faith thou needest, and must dare thee,
> Since Heav'n leaves no pledge in hand;
> Only wonder can safe bear thee
> To the beauteous wonderland.—*Ed.*

599. Dum vitant stulti vitia, in contraria currunt.   Hor. S. 1, 2, 24.

> To cure a fault, fools rush into extremes.—*Ed.*

600. Dum vivimus vivamus.—While we live, let us enjoy life.

> Live while you live, the epicure would say,
> And seize the pleasures of the present day.—*Doddridge*, Epigr.

The original, if so it may be called, of this hedonistic maxim is preserved in the *Inscriptiones Antiquæ*, etc., of Jan. Grüter (Amsterdam, 1707), where, in vol. 1, Pag. DCIX., 3, is an inscription, discovered at Narbonne, and apparently erected by some freedman of the Imperial Household, which concludes with these words,

AMICI · DVM · VIVIMVS · VIVAMVS.

(1.) Comedamus et bibamus, cras enim moriemur.   Vulg., Isa. xxii. 13.— *Let us eat and drink, for to-morrow we die.*

(2.) Bibamus, moriendum est.   Sen. Controv. ii. 14.—*Let us drink, for we must die.*

(3.) Dum licet, in rebus jucundis vive beatus,
Vive memor quam sis ævi brevis.   Hor. S. 2, 6, 96.

Then take, good sir, your pleasure while you may,
With life so short, 'twere wrong to lose a day.—*Conington.*

(4.) Dum fata sinunt, vivite læti.   Sen. Herc. Fur. 177.—*While fate
allows, live happily.*

(5.) Sapias, vina liques et spatio brevi
Spem longam reseces.   Dum loquimur, fugerit invida
Ætas: carpe diem, quam minimum credula postero.   Hor. C. 1, 11, 6.

Strain your wine, and prove your wisdom: life is short, should hope
be more ?
In the moment of our talking, envious time has slipped away.
Seize the present; trust to-morrow e'en as little as you may.—*Conington.*

(6.) Indulge genio, carpamus dulcia; nostrum est
Quod vivis: cinis et manes et fabula fies.
Vive memor leti: fugit hora; hoc, quod loquor, inde est.   Pers. 5, 151.

Stint not then your inclination, pluck the rose-bud while you may;
It is ours the living moment, soon you'll be but dust and clay.
Think of death: the hour's flying; what I speak is sped away.—*Ed.*

601. D'un dévot souvent au chrétien véritable
La distance est deux foix plus longue, à mon avis,
Que du pôle antarctique, au détroit de Davis.   Boil. Sat. 11, 114.

'Twixt a true Christian and a devotee,
The distance, to my mind, is twice as great
As from the Antarctic Pole to Davis' Strait.—*Ed.*

602. Dura aliquis præcepta vocet mea; dura fatemur
Esse; sed, ut valeas, multa dolenda feres.   Ov. R. A. 225.

Hard precepts these, one says; I own they are:
But health to gain much hardship must you bear.—*Ed.*

603. Dura Exerce imperia, et ramos compesce fluentes.   Virg. G. 2, 370.

Exert a rigorous sway,
And lop the too luxuriant boughs away.—*Dryden.*

Very necessary advice to an inexperienced author.

604. Durum! Sed levius fit patientia,
Quicquid corrigere est nefas.   Hor. C. 1, 24, 19.

'Tis hard, but what's impossible to cure,
Patience will make more light.—*Ed.*

605. Du sublime au ridicule il n'y a qu'un pas.   Napoleon I., in
De Pradt's Hist. de l'Ambassade, etc., Ed. 1815, p. 215.—
There is but one step from the sublime to the ridiculous.

The saying is attributed to Napoleon I., with reference to the Retreat
from Moscow in 1812, a phrase which, in conversation with his ambassador,
De Pradt, at Warsaw, he kept on repeating five or six times over.   See
also *Mémoires de Mme. de Rémusat*, Paris, 1880, vol. iii. pp. 55-6.   The *mot*
is, however, of an earlier origin.   Marmontel (Œuvres, vol. 5, p. 188) has,
"En général, le ridicule touche au sublime."—*In general the ridiculous
approaches the sublime:* Tom Paine (*Age of Reason*, 1794, pt. 2, fin, note)
says, "One step above the sublime makes the ridiculous, and one step
above the ridiculous makes the sublime again." [Büchm. pp. 489-90, and
Harb. p. 202.]

606. Dux fœmina facti.   Virg. A. 1, 364.

A woman's daring wrought the deed.—*Conington.*

E.*

607. Ea quoque quæ vulgo recepta sunt, hoc ipso quod incertum auctorem habent, velut omnium fiunt; quale est, Ubi amici, ibi opes. Quint. 5, 11, 41.—*Sayings in proverbial use, from the fact of their author being unknown, become common property, like "Where friends are, riches are," etc.*

608. Ea sola voluptas, Solamenque mali.   Virg. A. 3, 660.—*His " sole remaining joy " and solace of his woes.*   Said of the flocks of the Cyclops Polyphemus after he was blinded by Ulysses.

609. E cælo descendit γνῶθι σεαυτόν. Juv. 11, 27.—*From heaven descends the precept, Know thyself.*   Admonition of the oracle of Apollo at Delphi.   Quum igitur, *Nosce te,* dicit, hoc dicit, Nosce animum tuum. Cic. Tusc. 1, 22, 52.—*When the god says, Know thyself, he means, Know thy own mind.*

The saying is ascribed to Thales (Diog. Laert. 1, 40), who, in another part of the same author (1, 35), is represented as having replied to the question, What is difficult?—τὸ ἑαυτὸν γνῶναι ("to know oneself").   What was *easy,* he added, was "to give advice to another" (τὸ ἄλλῳ ὑποτίθεσθαι). Menander (p. 913) has a very natural reflection on Thales' maxim:

Κατὰ πόλλ' ἄρ' ἐστὶν οὐ καλῶς εἰρημένον
τὸ Γνῶθι Σαυτόν· χρησιμώτερον γὰρ ἦν
τὸ γνῶθι τοὺς ἄλλους.

The "Know thyself" is not quite wisely said:
Give me the knowledge of others instead.—*Ed.*

610. Ecce iterum Crispinus! et est mihi sæpe vocandus
Ad partes, monstrum nulla virtute redemptum
A vitiis, æger, solaque libidine fortis.   Juv. 4, 1.

Lo! Crispinus in a new part;
This unmitigated scoundrel,
Great alone in sensuality.—*Shaw.*

Ecce iterum Crispinus is commonly said of any one who is for ever "turning-up." What, here again! *Ecce iterum Crispinus!*

611. Ecce par Deo dignum (*sc.* spectaculum), vir fortis cum fortuna mala conpositus. Sen. Prov. cap. 2, 6.—*A brave man battling with misfortune is a spectacle worthy of the gods.*

612. Ἐχθρῶν ἄδωρα δῶρα κοὐκ ὀνήσιμα.   Soph. Aj. 665.

A foeman's gifts are no gifts, but a curse.—*Calverley.*

613. Ἐχθρὸς γάρ μοι κεῖνος ὁμῶς Ἀΐδαο πύλῃσιν,
Ὅς χ' ἕτερον μὲν κεύθῃ ἐνὶ φρέσιν, ἄλλο δὲ εἴπῃ. Hom. Il. 9, 312.
Duplicity.

Who dares think one thing, and another tell,
My heart detests him as the gates of hell.—*Pope.*

* Including the Greek H (long E).

614. E compie' mia giornata innanzi sera.   Petrarch, Son. 261.—*My day was finished before eventide.*

615. Écrasez (*or* Écrasons) l'infâme.—*Crush the infamous thing.*

It is said, or it has been said, that Voltaire, in using this expression in his correspondence (1759-68) with Frederick II., Diderot, D'Alembert, Damilaville, etc., intended by "*L'Infâme*," the world's Redeemer; and even Lacordaire, in his *Conférences de N. Dame*, understood him to be so speaking. But let us give his due even to Voltaire. He was attacking not Christ or Christianity, but that detestable bigotry of the time, which in 1762-66 sent Calas, La Barre, the Greniers, and other Protestant victims to the block and to the wheel. Whose heart would not have burnt with indignation at such atrocities? In his letters of that date, Voltaire used often to substitute the phrase in abbreviated form—*Écr. l'inf.*, or *Écrlinf.*—for his own sign-manual. Büchm. p. 280; Fumag. No. 1250; Lar. pp. 199-201.

616. Églé, belle et poëte a deux petits travers,
 Elle fait son visage, et ne fait pas ses vers.
                              P. D. Écouchard Lebrun, Epigr. 1, 9.

Mme. F. de Beauharnais.
Églé, beauty and poet, has two little crimes:
She makes her own face, and does not make her rhymes.—*Byron.*

Impromptu of Lebrun on Mme. Fanny de Beauharnais, a literary lady of the First Empire, who revenged herself by inviting the author of the lines to dinner and there exhibiting the couplet to her company, with the addition, in her own hand, of "*Vers faits contre moi par M. Lebrun, qui dîne aujourd'hui chez moi!*" Fourn. *L.D.A.*, 279-81.

617. Ἡ γλῶσσ' ὀμώμοχ', ἡ δὲ φρὴν ἀνώμοτος.   Eur. Hipp. 612 (tr. by Cic. Off. 3, 29, 108, Juravi lingua, mentem injuratam gero).— *My tongue has sworn it, but my mind's unsworn.*   Mental reservation.

618. Ego cogito, ergo sum.   R. Descartes, Princip. Philosoph., Amsterdam, 1644, Pt. 1, § 7.—*I think, therefore I am.*

The fact of consciousness proves the fact of existence—one of the first principles of the Cartesian philosophy in the pursuit of certain truth. The identical theory had been broached in the 6th century B.C. by Epimenides the Eleatic, as qu. in Clem. Alex. Strom. vi. (266) τὸ γὰρ αὐτὸ νοεῖν ἐστί τε καὶ εἶναι, *to think is the same thing as to be.* The connection between conscious thought and conscious existence occurs also in S. Augustine's *Soliloquia*, 2, 1 (vol. i. p. 275 C), where it is implied that there are no grounds for the certainty of being, except in the faculty of thought.— "Unde scis (te esse)?—Nescio. . . . Cogitare te scis?—Scio.—Ergo verum est cogitare te?—Verum."

619. Ego deum genus esse semper dixi et dicam cœlitum,
 Sed eos non curare opinor, quid agat humanum genus.
 Nam si curent, bene bonis sit, male malis, quod nunc abest.
                                        Enn. Trag. i. 61.
I have always said and will say that there is a race of gods,
But, I fancy, that what men do, is to them but little odds.
If they cared, good men would prosper, bad would suffer—not the case.—*Ed.*

620. Ego ero post principia.   Ter. Eun. 4, 7, 11.—*I'll take my stand in the rear.*   Prudence is the better part of valour.

621. Ego et rex meus.—*I and my king.*

> Style used by Cardinal Wolsey in official documents, and made one of the counts against him on his fall. In Hen. VIII. 3, 2, Norfolk says,

> > Then, that, in all you writ to Rome, or else
> > To foreign princes, *Ego et Rex meus*
> > Was still inscribed ; in which you brought the king
> > To be your servant.

> It is difficult to say what else the poor Cardinal could have written. *Rex meus et ego* would not even have been Latin.

622. Ego pretium ob stultitiam fero. Ter. And. 3, 5, 4.—*I am well rewarded for my folly.*

623. Ego primam tollo, nominor quia Leo. Phædr. 1, 5, 7.—*I take the first share by my title of Lion.* The Lion hunting in partnership with Sheep, Cow, and Goat, secures all four quarters of the booty for himself : hence *Societas Leonina*, Dig. 17, 2, 29, § 2, (*Lion's partnership*), stands for any combination in which one party gets all the profits, and the others all the loss. It may also be used of any company or assembly, where the "Lion" of the hour engrosses all the attention to himself.

624. Eheu fugaces, Postume, Postume,
Labuntur anni ; nec pietas moram
Rugis et instanti senectæ
Afferet, indomitæque morti.   Hor. C. 2, 14, 1.

> > Ah ! Postumus, they fleet away
> > Our years, nor piety one hour
> > Can win from wrinkles and decay
> > And Death's indomitable power.—*Conington.*

625. Eheu ! quam brevibus pereunt ingentia fatis ! Claud. Rufin. 2, 49.—*Alas ! what trifling events serve to overthrow great powers !* So Pope, *Rape of the Lock*, 1, 2, "What mighty contests rise from trivial things !"

626. Eheu Quam temere in nosmet legem sancimus iniquam !
Nam vitiis nemo sine nascitur ; optimus ille est,
Qui minimis urgetur.   Hor S. 1, 3, 66.

> > Alas ! what hasty laws against ourselves we pass !
> > For none is born without his faults : the best
> > But bears a lighter wallet than the rest —*Conington.*

627. Ehret die Frauen ! sie flechten und weben
Himmlische Rosen ins irdische Leben.
                              Schiller, Würde der Frauen.

> > Honour to women ! they twine and they wreathe
> > Roses of heaven round life's earthly path !—*Ed.*

628. Εἰ γάρ κεν καὶ σμικρὸν ἐπὶ σμικρῷ καταθεῖο,
καὶ θ' ἅμα τοῦτ' ἔρδοις, τάχα κεν μέγα καὶ τὸ γένοιτο. Hes. Op. 359.—*If you only keep adding little to little, it will soon become a big heap.* Adde parum parvo magnus acervus erit.—*Mony a little mak' a mickle.*

F

629. Εἰκόνας εἶναι τῆς ἑκάστου ψυχῆς τοὺς λόγους. Dion. Hal. Antiq.
Rom. 1, 1.—*Each man's words are the reflection of his mind.*

630. Ein ächter deutscher Mann mag keinen Franzen leiden,
Doch ihre Weine trinkt er gern.
>   Goethe, Faust, Auerbachs Keller.
> No thorough German can abide the French,
> Although he's glad enough to drink their wine.—*Ed.*

631. Ein Augenblick, gelebt im Paradiese,
Wird nicht zu teuer mit dem Tod gebüsst. Schiller, D. Carlos, 1, 5.
> One moment spent in Paradise,
> Were not too dearly bought with Death.—*Ed.*

632. Ein einz'ger Augenblick kann Alles umgestalten. Wieland,
Oberon, 7, 75.—*A single moment can change all.*

633. Eine schöne Menschenseele finden ist Gewinn. J. G. Herder,
Der gerettete Jüngling (1797).—*It is a gain to find a beautiful
human soul.*

634. Eine Versöhnung
Ist keine, die das Herz nicht ganz befreit.
Ein Tropfen Hass, der in dem Freudenbecher
Zurückbleibt, macht den Segenstrank zum Gift. Schiller, Maid
of Orleans, 3, 4 (Joan loq.).—*A reconciliation that does not completely free the heart, is none at all. One drop of hate left in the
cup of joy renders the blissful drink a poison.*

635. Ein Kaiserwort soll man nicht dreh'n, noch deuteln. G. A.
Bürger, Die Weiber von Weinsberg (1774), str. 11.—*An emperor's
word may no man wrest, nor garble.*

636. Ein Traum, ein Traum ist unser Leben
    Auf Erden hier;
Wie Schatten auf den Wogen, schweben
    Und schwinden wir;
Und messen uns're trägen Tritte
    Nach Raum und Zeit,
Und sind, und wissen's nicht, in Mitte
    Der Ewigkeit!   Joh. G. von Herder, 1796.
>   *Amor und Psyche.*
> A dream, a dream is all our lifetime here!
> Shadow on wave we toss and disappear;
> And mark by time and space our weary way,
> And are, but know not, in eternity!—*Ed.*

637. Ein unnütz Leben ist ein früher Tod. Goethe, Iphigenia, 1, 2
(Iph. loq.).—*A useless life is a premature death.*

638. Ein Wahn, der mich beglückt,
    Ist eine Wahrheit wert, die mich zu Boden drückt.
>   C. M. Wieland, Idris und Zenide (1768), 3, 10.

Where Ignorance is Bliss.

A fallacy that makes me glad,
Is worth a truth that leaves me sad.—*Ed.*

639. Εἷς οἰωνὸς ἄριστος, ἀμύνεσθαι περὶ πάτρης.   Hom. Il. 12, 243.—
The one best omen is, to fight for one's country. The patriot has
no need to consult auguries when his country is in danger.

640. Εἴθ', ὦ λῷστε, σὺ τοιοῦτος ὢν φίλος ἡμῖν γένοιο.   Xen. Hell. 4, 1, 38.
—*Would to heaven that a man of your noble sentiments were our
friend!* Speech of Agesilaus, King of Sparta, to the Persian
general, Pharnabazus (396 B.C.). Hence the saying, *Talis quum
(or* quum talis) *sis, utinam noster esses!* Generous recognition
of an enemy's work.

641. Eligito tempus, captatum sæpe, rogandi.   Ov. Ep. 3, 1, 129.—
*Choose your opportunity for making the request, after having
long watched for it.*

642. Ἑλοῦ βίον ἄριστον, ἡδὺν δὲ αὐτὸν ἡ συνήθεια ποιήσει.   Plut. Mor.
p. 727 (de Exilio, c. 8).—*Choose the best life, and habit will make
it sweet;* tr. by Bacon (Sermones 7, fin.). Optimum elige : suave
et facile illud faciet consuetudo.

643. Ἐλπὶς καὶ σὺ τύχη, μέγα χαίρετε · τὸν λιμέν' εὗρον.
Οὐδὲν ἐμοί χ' ὑμῖν · παίζετε τοὺς μετ' ἐμέ.   *V.* Dubner's Epigr.
Anthol. Palatina, Paris, 1864-72, vol. ii. p. 10. (Cap. ix. 49).

> Fortune and Hope, farewell! I'm here in port
> And finished with you. Now with others sport.—*Ed.*

Or,

> I've entered port; Fortune and Hope, adieu!
> Make game of others, for I've done with you.—*Ed.*

Latin versions abound; *e.g.,* the following, from Sir T. More's *Opera,*
Frankfurt, 1689, p. 233 (*Progymnasmata*):—

> Jam portum inveni: Spes et Fortuna valete;
> Nil mihi vobiscum est : ludite nunc alios.

Le Sage (Gil Blas, Bk. 9, 10, fin.) makes his hero inscribe the distich (in
the form *Inveni portum,* etc., and *Sat me lusistis,* etc.) on his castle of
Lirias on the conclusion of his wanderings; and Lord Brougham had the
words written on his villa at Cannes. For these, and further particulars, the
reader is referred to the exhaustive note on the subject by Mr R. Horton
Smith, in *N. and Q.,* 9th ser., ii. 29.

644. E mangia e bee e dorme e veste panni.   Dante, Inf. 33, 141.—
He eats, and drinks, and sleeps, and dons his clothes. Said of
Branca Doria, whom Dante seems to have put into hell before
he was dead.

645. Emas, non quod opus est, sed quod necesse est: Quod non opus
est, asse carum est.   Cato ap. Sen. Ep. 94, 28.—*Buy what you
need, not what you want: what you don't need is dear at a gift.*

646. Ἡμεῖς τοι πατέρων μέγ᾽ ἀμείνονες εὐχόμεθ᾽ εἶναι. Hom. Il. 4, 405.— *We pride ourselves on being far better men than our fathers.*

647. Encore une étoile qui file,
Qui file, file et disparait! Beranger, Étoiles qui filent (1820), Paris, 1821, vol. 2, 193.—*Yet another shooting-star! which falls, falls, and disappears!* Refrain of song.

648. Ἐν δὲ φάει καὶ ὄλεσσον. Hom. Il. 17, 647.—*Slay in the open daylight, if one needs must fall.* Ajax' prayer to Jove to dispel the darkness shrouding the field of battle.

Clear the sky
That we may see our fate, and die at least,
If such Thy will, in th' open light of day.—*Earl of Derby.*

649. En ego campana; nunquam denuntio vana.
Laudo Deum verum, plebem voco, congrego clerum;
Defunctos ploro, pestem fugo, festa decoro.
Vox mea, vox vitæ; voco vos, ad sacra venite!
Sanctos collaudo, tonitrua fugo, funera claudo.
Funera plango, fulgura frango, Sabbata pango;
Excito lentos, dissipo ventos, paco cruentos.
A helpe to Discourse, Lond., 1668.

The Bells.

I am the Bell; and no vain message do I tell,
True God I praise, collect the flock and call the priests.
The dead I mourn, and ban the plague, and gladden feasts.
The voice of life is mine; I bid to things divine.
Saints' prayers I crave, from thunder save, and close the grave.
Funerals knelling, lightnings quelling, Sundays telling;
Sluggards waking, tempests breaking and peace-making. – *Ed.*

N.B.—Another reading of line 3 is *Defunctos ploro, vivos voco, fulmina frango.* The famous Münster bell, cast at Basle 1486, and now in the Cantonal Museum of Schaffhausen, is pop. known as Schiller's bell, from having furnished the poet with the motto (and idea) for his *Lied von der Glocke.* Its legend is 𝔙𝔦𝔳𝔬𝔰 · 𝔙𝔬𝔠𝔬 · 𝔐𝔬𝔯𝔱𝔲𝔬𝔰 · 𝔓𝔩𝔞𝔫𝔤𝔬 · 𝔉𝔲𝔩𝔤𝔲𝔯𝔞 · 𝔉𝔯𝔞𝔫𝔤𝔬.

650. En ego, quum patria caream, vobisque, domoque,
Raptaque sint, adimi quæ potuere, mihi:
Ingenio tamen ipse meo comitorque fruorque;
Cæsar in hoc potuit juris habere nihil. Ov. T. 3, 7, 45.

The Poet in Exile.

When of my country, home, and you bereft,
And all that could be ta'en, was ta'en from me;
My art, t'accompany and cheer, was left;
Cæsar in this could claim no right nor fee.—*Ed.*

651. En hæc promissa fides est? Virg. A. 6, 346.—*Is this the fulfilment of his promise?*

652. En! hic declarat, quales sitis judices. Phædr. 5, 5, 38.—*This shows what good judges you are!*

653. Ἐν μύρτου κλαδὶ τὸ ξίφος φορήσω,
ὥσπερ Ἁρμόδιος καὶ Ἀριστογείτων,
ὅτε τὸν τύραννον κτανέτην,
ἰσονόμους τ᾽ Ἀθήνας ἐποιησάτην.   Callistr. p. 1290, Brunck's
Analecta Vet. Poet. Gr., 1776, i 155.

Harmodius and Aristogeiton.
In branch of myrtle will I wreathe my sword,
    Like Aristogeiton and Harmodius,
When they destroyed their country's tyrant lord,
    And gained for Athens equal rights and dues.—*Ed.*

These two young Athenian patriots, in 514 B.C., slew Hipparchus, brother
of the tyrant Hippias, to avenge an insult offered to Harmodius' sister and
destroy the line of the Pisistratidæ. Failing to reach Hippias, they rushed
back and killed the brother, with daggers hidden in the myrtle bough they
were carrying in the day's Panathenaic festival. Both suffered for the
deed, and were afterwards raised to "divine" honours by a grateful country.

All that most endears
Glory, is when the myrtle wreathes a sword,
Just as Harmodius drew on Athens' tyrant lord.—*Byron,* "Ch. Har." 3, 20.

"Hence," says Mr Tozer in his ed. of *Ch. Harold* (Lond., 1885, p. 262),
"the sword in myrtles drest" (*Christ. Year,* 3rd Sun. in Lent) "became
the emblem of the assertion of liberty." Card. Newman, in his *Letter to
Dr Pusey on his recent Eirenicon* (Lond., 1866, p. 9), says, "We at least
have not professed to be composing an Irenicon, when we treated you as
foes. There was one of old time who wreathed his sword in myrtle; excuse
me—you discharge your olive-branch as if from a catapult."

654. En pudet, et fateor, jam desuetudine longa
    Vix subeunt ipsi verba Latina mihi.   Ov. T. 5, 7, 57.
    I own with shame that discontinuance long
    Makes me well nigh forget the Latin tongue.—*Ed.*

655. Ἐν τῷ φρονεῖν γὰρ μηδὲν ἥδιστος βίος. Soph. Aj. 554.—*Unconscious
    childhood is life's sweetest age.*

656. En toute chose il faut considérer la fin. La Font. 3, 5 (Le Renard
    et le Bouc).—*In everything one must consider the end.*

    The "moral" of Æsop's Fab. 45, is, τῶν ἀνθρώπων τοὺς φρονίμους δεῖ
    πρότερον τὰ τέλη τῶν πραγμάτων σκοπεῖν, εἶθ᾽ οὕτως αὐτοῖς ἐπιχειρεῖν.—
    *Prudent men ought to consider beforehand the end of anything before proceed-
    ing to take it in hand.* Cf. Quidquid agas, prudenter agas, et respice finem.
    Gesta Romanorum, cap. 103 init.—*Whatever you do, act with caution, and
    consider the end;* and, In omnibus operibus tuis memorare novissima tua,
    et in æternum non peccabis. Vulg. Ecclus. 7, 40.—*Whatsoever thou takest in
    hand, remember the end and thou shalt never do amiss.*

657. Entre chien et loup. Prov.—*Between dog and wolf.* Twilight:
    the interval after sunset, so Quitard explains it (p. 227), when
    the wolf comes prowling round the sheep-fold before the
    shepherd's dog is placed on guard. Writing to Mme. de
    Grignan (Letter 826, ed. A. Regnier, 1862, vi. 505), Mme. de
    Sévigné says, "J'essaye d'éclaircir mes 'entre chiens et loups'
    (the obscure passages in my letters), autant qu'il m'est possible."

658. Entre nos ennemis
Les plus à craindre sont souvent les plus petits.   La Font. 2, 9.
Lion et Moucheron.—*Among our enemies, the most to be dreaded
are often the smallest.*

**659. Entre tard et trop tard, il y a, par la grâce de Dieu, une distance
incommensurable.**   Mme. Swetchine, vol. 1, Pensée xlv.—
*The difference between late and too late is, by God's mercy,
immeasurable.*

660. Ἔπεα πτερόεντα.   Hom. Il. 1, 201.—*Winged words.*

661. Eppur si muove!—*And yet it* (the Sun) *moves!*
Reputed saying of Galileo Galilei on his abjuration of his celebrated
Dialogue on Sun spots and the Sun's rotation (*Dialogo sopra i due massime
sistemi*) before the Inquisition on June 22, 1633.   The original copy of the
document is now to be seen in the Bibliotheca del Seminario at Padua,
and shows no sign of any such reservation on the part of the author; nor
has the minutest research succeeded in substantiating the fable.   The
earliest mention of the legend, acc. to Fumagalli, is Baretti's *Italian Library*
(Lond., 1757, p. 52), to which Büchmann adds Lacombo's *Dict. des portraits
historiques*, etc., Paris, 1768-9, vol. 2 (no page).   It is now universally
rejected as unauthentic. [Fumag. No. 309; Büchm. p. 467.]

662. Era già l'ora che volge il disio
A' naviganti, e intenerisce il cuore
Lo dì c' han detto a' dolci amici addio;
E che lo nuovo peregrin d'amore
Punge, se ode squilla di lontano,
Che paia il giorno pianger che si muore.   Dante, Purg. 8, 1.
                    The Sunset Hour.
            Now was the hour that wakens fond desire
            In men at sea, and melts their thoughtful heart
            Who in the morn have bid sweet friends farewell;
            And pilgrim, newly on his road, with love
            Thrills if he hear the vesper bell from far
            That seems to mourn for the expiring day.—*Cary.*
       Cf. Statius, S. 4, 6, 3, *Jam moriente die;* and Gray (Elegy), "The curfew
tolls the knell of parting day."

663. Era la notte, e non si vedea lume.   Ariosto, Orl. Fur. cant. 40,
st. 6.—*'Twas night, and not a glimmer to be seen.*

664. Ἔργα νέων, βουλαὶ δὲ μέσων, εὐχαὶ δὲ γερόντων.   Hes. Fr. 65.
            Let youth in deeds, in counsel man engage;
            Prayer is the proper duty of old age.—*Boswell.*

       Another form of the saying, Νέοις μὲν ἔργα, βουλὰς δὲ γεραιτέροις.   Paroem.
Gr., vol. i. p. 436 (App. 4, 6).— *Works for the young, and counsels for their
elders,* seems to be an echo of Eur. Fr. 497,

                 παλαιὸς αἶνος· ἔργα μὲν νεωτέρων,
                 βουλαὶ δ' ἔχουσι τῶν γεραιτέρων κράτος.

       Also cf. Macarius, *Centuriæ*, 4, 11 (Paroem. Gr., vol. ii. p. 167), for the
older, and apparently original, reading, Ἔργα νέων, βουλαὶ δὲ υέσων, πορδαὶ
δὲ γερόντων.

665. Eripuit cælo fulmen, mox sceptra tyrannis. A. R. J. Turgot, in Condorcet's *Vie de M. Turgot*, Lond., 1786, p. 200, Harb. Often qu. as, "Sceptrumque tyrannis."—*He robbed Heaven of its bolts, and tyrants of their sceptres.*

> Inscription for Houdon's bust of Franklin, with allusion to the discovery of the lightning conductor and the American War of Independence. The line is partly an adaptation of Manilius Astr. 1, 104, *Eripuitque Jovi fulmen viresque tonandi;* and partly of the *Eripuit fulmenque Jovi Phœboque sagittas* of Polignac's *Anti-Lucretius*, 1, 96.

666. Ernst ist das Leben, heiter ist die Kunst. Schiller, Wall. Lager. Prol., fin. (1798).—*Life is earnest, art is cheerful.*

667. Errare humanum est. Polignac, Anti-Lucretius, 5, 58.—*To err is human.* Cf. Pope (*Essay on Criticism*, Pt. ii. 325), "To err is human, to forgive divine."

> Hieron. (Ep. 57, 12) has, "errasse humanum est, et confiteri errorem, prudentis": and Cic. Phil. 12, 2, 5, "Cujusvis hominis est errare; nullius, nisi insipientis, in errore perseverare. Posteriores enim cogitationes (ut aiunt) sapientiores solent esse.—*Any man is liable to err, but no one but a fool will persist in his error. As they say, second thoughts are generally the wisest.* Hence, perhaps, the med. prov., "Humanum est peccare sed perseverare diabolicum." Chil. p. 518.—*To sin is human; to continue in sin is devilish.*
>
>> Man-like it is to fall into sin;
>> Fiend-like it is to dwell therein.—*Longfellow* (Aphorisms).
>
> Also:
>
>> Errare est hominis, sed non persistere: sæpe
>> Optimus est portus vertere consilium. Verinus, Chil. 518.
>
>> To err, not to persist in it, is man's:
>> The best escape is oft a change of plans.—*Ed.*

668. Errare, mehercule, malo cum Platone, . . . quam cum istis vera sentire. Cic. Tusc. 1, 17, 39.—*I would much rather err in company with Plato, than to think rightly with men of those opinions* (Pythagoreans).

669. Es bildet ein Talent sich in der Stille,
Sich ein Charakter in dem Strom der Welt. Goethe, Tasso, 1, 2.
—*A talent is developed in quietude: character is formed in the turmoil of the world.*

670. Es ist bestimmt in Gottes Rat
Dass man vom Liebsten, was man hat,
    Muss scheiden.

> Ed. von Feuchtersleben, "Nach altdeutscher Weise," as altered by Mendelssohn for his musical setting of the words.

>> It is ordained by God above
>> That from the thing he most doth love,
>> Man needs must sever.—*Ed.*

671. Es ist eine alte Geschichte,
     Doch bleibt sie immer neu.

          H. Heine, " Ein Jüngling liebt' ein Mädchen."

                    Love-making.
               It is an old-world story,
                 And yet 'tis ever new.—*Ed.*

672. Es kostet nichts, die allgemeine Schönheit
     Zu sein, als die gemeine sein für alle. Schiller, Maria Stuart, 3, 4.

     Elizabeth. She who to all is "common" may with ease
               Become the "common" object of applause.—*Bohn's Stand. Library.*

          ₊ This cruel fling of Elizabeth's at Mary's successive marriages is
     difficult to render into English, based as it is on a *jeu de mots*—"allgemein"
     and "gemein für alle."

673. Esse bonam facile est, ubi quod vetet esse remotum est. Ov. T. 5,
     14, 25.—*It is easy for a woman to be good, when all that hinders
     her from being so is removed.*

674. Esse oportet ut vivas, non vivere ut edas. Auct. Her. 4, 28, 39.
     —*One should eat to live, not live to eat.* Socrates says (Diog.
     Laert. 2, 34), τοὺς μὲν ἄλλους ἀνθρώπους ζῆν ἵν' ἐσθίοιεν· αὐτὸν δὲ
     ἐσθίειν ἵνα ζώῃ.—*Other men lived but to eat, while he ate to live.*

675. Esse quam videri, bonus malebat. Sall. Cat. 54.—*He preferred to
     be, rather than seem, an honest man.* Said of Cato Major. Cf. οὐ
     γὰρ δοκεῖν ἄριστος, ἀλλ' εἶναι θέλει. Æsch. Theb. 592.—*He would
     not seem just only; he would be so.* Plut. says (Aristides, c. 3),
     that when the actor came to this line the whole audience looked
     at Aristides, "the Just."

676. Esse quid hoc dicam, vivis quod fama negatur,
         Et sua quod rarus tempora lector amat?
     Hi sunt invidiæ nimirum, Regule, mores,
         Præferat antiquos semper ut illa novis.   Mart. 5, 10, 1.

                    Old and New Authors.
               Why, pray, to living men is fame denied,
                 And readers mostly their own age eschew?
               It is the freak of envy or of pride
                 Always to rate the old above the new.—*Ed.*

677. Esse quoque in fatis reminiscitur affore tempus,
     Quo mare, quo tellus, correptaque regia cœli
     Ardeat; et mundi moles operosa laboret.   Ov. M. 1, 256.

                    The Day of Doom.
               He calls to mind a presage of the fates,—
               That sea, and earth, and Heaven's high palaces
               Should burst in flame. and totter to its base
               All the laborious fabric of the world.—*Ed.*

678. Est aliquid quo tendis, et in quod dirigis arcum? Pers. 3, 60.—
     Have you any aim in view, and at what do you point your bow?

679. Est brevitate opus ut currat sententia.   Hor. S. 1, 10, 9.—*Terseness there wants to make the thought ring clear.*—Conington.
Need of a concise style.

680. Est deus in nobis, et sunt commercia cœli.   Ov. A. A. 3, 549.—
We poets have a god within, and hold communion with the sky.

681. Est genus hominum qui esse primos se omnium rerum volunt,
Nec sunt : hos consector.   Hisce ego non paro me ut rideant ;
Sed his ultro arrideo, et eorum ingenia admiror simul.
Quicquid dicunt, laudo : id rursum si negant, laudo id quoque.
Negat quis ? Nego. Ait ? Aio. Postremo imperavi egomet mihi
Omnia assentari.   Is quæstus nunc est multo uberrimus.
                                                      Ter. Eun. 2, 2, 17.

The Parasite.

Gnatho. Some men there are who would be first in every thing,
     And are not.   These are my game ; but not to make 'em laugh ;
     Rather, to laugh with them, astounded at their wit.
     They speak, and I applaud ; or, should they contradict,
     I praise that too.   If they deny, why so do I ;
     Affirm ?   My affirmation 's ready—in a word,
     I've schooled myself to yield assent on every point.
     'Tis the most paying occupation that I know.—*Ed.*

682. Est-il aucun moment
Qui vous puisse assurer d'un second seulement?   La Font. 11, 8.
(Vieillard et les trois jeunes hommes.)

     Can with certainty any one moment be reckoned
     That can give you th' assurance of passing a second ?—*Ed.*

683. Est locus unicuique suus.   Hor. S. 1, 9, 51.—*Each man finds his place.*   There is room for all.

684. Est modus in rebus ; sunt certi denique fines,
Quos ultra citraque nequit consistere rectum.   Hor. S. 1, 1, 106.

     Yes, there's a mean in morals ; life has lines,
     To north or south of which all virtue pines.—*Conington.*

Society is (or should be) inspired by that golden mean which is called good
taste, and woe to the man who oversteps the boundary.   Let your moderation be known unto all men.

685. Est multi fabula plena joci.   Ov. F. 6, 320.—*The story is full of fun.*

686. Est natura hominum novitatis avida.   Plin. 12, 5.—*It is the nature of man to love novelty.*

     Cf. Est quoque cunctarum novitas carissima rerum ;
        Gratiaque officio, quod mora tardat, abest.   Ov. Ep. 3, 4, 51.
     The dearest of all things is novelty ;
     And favours lose their value by delay.—*Ed.*

687. Estne Dei sedes nisi terra, et pontus, et aër,
Et cœlum, et virtus?   Superos quid quærimus ultra?
Jupiter est, quodcunque vides, quocunque moveris.   Luc. 9, 578.
—*Is not the Deity's dwelling the earth and sea and air and heaven*

and virtue ? Why seek the gods elsewhere ? Jupiter is, in truth, whatever you see, and wheresoever you are. The doctrine of Pantheism, which the concluding line well sums up.

688. Esto peccator et pecca fortiter, sed fortius fide et gaude in Christo, etc. Luther, Ep. ad Melanchthon, ex. Epp. R. P. M. Lutheri (Ienæ, 1556, Tom. i. p. 345).—*Be a sinner, and sin hardily, but believe and rejoice in Christ more mightily still, etc.*

689. Esto perpetua!—*Mayest thou endure for ever!* The supposed dying apostrophe of Pietro Sarpi (Fra Paolo) in speaking of his beloved Venice.

690. Esto, ut nunc multi, dives tibi, pauper amicis.   Juv. 5, 113.

> Adopt the way the present fashion tends;
> Indulge yourself, be saving tow'rds your friends.—*Ed.*

691. Est profecto deus, qui quæ nos gerimus auditque et videt.

. . . .

Bene merenti bene profuerit, male merenti par erit. Plaut. Capt. 2, 2, 63 and 65.—*Certainly there is a God who sees and hears what we do. . . . Well will it be for the well-deserving, and the evil-doer will get his deserts.*

692. Est quadam prodire tenus, si non datur ultra. Hor. Ep. 1, 1, 32.—*All may make some progress, though it be not allowed them to go beyond a certain point.*

693. Est quiddam gestus edendi. Ov. A. A. 3, 755.—*There is much in a person's mode of eating.*

694. Est rosa flos Veneris : cujus quo furta laterent
    Harpocrati matris dona dicavit Amor.
Inde rosam mensis hospes suspendit amicis,
    Convivæ ut sub eâ dicta tacenda sciant.
             Lemaire's *Poetæ Lat. Minor.* vii. p. 125.

Sub rosa.

> The rose is Venus' flower; her thefts to aid
> Love to Harpocrates the gift conveyed.
> 'Tis why each host hangs o'er his board a rose,
> That what's said under it may none disclose.—*Ed.*

Harpocrates was the God of Silence.—Burman's *Anthologia* (1773), lib. 5, epigr. 217, reads *amici.*

695. Est virtus placitis abstinuisse bonis. Ov. H. 17, 98.—*'Tis virtue to abstain from things that please.*

696. Et amârunt me quoque Nymphæ. Ov. M. 3, 456.—*I too have been loved by the Nymphs.* I too have found women to love me. Words of Narcissus on being unable to grasp his own reflection in the water.

697. Ἦ τὰν, ἢ ἐπὶ τᾶς. Plut. Lacœnar. Apophthegm. 15 (Mor. p. 299).
—*Either this, or upon this!* Parting words of the Spartan
mother on handing her son the shield he was to carry into
battle. He was to bring it back, if not brought back upon it.

698. Et c'est être innocent que d'être malheureux. La Font. Elégie
(Nymphes de Vaux., fin.).—*Misfortune's the proof of a man's
innocence.*

> Nicholas Fouquet (1615-80), appointed Superintendent of Finance on
> Mazarin's death, was in 1661 charged with malversation of the public
> funds, and imprisoned for life in the Fortress of Pignerol. Just previous
> to his fall, he had entertained the King in munificent style at his country
> seat, Vaux-Praslin, near Melun. It was in exculpation of his patron's
> errors that La Fontaine composed his Ode.

699. Et genus et virtus, nisi cum re, vilior alga est. Hor. S. 2, 5, 8.

> Yet family and worth, without the staff
> Of wealth to lean on, are the veriest draff.—*Conington.*

700. Etiam capillus unus habet umbram suam. Syr. 159.—*Even a
single hair casts a shadow.* The slightest clue is of importance.

701. Etiam celeritas in desiderio mora est. Syr. 149.—*When we long
for a thing, haste itself is slow.*

702. Etiam oblivisci quid sis, interdum expedit. Syr. 152.—*It is
sometimes expedient to forget who you are.*

703. Etiam sapientibus cupido gloriæ novissima exuitur. Tac. H. 4, 6.
—*Ambition is the last passion to be laid aside, even by the wise.*

> Plato (ap. Athenæus, 11, 116, p. 507) says, Ἔσχατον τὸν τῆς δόξης χιτῶνα
> ἐν τῷ θανάτῳ αὐτῷ ἀποδυόμεθα.—*Glory (ambition) is the last garment of which
> we divest ourselves, and that only with death itself.* Cf. Milton, *Lycidas*, 70,

> > Fame is the spur that the clear spirit doth raise
> > (That last infirmity of noble mind).

704. Et jam summa procul villarum culmina fumant,
Majoresque cadunt altis de montibus umbræ. Virg. E. 1, 83.

> *Approach of Evening.*
> Far off the smoke of farmsteads now ascends;
> The mountain's brow its lengthening shadow bends.—*Ed.*

705. Et le combat cessa, faute de combattants. Corn. Cid. (1636), 4, 3.
—*The combat ceased, for want of combatants.*

706. Et nati natorum, et qui nascentur ab illis. Virg. A. 3, 98.—*The
children of our children, and those who shall be born of them.*
Our posterity to the latest period.

707. Et nulli cessura fides, sine crimine mores,
Nudaque simplicitas, purpureusque pudor. Ov. Am. 1, 3, 13.

> Trusty good faith, a life without a stain,
> Of blushing purity, of manners plain.—*Ed.*

708. Et nunc omnis ager, nunc omnis parturit arbos;
     Nunc frondent sylvæ, nunc formosissimus annus.   Virg. E. 3, 56.

> *Spring.*
> Now fields and trees all blossoming appear,
> Leafy the woods, and loveliest the year.—*Ed.*

709. Et pudet, et metuo, semperque eademque precari,
     Ne subeant animo tædia justa tuo.   Ov. Ep. 4, 15, 29.—*I am
     ashamed and fear to be always making the same requests, lest you
     should conceive a well-deserved disgust of me.*

710. Et quando uberior vitiorum copia?   Quando
     Major avaritiæ patuit sinus?   Alea quando
     Hos animos?   Juv. 1, 87.

> What age so large a crop of vices bore,
> Or when was avarice extended more,
> When were the dice with more profusion thrown?—*Dryden.*

711. Et, quasi cursores, vitaï lampada tradunt.   Lucr. 2, 78.—*Like
     runners, they hand on the torch of life.*   Cf. Plat. Leges 6,
     776, γεννῶντάς τε καὶ ἐκτρέφοντας παῖδας, καθάπερ λαμπάδα
     τὸν βίον παραδιδόντας ἄλλοις ἐξ ἄλλων.—*Begetting and rearing
     children, they hand on life from one generation to another, like the
     torch in the race.*   Fig. taken from the "Torch-Race" at the
     Athenian festivals of Prometheus, Vulcan, etc.

712. Et quisquam ingenuas etiamnum suspicit artes,
     Aut tenerum dotes carmen habere putat?
     Ingenium quondam fuerat pretiosius auro:
     At nunc barbaries grandis, habere nihil.   Ov. Am. 3, 8, 1.

> Is there any one nowadays honours the arts,
> Or thinks that sweet verse has its due recompense?
> More than gold were prized formerly talents and parts:
> But now they're a drug in this sad decadence.—*Ed.*

713. Être aimable, charmer, ce n'est pas si facile,
     Quand on se fait aimer, on n'est pas inutile.   Louis Ratisbonne,
     Coméd. Enfantine, xxiii. (Le Charme), Paris, 1861, 8°, p. 72.

> To be amiable, charming 's not done with such ease;
> They've a useful career who have learnt how to please.—*Ed.*

714. Être rigoureux pour les particuliers qui font gloire de mépriser
     les Loix and les Ordonnances d'un État, c'est être bon pour le
     Public.   Et on ne fcauroit faire un plus grand Crime contre les
     Intérêts publics, qu'en fe rendant Indulgent envers ceux qui les
     violent.   Richelieu, Test. Pol. La Haye, 1740, 8°, 8th ed., vol. 2,
     cap. 5, p. 25.—*To act with rigour towards those individuals who
     glory in despising the laws, is to consult the public good; and one
     could not commit a greater crime against public interests, than to
     show indulgence to those who violate them.*

715. Et sæpe usque adeo, mortis formidine, vitæ
Percipit humanos odium lucisque videndæ,
Ut sibi consciscant mœrenti pectore lethum. Lucret. 3, 79.

Suicide.

Often, through fear of dying, men conceive
Hatred of life and to behold the light:
So much that they with sorrow-laden hearts
Inflict their deaths upon themselves!—*Ed.*

716. Et tenuit nostras numerosus Horatius aures,
Dum ferit Ausonia carmina culta lyra.
Virgilium vidi tantum: nec amara Tibullo
Tempus amicitiæ fata dedere meæ. Ov. T. 4, 10, 49.

With rhythmic numbers Horace charmed our ears,
Tuning th' Ausonian lyre to polish'd verse.
Virgil I did but see; and fate unkind
Vouchsafed me not to call Tibullus friend.—*Ed.*

Ovid's recollection of the chief poets of his day—beginning of the first
century of our era. "As for Burns, I may truly say, *Virgilium vidi tantum.*
I was a lad of fifteen in 1786-7, when he first came to Edinburgh," etc.
Sir Walter Scott, qu. in T. Carlyle's *Miscellanies*, London, 1869, vol. 2, p. 48.

717. Et veniam pro laude peto: laudatus abunde,
Non fastiditus si tibi, lector, ero. Ov. T. 1, 7, 31.

Pardon, not praise, I seek ; enough I'm praised,
If, on perusal, no disgust be raised.—*Ed.*

718. Et voilà justement comme on écrit l'histoire! Volt. Charlot, 1,
7.—*That is precisely how history is written!* A jumble of errors,
probabilities, and partial narration. "Don't read history to
me, that can't be true" Sir Robert Walpole to his son Horace.
Prior's *Life of Malone* (1860), p. 387.

In the play, the Countess's steward runs in to announce that the
villagers had taken the troupe of acrobats she had hired for the King's
amusement, for the King himself.

Tout le monde a crié le Roi ! sur les chemins ;
On le crie au village et chez tous les voisins ;
Dans votre basse-cour on s'obstine à le croire :
Et voilà justement comme on écrit l'histoire.

The play appeared in 1767, and on Sept. 24, 1766, Voltaire had made use
of the expression in writing to Mme. du Deffand. On a friend defending
him in the presence of the same lady, and maintaining that at least he had
invented nothing, "Rien?" repliquait-elle, "et que voulez-vous de plus." *Il
a inventé l'histoire!* Fourn. *L.D.L.*, p. 300.

719. Euge poeta! Pers. 1, 75.—*Bravo, poet!*

720. Eventu rerum stolidi didicere magistro. Claud. Eutr. 2, 489.—
—*Fools learn by the event.* Eventus hoc docet ; stultorum iste
magister est. Liv. 22, 39.—*The event, which is always your
fool's teacher, proves it.*

721. Ex abundantia enim cordis os loquitur. Vulg., Matt. xii. 34.—
Out of the abundance of the heart the mouth speaketh.

722. Excidat illa dies ævo, nec postera credant
     Sæcula; nos certe taceamus, et obruta multa
     Nocte tegi propriæ patiamur crimina gentis.   Stat. S. 5, 288.—
     *Let that day be blotted out of the record of time, and future ages
     know it not.   Let us at least be silent, and allow the crimes of our
     nation to be buried in the grave of night.*   Quoted by President
     Christophe de Thou *à propos* of the St Bartholomew massacres.
     See the *Mémoires de la Vie*, etc., Rotterdam, 1711, p. 10, by
     his son, J. A. de Thou, the historian.

723. Exeat aula Qui volet esse pius.   Virtus et summa potestas
     Non coeunt: semper metuet, quem sæva pudebunt.   Luc. 8, 493.

> Let all who prize their honour quit the court:
> Virtue with sovereign power seldom mates,
> And he's not safe who still can blush at blood.—*Ed.*

724. Exegi monumentum ære perennius,
     Regalique situ pyramidum altius;
     Quod non imber edax, non Aquilo impotens,
     Possit diruere, aut innumerabilis
     Annorum series aut fuga temporum.
     Non omnis moriar; multaque pars mei
     Vitabit Libitinam.   Usque ego postera
     Crescam laude recens, dum Capitolium
     Scandet cum tacita virgine pontifex.
     Dicar, qua violens obstrepit Aufidus,
     Et qua pauper aquæ Daunus agrestium
     Regnavit populorum, ex humili potens,
     Princeps Æolium carmen ad Italos
     Deduxisse modos.   Sume superbiam
     Quæsitam meritis, et mihi Delphica
     Lauro cinge volens, Melpomene, comam.   Hor. C. 3, 30, 1.

The Poet's Immortality.

> Finished my monument of song,
> Than pyramid high'r, than bronze more strong.
> Nor shall the rain, or North wind's rage,
> Years immemorial—age on age—
> Wholly destroy it: much I've said
> Shall 'scape the goddess of the dead.
> Long as the priest and maid ascend
> The Capitol, my fame 'll extend
> With growth of time.   Ofanto's roar,
> Where Daunus from his arid shore
> Ruled o'er his rustic populace—
> Men shall point out my natal place.
> "There was he born," they'll say; "grown great
> "From nothing, and the first to mate
> "Greek lyrics with the western muse."
> Melpomene, do not refuse
> The proud acclaim by honour won,
> And crown with Delphic bays thy son.—*Ed.*

725. Exemplo quodcunque malo committitur ipsi
Displicet auctori; prima hæc est ultio, quod se
Judice nemo nocens absolvitur.   Juv. 13, 1.

Sin its own Avenger.

Each act of sin, in the remorse it brings
Deals its first vengeance ; i' the court of conscience
The guilt remains, and cannot be discharged.—*Ed.*

726. Exemplumque Dei quisque est in imagine parva.   Manil. Astr. 4,
895.—*Each man is the image of his God in small.*

727. Exigui numero, sed bello vivida virtus.   Virg. A. 5, 754.

A gallant band, in number few,
In spirit resolute to dare.—*Conington.*

728. Exilioque domos et dulcia limina mutant,
Atque alio patriam quærunt sub sole jacentem.   Virg. G. 2, 511.

The Emigrants.

Forth from familiar scenes the exiles roam,
To seek 'neath other skies another home.—*Ed.*

729. Exilis domus est, ubi non et multa supersunt,
Et dominum fallunt, et prosunt furibus.   Hor. Ep. 1, 6, 45.

It's a poor house which not great substance leaves,
To 'scape the master's eye, and fatten thieves.—*Ed.*

730. Eximia veste et victu convivia, ludi,
Pocula crebra, unguenta, coronæ, serta parantur;
Nequidquam: quoniam medio de fonte leporum
Surgit amari aliquid, quod in ipsis floribus angat.   Lucr. 4, 1127.

Surgit amari aliquid.

Go, deck the board with damask fine,
Cheer of the best, and mirth and wine:
Fill fast the cups, and in their train
Bring perfumes, wreaths——'Tis all in vain :
'Mid the full flood of revelries,
Some drop of bitterness will rise
To dash the pleasure of the hour,
And poison each delightsome flower.—*Ed.*

Byron (*Childe Harold*, Cant. 1, St. 82) has,

Full from the fount of joy's delicious springs
Some bitter o'er the flowers its bubbling venom flings.

731. Existimo in summo imperatore quatuor has res inesse oportere;
scientiam rei militaris, virtutem, auctoritatem, felicitatem.
Cic. Manil. 10, 28.

Qualifications of a General.

A Commander-in-chief ought to possess these four qualifications—knowledge of warfare, courage, authority, and a lucky star.

732. Exitus acta probat.   Ov. H. 2, 85.—*The event justifies the deed.*

733. Exitus in dubio est: audebimus ultima, dixit;
Viderit audentes forsne Deusne juvet.   Ov. F. 2, 781.

> Doubt shrouds th' event; but we'll dare all, he said,
> And see if chance or God the daring aid.—*Ed.*

734. Ex luce lucellum.—*A small profit derived from light.*

> Originally said of the obsolete window-tax, the phrase was revived by
> Mr Lowe in 1871 as motto for his projected Government stamp on match-
> boxes. The Match-Tax Bill was introduced on April 20, and withdrawn on
> April 25. Some wit suggested to the defeated Chancellor the transference
> of the duty to photographs, with the motto, *Ex sole solatium.*

735. Ex magna cœna stomacho fit maxima pœna;
Ut sis nocte levis, sit tibi cœna brevis.   Coll. Salern. i. p. 451, l. 194.

> Who sups too well pays vengeance fell;
> From supper light comes quiet night.—*Ed.*

736. Exoriare aliquis nostris ex ossibus ultor.   Virg. A. 4, 625.

> Rise from my ashes, some avenger rise!—*Ed.*

> Dying imprecation of Dido upon the false Æneas. The line is said to
> have been written with the point of his sword on the walls of his dungeon
> by Philip Strozzi before killing himself, when imprisoned by Cosmo I. de'
> Medici, for complicity in the murder of Duke Alexander, his predecessor,
> in 1537. *V.* Fumag. 681.

737. Ex pede Herculem. Prov.—*You can judge of Hercules's stature by
his foot.* The whole of anything may be inferred from the part. Cf.
Ex ungue leonem; or in Gr.,ἐξ ὄνυχος λέοντα (sc. γράφειν). Alcæus
ap. Plut. de Defectu Orac. 3 (Mor. p. 500).—*To draw a lion
from a lion's claw, i.e.,* from a small but characteristic part.

738. Expende Hannibalem: quot libras in duce summo
Invenies?   Juv. 10, 147.

> Weigh out Hannibal: see how many
> Pounds there'll be in that great captain!—*Shaw.*

Motto of Byron's *Ode to Napoleon Buonaparte,* 1814.

739. Experientia docet. Prov.—*Experience teaches.* We learn by
experience. Cf. Usus, magister egregius. Plin. Ep. 1, 20, 12.
—*That excellent master, Experience.* Cujus usum, ut ceteras
artes, experientia docuit. Tac. H. 5, 6.—*Proficiency in which, as
in other arts, is taught by experience.*

740. Experimentum crucis.—*A decisive experiment.*

> In the absence of more precise information on the source and meaning of
> this phrase, attention may be called to the anon. suggestion in *N. and Q.*
> (3rd ser., ii. 396), that it is derived from Bacon's *instantiœ crucis* (Nov.
> Org. 2, 36; vol. 8, 143), or "logical finger-posts" (from *crux,* a sign-post),
> showing the right way from the wrong, demonstration from conjecture.
> An *experimentum crucis* would be such an experiment in natural science,
> etc., as would afford an *instantia crucis.* Men must learn, Bacon adds
> *(ibid.,* fin.), to examine nature by examples that show the way and by
> experiments that throw light, and not by reasoning from probabilities:
> ("de natura judicare *per instantias crucis, et experimenta lucifera,* et non
> per rationes probabiles").

741. Experto credite. Virg. 11, 283.—*Believe one who speaks from experience.*

Cf. Crede experto, non fallimus, Sil. 7, 395; experto credite, Ov. A. A. 3, 511; experto crede, St Bernard, Ep. 106, 110. Büchm. (p. 391) qu. Antonius de Arena († 1544), *Ad compagnones* ("Consilium pro dansatoribus," ver. 3), for the prov. "Experto crede Roberto."

742. Expliquera, morbleu! les femmes qui pourra! Barthe, Fausses Infidélités, sc. 17, fin. Œuvr. Choisies, Paris, 1811, p. 51.

Mondor. Explain the women? Zounds! let him who can!

743. Exploranda est veritas. Phædr. 3, 10, 5.—*The truth must be investigated.*

744. Explorant adversa viros, perque aspera duro
Nititur ad laudem virtus interrita clivo.   Sil. 4, 605.

Adversity's man's test; unterrified
True worth fights up the rugged steep to fame.—*Ed.*

745. Ex quovis ligno non fit Mercurius. Prov. *See* App. Apol. cap. 43.
—*A Mercury is not to be made out of any piece of wood.* You can't make a silk purse out of a sow's ear.

746. Exsulis hæc vox est; præbet mihi litera linguam;
Et, si non liceat scribere, mutus ero.   Ov. Ep. 2, 6, 3.

Foreign Letters.
The voice of the exile, his pen is his word:
And were't not for letters, I should not be heard.—*Ed.*

747. Extra Ecclesiam nulla salus.—*Outside the Church there is no salvation.*

Like other terse epitomes of general truths, this axiom cannot be traced, *verbum verbo*, to any one author, being but the proverbial shape into which many analogous sayings of the kind have been finally cast. Origen, in the first half of the 3rd century, says (Homily 3 on Josue, Bened. Ed., 1733, p. 404A), Nemo semetipsum decipiat . . . extra ecclesiam nemo salvatur. —*Let no one deceive himself, outside the Church no one can be saved.* Fifty years later, St Cyprian echoes the great Alexandrian father with *Salus extra ecclesiam non est.* Ep. 73, 18. (Caillau's Patres Apost., vol. 14, p. 273); and cf. id. Ep. 62, 4. (Migne, vol. 4, p. 371.) St Augustine, in the next century, writes more fully: Extra Ecclesiam Catholicam totum potest præter salutem. Potest habere honorem, potest habere sacramentum, potest cantare Halleluia, potest respondere Amen, potest Evangelium tenere, potest in nomine Patris et Filii et Spiritus Sancti fidem et habere et prædicare: sed nusquam nisi in Ecclesia Catholica salutem poterit invenire. Serm. ad Cæsar. Eccl. Plebem. c. 6 (vol. ix. 422D).—*Outside of the Catholic Church everything may be had except salvation. You may have Orders and Sacraments, you may sing Alleluia and answer Amen, you may hold the Gospel and have and preach the faith in the name of the Father, the Son, and the Holy Ghost: but nowhere except in the Catholic Church can salvation be found.*

748. Extra fortunam est, quidquid donatur amicis;
Quas dederis, solas semper habebis opes.   Mart. 5, 42, 7.

Who gives to friends so much from Fate secures,
That is the only wealth for ever yours.—*Hay.*

G

Cf. the Epitaph of Wm., Earl of Devonshire († 1216), and of Mabel his wife, in E. Cleaveland's *Geneal. Hist. of the Courtenays*, Exon., 1735, fol. p. 142.

> What we gave, we nave;
> What we spent, we had;
> What we left, we lost.

749. Ex umbris et imaginibus in veritatem. Card. Newman, his own epitaph.—*From shadows and figures to the reality.*

F.

750. Faber est suæ quisque fortunæ. Appius Cl. Cæcus (307 B.C.) ap. Sall. de Rep. Ord. 1, 1 (in oblique narration—*Fabrum esse*, etc.). —*Each man is the architect of his own fortunes.*

> Sapiens . . . ipse fingit fortunam sibi. Plaut. Trin. 2, 2, 84.—*A clever man shapes his fortune for himself.* Sui cuique mores fingunt fortunam. Nep. Att. 11, 6.—*It is our character that determines our fortunes.* Chacun est artisan de sa bonne fortune. Régnier, Sat. 13, "Macette."—*Each is the architect of his good fortune.*

751. Fabula (nec sentis) tota jactaris in urbe. Ov. Am. 3, 1, 21.— *You don't know it, but you are the talk of the town.*

752. Faciendi plures libros nullus est finis: frequensque meditatio carnis afflictio est. Vulg. Eccles. xii. 12.—*Of making many books there is no end; and much study is a weariness of the flesh.*

753. Facies non omnibus una,
Nec diversa tamen; qualem decet esse sororum. Ov. M. 2, 13. —*The features were not the same in all, nor yet the difference great: but such as is the case between sisters.* A family likeness.

754. Facile largiri de alieno. Just. 36, 3, 9.—*It is easy to be generous with other people's property.* (The text is, "Facile tunc Romanis de alieno largientibus.")

755. Facile princeps. Cic. Div. 2, 42, 87.—*Easily the first.* By far the best.

756. Facilis descensus Averno;
Noctes atque dies patet atri janua Ditis;
Sed revocare gradum superasque evadere ad auras,
Hoc opus, hic labor est. Virg. A. 6, 126.

The Descent to the Lower World.

> Smooth the descent and easy is the way;
> (The Gates of Hell stand open night and day):
> But to return, and view the cheerful skies,
> In this the task and mighty labour lies.—*Dryden.*

> Applicable to the ease with which men fall into vicious habits, and the difficulty of retracing their steps. Cf. Vulg., Matt. vii. 13. Lata porta, et spatiosa via est quæ ducit ad perditionem, et multi sunt qui intrant per eam.—*Wide is the gate*, etc.

757. Facinus est vincire civem Romanum, scelus verberare, prope
parricidium necare: quid dicam in crucem tollere? verbo satis
digno tam nefaria res appellari nullo modo potest. Cic. Verr. 2,
5, 66, § 170.—*It is an offence even to bind a Roman citizen, a crime
to flog him, almost the act of a parricide to put him to death: what
shall I then call crucifying him? Language worthy of such an
enormity it is impossible to find.*

The interest attaching to this quotation arises from the infliction of the
particular penalty that Cicero condemns—about eighty years later—upon
the world's Redeemer,—"*Crucifixus etiam pro nobis sub Pontio Pilato, etc.*"

758. Facinus majoris abollæ.   Juv. 3, 115.—*A crime committed by one
in high station.*

He is speaking of a murder committed by a stoic who wore the *abolla*, or
philosopher's robe. Improperly, it might stand for "a crime of *deeper dye*."

759. Facinus quos inquinat æquat.   Luc. 5, 290.
Crime, where it stains, brands all with level rank.—*Ed.*

760. Facis de necessitate virtutem.   Hier. adv. Ruf. 3, 2.—*You are
making a virtue out of necessity.*

761. Facito aliquid operis, ut semper te diabolus inveniat occupatum.
Hier. Ep. 125, § 11; Migne, vol. 22, 939 (Harb.).—*Always be
doing something, that the devil may find you engaged.*

762. Faciunt næ intelligendo, ut nihil intelligant.   Ter. And. Prol. 17.
—*They are so knowing, that they know nothing at all.*

763. Fac plurima mediocriter, si non possis unum aliquid insigniter.
Plin. Ep. 9, 29, 1.—*Be content with many moderate successes,
if a signal triumph be denied you.*

764. Facta canam; sed erunt qui me finxisse loquantur.   Ov. F. 6, 3.
—*I speak of facts, though some will say that I am inventing.*

765. Facta ducis vivent, operosaque gloria rerum;
Hæc manet; hæc avidos effugit una rogos.   Ov. Liv. 265.
The hero's deeds and hard-won fame shall live;
They can alone the funeral fires survive.—*Ed.*

766. Fac tantum incipias, sponte disertus eris.   Ov. A. A. 1, 610.—
Only begin, and you will become eloquent of yourself.

767. Factis ignoscite nostris,
Si scelus ingenio scitis abesse meo.   Ov. F. 3, 309.—*Forgive the
deed, since you know that all wicked intent was far from my mind.*

768. Factum abiit, monumenta manent.   Ov. F. 4, 709.—*The event is
past, the memorial of it remains.*   Motto of London Numismatic
Society.

769. Factum est illud; fieri infectum non potest.   Plaut. Aul. 4, 10,
11.—*The deed is done and cannot be undone.*

Μόνου γὰρ αὐτοῦ καὶ θεὸς στερίσκεται
ἀγένητα ποιεῖν ἄσσ' ἂν ᾖ πεπραγμένα.   Agathon ap. Arist. Eth. N. 6, 2, 6.

E'en Heaven itself commands not this one grace—
To make undone what once has taken place.—*Ed.*

770. Faites votre devoir, et laissez faire aux dieux.   Corn. Horace, 2, 8
(Horace père loq.).—*Do your duty, and leave the rest to God.*

771. Fallacia Alia aliam trudit.   Ter. And. 4, 4, 39.—*One lie begets
another.*

772. Fallere credentem non est operosa puellam
Gloria.   Simplicitas digna favore fuit.   Ov. H. 2, 63.

To dupe a trustful girl is small renown;
To one so simple, kindness should be shown.—*Ed.*

773. Fallite fallentes: ex magna parte profanum
Sunt genus; in laqueos quos posuere, cadant.   Ov. A. A. 1, 645.

The cheaters cheat, mostly a godless gang;
In their own nooses let the scoundrels hang.—*Ed.*

Büchm. qu. "Le trompeur trompé" (*The Cheater Cheated*), title of a
comic opera of Guilet and Gaveaux, 1799: and the *Betrogene Betrüger* (same
meaning) of G. E. Lessing, *Nathan*, 3, 7.

774. Fallit enim vitium, specie virtutis et umbra,
Quum sit triste habitu, vultuque et veste severum.   Juv. 14, 109.

Vice can deceive, ape virtue's mien and air
By sad demeanour, face and dress severe.—*Ed.*

775. Fallitur, egregio quisquis sub principe credit
Servitium.   Nunquam libertas gratior extat
Quam sub rege pio.   Claud. Cons. Stil. 3, 113.

He errs who deems it servitude to live
Under a noble prince: for liberty
Is never sweeter than with pious kings.—*Ed.*

776. Familiare est hominibus omnia sibi ignoscere, nihil aliis remittere;
et invidiam rerum non ad causam, sed ad voluntatem personasque
dirigere.   Vell. 2, 30, 3.—*Men as a rule pardon all their own
faults, make no allowance for others, and fix the whole blame upon
the individual, without any regard for the circumstances of the case.*

777. Familiaris rei communicatio mater contemptus existit.   Alanus
de Insulis, Lib. de Planctu Naturæ.   (*Anglo-Saxon Satirists*, ed.
T. Wright, Record Series, vol. 2, p. 454).—*Familiar communi-
cation is the mother of contempt.*

778. Fari quæ sentiat.   Hor. Ep. 1, 4, 9.—*To speak as you think.*
Motto of the Earl of Orford, and stamped by Horace Walpole
on the books printed at his private press at Strawberry Hill.

779. Fastidientis stomachi est multa degustare.   Sen. Ep. 2, 3.—*It
shows a delicate stomach to be tasting so many dishes.*   Said of
reading too many kinds of books.

780. Fata obstant. Virg. A. 4, 440.—*The Fates are against it.*

781. Faut d'la vartu, pas trop n'en faut;
L'excès partout est un défaut.
> Boutet de Monvel, L'erreur d'un moment, Sc. 1.
Comedy in one act (1773), the music by Des Aides (Dezède);
and the qu. is the refrain of "Catau," the village girl's song,
pronounced in broad Auvergnat. Alex. p. 527.

> *Est modus in rebus.*
> Be virtuous: not too much; just what's correct:
> Excess in anything is a defect.—*Ed.*

> Cf. Mol. Misanthr. 1, 1 (Philinte loq.):
>> La parfaite raison fuit toute extrémité,
>> Et veut que l'on soit sage avec sobriété.

>> Perfect good sense in all things shuns extremes,
>> And sober wisdom the true wisdom deems.—*Ed.*

782. Fay ce que vouldras. Rab. 1, 57.—*Do as you please.* Rule of
Gargantua's Abbey of Thélème, and the motto of the Club of
wits and *literati* called St Franciscans (after Sir Francis Dash-
wood, the President), assembling at Medmenham Abbey—middle
of 18th century,—adopted from the words inscribed over the
Abbey gates.

783. Fecisti nos ad te, et inquietum est cor nostrum donec requiescat in
te. Aug. Conf. 1, 1 (vol. i. 49 A).—*Thou hast made us for Thyself,
and the heart is restless until it finds its rest in Thee.*

784. Fecundi calices quem non fecere disertum,
Contracta quem non in paupertate solutum? Hor. Ep. 1, 5, 19.
> What tongue hangs fire when quickened by the bowl?
> What wretch so poor but wine expands his soul?—*Conington.*

785. Felices ter et amplius,
Quos irrupta tenet copula, nec, malis '
Divulsus querimoniis,
Suprema citius solvet amor die.   Hor. C. 1, 13, 17.
> Happy, happy, happy they
> Whose living love, untroubled by all strife,
> Binds them till the last sad day,
> Nor parts asunder but with parting life!—*Conington.*

786. Feliciter is sapit, qui periculo alieno sapit. Plaut. Merc. 4 [7, 40.
Supposita].—*He is lucky who learns wisdom at another man's
expense.*
> Felix quicunque dolore
> Alterius disces posse carere suo. Tib. 3, 6, 43.—*You are happy if you learn
> by another's suffering to escape it yourself.*

787. Fere libenter homines id quod volunt credunt. Cæs. B. G. 3, 18.
—*Men in general believe that which they wish.* The wish is
father to the thought.

Cf. Quæ volumus et credimus libenter, et quæ sentimus ipsi, reliquos
sentire speramus, id. *B. C.* 2, 27.—*What we desire we readily believe, and
what we think ourselves, we imagine others to think also;* and, Quod nimis
miseri volunt, Hoc facile credunt. Sen. Herc. Fur. 313.—*What the wretched
anxiously wish for, that they easily believe.*

788. Ferme acerrima proximorum odia sunt.   Tac. H. 4, 70.—*Hatred
between relations is generally the most bitter of all.*

789. Ferme fugiendo in media fata ruitur. Liv. 8, 24.—*Men generally
rush into the very dangers they are endeavouring to avoid.*

790. F.E.R.T.—*He bears.*   Device of the House of Savoy and of the
Order of the SSma Annunziata.

> Many explanations of the motto have been propounded, mainly acrostical
> —*e.g., Fortitudo Ejus Rhodum Tenuit*, with ref. to Amadeus' (Fifth) sup-
> posed relief of Rhodes in 1310: *Fœdere Et Religione Tenemur*, the legend
> of a gold doubloon of Victor Amadeus I. (1718-30); while others derive the
> letters from a medal of Charles Emmanuel (1590), bearing the Virgilian
> hemistich *Fertque refertque* (A. 12, 866).   *V.* Fumagalli, No. 1070, and
> authorities there cited.   A. Wiel's *Romance of the House of Savoy*, Lond.,
> 1898, vol. i. p. 227.

791. Fertilior seges est alienis semper in agris;
     Vicinumque pecus grandius uber habet.   Ov. A. A. 1, 349.

> Crops are e'er richer in a neighbour's field;
> And neighbours' kine produce a fuller yield.—*Ed.*

792. Fervet olla, vivit amicitia (or, ζεῖ χύτρα, ζῇ φιλία).   Chil. (*Amicitia*) p. 47; Theogn. 115.—*As long as the pot boils, the friendship lasts.*   False friends.   Dinner-acquaintance, parasites.

793. Festina lente.   Chil. p. 240.—*Hasten slowly.*   On Slow.   Punning
motto of the Onslow family.

> Lit. transl. of σπεῦδε βραδέως, one of the maxims which Suetonius (Aug. 25)
> records as being freq. cited by Augustus with ref. to the tactical qualities
> of a good general.   The others were the line of Euripides (Phæn. 599),
> ἀσφαλὴς γάρ ἐστ' ἀμείνων ἢ θρασὺς στρατηλάτης (*A steady general is better than
> a dashing one*); and, "Sat celeriter fieri quidquid fiat satis bene" (*Soon
> enough if well enough*)—by some attrib. to P. Syrus; *see* Ribb. ii. p. 150.
> The motto (in Gk.) was even stamped upon certain coins of Augustus, as
> they were later upon those of Titus and Vespasian.   "Sat cito, si sat
> bene"—*Quick enough, if good enough*—is referred to Cato Major, ap.
> Hieron. Ep. 66, § 9.   Cp. also the words of Q. Fabius Maximus (the
> Cunctator) to L. Æmilius Paullus before Cannæ—Omnia non properanti
> clara certaque erunt: festinatio improvida est et cæca. Liv. 22, 39, 14.—
> *To the man who takes his time, everything will come out clear and sure,
> while haste is not only aimless but blind.*   A number of cognate sayings will
> occur to the reader: the σχολῇ ταχύς, *leisurely swift*, of Soph. Ant. 231;
> the German "Eile mit Weile," and "Ohne Hast, doch ohne Rast,
> *unhasting, unresting*—said of the sun, and also associated with the name
> of Goethe; the "Hâtez-vous lentement" of Boileau (*q.v.*); the prov.,
> Pas à pas on va bien loin, *Slow and sure go far in a day*, etc.

794. Festinat enim decurrere velox
     Flosculus angustæ miseræque brevissima vitæ
     Portio: dum bibimus, dum serta, unguenta, puellas
     Poscimus, obrepit non intellecta senectus.   Juv. 9, 126.

Our fleeting prime, the too brief flower
Of life's unhappy, anxious hour,
Hastes to run out its race:
'Mid flowing cups and garlands gay,
Perfumes and girls, its stealthy way
Old age steals on apace.—*Ed.*

795. Fiat experimentum in corpore vili.—*Let the experiment be made upon some common body.*

Saying originating in an incident in the life of M. A. Muret (Muretus), the humanist (1526-85), as related by Antoine du Verdier, Prosopographie etc., des Hommes Illustres, Lyon, 1603, vol. 3, pp. 2542-3. Imprisoned in the Paris Châtelet on some abominable charge, Muret was released (1554) on condition of instantly quitting the kingdom. He had hardly crossed the Italian frontier when he fell seriously ill. The physicians who were called in wished to try the effect of a novel remedy, and, taking their patient for an illiterate man, said to each other, *Faciamus periculum in corpore vili.* Muret made no sign, but, as soon as the doctors were gone, effected a hurried departure from the inn, the fright which he had received having completely cured the ailment. The rhetorical version of the story adopted by Dean Farrar (Hulsean Lectures) and others is devoid of foundation.

796. Fiat justitia, ruat cœlum.—*Justice must be done, though the heavens should fall.*

Mr Bartlett (*Quotations*) points out that the words are to be found in Ward's *Simple Cobbler of Aggawam in America.* Printed 1647. (2) Ruat cœlum, fiat Voluntas Tua. Sir T. Browne, *Rel. Med.* Pt. 2, sect. 11.—*Let Thy will be done, if Heaven fall;* and Büchm. gives the version—(3) Fiat justitia, et pereat mundus, from Joh. Manlius' Loci Communes (1563), vol. ii. p. 290.—*Let justice be done, and the world perish,* as the saying of the Empe·or Ferdinand I. (1556-1564).

797. Ficus ficus, ligonem ligonem vocat. Chil. p. 451 (Libertas, Veritas).—*He calls figs figs, and a spade a spade.*

When we "call a spade a spade," we repeat a prov. which must have been current at least five hundred years ago in the Low Countries and Germany, no less than here, and which Erasmus' rendering (above) would seem to derive from classic times. Lucian, whose citation from a "comic" writer (de Hist. conscribend. 41) appears to have been in Erasmus' mind, does not, however, use "spade" but "tub," as an instance of a plain thing being called by its plain name,—τὰ σῦκα σῦκα, τὴν σκάφην σκάφην λέγων (*calling figs figs, and a tub a tub*). In Meineke also (p. 1223) is, ἄγροικός εἰμι τὴν σκάφην σκάφην λέγων, *I'm a plain man, and call a tub a tub:* and Plut. Mor. p 212(Philipp. Apophth. 15), remarks that the "boorish" Macedonians said "tub" when they meant "tub." The French, in the same sense, "call a cat a cat," so that to search for equivocal meanings underlying the words is beside the question.

798. Fidem qui perdit, quo se servet relicuo? Syr. 166.—*How shall the man maintain himself whose character is gone?*

Who steals my purse, steals trash; 'tis something, nothing;
'Twas mine, 'tis his, and has been slave to thousands;
But he that filches from me my good name,
Robs me of that which not enriches him.
And makes me poor indeed.—*Shakesp.* "Othello," 3, 3.

799. Fidus Achates. Virg. A. 1, 188.—*Faithful Achates.* Said of any trusty henchman or personal attendant.

800. Fille de la douleur, harmonie! harmonie!
Langue que pour l'amour inventa le génie,
Qui nous vins d'Italie, et qui lui vins des cieux.

A. de Musset, *Lucie.*

> Daughter of sorrow, O harmony! harmony!
> Language that genius invented for love!
> Thou travelledst hither from musical Italy,
> And to Italy camest from Heaven above!—*Ed.*

801. Fils de Saint Louis, montez au ciel!—*Son of St Louis, ascend to heaven!*

Imaginary speech of the Abbé Edgeworth at the death of Louis XVI., invented the night of the execution by Charles Lacretelle, writer on the staff of the *Républicain Français.* In his *Dix années d'épreuves* (Paris, 1842, p. 134), he himself says of the celebrated *mot,* "J'en ai cherché vainement l'auteur . . . et il me semble que le souvenir d'une telle *invention* ne doit point se perdre." At the actual moment of death, and for some moments previous, Father Edgeworth seems to have been kneeling by the king in a semi-conscious state (vide *Journal of Mary Frampton,* p. 89; and Fourn. *L.D.L.,* chap. lvii. pp. 379-82).

802. Fin de siècle.—*End of the century.* Title of a play of Micard and de Jouvenot, first represented at Château d'Eau, April 17, 1888, and supposed to be the first instance of the well-worn phrase. Alex. pp. 480-1.

803. Finge datos currus, quid agas? Ov. M. 2, 74.—*Suppose the chariot were granted you, what would you do?* Apollo to Phæthon requesting the chariot of the Sun. Suppose you gained the object of your ambition, what then?

804. Finis (*or* F. regni) Poloniæ—Cᵗᵉ L. P. de Ségur, Hist. de Frédéric-Guillaume II., Paris, 1800; and Süd-Preussischen Zeitung, Oct. 25, 1794.—*The end [of the kingdom] of Poland!*

Words placed in the mouth of Kosciusko by the above, after the defeat of Maciejowice, Oct. 10, 1794, and formally repudiated by K. himself to Ségur in a letter of Nov. 12, 1803. *V.* Amédée Renée's tr. of Cesare Cantu's "Storia di cento anni"—*Histoire de cent ans,* Paris, 1852, vol. 1, p. 419 n. [Fourn. *L.D.L.,* chap. lxii. p. 414 note; and Büchm. p. 470.]

805. Flamma fumo est proxuma.
Fumo comburi nihil potest, flamma potest. Plaut. Curc. 1, 1, 53.
—*Where there is smoke there is fire: smoke can't burn, but fire can.* "The least approach to impropriety leads to vice." Lew. and S., *s.v.* "Flamma."

806. Fleque meos casus : est quædam flere voluptas :
Expletur lacrimis egeriturque dolor.   Ov. T. 4, 3, 37.

> Weep o'er my woes: to weep is some relief,
> For that doth ease and carry out our grief.—*Dryden.*

807. Fluctus in simpulo, ut dicitur. Cic. Leg. 3, 16, 36.—*A tempest in a teacup, as the saying is.*

808. Fœdius hoc aliquid quandoque audebis amictu.
   Nemo repente venit turpissimus.   Juv. 2, 82.

> Thus, you'll proceed to greater lengths of evil:
> No man was all at once a perfect devil.—*Shaw.*

Cf. id. 14, 123, Sunt quædam vitiorum elementa.—*Vice has its rudiments like other things;* and Sen. Agam. 153, Extrema primo nemo tentavit loco.— *None ever went to extremes at the first attempt.*   Beaumont and Fletcher have (*King and No King*, 5, 4),

> There is a method in man's wickedness:
> It grows up by degrees.

In Racine's Phèdre, 4, 2, Hippolytus says to Theseus, "Ainsi que la vertu, le crime a ses degrés."—*Like virtue, crime has its successive steps;* and, three lines above, is, "Quelques crimes toujours précèdent les grands crimes."

809. Fol à vingt et cinq Karats dont les vingt et quatre font le tout.
   J. Bonaventure Des Périers, Contes et Joyaux Devis, Nouvelle
   2, fin.—*A twenty-five carat madman, when twenty-four is the highest ratio known.*   An unalloyed ass, lunatic.

Cf. Rab. Bk. 3, cap. 38.—"Triboulet, dist Pantagruel, me semble compétentement fol.   Panurge respondit ; Proprement et fatalement fol." Then follow some 200 different kinds of lunacy, from all of which poor Triboulet is pronounced to be suffering, and, about three parts down the list, comes—"Fol à 24 carats." La Font. 7, 15 (Devineresses), also has "quoiqu' ignorante à vingt et trois carats, Elle passait pour un oracle."

810. Folia sunt artis et nugæ meræ.   App. Met. 1, 8, fin.—*Only the fringe and trifling of art.*   Dilettanteism.   Artistic trifles.

811. Foris ut mos est: intus ut libet.   Prov.—*Abroad, say what is expected of you: at home, think as you please.*

812. Forma bonum fragile est, quantumque accedit ad annos
   Fit minor: et spatio carpitur ipsa suo.
   .   .   .   .
   Et tibi jam cani venient, formose, capilli:
   Jam venient rugæ, quæ tibi corpus arent.
   Jam molire animum, qui duret, et adstrue formæ.
   Solus ad extremos permanet ille rogos.   Ov. A. A. 2, 113.

Fragile is Beauty.

> Fragile is beauty: with advancing years
> 'Tis less and less and, last, it disappears.
> Your hair too, fair one, will turn grey and thin;
> And wrinkles furrow that now rounded skin;
> Then brace the mind and beauty fortify,
> The mind alone is yours, until you die.—*Ed.*

813. Forma viros neglecta decet.   Ov. A. A. 1, 509.—*An unstudied dress is most becoming to men.*

814. Formosa facies muta commendatio est.   Syr. 169.—*A beautiful face is a mute recommendation.*

815. Forsan et hæc olim meminisse juvabit. Virg. A. 1, 203.—*One day, perhaps, 'twill please us to remember even this.* Eur. (Fragm. Andromeda, 36) has, ἀλλ' ἡδύ τοι σωθέντα μεμνῆσθαί πόνων.—'*Tis sweet to remember past troubles when one is safe.*

816. Fors et virtus miscentur in unum. Virg. A. 12, 715.—*Chance and force unite together.* Said of the combat between **Turnus** and **Æneas**, the words may be applied to any contest in which it is uncertain which side will prevail. Mr Conington renders it,
   "Chance joins with force to guide the steel."

817. Forsitan hæc aliquis, nam sunt quoque, parva vocabit:
   Sed, quæ non prosunt singula, multa juvant. Ov. R. A. 419.—
   Some perhaps will call these slight matters, and so they are; yet what is of little use by itself, when multiplied effects much. Power of small things. From the second line has been formed the Law Maxim—Quæ non valeant singula, juncta juvant, *i.e.,* "*Words which are inoperative,* in the interpretation of deeds and instruments, *when taken by themselves, become effective when taken conjointly.*"

818. Fortem posce animum, mortis terrore carentem,
   Qui spatium vitæ extremum inter munera ponat
   Naturæ, qui ferre queat quoscunque labores,
   Nesciat irasci, cupiat nihil, et potiores
   Herculis ærumnas credat sævosque labores
   Et Venere, et cænis, et pluma Sardanapali.   Juv. 10, 357.
   Ask strong resolve, freed from the fears of death,
   That counts 'mid Nature's gifts our latest breath:
   That can with courage any toil support;
   That knows not anger, and that covets naught:
   Preferring the hard life Alcides led
   To Love, or feasts, or luxury's downy bed.—*Ed.*

819. Fortes indigne tuli
   Mihi insultare: te, naturæ dedecus,
   Quod ferre certe cogor, bis videor mori.   Phædr. 1, 21, 10.
   The Dying Lion to the Ass that kicked him.
   Ill have I brock'd that nobler foes
   Should triumph o'er my dying woes:
   But, scorn of nature, forced to lie
   And take thy taunts, is twice to die.—*Ed.*

820. Fortissima Tyndaridarum. Hor. S. 1, 1, 100.—*Brave as the daughter of Tyndarus.* A second Clytemnestra, Lady Macbeth, Judith, Jael.

821. Fortitudo in laboribus periculisque cernatur, temperantia in prætermittendis voluptatibus, prudentia in dilectu bonorum et malorum, justitia in suo cuique tribuendo.   Cic. Fin. 5, 23, 67.
   The Cardinal Virtues.
   Fortitude is shown in toil and danger: Temperance in declining sensual enjoyments: Prudence in the choice between good and evil: Justice in awarding to every one his due.

823. FORTUNA.—*Fortune*, personified as the Goddess of Chance, Luck, Fate.

(1.) Fortuna quum blanditur, captatum venit. Syr. 167.—*When Fortune comes fawning, it is to ensnare.* (2.) Fortunam citius reperias, quam retineas. Syr. 168.—*It is easier to meet with Fortune, than to keep her.* (3.) Fortuna multis dat nimis, satis nulli. Mart. 12, 10, 2.—*Fortune gives many too much, enough to none.* (4.) Fortuna obesse nulli contenta est semel. Syr. 183.—*Fortune is never content with doing a man one injury only.* (5.) Non est tuum, fortuna quod fecit tuum. C. Lucilius (ii. 373).— *Count not that thine which fortune has made thine.* (6.) Fortuna vitrea est, tum quum splendet, frangitur. Syr. 189.—*Fortune is of glass; she glitters just at the moment of breaking.* "My hour is not come; when it does, I shall break like glass." Reported saying of Napoleon III. Cf. *Et comme elle a l'éclat du verre, Elle en a la fragilité* ("As glory has the brilliancy of glass, it has also its brittleness"). Godeau, Ode Au Roy (Biblioth. Poét., Paris, 1745, 4°, vol. 2, p. 77). The couplet, it may be added, was reproduced word for word by Corneille in Polyeucte (1640), 4, 2.

824. Fortunæ filius. Hor. S. 2, 6, 49.—*A son of fortune.* Fortune's favourite. A lucky fellow. In Gr., παῖς τῆς τύχης.

Quia tu gallinæ filius albæ,
Nos viles pulli, nati infelicibus ovis. Juv. 13, 141.—*Because you are "a white hen's chick;" and we a common brood hatched from unlucky eggs.* Born with a silver spoon in his mouth.

825. Fortuna miserrima tuta est. Ov. Ep. 2, 2, 31.—*A poor fortune is the safest.*

826. Fortunato omne solum patria est. Prov.—*Every soil is the home of the fortunate.*

Cf. Patria est, ubicumque est bene. Poeta ap. Cic. Tusc. 5, 37, 108.— *One's country is wherever one is well;* or shorter, *Ubi bene, ibi patria.* Πατρὶς γάρ ἐστι πᾶσ' ἵν' ἂν πράττῃ τις εὖ. Ar. Plut. 1151.—*A man's country is wherever he does well.* So also Men. Mon. 716, Τῷ γὰρ καλῶς πράσσοντι πᾶσα γῆ πατρίς. On this theme, John Owen composed the following epigram, Liber *Ad Carolum Eboracensem* (Charles I.), 3, 100.

VVhere I do vvell,
There I dvvell.

Illa mihi patria est ubi pascor, non ubi nascor;
Illa ubi sum notus, non ubi natus eram.
Illa mihi patria est mihi quæ patrimonia præbet;
Hic ubicunque habeo quod satis est, habito.

827. Fortunatus et ille deos qui novit agrestes. Virg. G. 2, 493.— *Happy is the man who knows the country gods.* Felicities of a country life.

828. Freiheit ist bei der Macht allein. Schiller, Wall. Lager, Sc. 11.— *Freedom must ever ally with force.*

829. Freiheit ist nur in dem Reich der Träume,
Und das Schöne blüht nur im Gesang.
Schiller, Der Antritt des neuen Jahrhunderts (1801).

Freedom lives only in the realm of dreams,
And in song only blooms the beautiful.—*Ed.*

830. Frei will ich sein im Denken und im Dichten ;
　　　Im Handeln schränkt die Welt genug uns ein.　　Goethe, Tasso,
　　　4, 2 (Tasso loq.).—*Free will I be in thought and in my poetry;
　　　in conduct the world trammels us enough.*

831. Frons, oculi, vultus persæpe mentiuntur ; oratio vero sæpissime.
　　　Cic. Q. Fr. 1, 1, 5.—*The forehead, eyes, and face often belie the
　　　thoughts, but the speech most of all.*　　Cf. Fronti nulla fides. Juv.
　　　2, 8.—*Trust no man's countenance.*

832. Fructus matura tulissem.—*With maturity I should have borne
　　　fruit.*　　Written on the wall of his cell in the prison of S. Lazare
　　　(Jan.-July 1794) by Marie André Chénier, with a storm-
　　　shattered tree for emblem.　　Fourn. *L.D.L.*, cap. 59, p. 395 and
　　　note, and Loizerolles' *La Mort de Loizerolles*, Paris, 1813,
　　　p. 176 n.

833. Früh übt sich, was ein Meister werden will.
　　　Die Axt im Haus erspart den Zimmermann.
　　　Wer gar zu viel bedenkt wird wenig leisten.　　Schiller, W. Tell, 3, 1.
　　　(Three sayings of Tell in this scene of the play.)

> The early practice 'tis that makes the master.
> An axe i' th' house oft saves the carpenter.
> He that is over-cautious will do little.—*Ed.*

834. Fuge magna ; licet sub paupere tecto
　　　Reges et regum vita præcurrere amicos.　　Hor. Ep. 1, 10, 32.

> Keep clear of courts: a homely life transcends
> The vaunted bliss of monarchs and their friends.—*Conington.*

835. Fulgente trahit constrictos gloria curru,
　　　Non minus ignotos generosis.　　Hor. S. 1, 6, 23.

> *The Race for Glory.*
> Chained to her glittering car Fame drags along
> Both high and lowly born, a motley throng.—*Ed.*

836. Fumum et opes strepitumque Romæ.　　Hor. C. 3, 29, 12.

> The smoke, the wealth, and noise of Rome.—*Conington.*

837. Fungar vice cotis, acutum
　　　Reddere quæ ferrum valet, exsors ipsa secandi.
　　　Munus et officium, nil scribens ipse, docebo.　　Hor. A. P. 304.

> Mine be the whetstone's lot
> Which makes steel sharp, though cut itself will not.
> Although no writer, I may yet impart
> To writing folk the precepts of their art.—*Conington.*

G.

838. Gallum in sterquilinio suo plurimum posse.　Sen. Apocol. 7, 3.—
　　　Every man is cock of his own dunghill.　　Lew. and S.

839. Γαμεῖν ὁ μέλλων εἰς μετάνοιαν ἔρχεται.　Men. Monost. 91.—*He
　　　who is going to marry is on the road to repentance.*

840. Γάμος γὰρ ἀνθρώποισιν εὐκταῖον κακόν. Men. Monost. 102.—
Marriage is an evil that men pray for.

841. Gaudia principium nostri sunt, Phoce, doloris. Ov. M. 7, 796.—
Joy is the source, Phocus, of all our pain.

842. Gedanken sind zollfrei. Prov. ap. Luther, Von Weltlicher Oberkeit, u.s.w., 1523.—*Thoughts are toll-free.*

> Büchm. qu. Cic. Mil. 29, 79, Liberæ sunt nostræ cogitationes; and Dig.
> 48, 19, 18, Cogitationis pœnam nemo patitur.—*No one can be punished for
> his thoughts.* On the other hand, the moral responsibility of thought is
> well expressed in the qualification sometimes added to the quot.—*aber nicht
> höllenfrei*—"but not hell-free."

843. Geduld! Geduld! wenn's Herz auch bricht. Bürger, Lenore (fin).
—*Patience! patience! though heart should break.*

844. Γέλως ἄκαιρος ἐν βροτοῖς δεινὸν κακόν. Men. Monost. 88.—*Ill-
timed laughter in men is an awful curse.*

845. Γῆν ὁρῶ. Diogenes, in Diog. Laert. 6, 38.—*I see land* (or *Land
at last*)! Remark of Diogenes on approaching the end of a long
and tedious book.

846. Genus immortale manet, multosque per annos
Stat fortuna domus, et avi numerantur avorum. Virg. G. 4, 208.

> In endless line the fortunes of the race
> Go back for years, and grandsires' grandsires trace.—*Ed.*

> Motto of Addison's paper (*Spectator* 72) on the *Everlasting Club* of 100
> members who relieve each other, one always being in attendance. Borrowed
> from the above is the *Stet fortuna domus* (May the fortunes of the house
> stand firm), often given as a toast or sentiment. The motto of Harrow
> School.

847. Geteilte Freud' ist doppelt Freude,
Geteilter Schmerz ist halber Schmerz. C. A.Tiedge, Urania, 4, 223.

> Joy, when it's shared, its pleasure doubles,
> And sorrow, loses half its troubles.—*Ed.*

848. Gewöhnlich glaubt der Mensch, wenn er nur Worte hört,
Es müsse sich dabei doch auch was denken lassen.
  Goethe, Faust, Hexenküche.

> *Mephist.* If only words they hear, most men suppose
>   That with the sound some kind of meaning goes.—*Ed.*

849. Γλυκὺ δ' ἀπείροισι πόλεμος· πεπειραμένων δέ τις
ταρβεῖ προσιόντα νιν καρδίᾳ περισσῶς. Pind. Fr. 110.

> To th' inexperienced war is sweet: but he
> Who knows, at heart dreads greatly its approach.—*Ed.*

850. Γνοῖεν δ', ὡς δὴ δηρὸν ἐγὼ πολέμοιο πέπαυμαι. Hom. Il. 18, 125.

> Then shall all men know
> How long I have been absent from the field.—*Earl of Derby.*

Achilles, on returning to "the front" after long retirement, thus predicts the "difference" that would ensue upon his reappearance in the field; and the sentiment was chosen to figure on the forefront of the *Lyra Apostolica*, which in verse discharged the same interpretative office to the "Oxford Movement" that the famous "Tracts" rendered in prose. In his *Apologia* (1878, p. 34), Newman, who was travelling in Italy with Hurrell Froude at the time (Spring, 1833), makes an allusion to the circumstance. "It was in Rome that we began the *Lyra Apostolica*, and . . . the motto shows the feeling both of Froude and myself at the time. We borrowed from M. Bunsen a Homer, and Froude chose the words in which Achilles, on returning to battle, says, 'You shall know the difference now that I am back again.'"

851. Gott macht gesund, und der Doktor bekommt das Geld.   Prov.
—*God makes us well, and the doctor gets the money.*

852. Græcia capta ferum victorem cepit, et artes
     Intulit agresti Latio.   Hor. Ep. 2, 1, 156.

     Greece, conquered Greece her conqueror subdued,
     And Rome grew polished, who till then was rude.—*Conington.*

853. Græcia Mœonidem, jactat sibi Roma Maronem,
     Anglia Miltonum jactat utrique parem.
                           Selvaggi, pref. to the Lat. Poems.

               Ad Joannem Miltonum.
     Greece boasts her Homer, Rome can Virgil claim;
     England can either match in Milton's fame.—*Ed.*

854. Grammatici certant et adhuc sub judice lis est.   Hor. A. P. 78.—
The grammarians are at variance, and the controversy is still undetermined.   The question was, who invented Elegiac verse!

855. Grammaticus Rhetor Geometres Pictor Aliptes
     Augur Schœnobates Medicus Magus—omnia novit.   Juv. 3, 76.

     Grammarian, Orator and Geometrician,
     Painter, Gymnastic-teacher and Physician,
     Augur, Rope-dancer, Conjurer—he was all.—*Ed.*

               Buckingham.
     A man so various, that he seemed to be
     Not one, but all mankind's epitome:
     .   .   .   .
     Was everything by starts, and nothing long,
     But in the course of one revolving moon,
     Was Chymist, Fiddler, Statesman, and Buffoon.
                     —*Dryden,* "Abs. and Ach.," 1, 545.

856. Grattez le Russe et vous trouverez le Cosaque (*ou* le Tartare).
Prince de Ligne, *v.* Hertslet's *Treppenwitz*, etc., 4th ed., Berlin, 1895, p. 360.—*Scratch the Russian and you will find the Cossack (or the Tartar).*

857. Grau, teurer Freund, ist alle Theorie,
     Und grün des Lebens goldner Baum. Goethe, Faust, Schülerscene.

     Mephist. Grey, my dear friend, is every theory,
     And green the golden tree of life.—*Ed.*

858. Grave pondus illum, magna nobilitas, premit.　　Sen. Troad. 492.

The New Peer.
A heavy burden on his back doth lie.
Th' oppressive sense of his nobility.—*Ed.*

859. Gravis ira regum est semper.　Sen. Med. 494.—*The anger of kings is always a grave matter.*

860. Grosse Seelen dulden still.　Schiller, Don Carlos, 1, 4.—*Great souls suffer in silence.*

861. Guerra al cuchillo.—*War to the knife!*　A war of extermination (*à outrance*).　Byron, Ch. Harold, 1, 86, gives the reply of Palafox, Governor of Saragoza, when summoned to surrender by the French in 1808:

" War, war is still the cry, war even to the knife!"

862. Guerre aux châteaux, paix aux chaumières!　Chamf. Œuvres Compl. (ed. Ginguéné), l'an 3 de la Rép. (1795), vol. 1, *Notice*, p. lviii.—*War to the castles, peace to the cottages!*　Proposed as battle-cry of the Rep. armies in the campaign against the Allied Powers in 1792-3. Berchoux, in his *Épitre Politique*, etc., *à Euphrosine* (Œuvres, 4 vols., Paris, 1829, vol. 4, p. 127), gave a humorous turn to the fierce denunciation by adding,

Attendu que dans ces dernières
Le pillage serait sans prix.

863. Γυναικὶ κόσμος ὁ τρόπος, οὐ τὰ χρυσία.　Men. Monost. 92.—*Manners, not jewels, are a woman's ornament,* qu. by Addison in *Spectators* 265 and 271.

864. Γυναικὸς οὐδὲν χρῆμ' ἀνὴρ ληΐζεται
'Εσθλῆς ἄμεινον, οὐδὲ ῥίγιον κακῆς.　Simonid. Amorg. 6 (7), p. 446.
—*A man cannot have a better possession than a good wife, nor a more miserable than a bad one.*　Also,

οὕτω γυναικὸς οὐδὲν ἂν μεῖζον κακὸν
κακῆς ἀνὴρ κτήσαιτ' ἄν, οὐδὲ σώφρονος
κρεῖσσον· παθὼν δ' ἕκαστος ὧν τύχῃ λέγει.　Soph. Fr. 608.

No greater evil can a man endure
Than a bad wife, nor find a greater good
Than one both good and wise; and each man speaks
As judging of the experience of his life.—*E. H. Plumptre.*

H.

865. Habeas, ut nactus: nota mala res optuma 'st.　Plaut. Trin. 1, 2, 25.—*Keep what you've got.　The evil that we know is the better of the two.*　So Shakes ., Haml. 3, 1, says:

Rather bear those ills we have,
Than fly to others that we know not of.

866. Habemus confitentem reum. Law Max.—*We have the best possible witness in the confession of the accused.*

"The plea of guilty by the party accused shuts out all further inquiry. *Habemus confitentem reum* is demonstrative, unless indirect motives can be assigned" (Lord Stowell, *Mortimer* v. *Mortimer*, 2 Hagg. 315).

867. Habeo senectuti magnam gratiam, quæ mihi sermonis aviditatem auxit, potionis et cibi sustulit. Cic. Sen. 14, 46.—*I owe great thanks to old age for increasing my avidity for conversation, and diminishing my appetite for meat and drink.*

868. Habet enim præteriti doloris secura recordatio delectationem. Cic. Fam. 5, 12, 4.—*It is pleasant to recall in happier days the troubles of the past*

869. Hac quoque de causa, si te proverbia tangunt,
Mense malas Maio nubere vulgus ait.   Ov. F. 5, 489.

That's why—if proverbs move you—people say,
Unlucky is the bride who weds in May.—*Ed.*

The Roman festival of the Lemuria, held to appease the spirits of the departed, was kept on the 9th, 11th, and 13th of May, and the month, in consequence, was not considered propitious for marriage. Romulus instituted it to conciliate Remus' shade.

870. Hac sunt in fossa Bedæ venerabilis ossa.—*In this vault lie the bones of Venerable Bede.* Inscription (1830) on Ven. Bede's tomb in Durham Cathedral.

871. Hac urget lupus, hac canis, aiunt. Hor. S. 2, 2, 64.—*A wolf on one side, a dog on the other, as they say.* Between two fires.

Cf. Inter malleum et incudem. Chil. p. 206.—*Between the hammer and the anvil.* Inter sacrum saxumque sto: nec quid faciam scio. Plaut. Capt. 3, 4, 84.—*I stand between the victim and the knife, and what to do, I know not.* Between the devil and the deep sea. A fearful predicament.

872. Hæc brevis est nostrorum summa malorum. Ov. T. 5, 7, 7.—*This is the short sum total of our troubles.*

873. Hæc faciant sane juvenes: deformius, Afer,
Omnino nihil est ardelione sene.   Mart. 4, 79, 9.

Leave such pursuits to youths; for certainly
There's nought so odious as an old Paul Pry.—*Ed.*

874. Hæc studia adolescentiam alunt, senectutem oblectant, secundas res ornant, adversis perfugium ac solatium præbent, delectant domi, non impediunt foris, pernoctant nobiscum, peregrinantur, rusticantur. Cic. Arch. 7, 16.—*These studies are the food of youth, and the solace of age; they adorn prosperity, and are the comfort and refuge of adversity; they amuse us at home, and are no encumbrance abroad; they accompany us at night, on our travels, and in our rural retirement.*

875. Hæc sunt jucundi causa cibusque mali. Ov. R. A. 138.—*These things are at once the cause and food of the agreeable malady (Love).*

876. Hæ nugæ seria ducent In mala.   Hor. A. P. 451.—*These trifles will lead to serious mischief.*

877. Hæret lateri lethalis arundo.   Virg. A. 4, 73.

> The fatal dart
> Sticks in her side, and rankles in her heart.—*Dryden.*
>
> Said of the hapless Dido, in love with Æneas.

878. Hanc personam induisti, agenda est. Sen. Ben. 2, 17, 2.—*Now that you have assumed this character, you must go through with it.*

879. Has patitur pœnas peccandi sola voluntas.
Nam scelus intra se tacitum qui cogitat ullum,
Facti crimen habet.   Juv. 13, 208.

> *Sins of the Intention.*
> Such blame the mere desire to sin incurs.
> For he who inly plans some wicked act,
> Has as much guilt, as though the thought were fact.—*Ed.*

880. Hâtez-vous lentement; et sans perdre courage,
Vingt fois sur le métier remettez votre ouvrage:
Polissez-le sans cesse et le repolissez;
Ajoutez quelquefois, et souvent effacez.   Boil. L'A. P. 1, 171.

> Hasten then, but full slowly: don't lose heart of grace;
> And your work twenty times on the easel replace.
> Be continually polishing; polish again;
> Add something to this part; through that draw your pen.—*Ed.*

881. Haud facile emergunt quorum virtutibus obstat
Res angusta domi.   Juv. 3, 164.

> Slow rises worth by poverty oppressed.—*Johnson,* "Vanity of Human Wishes," 177.

882. Hectora quis nosset, si felix Troja fuisset?
Publica virtuti per mala facta via est.   Ov. T. 4, 3, 75.

> Had Ilium stood, who'd known of Hector's name?
> Misfortune is the royal road to fame.—*Ed.*

883. Hei mihi, difficile est imitari gaudia falsa!
Difficile est tristi fingere mente jocum.   Tib. 3, 6, 33.

> How hard to feign the joys one does not feel,
> Or aching hearts 'neath show of mirth conceal!—*Ed.*

884. Hei mihi, qualis erat! quantum mutatus ab illo
Hectore, qui redit exuvias indutus Achilli.   Virg. A. 2, 274.

> Ah! what a sight was there! how changed from him,
> The Hector we remember, as he came
> Back with Achilles' armour from the fray!—*Ed.*

885. Hei mihi! quam facile est, quamvis hic contigit omnes,
Alterius luctu fortia verba loqui.   Ov. Liv. 9.

> How easy 'tis, as all experience shows,
> To give brave comfort for another's woes.—*Ed.*

H

886. Henri IV. fut un grand roi; Louis XIV. fut le roi d'un beau règne.
Voisenon, ap. Chamf. Caractères, etc. (i. p. 131).—*Henry IV. was
a great king, Louis XIV. the king of a grand reign.*

887. Heredis fletus sub persona risus est.   Syr. 221.—*The tears of an
heir are really disguised laughter.*

888. Heu facinus! non est hostis metuendus amanti.
Quos credis fidos, effuge; tutus eris.   Ov. A. A. 1, 751.

> Strange, that the lover ne··d not fear a foe!
> Beware of friends! you'll then be safe, I know.—*Ed.*

Cf. the prov. Da chi mi fido, guardi mi Dio: da chi non mi fido, mi
guarderò io.—*God protect me from those I trust: from those I don't trust, I'll
protect myself.*

889. Heu! melior quanto sors tua sorte mea!   Ov. Am. 1, 6, 46.—
Alas! how much superior is your lot to mine.

890. Heu pietas, heu prisca fides, invictaque bello
Dextera!   Virg. A. 6, 879.

> O piety! O ancient faith!
> O hand untam'd in battle scathe.—*Conington.*

891. Heu! quanto minus est
Cum reliquis versari,
Quam tui meminisse!   Shenstone's epitaph on the tomb of his
cousin, Maria Dollman, at the Leasowes.

Cf. Moore, "*I saw thy form :*"

> To live with them is far less sweet
> Than to remember thee!

892. Heu quantum fati parva tabella vehit!   Ov. F. 2, 408.—*Ah! what
destinies hang upon that little vessel!*   Said of the "ark" in which
Romulus and Remus were exposed.   *Tabella* also = letter, book,
picture, voting-ticket.

893. Heureux qui, dans ses vers, sait d'une voix légère,
Passer du grave au doux, du plaisant au sévère.   Boil. L'A.P.1,75.

Happy who in his verse can gently steer
From grave to light, from pleasant to severe.—*Dryden*, "Art of P.," 1, 75.

Pope, in his *Essay on Man*, Ep. 4, 379, has:

> Happily to steer
> From grave to gay, from lively to severe.

894. Hic, ait, hic pacem temerataque jura relinquo;
Te, Fortuna, sequor: procul hinc jam foedera sunto:
Credidimus fatis, utendum est judice bello.   Luc. 1, 225.

The Rubicon.

> Here, here I bid all peace and law farewell!
> With treaties hence—Fortune, I turn to thee
> ·And Fate, and to th' arbitrament of war.—*Ed.*

895. Hic cineres, ubique nomen.—*His ashes are here; his name everywhere.* Inscription on Gen. Marceau's (1769-96) tomb at Ehrenbreitstein.

896. Hic et ubique.—*Here and everywhere.* Ubiquitous.

> *Ghost.* (Beneath) Swear!
> *Ham. Hic et ubique?* Then we'll shift our ground:—
> Come hither, gentlemen, etc.—*Shakesp.* "Hamlet," 1, 5.

897. Hic gelidi fontes, hic mollia prata, Lycori,
Hic nemus; hic toto tecum consumerer ævo.   Virg. E. 10, 42.

> Here are cool founts, Lycoris; mead and grove:
> Here could I live for aye with thee to love.—*Ed.*

898. Hic illius arma, Hic currus fuit.   Virg. A. 1, 16.—*Here were her (Juno's) arms, her chariot here.*   Conington.

> Applicable to relics of any famous man. "The Ferrarese possess Ariosto's bones; they show his armchair, his inkstand, his autograph—*hic illius arma*, etc." Hobhouse's Notes to *Ch. Harold*, Cant. 4; *Byron's Works*, E. H. Coleridge ed., Lond., 1897, vol. ii. p. 487.

899. Hic jacet hujus sententiæ primus author.
Disputandi pruritus fit Ecclesiarum scabies.
Nomen alias quære.

> Here lies the original author of the saying,
> *The itch for controversy is the scab of the Church.*
> Seek his name elsewhere.

Inscription on sepulchral slab of Sir H. Wotton († 1639) on the choir steps of Eton College Chapel.

900. Hic manebimus optime.   Liv. 5, 55.—*This is the best place to halt.* We can't do better than remain here.

> In the sack of Rome by Brennus (390 B.C.), when it was being debated in Senate whether the government should not be transferred to Veii, it so happened that the guard of the day passed through the Forum, and the captain ordered the ensign, "Plant the colours here! This is the best place to stop." (*Signifer, statue signum, hic manebimus optime.*) The word of command reached the ears of the senators in the Curia, and was at once interpreted as an omen in favour of remaining in the city.

901. Hic murus aëneus esto
Nil conscire sibi, nulla pallescere culpa.   Hor. Ep. 1, 1, 60.
A Good Conscience.

> Be this your wall of brass, your coat of mail,
> A guileless heart, a cheek no crime turns pale.—*Conington.*

On Feb. 11, 1741, this qu. formed the subject of a House of Commons wager. Sir R. Walpole used the line in defence of his own political integrity, but inaccurately—*nulli culpæ.* Pulteney at once jumped up to dispute both the Latin and the logic of the minister, and laid a guinea that Horace had never written such a line. The Clerk of the House, Sir N. Hardinge, was made umpire, and he decided against the Prime Minister, who thereupon threw a guinea to Pulteney. On catching it, Pulteney held it up to the House, saying, "This is the only money I have received from the Treasury for many years, and it shall be the last." The identical guinea, with a memorandum of the circumstance in Pulteney's hand, is now in the British Museum. On Feb. 26, 1896, this historical wager was referred to in Parliament and explained. *V.* Hansard *in l.*, and Mr Swift MacNeill's letter to the *Daily Chronicle* of Feb. 28, 1896.

902. Hic nigræ succus loliginis, hæc est
.Ærugo mera.   Hor. S. 1, 4, 100.

> Here is the poison-bag of malice, here
> The gall of fell detraction, pure and sheer.—*Conington.*

903. Hic Rhodus, hic salta (*or* saltus)!   Chil. p. 63 (*Arrogantia*): a tr. of Æsop's fable, Κομπαστής (203, ed. Halm.), ἰδοὺ ἡ Ῥόδος, ἰδοὺ καὶ τὸ πήδημα.—*Here is Rhodes, make your jump here!*

> In the fable, some vapouring fellow was bragging of the extraordinary jump that he had made at Rhodes. "All right," interposed one of his hearers, "suppose this to be Rhodes, and do you repeat the performance." The qu. is used to bring to book any similar gasconades by practical demonstration.   Ajax says, *à propos*, in Ov. M. 13, 14,

> > Sua narret Ulixes
> > Quæ sine teste gerit, quorum nox conscia sola est.

> Well may Ulysses tell the feats he's done
> With none else by, and known to night alone.—*Ed.*

904. Hic ubi nunc urbs est, tum locus urbis erat.   Ov. F. 2, 280.—*Where the city is now, was then only its future site.*

905. Hic ver assiduum atque alienis mensibus æstas.   Virg. G. 2, 149.
—*Here it is one perpetual spring, and summer extends to months not properly her own.*   The climate of Italy.

906. Hic victor cæstus artemque repono.   Virg. A. 5, 484.

> *Entellus.* I here renounce as conqueror may,
> The gauntlets and the strife.—*Conington.*

> The successful artist, actor, singer, etc., retires from public life, laying down his profession and its accessories at once.

907. Hic vigilans somniat.   Plaut. Capt. 4, 2, 68.—*He is dreaming wide-awake.*   Castle-building.   A very absent person.

908. Hier stehe ich! Ich kann nicht anders.   Gott helfe mir, Amen!   Luther before the Diet of Worms, April 18, 1521, when invited to retract his heretical doctrines.—*Here I take my stand! I cannot do otherwise.   God help me! Amen.*   The oldest version, however, credits Luther with the last four words only: and it is probable that the dramatic *Hier stehe ich* u.s.w. is a later addition.   *V.* Buchm. p. 512.

909. Hi mores, hæc duri immota Catonis
Secta fuit, servare modum finemque tenere,
Naturamque sequi, patriæque impendere vitam:
Nec sibi, sed toti genitum se credere mundo.   Lucan. 2, 380.

The Younger Cato.

Stern Cato's rule and plan was this—
To fix a limit, shun excess;
Dame Nature for his teacher take,
Spend and be spent for country's sake,
And deem his energies designed
Not for himself but all mankind.— *Ed.*

910. Hi motus animorum atque hæc certamina tanta
Pulveris exigui jactu compressa quiescent.   Virg. G. 4, 86.

These quivering passions and these deathly throes,
A handful of earth's dust will soon compose.—*Ed.*

Said of the battles of the bees, these lines have been applied both to
the scattering of dust at funerals, and to the termination of the frolics of
the Carnival with the symbolic Ashes of the First day of Lent.

911. Ili narrata ferunt alio; mensuraque ficti
Crescit, et auditis aliquid novus adjicit auctor.   Ov. M. 12, 57.—
*These carry the tale elsewhere; the fiction increases in size, and
every fresh narrator adds something to what he hears.*

912. Hinc illæ lachrymæ.   Ter. And. 1, 1, 99.—*Hence those tears!* This
is the reason of all these complaints.

Simo is explaining the unwonted display of feeling by his son Pamphilus
on the death of their neighbour, Madame Chrysis. The young man's
interest, it turned out, was all on account of Madame's pretty sister, who
had by no means departed this life. "At at! hoc illud est! *Hinc* illæ
lachrymæ, etc." (Aha! That is it! *That* explains those tears, that sym-
pathy.) The words are qu. by Hor. Ep. 1, 19, 41; and Cic. Cæl. 25, 61.

913. Hinc lucem et pocula sacra.—*Hence light and draughts divine.*
Motto of Cambridge University, and device of the Univ. Press,
with crowned figure holding a Sun in one hand and a Cup in
the other.

914. Hinc subitæ mortes atque intestata senectus.   Juv. 1, 144.—*Hence
sudden deaths, and intestate old age,* viz., from over indulgence.

915. Hinc totam infelix vulgatur fama per urbem.   Virg. A. 12, 608.—
Hence the sad news is propagated through the whole city.

916. Hinc usura vorax, avidumque in tempore fænus,
Et concussa fides, et multis utile bellum.   Luc. 1, 181.—*Hence
(from Cæsar's ambition) arise ruinous usury, extortionate interest,
shaken credit, and war welcome to many.*

917. Hippocrate dit oui, mais Galien dit non.   Regnard, Les Folies
Amoureuses, 3, 7 (Crispin loq.).—*Hippocrate says Yes, but
Galienus says No.* Erastus's valet, Crispin, posing for the nonce
as a man of science, undertakes to explain the cause of Agatha's
(pretended) madness.

918. His saltem accumulem donis, et fungar inani
Munere.   Virg. A. 6, 886.—*I will at least lay this tribute upon
his tomb, and discharge a duty, though it avails him not now.*

919. Historia vero testis temporum, lux veritatis, vita memoriæ, magistra vitæ, nuntia vetustatis.   Cic. De Or. 2, 9, 36.—*History—
that testimony of time, that light of truth, that embodiment of
memory, that guide of life, that record of antiquity!*

920. Hoc erat in votis; modus agri non ita magnus;
Hortus ubi; et tecto vicinus jugis aquæ fons,
Et paullum silvæ super his foret.   Hor. S. 2, 6, 1.

> This used to be my wish—a bit of land,
> A house and garden with a spring at hand,
> And just a little wood.—*Conington.*

921. Hoc illi garrula lingua dedit.   Ov. Am. 2, 2, 44.—*This penalty his
chattering tongue has paid.*   Said of Tantalus for revealing the
secrets of the gods.

922. Hoc illis narro qui me non intelligunt.   Phædr. 3, 12, 8.—*I speak
to those who understand me not.*

923. Hoc si crimen erit, crimen amoris erit.   Prop. 2, 30, 24.—*If this
be crime, it is the crime of love.*

924. Hoc volo; sic jubeo, sit pro ratione voluntas.   Juv. 6, 223.—*This
is my will, thus I command, let my wishes be reason enough!*

925. Hodie homo est, et cras non comparet.   Quum autem sublatus
fuerit ab oculis, etiam cito transit a mente.   A Kempis, 1, 23, 1.
—*Man is here to-day and gone to-morrow; and when he is once
out of sight, he is as soon out of mind.*   Bartlett (Quotations,
1890, p. 5) cites "Out of syght, out of mynd," Googe's *Eclogs,*
1563 ; and Lord Brooke, Sonnet 56, "And out of mind as soon
as out of sight."

926. Hodie mihi, cras tibi.—*To-day for me, to-morrow for thee.*
Epitaph of the elder Wyatt (1503-41) at Ditchley.   Ecclus, 38,
23, Mihi heri, et tibi hodie.—*Yesterday for me, to-day for thee.*

927. Hombre pobre todo es trazas.   Prov.—*A poor man is all schemes.*

928. Homicidium quum admittunt singuli, crimen est, virtus vocatur
quum publice geritur.   Impunitatem sceleribus acquirit non
innocentiæ ratio, sed sævitiæ magnitudo. St Cypr. Ep. 1, 6.—
*Murder is a crime, when committed by individuals: a fine deed
when it is done wholesale.   It is the scale on which the violence is
dealt, and not the innocence of the perpetrators, that procures
impunity.*   Quicquid multis peccatur, inultum est. Luc. 5, 260.
—*Crime goes unpunished when it is the work of many.*   "And
all go free when multitudes offend."—*Rowe.*

> One murder made a villain,
> Millions a hero.   Princes were privileged
> To kill, and numbers sanctified the crime.—*B. Porteus,* "Death," 154.

929. Homine imperito nunquam quicquam injustius,
Qui, nisi quod ipse fecit, nihil rectum putat. Ter. Ad. 1, 2, 18.
—*Nothing so unreasonable as your ignorant man, who thinks nothing right but what he does himself.*

930. Hominem pagina nostra sapit. Mart. 10, 4, 10.—*My pages are about men and women.*

931. Homines dum docent discunt. Sen. Ep. 7, 8.—*Teaching others, we learn ourselves.*

932. Homines plus in alieno negotio videre, quam in suo. Sen. Ep. 109, 14.—*It is said that* (Aiunt) *men know more of other people's business than they do of their own.* Lookers-on see most of the game.

933. Hominibus plenum, amicis vacuum. Sen. Ben. 6, 34, 2.—*Crowded with men, yet bare of friends.* Said of kings' courts.

934. Homo antiqua virtute ac fide. Ter. Ad. 3, 3, 88.—*A man of the old-fashioned virtue and sense of honour.*

935. Homo homini lupus. Chil. (*Diffidentia*) p. 180.—*Man is to man a wolf.*

This prov. of "man's inhumanity to man" seems to be an abbrev. form of Plaut. As. 2, 4, 88, Lupus est homo homini, non homo; quum qualis sit non novit—*Man to his brother man is but a wolf, as long as he knows him not.* On the other hand, Cæcilius Statius, 265, says, Homo homini deus est si suum officium sciat—*A god is man to man if he but know his duty.* Hence the saying, "Homo homini aut deus aut lupus." *See* also Owen (Jno), Epigr. iii. 23.

936. Homo Latinissimus. Hier. Ep. 50, 2.—*A most perfect Latin scholar.*

937. Homo trium literarum. *See* Plaut. Aul. 2, 4, 46.—*A man of three letters, i.e.,* Fur, *a thief.*

937A. Homunculi quanti sunt, quum recogito. Plaut. Capt. Prol. 51.—*What poor creatures we are, when I think on 't !*

938. Honestus rumor alterum est patrimonium. Syr. 217.—*A good name is a second patrimony.*

939. Honi soit qui mal y pense.—*Disgraced be he who thinks evil of it.* Supposed to refer to the campaign against France, led in person by Ed. III., which terminated in the battle of Crécy, Aug. 26, 1346. Motto of the Crown of England, and also of the Order of the Garter.

940. Honteux comme un renard qu'une poule aurait pris. La Font. 1, 18 (Le Renard et la Cigogne).—*As sheepish as a fox that had been caught by a fowl.* Outwitted.

941. Horas non numero nisi serenas.—*I only mark the shining hours.* Common inscription on sun-dials.

942. Horrenda late nomen in ultimas
    Extendat oras, qua medius liquor
    Secernit Europen ab Afro
        Qua tumidus rigat arva Nilus;

    Aurum irrepertum, et sic melius situm,
    Quum terra celat, spernere fortior,
    Quam cogere humanos in usus,
        Omne sacrum rapiente dextra.   Hor. C. 3, 3, 45.

England's African Empire.
Ay, let her scatter far and wide
  Her terror, where the land-locked waves
Europe from Afric's shore divide,
  Where swelling Nile the cornfield laves—

Of strength more potent to disdain
  Hid gold, best buried in the mine,
Than gather it with hand profane
  That for man's greed would rob a shrine.—*Conington.*

  ** These lines were applied to the British in S. Africa by Prof. E. G. Ramsay (Letter to the *Times*), Jan. 13, 1896.

943. Horresco referens. Virg. A. 2, 204.—*I shudder to tell it.*

944. Horridus miles esse debet, non cœlatus auro argentoque, sed ferro et animis fretus. Virtus est militis decus. Liv. 9, 40, 4.— *A soldier should be of fierce aspect, not tricked out with gold and silver, but relying on his courage and his sword. Manliness is the soldier's virtue.*

945. Horror ubique animos, simul ipsa silentia terrent. Virg. A. 2, 755.

    All things were full of terror and affright,
    And dreadful e'en the silence of the night.—*Dryden.*

946. Hos ego versiculos feci, tulit alter honores.
    Sic vos non vobis nidificatis aves,
    Sic vos non vobis vellera fertis oves,
    Sic vos non vobis mellificatis apes
    Sic vos non vobis fertis aratra boves.   Virg. ap. Don. Vit. Virgili, 17 (Pref. to Delphin ed.).— *I wrote these verses, another got the credit of them. Thus do ye birds build nests, but not for yourselves; thus, too, ye sheep grow fleeces, but not for yourselves; ye bees also make honey, and ye oxen draw the plough, and others get the benefit of your labours.*

    The story goes that after the victory of Actium (31 B.C.), Virgil posted a complimentary but anonymous couplet upon the portals of Cæsar's palace,

      Nocte pluit tota, redeunt spectacula mane;
      Divisum imperium cum Jove Cæsar habet.

    The authorship was claimed by Bathyllus, who thereupon was presented with an honorarium in token of the Imperial pleasure. The following night, *Sic vos non vobis* was found scored four times over in the same place, presenting a puzzle that none was able to solve, until Virgil came forward with a copy of the completed quatrain. "Sic vos non vobis" applies in any case where one person does the work and another gets the credit or profit of it.

947. Hospes nullus tam in amici hospitium devorti potest,
Quin ubi triduum continuum fuerit, jam odiosus siet.
Verum ubi dies decem continuos immorabitur,
Tametsi dominus non invitus patitur, servi murmurant. Plaut.
Mil. 3, 1, 146.—*No one can stay at a friend's house for three
whole days together without becoming a bore: if he stops ten, even
should his host be agreeable, the servants will grumble.*

948. Hos successus alit; possunt, quia posse videntur. Virg. A. 5, 231.

> Cheer'd by success they lead the van,
> And win because they think they can.—*Ed.*

949. Huic maxime putamus malo fuisse, nimiam opinionem ingenii
atque virtutis. Nep. Alc. 7, 7.

> *Alcibiades.*
>
> The cause of his fall was, I believe, an overrated estimate of his own
> powers.

950. Humanum amare est, humanum autem ignoscere est. Plaut.
Merc. 2, 2, 48.—*It is human to love, it is human also to forgive.*

951. Humanum facinus factum est.
Actutum Fortunæ solent mutarier: varia est vita. Plaut. Truc.
2, 1, 8.—*The usual thing has happened. Circumstances are apt
to change in an instant. Life is full of uncertainties.*

952. Hunc servare modum nostri novere libelli;
Parcere personis, dicere de vitiis.   Mart. 10, 33, 9.

> My writings keep to this restriction nice;
> To spare the man but scourge his special vice.—*Ed.*

I.

953. I benedico il loco, e'l tempo e l'ora. Petrarch, Sonetto in vita di
M. Laura, 12.—*I bless the place and time and hour* when first I
saw Laura.

954. Ibi omnis Effusus labor, atque immitis rupta tyranni
Fœdera.   Virg. G. 4, 491.

> *Orpheus and Eurydice.*
>
> There all his labour is lost, and forfeited
> His compact with th' inexorable king.—*Ed.*

955. Ich bin besser als mein Ruf. Schiller, *Maria Stuart*, 3, 4 (Mary
loq.).—*I am better than my reputation.* Ov. Ep. 1, 2, 143 says
of Claudia, Ipsa sua melior fama.—*She herself is better than report makes her.*

956. Ich dien.—*I serve.*

> Device of the Prince of Wales, and adopted first by the Black Prince,
> who took it, together with the crest of the Three Feathers, from the King
> of Bohemia, after killing him with his own hand on the field of Crécy,
> 1346.

957. Ich habe genossen das irdische Glück,
     Ich habe gelebt und geliebet.   Schiller, Piccol. 3, 7 (Thekla's song).—*I have tasted earthly happiness, I have lived and I have loved.*

958. Ich habe hier blos ein Amt, und keine Meinung.   Schiller, Wall. Tod. 1, 5 (Wrangel loq.).—*I have but an office here, and no opinion.*

959. Ich heisse der reichste Mann in der getauften Welt:
     Die Sonne geht in meinem Staat nicht unter.   Schiller, D. Carlos, 1, 6.

> *Philip II.* I am the richest man in Christendom;
> The sun ne'er sets in my dominions.—*Ed.*

> Büchm. (pp. 197-8) finds the origin of this in Hdt. 7, 8, where **Xerxes** says of the intended westerly extension of his dominions—οὐ γὰρ δὴ χώραν οὐδεμίαν κατόψεται ὁ ἥλιος ὅμουρον ἐοῦσαν τῇ ἡμετέρῃ—*The sun will look down on no country bordering our own;* and quotes the Prol. of Guarini's *Pastor Fido*—composed 1585 in honour of the nuptials of the Duke of Savoy with Catherine of Austria (dau. of Philip II.):—

> Altera figlia
> Di quel Monarca, a cui
> Nè anco quando annotta, il Sol tramonta.

> The second daughter of that King, for whom,
> Even when night falls, the sun never sets.—*Ed.*

960. Ich sag'es dir: ein Kerl, der speculiert
Ist wie ein Tier, auf dürrer Heide
Von einem bösen Geist im Kreis herumgeführt
Und rings umher liegt schöne grüne Weide.
                       Goethe, Faust, Studirzimmer.

> *Meph.* I tell you what—your speculating wretch
> Is like a beast upon a barren waste,
> Round, ever round by an ill spirit chased,
> Whilst all about him fair green pastures stretch.—*Sir T. Martin.*

961. Id arbitror adprime in vita esse utile ne quid nimis.   Ter. **Andr.** 1, 1, 33 (Sosia loq.).—*I consider it to be a leading maxim through life, never to go to extremes.*

> In Gr., μηδὲν ἄγαν has exactly the same prov. meaning as "Ne quid nimis," *i.e., Not too much of anything.* It is attrib. to Chilo, in Diog. Laert. 1, 41. Μηδὲν ἄγαν, καιρῷ πάντα πρόσεστι καλά.—*Never push a thing too far (don't overdo it): at the proper time all will come out right.* The same author also ascribes the saying to Solon (1, 63), and to Socrates (2, 32), the last of whom calls it "the virtue of youth." *V.* also Μηδὲν ἄγαν σπεύδειν· πάντων μεσ' ἄριστα, Theognis, 335, p. 149; and Pind. Fr. 216, p. 453. La Font., as usual, has a word on the subject,—

> . . . Il n'est âme vivante
> Qui ne pèche en ceci.   Rien de trop est un point
> Dont on parle sans cesse, et qu'on n'observe point.   Fab. 9, 11.

962. Id cinerem, aut Manes credis curare sepultos?   Virg. A. 4, 34.—*Do you suppose that the ashes and spirits of the departed concern themselves with such things?*

963. Id commune malum, semel insanivimus omnes. Ioh. Mantuanus, Eclog. 1, 217 (De honesto amore).—*It is a common complaint, we have all been mad once.* Giov. Battista Spagnuoli of Mantua wrote under the name of *Johannes Mantuanus.* The first line of the couplet is,

> Tu quoque, ut hic video, non es ignarus amorum;
> *Id commune malum,* etc.

964. Id demum est homini turpe quod meruit pati. Phædr. 3, 11, 7.— *That after all only disgraces a man which he has deserved to suffer.*

965. I, demens! et sævas curre per Alpes, Ut pueris placeas, et declamatio fias. Juv. 10, 166.

> *Hannibal.*
>
> Haste! madman, haste to cross the Alpine height,
> And make a theme for schoolboys to recite.—*Ed.*

966. Idem velle atque nolle, ea demum firma amicitia est. Sall. Cat. 20, 5.—*An identity of likes and dislikes is after all the only basis of friendship.*

> Nep. Att. 5, Plus in amicitia valere similitudinem morum, quam affini-tatem.—*A similarity of tastes has much more to do with friendship than affinity.* Cf. Cic. Off. 1, 16, 51; id. Am. 4, 15; and Planc. 2, 5. "A question was started, how far people who disagree in a capital point can live in friendship together. Johnson said they might. Goldsmith said they could not, as they had not the same *idem velle atque idem nolle*—the same likings and the same aversions."—Croker's *Boswell* (1853), p. 240.

967. Ideo regnum Ecclesiæ manebit in æternum, quia individua fides, corpus est unum. S. Ambrose, In Luc. lib. vii., n. 91.—*Therefore shall the kingdom of the Church endure for ever, because the faith is undivided and the body one.*

968. Ie congnois tout, fors que moy mesmes. F. Villon, refrain of "Ballade des menus propos," p. 136.—*I know everything except myself.*

969. Ignavis semper feriæ sunt. Chil. p. 286: tr. of ἀεργοῖς αἰὲν ἑορτά. Theocr. Id. 15, 26.—*With the idle it is always holiday.*

970. Ignis aurum probat, miseria fortes viros. Sen. Prov. 5, 8.—*As fire tries gold, so misfortune is the test of fortitude.* "Calamity is man's true touchstone." Beaum. & Fletcher's *Triumph of Honour,* Sc. 1.

971. Ignoscas aliis multa, nihil tibi. Aus. Sap. 3, 4.—*Forgive much to others, yourself nothing.*

972. Ignoti nulla cupido. Ov. A. A. 3, 397.—*No one desires the un-known.* On ne peut désirer ce qu'on ne connait pas. Volt. Zaire, 1, 1.

973. Ignotis errare locis, ignota videre Flumina gaudebat, studio minuente laborem. Ov. M. 4, 294.—

He loved to wander amid unknown places, to visit unknown
rivers, the pursuit lessening the fatigue.

> He sought fresh fountains in a foreign soil,
> The pleasure lessen'd the attending toil.—*Addison.*

974. Il a jeté des pierres (*or* une pierre) dans votre jardin. Quit.
p. 471.—*That* (remark, etc.) *was aimed at you.*

975. Il arrive comme Mars en Carême. Prov.—*He arrives like March*
in Lent. Said of any invariable occurrence which calls for no
remark. On the other hand, "Comme marée en Carême" (*Like*
fish in Lent) is tantamount to an opportune arrival. Quit. p. 192.

976. Il a travaillé, il a travaillé pour le roi—de Prusse.— *He has worked,*
he has worked for the King—of Prussia. Sung in Paris of Marshal
Soubise, after his defeat at Rossbach by Frederick the Great,
Nov. 3rd, 1757. Hence *travailler pour le roi de Prusse* means
to labour in vain. Plötz, *Vocabulaire Systématique*, 15th ed.,
p. 377, *s.v.* "Umsonst." Quit. (p. 633), on the other hand, makes
the saying refer to Fredk. William I. (1688-1740), notorious
for his niggardliness and parsimony.

977. Il bel paese
Ch' Appenin parte, e'l mar circonda e l'Alpe. Petrarch, Son. in
vita di M. Laura, 114.—*The lovely land ridged by the Apennines,*
that sea and Alps environ. Italy.

978. Il compilait, compilait, compilait. Volt., Le Pauvre Diable, 1758.
—*He compiled, he compiled, he compiled.* In the poem, L'Abbé
Trublet figures as a typical bookmaker; a laborious scribe
without a particle of originality.

> Il entassait adage sur adage;
> Il compilait, compilait, compilait, etc.

V. Fumag. 649 *ad hoc*, who with no less grace than truth describes his
brother-compilers as *codesta razza di eunuchi scribacchianti*, that wretched
race of scribbling eunuchs!

979. Il connaît l'univers, et ne se connaît pas. La Font. 8, 26 (Démo-
crite et les Abdéritains).—*He knows the whole world, yet does*
not know himself.

> Qu'un homme est misérable, à l'heure du trespas
> Lors qu' ayant negligé le seul point necessaire,
> Il meurt connu de tous et ne se connoist pas! Nicolas Vauquelin
des Yvetaux, *Addition à . . . les œuvres de N. V. d. Y.* par Julien Travers,
Caen, 1856, 8º, p. 12, Sonnet II.—*How wretched the case of any one at the*
point of death, when thro' neglect of the one thing necessary, he dies known to
everyone excepting himself! Travers himself doubts the authenticity of the
lines, and suspects them to be Hesnault's.

980. Il dolce far niente.—*The sweet occupation of doing nothing.*

> Strange that it should have been reserved for the most laborious people
of Europe to have stereotyped the felicity of idleness into a "world
proverb"! When Goldoni, in *La Metempsicosi*, 2, 3 (*v.* Harb. p. 402),
praises *Quel dolce mestier di non far niente* ("That agreeable pursuit of

doing nothing"), he is literally reproducing the "national" sentiment of nearly 2000 years previous—in the *Nil agere delectat* of Cic. Or. 2, 24 ; and the *Illud iners quidem, jucundum tamen, nihil agere* of Plin. Ep. 8, 9.

Ah ! qu'il est doux
De ne rien faire,
Quand tout s'agite autour de nous !   Barbier and Carré,
Galathée, 2, 1.   Com. Opera, music by V. Massé, 1852.   *V.* Alex. p. 148.

981. Il en est du véritable amour comme de l'apparition des esprits : tout le monde en parle, mais peu de gens en ont vu. La Rochef. Max. 76, p. 41.— *True love resembles apparitions : everyone talks of them, though few have ever seen them.*

982. Il en est pour les choses littéraires comme pour les choses d'argent : on ne prête qu'aux riches. Fourn. *L.D.A.*, chap. iv. p. 15.—*It is the same in literary as in pecuniary matters: one only lends to the rich.* A fine line, unknown, is, *e.g.*, immediately set down to Shakespeare.

983. Il est beau qu'un mortel jusques aux cieux s'élève, Il est beau même d'en tomber. Quinault, Phaéton, 4, 2.—*'Tis a fine thing for a mortal to raise himself to the skies, fine even to fall from thence.* Phaeton speaks of his own disaster in terms which might be applied to modern aeronautics.

984. Il est bien difficile de garder un trésor dont tous les hommes ont la clef. Trésor du Monde (Paris, 1565, 12mo, Bk. ii. p. 59).—*It is very difficult to guard a treasure of which all men have the key.* In the *Chevræana* (vol. i. p. 350), the saying is attrib. to Bassompierre.

985. Il est bon de parler, il est bon de se taire; Mais il faut parler juste et surtout à propos. Aug. Rigaud, Fables Nouv. (1823-24), 12, 12   Alex. p. 373.

Speech and silence, at times, are both equally just,
But speak well, and ('fore all) to the point, if you must.—*Ed.*

La Font. 8, 10 (L'Ours et l'Amateur, etc.), has, " Il est bon de parler, et meilleur de se taire."

986. Il est bon de tuer de temps en temps un amiral pour encourager les autres. Volt. Candide, cap. 23.—*It is a good thing every now and then to kill an admiral in order to encourage the others* Written about three years after Admiral Byng's execution.

987. Il faut avoir pitié des morts. Victor Hugo, Prière pour tous.— *One must have pity on the dead.*

988. Il faut qu'une porte soit ouverte ou fermée. De Brueys et de Palaprat, Grondeur, 1, 6.   Œuvres de Théatre, Paris, 1755-65. Produced at the Théatre Fr., Feb. 3, 1691.—*A door must either be open or shut.* Said on any occasion where there is only one alternative.

In the play, Dr Grichard, the " Grondeur," is furious at having been kept waiting outside his door; upon which Lolive, the servant, after admitting him, says, "Oh ça, monsieur, quand vous serez sorti, voulez-vous que je laisse

la porte ouverte ? *M. Grichard.* Non. *L.* Voulez-vous que je la tienne
fermée? *M. G.* Non. *L.* Si faut-il monsieur ! . . . *M. G.* Te tairas-tu?
L. Monsieur, je me ferais hacher: *il faut qu'une porte soit ouverte ou fermée ;*
choisissez; comment la voulez-vous ? "—Title of one of Alfred de Musset's
Proverbes.

989. Il faut rire avant que d'être heureux, de peur de mourir sans
avoir ri. La Bruy., chap. 4 (Du Cœur).—*One has to laugh before
one is merry for fear of dying without having laughed.*

990. Ilicet infandum cuncti contra omina bellum,
Contra fata deum, perverso numine poscunt.　　Virg. A. 7, 583.

Ill-advised War.
'Gainst omens flashed before their eyes,
'Gainst warnings thundered from the skies,
They cry for war.—*Conington.*

991. Illa est agricolæ messis iniqua suo. Ov. Her. 12, 48.—*That is a
harvest which pays the labourer badly.* A losing game: a bad
trade.

992. Illam, quicquid agit, quoquo vestigia flectit,
Componit furtim, subsequiturque decor.　　Tibull. 4, 2, 8.

Sulpicia.
Whate'er she does, where'er her steps she bends,
Grace on each action silently attends.—*Ed.*

993. Illa placet tellus in qua res parva beatum
Me facit, et tenues luxuriantur opes.　　Mart. 10, 96, 5.

Happiness.
Where on a little you can happy be,
And small incomes abound, 's the land for me.—*Ed.*

994. Ille dies primus leti primusque malorum
Causa fuit.　　Virg. A. 4, 169.—*That day was the beginning of
death and disaster.*

995. Ille igitur nunquam direxit brachia contra
Torrentem; nec civis erat qui libera posset
Verba animi proferre, et vitam impendere vero.　　Juv. 4, 89.

The Time-Server.
He never tried to swim against the stream,
Nor dared, as citizen, to speak his mind,
And stake his life, at all costs, on the truth.—*Ed.*

This is your safe man who is never guilty of indiscreet verities, and
always contrives to be in with the winning side; as, in fact, Crispus did;
and, as Juvenal goes on to say, lived to see fourscore years even at the
Court of Domitian. Cf. καιρῷ λατρεύειν, μηδ' ἀντιπλέειν ἀνέμοισιν. Pseudo-
phocylid. 121, p. 98.—*Go with the times; don't sail against the wind.*

996. Ille mi par esse Deo videtur,
Ille (si fas est) superare Divos,
Qui, sedens adversus, identidem te
　　Spectat et audit
Dulce ridentem.　　Cat. 51, 1.

To Lesbia.

Blest as the immortal gods is he,
Or (may I say it ?) still more blest,
Who sitting opposite to thee
Sees thee, and hears thy laugh and jest.—*Ed.*

997. Ille sinistrorsum, hic dextrorsum, abit: unus utrique
Error, sed variis illudit partibus.   Hor. S. 2, 3, 50.

This to the right, that to the left hand strays,
And all are wrong, but wrong in different ways.—*Conington.*

998. Ille terrarum mihi præter omnes
Angulus ridet.   Hor. C. 2, 6, 13.—*That little nook of earth
charms me more than any other place.*

999. Ille, velut pelagi rupes immota, resistit;
Quæ sese, multis circumlatrantibus undis,
Mole tenet; scopuli nequidquam et spumea circum
Saxa fremunt, laterique illisa refunditur alga.   Virg. A. 7, 586.

Latinus.

He stands just like some sea-girt rock,
Moveless against the ocean-shock ;
Fast anchored by the ponderous form
Its mass opposes to the storm.
The wild waves bellow all around,
And spray-drenched cliffs return the sound ;
But, nothing heeding, it flings back
The broken wreaths of floating wrack.—*Ed.*

1000. Illic et cantant quicquid didicere theatris;
Et jactant faciles ad sua verba manus.   Ov. F. 3, 535.—*They
sing snatches of the songs learnt at the theatre, and accompany the
words with ready gestures of the hand.*

1001. Il lit au front de ceux qu'un vain luxe environne
Que la Fortune vend ce qu'on croit qu'elle donne.
La Font. Contes (Philemon and Baucis), 5, 9, 11.

'Tis writ on the palace where luxury dwells,
That fortune in seeming to give, really sells.—*Ed.*

Cf. Voiture (to the Comte du Guiche, Oct. 15, 1641): "Pour l'ordinaire
elle (la Fortune) vend bien chèrement les choses qu'il semble qu'elle nous
donne." *Lettres choisies de Voiture et Balzac,* 2 vols., Paris, 1807, vol. 1,
p. 114.

1002. Illud amicitiæ sanctum et venerabile nomen,
Re tibi pro vili sub pedibusque jacet.   Ov. T. 1, 8, 15.

And Friendship's sacred, venerable name
Lies trodden 'neath your feet, a thing of shame.—*Ed.*

1003. Il maestro di color che sanno. Dante, Inf. 4, 131.—*The master of
the wise.*   Said of Aristotle ; Socrates and Plato being placed
next below.   Petrarch, *Triumph of Fame,* c. 3, gives the first
place to Plato.

1004. Il me faut du nouveau, n'en fût-il point au monde. La Font., Clymène (1674), line 35 (Apollo to the Muses).—*I must have something new, if there were none in the world.*

1005. Il meglio è l'inimico del bene, or (in Fr.), Le mieux est l'ennemi du bien. V. Volt. Dict. Philosophique, *art.* ART DRAMATIQUE.— *Better is the enemy of well.*   Skakesp. *King Lear*, 1, 4, has,

> "Striving to better, oft we mar what's well."   Cf. the Italian epitaph, Stavo ben, ma per star meglio, sto qui.—*I was well; I would be better; and here I am:* and its English counterpart,—
>> Here lie I and my three daughters,
>> Died of drinking the Cheltenham waters.
>> If we'd stuck to the Epsom salts,
>> We shouldn't be lying in these here vaults.

1006. Il mondo invecchia, e invecchiando intristisce. Tasso, Aminta, 2, 2, 71.—*The world grows old, and growing old grows worse.*

1007. Il n'appartient qu'aux grands hommes d'avoir de grands défauts. La Rochef., § 195, p. 55.—*It is only great men who can afford to display great defects.*

1008. Il ne faut jamais hasarder la plaisanterie, même la plus douce et la plus permise, qu'avec des gens polis, ou qui ont de l'esprit. La Bruy. Car., La Société (vol. i. p. 92).—*It never does to risk a joke, even of the mildest and most unexceptionable character, except in the company of witty and polished people.*

1009. Il ne faut pas parler Latin devant les Cordeliers. Prov. Quit. p. 260.—*It doesn't do to talk Latin before the Cordeliers* (Franciscan Observantines).   Be careful not to speak too confidently before those who are masters of the subject.

1010. Il ne faut point parler corde dans la famille (*or* la maison) d'un pendu. Prov. Quit. p. 592.—*Don't talk rope in the family of one who has been hanged.*

1011. Il ne s'agit pas de consuls, et je ne veux pas être votre aide-de-camp. Sainte Beuve, Causeries du Lundi, v. 215.—*It is no question of consuls, and I don't choose to be your aide-de-camp.* Sieyès to Bonaparte in 1800 on resigning the post of Second Consul.

1012. Il ne se faut jamais moquer des misérables,
> Car qui peut s'assurer d'être toujours heureux ?
>> La Font. Renard et L'Écureuil.

(Œuvres inédites, recueillies par Paul Lacroix, Paris, 1863, 8°, pp. 3, 4.)
> Of men in misfortune no ridicule make,
> For who can be sure of good luck without break ?—*Ed.*

In the end the bragging Fox is killed, the Squirrel looking on :—

> Il le voit, mais il n'en rit pas,
> Instruit par sa propre misère.

These last lines are quoted in circumstances which, though ridiculous in themselves, touch one too nearly to be made subjects of joking.

1013. Il n'est bon bec que de Paris. F. Villon, Ballade des Femmes de Paris, p. 85.—*No place like Paris for sharp tongues.* The ballad's title should not be overlooked, the *bavardes* rather than the *bavards* being the subject of the poet's comment. Its last verse goes:

> Prince, aux dames parisiennes
> De bien parler donnez le prix ;
> Quoi qu'on die d'Italiennes,
> *Il n'est bon bec que de Paris.*

1014. Il n'est pas besoin de tenir les choses pour en raisonner. Beaum. Figaro, Act v. Sc. 3 (Figaro loq.).—*It is not necessary to believe things, in order to argue about them.*

1015. Il n'est pas encore temps de le dire, les vérités sont des fruits qui ne doivent être cueillis que bien mûrs. Voltaire, Lettre à la Comtesse de Bassewitz, 24th Dec. 1761.—*The time has not yet arrived for saying it: truth is a fruit which ought not to be gathered until it is full ripe.*

1016. Il ne sut que mourir, aimer, et pardonner,
S'il avait su punir, il aurait du régner. Cte. de Tilly, Œuvres mêlées, Berlin, 1803, 8vo, p. 178.

Louis Seize.

He could die, love, forgive : but it all was in vain,
Since punish he could not, and so could not reign.—*Ed.*

1017. Il n'y a au monde que deux manières de s'élever: ou par sa propre industrie, ou par l'imbécillité des autres. La Bruy. cap. vi. (vol. 1, p. 114).—*There are only two ways of rising in the world: either by one's own exertions, or by the imbecility of others.*

1018. Il n'y a de nouveau que ce qui a vieilli. Motto of *Revue Rétrospective* (1st ser., 1833, ed. M. J. Tascherau), Alex. p. 347.— *There is nothing new except that which has become antiquated.* Also, Il n'y a de nouveau que ce qui est oublié.—*There is nothing new except what is forgotten.* Attributed to Mdlle. Bertin, milliner to Marie Antoinette. Fourn. *L.D.A.*, chap. xii. pp. 149-50.

1019. Il n'y a de place dans l'histoire que pour le vrai, et tout ce qui n'est que vraisemblable doit être renvoyé aux espaces imaginaires des romans et des fictions poétiques. Le Père Griffet, *Traité des différentes sortes de preuves,* etc., p. 42. (Fourn. *L.D.L.*, cap. iv.)—*History can only admit what is true, and mere probabilities must be relegated to the imaginary field of romance and poetical fiction.*

1020. Il n'y a pas de gens plus affairés que ceux qui n'ont rien à faire. Prov.—*No people so busy as those who have nothing to do.*

I

1021. Il n'y a pas de héros pour son valet-de-chambre.   Mme. Cornuel,
Lettres de Mlle. Aïssé (1728), edit. J. Ravenel, Paris, 1853, p. 161.
—*No man is a hero to his valet de chambre.*

> Montaigne says (*Essais*, 3, 2), Peu d'hommes ont esté admirez par leurs
> domestiques—*Few men have been admired by their servants;* upon which
> his commentator, Pierre Coste, qu. a recorded saying of Marshal de
> Catinat, "Il faut être bien héros pour l'être aux yeux de son valet de
> chambre"—*One must be a hero indeed to be so in the eyes of one's valet.*
> M. de Créqui says of Catinat, who was adored by his servants, "D'anciens
> auteurs ont dit qu'il n'y avoit jamais eu de héros pour ses gens. Il semble
> que le Maréchal de Catinat ait démenti cette maxime" (Mémoires pour
> servir à l'histoire de Nicolas de Catinat, Paris, 1775, p. 284).   Claudian,
> Bell. Gild. 385, has, Minuit præsentia famam—*Proximity lessens respect.*
> Alex. p. 240.

1022. Il n'y a pas moins d'esprit ni d'invention à bien appliquer une
pensée que l'on trouve dans un livre, qu'à être le premier auteur
de cette pensée . . . On a oui dire au Cardinal du Perron, que
l'application heureuse d'un vers de Virgile était signe d'un
talent.   Bayle Dict. ART. *Epicure*, p. 1132, note.—*There is as
much successful ingenuity in making an apt application of a
sentiment discovered in some author, as in being the first to conceive it. . . . One has heard the Cardinal du Perron say that a
felicitous adaptation of a line of Virgil was a talent in itself.*

1023. Il n'y a plus de Pyrénées.   Volt. Siècle de Louis XIV. cap. 28.—
There are no more Pyrenees.   Mot with which Louis XIV. is
credited on the departure of the Duke of Anjou from Paris,
Nov. 16, 1700, to ascend the throne of Spain as Philip V.

> Acc. to the *Journal du Marquis de Dangeau* (ed. Didot, Paris, 1853-60,
> vol. vii. p. 419), the saying originated with the Spanish ambassador,
> who remarked that "présentement les Pyrénées étaient fondues" (*the
> Pyrenees had now melted away*).   The Mercure Galant (Nov. 1700. p. 237),
> on the other hand, repeats the ambassador's speech in Voltaire's words,
> "Quelle joie! il n'y a plus de Pyrénées! Elles sont abymées, et nous ne
> somme plus qu'un."   The saying had, however, been anticipated on the
> occasion of the marriage of Louis XIII. with Anne of Austria (1615), of
> which Malherbe wrote (Œuvres, vol. 1, p. 215, ed. Lud. Lalanne):

> > Puis quand ces deux grands hyménées,
> > Dont le fatal embrassement
> > Doit aplanir les Pyrénées.   Poésies, lxiv., l. 151.

1024. Il n'y a point au monde un si pénible métier que celui de se faire
un grand nom.   La vie s'achève que l'on a à peine ébauché son
ouvrage.   La Bruy. vol. i. cap. 2 (Mérite personnel).—*There is
not a more arduous task in the world than that of making a great
name: life comes to an end before one has hardly sketched out
one's work.*

1025. Il n'y a point de patrie dans le despotique; d'autres choses y
suppléent, l'intérêt, la gloire, le service du prince.   La Bruy.
chap. 10, Du Souverain (vol. i. p. 186).—*Under a despotic government the idea of country drops out altogether, and its place is*

supplied in other ways, by private interests, public fame, and the service of the sovereign.

1026. Il n'y a que ceux qui ne font rien, qui ne se trompent pas. A. Favre, Recherches Géologiques, Paris, 1867, vol. 3, p. 76.— *It is only those who never do anything who never make mistakes.* Harb. qu. *à propos* the "Solo chi non fa niente è certo di non errare" of M. d'Azeglio in his *I miei Ricordi*, chap. xvi.

1027. Il n'y a que le premier pas qui coûte. Prov. ap. Quit. p. 584.—*It is only the first step which matters.*

This celebrated saying originates with the traditional account of the martyrdom of S. Dionysius, who is reported to have carried his head from Montmartre, the scene of his decapitation, to S. Denis, the place of his interment. Quitard even adds (*in l.*) that, "Pour qu'on ne m'accuse pas de vouloir rien ôter à la gloire de S. Denis, j'ajouterai (d'après Helduin, son biographe) qu'il *baisa* plusieurs fois sa tête sur la route, en présence des anges qui l'accompagnaient en chantant: *Gloria tibi, Domine, Alleluia!* Acc. to the same author, ibid., the Card. de Polignac was objecting to the length of the journey to be traversed by the saint, upon which Mme. du Deffand replied, "Monseigneur, il n'y a que la premier pas qui coûte." *V.* her letter to D'Alembert, claiming the authorship of the *mot*, of July 7, 1763—*Trois mois à la Cour de Frédéric, Lettres inédites de D'Alembert,* Gaston Maugras, Paris, 1886, p. 28.

Finally, the great Gibbon comes in to give classic rank to the *dicton.* It is even admitted into his *Decline*, etc., vol. 7, cap. 39 n., where he remarks that "a lady of my acquaintance (presumably Mme. du Deffand)," observed thereupon: "La distance n'y fait rien; il n'y a que le premier pas, etc." In her younger days Mme. du Deffand had been a "femme galante," who in the autumn and winter of her life found her vocation in the salon rather than in the exercises of the *dévote.* During the latter part of the reign of Louis XV., her house in the Rue St Dominique became the general rendezvous where all the celebrities of the day used to meet. Marie Antoinette's brother, the Emperor Joseph II., was one of her guests, of whom Mme. du D. wrote to Horace Walpole, "Il est d'une familiarité dont on est charmé." Gibbon was another, and his introduction was attended by a comical incident enough. The hostess being now blind, had to resort to her sense of touch in order to get an idea of the looks, and even the character of a newcomer; and Gibbon's face, as his pictures show, was fabulously expansive and puffy. "Au premier contact, madame rougit, et, se réculant vivement sur son fauteuil, s'écria avec indignation, 'Voilà une infame plaisanterie!' Elle s'était figurée que Gibbon s'était présenté à rebours, et qu'elle avait pris pour les 'joues de derrière' ce qui était bien et dûment le visage de Gibbon." *Correspondance compl. de la Marquise du Deffand.* Paris, 1865, vol. i. p. 210.

1028. Il n'y a que les morts qui ne reviennent pas. Bertrand Barère, *Moniteur,* 29 Mai 1794.—*It is only the dead that never come back.*

The history of this saying has a peculiar interest, having been originally uttered with reference to Englishmen by the most finished liar of his age. B. Barère presided at the mock trial of Louis XVI., and a year later (May 26, 1794) proposed, and carried, in National Convention, the resolution that no quarter should be given to any English or Hanoverian soldier. "He had many associates in guilt," says Macaulay, "but he distinguished himself from them all by the bacchanalian exaltation which he seemed to feel in the work of death" (*Edin. Rev.,* April '44).

1029. Il n'y a rien de changé en France : il n'y a qu'un Français de plus. Comte Beugnot, see below.—*Nothing is changed in France, there is only one Frenchman more than before.*

Celebrated but fabulous reply of the Comte d'Artois (Charles X.) to Talleyrand on his reception at the Barrière de Bondy, April 12, 1814. The Prince, as a fact, was too much moved at the moment to do more than stammer out his thanks, but as it was imperative that next day's *Moniteur* should contain "*la réponse de Monsieur*," Talleyrand deputed the *ad interim* minister of the Interior, Beugnot, to compose a "reply." Late that night, and after several failures, Beugnot himself says, "Enfin j'accouche de celle qui est au *Moniteur*, où je fais dire au prince : Plus de divisions, la paix et la France . . . et rien n'y est changé, si ce n'est qu'il s'y trouve un Français de plus." With this Talleyrand was satisfied, and the copy was sent off at once to the ministerial organ. V. *Mémoires du Comte Beugnot*, 2nd ed., 1868, vol. 2, chap. 16, pp. 126-31. Alex. pp. 209-11.

1030. Il plaît à tout le monde, et ne sauroit se plaire. Boil. Sat. 2, fin. —*He pleases all the world, but cannot please himself.* Said of Molière.

1031. Il savait de la métaphysique, ce qu'on en a su dans tous les âges— c'est à dire, fort peu de chose. Volt. *Zadig*, chap. 1.—*He knew as much of metaphysics as men have known at all times—that is to say, very little indeed.*

1032. Il savait se faire entendre, à force de se faire écouter.—*He makes himself understood, by making men listen to him.* Said by M. Villemain of Andrieux, the Professor of Literature at the Collége de France, 1800, and qu. by A. H. Taillandier, *s.v.* ANDRIEUX, in Didot's *N. Biog. Générale*: but Beaumarchais had forestalled him in his *Deux amis*, 1, 1 (1770); "Une jeune actrice se fait toujours assez entendre, lorsqu'elle a le talent de se faire écouter."

1033. Il segretto per esser felici
So per prova e l'insegno agli amici. Felice Romani, Lucrezia Borgia, 2, 4 (Music by Donizetti).—Orsini sings : *The secret of happiness I know by experience, and teach it to my friends* (to play, drink, and laugh at care).

1034. Il s'est coupé le bras gauche avec le bras droit. J. Bapt. Say, Traité d'économie politique, Bk. i. cap. 20 (ed. 1814, vol. i. p. 301).—*He has cut off his left arm with his right.* Attributed to Queen Christina of Sweden *à propos* of the revocation of the Edict of Nantes by Louis XIV.

1035. Ils n'ont rien appris, ni rien oublié. Talleyrand, Album Perdu, p. 147.—*They have learnt nothing, and forgotten nothing.*

M. de Talleyrand (says the *Album, in l.*) described the émigrés as, "des gens qui n'ont rien appris, ni rien oublié depuis trente ans," and the *mot* has been accordingly fathered upon him, with quite as much justice as other of his attributions. It must have been said ("trente ans") some-where about 1820, whereas Lafayette (in his *Mémoires, Correspondance, etc.*, Paris, 1838), writing at the time of the Restoration (1814), says of the

Comte d'Artois that he did not conceal the fact that, "en loyal émigré, il n'avait rien appris, rien oublié" (vol. 5, p. 346). In the same year, in conversation with Alexander of Russia, Lafayette expressed the hope that their late misfortunes might have taught (*corrigé*) the Bourbons a lesson. "Corrigés? me dit-il. Ils sont incorrigés et incorrigibles!" (id., ibid. vol. 5, p. 311). To go back much farther in the fortunes of the *émigrés* and their characteristic indifference to the teachings of history, we come upon a letter of the Chevalier de Panat to Mallet du Pan, dated London, Jan. 1796, in which, speaking of the Count of Provence and his entourage, he says, "Personne n'est corrigé; personne n'a su ni rien oublier, ni rien appendre." *Mémoires et Corresp. de Mallet du Pan, receuillis par M. A. Sayous* (Paris. 1851, 8vo, vol. 2, p. 197).—*No one is altered; no one has learnt either to forget the past, or to be wiser for the future.* In 1828, Béranger proved the truth of the saying, when his third series of political songs procured him a fine of 10,000 francs and imprisonment for nine months at La Force, where he wrote *Denys, maître d'école*, with its refrain of "Jamais l'exil n'a corrigé les rois."

1036. Il sont passés ces jour de fêtes,
Ils sont passés, ils ne reviendront plus.
Anseaume, Tableau parlant (1769), sc. 5.

> Music by Grétry. Columbine loq.: *They are gone by those happy festive days: they are past and never will return.* In Schiller's "Don Carlos," 1, 1, Domingo enunciates a similar sentiment in,
>
> Die schönen Tage in Aranjuez
> Sind nun zu Ende.—*The happy days of Aranjuez are now ended.*

1037. Ils sont trop verts, dit-il, et bons pour des goujats! La Font. 3, 11 (Le Renard et les Raisins).—*They are too green, said he, and only good for fools!*

1038. Il tombe sur le dos et se casse le nez. Chamf. Car. (i. 155).—*He falls on his back and breaks his nose.* Said of a notoriously unlucky man. *See* Quit. p. 325.

1039. Il trouvait la nature trop verte et mal éclairée. Et son ami, Lancret, le peintre des salons à la mode, lui répondait; Je suis de votre sentiment, la nature manque d'harmonie et de séduction. Charles Blanc's "Histoire des Peintres de toutes les écoles," Paris, 1862, fol. *École Francaise*, vol. 2, art. BOUCHER, init.—*He (Boucher) considered nature too green and badly lighted: and his friend, Lancret, the fashionable painter of the day, added: "I am of your opinion. Nature is wanting in harmony and seductiveness."*

1040. Il y a de bons mariages; mais il n'y en a point de délicieux. La Rochef. Max. 113, p. 45.—*There are good marriages, but there are none that can be called delicious.*

1041. Il y a fagots et fagots. Mol. Méd. malgré lui, 1, 6.—*There are faggots and faggots.*

1042. Il y a mes amis qui m'aiment, mes amis qui ne se soucient pas du tout de moi, et mes amis qui me détestent. Chamf. in Didot's *Nouv. Biogr. Gén.*, art. CHAMFORT, by von Rosenwald.—*There are*

*my friends who love me, my friends who don't care a farthing
about me, and my friends who detest me.*

1043. Imago animi vultus, indices oculi.   Cic. de Or. 3, 221.—*Faces
reflect character; and the eyes are the chief witness.*

1044. Im engen Kreis verengert sich der Sinn,
    Es wächst der Mensch mit seinem grössern Zwecken.
                                    Schiller, Wall. Lager. Prol.

> The mind grows narrow in its narrow round,
> But as his aims enlarge, the man expands.—*Ed.*

1045. Immensa Romanæ pacis majestate.   Plin. 27, 1, 1.—*The world-
wide sovereignty of the Roman empire.*   Similarly, the term *Pax
Britannica* is used to express a dominion of wider extent even
than that enjoyed by the Cæsars.

1046. Immo id quod aiunt, auribus teneo lupum.
    Nam neque quomodo a me amittam, invenio: neque, uti retineam,
    scio.   Ter. Phorm. 3, 2, 21.—*Indeed it is as they say, I've got a
    wolf by the ears.   How to loose him I don't see; how to hold him
    I can't tell.*   A fearful predicament.   Catching a Tartar.

1047. Immortale odium, et nunquam sanabile vulnus
    Ardet adhuc Coptos et Tentyra.   Summus utrimque
    Inde furor vulgo, quod numina vicinorum
    Odit uterque locus: quum solos credat habendos
    Esse Deos, quos ipse colit.   Juv. 15, 34.

> *Religious Controversies.*
>
> A deathless hatred and a fatal wound
> Still rankles 'twixt Coptos and Tentyra.
> The fiercest rage on both sides fills the mob,
> Since each detests his neighbour's deities,
> Convinced that only those are to be held
> As gods, whom they especially adore.—*Ed.*

1048. Impar congressus Achilli.   Virg. A. 1, 475.—*No match for a
contest with Achilles.*   Said of Troilus.

1049. Imperat aut servit collecta pecunia cuique.   Hor. Ep. 1, 10, 47.—
A man's money is either his master or his slave.

1050. Imperium et libertas.   *Empire and freedom.*

> Phrase employed by Lord Beaconsfield at Lord Mayor's dinner, November
> 10, 1879.   "One of the greatest of Romans, when asked what were his
> politics, replied, *Imperium et Libertas.*   That would not make a bad
> programme for a British Ministry."   Mr Gladstone a fortnight later in
> Midlothian characterised the quotation as "an unhappy and ominous
> allusion," and said that the words meant simply this, "Liberty for our-
> selves, Empire over the rest of mankind" (see *Times*, November 11 and 28,
> 1879).   In Cic. Philipp. 4, 4, 8, is, Decrevit senatus D. Brutum optime de
> re publica mereri, quum senatus auctoritatem, populique R. *libertatem
> imperiumque* defenderet.—*The senate passed a resolution to the effect that
> Decius Brutus deserved well of the Republic, for his defence of the senate's
> authority, and the liberty and empire of the R. people.*   In *N. and Q.*

(8th series, vol. x. p. 453) Mr R. Pierpont suggests, as the ground of Lord Beaconsfield's remarks, the *Divi Britannici*, etc., of Sir Winston Churchill. Kt., London, 1675, p. 349, where it is said, "Here the two great interests, IMPERIUM and LIBERTAS, res olim insociabiles (saith Tacitus), began to Incounter each other." The ref. is to Tac. Agr. 3, *res olim dissociabiles . . . principatum ac libertatem.*

1050A. Imperium in imperio.—*An empire (or government) existing within an empire.*

The Catholic Church, extending to all countries independently of national distinctions, presents everywhere the appearance of an *imperium in imperio* —a spiritual kingdom subsisting within the temporal. "The Church, an *imperium in imperio* . . . was aggressive as an institution, and was encroaching on the State with organised system." (Froude, *Life and Times of Thos. Becket.*)

1051. Impossible est un mot que je ne dis jamais.   Collin d'Harleville, Malice pour malice, 1, 8.—*"Impossible" is a word which I never pronounce.* Napoleon (Lettre à Lemarois, July 9, 1813) says, "'Ce n'est pas possible,' m'écrivez-vous: cela n'est pas Français."

1052. Im wunderschönen Monat Mai.   H. Heine, *Lyrische Intermezzo*, 1.—*In beautifullest month of May!*

1053. In amore hæc sunt mala; bellum,
Pax rursum: hæc si quis, tempestatis prope ritu
Mobilia et cæca fluitantia sorte, laboret
Reddere certa sibi, nihilo plus explicet, ac si
Insanire paret certa ratione modoque.   Hor. S. 2, 3, 267.

> Now love is such a thing; first war, then peace,
> For ever heaving like a sea in storm,
> And taking every hour some different form.
> You think to fix it? Why, the job's as bad
> As if you tried by method to be mad.—*Conington.*

The passage in the *Eunuchus* of Terence, Act i. sc. 1, which Horace is imitating here, concludes with, "nihilo plus agas, quam si des operam ut cum ratione insanias."— *You would get no further than if your object was to be mad by the rules of reason* "Though this be madness," says Polonius (*Hamlet*, 2, 2), "yet there's method in it."

1054. Inanis verborum torrens.   Quint. 10, 7, 23.—*An unmeaning torrent of words.*

1055. In aurem ultramvis dormire.—*To sleep on either ear, soundly.* Ademtum tibi jam faxo omnem metum, In aurem utramvis otiose ut dormias. Ter. Heaut. 2, 3, 100.—*I will rid you of all your fears, so that you may sleep as soundly as you please.   See* Gell. 2, 23, 9; and Menand. Plocium, I. 1 (p. 944). Ἐπ' ἀμφότερα νῦν ἅτ' ἐπίκληρος οὖσα δὴ μέλλει καθευδήσειν.

1056. In causa facili cuivis licet esse diserto;
Et minimæ vires frangere quassa valent.   Ov. T. 3, 11, 21.

> In easy matters every one can speak,
> And little strength a bruised thing can break.—*Dryden.*

1057. Inceptis gravibus plerumque et magna professis,
Purpureus, late qui splendeat, unus et alter
Adsuitur pannus.   Hor. A. P. 14.

Purple Patches.

When poets would affect the lofty stave,
With pompous opening and with prelude brave;
It is a common trick, the eye to catch,
To sew on here and there a purple patch.—*Ed.*

1058. Incidis in Scyllam, cupiens vitare Charybdim. Gualterus de
Castellione (Philip Gauthier de Châtillon, or de Lisle), Gesta
Alexandri, lib. 5, ver. 297 (Rouen, 1487).—*In grave anxiety to
avoid Charybdis, you fall into Scylla.*

" Out of the frying pan," etc.   A choice of evils.   " Thus when I shun
Scylla, your father, I fall into Charybdis. your mother " (Launcelot to
Jessica), *Merch. of Venice*, 3, 5.   The generally received *Incidis* does not
appear in the black letter ed. of 1487 (B.M.), which is as follows:—

Quo tendis ferte
Rex periture fugă ? nescis heu perdite nescis
Quẽ fugias: hostes incurris dũ fugis hostem.
Corruis in syllam cupiens vitare caribdim.

Darius' Flight.

Why, fated king, a tame evasion try?
You know not, lost one, whom or where to fly.
You meet the foe you dread; and, pressed by all,
Shunning Charybdis into Scylla fall.—*J. W. Croker.*

** The rock of Scylla and whirlpool of Charybdis, represented by the
ancients as dangerous sea-monsters, are thought to be poetical figures for
the strong races running off Scilla and Faro at the N. extremity of the
Straits of Messina.

1059. Inde datæ leges ne fortior omnia posset.   Law Max.—*Laws were
made for this purpose, that the stronger might not always prevail.*

1060. In deiner Brust sind deines Schicksals Sterne.
Schiller, *Piccol.* 2, 6.

Illo: (*You'll wait upon the stars and on their hours,
Till th' earthly hour escapes you.   O. believe me,*)
In your own bosom are your destiny's stars!—*Coleridge.*

1061. Index animi sermo.   Law Max.—*Words are the index or interpretation of the intention*   The meaning of an Act of Parl. is
best explained by the direct words of its framers.

1062. Indica tigris agit rabida cum tigride pacem
Perpetuam : sævis inter se convenit ursis
Ast homini ferrum letale incude nefanda
Produxisse parum est.   Juv. 15, 163.

Tiger with tiger keeps perpetual peace,
And, *inter se*, fierce bears from conflict cease;
Yet man is not afraid to forge the sword
On impious anvils.—*Ed.*

Pliny (7, 1, 16) says: Cœtera animantia in suo genere probé degunt . . .
Leonum feritas inter se non dimicat: serpentium morsus non petit serpentes
. . . at hercule homini plurima ex homine sunt mala.—*All other creatures
conduct themselves well with their own kind; the fierceness of lions is not
vented on themselves; the serpents fangs are not aimed at other serpents;
yet much of men's sufferings come from their fellow-men!* Cf. Boileau,
Sat. 8, 125:—

> Voit-on des loups brigands comme nous inhumains,
> Pour détrousser les loups courir les grand chemins?—

*Does one see wolves taking to the road in order to plunder other wolves, as
does inhuman man?*

1063. Indignor quidquam reprehendi, non quia crasse
Compositum illepideve putetur, sed quia nuper.   Hor. Ep. 2, 1, 76.

> I chafe to hear a poem called third-rate
> Not as ill-written, but as written late.—*Conington.*

1064. Indocilis pauperiem pati.   Hor. C. 1, 1, 18 —*Incapable of bearing
straitened means.*   Motto of the Merchants of Bristol.

1065. Indocilis privata loqui.   Lucan. 5, 539.—*Incapable of divulging
secrets.*

1066. Indocti discant, et ament meminisse periti.   Transl. by President
Hénault (*Abrégé Chronologique,* 1749, *Avertissement,* p. viii) of
Pope (Essay on Criticism, line 741).

> Content, if hence th' unlearn'd their wants may view,
> The learned reflect on what before they knew.

1067. Indole pro quanta juvenis, quantumque daturus
Ausoniæ populis ventura in sæcula civem!
Ille super Gangen, super exauditus et Indos
Implebit terras voce, et furialia bella
Fulmine compescet linguæ, nec deinde relinquet
Par decus eloquio cuiquam sperare nepotum.   Sil. 8, 408.

> *Cicero.*
>
> What youthful genius, what a mighty name
> To add t' Ausonia's crowded scroll of fame!
> He beyond Ind and Ganges shall be heard,
> And fill the countries with his voice and word;
> Repressing wars of cruelty and wrong
> By the mere lightning of his vivid tongue:
> Nor may posterity hope in ages hence
> To match the splendour of his eloquence.—*Ed.*

The lines were quoted by Mr Burke (speech on the India Bill, 1783),
applying them to Mr Fox, the minister in charge of the measure.

1068. Inexpiabilis et gravis culpa discordiæ nec passione purgatur.   Esse
martyr non potest qui in ecclesia non est. . . . Occidi talis
potest, coronari non potest.   S. Cyprian, de Unitate, 14.

> *No Martyrs out of the Church.*
> The inexpiable sin of schism is not done away with even by suffering.
> No one can be a martyr who is not in the Church. . . . He may be slain,
> crowned he cannot be.

1069. Infelix operam perdas; ut si quis asellum
    In Campo doceat parentem currere frænis.   Hor. S. 1, 1, 90.
>   'Twere but lost labour, as if one should train
>   A donkey for the course by bit and rein.—*Conington.*

1070. Infinita è la schiera degli sciocchi.   Petrarch, *Trionfo del Tempo*,
    84.—*The battalions of fools are infinite.*

1071 Infirmi est animi exiguique voluptas Ultio.   Juv. 13, 190.—
    Revenge's the joy of starved and puny souls.

1072. In flagranti crimine comprehensi.   Just. Cod. 9, 13, 1.—*Caught
    in the very act:* or, "*in flagrante delicto*"—*in the very com-
    mission of the offence.*

1073. In flammam flammas, in mare fundis aquas.   Ov. Am. 3, 2, 34.—
    You are adding fire to flames, and water to the sea.

1074. Inflatum, plenumque Nerone propinquo.   Juv. 8, 72.—*Full to
    bursting of his relationship to Nero.*   Of any who talk much of
    their smart relations.

1075. Ingeniis patuit campus, certusque merenti
    Stat favor: ornatur propriis industria donis.
                                            Claud. Cons. Mall. 262.

> *Fair Field and no Favour.*
> The field is free to talent; merit's sure
> Of its applause, and industry is crowned
> With the reward that's due to its own pains.—*Ed.*

1076. Ingenio arbusta ubi nata sunt, non obsita.   Næv. Trag., Lycurgus
    (*V.* Ribb. i. 11).—*Wherein the copsewood is sown by natural
    process, not planted.*   "A definition, more than 2000 years old,
    of the strange spell which lifts verse into poetry, which it would
    be difficult to improve."   F. T. Palgrave, *Gold. Treasury*, Pref.,
    2nd series, 1897.

1077. Ingenio facies conciliante placet.   Ov. Med. Fac. 44.—*The face
    pleases, if the disposition charms.*

1078. Ingenium eum in numerato habere.   Quint. 6, 3, 111.—Of a
    certain advocate who had the gift of clever *extempore* speaking,
    Augustus said that "*he kept his wit in ready money.*"   The
    French have transl. the words into a prov., *Avoir de l'esprit
    argent comptant.*

1079. Ingenium mala sæpe movent.   Ov. A. A. 2, 43.—*Misfortune
    often quickens genius.*

> Cf. Sed convivatoris, uti ducis, ingenium res
>   Adversæ nudare solent, celare secundæ.   Hor. S. 2, 8, 73.
>
> Good fortune hides, adversity brings forth
> A host's resources, and a general's worth.—*Francis.*

1080. Ingenium par materiæ. Juv. 1, 151.—*Talents equal to the subject.*

1081. Ingentes animos angusto in corpore versant. Virg. G. 4, 83.— *A mighty spirit fills that little frame.* True of Alexander, Napoleon I., and Nelson, all men of short stature.

1082. Ingenuas didicisse fideliter artes
Emollit mores, nec sinit esse feros. Ov. Ep. 2, 9, 47.—*A careful study of the liberal arts refines the manners, and prevents their becoming rude.*

1083. Ingenui vultus puer, ingenuique pudoris. Juv. 11, 154.—*A boy as frank and shy as nature can produce.*

1084. Inglese Italianizato, Diavolo incarnato. Prov.—*An Italianised Englishman is a devil incarnate.*

1085. Ingrata· Patria: Nè· Ossa· Quidem· Mea· Habes. Val. Max. 5, 3, 2. —*Ungrateful country,thou canst not boast even my bones.* Inscription ordered to be placed on his tomb by Scipio Africanus (236-183 B.C.), at Liternum in Campania, in revenge for the unworthy partisan persecution which embittered his last days.

1086. Ingratus.—*Ungrateful.* Sayings respecting ingratitude:

(1.) Dixeris maledicta cuncta, quum ingratum hominem dixeris. Syr. 126.—*If you say a man is ungrateful, you can call him no worse name.* (2.) Ingratus est qui remotis arbitris agit gratias. Sen. Ben. 2, 23.—*He is an ungrateful man who returns thanks in secret.* (3.) Nil homine terra pejus ingrato creat. Auson. Epigr. 140, 1.—*The earth does not produce a worse thing than an ungrateful man.* (4.) Ingratus unus omnibus miseris nocet. Syr. 243.—*One ungrateful man does an injury to all poor people.*

1087. In hoc signo vinces, *or* Τούτῳ νίκα. Euseb. vit. Constantin. 1, 28. —*In this sign,* i.e., of the Cross, *thou shalt conquer.*

The words were assumed as motto by the Emperor Constantine the Great, and attached to the Imperial Standard (*Labarum*), in memorial of the luminous Cross which appeared to him in the heavens on the eve of his defeat of Maxentius and victorious entry into Rome, 312 A.D.

1088. Inhumana crudelitas, perfidia plus quam Punica, nihil veri, nihil sancti, nullus deorum metus, nullum jusjurandum, nulla religio. Liv. 21, 4.

Character of Hannibal.

An inhuman cruelty and a more than Punic perfidy stained his reputation, leaving him without regard either for truth or honour, and without any respect for the gods, for the sanctity of an oath, or for plighted faith.

1089. Inimici famam, non ita ut nata est, ferunt. Plaut. Pers. 3, 1, 23. —*Enemies circulate stories in another form than that they had originally.*

1090. Iniquissima hæc bellorum conditio est: prospera omnes sibi vindicant, adversa uni imputantur. Tac. Agr. 27.—*The most unjust circumstance in war is this, that while all take the credit for any success achieved, they throw all the blame for reverses upon one pair of shoulders.*

1091. Initia magistratuum nostrorum meliora ferme, et finis inclinat. Tac. A. 15, 21.—*Office, as a rule, is well enough discharged at the outset: it is towards the end that it declines in vigour.* New brooms sweep clean.

1092. Initium est salutis, notitia peccati. Sen. Ep. 28, 7.—*The first step towards recovery, is the knowledge of the sin committed.*

1093. Injuriæ qui addideris contumeliam. Phædr. 5, 3, 5.— *Who hast added insult to injury.*

1094. Injuriarum remedium est oblivio. Syr. 250.—*Oblivion is the best remedy for insults.*

1095. In meinem Staate kann jeder nach seiner Façon selig werden. Frederick II. ap. Büchm. p. 518.—*In my kingdom every one can go to heaven after his own fashion.*

> Only a month after his accession, June 22, 1740, Frederick penned a memorandum on the education of the children of his Catholic soldiers. The king was all in favour of toleration and religious liberty, his Note declaring that "hier mus ein jeder nach seiner Fasson selich werden," which Büchmann puts into the pop. form given above. He cites Busching's *Charakter Friedrichs II.* as authority, but without further particulars, and adds an apposite parallel in Fr. history from the mouth of Henry IV.:—"Plut à Dieu . . . que vous fussiez si prudent que de laisser à chacun gagner Paradis comme il l'entend."

1096. In nocte consilium, Chil. p. 199 ; *or,* La nuit porte conseil, Quit. p. 253. Prov.—*The night brings counsel.* Sleep upon it. Cf. Menand. *Monost.* 150, ἐν νυκτὶ βουλή τοῖς σοφοῖσι γίνεται.— *Counsel cometh to the wise in the night.*

1097. Innocui vivite, numen adest. Ov. A. A. 1, 640.—*Lead innocent lives, for God is here.*

> Inscribed over his Lecture Room by Linnæus. (*V. D. H.* Stoever's "Life of Linnæus," tr. by J. Trapp, Lond., 1794, p. 269.)

1098. Innumerabilibus Constantinŏpolītani
Conturbabantur sollicitudinibus.
Joannes Buchlerus, *Sacr. Profanumque Phrasium Poet. Thesaurus*, 18th ed., London (Thos. Newcomb), 1679, pp. 352-3.—*The people of Constantinople were perturbed by innumerable anxieties.* Specimen of *versus macroculus* or *tardigradus*, a line composed of the longest possible words, like the *honorificabilitudinitatibus* of Costard in "Love's Labour Lost,"5,1.

1099. In omnibus requiem quæsivi sed non inveni, nisi in angellis et libellis. Thos. à Kempis, de Imit., Præf. vi.—*I have sought rest everywhere, and found it not, save in little nooks and little books.* A saying frequent on à Kempis' lips in praise of the retirement of the monastic cell.

1100. Inopem me copia fecit. Ov. M. 3, 466.—*Plenty has made me poor.* Said by Narcissus, in love with his own reflection. Excessive wealth often leaves its owner as perplexed as excessive poverty; and copiousness of ideas often embarrasses a due flow of language.

1101. Inopiæ desunt multa, avaritiæ omnia   Syr. 236.—*Poverty is in need of much, avarice of everything.*

1102. In pace leones, in prælio cervi. Tert. Coron. Mil. 1.—*Lions in time of peace, deer in time of war.* A courageous person. Cf. In prætoriis leones, in castris lepores. Sid. Ep. 5, 7.—*Lions in barracks, hares in the field:* Domi leones, foras vulpes. Petr. 44, 4.—*Lions at home, foxes abroad.*

1103. In pretio pretium nunc est; dat census honores
    Census amicitias: pauper ubique jacet.   Ov. F. 1, 217.

> Worth nowadays means wealth; friends, place, power—all
> Money can buy: the poor goes to the wall.—*Ed.*

1104. In principatu commutando sæpius
    Nil præter domini nomen mutant pauperes. Phædr. 1, 15.—*In a change of rulers (government) the poor often change nothing but their master's name.*

1105. In quella parte
    Di mia età, dove ciascun dovrebbe
    Calar le vele e raccoglier le sarte.   Dante, Inf. 27, 79.

> At that part of my life when it behoves
> Each one to lower sail, and haul in sheet.—*Ed.*

1106. Insanire putas sollennia me, neque rides. Hor. Ep. 1, 1, 101.—*You think me bitten with the prevailing madness, and you do not laugh.*

1107. Insani sapiens nomen ferat, æquus iniqui,
    Ultra quod satis est virtutem si petat ipsam. Hor. Ep. 1, 6, 15.—*Let the wise be called fool, and the just unjust, if his pursuit even of Virtue herself be carried beyond the bounds of prudence.*

1108. In se magna ruunt: lætis hunc numina rebus
    Crescendi posuere modum; nec gentibus ultra
    Commodat in populum terræ pelagique potentem
    Invidiam Fortuna suam.   Lucan. 1, 81.

> *The Second Civil War.*
> Greatness brings its own fall. The very fates
> Impose this limit on too prosperous states.
> 'Twas Fortune's envy overthrew the lords
> Of land and sea, sans aid of barb'rous hordes.—*Ed.*

1109. In silvam non ligna feras insanius. Hor. S. 1, 10, 34.—*It would be as silly as to carry sticks into the wood.*

> A saying equivalent to ours of "carrying coals to Newcastle," or any other superfluous labour. The Greeks have a proverb to the same effect, Γλαῦκ' Ἀθήναζε, Ar. Av. 301 (or γλαῦκ' εἰς Ἀθήνας, ap. Cic. Fam. 9, 3, 2), *Owls to Athens,* the owl being Athene's bird; so too ἰχθῦς εἰς Ἑλλήσποντον, *Fish to the Hellespont.*

1110. In solo vivendi causa palato est.   Juv. 11, 11.—*Their palate is the sole object of their existence.*

> Men whose sole bliss is eating, who can give
> But that one brutal reason why they live.

1111. Insperata accidunt magis sæpe quam quæ speres.   Plaut. Most. 1, 3, 40.—*The unexpected happens more frequently than that which one hopes for.*

1112. In stomacho . . . ridere.   Cic. Fam. 2, 16, 7.—*To laugh in one's sleeve.*

1113. Integer vitæ scelerisque purus
Non eget Mauri jaculis neque arcu.   Hor. C. 1, 22, 1.

> Pure lives and upright have no need
> For Moorish arms of lance or bow.—*Ed.*

1114. In tenui labor, at tenuis non gloria.   Virg. G. 4, 6.

> Slight is the subject, but the praise not small.—*Dryden.*

1115. In te omnis domus inclinata recumbit.   Virg. A. 12, 59.—*On thee repose all the hopes of your family.*   Speech of Amata to her son Turnus, dissuading him from engaging in single combat with Æneas.

> Since on the safety of thy life alone
> Depends Latinus, and the Latian throne.—*Dryden.*

1116. Inter cetera mala, hoc quoque habet stultitia proprium, semper incipit vivere.   Sen. Ep. 13, 15.—*Among other evils, folly has this special peculiarity, it is always beginning to live.*

1117. Interdum lacrymæ pondera vocis habent.   Ov. Ep. 3, 1, 158.— *Tears have sometimes the force of words.*

1118. Interdum vulgus rectum videt; est ubi peccat.   Hor. Ep. 2, 1, 63.

> Sometimes the crowd a proper judgment makes,
> But oft they labour under great mistakes.—*Francis.*

1119. Interea dulces pendent circum oscula nati;
Casta pudicitiam servat domus.   Virg. G. 2, 523.

> His little children, climbing for a kiss,
> Welcome their father's late return at night;
> His faithful bed is crown'd with chaste delight.—*Dryden.*

1120. Interea gustus elementa per omnia quærunt,
Nunquam animo pretiis obstantibus; interius si
Attendas, magis illa juvant, quæ pluris emuntur.   Juv. 11, 14.

> *The Gourmet.*
> Heaven and the earth are ransacked
> For the most expensive dainties;
> In his heart he likes the dish best
> Which has cost the most.—*Shaw.*

> Cf. Dii boni! quantum hominum unus venter exercet! Sen. Ep. 95, 24. —*Good God! to think of the army of people that a single stomach will keep to do its bidding!*

1121. Inter eos rursum si reventum in gratiam est,
Bis tanto amici sunt inter se, quam prius.   Plaut. Am. 3, 2, 61.
—*If they yet reconciled to each other again, they become twice the
friends they were before.*

1122. Interest reipublicæ ut sit finis litium.   Law Max.—*It is for the
interest of the State that there be an end to litigation.*   The public
good is concerned in fixing a limit to lawsuits, which in some
cases might be almost indefinitely prolonged.

1123. Inter nos sanctissima divitiarum
Majestas.   Juv. 1, 112.—*Riches, among ourselves, the reverence
get that's due to God.*

> Cf. Dea Moneta, *the goddess Money.* The "Almighty Dollar," as Wash-
> ington Irving was the first to call it (*see* his "*Creole Village*").   Moneta or
> Mnemosyne (*Remembrance*), the mother of the Muses, was also a title of
> Juno, and from the circumstance of her temple in Rome being used for
> coining public money, comes the use of the words, *moneta,* money, and
> mint.   A curious derivation.

1124. Inter os et offam.   Cato ap. Gell. 13, 17, 1.—*Between mouth and
morsel,* much may happen.

> The English equivalent, "There's many a slip between cup and lip," is
> the translation of the Greek, Πολλὰ μεταξὺ πέλει (H. Stephanus reads πέτει)
> κύλικος, καὶ χείλεος ἄκρου. Anth. Pal. 10, 32, and the Latin, *Multa cadunt
> inter calicem supremaque labra.*   The saying is traced to Ancæus, mythic
> king of Arcadia, and son of Neptune, who was warned that he would never
> taste of the vines that he planted.   The grapes ripened, the wine was made,
> and Ancæus was lifting the cup to his lips when he was told that a boar was
> ravaging the vineyard.   He ran out, and met his death.   Dict. of Class.
> Biography, *s.v.* ANCÆUS.   An old French prov. (Quit. p. 167) expresses the
> same truth in, "Entre bouche et cuillier avient souvent grant encombrier."

1125. Inter spem curamque, timores inter et iras,
Omnem crede diem tibi diluxisse supremum;
Grata superveniet quæ non sperabitur hora.   Hor. Ep. 1, 4, 12.

> Let hopes and sorrows, fears and angers be,
> And think each day that dawns the last you'll see:
> For so the hour that greets you unforeseen
> Will bring with it enjoyment twice as keen.—*Conington.*

1126. Intolerabilius nihil est quam fœmina dives.   Juv. 6, 460.—*Nothing
so intolerable as a rich woman.*

1127. In vetere [testamento] novum late(a)t, et in novo vetus pate(a)t.
St Aug. Quæst. in Exod. lib. 2, quæst. 78 (vol. 3, Pt. I. 333 C).
—*In the Old Testament the New lies hid: in the New Testament
the Old is revealed.*

1128. Invidus, iracundus, iners, vinosus, amator;
Nemo adeo ferus est, ut non mitescere possit,
Si modo culturæ patientem commodet aurem.   Hor. Ep. 1, 1, 38.

> Run through the list of faults: whate'er you be,
> Coward, pickthank, spitfire, drunkard, debauchee—
> Submit to culture patiently, you'll find
> Her charms can humanise the rudest mind.—*Conington.*

1129. In vino veritas.   Prov.—*Wine tells truth.*

Cf. the following:—Vulgoque veritas jam attributa vino est. Plin. 14, 28.
—"*Truth in wine*" *is an old proverb.* Ἀνδρὸς δ᾽οἶνος ἔδειξε νόον. Theognis,
500.— *Wine reveals man's thoughts.* Κάτοπτρον εἴδους χαλκός ἐστ᾽, οἶνος δὲ
νοῦ. Aesch. Fr. 274.—*Brass is the mirror of the form, wine of the heart:*
and ἐν οἴνῳ ἀλήθεια. Apost. Cent. vii. 37.—*In wine lies truth.*   Theocritus
(Id. 29, 1) says amusingly,

> οἶνος, ὦ φίλε παῖ, λέγεται καὶ ἀλάθεα·
> κἄμμε χρὴ μεθύοντας ἀλαθέας ἔμμεναι.

If wine be truth, dear child, then I and you,
Being both intoxicated, must be "true."—*Ed.*

1130. Invisa nunquam imperia retinentur diu.   Sen. Phœn. 660.—
Hated governments never last long.

1131. Invisurum aliquam facilius quam imitaturum.   Plin. 35, 36.—
A man will sooner find fault with anything than imitate it.   Tr.
of μωμήσεταί τις μᾶλλον ἢ μιμήσεται ("sooner *carp* than *copy*"),
Bergk, ii. p. 318; said to have been written by Zeuxis under-
neath one of his best pictures.

1132. Invitat culpam qui peccatum præterit.   Syr. 238.—*He allures to
sin who condones a transgression.*

1133. In vitium ducit culpæ fuga.   Hor. A. P. 31.—*Avoiding one fault
leads to another.*

1134. I pensieri stretti, ed il volto sciolto.   Prov.—"*Thoughts close, and
looks loose.*" Johnson tr. (*Life of Milton*).   Concealing one's
thoughts under an amiable exterior; the "precept of prudence," given to Milton on embarking on his travels in 1638.

1135. Ipsa quidem virtus pretium sibi, solaque late
Fortunæ secura nitet, nec fastibus ullis
Erigitur, plausuve petit clarescere vulgi.   Claud. Cons. Mall. 1, 1.

Virtue, her own reward.

Virtue's her own reward.   Her star shines bright,
And her's alone, in Fortune's own despite:
Pomp cannot dazzle her, nor is her aim
To make the plaudits of the mob her fame.—*Ed.*

1136. Ipsa quoque assiduo labuntur tempora motu,
Non secus ac flumen.   Neque enim consistere flumen,
Nec levis hora potest: sed ut unda impellitur unda,
Urgeturque prior veniente, urgetque priorem ;
Tempora sic fugiunt pariter, pariterque sequuntur:
Et nova sunt semper: nam quod fuit ante relictum est,
Fitque quod haud fuerat, momentaque cuncta novantur.
                                               Ov. M. 15, 179.

Time compared to a River.

Time glides along with constant motion
Just like a river to the ocean.
For neither may the waters stay,
Nor the wing'd hour its flight delay.
But wave by wave is urged along,
Down hurrying in tumultuous throng;
This one by that behind it sped,
Itself impelling those ahead—
So time pursues and is pursued,
And every instant is renewed.
What was the future is the past,
And hours unborn are born at last:
And as they're distanced in the race,
Others succeed to take their place.—*Ed.*

1137. Ipsa scientia potestas est. Bacon, De Hæresibus, x. 329.—
Knowledge itself is power. Cf. id. Nov. Org. Aphor. 3 (vol. viii. 1),
Scientia et potentia in idem coincidunt; and Vulg. Prov. 24, 5,
Vir sapiens fortis est, et vir doctus robustus et validus.

1138. Ipse dixit (or Αὐτὸς ἔφα).—*He said so himself.* Assertion without proof.

Diog. Laert. (8, 46) traces the expression as a prov. to Pythagoras of
Zante, from whom the αὐτὸς ἔφα ("The master said so") passed into
a common saying. So Cicero (N.D., 1, 5, 10) says of the Pythagoreans,
that when asked the reason of their doctrines, they used to reply, "*Ipse
dixit : ipse* autem erat Pythagoras."

1139. Ipse docet quid agam : fas est et ab hoste doceri. Ov. M. 4, 428.

He shows the way himself; 'tis right, you know,
To learn a lesson even from a foe.—*Ed.*

We should not be above taking a leaf even from an enemy's book.

1140. Ipse pavet; nec qua commissas flectat habenas,
Nec scit qua sit iter, nec, si sciat, imperet illis. Ov. M. 2, 169.

A Runaway Team.

Scared, he forgets which rein, which way the course is;
Nor, if he knew, could he control his horses.—*Ed.*

1141. Ira furor brevis est : animum rege, qui, nisi paret,
Imperat : hunc frenis, hunc tu compesce catena.
Hor. Ep. 1, 2, 62.

Anger's a short-lived madness: curb and bit
Your mind : 'twill rule you if you rule not it.—*Conington.*

1142. Irarum tantos volvis sub pectore fluctus ? Virg. A. 12, 831.—
Stir you such waves of wrath beneath that breast? Jove to Juno,
desiring to appease her rage over the successes of the Trojans in
Italy.

1143. Ire domum atque Pelliculam curare jube. Hor. S. 2, 5, 37.

Bid him go home and nurse himself.—*Conington.*

K

1144. Ire tamen restat, Numa quo devenit et Ancus.   Hor. Ep. 1, 6, 27.
> At length the summons comes, and you must go
> To Numa and to Ancus down below.—*Conington.*

Motto of *Spectator* (329) on Sir Roger's visit to the Abbey.

1145. Irritabis   crabrones.   Plaut. Am. 2, 2, 75.—*You   will   bring   a hornet's nest about your ears.*

1146. Is minimo eget mortalis qui minimum cupit.   Incert., in Ribb. ii. 147.   Qu. by Sen. Ep. 108, 11.—*That man wants least who least desires.*

1147. Is ordo vitio vacato, cæteris specimen esto.   Cic. Leg. 3, 3, 10.— *Let that order* (senators) *be free from vice, and an example to the rest.*   Precept contained in the Twelve Tables.

1148. Ista decens facies longis vitiabitur annis,
> Rugaque in antiqua fronte senilis erit.
> Injicietque manum formæ damnosa senectus,
> Quæ strepitum passu non faciente venit.   Ov. T. 3, 7, 33.

> *Tu vieilliras, ma belle!*
> That comely face will fade as years expand,
>   And wrinkles on thy brow their witness trace;
> Age on thy beauty lay his ruthless hand,
>   As, step by step, he comes with noiseless pace.—*Ed.*

1149. Istæc in me cudetur faba.   Ter. Eun. 2, 3, 89.—*I shall have to smart for it;* lit., "that bean will be pounded on me."

1150. Istam
> Oro (si quis adhuc precibus locus), exue mentem.   Virg. A. 4, 318.

> I pray (if prayer can touch you), change your will.—*Conington.*

1151. Istuc est sapere, non quod ante pedes modo 'st
> Videre, sed etiam illa quæ futura sunt
> Prospicere.   Ter. Ad. 3, 3, 32.—*That is to be wise, not merely to see what is under your nose, but to forecast those things which are to come.*

1152. Ita amicum habeas, posse ut facile fieri hunc inimicum putes.
> Syr. 245.—*Consider a friend in the light of one who may easily become a foe.*

> Cp. Cic. (Am. 16, 59): Ita amare oportere, ut si aliquando esset osurus.
> —*One ought so to love as to be prepared for love changing to hate*—derived
> from the φιλεῖν ὡς μισήσοντας of Bias (Diog. Laert. 1, 87); and Soph. Aj. 679,

> ὅ τ' ἐχθρὸς ἡμῖν ἐς τοσόνδ' ἐχθαρτέος,
> ὡς καὶ φιλήσων αὖθις, ἔς τε τὸν φίλον
> τοσαῦθ' ὑπουργῶν ὠφελεῖν βουλήσομαι
> ὡς αἰὲν οὐ μενοῦντα.

> Who is my foe, I must but hate as one
> Whom I may yet call friend; and him who loves me
> Will I but serve and cherish as a man
> Whose love is not abiding.—*Calverley.*

> Cf. also, Hac fini ames, tanquam forte fortuna osurus. Gell. 1, 3, 30;
> and Chil., p. 41, Ama tanquam osurus.

1153. Italia, Italia! o tu cui feo la sorte
Dono infelice di bellezza, ond' hai
Funesta dote d'infiniti guai
Che in fronte scritti per gran doglia porte:
Deh fossi tu men bella o almen piu forte,
Onde assai più ti paventasse, o assai
T'amasse men, chi dal tuo bello a' rai
Par che si strugga, e pur ti sfida a morte.

Vinc. Filicaja, *Sonnet* 87.

All' Italia.

Italia! oh Italia! thou who hast
The fatal gift of beauty, which became
A funeral dower of present woes and past,
On thy sweet brow is sorrow ploughed by shame,
And annals graved in characters of flame.
O God! that thou wert in thy nakedness
Less lovely or more powerful, and couldst claim
Thy right, and awe the robbers back who press
To shed thy blood, and drink the tears of thy distress.

Byron, "Ch. Harold," 4, 42.

1154. Ita vita 'st hominum, quasi quum ludas tesseris;
Si illud quod maxime opus est jactu non cadit,
Illud, quod cecidit forte, id arte ut corrigas.   Ter. Ad. 4, 7, 21.

The life of man is but a game of dice:
And, if the throw you most want does not fall,
You must then use your skill to make the best
Of whatsoever has by chance turned up.—*Ed.*

J.

1155. Ja, Bauer! das ist ganz was Anders! Karl W. Ramler, *Fabellese,*
Berlin (1783-90), 1, 45, Der Junker u. der Bauer.—*Ah ! yokel,
that is quite another thing !* Quite another pair of shoes.

1155A. J'ai failli attendre. —*I was all but kept waiting.* Told of Louis
XIV. upon some trifling unpunctuality being shown him, and
rejected by Fournier (*L.D.L.,* 310-11) as contrary to the King's
habitual and well-known patience.   On the other hand,
Alexandre cites the opposite testimony of the Duchesse
(Elizabeth Charlotte) of Orleans, " Il ne pouvait souffrir que l'on
se fît attendre" (Mémoires, Fragments, etc., Paris, 1832, p. 38).

1156. J'aime à revoir ma Normandie,
C'est le pays qui m'a donné le jour.   Fred. Bérat (music and
words), 1835.—*I love to revisit my own Normandy, the land that.
gave me birth.*

1157. J'aime mieux un vice commode qu'une fatigante vertu.   Mol`.
Amph. 1, 4.—*I prefer an easy vice to a tiresome virtue.*

1158. J'ai ri, me voilà désarmé! A. Piron, La Métromanie, 3, 7 (Œuvres,
1855, p. 128).—*I have laughed, and so have disarmed myself.*

While Damis is being lectured by his uncle, Baliveau, for his absurd notion of making poetry his profession, the former lets fall some humorous repartee, which makes his uncle laugh, and brings the argument to an end.

1159. J'ai vécu.—*I lived.*

Famous *mot* of Sieyès when asked what "he did" during the "Terror" of the Revolution. "Ce que j'ai fait? lui répondit M. Sieyès, j'ai vécu." Il avait en effet résolu le problème pour lui le plus difficile de ce temps, celui de ne pas périr (Mignet, *Notice historique sur la vie, etc.*, de M. de Sieyès, in "Institut de France," Pièces diverses, vol. for 1836, p. 70). It appears that, as in the case of "La mort sans phrase," more has been made of Sieyès' words than he intended. "Il s'indignait qu'on attribuât a ce mot *j'ai vécu*, qu'il avait dit pour résumer sa conduite sous la Terreur, un sens d'égoisme et d'insensibilité qu'il n'y avait pas mis." Sainte Beuve, Causeries du Lundi, 3rd ed., vol. 5, p. 215. More appropriate to that awful time would be the passage in Victor Hugo's *Marion Delorme*, 4, 8, "*Le Roi.*—Pourquoi vis-tu? *L'Angély.*—Je vis par curiosité."

1160. Jamais on ne vaincra les Romains que dans Rome. Rac. Mithridate, 3, 1 (Mithridates loq.).—*Never will the Romans be conquered but in Rome.*

1161. Jam color unus inest rebus, tenebrisque teguntur
Omnia: jam vigiles conticuere canes.　　Ov. F. 4, 489.

Midnight.

Nature is now one hue ; a veil of dark
Shrouds all : the watchdogs e'en have ceased to bark.—*Ed.*

1162. Jam dudum animus est in patinis. Ter. Eun. 4, 7, 46.—*My belly has long been crying cupboard.*

1163. Jam non ad culmina rerum
Injustos crevisse queror: tolluntur in altum
Ut lapsu graviore ruant.　　Claud. Ruf. 1, 21.

Prosperity of the Wicked.

I grieve no longer that ungodly men
Are rais'd to Fortune's highest pinnacle:
They're lifted high, on purpose, that they may
Be hurled with crash more awful to the ground.—*Ed.*

1164. Jam pauca aratro jugera regiæ
Moles relinquent.　　Hor. C. 2, 15, 1.

Few roods of ground the princely piles we raise
Will leave to plough.—*Conington.*

Said of the tracts of land withdrawn from cultivation to form demesnes around the mansions of the rich. "It is a melancholy thing to stand alone in one's county," said Lord Leicester, when complimented on the completion of Holkham: "I look around, and not a house is to be seen but mine. I am the giant of Giant Castle, and have ate up all my neighbours." Dr H. Julian Hunter's "Inquiry into Dwellings of Rural Labourers," n.d. (?1870), p. 135 n.

1165. Jamque faces et saxa volant: furor arma ministrat.

Virg. A. 1, 15).

And brands and stones already fly,
For rage has always weapons nigh.—*Conington.*

1166. Jamque opus exegi quod nec Jovis ira, nec ignes,
Nec poterit ferrum, nec edax abolere vetustas. Ov. M. 15, 871.

Completion of the Metamorphoses.

I've finished now a work that not Jove's rage
Nor fire nor sword can kill, nor cank'ring age.—*Ed.*

1167. Jamque quiescebant voces hominumque canumque;
Lunaque nocturnos alta regebat equos. Ov. T. 1, 3, 27.

Midnight.

Now men and dogs were silent; in the height
The Moon drove on the horses of the night.—*Ed.*

1168. Jam redit et Virgo, redeunt Saturnia regna. Virg. E. 4, 6.

Return of the Golden Age.

The Virgin now returns, and Saturn's blissful reign.—*Ed.*

1169. Jam seges est ubi Troja fuit, resecandaque falce
Luxuriat Phrygio sanguine pinguis humus. Ov. H. 1, 53.

The Site of Troy.

The scythe now reaps the corn where Ilion stood,
And fields that fatten on the Trojans' blood.—*Ed.*

1170. J'appelle un chat un chat, et Rolet un fripon. Boil. Sat. 1, 52.
—*I call a cat a cat, and Rolet a rogue.* "Call a spade a spade."

Charles Rolet was a Proctor (Procureur) of the Paris Parliament (temp. Louis XIV.) of so unenviable a reputation that De Lamoignon, the President, was in the habit of saying, "He's a regular Rolet," in speaking of any notorious cheat; and in 1681 the man was heavily fined and banished for nine years. He was commonly known as *L'Ame damnée*, and is the *Volichon* of Furetière's romance. In the 2nd ed. of the *Satires* (ed. de La Haye, 1722, vol. 1, p. 19), Boileau, in order to protect himself against the attorney, appended a footnote to the name, "C'est un hôtelier du pays Blaisois"; but this made matters no better, since there happened to be an innkeeper in the neighbourhood of Blois of the same name, who threatened the poet with legal proceedings. The whole passage is—

Je suis rustique et fier, et j'ai l'âme grossière,
Je ne puis rien nommer, si ce n'est par son nom,
J'appelle un chat un chat, et Rolet un fripon.

[*See* Alex. p. 88; Quit. pp. 212-13.]

1171. J'avois un jour un vallet de Gascongne,
Gourmand, yvrogne et asseuré menteur,
Pipeur, larron, jureur, blasphémateur,
Sentant la hart de cent pas à la ronde;
Au demourant, le meilleur filz du monde. Clément Marot, 1531.

Au Roy pour avoir esté dérobé.

I'd a varlet of Gascony once on a time;
A glutton, a drunkard, an impudent liar,
Cheat, thief, and blasphemer, a cursing spitfire,
Who smelt of the halter at a hundred yards—
But the best chap alive in all other regards.—*Ed.*

₊ *Le meilleur fils* (or *le meilleur enfant*) *du monde* has passed into a prov., "qui se place comme un *Gloria Patri* à la suite des critiques qu'on fait de quelqu'un." Quit. pp. 397-8.

1172. J'ay vescu sans nul pensement,
      Me laissant aller doucement
      A la douce loy naturelle;
      Et ne fcaurois dire pourquoy
      La Mort daigna penser à moy
      Qui n'ay daigné penser en elle.— M. Régnier.

His own Epitaph.

Careless I lived, and easily
    (As nature bade) indulged each whim;
I wonder, then, Death thought of me
    Who never thought of him.—*Ed.*

Is it possible that Regnier could have got the idea of his Epitaph from the "ancients"? He was hardly the man to dabble in inscriptions: yet here is the precise sentiment, expressed in hardly more words than he has lines, in the brief sepulchral record of Sextius Perpenna, composed some fifteen hundred years before (Grüter, page 920, 9);—VIXI · QVEMADMODVM · VOLVI · QVARE · MORTVVS · SIM · NESCIO (*I lived as I liked, and why I am dead I don't know*). Regnier lived a more than "easy" life, being at thirty already an old man, and dying quite worn out ten years later in 1613. Boileau, however, recognised his poetical gifts, saying of him, "Dans son vieux style encore il y a des grâces nouvelles;" as, *e.g.*, in his satire of *Les Grands Seigneurs.*

The above version of the Epitaph comes from E. Courbet's edition of Regnier's Works (Paris, 1875), where in Note, p. 275, will be found a variant of the last three lines, viz.—

Et si m'estonne fort pourquoy,
La mort oza songer en moy
Qui ne songeay iamais en elle.

1173. Jean s'en alla comme il était venu,
      Mangeant le fonds avec le revenu.

                La Font. *Œuvres*, Paris, 1892 (ix. p. 81).

Épitaphe d'un Paresseux.

John went home as he had come,
Spending capital and income.—*Ed.*

1174. J'écarte ce qui me gêne. Mme. de Rémusat, Mémoires, etc., Paris, 1880, vol i. p. 389.—*I push aside everything that stands in my way.* Bonaparte's characteristically frank account of his assassination of the Duc D'Enghien.

1175. Je dirais volontiers des métaphysiciens ce que Scaliger disait des Basques: "on dit qu'ils s'entendent; mais je n'en crois rien." Chamf. Max. et Pensées, cap. vii. (vol. 2, p. 84).—*I am quite prepared to say of metaphysicians what Scaliger used to say of the Basques: "People declare that they understand one another, but I don't believe a word of it."* This accords with a remark (made by I forget whom) to the effect that when one man is attempting to explain a point which he does not himself understand, to another who does not comprehend what he is saying, *that* is "metaphysics."

1176. Jejunus raro stomachus vulgaria temnit.   Hor. S. 2, 2, 38.—
A hungry stomach does not often despise coarse food.

1177. Je maintiendray.   Motto of William III.—*I will maintain them.*
"The ellipsis in his ancestral device, *Je maintiendray*, is
supplied by the words, 'the liberties of England and the Protestant religion.'"   F. A. Clarke, "Life of Bp. Ken," 1896, p. 121.

1178. J'embrasse mon rival, mais c'est pour l'étouffer.   Raç. Brit. 4, 3.
—*I embrace my rival, but it is in order to choke him.*   Nero to
Burrus, on his pretended reconciliation with Britannicus.

> Montaigne (*Essays*, Bk. i. ch. 38) says, "La pluspart des plaisirs, disent-
> ils (les sages), nous chatouillent et *embrassent pour nous estrangler;* comme
> faisaient les larrons que les Ægyptiens appeloient Philistas"; evidently
> quoting Sen. Ep. 51, 13, Voluptates . . . latronum more, quos *philetas*
> Ægyptii vocant, in hoc nos amplectuntur ut strangulent.—*Pleasures, like
> the robbers the Egyptians call "Kissers," embrace their victim only to strangle
> him.*

1179. Je m'en vais chercher un grand peut-être.   Rabelais.—*I am off
in search of a great May-be.*

> Rabelais, on his deathbed in Paris, on the Cardinal du Bellay (others
> say the Card. de Châtillon) sending a page to inquire of his state, is
> reported to have answered, " Dis à Monseigneur l'état où tu me vois. Je
> m'en vais chercher un grand peut-être. Il est au nid de la pie! dis-lui
> qu'il s'y tienne ; et pour toi tu ne seras jamais qu'un fou. Tire le rideau,
> la farce est jouée" (*Biographie* Michaud).—*Tell my lord the state in which
> you find me. I am off in search of a great may-be. He is at the top of the
> tree: tell him to keep there. As for you, you'll never be aught but a fool.
> Let the curtain fall, the farce is played out.* Sometimes qu. as, *Je vais
> querir un grand*, etc., as in *Œuvres de Rabelais*, ed. Dupont, Paris, 1865,
> 8vo, vol. i. p. xvii. He is also credited with adding, on the same occasion,
> *Beati qui in Domino moriuntur*, as he drew his domino over his head and
> expired in a fit of laughter. *See* Lombroso's *Man of Genius*, p. 31, Eng.
> transl. An echo of Rabelais is heard more than a cent. later in the tradi-
> tional "last words" of Thomas Hobbes (Dec. 4, 1679)—"I am going to
> take a great leap into obscurity;" allusion to which occurs in Vanbrugh's
> *Provoked Wife* (5, 6), where Heartfree says: "Now, I am in for Hobbes'
> Voyage—a great leap in the dark." On Dec. 31, 1889, the last words of
> W. T. H., executed within Maidstone Gaol, were, "Now for the great
> secret ! "

1180. Je me presse de rire de tout, de peur d'être obligé d'en pleurer.
Beaum., Barb. de Séville, 1, 2 (Figaro).—*I make haste to laugh
at everything for fear of being obliged to weep over it.*

1181. Je mourrai seul.   Pascal, Pens. 2, 7, 1 (Panthéon Bibliothèque).—
I shall die alone.

> Why should we faint and fear to live alone,
> Since all alone, so Heaven has willed, we die ?
>   Keble, Christian Year, 24th S. aft. Trinity.

1182. Je n'ai fait celle-ci plus longue que parce que je n'ai pas en le
loisir de la faire plus courte.   Pasc. Lettres Prov. 16.—*My
letter is longer than usual, because I hadn't the time to make it
shorter.*

1183. Je n'ai mérité Ni cet excès d'honneur, ni cette indignité. Raç. Brit. 2, 3 (Junia loq.).—*I have deserved neither this excessive honour, nor this indignity.*

1184. Je n'en vois pas la necessité.—*I don't see the necessity of it.*

> The Abbé Desfontaines, scribbler and libellist (1685-1745), on being brought up before Comte d'Argenson, the Intendant of Paris, for some grave literary indiscretion, pleaded, by way of excuse, "Il faut bien que je vive" (*I must live somehow*). To this Argenson replied, "Je n'en vois pas la necessité." V. *Commentaire historique sur les œuvres de l'auteur de lc Henriade*, in Voltaire's *Œuvres complètes*, Gotha, 1776, vol. 48, p. 99; and his Letter to Albergati Capacelli of Dec. 23, 1760. Quit. 698, points out the origin of the saying in Tertullian, *Idolat.* 5, where, with reference to the Church's condemnation of the trade of idol-making, he meets an identical objection on the part of the Christian artificer in the same way. *Jam illa objici solita vox: non habeo aliquid quo vivam.—Districtius repercuti potest: vivere ergo habes?* "Of course the usual objection is made, 'I have no other means of living':" to which may be somewhat sharply retorted, "Is there any necessity why you should live?"

1185. Je ne voyage sans livres, ny en paix, ny en guerre . . . c'est la meilleure munition que j'aye trouvé a cet humain voyage. Montaigne, Bk. iii. cap. 3.—*I never travel without books, whether in peace or in war: they are the best provender I know of for man's earthly journey.*

1186. J'en passe et des meilleurs. V. Hugo, Hernani (1830), 3, 6.— *I pass over some, including even some of the best.*

> In the scene, Don Ruy Gomez is showing Charles Quint the portraits of his ancestors, some of which he stops to notice and explain, passing over the rest.
>> Voila don Vasquez, dit le Sage.
>> Don Jayme, dit le Fort. Un jour, sur son passage,
>> Il arrêta Zamet et cent Maures tout seul.
>> *J'en passe et des meilleurs.*

> No single line of Hugo has perhaps attained such popularity (in quotation, application, and parody) among the world's *volitantia verba* as this. It has much the force of the phrase, "To name only a few examples," where other and stronger cases in point might be cited, if necessary.

1187. Je pardonne aux autres de ne pas être de mon avis, mais je ne leur pardonne pas de ne pas être du leur. Talleyrand, in Mrs Bishop's *Life of Mrs Augustus Craven*, Lond., 1895, vol. ii. p. 116.—*I freely forgive others for not sharing my opinions, but I cannot forgive them for not being true to their own.*

> "How bitterly these words apply" (Mrs Craven remarks, Feb. 1882) "to the men who are outraging every notion of liberty, whilst having its name written on all the walls of Paris!" The allusion is, of course, to Jules Ferry's "Laws" expelling the Jesuits and certain other religious communities of that year, a mere flea-bite compared with the drastic "Associations" bill of M. Combes in 1902-3.

1188. Je plie, et ne romps pas. La Font. 1, 22 (Chêne et Roseau).— *I bend, but do not break.* Said of one who is obliging, without being weak.

1189. Je prends mon bien où je le trouve.—*I take what is mine wherever I find it.* Defence often offered by those who, under the shelter of a memorable precedent, borrow their ideas from others; being possessed of *beaucoup de mémoire, et peu de jugement*, "a good memory and little wit."

> The orig. saying is Molière's, who employed it to justify himself in transplanting bodily two scenes from the *Pédant Joué* of Cyrano de Bergerac (1654) to his own *Fourberies de Scapin* of seventeen years afterward. Grimarest, in his *Vie de Molière*, Paris, 1705, pp. 13-14, recounting the incident, says that Cyrano had utilised for a scene of his own comedy, ideas and language which he had overheard from Molière (*c.* 1653) at some reunion of the day at Gassendi's; and that, in reproducing the scenes in question in the *Fourberies de Scapin*, Molière was, after all, only appropriating his own property. "Il m'est permis," disoit Molière, "de reprendre mon bien où je le trouve." Büchm. (p. 275) cites *à propos* a parallel from the Digests, Ubi rem meam invenio, ibi vindico. Dig. 6, 1, 9. —*Where I find what is mine, I appropriate it.*

1190. Je suis assez semblable aux girouettes, qui ne se fixent que quand elles sont rouillées. Volt. Lettre à M. d'Albaret, April 10, 1760.—*I am very like the weathercocks, which only cease to work when they are rusty.*

1191. Je t'aime d'autant plus que je t'estime moins. Collé (C), Cocatrix, Tragédie Amphigouristique en un Acte (1731), sc. i. (Théatre de Société, Nouv. Ed. La Haye, 1777, vol. 3, p. 190). Amatrox to Vortex, as they dismount from their asses.—*The less I esteem you, the more I love you.*

1192. J'étais pour Ovide à quinze ans,
Mais je suis pour Horace à trente.

> Le P. Ducerceau, La Valise du Poète, Œuvres (Poésies), Paris, 1828, p. 140.—*I was all for Ovid at fifteen, but I am for Horace at thirty.* Ducerceau was tutor to Prince de Conti (Jean Fr. de Bourbon), by whom he was accidentally shot, July 4, 1730, in the boy's thirteenth year.

1193. Judex damnatur ubi nocens absolvitur. Syr. 257.—*The judge is censured when the guilty are acquitted.*

> . Motto of the *Edinburgh Review*, founded 1802. Sydney Smith, who was one of its original staff, says, "The motto I proposed for the *Review* was *Tenui musam meditamur avena* ('We cultivate literature upon a little oatmeal'). But this was too near the truth to be admitted, and so we took our present grave motto from Publius Syrus, of whom none of us, I am sure, had ever read a single line."—Lady Holland's *Memoir of the Rev. S. Smith*, London, 1855, 8vo, vol. i. p. 23.

1194. Judicio perpende, et, si tibi vera videntur,
Dede manus: aut, si falsum est, accingere contra. Lucr. 2, 1042.

Pros and Cons

Ponder it closely; if you think it true,
Then yield: if false, attack it hardily.—*Ed.*

1195 Judicis officium est, ut res, ita tempora rerum Quærere. Ov. T. 1, 1, 37.—*It is a judge's duty to examine not only the facts, but the circumstances of the case.*

1196. Judicium subtile videndis artibus. Hor. Ep. 2, 1, 242.—*A discriminating taste (or judgment) in understanding the arts.*

1197. Jugez un homme par ses questions, plutôt que par ses réponses. Prov.—*Form your opinion of a man from his questions, rather than from his answers.*

1198. Junius Aprilis Septemque Novemque tricenos,
Unum plus reliqui: Februs tenet octo vicenos;
At si bissextus fuerit, super additur unus.

Harrison's *Descript. of Britaine*,
prefixed to Holinshed's Chron., 1577.

Thirty days hath September,
April, June, and November,
February eight and twenty all alone,
And all the rest have thirty-one.
Unless that Leap-year doth combine
And give to February twenty-nine.
—*The Return from Parnassus*, Lond., 1606.

1199. Jura neget sibi nata, nihil non arroget armis. Hor. A. P. 122.

All laws, all covenants let him still disown,
And test his quarrel by the sword alone.—*Conington.*

1200. Jurgia præcipue vino stimulata caveto:
Aptior est dulci mensa merumque joco. Ov. A. A. 1, 591, 594.

All brawls and quarrels strictly shun,
And chiefly those in wine begun:
For harmless mirth and pleasant jest
Befit the board and bottle best.—*Ed.*

1201. Jus et fas multos faciunt, Ptolemæe, nocentes:
Dat pœnas laudata fides, quum sustinet, inquit,
Quos Fortuna premit. Fatis accede Deisque,
Et cole felices, miseros fuge. Sidera terra
Ut distant, et flamma mari, sic utile recto. Luc. 8, 484.

Justice and law make many criminals.
Men of approved worth ere now have suffered
When Fortune frowned. Then, yield to fate and God!
Honour the lucky, shun th' unfortunate!
Not earth from heav'n more distant, fire to flood
More opposite, than expediency and right.—*Ed.*

1202. Jusqu'où les hommes ne se portent-ils point par l'intérêt de la religion, dont ils sont si peu persuadés, et qu'ils pratiquent si mal? La Bruy. ch. xvi. (Esprit forts), vol. ii. p. 171.—*Men will go any lengths in the cause of religion, although their belief of its truths may be little, and their practice of its precepts less.*

1203. Juste milieu.—*A strict middle-course.*

Reply of Louis Philippe to a deputation from the town of Gaillac, Dept. Tarn, Jan. 29, 1831, after the disturbances of the month previous. "Nous chercherons à nous tenir, dans un *juste milieu*, également éloigné des excès du pouvoir populaire, et des abus du pouvoir royal" (*Moniteur*, Jan. 31, 1831). —*We shall endeavour to observe a strict middle-course, equally removed from the past abuses of the royal power and from the excesses of the power of the people.* Pasc. (*Pens.* 25, 14) employs the phrase (*le juste milieu*) to denote the precise line that separates truth from error.

1204. Justitia . . . erga Deos, religio, erga parentes pietas, creditis in rebus fides . . . nominatur. Cic. Part. Or 22. 78.—*The discharge of our duty towards God, is called Religion; towards our parents, Piety; and in matters of trust, Good Faith.*

1205. Justitia est constans et perpetua voluntas jus suum cuique tribuens. Justin. Inst. 1, 1, 1.—*Justice is the constant and perpetual wish to render to every one his due.* Thus, *suum cuique* = Give every man his due.

1206. Justum et tenacem propositi virum,
Non civium ardor prava jubentium,
Non vultus instantis tyranni
Mente quatit solida. Hor. C. 3, 3, 1.

The Happy Warrior.
The man of firm and righteous will,
No rabble, clamorous for the wrong,
No tyrant's brow, whose frown may kill,
Can shake the strength that makes him strong.—*Conington.*

1207. J'y suis, et j'y reste.—*Here I am, and here I stay.*

Celebrated reply of the French General (afterwards Marshal) MacMahon after his capture of the Malakhoff (Sept. 8, 1855), when the English commander-in-chief sent an A.D.C. asking if M. could maintain his position, and warning him of the undermining of the fort by the enemy—*Dites a votre général*, répondit-il, *que j'y suis et j'y reste!* V. *Figaro* of Oct. 28, 1893, article by Germain Bapst, published a few days after MacMahon's death; and Alex. pp. 436-8. Büchm., p. 498, makes it to have been a pencilled message sent to his own commanding officer.

K.

1208. Καὶ βρέφος διδάσκεται
λέγειν ἀκούειν θ' ὧν μάθησιν οὐκ ἔχει.
ἃ δ' ἂν μάθῃ τις, ταῦτα σώζεσθαι φιλεῖ
πρὸς γῆρας· οὕτω παῖδας εὖ παιδεύετε. Eur. Suppl. 914.

Educate! Educate!
E'en babes are taught
To hear and speak of things they never knew;
And what one learns, one carries to old age:
So, give good education to your boys.—*Ed.*

1209. Καιρὸν γνῶθι.　Diog. Laert. 1, 79.　(Nosce tempus.　Chil. p. 687).
—*Know your opportunity.*　Apophthegm of Pittacus, one of the
Seven Sages.

> Ansonius (Sap. Pittacus, 3) explains it thus:—
>> Sed iste καιρὸς, tempus ut noris, monet;
>> Et esse καιρὸν, tempestivum quod vocant.
>> Romana sic est vox, Venito in tempore.

1210. Καιρὸς πρὸς ἀνθρώπων βραχὺ μέτρον ἔχει.　Pind. Pyth. 4, 508.—
Time and tide wait for no man: lit., "time allows men but
short measure."

1211. Καὶ τόδε Φωκυλίδεω· Λέριοι κακοί· οὐχ᾽ ὁ μεν, ὅς δ᾽ οὔ·
Πάντες, πλὴν Προκλέους· καὶ Προκλέης Λέριος.　　Phocyl. i.

> This of Phocylides: bad are the Lerians, not this or that one:
> All, excepting Procles: and Procles's a Lerian.—*Ed.*

> Rejoinder of Phocylides to Demodocus of Leria on his satire of the
> Miletans. The lines were imitated by Porson in the well-known parody:
>> The Germans in Greek
>> Are sadly to seek;
>> Not five in five score,
>> But ninety-five more:
>> All, save only Hermann,
>> And—Hermann's a German.

1212. Κακοῦ κόρακος κακὸν ὠόν.　Paroem. Gr., ii. p. 466.—*A bad crow
lays a bad egg.*　"Ne'er was good son of evil father born," as
runs the saying, quoted by Euripides, Fr. 342 (*Dictys*, 11).

> φευ φεῦ, παλαιὸς αἶνος ὡς καλῶς ἔχει,
> οὐκ ἂν γένοιτο χρηστὸς ἐκ κακοῦ πατρός.

1213. Καππαδόκην ποτ᾽ ἔχιδνα κακὴ δάκεν· ἀλλὰ καὶ αὐτή
κάτθανε, γευσαμένη αἵματος ἰοβόλου.　　Demodocus, 4.

> A noxious snake once bit a Cappadocian
> And died: the man's blood prov'd the deadlier potion.—*Ed.*

> Imitated in Latin, Epigr. Delectus, p. 331:
>> Vipera Cappadocem mala sana momordit: at ipsa
>> Gustato periit sanguine Cappadocis.

> In French (Fourn. *L.D.A.*, p. 288):
>> Un gros serpent mordit Aurelle;
>> Que croyez-vous qu'il arriva?
>> Qu' Aurelle en mourût? Bagatelle!
>> Ce fut le serpent qui creva.

> And by Goldsmith, "Elegy on a Mad Dog":
>> The man recovered of his bite,
>> The dog it was that died.

1214. Kein Talent, doch ein Charakter.　Heine, Atta Troll, cap. 24.—
No talent, but a character for all that.

1215. Kennst du das Land, wo die Citronen blüh'n?　Goethe, Wilhelm
Meisters Lehrjahre, 3, 1.—*Know'st thou the land where the lemon
trees bloom?*

1216. Κρεῖττον γὰρ ὀψὲ ἄρξασθαι τὰ δέοντα πράττειν ἢ μηδέποτε. Dion. Halic. Antiq. Rom. 9, 9.—*Better to begin to do your duty late than never.*

1217. Κτῆμα ἐς ἀεί. Thuc. 1, 22.—*A perpetual possession.* Said by Thucydides of his own history, which he bequeathed as an "imperishable treasure" to posterity.

1218. Kurz ist der Schmerz, und ewig ist die Freude! Schiller, Jungfrau v. Orleans, fin. (Joan loq.).—*Short is the pain, and eternal is the joy!*

L.

1219. Labitur occulte, fallitque volubilis ætas. Ov. Am. 1, 8, 49.— *Time glides away unnoticed, and eludes us in his flight.*

1220. Laborare est orare.—*To work is to pray.*

> "Admirable was that of the old monks, *Laborare est orare*, Work is worship. . . . All true work is sacred: in all true work there is something of divineness." Carlyle, *Past and Present*, Bk. 3, cap. 12, init. Spite, however, of Carlyle and current tradition, it does not appear that the qu. obtains as maxim or motto of any existing religious order; and it is possible, as Mr Ed. Marshall points out in *Notes and Q.*, vol. xi. 472, that the popular "jingle" may have been derived from the "laborare *et* orare" of Pseudo-Bernard, *Opera*, vol. ii., col. 866, Paris, 1690. He says: "Qui orat et laborat, cor levat ad Deum cum manibus; qui vero orat et non laborat, cor levat ad Deum sed non manus."

1221. Labor est etiam ipse voluptas. Manil. Astr. 4, 155.—*Even the toil itself is a pleasure.*

1222. Labor omnia vicit
Improbus, et duris urguens in rebus egestas. Virg. G. 1, 145.— *Unremitting toil and the exigencies of want have conquered all things.*

1223. Laborum Dulce lenimen. Hor. C. 1, 32, 14.—*Sweet solace of my toil.*

1224. L'absence est à l'amour, ce qu'est au feu le vent,
Il éteint le petit, il allume le grand.
> Bussy Rabutin, Maximes d'Amour (Amours des Dames, Cologne, 1717, p. 219).

Love in Absence.

Absence acts upon Love as wind acts upon fire ;
It quenches the faint, makes the ardent burn higher.—*Ed.*

> "Ce sont les grands feux qui s'enflamment au vent, mais les petits s'esteignent si on ne les y porte à couvert." St Franç. de Sales, *Introd. à la Vie Dévote* (1610), Pt. 3, chap. 34: and "L'absence diminue les médiocres passions, et augmente les grandes, comme le vent éteint les bougies, et allume le feu. La Rochef., § 284, p. 68.

1225. La Charte sera désormais une vérité. - *The Charter shall be hence-forward a reality.*

> Closing words of the Proclamation of Louis Philippe, July 31, 1830. The effect of this announcement was all but ruined by the substitution of the indefinite article for the definite in the *Moniteur's* account of the proceedings ("*Une* Charte," etc.); similarly, the printer's error in making Sieyès say in a public statement of his political principles, "J'ai *abjuré* la Republique" (instead of "J'ai *adjuré*"), constituted a mistake sufficient at the time to bring a man to the guillotine. Fourn. *L. D. L.*, chap. 58; and Alex. p. 86.

1226. La confiance fournit plus à la conversation que l'esprit. La Rochef., § 1, p. 178. —*Confidence contributes more to conversation than wit.* On this Mme. de Sablé, to whom La Rochefoucauld communicated the thought, remarks that mere "self-confidence" must not be mistaken, under the name of *confiance*, for that perfect ease of situation which is the necessary element of good conversation.

1227. La cour du roi Pétaud. Prov.(Quit.p.597).—*King Pétaud's Court.* —All confusion, noise, and disorder, as in Mol. Tartaffe 1, 1.

> On n'y respecte rien, chacun y parle haut,
> Et c'est tout justement la cour du roi Pétaud.

1228. Lacrimæque decoræ
Gratior et pulchro veniens in corpore virtus.   Virg. A. 5, 343.

> So well the tears beseem his face,
> And worth appears with brighter shine
> When lodged within a lovely shrine.—*Conington.*

1229. La critique est aisée, et l'art est difficile. Destouches, Glorieux, 2, 5. *Chefs d'œuvres des auteurs comiques* (Destouches, Fagan. etc.), Paris, 1845, pp. 128-9.—*Criticism is easy, art is difficult.* The passage is as follows:

> Mais, on dit qu'aux auteurs la critique est utile.
> *La critique est aisée et l'art est difficile :*
> C'est là ce qui produit ce peuple de censeurs,
> Et ce qui rétrécit le talent des auteurs.

1230. La défense est un charme: on dit qu'elle assaisonne
Les plaisirs, et surtout ceux que l'amour nous donne.
La Font. Contes, 5, 10, 53 (Les Filles de Minée).

> *Stolen Waters are Sweet.*
> What's forbid is e'er charming, and, all things above,
> Is the zest that it gives to the pleasures of Love.—*Ed.*

1231. La dernière chose qu'on trouve en faisant un ouvrage, est de sçavoir celle qu'il faut mettre la première. Pasc. Pens. 31, 42.—*In writing a book, the last thing that one learns is to know what to put first.*

1232. La donna è mobile
Qual pium' al vento,
Muta accento, e di pensier.   F. M. Piave, Rigoletto, 3, 2.
(Music by Verdi).—*Woman is as light as a feather before the*

breeze. Her tone and thoughts are ever changing. Cf. Varium et mutabile semper Femina. Virg. A. 4, 569.

1233. La douleur est un siècle, et la mort un moment. Gresset, Ep. sur ma Convalescence, l. 92.—*Pain seems an age, while death is but a moment.*

1234. La durée de nos passions ne dépend pas plus de nous que la durée de notre vie. La Rochef. Max , § 5, p. 31.—*The duration of our passions no more depends upon our own will, than does the continuance of our lives.*

1235. Lætus sum laudari me abs te, pater, a laudato viro. Næv.Trag.15, (Hector loq.).—*I am glad to be praised by thee, father, a man whom all men praise.*

1236. La façon de donner vaut mieux que ce qu'on donne Corn. Menteur, 1, 1 (Cliton loq.).—*The way in which a thing is given is worth more than the gift.*

1237. La faiblesse est plus opposée à la vertu que le vice. La Rochef., § 14, p. 179.—*Weakness is a greater enemy to virtue even than vice.*

1238. La feuille tombe à terre, ainsi tombe la beauté Prov.—*The leaf falls to earth, and so does beauty.*

1239. La foi qui n'agit point, est-ce une foi sincère? Raç. Ath. 1, 1 (Joad loq.).—*The faith that acts not, is it truly faith?*

1240. La garde meurt et ne se rend pas.—*The guard dies but does not surrender.*

Legendary speech of Lt.-Gen. Pierre Jacques, Baron de Cambronne, and General of division at Waterloo, when summoned to surrender with the remains of the Imperial Guard by Col. Hugh Halkett, King's German Legion. At a banquet given in his honour at Nantes (1835), Cambronne himself publicly disavowed the saying, which he further showed to be contradicted by facts. "In the first place," he would remark, "we did not die, and, in the second, we did surrender." Others have pretended that Cambronne's actual reply consisted of a single word (*les cinq lettres*), more forcible than polite, which V. Hugo had the courage to print in full in "Les Miserables" (vol. iii. Bk. 1, ch. 15). This account, however, appears to be as devoid of foundation as the other. In Jan. 1842 Cambronne died, and the city of Nantes voted a statue to its illustrious townsman with the quotation for inscription. On this the two sons of Lt.-Gen. Michel entered a counter-claim (and again in 1862) to the authorship of the celebrated speech on behalf of their father, who was killed at C.'s side on the field of Waterloo; but with so little success that the Nantes statue bears the lying legend to this day. Of the various solutions of the question, that of Fournier seems the most probable—that the *mot* was invented the night of the battle by Rougemont, a noted *faiseur de mots*, then correspondent of the *Indépendant*, in which it appeared the next day, being repeated in the *Journal Général de France* on June 24. Certain it is that, whoever invented the saying, there never was one so felicitous or that so immediately *fit fortune.* It was the swan-song of "La Grande Armée," and the last expression of French heroism. It retrieved even Waterloo itself after a fashion, and irradiated the terrible disaster with a sentimental limelight glory. *See* Fourn. *L. D. L.*, pp. 412-15 and note; Lar. pp. 440-7; Büchm. p. 493 n.; Alex. 219-20; Brunschwigg's "Cambronne," Nantes, 1894; Fumag. 322-3, and the authorities cited by them.

1241. L'âge d'or était l'âge où l'or ne régnait pas. Lézay-Marnésia, Épître à mon curé, Les Paysages, etc., Paris, 1800, p. 176.—*The golden age was the age when gold did not reign.*

1242. La gloire est le but où j'aspire,
    On n'y va point par le bonheur.   V. Hugo, Ode 1.

> Glory's the goal that I aspire to reach,
> But happiness will never lead me there.—*Ed.*

1243. La grammaire, qui sait régenter jusqu'aux rois. Mol. Fem. Sav. 2, 6 (Philaminte loq.).—*Grammar, that lords it even over kings.*

> Suetonius (de Ill. Gramm. 22) says that M. P. Marcellus the grammarian rebuked even Tiberius himself for some solecism, and that, on one of the courtiers present, Ateius Capito, remarking that if the word was not good Latin it would be so in future, Marcellus gave Capito the lie, adding (to the Emperor), *Tu enim Cæsar civitatem dare potes hominibus, verbis non potes*— "Cæsar, you can grant citizenship to men, but not to words." Hence the saying, *Cæsar non supra grammaticos*—"Cæsar is not above the grammarians." A later Emperor, however, Sigismund I., disclaimed any such absurd limitations, and, at the Council of Constance, 1414, replied to a prelate who had objected to some point in H.I.M.'s locution, *Ego sum Rex Romanus et supra grammaticam*—"I am the Roman Emperor and am above grammar." (See Menzel, *Geschichte der Deutschen*, 3rd ed cap. 325; Zincgref's Apophthegmata, Strassburg, 1626, p. 60; and Büchm. pp. 508-9.)

1244. La grandeur a besoin d'être quittée pour être sentie. Pasc. Pens. 31, 19.—*Greatness has to be resigned in order to be properly appreciated.*

1245. L'aigle d'une maison, n'est qu'un sot dans une autre. Gresset, Le Méchant, 4, 7 (Cléon loq.).—*The eagle of one family is a fool in another.* One man's swan is another man's goose.

1246. Laissez dire les sots: le savoir a son prix. La Font. 8, 19 (L'Avantage de la Science).—*Let ignorance talk as it will, learning has its value.*

1247. Laissez faire, laissez passer!—*Let us alone, let us have free circulation* for the products of labour and commerce!

> Axiom of the "Physiocratic" school of French economists of the middle eighteenth century—Quesnay (1694-1774), de Gournay (1712-1759), and Turgot (1727-1781),—who, in their wish to abolish all differential duties and bounties, anticipated the Free-traders of a hundred years later. Gournay is generally credited with the second half of the saying, the former part having originated in this connection, in a conversation between Colbert and a leading merchant of the name of Legendre, as far back as 1680. The minister asked the man of business, "Que faut-il faire pour vous aider ?—*Nous laisser faire.*" Martin, in relating the incident, adds by way of comment, "Laissez faire et laissez passer! c'est à dire, plus de règlements qui enchaînent la fabrication, et font du droit de travailler un privilége : plus de prohibitions qui empêchent les échanges, plus de tarifs qui fixent les valeurs des denrées et des merchandises." (H. Martin, Hist. de la France (1853), vol. 18, pp. 429 and 432-33.) In later days the *Laissez faire* principle has been chiefly associated with the name of Adam Smith, though it would be absurd to reduce his teaching to so purely negative a doctrine. State intervention, according to the *Wealth of Nations*, is imperative when the

individual is unequal to the occasion; but where he can act for himself, government must stand aside, and *laisser le faire.*   V. Dupont de Nemours, *Économistes du XVIIIᵉ siècle,* where the saying is attributed to Vincent de Gournay; and Alex. p. 274.

1248. La langue des femmes est leur épée, et elles ne la laissent pas rouiller.   Prov. (Quit. p. 381).—*Women's tongue is their sword, and they don't let it rust.*

1249. La légalité nous tue.   M. Viennet in the Chamber of Deputies, Mar. 29, 1833.   (Fourn. *L.D.L.,* cap. 63).—*We are being killed by "legality."*

1250. Λαλήσας μὲν πολλάκις μετενόησα, σιωπήσας δὲ οὐδέποτε.   Simonides in Plut. Mor. 515 A, Dübner, Paris ed., p. 623 (De garrulitate, cap. 23, fin.).—*I have often repented of speaking, never of holding my tongue.*

1251. La libéralité consiste moins à donner beaucoup, qu'à donner à-propos.   La Bruy. (Du Cœur), vol. 1, cap. 4.—*Liberality consists less in giving profusely than seasonably.*

1252. L'Allégorie habite un palais diaphane.   Lemierre, Peinture, Chant 3ᵉ.—*Allegory inhabits a transparent palace.*

1253. La loi permet souvent ce que défend l'honneur.   Saurin, Blanche et Guiscard (1763), 5, 6 (Blanche loq.).—*Law oft allows what honour must forbid.*

1254. La manière d'être reçu dépend beaucoup de la manière dont on se présente.   Beudant, *Voyage en Hongrie,* qu. in *The Gypsy Road* (G. A. J. Cole, 1894, p. 77).—*The kind of reception one meets with depends much on the way in which one presents oneself.*

1255. La mémoire est une Muse, on plutôt, c'est la mère des Muses que Ronsard fait parler ainsi:

> Grèce est notre pays, Mémoire est notre mère.

Chateaubriand, in *Chateaubriand et son temps,* Cte. de Marcellus, Paris, 1859, p. 286.—*Memory is a Muse in herself, or rather the mother of the Muses, whom Ronsard represents saying,*

> Greece is our country, Memory is our Mother.

> Cf. Usus me genuit, mater peperit memoria:
> Sophiam vocant me Grai, vos sapientiam.   Afran. 298.—*Practice is my father, Memory my mother: the Greeks call me Sophia, and ye call me Wisdom.*

1256. La mère en prescrira la lecture à sa fille.   Piron, Métromanie, 3, 7.—*Mothers will give it to their daughters to read.*   Damis urges the highly moral character of his poetry, in reply to his uncle Baliveau's ridicule of so impractical a career.

L

1257. L'amitié est l'Amour sans ailes. Prov.—"*Friendship is Love without his wings;*" title of stanzas in Byron's "Hours of Idleness," and repeated, in the form, "Love's image upon earth without his wing," in the Dedication (to Ianthe) of Childe Harold (Canto I.), st. 2.

1258. La Mode est un tiran dont rien nous délivre,
A son bisare goût il faut s'acommoder:
Et sous ses foles loix étant forcé de vivre,
Le sage n'est jamais le premier à les suivre,
    Ni le dernier à les garder.

> Étienne Pavillon, Poésies Morales, xvi., Stances, Conseils à une jeune Démoiselle. (Œuvres, Amsterdam, 1750, vol. 2, p. 292.)
>
> *The Tyranny of Fashion.*
> A tyrant is fashion whom none can escape,
> To his whimsical fancies our tastes we must shape:
> We are forced to conform to the mode, it is true,
> But it's never the wise who first follow the new,
>   Nor the last to abandon the old.—*Ed.*

1259. La moquerie est souvent indigence d'esprit. La Bruy. chap. v. (La Société), vol. i. p. 93.—*Ridicule is frequently a sign of lack of wit.*

1260. La mort cache un délicieux mystère.—*Death hides a delightful secret.* Said by Alexandrine de la Ferronays. *V.* Mrs Bishop's *Memoir of Mrs Augustus Craven*, Lond., 1895, vol. 2, p. 203.

1261. La mort est plus aisée à supporter sans y penser, que la pensée de la mort sans péril. Pasc. Pens. 31, 3.—*Death is easier to bear when it comes unlooked for, than the bare thought of it when all is well.*

1262. La mort ne surprend point le sage:
Il est toujours prêt à partir,
S'étant su lui-même avertir
Du temps où l'on se doit résoudre à ce passage.

> La Font. 8, 1 (La Mort et le Mourant).—*Death never takes the wise unawares; he is always ready to depart, having learnt to anticipate the time when he must perforce make this last journey.*

1263. La mouche du coche. Prov. (Quit. p. 544).—*The fly of the coach.* A busybody, all fuss and no work. *V.* La Font. (7, 9), Le Coche et La Mouche, and Æsop's Fables, 217, κώνωψ καὶ βοῦς (*Culex et bos*), of which it is an imitation.

1264. L'amour-propre offensé ne pardonne jamais. Vigée, Aveux Difficiles, sc. 7. Bibliothèque Dramatique, Paris, 1824, p. 259, (Cléante loq.).—*Wounded self-love never forgives.*

1265. La naissance n'est rien où la vertu n'est pas. Mol. Fest. de P. 4, 6, (Don Louis).—*Birth is nothing without virtue.*

1266. L'anime triste di coloro
Che visser senza infamia, e senza lodo,
Mischiate sono a quel cattivo coro
Degli angeli, che non furon ribelli,
Nè fur fedel a Dio, ma per se foro.   Dante, Inf. 3, 35.

> The wretched souls of those, who lived
> Without or praise or blame, with that ill band
> Of angels mix'd, who nor rebellious proved,
> Nor yet were true to God, but for themselves
> Were only.—*Cary.*

And *ibid.* l. 62,

> La setta de' cattivi
> A Dio spiacenti ed a nemici sui.

Dante places these characterless souls just within the gate of Hell.

1267. **La nuit tous les chats sont gris.** Prov. (Quit. p. 214).—*At night all cats are grey.* Darkness hides defects, and obliterates distinctions.

1268. **La parole a été donnée à l'homme pour déguiser sa pensée.**—*Speech has been given to man to conceal his thoughts.*

This celebrated saying (and sentiment), in the form in which it stands above, was probably derived from Molière's *La parole a été donnée à l'homme pour expliquer sa pensée* (Le Mariage forcé, 1664, sc. 6), but who may have been the cynic who so cleverly travestied the highly moral sentence of Doctor Pancrace it is not easy to determine. According to Barère's *Mémoires*, (Paris, 1842, vol. 4, p. 447), the words were spoken by Talleyrand in conversation with the Spanish ambassador, Izquierdo, in 1807, and the ascription has much in its favour. Others confidently award the *dicton*, not to Talleyrand, but to Talleyrand's *âme damnée*, Montrond; while Heine (*Ideen, Das Buch Le Grand*, 1826, cap. 15, Complete Works, i. 296), with the substitution of *cacher* for *déguiser*, represents it as Fouché's. In the way of variants and parallels, more than one apposite instance is forthcoming. Voltaire, in his *Dialogues*, XVII. (Le Chapon et la Poularde, 1762), makes the misanthropic capon say of men in general that, *"Ils . . . n'employent les paroles que pour déguiser leurs pensées;"* with which may be compared the lines of Young (1681-1765) in his *Love of Fame, the Universal Passion* (vv. 207-8),

> Where nature's end of language is declined,
> And men talk only to conceal the mind.

Earlier still, Swift describes a first minister of state as a "creature" who "applies his words to all uses, except to the indication of his mind; and that he never tells a truth, but with an intent that you should take it for a lie," etc., etc. *Voy. to the Houyhnhnms*, chap. vi. (Works, ed. T. Sheridan, J. Nichols, Lond., 1801, vol. 6, p. 301).
Campistron (*Œuvres de M. de C.*, 1750, vol. 3, p. 36), in his *Pompeia*, 2, 5, makes Clodius say to Felix, "Le cœur sent rarement ce que la bouche exprime."—*It is rare for the mouth to utter the heart's true sentiments.*
From the classics Büchm. cites two instances—Dionysius Cato (lib. 4, Dist. 26),

> Perspicito tecum tacitus quid quisque loquatur:
> Sermo homines mores et celat et indicat idem.

> Consider inwardly what each man says:
> His talk both hides and shows man's secret ways.—*Ed.*

And Plutarch (*De recta ratione audiendi*, cap. 7, p. 41 D), who remarks that the majority of the sophists, τοῖς ὀνόμασι παραπετάσμασι χρῶνται τῶν διανοημάτων—*employ their words as so much concealment of their thoughts.*

It may be added that Harel, in the *Siècle* of August 24, 1846, attributes "La parole," etc., definitely to Talleyrand; and the *Derniers Souvenirs* of Cte. J. d'Estourmel (Paris, 1860, p. 319), says its real author was Montrond. [For the above, see Büchm. pp. 487-8; Alex. pp. 375-6; Fourn. *L.D.L.*, pp. 441-2, and the authorities, references, and additional matter there quoted.]

1269. La pire de toutes les mésalliances est celle du cœur.   Chamf. Maximes, vol. 2, p. 80.—*The worst misalliance of all is the misalliance of affections.*

1270. La plupart des hommes emploient la première partie de leur vie à rendre l'autre misérable.   La Bruy. ch. xi. De l'homme, (vol. ii. p. 48).—*Most men spend the first part of their lives in making the latter part miserable.*

1271. La plupart des livres d'à present ont l'air d'avoir été faits en un jour, avec des livres lus de la veille.   Chamf. Maximes, vol. 2, p. 85.—*Most works of the present day look as if they had taken a day to write, with the help of books that it had taken a day to read.*

1272. La plupart des nobles rappellent leurs ancêtres, à peu près comme un *cicerone* d'Italie rappelle Cicéron.   Chamf. Maximes, vol. 2, p. 10.—*Most of our present nobles bear as much resemblance to their ancestors, as an Italian cicerone bears to Cicero.*

1273. La plus belle victoire est de vaincre son cœur.   La Font. Élégie, Nymphes de Vaux, fin.—*The finest victory is to conquer one's own heart.*

1274. La popularité? c'est la gloire en gros sous.   V. Hugo, Ruy Blas, 3. 5 (Don Salluste to Ruy Blas).—*Popularity? Why, that means glory in copper coinage.*

1275. L'appétit vient en mangeant, disoit Angeston, mais la soif s'en va en beuvant.   Rab. 1, 5.—*The appetite grows with eating, said Angeston, but thirst is quenched by drinking.*

Angeston stands for Jerome de Hangest († 1538), doctor of the Sorbonne and well-known for his attacks on Luther and the Lutherans.   The first half of the qu. is supposed to have been pleaded by Jacques Amyot (1513-1593), translator of Plutarch, and sometime tutor to Charles IX., on the latter expressing surprise at Amyot's greediness in asking for a bishopric instead of being content with the benefice he already enjoyed.   Quit. points out (p. 65) a parallel in Ovid (Met. 8, 841), *Cibus omnis in illo causa cibi est* ("With him all food only produces a craving for more"), said of Erysich-thon, condemned to perpetual hunger for destroying the sacred grove of Ceres.

1276. La propriété c'est le vol.   P. J. Proudhon.—*Property is theft.*

In 1840 Proudhon, economist and socialist, brought out his treatise, *Qu'est ce que la propriété?* ("What is property?"), the first page of which ("Recherches sur le principe du droit et du gouvernement") in its opening sentence answered the question with the paradox, "*C'est le vol*," *i.e.*, property cannot be justly enjoyed without an adequate equivalent for the labour which gives it its value. Brissot de Warville, in his *Recherches sur le droit de propriété et le vol* (Biblioth. Philosoph. du législateur, 1782, vol. vi. p. 293), had anticipated Proudhon by more than half a century, with his "La propriété exclusive est un vol dans la nature." Alex. pp. 406-7; Fourn. *L.D.L.*, cap. 56.

1277. La Prusse, le pays classique des écoles et des casernes. Ascribed to Victor Cousin, ap. Fumag No. 869.—*Prussia, the classic land of schools and barracks.* Büchm. (p. 497) also attributes the saying to Cousin, giving as authority J. Jacoby's "Henri Simon," 2nd ed., p. 110; but, strange to state, makes Cousin to have uttered the apophthegm in German.

1278. La raison du plus fort est toujours la meilleure. La Font. 1, 10 (Le Loup et l'Agneau).—*The argument of the strongest is always the best.* Might *v.* Right. Parallels abound—"La force prime le droit," (*Might is Right*); "Le droit du plus fort est toujours le meilleur;" "Macht geht vor Recht;" and so forth.

1279. L'argent est un signe d'une chose, et le réprésente. Montesquieu, L'esprit des Lois, Bk. 22, cap. 2.—*Money is a token of a certain thing, and represents it.*

1280. Largior hic campos æther et lumine vestit
Purpureo: solemque suum, sua sidera norunt. Virg. A. 6, 640.

The Elysian Fields.

Around the champaign mantles bright
The fulness of purpureal light;
Another sun and stars they know,
That shine like ours, but shine below.—*Conington.*

1281. Largitionem fundum non habere. Prov. ap. Cic. Off. 2, 15, 55.—*Giving has no bottom to its purse.*

1282. Largus opum, et lingua melior, sed frigida bello
Dextera, consiliis habitus non futilis auctor. Virg. A. 11, 338.

Drances.

Wealthy, and dowered with wordy skill,
In battle spiritless and chill;
At council-board a name of weight,
Powerful in faction and debate.—*Conington.*

1283. La roche Tarpéienne est près du Capitole. Jouy, La Vestale, 3, 3. (1807); Music by Spontini.—*The Tarpeian rock is close to the Capitol.* The seat of power is close to the scene of execution. It is no great distance from Westminster to the Tower. [Büchm. p. 484.]

1284. L'art de faire des vers, deust on s'en indigner,
Doit etre a plus haut prix que celui de regner.
Tous deux egalement nous portons des couronnes;
Mais, roi, je la reçus; et poete, tu les donnes.

"Charles IX.," in Ronsard, (Œuvres compl. ed. Prosper Blanchemain, Paris, 1858, vol. 3, p. 261).

Vers du roy à Ronsard.

The art of verse-making (should one be complaining)
Is higher at least than the talent of reigning:
We each boast a crown, both the monarch and poet,
Yet kings but receive it, while authors bestow it.—*Ed.*

Beginning of a dozen justly-admired Alexandrines, supposed to have been addressed by Charles IX. to Ronsard, but generally considered supposititious. Fournier (*L.D.L.*, pp. 185-191 and Notes) ascribes the lines to Jean Le Royer, Sieur de Prades, on account of their first appearance in his *Sommaire de l'histoire de France*, Paris, 1651, p. 548.

1285. Lasciate ogni speranza, voi ch'entrate.   Dante, Inf. 3, 9.

The Gates of Hell.

All hope abandon, ye who enter here!

With this cp. the following from Plaut. Bacch. 3, 3, 1:

Pandite atque aperite januam hanc Orci, obsecro!
Nam equidem haud aliter esse duco, quippe quo nemo advenit
Nisi quem spes reliquere omnes esse ut frugi possiet.

Wide, open wide this gate of Hell, I pray!
For such I take it—whither no man comes
Unless he's lost all hope of being reformed.—*Ed.*

1286. Lascivi soboles gregis.   Hor. C. 3, 13, 8.—*Offspring of a wanton race.*

1287. La Société de Jésus est une épée dont la poignée est à Rome, et la pointe partout.   L'Abbé Raynal (G. F. T.), qu. in Diderot's *Œuvres choisies* (ed. F. Génin), 1856, p. 298.—*The Society of Jesus is a sword, the handle of which is in Rome, and its point everywhere.*

André Dupin, lawyer and statesman, repeated the *mot* as though it had been an original saying, when defending the *Constitutionnel* before the Cour Royale, Nov. 26, 1825, and even reproduced it in his "Memoirs," vol. i. p. 215.   In the *Anti-Coton* of T. A. D'Aubigné (1610, 18mo, p. 73), the Society is spoken of as *une épée dont la lame est en France et la poignée à Rome.* V. Fourn. *L.D.L.*, pp. 433-5; and Alex. p. 496.

1288. La société n'est pas le développement de la nature, mais bien sa décomposition et sa refonte entière.   Chamf. Maximes (vol. 2, p. 6).—*Society (1788), so far from being the development of nature, is its decomposition, leading to a complete reconstruction.*

1289. Lateat scintillula forsan.—*Perchance some tiny spark (of life) may still lie hid.*   Motto of the R. Humane Society.

1290. Laterem lavem.   Ter. Phorm. 1, 4, 9.—*As good wash a brickbat.* Cf. λίθον ἕψεις. Ar. Vesp. 280.—*You're boiling a stone.* Labour lost.

1291. Latet anguis in herba.   Virg. E. 3, 93.—*A snake is lurking in the grass.*

1292. Laudamus veteres, sed nostris utimur annis,
Mos tamen est æque dignus uterque coli.   Ov. F. 1, 225.

We laud the old, but live in modern days:
Yet, old or new, each fashion's worthy praise.—*Ed.*

1293. Laudatis semper antiquos, sed nove de die vivitis. Tert. Apol. 6.
—*You are ever lauding the old ways, yet daily fashioning your lives anew.*

1294. Laudato ingentia rura, Exiguum colito. Virg. G. 2, 412.—
Praise a large estate; but choose a small one for yourself. In every thing moderate your aims, hopes, and desires.

1295. Laudatur ab his, culpatur ab illis. Hor. S. 1, 2, 11.—*He is praised by these, blamed by those.*

1296. Laudat venales qui vult extrudere merces. Hor. Ep. 2, 2, 11.—
The man who wants to get his wares off his hands, praises their excellence.

1297. Laudibus arguitur vini vinosus Homerus. Hor. Ep. 1, 19, 6.

> The praises heap'd by Homer on the bowl
> At once convict him as a thirsty soul.—*Conington.*

1298. Laudo manentem; si celeres quatit
Pennas, resigno quæ dedit, et meâ
Virtute me involvo probamque
Pauperiem sine dote quæro. Hor. C. 3, 29, 53.

> *Fortune.*
> She stays, 'tis well: but let her shake
> Those wings, her presents I resign,
> Cloak me in native worth and take
> Chaste Poverty undowered for mine.—*Conington.*

A fallen minister, at the time of the Restoration (1814), applied the lines to himself. *V.* Fourn. *L.D.A.*, cap. 28, fin. He said:

> Je vais, victime de mon zèle,
> M'envelopper dans ma vertu.

To which it was instantly replied:

> Voilà, voilà ce qui s'appelle
> Etre légèrement vêtu!

> A Martyr to my zeal, I fold
> Me in my virtue, and retire.
> Indeed, indeed! That must be called
> A very light and scant attire.—*Ed.*

1299. La vertu n'iroit pas si loin, si la vanité ne lui tenoit compagnie.
La Rochef. Max., § 205, p. 56.—*Virtue would not go so far, if vanity did not keep her company.*

1300. La vraye science et le vray estude de l'homme, c'est l'homme.
Charron, Traité de la Sagesse, Bk. i., Pref. (Bordeaux, 1601).—
The real science and the real study for man is man himself.

Cf. Pope, *Essay on Man*, Ep. 2, 1:

> The proper study of mankind is man.

1301. La vue d'un tel monument est comme une musique continuelle et
fixée. Mme. de Stael, Corinne (1807), 4, 3.—*The view of such a
building* (St Peter's) *has the effect of continuous music fixed in
concrete shape.* Schelling (" Vorlesungen über Philosophie der
Kunst," 1807, pp. 576 and 593) twice uses the expression, " Die
Architektur ist die erstarrte Musik" (*Architecture is petrified
Music*); which Schopenhauer, in his " Welt als Wille u. Vorstel-
lung" (1819), 2, 519, improved into "gefrorne Musik" (*frozen
music*); and as such the expression is gen. cited. Büchm.
pp. 337-8.

1302. Le bestemmie fanno come le processioni; ritornano donde par-
tirono. Prov.— *Curses are like religious processions; they return
whence they set out.*

1303. Le bonheur des méchants comme un torrent s'écoule. Raç.
Athalie, 2, 7 (Joas loq.).—*The happiness of the wicked runs dry
like a torrent.*

1304. Le bonheur et le malheur vont d'ordinaire a ceux qui ont le plus
de l'un et de l'autre. Abbé de St Réal, Max. 18. (Harb.)—*Both
good and bad fortune generally fall to the lot of those that have
the greatest share of either.*

1305. Le bonheur semble fait pour être partagé. Raç. Études littér. et
morales, Pt. ii. 4 (Ed. de la Rochefoucauld, Paris, 1855, p. 33).
—*Happiness seems made to be shared.*

1306. Le bruit est pour le fat, la plainte est pour le sot,
L'honnête homme trompé s'éloigne et ne dit mot.
De la Noue, La Coquette corrigée, 1, 2,
Œuvres de Théâtre, Paris, 1765, p. 23.   (Clitandre loq.) :

> The fop begins to bluster and the fool begins to whine;
> The man of sense, when taken in, goes off and gives no sign.—*Ed.*

> Lines often quoted by Lord Macaulay when he found that advantage had
> been taken of his confidence or his generosity. " Odd," he remarks, " that
> two lines of a damned play—and, it should seem, of a justly damned play
> —should have lived near a century and have become proverbial."
> "Journal," Feb. 15, 1851, in *Life and Letters*, etc., by G. O. Trevelyan,
> London, 1881, p. 89 and n.

1307. Le but de mon ministère a été celui-ci; rétablir les limites natu-
relles de la Gaule: identifier la Gaule avec la France, et partout
où fut l'ancienne Gaule constituer la nouvelle. Richelieu, Test.
Politique, in Labbe's *Elogia Sacra*, 1706, p. 253.—*The aim of
my ministry has been this: to re-establish the natural boundaries
of Gaul; identify Gaul with France; and everywhere replace
ancient Gaul with its modern counterpart.*

1308. Le cabaret est le salon du pauvre. Gambetta, when President
of the Fr. Chamber in 1881, in Mrs Bishop's *Memoir of Mrs
Augustus Craven*, Lond., 1895, ii. p. 100.—*The public-house is the
poor man's club.*

1309. Le ciel défend, de vrai, certains contentements,
Mais il est avec lui des accommodements.

Mol. Tart. 4, 5 (Tartuffe loq.).—*Heaven, it is true, forbids certain gratifications, but even in that quarter arrangements may be made.*

1310. Le cœur a ses raisons, que la raison ne connoist pas. Pasc. Pens. 28, 58.—*The heart has its reasons, of which the reason takes no cognisance.*

1311. Le congrès ne marche pas, il danse.—*If the Congress does not march, at least it dances.*

Said of the Vienna Congress which assembled in Sept. 1814, and was made the occasion for a prolonged succession of festivities all through the winter, culminating in Prince Metternich's ball of March 7, which was rudely interrupted by the news of Bonaparte's successful landing in the S. of France! The "Correspondence of the brothers Grimm" (Weimar, 1881) gives under the date of Nov. 23, 1814, a reported saying of the day, attributed to Charles Joseph, Prince de Ligne, "Le congrès danse beaucoup, mais il ne marche pas." Büchm. p. 528; Fourn. *L.D.L.*, pp. 427-8.

1312. Le crime fait la honte, et non pas l'échafaud. Thos. Corneille, "Comte d'Essex," 4, 3 (Essex loq.).—*Crime, not the scaffold, is the real disgrace.* Qu. by Charlotte Corday, a scion of the poet's family, in a letter written on the eve of her execution, July 16, 1793. St Aug. has (Enarr. in Ps. 34, vol. 4, 183A), Martyres non facit pœna sed causa—*It is not the punishment, but the cause, that makes the martyr.*

1313. Le diable était beau quand il était jeune. Prov.—*The devil was good-looking when he was young, i.e.,* before his fall. Quit. (p. 301) defines *La beauté du diable* to be "la fraicheur de la jeunesse qui prête quelque agrément à la figure la moins jolie."

1314. Le droit est au plus fort en amour comme en guerre,
Et la femme qu'on aime aura toujours raison.

A. de Musset, Idylle.

The law sides with the strongest, in love as in war,
And the woman I worship will always be right.—*Ed.*

1315. "L'égalité"! ce mot stérile et chimérique,
Qu'on répète toujours, que jamais on n'explique,
De tous les préjugés renferme le plus grand;
Et la nature humaine est pour premier garant.

M. J. Chénier, Caius Gracchus (1792), 3, 2.

"Equality"! that idle word, and vain—
Which all repeat but no one will explain—
Of all sheer fallacies contains the worst,
And, for disproof, nature itself stands first.—*Ed.*

1316. Le génie n'est qu'une plus grande aptitude à la patience. Buffon, ap. Hérault de Séchelles, "Voyage à Montbar," 1801, p. 15. (E. Latham in *N. and Queries*, 9th ser., xi. p. 374).— *Genius is only an unusual aptitude for patience.* Carlyle in his

"Frederick the Great," Bk. 4, cap. 3 (vol. i. p. 415), says, "Genius, which means transcendent capacity for taking trouble."

1317. Leges bonæ ex malis moribus procreantur. Macr. Saturn. 2, 13. —*Good laws are the product of bad morals.* Cf. Probatum est . . . leges egregias . . . ex delictis aliorum gigni. Tac. Ann. 15, 20.

1318. Leges mori serviunt. Plaut. Trin. 4, 3, 36.—*Laws are subservient to custom.* Usage modifies the law.

1319. L'Église! c'est la question de la vérité sur la terre. Mme. Swetchine, vol. i. Pensée lvii.—*The Church! that means the existence of the truth on earth, or not.*

1320. Λέγουσιν ἅ θέλουσιν· λεγέτωσαν· οὐ μελ[ε]ι μοι· συ φίλ[ε]ι με· συμφερ[ε]ι σοι.   Inscr. on antique gem, (No. 2154 in A. H. Smith's Cat. of Engraved Gems in the Brit. Museum. Cf. Corpus Inscr. Græc., No. 7293).—*They say what likes them; let them say, I care not I.   But love thou me; 'tis good for thee.*

Prof. J. H. Middleton ("Engraved Gems of Classical Times," p. 95) says this maxim is specially common on late Roman gems; and Dean Burgon ("Letters from Rome," p. 288) speaks of the sentiment as being the favourite "posy" on rings found at Pompeii. Without its second half, the motto may be taken only to express a philosophic superiority to the cackling of idle tongues, as in the kindred inscription now in the entrance hall of Marischal Coll., Aberdeen, and probably inscribed by the founder, George, fifth Earl Marischal, in 1593. It is as follows:

> They haif said.
> Quhat say they?
> Lat thame say.

1321. Le gouvernement de France est une monarchie absolue, tempérée par des chansons. Chamf. Caractères, vol. i. p. 74.—*The French government is an absolute monarchy, qualified by epigrams.*

A case in point presents itself in the saying of Mazarin: "Ils chantent, ils payeront"—*Let them sing, they will have to pay*—when the populace, incensed by some new form of extortion, vented their anger against the Minister in appropriate *Mazarinades.*   Fournier (*L.D.L.*, p. 267) quotes from the *Nouvelles Lettres de la Duchesse d'Orléans, née Princesse Palatine,* Paris, 1853, p. 249: "Le Cardinal Mazarin disoit, 'La Nation Française est la plus folle du monde: ils crient et chantent contre moi, et me laissent faire: moi, je les laisse crier et chanter, et je fais ce que je veux '"   Alex. (p. 83) refers the reader to the *Encyclopédiana* (Encyclopédie Méthodique du 18e siècle, p. 63) for the Cardinal's rejoinder to the protests against his new taxes: "Tant mieux; s'ils cantent la cansonette, ils pagaront." Voltaire reports the saying as, "Laissons-les dire et qu'ils nous laissent faire." Lettre à M. Hénin, 13th Sept. 1772. *V.* Fourn. *L.D.L.*, cap. 43. This characteristic levity of his compatriots is well touched off by Beaumarchais (Mariage de Figaro, fin.), where Bridoison sings:

> Qu'on l'opprime, il peste, il crie,
> Il s'agite en cent façons;
> *Tout finit par des chansons.*

On this Alphonse Karr regretfully remarks (*L'Esprit d'Alphonse Karr,* Paris, 1877, p. 84), "Où est l'heureux temps signalé par Beaumarchais où tout finissait par des chansons?   Hélas! aujourd'hui tout finit par des discours."   In the Empire of the Tsar this proverbial limitation of absolutism takes a more tragic shape, which received due epigrammatic definition in the words of a Russian noble addressed to Count Ernst Friedrich Münster, Hanoverian Minister at Petersburg, *à propos* of the murder of the Emperor Paul on Mar. 23, 1801. "Le despotisme," he said, "temperé par l'assassinat, c'est notre Magna Charta." *V.* Büchm. p. 483, Alex. p. 319, and the parallels and variants there cited.

1322. Lehrstand, Nährstand, Wehrstand—*Teaching-class, Working-class, Soldier-class.* Erasmus Alberus in his "Predigt vom Ehestand," 1546, fol. 6, says, Der Priester muss lehren, die Oberkeit wehren, die Bauerschaft nähren—*The priest must teach, the nobles bear arms, and the peasantry labour.* Büchm. p. 130.

1323. Le jeu ne vaut pas la chandelle. Prov. (Quit. p. 477).—*The game is not worth the candle.*

> This prov. receives its simplest (and therefore its best) explanation as a reference to any game played after dark, which was (or was not) worth the farthing dip that lighted the players. When used in the transferred sense —"it is not worth while"—some would have it that the *ne* changes to *n'en:* as, *e.g.,* "De sorte que bien souvent ils acheptent bien cher ce qu'on leur donne; et le jeu *n'en* vaut pas la chandelle." Brantôme, Dames Gallantes, i. (Œuvres, Paris, 1848, vol. 2, p. 273); and,
>
> Loin de passer son temps, chacun le perd chez elles,
> Et le jeu, comme on dit, *n'en* vaut pas les chandelles. Corn. Menteur, 1, 1.

1324. Le Latin dans les mots brave l'honnêteté,
Mais le lecteur français veut être respecté. Boil. L'A. P. 2, 175.
—*What is written in Latin may defy propriety, but respect must be shown to the reader in French.*

1325. Le leggi son, ma chi pon mano ad esse? Dante, Purg. 16, 97.—*Laws indeed there are, but who observes them?*

1326. Le méchant n'est jamais comique. De Maistre, Comte J., *Soirées de St Pétersbourg,* Lyon, 1872, vol. 1, p. 240.—*A bad man is never comic.* His estimate of Voltaire. "Dans les genres qui paraissent les plus analogues à son talent naturel, il se traine; il est médiocre, froid, et souvent (qui le croirait?) lourd et grossier dans la comédie; *car le méchant n'est jamais comique.*" The converse is also true that *Le comique—le vrai comique n'est jamais méchant,* "The really amusing man cannot be a bad man."

1327. Le monde, chère Agnès, est une étrange chose! Mol. l'École des Femmes, 2, 4.
> The world, dear Agnes, is a strange affair!—*Ed.*

1328. Le monde est plein de fous, et qui n'en veut pas voir
Doit se tenir tout seul et casser son miroir. Anon.

> The world is full of madmen, and who would not see one pass,
> Must keep himself shut up at home, and break his looking-glass.—*Ed.*

> Epigram of the seventeenth century, forming the motto of an engraving of that date representing "Le Chariot de la Mère Folle"—*see* Fourn. (*L.D.A.,* cap. 33, *init.*), who discovered the print in question.

1329. Le *moy* est haïssable.   Pasc. Pens. 29, 27.—*"I" is hateful.*

1330. L'Empire c'est la Paix.—*The Empire means Peace.*

> Celebrated apothegm of Napoleon III., summing up the benefits of the Second Empire (Speech at a banquet in the Chamber of Commerce, Bordeaux, October 9, 1852).   The saying was parodied by *Punch* to signify *L'Empire c'est la "pay"* (with allusion to the excessive taxation under the new régime), and by *Kladderadatsch* to "*L'Empire c'est l'épée,*" The Empire means the sword.

1331. L'Empire est fait.—*The Empire is an accomplished fact.*   Said by Thiers, Jan. 17, 1851.   *Moniteur*, Jan. 18, 1851, p. 187, col. 1: (Thiers, *Discours Parlementaires*, vol. ix. p. 114.   Alex. pp. 155-6).

1332. Leniter, ex merito quicquid patiare, ferendum est;
Quæ venit indignæ pœna, dolenda venit.   Ov. H. 5, 7.

> *Undeserved Punishment.*
> To suffer for misdoing 's an easy thing;
> But when one's innocent—there lies the sting !—*Ed.*

1333. L'ennui est entré dans le monde par la paresse.   La Bruy. cap. xi. (De l'homme), vol. 2, p. 48.—*Tedium came into the world through idleness.*

1334. L'ennui naquit un jour de l'uniformité.   La Motte Houdard, Fables Nouvelles, Paris, 1719: Bk. 4, fab. 15.   (Les Amis trop d'accord).—*Boredom was born one day of uniformity.*   Nothing is more tiresome than monotony.

> It is recorded of Mme. de Chateaubriand that, wearied one day of the eternal educational "shop" that was monopolising the conversation in her *salon*—Joubert and Fontanes being the chief sinners—she improvised an alteration of the original—
> "L'ennui naquit un jour de *l'université.*"
> [*See* Alex. p. 161; and Fourn. p. 140.]

1335. L'enseigne fait la chalandise.   La Font. (Les Devineresses) 7, 15. —*A good sign brings in customers.*   A reason for advertising.

1336. Le plaisir le plus délicat est de faire celui d'autrui.   La Bruy. cap. 5 (La Société), vol. 1, p. 83.—*The most exquisite pleasure consists in giving pleasure to others.*

1337. Le plus beau livre qui soit parti de la main d'un homme, puisque l'Évangile n'en vient pas.   Bernard de Fontenelle, Vie de Corneille.—*The finest work which has ever issued from the hands of man, for the Gospel is not a human composition.*   Said of "*The Imitation.*"   (Théatre de P. Corneille. Nouv. ed., Genève, 1774, vol. 8, p. 508.)

1338. Le plus semblable aux morts meurt le plus à regret.   La Font. 8, 1 (La Mort et le Mourant).—*He who most resembles the dead dies the most reluctantly.*   Cf. the *Agli infelici difficile è il morir* (To the unfortunate, death is hard) of Metastasio's "Adriano," 1, 15.

1339. Le premier qui fut roi fut un soldat heureux;
Qui sert bien son pays n'a pas besoin d'aieux.   Volt. Mérope,
1, 3 (Polyphonte loq.).—*The first king was a successful soldier;
he who serves his country well needs no ancestors.*

> Borrowed from Lefranc de Pompignan's *Didon* (1734): "Le premier qui fut roi fut un usurpateur" (*The first man to be king was an usurper*), a line which the Censorship suppressed (Fourn. *L.D.A.*, p. 255).   Sir W. Scott, Woodstock. 2, 37, says: "What can they see in the longest kingly line in Europe, save that it runs back to a successful soldier?"

1340. Le proufit (profit) de l'un est dommage de l'aultre.   Montaigne, 1, 21.—*One man's profit is another man's loss.*

1341. Le public! le public! combien faut-il de sots pour faire un public? Chamfort, Caractères, etc. (vol. 1, pp. 16-17).—*"The public! the public!" How many fools does it take to make the public?*

1342. Le quart d'heure de Rabelais.   Alex. p. 421.—*Rabelais' quarter of an hour.*   The *mauvais quart d'heure* spent in settling accounts of all kinds, or in any other equally unpleasant situation.

> According to the story, Rabelais, on his way back from Rome, found himself at Lyons without the means of prosecuting his journey any farther.   He therefore confided to certain physicians of the city that he was carrying a poison of the most deadly description, with which he purposed putting a speedy end to the tyrant on the throne—Henry II.   He was, of course, instantly arrested and escorted to Paris, where he amused the King with the story of his ruse and the success that had attended it.   The tale is generally considered apocryphal, but may be read in the MS. *Rabelaesina Elogia* of Antoine le Roy, in the Bibliothèque Nationale, Nº. Lat. 8704, p. 16.

1343. Le roi de France ne venge pas les injures du duc d'Orléans.— *The King of France does not avenge the wrongs of the Duke of Orleans.*

> Trad. reply of the D. of Orleans, on succeeding to the throne as Louis XII. (1498), to the Orleans deputies, who hastened to make good all differences between them in the past by prompt submission to the new sovereign.   According to the MS. chronicle of Humbert Velay and the *Prologue* of the translator, Nicolas de Langes, the King replied, "Il ne seroit décent et à honneur à un roi de France de venger les querelles d'un duc d'Orléans."   Philip, Count of Brescia, on succeeding to the Duchy of Savoy in 1464, had made a similar answer: "Il serait honteux au duc de venger les injures faites au comte."   A much more remote parallel is pointed out by Suard in the *Evasisti*, (You have escaped), of the Emperor Hadrian on meeting a political opponent immediately after accession to imperial honours.   Hist. Aug. Script. *Adrianus Cæsar*, c. 17.   [Fourn. *L.D.L.*, 140-1; Suard, Notes sur l'Esprit d'imitation, *Revue Française*, Nouv. Série, vol. 6, p. 202.]

1344. Le roi d'un peuple libre est seul un roi puissant.   Gudin de la Brenellerie, Sur l'abolition de la servitude, Paris, 1781, p. 5.— *The king of a free people is the only powerful king.*

1345. Le roi qui régne est toujours le plus grand.   Boursault, Ésope à la cour.—*The reigning sovereign is always the greatest;* a line which was removed by the censorship.   Lettres Choisies de Voiture, Balzac, Boursault, etc., Paris, 1807, vol. 2, p. xvi (Biogr. Notice).

1346. Le roi régne et ne gouverne pas.   L. A. Thiers.—*The king reigns but does not govern.*

> Constitutional maxim of Thiers, enforced by him in his opposition paper, *Le National*, which he started (beginning of 1830), in conjunction with Mignet and A. Carrel, to combat the government of Charles X. (*see* the *National* for Jan. 18, Feb. 4, 19, and July 1 of that year). The saying appeared much earlier in the *Rex regnat sed non gubernat*, said by Jan Zamoyski, the famous Polish statesman, of Sigismond III. [Alex. p. 452; Fumag. No. 1152; Büchm. p. 470.]

1347. Les absents ont toujours tort.   Prov. (Quit. p. 8).—*The absent are always wrong.*

1348. Les affaires ?   C'est bien simple: c'est l'argent des autres.   Alex. Dumas fils, Question d'argent (1857), 2, 7.—*Business?   It is easily explained: it is other people's money.*

> In the play, Réné asks: *Qu'est-ce que c'est que les affaires, Monsieur Giraud?* to which Giraud replies in the words of the quotation (Théâtre Complet d'Alex. Dumas fils., 2e Série, Paris, 1868).   But the identical words had already occurred in the *Marguerite, ou Deux Amours* of Mme. de Girardin, where (ed. Bruxelles, 1852, vol. 2, p. 104) she makes Montrond (Talleyrand's *âme damnée*) say: " Je sais très bien ce que c'est que les affaires: les affaires, c'est l'argent des autres!" Alex. p. 3.   Béroalde de Verville's "Moyen de Parvenir" (Paris, 1879, p. 106) has, "PÉTRARQUE. —Mais de quoy sont composées les affaires du monde? QUELQU'UN.—Du bien d'autruy."

1349. Les amis de l'heure présente
    Ont le naturel du melon;
    Il faut en essayer cinquante
    Avant qu'en rencontrer un bon.

>   Claude Mermet, Le temps passé, Lyon, 1601, p. 42.— *Friends of the passing hour much resemble a melon: you must try fifty before you get a good one.*

1350. Les beaux (*or* Les grands) esprits se rencontrent.   Quit. p. 359.— *"Great wits jump."*   Sterne, Tristram Shandy, vol. 3, cap. 9 (orig. edition).

1351. Les beaux yeux de ma cassette.   Mol. L'Avare, 5, 3 (Harpagon).— *The lovely eyes of my money-box*, scil. its contents.

1352. Les belles actions cachées sont les plus estimables.   Pasc. Pens. 29, 25.—*Good actions should be secret to be really admirable.*

1353. Les cœurs aimants sont comme les indigents: ils vivent de ce qu'on leur donne.   Mme. Swetchine, Airelles, 63.—*Loving hearts are like beggars: they live on what people give them.*

1354. Les dieux s'en vont!   Chateaubriand, Les Martyrs (1809), fin. (Œuvres, Paris, 1836, vol. 21, p. 132).—*The gods are departing!*

> On the martyrdom, at Rome, of Eudorus and Cymodocea by wild beasts, the author represents the whole arena being shaken by sudden thunder,

above the echoes of which were heard these words, proclaiming the down-fall of paganism. The idea was borrowed from the history of Josephus (6, 5, 31), who relates that on the eve of Pentecost, 65 A.D., the priests, on entering the Temple to execute their ministrations, were startled by a loud noise, succeeded by a cry as of many voices in chorus, "Depart we hence!" Μεταβαίνωμεν ἐντεῦθεν.

1355. Le secret d'ennuyer est celui de tout dire. Volt. VIe Discours sur l'homme, 172.—*The surest way of wearying your readers is to say everything that can be said on the subject.* The couplet runs,

> Mais malheur à l'auteur qui veut toujours instruire,
> Le secret d'ennuyer, etc.

Boileau had already enunciated the same truth in L'Art Poét. 1, 63, "Qui ne sait se borner ne sut jamais écrire"—*The man who cannot keep himself within bounds will never write anything.*

1356. Les envieux mourront, mais non jamais l'envie. Mol. Tart. 5, 3.— *The envious will die, but envy never.* Prov. utilised by Molière either from the Lat. *Invidus acer obit, sed livor morte carebit* (The most envious man dies at last, but envy is immortal) of Phil. Garnier's Thesaurus Adagiorum, Frankfurt, 1612, 12mo, p. 260: or from Adrien de Montluc's *Comédie de Proverbes*, Paris, 1633, 3, 7 (p. 161).—"L'enuie ne mourra jamais, mais les enuieux mourront."

1357. Les esprits médiocres condamnent d'ordinaire tout ce qui passe leur portée. La Rochef., § 76, p. 78.—*Men of inferior intelligence generally condemn everything that is above the level of their understanding.*

1358. Les extrêmes se touchent. Mercier, Tableau de Paris, Amster-dam, 1782, vol. iv. p. 155. Title of cap. 348.—*Extremes meet.*

Pascal (Pens. 31, 27), comparing first principles with their most widely extended effects, says: *Les extrémitez se touchent, et se réunissent à force de s'estre éloignées, et se retrouvent en Dieu, et en Dieu seulement.* In La Bruy. ch. xii. (Jugements), vol. ii. p. 76, we have, "Une gravité trop étudiée devient comique; ce sont comme des extrémités qui se touchent, et dont le milieu est dignité."

1359. Les femmes ont toujours quelque arrière-pensée. Destouches, Dissipateur, 5, 9 (Le Marquis loq.).— *Women always speak with reservation.* The first use of "arrière-pensée" (c. 1730), says Fournier, *L.D.L.*, p. 390 n.

1360. Les femmes sont extrêmes: elles sont meilleures ou pires que les hommes. La Bruy. cap. iii. (*Des femmes*), vol. i. p. 58.—*Women, ever in extremes, are always either better or worse than men.*

> For men at most differ as Heaven and Earth,
> But women, worst and best, as Heaven and Hell.
> —*Tennyson*, Merlin and Vivien.

1361. Les fous font des festins, et les sages les mangent. Prov.— *Fools make feasts, and wise men eat them.* Fools build houses and wise men live in them.

1362. Les grands ne sont grands que parce que nous sommes à genoux; relevons-nous! L. Prudhomme.—*The great are only great because we are on our knees. Let us stand up!*

> Motto of Louis Prudhomme's *Journal des Révolutions de Paris* (July 1789), the authorship being variously ascribed to P. and to his editor, Loustalot. Fournier cites (in C. Moreau's *Bibliogr. des Mazarinades*, Paris, 1850, 8vo, i. p. 31, and ii. p. 359 and n.), Duboscq-Montandré's pamphlet of *Le point de l'Ovale* of 1652, in which occurs a similar expression: "Les grands ne sont grands que parceque nous les portons sur les épaules; nous n'avons qu'à les secouer pour en joncher la terre." [Fourn. *L.D.L.*, pp. 376-7.]

1363. Les hommes font les lois. Les femmes font les mœurs. Guibert, Connétable de Bourbon, Trag. in 5 Acts (Aug. 27, 1775), 1. 4.—

> *Adelaide.* Men make the laws:
> *Bayard.*   The morals women make.

1364. Les hommes sont cause que les femmes ne s'aiment point. La Bruy. cap. iii. (*Des Femmes*), vol. i. p. 58.—*Men are the reason why women do not love each other.*

1365. Les honneurs changent les mœurs. Prov. (Quit. p. 458).—*Honours change manners,* and not always for the better.

1366. Le silence du peuple est la leçon des rois. Sermons de Messire J. B. Charles Marie de Beauvais, Evêque de Senez, Paris, 1807, vol. iv. p. 243 (Oraison Funèbre de Louis XV., le Bien-aimé, S. Denis, Juillet 27, 1774).—*A people's silence is a lesson to their kings.*

> The passage is as follows :—"Le peuple n'a pas, sans doute, le droit de murmurer; mais, sans doute aussi, il a le droit de se taire; et son silence est la leçon des rois." — *The people, no doubt, has not the right to murmur; but, as certainly also, it has the right to hold its peace, and the people's silence is a lesson to its king.* The preacher was contrasting the unpopularity of the king's latter years with the earlier part of his reign. On the Good Friday previous (April 1/74), the same prelate in the course of his sermon had said, "Sire, mon devoir de ministre d'un Dieu de vérité m'ordonne de vous dire que vos peuples sont malheureux, que vous en êtes la cause, et qu'on vous le laisse ignorer."—*Sire, my duty as minister of the God of Truth compels me to tell you that your people are wretched, that you are the cause of their misery, and that you are left in ignorance of the fact.* His text was Jonas iii. 4: "Yet forty days, and Ninive shall be destroyed"; and forty days (to a day) afterwards, May 10th, Louis died—a literal fulfilment to which the orator refers in the Funeral Discourse (ibid. p. 217). V. *Nouvelle Biog. Gén.* (Didot), s.v. BEAUVAIS. The good bishop's words were not forgotten, and on the morrow of the taking of the Bastille, July 15/89, when the National Assembly (Versailles) was momentarily expecting, with feelings of relief and even of joy, the entry of the King, "one of the members" observed, "Qu'un morne respect soit le premier accueil fait au monarque dans un moment de douleur. *Le silence des peuples est la leçon des rois.*" Hugou (N. J.), *Mémoires de la Révol. de France*, Paris, 1790, vol. 3, p. 269. Thiers, in his *Révol. Française* (vol. 1, chap. 2), quotes Hugou's words, and makes the "member" to be Mirabeau.

1367. Le silence est l'esprit des sots,
    Et l'une des vertus du sage.

> Bernard de Bonnard, Moralité (Poésies diverses, 1824, p. 251). Alex. p. 483.

> Silence is the wit of fools,
> And a virtue in the wise.—*Ed.*

The preceding lines are :

> Ne parler jamais qu' à propos,
> Est un rare et grand avantage.
> *Le silence est,* etc.

1368. Les jours se suivent et ne se ressemblent pas. Prov. (Quit. p. 483).
—*The days follow, but do not resemble each other.* Fair or foul,
lucky or unlucky, no two alike. Hes. (Op. 823) has, ἄλλοτε
μητρυιὴ πέλει ἡμέρη, ἄλλοτε μήτηρ—*One day is like a stepmother
to us, another like a mother.*

1369. Les meilleurs livres sont ceux que chaque lecteur croit qu'il aurait
pu faire. Pasc. Pens, 1, 2 (*Biblioth. Nationale* Ed., p. 28).—*The best
books are those that everyone thinks he could have written himself.*

1370. Les miracles sont les coups d'état de Dieu. Mme. Swetchine,
vol. i. Pensée lxiv.—*Miracles are God's coups d'état.*

1371. Le soleil ni la mort ne se peuvent regarder fixement. La Rochef.,
§ 26, p. 34.—*Neither the sun nor death can be looked at full in
the face.*

1372. Le sort fait les parents, le choix fait les amis. Delille, La Pitié,
Chant 1.—*'Tis fate gives us kindred, and choice gives us friends.*

1373. Les passions sont les seuls orateurs qui persuadent toujours.
La Rochef., § 8, p. 32.—*The passions are the only orators that
never fail to convince us.*

1374. L'espérance est le songe d'un homme éveillé. Prov. (Quit. p. 356).
—*"For hope is but the dream of those that wake,"* Prior, *Solomon,*
etc., Bk. 3, 102. A saying of Aristotle (Diog. Laert. 5, 18),
ἐρωτηθεὶς τί ἐστιν ἐλπίς; Ἐγρηγορότος, εἶπεν, ἐνύπνιον—*Asked
what Hope was: the dream, said he, of a waking man.*

1375. L'esprit de la conversation consiste bien moins à en montrer
beaucoup, qu'à en faire trouver aux autres. La Bruy. cap. v.
(La Société), vol. i. p. 83.—*The art of conversation consists much
less in being witty oneself than in making others appear so.*

1376. L'esprit et les talents sont bien ;
Mais sans les Graces, ce n'est rien.
      Fs. de Neuf-Château, Almanach des Muses, 1775, p. 215.

> Wit and Talent are good in their places,
> But they're nothing without the Graces.—*Ed.*

1377. L'esprit qu'on veut avoir gâte celui qu'on a. Gresset, Le Méchant,
(1745), 4, 7 (Ariste to Cléonte).—*The wit one aims at spoils the
wit one has by nature.*

1378. Les rivières sont des chemins qui marchent et qui portent où l'on
veut aller (Pasc. Pensées, Art. vii. 37, in Ernest Havet's ed.,
Paris, 1866, 8vo, p. 106).—*Rivers are moving roads, which carry*

M

one whither one would go. "Oui," adds M. Havet in a note, "pourvu qu'on veuille aller où elles portent."

Viam qui nescit qua deveniat ad mare
Eum oportet amnem quærere sibi.   Plaut. Poen. 3, 3, 14.

He who knows not his way unto the sea,
Should keep a river in his company.—*Ed.*

1379. Les soldats d'Alexandre érigés tous en rois. Volt. Olympie, 2, 2.
—*Alexander's soldiers promoted to be so many kings.* Applicable to the titles, princely and royal, bestowed by Napoleon I. on his generals.

1380. Les sots depuis Adam sont en majorité. C. Delavigne, Épître à MM. de l'Acad. Fr. sur la question, *"L'Étude fait-elle le bonheur?"* ver. 112.—*Since Adam's time fools have been in the majority:* and, unfortunately, it is the majority that governs.

1381. Les succès produisent les succès, comme l'argent produit l'argent. Chamf. Maximes, vol. 2, p. 89.—*Success produces success, like money makes money.*

1382. Les trente-six raisons d'Arlequin. Quit. p. 75.—*Harlequin's thirty-six reasons.* Harlequin arrives with thirty six reasons why his master is unable to accept the invitation sent him. The first is, that he is dead.

1383. Les uns disent que le roi d'Angleterre est mort, les autres disent qu'il n'est pas mort; pour moi, je ne crois ni les uns, ni les autres; je vous le dis en confidence, mais surtout ne me compromettez pas. Talleyrand, *Album Perdu*, p. 36.—*Some say that the King of England (George III.) is dead, some that he isn't. I believe neither the one nor the other. I only tell you in confidence, but for Heaven's sake don't make me responsible.*

1384. Le superflu, chose très nécessaire. Volt. Le Mondain (1736), v. 22.—*Superfluities! a very necessary article.* Marivaux in his *Jeu de l'Amour et du Hasard* (1730), 1, 1, has—

Silvia. De beauté et de bonne mine, je l'en dispense; ce sont là des agréments superflus.

Lisette. Vertuchoux! si je me marie jamais, ce superflu-là sera mon necessaire. (Alex. pp. 498-9.)

1385. L'État c'est moi! Chéruel, Hist. de l'Administration Monarchique, Paris, 1855, p. 32.—*I am the State.*

Reply attributed to Louis XIV. in his seventeenth year, and supposed to have been addressed to the President of the Parliament of Paris, April 13, 1655, on the latter offering some objections "in the interests of the State," to the fiscal demands of the sovereign. "The State," Louis is supposed to have interjected at this point; "the State is myself." To give full picturesqueness of insolence to the scene, the boy king is represented as having come to Parliament directly from the chase in the Forest of Vincennes, to which, when the necessary business had been transacted, he afterwards returned. He makes his appearance before the assembly in full hunting-dress, "justaucorps rouge, chapeau gris, et grosses bottes"; to which imagination may add an impatient slapping of the *grosses bottes* with the whip that formed part of the royal equipment, while awaiting the registering of the royal edicts. Such is the tradition; a pretty enough one in its way, and if the critics have succeeded in demolishing the wording of it as matter of authentic record, it is only to admit its essential truth as typical of the autocratic spirit that was to control the affairs of France until the Revolution swept everything away. The king, says Chéruel, quoting from a contemp. diary in the Bibliothèque Nat. (*Hist. de l'Administration Monarchique*, etc., 1855, vol. ii. pp. 32-4), suppressed at once all initiative or action of any kind on the part of the Parliament, "sous prétexte de délibérer sur les édits qui naguères ont été lus et publiés en ma presence," and left the house in silence. It was not so much a *Lit de justice* as a dissolution that was thus inflicted on the Parliament, and the royal behests were less resented than the cavalier tone in which they were delivered. Some thirty years later, Bossuet confirms with his episcopal sanction the absolutism of his royal master: "Tout État est en lui, la volonté de tout le peuple est renfermée dans la sienne. Comme en Dieu est réunie toute perfection, etc., ainsi toute la puissance des particuliers est réunie en la personne du prince" (*Politique tirée de l'Écriture Sainte*, Bk. 5, art. 4). La Bruyère (chap. 10, Du Souverain), writing about the same date, says, "Il n'y a point de patrie dans le despotique; d'autres choses y suppléent: l'interêt, la gloire, le service du prince": and, in the treatise on Common Law, drawn up by de Torci at Louis the Fourteenth's orders for the instruction of the D. of Burgundy, occurs the passage, "La nation ne fait pas corps en France: elle réside toute entière dans la personne du roy." Lémontey (P. E.), *Essai sur la Monarchie de Louis XIV.*, 1818, p. 327 n.

1386. Le temps est un grand maître, il règle bien des choses. Corn. Sertor. 2, 4.—*Time is a great master, he sets many things right.*

1387. Le temps n'épargne pas ce qu'on a fait sans lui. Fayolle, Disc. sur la littérature, etc., Paris, 1801, stanza 7.—*Time preserves nothing that has not taken time to do.*

1388. Le temps, qui change tout, change aussi nos humeurs; Chaque âge a ses plaisirs, son esprit et ses mœurs.
Boil. L'A. P. 3, 373.

Our tastes e'en take with time a different phase:
Each age has its own pleasures, wit, and ways.—*Ed.*

1389. Le trident de Neptune est le sceptre du monde. Lemierre, Le Commerce (1756).—*The trident of Neptune is the sceptre of the world.* A good motto for a naval and commercial power like Great Britain.

1390. Leurs écrits sont des vols qu'ils nous ont faits d'avance. Piron, La Métromanie (1738), 3, 6.—*Their writings* (our predecessors') *are thoughts stolen from us by anticipation.* Said of the thoughts of men of genius that find their echo in every age. *V.* Alex. p. 541.

The Chevalier de Cailly ("d'Aceilly") has some lines (*Diverses petites poésies*, 1667, p. 160) to the same effect:

Dis-je quelque chose assez belle,
L'Antiquité, toute en cervelle,
Me dit, je l'ay dite avant toy.
C'est une plaisante donzelle;
Que ne venoit-elle après moy,
J'aurois dit la chose avant elle.

And de Musset's witty expression of the sentiment (Namouna, Chant 2, 9) will be familiar to many:

> Rien n'appartient à rien, tout appartient à tous;
> Il faut être ignorant comme un maître d'école
> Pour se flatter de dire une seule parole
> Que personne ici-bas n'ait pu dire avant nous.
> C'est imiter quelqu'un que de planter des choux.

1391. Leve fit quod bene fertur onus. Ov. Am. 1, 2, 10.— *The burden which is borne with cheerfulness becomes light.*

1392. Le véritable Amphitryon est l'Amphitryon où l'on dîne. Mol. Amph. 3, 5 (Sosie loq.).—*The true Amphitryon is the Amphitryon where one dines.*

1393. Levia perpessæ sumus,
Si flenda patimur.   Sen. Troades, Act. iii. 412 (Andromache loq.).—*Light are our woes, if tears can comfort them.*

1394. Levis est dolor qui capere consilium potest. Sen. Med. 155.— *That grief is light which is able to take advice.*

1395. Le vrai est le sublime des sots. Le P. Griffet, Études de l'hist. réligieuse, 2nd Éd., p. 271.—*Truth is a fool's idea of the sublime.*

1396. Le vrai moyen d'être trompé, c'est de se croire plus fin que les autres. La Rochef., § 127, p. 47.—*The surest way to be taken in is to think one's self more clever than others.*

1397. L'exactitude de citer. C'est un talent plus rare que l'on ne pense. Bayle, Dict. Art. SANCHEZ, *Remarques.*—*Exactness of quotation is a rarer talent than is commonly supposed.* Yet the most absolute correctness in quoting stands on a lower level than the gift of felicitous application, for which wit and a well-stored memory are essential. "C'est l'inspiration," says Chateaubriand, "qui donne les citations heureuses." (*Chateaubriand et son temps,* par le Cte. de Marcellus, Paris, 1859, p. 286.)

1398. L'exactitude est la politesse des rois.—*Punctuality is the politeness of kings.* Attributed to Louis XVIII. Souvenirs de J. Lafitte, Paris, 1844, i. p. 150. (Büchm. p. 494.)

1399. L'expérience est un habit qui ne se fait que sur mesure. Prov.— *Experience is a coat that must be made to measure.* It is little good at second-hand.

1400. L'histoire n'est que le tableau des crimes et des malheurs. Volt. L'Ingénu, ch. 10.—*History is little else than a picture of crime and misfortune.* Gibbon (ch. 3) says: "History, which is, indeed, little more than the register of the crimes, follies, and misfortunes of mankind."

1401. L'homme absurde est celui qui ne change jamais. A. M. Barthélémy, Ma Justification (1832).—*It is the absurd man who never changes his opinion.* Barthélémy himself, who flattered and attacked by turns the Bourbons and the Orleanists, and ended his variegated career as a pronounced adherent of the Second Empire, certainly had ample reasons for the truth of this sentiment. The passage runs:—

> J'ai pitié de celui qui, fort de son système,
> Me dit, Depuis trente ans ma doctrine est la même;
> Je suis ce que je fus; je crois ce que je croyais.
> *L'homme absurde,* etc.

1402. L'homme est de glace aux vérités,
Il est de feu pour les mensonges. La Font., Le Statuaire, 9, 6 *(fin.).*

> Where truth's concerned men are as ice,
> But fire, when they are telling lies.—*Ed.*

1403. L'homme n'est qu'un roseau le plus faible de la nature; mais c'est un roseau pensant. Pasc. Pens. 23, 6.—*Man is the weakest reed in the world, but it is a reed that thinks.*

1404. L'homme propose et Dieu dispose. Montluc, Coméd. de Proverbes, 3, 7; tr. from the "Homo proponit, sed Deus disponit," of à Kempis, 1, 19, 2.—*Man proposes and God disposes.*

> Cor hominis disponit viam suam; sed Domini est dirigere gressus ejus. Vulg. Prov. xvi. 9.—*A man's heart deviseth his way, but the Lord directeth his steps.* Fénelon, in his Epiphany sermon (1685), says of the discovery of America and of the planting of the faith there, that the enterprise was man's but the design God's: *Ainsi,* he adds, *l'homme s'agite, mais Dieu le mène.* Publ. Syrus, 216, has, *Homo semper aliud, Fortuna aliud cogitat*—"Man has one thing in view, and Fate has another."

1405. L'homme se croit toujours plus qu'il n'est, et s'estime moins qu'il ne vaut. Mme. Swetchine, vol. 2, Pensée 4.—*We always think ourselves greater than we are, and respect ourselves less than we deserve.*

1406. L'homme, "subject . . . vain, divers et ondoyant." Montaigne, Essays, 1, 1.—*Man is a vain, wayward, and wavering thing.*

1407. L'homme vit souvent avec lui même, et il a besoin de vertu; il vit avec les autres, et il a besoin d'honneur. Chamf. Maximes, vol. 2, p. 18.—*Man needs virtue because he must be often alone; and he needs honour also because he has to mix with others.*

1408. L'hypocrisie est un hommage que le vice rend à la vertu. La Rochef., § 223, p. 60.—*Hypocrisy is the homage which vice renders to virtue.*

1409. Libera chiesa in libero stato.—*A free church in a free State.* The maxim of Cavour, and his last audible words on his deathbed, June 6, 1861.

> They were addressed to the priest, Fra Giacomo, who was with him at the time. Pressing the friar's hand in token of recognition, the dying man murmured, *Frate, libera chiesa in libero stato.* For all particulars and authorities, *v.* Fumag. No. 592.

1410. Libera Fortunæ mors est: capit omnia tellus
    Quæ genuit: cælo tegitur qui non habet urnam.   Luc. 7, 818.

> Death's beyond Fortune's reach: the earth finds room
> For all she bare: and he that has no urn
> Has heav'n to cover him.—*Ed.*

1411. Liberavi animam meam.   St Bernard, Ep. 371.—*I have delivered
    my soul.*   I have relieved my conscience by speaking, and am
    no longer responsible.

> Evidently derived from Ezekiel iii. 19: "If thou give warning to the
> wicked, and he be not converted from his wickedness . . . he shall die in
> his iniquity, but thou hast delivered thy soul" (*tu autem animam tuam
> liberasti*).   St Bernard (1147 A.D.) is telling the Abbé Suger the words in
> which he had cautioned Louis VII.. dit Le Jeune (1137-1180), against giving
> his daughter Marie in marriage to Fulk, Count of Anjou, for reasons of con-
> sanguinity.   After entering his protest against the prohibited act, he adds:
> "*Liberavi animam meam: liberet et vestram Deus labiis iniquis et a lingua
> dolosa.*

1412. Liber indicium est animi.   Ov. T. 2, 357.—*Books are the index of
    the writer's mind.*

> Well would it be if authors bore this truth in mind !   It is nothing to
> the purpose that Ovid only states the proposition to deny it, and that, like
> every lascivious writer, from Catullus downwards, he excuses his literary
> improprieties on the ground that his own morals were unexceptionable.
> Impertinence indeed !   Even were the plea true, it were nothing *ad rem*,
> since an author's influence is derived from his published writings, and not
> from his private history.

1413. Liberi, quo nihil carius humano generi est.   Liv. 1, 9.—*Children
    —the dearest treasure of our race.*

1414. Libertas est potestas faciendi id quod jure licet.   Law Max.—
    Liberty consists in the power of doing that which the law permits.

1415. Libertas scelerum est, quæ regna invisa tuetur,
    Sublatusque modus gladiis.   Luc. 8, 491.

> Full range of crime, and daggers freely drawn—
> These are the props of hated governments.—*Ed.*

1416. Libertas ultima mundi
    Quo steterit ferienda loco.   Lucan, 7, 580.

> *Liberty.*

> Where Liberty had made her final stand,
> There must she be assailed with impious hand.—*Ed.*

1417. Libito fè lecito.   Dante, Inf. 5, 56.—*What she liked, that made
    she law.*   Said of Semiramis.

> Cf. Chaucer, Monkes Tale:

> His lustes were as a law in his degree.

> And Goethe, Tasso, 2, 1 (Tasso loq.): "Erlaubt ist, was gefällt."—*All's
> lawful, so it please.*   A much earlier instance is found in Caracalla's
> incestuous passion for the voluptuous beauty of his stepmother, Julia.

Vellem, si liceret (" I'd marry you but for the law"), he is said to have told her; to which the lady replied: *Si libet, licet. An nescis te impera- torem esse, et leges dare, non accipere?* (" What you like is the law. Do you forget that you are Emperor, and give laws, not receive them?")— Spart. Caracalla, 10.

1418. Licet superbus ambules pecunia,
    Fortuna non mutat genus.   Hor. Epod. 4, 5.

> *Nouveau Riche.*
> Your money cannot change your blood,
> Although you strut as though it could.

1419. Liebe kennt der Allein, der ohne Hoffnung liebt.   Schiller,
    D. Carlos, 2, 8.—*He only knows what love is, who loves without hope.*

1420. Lieb Vaterland, magst ruhig sein!   Max Schneckenburger,
    Wacht am Rhein.—*Dear Fatherland, may peace be thine!*

1421. Limæ labor ac mora.   Hor. A. P. 291.—*The labour and tedious- ness of polishing* (any work of art, poetry, painting, etc.) *as though with a file.*

1422. L'impossibilité où je suis de prouver que Dieu n'est pas, me découvre son existence.   La Bruy. ch. xvi. (Esprits forts), vol. 2, p. 167.—*The impossibility which I feel of proving that God is not, proclaims His existence.*

1423. L'ingratitude est l'indépendance du cœur.   Nestor Roqueplan (*fl.* 1840).—*Ingratitude is* (merely) *independence of spirit.*

> Other of R.'s ironical paradoxes are *Qui oblige, s'oblige* (To oblige is to lay oneself under an obligation), and, which is the same, *Un service n'oblige que celui que le rend.*   (Lud. Halévy, in *Intermédiaire des Chercheurs*, vol. 2, col. 663; and Alex. p. 258.)

1424. Lingua, sile; non est ultra narrabile quicquam.   Ov. Ep. 2, 2, 61.
    —*Silence, my tongue! not a word more must be spoken.*

1425. L'iniure se graue en métal;
    Et le bienfait s'escrit en l'onde.

    Jean Bertaut, Défense de l'amour, Œuvres, ed. Chenevière, Paris, 1891, 12mo, p. 365.—*Wrongs are engraved on metal, and kindnesses written in water.*

> Cf. Shakesp. "Hen. VIII." 4, 2:
> > Men's evil manners live in brass: their virtues
> > We write in water.
> And Sir Thos. More, "Hist. of K. Rycharde III." (1513): " For men use if they have an evil turne, to write it in marble; and whoso doth us a good tourne, we write it in duste."   Pitt Press Series, reprint (1883, p. 35, 20) from the London ed. of 1557.

1426. L'insurrection est le plus saint des devoirs. Lafayette, Mémoires, Corresp. et MSS. du Général Lafayette, Paris, 1837, vol. 2, p. 382.—*Insurrection is the most sacred of duties.*

> Although much qualified when read with its context, this sentiment, occurring in a speech delivered in Nat. Assembly during the early days of

the Revolution (Feb. 20, 1790), was sure to be cited afterwards, and was cited, as a justification of general lawlessness. An echo of the words will be found in Art. xxxv. of the "Declaration des droits de l'homme" (*Moniteur*, June 27, 1793): "Quand le gouvernement viole les droits du peuple, l'insurrection est, pour le peuple et pour chaque portion du peuple, le plus sacré des droits et le plus indispensable des devoirs." Alex. pp. 260-1; and Chamf. vol. 3, p. 174.

1427. L'Italia farà da se.—*Italy will act by herself.*

The paternity of this phrase—the watchword of the Italian liberationists of 1848-9—is much disputed. Fumag. produces the text of Charles Albert's "Proclamation to the people of Lombardy and Venice," of Mar. 23, 1848—only two days before the Piedmontese troops crossed the Ticino—in which the king showed how wonderfully Providence had *pose l'Italia in grado di far da se* ("put Italy in a position to act by herself"). On the other hand, the king himself (*v.* Piersilvestro Leopardi, *Narrazioni storiche*, Torino, 1856, cap. 49, p. 230) honestly disavowed the authorship of the words, though he admitted that they were most *à propos*. The words have also been ascribed to Gioberti and others, for which see Fumag. 1008; Büchm. pp. 467-8.

1428. L'Italie est une expression (*or* un nom) géographique. Prince von Metternich.—*Italy is a geographical expression.*

It would seem that Metternich let fall this remark while discussing the Italian question with Palmerston in the summer of 1847, and added that, "more or less," the description would equally apply to Germany. *V.* "Aus dem Nachlasse des Grafen Prokesch-Osten, Briefwechsel mit Herrn von Gentz und Fürsten Metternich," Wien, 1881, vol. 2, p. 343; Büchm. p. 538; and the "Mémoires, Documents, etc., de Metternich publiés par son fils," Paris, 1883, vol. 7, p. 415.

1429. Literæ Bellerophontis. Chil. p. 488.—*Bellerophon's letter.*

Bellerophon was sent by Prætus, at the instigation of his wife Sthenoboea, with a letter, called σήματα λυγρά (*baneful tokens*) in Il. 6, 168, to Iobates to put the bearer to death. Hence the bearer of any missive unfavourable to himself (like Uriah's letter to Joab, 2 Kings xi. 14) is called a "Bellerophon," and the letter, *literæ Bellerophontis.* Cf. Plaut. Bacch. 4, 7, 12.

1430. Litera enim occidit, spiritus autem vivificat. Vulg. Cor. 2, 3, 6.— *The letter killeth, the spirit giveth life.*

1431. Litera gesta docet: quid credas allegoria; Moralis quid agas: quo tendas anagogia.

Med. Latin.—*The letter (of Scripture) gives the facts: its allegorical meaning contains the doctrine; its morality furnishes a rule of life, and its mysticism shows whither you should aim.*

1432. Locus est et pluribus umbris. Hor. Ep. 1, 5, 28.

There's room enough, and each may bring his friend.—*Creech.*

The "*Umbra*" is the uninvited guest, brought to the feast by one of the *invités.*

1433. Lo giorno se n'andava, e l'aer bruno Toglieva gli animai che sono in terra Dalle fatiche loro   Dante, Inf. 2, 1.

The day was failing, and the dusky hour Of twilight loosed all creatures from their toil.—*Ed.*

Imitated in Chaucer's *Assemble of Foules:*

The day 'gan failin; and the darke night,
That revith bestis from their businesse.

1434. L'on espère de vieillir et l'on craint la vieillesse; c'est à dire l'on
aime la vie et l'on fuit la mort. La Bruy. ch. xi. (L'homme),
vol. ii. p. 32.—*We hope to grow old, yet we dread old age; that
is, we love life, and wish to avoid death.*

Ὦ γῆρας, οἵαν ἐλπίδ' ἡδονῆς ἔχεις,
καὶ πᾶς τις εἰς σὲ βούλετ' ἀνθρώπων μολεῖν·
λαβὼν δὲ πεῖραν μεταμέλειαν λαμβάνει·
ὡς οὐδέν ἐστι χεῖρον ἐν θνητῷ γένει.   Eur. Fr. 904.

Old Age.

What pleasurable hopes are thine, Old Age!
And every man desires to reach that stage;
But, with experience, changes soon his mind,
Deeming there's nothing worse for poor mankind.—*Ed.*

1435. Longa est injuria, longæ
Ambages, sed summa sequar fastigia rerum.   Virg. A. 1, 341.

Long
And dark the story of her wrong:
To thread each tangle time would fail,
So learn the summits of the tale.—*Conington.*

1436. Longe mea discrepat istis
Et vox et ratio.

Hor. S. 1, 6, 92.—*Both my words and feelings differ widely
from theirs.*

1437. Longum iter est per præcepta, breve et efficax per exempla.
Sen. Ep. 6, 5.—*It is a long way of teaching by precepts, short and
efficacious by example.*

1438. L'on se repent rarement de parler peu, très souvent de trop
parler: maxime usée et triviale que tout le monde sait, et que
tout le monde ne pratique pas.   La Bruy. ch. xi. (L'homme),
Car. vol. ii. p. 63.—*We rarely repent of having spoken too little,
often of having said too much—a well-worn maxim which every
one knows, but which every one does not practise.*

1439. L'ordre règne à Varsovie.—*Order reigns at Warsaw.*

On Sept. 7 and 8, 1831, Poland made its last determined struggle for
freedom, which was crushed in a few days, with tremendous losses on the
Polish side, by the Russian general Paskiewitch; and Sébastiani, the
French Minister for Foreign Affairs, was able to announce in the Chamber
of Deputies, on Sept. 16, the occupation of Warsaw by the Tsar's forces.
In the *Moniteur* of Sept. 17 (p. 1601, col. 2) he is reported to have said,
"Le gouvernement a communiqué tous les renseignements qui lui étaient
parvenus sur les événements de la Pologne . . . au moment où l'on
écrivait, la tranquillité régnait à Varsovie." The word "*l'ordre*" (order),
with which the saying is proverbially connected, is probably due to the
Moniteur of the day before, which reported that "*L'ordre* et la tranquillité

sont entièrement rétablis dans la capitale." In the *Caricature* of the day a cartoon appeared (by Grandville and Eugène Forest), of a Russian soldier surrounded by a mound of Polish corpses, and entitled "L'ordre règne à Varsovie," which accounted in no small measure for the perpetuation of the epigram.

1440. L'oreille est le chemin du cœur. Volt. Ep. 46, Réponse au roi de Prusse.—*The ear is the road to the heart.* The same has been said, though not in poetry, of the stomach.

1440A. Λύχνου ἀρθέντος, γυνὴ πᾶσα ἡ αὐτή. Apost. Cent. 10, 90.—*When the light is removed, every woman is the same.* "Joan's as good as my lady in the dark."

1441. Lucri bonus est odor ex re
Qualibet. Illa tuo sententia semper in ore
Versetur, dis atque ipso Jove digna, poetæ:
Unde habeas, quærit nemo; sed oportet habere. Juv. 14, 204.

> "Profit smells sweet from whatsoe'er it springs."
> This golden sentence, which the powers of Heaven
> Or Jove himself might glory to have given,
> Will never, poets, from your thoughts, I trust;
> None question whence it comes, but come it must.—*Gifford.*

The "golden maxim," here referred to, came from Vespasian's lips when his son Titus expostulated with him on the tax levied on latrines. Suet. *Vesp.* 23.

1442. Lucus a non lucendo.—*A grove* (is so called) *from its not giving light* (lux).

> Quint. (1, 6, 34) says, Etiamne a contrariis aliqua sinemus trahi? ut lucus, quia umbra opacus, parum luceat?—*Shall we go so far as to derive words from their contraries, like* Lucus, *from the absence of* Lux *caused by its thick shade?* Cf. St August. Doctr. Christ., lib. 3, cap. 41 (vol. 3, Pt I. p. 43 F). So also Bellum, a nulla re bella; Canis, a non canendo, etc. To the *Lucus a non* principle, as it is called, are referred all such paradoxical derivations and descriptions which involve a contradiction in the mere stating of them.

1443. Lugete o Veneres Cupidinesque
Et quantum est honinum venustiorum!
Passer mortuus est meæ puellæ:
Passer, deliciæ meæ puellæ,
Quem plus illa oculis amabat. Cat. 3, 1.

> *Lesbia's Sparrow.*
> Queens of Beauty, saucy Cupids,
> Handsome folk all the world over,
> Come and join me in my sorrow;
> My own darling's lost her sparrow;
> He was her pet, her own darling;
> Better than her eyes she loved him.—*Shaw.*

1444. Lumen in Cœlo.—*Light in the Heavens.* Motto assigned to the Pontificate of Leo XIII. in the "Prophecies of St Malachy."

> Those prophecies were first published in Venice, 1591 (and again in 1595), by the Benedictine Arnold Wyon (or Wion), who himself suspected their genuineness. The list, designed to reach to the end of the world, is not yet exhausted, and allows Pius X. nine successors, extending to about the

end of the century: the remaining Popes being respectively indicated by
the mottoes *Religio depopulata, Fides intrepida, Pastor angelicus, Pastor et
nauta, Flos florum, De medietate lunæ, De labore solis,* and the *Gloria
olivæ* of a "Peter the Second," who will assist at the destruction of
Rome and the consummation of all things generally. Occasionally, but
only occasionally, "St Malachy" makes a lucky shot. *Peregrinus apos-
tolicus* aptly describes the enforced "wanderings" of Pius VI., until his
death, in a foreign land, at Valence in 1799. "*Aquila rapax*" falls in
with the carrying off to Paris of Pius VII. by (the "Eagle") Napoleon in
1804; and Pio Nono's "*Crux de Cruce*" found interpretation in the "cross"
which he suffered from the heraldic "Cross" of the house of Savoy. The
flaming comet borne in the Pecci family arms presents another curious coincidence in the *Lumen de cœlo* of Leo XIII. The *devise* of Pius X. is *Ignis
ardens*, regarding which no satisfactory explanation has as yet been found.

1445. L'une des marques le la médiocrité d'esprit, est de toujours
conter. La Bruy. ch. xii. (*Jugements*), vol. 2, p. 79.—*It is a
sign of mediocrity of wit to be always telling anecdotes.*

1446. L'univers est une espèce de livre, dont on n'a lu que la première
page quand on n'a vu que son pays. Fougeret de Monbron, Le
Cosmopolite, Lond., 1761, p. 3.—*The world is a book of which
the man has only read the first page who has seen but his own
country.* Motto of "Childe Harold."

1447. Lupus in fabula (*or sermone*).—*The wolf in the story.* Said of
the appearance of any one who is the immediate subject of
conversation. "Talk of the D——, etc."

> De Varrone loquebamur, lupus in fabula: venit enim ad me. Cic. Att.
> 13, 33, 4.— *We were talking about Varro, and (talk of the D——) in he came!*

1448. Lusisti satis, edisti satis, atque bibisti:
Tempus abire tibi est. Hor. Ep. 2, 2, 214.

> You've frolick'd, eaten, drunk to the content
> Of human appetite: 'tis time you went.—*Conington.*
> Cf. "Affatim Edi, bibi, lusi."—Liv. Andronicus Trag. (Ribb. ii. 4).

1449. Lyon fit la guerre à la liberté; Lyon n'est plus.—*Lyons made
war upon liberty; Lyons is no more.*

> Inscription ordered to be written on a column marking the "site" of
> Lyons, after its siege and surrender to the forces of the infamous Conven-
> tion, Oct. 9, 1793. The very name of Lyons was to disappear under the
> new designation of "Commune Affranchie." The work of destroying the
> city (and of massacring its inhabitants) was faithfully carried out under
> the superintendence of three creatures of hideous memory, known on earth
> as Couthon. Collot d'Herbois, and Fouché; and the place was reduced to a
> heap of ruins. Couthon was sent to his account the year following, along
> with Robespierre, July 28, 1794; and his fellow-assassin, Collot d'Herbois,
> died in 1796 in the prisons of Cayenne. Fouché, the least abominable of
> the three, had better fortune: he rose to be "Duke of Otranto" under
> Napoleon, amassed an enormous fortune, and died, in exile, at Trieste in
> 1820. Chateaubriand, who saw Fouché enter the royal presence at S. Denis
> (July 1815), supporting Talleyrand on his arm, represents him as "Crime"
> personified—"le vice appuyé *sur le bras du crime.*" (*Mémoires d'Outre-tombe*,
> 1860, vol. 4, p. 25). Just a week (Oct. 16) after the fall of Lyons, the Queen
> of France passed into the heavenly kingdom to receive the martyr's crown.

M.

1450. Mach 'es Wenigen recht: Vielen gefallen ist schlimm.   Schiller,
Votivtafeln (Wahl).—*Be content to satisfy a few, to please many
is bad.*

1451. Macte nova virtute, puer, sic itur ad astra.   Virg. A. 9, 641.—
*Increase in new deeds of valour, my son!   That is the road to
fame!*

> Go on, and raise your glories higher!
> 'Tis thus that men to heaven aspire.—*Conington.*

The first half of the line is sometimes said ironically, and the latter has
been applied to ballooning.   Cf. Liv. 10, 40: Macte virtute diligentiaque
esto—*Persevere in virtue and diligence.*

1452. Madame cependant a passé du matin au soir, ainsi que l'herbe
des champs.   Le matin elle fleurissait: avec quelle grâce, vous
le savez: le soir nous la vîmes séchée.   Bossuet, Oraison
Funèbre de Henriette Anne d'Angleterre, Duchesse d'Orléans,
St Denis, Aug. 21, 1670.—*Her Highness passed, like the grass
of the field, from the morning to eventide.   At her dawn, she
bloomed with a grace that you all remember: at evening we saw
her withered.*   The Duchess, daughter of Charles 1., died
June 30, 1670, not without suspicions of poison.   The following
is also from the same "Oraison."

1453. Madame fut douce envers la mort, comme elle l'était envers tout
le monde.—*She was gentle in face of death, as she was indeed
with every one.*   Often qu. of a calm and resigned end.

1454. Ma foi! s'il m'en souvient, il ne m'en souvient guère.   Thos.
Corneille, Le Géolier, 2, 6 (Jodelet loq.).—*'Faith! if I remember
it, I remember it but seldom.*

In the play, Jodelet, a farcical serving-man, has been arrested in the
habiliments of Frederick, K. of Sicily, and brought before the latter's
mortal enemy, the King of Naples.   Octave, the equerry of Frederick,
pretends, in order to keep up the joke, that he is in the presence of his
sovereign, and reminds him of various acts of devotion rendered by his
(Octave's) family on behalf of the royal person.   To this, Jodelet replies in
the terms of the quotation.

1455. Magalia quondam.   Virg. A. 1, 421.—*Formerly cottages.*   Where
hovels once stood, splendid mansions stand.   The early history
of the outlying parts of most modern cities.

1456. Magis magnos clericos non sunt magis magnos sapientes.   Rab.
1, 39; and Montaigne, 1, 24.   (Brother Jean des Entommeures,
the monk, to Gargantua).—*The greatest churchmen are not always
the wisest of men.*   Régnier, Sat. 3, fin. (Œuvres compl. ed. Jannot,
Paris, 1867), puts the same sentiment in another form:

> N'en desplaise aux docteurs, Cordeliers, Jacobins,
> Pardieu! les plus grands clercs ne sont pas les plus fins.

> To divines of all kinds with due deference bowing.
> The greatest of churchmen are not the most knowing.—*Ed.*

1457. Magistratum legem esse loquentem, legem autem mutum magistratum. Cic. Leg. 3, 1, 2.—*The magistrate is the law speaking, the law is the magistrate keeping silence.*

1458. Magna civitas, magna solitudo. Tr. of the anon. ἐρημία μεγάλη 'στὶν ἡ μεγάλη πόλις, in Meineke, p. 1250.—*A great city is a great solitude;* and of no city is this more true than of London. Originally said of Megalopolis in Arcadia, the line is qu. by Strabo (xvi. 738, fin.) of Seleucia on the Tigris, the capital of the Seleucidæ, now El Modain, which during the third century B.C. surpassed Babylon in superficial area, although for the most part deserted.

1459. Magna mœnis mœnia. Plaut. Mil. 2, 2, 73.—*You are building great walls.* A great undertaking.

1460. Magnas inter opes inops. Hor. C. 3, 16, 28.—*Poor in the midst of wealth.* Description of a miser.

1461. Magno jam conatu magnas nugas. Ter. Heaut. 4, 1, 8.—*An extraordinary effort for a mere trifle.*

1462. Magnum pauperies opprobrium jubet
    Quidvis et facere et pati. Hor. C. 3, 24, 42.—

Poverty.

No shame too great, no hardship too severe,
That poverty won't urge, or won't endure.—*Ed.*

1463. Magnumque decus, ferroque petendum,
    Plus patria potuisse sua : mensuraque juris
    Vis erat. Lucan. 1, 174.

'Twere a proud boast indeed and one to win
At the sword's point—to force one's private aims
On an unwilling country and to make
Violence the rule of law.—*Ed.*

Lucan says here precisely what that eminent master of common sense, Bismarck, said in conference with Favre on the terms of peace in 1871. "The country," he remarked, "requires to be served, and not to be domineered over." Political consistency often becomes mere blundering wrongheadedness. *See* Moritz Busch's *Bismarck*, etc., vol. 2, p. 279, Engl. tr.

1464. Mais, au moindre revers funeste,
    Le masque tombe, l'homme reste,
    Et le héros s'évanouit. J. B. Rousseau, A la Fortune, 2, 6.

Fortune.

But, if perchance his fortune wanes,
The mask drops off, the man remains :
And the hero disappears.—*Ed.*

Cp. Eripitur persona, manet res. Lucr. 3, 58.—*The mask is snatch'd away, the man remains;* and, Vera redit facies, dum simulata perit. Petr. cap. 80.—*The real face returns, while the disguise disappears.* Said of actors on resuming their ordinary attire after the play.

1465. Mais c'est donc une révolte! Non, Sire, c'est une révolution. Vie du Duc de la Rochefoucauld Liancourt par le Comte (F. G.) de la Rochefoucauld Liancourt, Paris, 1827, p. 26.—*But this, then, is a revolt!*—*No, Sire, it is a revolution.*

> Famous reply of the Duc de Liancourt to Louis XVI., on reporting to his royal master, on the night of July 12, 1789 (and not on the fall of the Bastille, two days later, as is commonly said), the insurgent condition of Paris, consequent on the dismissal of Necker and the fatal and fatuous charge of the Prince de Lambesc's "Royal Allemand" cavalry on the crowd in the Tuileries gardens of the same day. Paris was roused on every side to a pitch of fury which henceforward carried all before it; and had it not been for the blunder of this unhappy Sunday, the march of history might have taken a different course. If there was a kindlier, more beneficent soul then living than the king it was Liancourt, yet such qualities make a poor breakwater against a "revolution." The quotation is, I believe, the earliest instance of the word in its modern typical (and violent) sense.

1466. Mais elle était du monde où les plus belles choses
      Ont le pire destin;
    Et rose, elle a vécu ce que vivent les roses,
      L'espace d'un matin.   Malherbe, Ode à du Périer.

> *An Early Death.*
>
> A world was hers where all that fairest blows
>   Meets with the cruellest doom:
> The rose had but the lifetime of a rose—
>   A single morning's bloom.—*Ed.*

1467. Mais où sont les neiges d'antan? Fr. Villon, refrain of the ballad, Des Dames Dv Temps Jadis.—*But where are last year's snows?* Said of those times and scenes in the past of which only the regretful memory remains.

1468. Major e longinquo reverentia. Tac. A. 1, 47.—*Respect is greater from a distance.* Said of the majesty which surrounds royalty. In this, as in many other cases, "distance lends enchantment to the view."

1469. Majore tumultu
    Planguntur nummi quam funera, nemo dolorem
    Fingit in hoc casu . . . . . .
    Ploratur lacrimis amissa pecunia veris.   Juv. 13, 130.

> Money's bewailed with much more harrowing scenes
> Than a man's death: for that none sorrow feigns.
> The loss of cash is mourned with genuine tears.—*Ed.*

1470. Major privato visus, dum privatus fuit, et omnium consensu capax imperii, nisi imperasset.   Tac. H. 1, 49.

> *Galba.*
>
> When he was a private individual he always seemed to be above his station; and, had he never come to the throne, he would have been deemed by common consent capable of the supreme power.

Cf. ἀμήχανον δὲ παντὸς ἀνδρὸς ἐκμαθεῖν
ψυχήν τε καὶ φρόνημα καὶ γνώμην, πρὶν ἂν
ἀρχαῖς τε καὶ νόμοισιν ἐντριβὴς φανῇ.   Soph. Ant. 175.

But who can penetrate man's secret thought,
The quality and temper of his soul,
Till by high office put to frequent proof,
And execution of the laws?—*Potter.*

The saying, ἀρχὴ ἄνδρα δεικνύει—*Power shows the man*—is ascribed by
Diog. Laert. (1, 77) to Pittacus.   Bacon (Essay XI.) also has, "A place
showeth the man." Epaminondas, in Plut. Mor. p. 990, 22 (Præcepta
Gerend. Reip. c. 15, 2), gave the maxim a new turn—οὐ μόνον ἡ ἀρχὴ
τὸν ἄνδρα δείκνυσιν, ἀλλὰ καὶ ἀρχὴν ἀνήρ—*Not only does office show the man,
but the man the office.*

1471. Major rerum mihi nascitur ordo,
     Majus opus moveo.

        Virg. A. 7, 44.—*A greater series of events now rise before
     me; I touch upon greater subjects.* Æneas' landing in Italy,
     and early history of Latium.

1472. Major sum quam cui possit fortuna nocere;
     Multaque ut eripiat, multo mihi plura relinquet.
     Excessere metum mea jam bona.   Ov. M. 6, 195.

                    Niobe's Luckless Boast.
        I am too great for fortune's injuries:
        Though she take much, yet must she leave me more.
        The blessings I enjoy can smile at fears.—*Ed.*

1473. Majus ab hac acie, quam quod sua sæcula ferrent,
     Vulnus habent populi: plus est quam vita salusque
     Quod perit: in totum mundi prosternimur ævum.   Lucan.7,638.

                    Pharsalia.
        Rome has received from this day's fight
        A deeper wound than meets the sight.
        'Tis more than loss of life and limb,
        We're crushed unto the end of time.—*Ed.*

1474. Malbrouck s'en va-t-en guerre,
     Mi ron ton, ton ton, mirontaine!
     Malbrouck s'en va-t-en guerre,
     Ne sçait quand reviendra, etc.

        *Marlborough is off to the wars, mi ron ton, ton ton, miron-
     taine, Marlborough is off to the wars and no one knows when he
     will return.*

        Old French song of the 18th cent., sung of Chas. Churchhill, third Duke
     of Marlborough, and his abortive expedition against Cherbourg in 1758.
     The air is of unknown origin and date.   It is the tune of "For he's a jolly
     good fellow," etc., and of an Arabic song beginning *Malbrook saffur lil
     harbi, Ya lail-ya, lail-ya, laila.*

1475. Maledicus a malefico non distat nisi occasione.   Quint. 12, 9, 9.—
     *An evil-speaker differs only from an evil-doer in the want of
     opportunity.*   "Willing to wound, and yet afraid to strike."
     Pope, Prol. to *Satires.*

1476. Male parta, male dilabuntur. Poeta ap. Cic. Phil. 2, 27, 65.—
Ill-gotten goods will come to nought. Cf. Plaut. Pæn. 4, 2, 22.
Male partum, male disperit.—*Light come, and light go.*

1477. Male secum agit æger, medicum qui hæredem facit. Syr. 332.—
A sick man does badly for himself who makes his doctor his heir.

1478. Male verum examinat omnis
Corruptus judex.   Hor. S. 2, 2, 8.

> The judge who soils his fingers by a gift
> Is scarce the man a doubtful case to sift.—*Conington.*

1479. Malheureuse France, malheureux roi!   Étienne Béquet, *Journal
des Débats,* Aug. 10, 1829.—*Unhappy France, unhappy king!*

Last words of an article provoked by the substitution of the reactionary
Polignac ministry for the moderate and conciliatory policy of Martignac's
cabinet. The culprit himself escaped punishment, Bertin, the editor of
the *Débats,* having taken the entire responsibility of the publication on
himself, for which he was sentenced to six months imprisonment and a fine
of 500 fr.

1480. Malum consilium consultori est pessimum. Gell. 4, 5, 2. A transl.
of Hes. Op. 264: ἡ δὲ κακὴ βουλὴ τῷ βουλεύσαντι κακίστη.—
Bad counsel is worst for the counsellor, like Haman's advice to
Ahasuerus.

1481. Malum est consilium, quod mutari non potest. Syr. 362.—*It is
a bad decision that cannot be altered.*

1482. Mal vêtus, logés dans les trous,
Sous les combles, dans les décombres,
Nous vivons avec les hiboux,
Et les larrons, amis des ombres.
> Pierre Dupont, Chant des Ouvriers, 1846.

> *The Proletariat.*
> In rags, and lodged in filthy holes,
> Up in the roof, in noisome plight;
> We herd along with thieves and owls,
> And such ill-omened birds of night.—*Ed.*

1483. Manet alta mente repostum
Judicium Paridis spretæque injuria formæ.
> Virg. A. 1, 26.—*Deep-seated in her heart remains the decision
of Paris, and the affront shown to her slighted beauty.* Juno
resenting the judgment of Paris in awarding the prize of beauty
to Venus.

1484. Man lebt nur einmal in der Welt. Goethe, Clavigo (1774), 1, 1
(Carlos loq.).—*Man has but one life in this world.*

1485. Man soll die Stimmen wägen und nicht zählen. Schiller, Demetrius. — *Votes should be weighed, not counted.* Plin. (Ep. 2, 12)
says, Numerantur enim sententiæ non ponderantur; nec aliud

in publico consilio potest fieri, in quo nihil est tam inæquale, quam æqualitas ipsa.—*Votes are counted not weighed, nor is anything else possible in a court of justice, where nothing is so unequal as equality itself.*

1486. Man spricht vergebens viel, um zu versagen;
Der andre hört von allem nur das Nein!
Goethe, Iphigenia, 1, 3 (Thoas loq.).—*In vain one adds words in making a refusal: the other, first and last, only hears the "No!"*

1487. Μάντις ἄριστος ὅστις εἰκάζει καλῶς. Eur. Fr. 944, Dind.—*He is the best divine who best divines.* He is the best prophet who makes the best guess. Motto of *Guesses at Truth*, by the brothers A. and J. Hare. *V.* Plut. de Defect. Orac. 432 C.

1488. Mantua me genuit, Calabri rapuere, tenet nunc
Parthenope. Cecini pascua, rura, duces.
Tib. Cl. Donatus, Vita Virgili (prefixed to Delph. Ed.).—*Mantua was my birthplace; Calabria carried me off; Naples holds me now. I sang pastures, fields, heroes.* Virgil's epitaph.

1489. Manum de tabula. Cic. Fam. 7, 25, 1.—*Hands off the picture! Add no more to your work! Enough!*

Apelles, comparing himself with the painter Protogenes, maintained that *Uno se præstare, quod manum ille de tabula nesciret tollere* (Plin. 35, 36, 10), "In one particular he had the advantage, because Protogenes never knew when to leave off."

1490. Manus hæc inimica tyrannis
Ense petit placidam sub libertate quietem.
Algernon Sidney (written in an album at Copenhagen).
Sworn foe to tyranny, this hand but draws
The sword in gentle peace' and freedom's cause.—*Ed.*

1491. Manus manum lavat. Sen. Apoc. 9, 9.—*One hand washes the other.* Mutual assistance. Cf. La Font. 8, 17 (L'Ane et le Chien), Il se faut entr'aider, c'est la loi de nature.—*It is our duty to assist each other; 'tis nature's law.*

In Menand. *Monost.* 543 is, χεὶρ χεῖρα νίπτει, δάκτυλοι δὲ δακτύλους— *Hand washes hand, and fingers fingers.* Büchm. p. 346, qu. a line of Epicharmus, Ἁ δὲ χεὶρ τὰν χεῖρα νίζει· δός τι, καί τι λάμβανε, Stob. 10, 13— *As one hand washes the other; so you must both give and take:* and,

Hand wird nur von Hand gewaschen;
Wenn du nahmen willst, so gieb. Goethe, *Wie du mir, so ich dir.*

Either hand must wash the other;
If you take, then you must give.—*Ed.*

1492. Marchand qui perd, ne peut rire. Mol. G. Dandin, 2, 9.—*The dealer who loses cannot afford to laugh.* Let those laugh who win.

1493. Marmoream se relinquere quam latericiam accepisset. Suet. Aug. 29.—*He had received a Rome of brick, and he left a Rome of marble.* Well known boast of Augustus with reference to

N

the palatial splendour with which he almost rebuilt the city during his long reign. Johnson says the same of the transformation effected in English poetry by the genius of Dryden. (*Life of Dryden*). Of Queen Victoria, on the other hand, it will be said that she found London stucco, and left it brick.

1494. Mars gravior sub pace latet. Claud VI. Cons. Hon. 307.—*More serious hostilities lie concealed under a semblance of peace.*

1495. Martyres veros non facit pœna, sed causa. St Aug. Ep. 89, 2 (vol. ii. p. 166 F) —*It is the cause, and not the penalty, that distinguishes the true martyr from the false.*

1496. Ma solo un punto fu quel che ci vinse. Dante, Inf. 5, 132.—*But there was one point only which was too much for us.* Francesca di Rimini, speaking of the passage in the romance of Lancelot —where he and Guinevere embrace—that she and Paolo read together.

1497. Mater artium necessitas, *or*, Necessitas rationum inventrix. Chil. p. 369. Prov.—*Necessity is the mother of invention.*

Cf. the Greek, Χρεία διδάσκει, κἂν βραδύς τις ᾖ, σοφόν. Eur. Telephus, Fr. 27.—*Necessity will put wits even into the dullest heads;* and, Χρεία διδάσκει κἂν ἄμουσος ᾖ σοφόν. Menand. Carchedon. 6.—*Necessity teaches wisdom even to the unlearned.*

1498. Materiem, qua sis ingeniosus, habes. Ov. A. A. 2, 34.—*You have materials with which to show your talent.*

1499. Materiem superabat opus. Ov. M. 2, 5.—*The workmanship surpassed in value the material.* Description of the Palace of the Sun, the silver doors of which were enriched with embossed work by Vulcan. Applicable to any object of art where the material falls out of sight and the workmanship is everything.

1500. Mature fieri senem, si diu velis esse senex. Prov. ap. Cic. Sen. 10, 32.—(The proverb says) *You must be an old man young, if you would be an old man long.*

1501. Maxima quæque domus servis est plena superbis. Juv. 5, 66.
Every big house has a crowd of
Supercilious servants.—*Shaw.*

1502. Mecum facile redeo in gratiam. Phædr. 5, 3, 6.—*I soon get on good terms again with myself,* as the bald man said after slapping his poll to drive off a fly.

1503. Μηδεὶς ἀγεωμέτρητος εἰσίτω. Chil. p. 710; and L. and S., *s.v.* ἀγεωμέτρητος.—*Let no one enter who is ignorant of geometry.* Inscr. over Plato's door.

1504. Medice, cura te ipsum. Prov. Vulg. Luc. 4, 33.—*Physician, heal thyself.*

1505. Médiocre et rampant, et l'on arrive à tout Beaum. Mariage de Fig. 3, 5 (Figaro loq.).—*Be second-rate, cringe, and you may attain to anything.* Cf. Omnia serviliter pro dominatione, Tac. H. 1, 36.—*Servile in all things, so it might lead him to power.* Said of the Emperor Otho.

1506. Mediocria firma.—*The middle station is the most secure.* Inscribed over his door at Gorhambury by Sir N. Bacon.

1507. Mediocribus esse poetis
Non Di, non homines, non concessere columnæ.   Hor. A. P. 372.
> But gods and men and booksellers agree
> To place their ban on middling poetry.—*Conington.*

1508. Medio tutissimus ibis.   Ov. M. 2, 137.—*You will go more safely in the middle.* Avoid extremes. Phœbus' directions to Phaethon for guiding the chariot of the Sun.

1509. Μὴ εἶναι βασιλικὴν ἀτραπὸν ἐπὶ γεωμετρίαν.   Proclus' Commentt. in Euclidem, etc.   Prol. II. 39. (Ed. Teubner, 1873, p. 68.)— *There is no royal road to geometry.* Reputed answer of Euclid to Ptolemy I. of Egypt on geometrical studies.

1510. Me focus et nigros non indignantia fumos
Tecta juvant, et fons vivus, et herba rudis.
Sit mihi verna satur: sit non doctissima conjux,
Sit nox cum somno, sit sine lite dies.   Mart. 2, 90, 7.
Earthly Bliss.
> Give me my hearth; my roof-tree all defiled
> With welcome reek; a spring, and herbage wild;
> A well-fed slave, and not too learn'd a wife;
> Sound sleep by night, and days devoid of strife.—*Ed.*

1511. Μέγα βιβλίον μέγα κακόν.—*A great book is a great evil.* Of Callimachus it is related, (in Athenæus, Deipnosoph. iii. p. 72, 1), τὸ μέγα βιβλίον ἴσον, ἔλεγεν, εἶναι τῷ μεγάλῳ κακῷ—*A great book, said he, was equivalent to a great evil.*

1512. Mehr Licht!—*More light!*
> Traditional "last words" of Goethe, March 22, 1832. Hertslet (Treppenwitz der Weltgeschichte, Berlin, 4th ed., 1895, p. 319), says that the poet's last intelligible words, addressed to his servant, were, "Macht doch den zweiten Fensterladen auch auf, damit *mehr Licht* herein komme." Both Sydney Smith (Feb. 22, 1845) and Lawrence Oliphant (Dec. 23, 1888) seem to have expired with almost the same words on their lips.

1513. Μὴ κακὰ κερδαίνειν· κακὰ κέρδεα ἶσ' ἄτῃσιν.   Hes. Op. 350.—*Make not dishonest gains: they are only equal to losses.*

1514. Μὴ κίνει Καμαρίναν, *or,* Ne moveas Camarinam.   Apost. 11, 49; and Chil. p. 489.—*Do not disturb Camarina.*
> Answer of the oracle to the inhabitants of Camarina (*Camarana*) in Sicily, when they asked Apollo if they should drain their lake to be rid of the malaria produced by it. Rejecting the deity's counsel, they filled up the lake and so allowed the enemy to capture the city. *V.* Servius in Virg. A. 3, 700, who speaks of the place as *fatis nunquam concessa moveri.* Hence the prov. *Quieta non movere* ("Leave well alone"), the motto of Sir R. Walpole, and, in principle, that of Lord Melbourne, as expressed in his characteristic objection, "Why can't you leave it alone?"

1515. Μελέτη τὸ πᾶν. Diog. Laert. 1, 99.—*Practice* (application) *is everything.* Saying of Periander, one of the seven Sages.

1516. Mel in ore, verba lactis,
Fel in corde, fraus in factis.

> Words of milk, and honied tongue:
> Heart of gall and deeds of wrong.—*Ed.*

Mediæval satire on hypocritical priests, probably derived from Plaut. Truc. 1, 2, 76.

> In melle sunt linguæ sitæ vostræ atque orationes
> Lacteque: corda felle sunt lita atque acerbo aceto.

With which comp. "Molliti sunt sermones ejus super oleum: et ipsi sunt jacula." Vulg. Ps. liv. 21.

1517. Melius omnibus quam singulis creditur. Singuli enim decipere et decipi possunt: nemo omnes, neminem omnes fefellerunt. Plin. Pan. 1, 62, 9.—*General testimony is more worthy of credence than particular. Individuals can mislead and be misled : but no one ever yet tricked all the world, nor does the world combine to deceive a particular individual.* The universal consent of mankind must be taken as the final decision on any given point.

1518. Melius, pejus; prosit, obsit; nihil vident nisi quod lubet. Ter. Heaut. 4, 1, 30.—*Better or worse, help or hurt—they see nothing but what suits their humour.*

1519. Me, me (adsum, qui feci) in me convertite ferrum,
O Rutuli: mea fraus omnis: nihil iste nec ausus,
Nec potuit; cælum hoc et conscia sidera testor.

Virg. A. 9, 427.

Nisus and Euryalus.

> Me! me, he cried, turn all your swords alone
> On me! The fact confess'd, the fault my own!
> He neither could nor durst, the guiltless youth:
> Yon heaven and stars bear witness to the truth.—*Dryden.*

1520. Même beauté, tant soit exquise,
Rassasie et soûle à la fin.
Il me faut d'un et d'autre pain:
Diversité, c'est ma devise.

La Font. Contes, 4, 12 (Pâté d'Anguille).

Variety.

> The same, same beauty every day
> Palls at last—to satiety.
> A fresh loaf for the stale one, pray!
> My motto is variety.—*Ed.*

1521. Memento mori.—*Remember thou must die.* A reminder of our latter end.

> The Egyptians used at their banquets to send round a servant with a miniature coffin containing the image of a mummy, painted so as to resemble the reality, which he presented to each guest, saying, ἐς τοῦτον ὀρέων, πῖνέ τε καὶ τέρπευ· ἔσεαι γὰρ ἀποθανὼν τοιοῦτος—*Gaze on this, and drink and enjoy yourself ; for when you are dead, such will you be.* V. Hdt. 2, 78, ed. Rawlinson, Lond., 1858, and Note.

Frange toros; pete vina: rosas cape: tingere nardo.
Ipse jubet mortis te meminisse Deus.   Mart. 2, 59, 3.

Crowd the couches, call for wine-cups, unguents bring and rosy wreath!
In your joyance God Himself commands you to remember death.—*Ed.*

Hoc etiam faciunt, ubi discubuere, tenentque
Pocula sæpe homines, et inumbrant ora coroneis,
Ex animo ut dicant: Brevis hicc' est fructus homulleis;
Jam fuerit; neque post unquam revocare licebit.   Lucr. 3, 925.

'Tis thus with guests who at the board carouse,
And pledge the wine-cup, twine with wreaths their brows—
Saying in fact, " Brief joy have mortal men;
Soon 'twill have gone, and cannot come again."—*Ed.*

Behind the Roman general in his triumphal chariot stood a slave, who, at this supreme moment of earthly glory, whispered in his ear, "Respice post te, hominem te memento," *Look behind you, remember that you are but mortal.* Tert. Apol. 33. This is confirmed by Arrian, Dissertat. Epict. iii. 24, 85; Plin. 28, 89 [28, 7, ed. Valpy]; and Hieron. Ep. 39, 2, ad fin. Cf. Mayor's Ed. of Juvenal, Sat. 10, 41-2, and Note. In the Office for Ash Wednesday the priest pronounces the words, "Memento, homo, quia pulvis es et in pulverem reverteris" (*Remember, man, that thou art dust and unto dust shalt return*), as he signs each person with the blest ashes; and the Russian Tsars used to be presented with specimens of marble at their coronation, from which to select one for their tombs, and a handful of human ashes to show what they should become.   *V.* Palmer's (W.) *Visit to the Russian Church*, London, 1882, p. 113.

1522. Meminerunt omnia amantes.   Ov. Her. 15, 43.—*Lovers remember everything.*

1523. Memini etiam quæ nolo: oblivisci non possum quæ volo. Themist. ap. Cic. Fin. 2, 32, 104.—*I remember things I had rather not: I am unable to forget those I would.*

1524. Memoria minuitur . . . nisi eam exerceas.   Cic. Sen. 7, 21.—*Without exercise memory loses its power.*

1525. Menace-moy de vivre et non pas de mourir. Sallebray, La Troade (1640), 2, 4, Œuvres, Paris (Quinet), p. 43.—*Threaten me with life and not with death!* Andromache, Hector's wife, thus retorts on Ulysses in words that might have been hurled in the face of Fouquier Tinville by the last survivor of some aristocratic house during the Reign of Terror.

1526. Mendacem memorem esse oportere. Quint. 4, 2, 91.—*A liar should have a good memory.* Corneille borrows the thought for his *Menteur*, 4, 5: " Il faut bonne mémoire, après qu'on a menti."

1527. Me nemo ministro Fur erit.   Juv. 3, 46.—*No man shall have my help to play the thief.*

1528. Mens æqua in arduis.—*Calmness in difficulties.*   Inscrip. under Warren Hasting's portrait in the Council Chamber of Calcutta.

1529. Mens cujusque is est quisque: non ea figura quæ digito demonstrari potest. Cic. Rep. 6, 24, 26.—*The mind is the man, not the person that can be pointed out with the finger.*

1530. Mens immota manet, lacrimæ volvuntur inanes.   Virg. A. 4, 449.

> *Æneas and Dido.*
> Unchanged his heart's resolves remain,
> And falling tears are idle rain.—*Conington.*

1531. Mens regnum bona possidet.   Sen. Thyest, 380.—*A good conscience is a kingdom.*

> My mind to me a kingdom is,
> Such perfect joy therein I find.—*Byrd,* Psalmes and Sonnets, 1588.

1532. Mentez, mes amis, mentez!   Volt. (in Fourn. *L.D.L.*, pp. 300-1, note).—*Lie, my friends, lie!* Voltaire wished to keep the authorship of *L'Enfant Prodigue* a secret: "mais si l'on vous devine?" disaient ses amis.—"Criez; l'on se trompe, ce n'est pas de Voltaire.   *Mentez, mes amis, mentez!*"

1533. Me quoque Musarum studium sub nocte silenti
Artibus adsuetis sollicitare solet.
> > > Claud. VI. Cons. Hon. (Præf. 11).

> Me too the study of the Muse invites
> With wonted charm upon the silent nights.—*Ed.*

1534. Mes iours font allez errant.   F. Villon, Grand Testament, St. 28, p. 28.—*My days are gone a-wandering.*   Cf. Vulg. Iob. vii. 6.

1535. Messer ohne Klinge, an welchem der Stiel fehlt.   Büchm. p. 153. —*A knife without handle and minus a blade.* A valuable possession.   Nothing.

> The words, Büchm. says, occurred in an 18th cent. Auction Catalogue of effects of a certain "Sir H. S.," which G. C. Lichtenberg thought worth inserting in the Göttingen "Taschen-Kalendar" of 1798. On the other hand, we recognise an old friend in the "Couteau de Janot"—"qui m'a déjà usé deux manches et trois lames, et c'est toujours le même"—of Dorvigny's *Les Battus paient l'amende*, sc. v. (1779); Alex. pp. 117-8. "According to the familiar illustration, the 'blade' and the 'handle' are successively renewed, and identity is lost without the loss of continuity." Card. Newman, "Essay on Development," etc., p. 3 (Lond., 1846).

1536. Messe tenus propria vive.   Pers. 6, 25.—*Live well up to your income.*

1537. Messieurs les gardes française, tirez!   Mis. de Valfons, Souvenirs, Paris, 1860, p. 143.—*Gentlemen of the French guard, fire!* Speech of Lord Chas. Hay, second son of the third Marquis of Tweeddale, at the battle of Fontenoy, May 11, 1745. But see below.

> It appears that early in the day, Hay, who, as acting Lt.-Col. was leading the First Regt. of Foot Guards, on turning the crest of a hill came suddenly upon the enemy, to the mutual astonishment of both parties, neither of whom were prepared for such a surprise though neither discovered the least want of composure. The interval between the two lines was so short as to be within speaking distance, and Lord Charles stepped forward from the ranks, and, after the courtly manner of the time, with gracefully-doffed hat and bow, and sword held at the "salute," politely invited the French commander, the Comte d'Auteroches, to "open the ball." *Monsieur, dit le*

capitaine, so de Valfons tells the story, *faites tirer vos gens! Non, Monsieur, répondit d'Auteroches, nous ne tirons jamais les premiers.* The English accordingly fired, and with such terrific effect as to inflict the loss of nearly a thousand dead and wounded on the enemy's side. But it is curious, and wholly characteristic of the French writers on the subject, that they should have claimed all the *honneur* and *courtoisie* of the incident for .their own side, entirely ignoring the fact that the initiative in such chivalrous action was taken by Hay, and that the advantage of "first fire" was offered to the enemy, in the first instance, by the English officer.

1538. Métier d'auteur, métier d'oseur.   Beaum. (*see* Fourn. *L.D.A.*, p. 94).
—*To be an author, means a daring man.*

1539. Μέτρον ἄριστον.   Diog. Laert. 1, 93.—*Moderation is best.*   Saying of Cleobulus, one of the Seven.   Cf. the ὁ μέσος βίος βέλτιστος of Arist. Pol. 4, 11; the "aurea mediocritas" (*golden mean*) of Hor. C. 2, 10, 5; and Cic. Off. 1, 25, 89.

1540. Mettre les points sur les i.   Quit. p. 462.—*Dotting one's i's.* Prov. implying extreme exactness, derived from early 16th cent. when the more precise copyists began dotting the *i* to avoid two consecutive *i's* being mistaken for *u* and other confusions.

1541. Meum est propositum in taberna mori,
Vinum sit appositum morientis ori;
Ut dicant quum venerint angelorum chori,
Deus sit propitius huic potatori.

Walter Map, Confessio Goliæ (de Nugis Curialium), v. 45, in Lat. Poems attrib. to W. Map (or Mapes), ed. T. Wright, Lond., 1841, p. 73.

In a tavern bar to die, it is my design, sir!
Handy to my parching lips put a cup of wine, sir!
So that when the angel-choirs come and find me mellow,
They may say, "The Lord have mercy on this honest fellow!"—*Ed.*

1542. Μία γὰρ χελιδὼν ἔαρ οὐ ποιεῖ.   Arist. Eth. Nic. 1, 7, 16.—*One swallow don't make a spring* (summer).

1543. Michel, più che mortale, Angel divino.   Ariosto, Orl. Fur. 33, 2.
—*Michael, more than mortal, angel divine!*   Michael Angelo.

1544. Mieux vaut goujat debout qu'empereur enterré.   La Font. (Contes), Matrone d'Éphèse, fin.—*A fool on his legs is better than a buried emperor.*   Cf. Eccles. ix. 4, Melius est canis vivus leone mortuo—*A live dog is better than a dead lion.*

1545. Mieux vaut voir un chien enragé, qu'un soleil chaud en Janvier. Prov.—*Better see a mad dog than a hot sun in January.*

Cf. R. Inwards' *Weather Lore*, Lond., 1893, p. 10:
In January if the sun appear,
March and April pay full dear.

And, Se Gennaio sta in camicia, Marzo scoppia dal riso—*If January work in his shirt-sleeves* (be mild), *March will burst with laughter* (will be very rough).

1546. Mihi istic nec seritur nec metitur.   Plaut. Epid. 2, 2, 80.—*There is neither sowing nor reaping in this affair for me.*   It will not redound to my profit any way.

1547. Mihi res, non me rebus, subjungere conor.   Hor. Ep. 1, 1, 19.

My aim's to rule events, not let events rule me.—*Ed.*

1548. Mihi tarda fluunt ingrataque tempora.   Hor. Ep. 1, 1, 23.—*Tedious and slow I find the time pass by.*

1549. Militat omnis amans, et habet sua castra Cupido:
Attice, crede mihi, militat omnis amans.
Quæ bello est habilis, Veneri quoque convenit, ætas;
Turpe senex miles, turpe senilis amor.   Ov. Am. 1, 9, 1.

Each lover's a soldier, believe me, Serenus;
Cupid too has his camp, for each lover must fight:
The best age for war is the best age for Venus;
Old soldiers, old lovers, are both a sad sight.—*Ed.*

Militiæ species amor est: discedite segnes;
Non sunt hæc timidis signa tuenda viris.   Ov. A. A. 2, 233.

Love is a kind of war: sluggards, depart!
Its ranks cannot be kept by craven heart.—*Ed.*

1550. Mille hominum species et rerum discolor usus;
Velle suum cuique est, nec voto vivitur uno.   Pers. 5, 52.

Countless the kinds of men, of countless hues:
With each his own, and not another's views.—*Ed.*

1551. Mille verisimili non fanno un vero.   Prov.—*A thousand probabilities don't make one truth.*

1552. Minima de malis.   Prov. ap. Cic. Off. 3, 29, 105.—*Of two evils choose the least.*

So also (id. ibid.), Ex malis eligere minima oportere—*Of evils one ought to choose the least;* De duobis malis minus est semper eligendum. A Kempis, Imitatio, 3, 12, 3—*Of two evils always choose the least;* and, in same sense, τὰ ἐλάχιστα ληπτέον τῶν κακῶν. Arist. Eth. Nic. 2, 9, 4.

1553. Minus aptus acutis Naribus horum hominum.   Hor. S. 1, 3, 29.—*Hardly fitted for such fastidious company.*   Description of an honest country fellow.

1554. Mira cano: Sol occubuit; nox nulla sequuta.   Wm. Camden's *Remains concerning Britain,* Lond., 1870, p. 351 ("Epigrams").—*I sing a prodigy: the sun set, yet no night followed.*   W. C. adds, " He that made the verse (some ascribe it to that Giraldus) could adore both the Sun setting and the Sun rising, when he could so cleanly honour K. Henry II. then departed, and K. Richard succeeding." *Nox nulla secuta est* is legend of Wm. and Mary's medal in commem. of the battle of La Hogue, 1692.

1555. Miremur te non tua.   Juv. 8, 68.—*Give us something to admire in yourself, not in your belongings.*   To one who boasts of his ancestry.

1556. Misce stultitiam consiliis brevem,
Dulce est desipere in loco.   Hor. C. 4, 12, 27.

> And be for once unwise.   While time allows,
> 'Tis sweet the fool to play.—*Conington.*

1557. Misera est magni custodia census.   Juv. 14, 304.—*The charge of a great estate is a miserable thing.*

1558. Misericordia Domini inter pontem et fontem.—*The Lord's mercy may be found between bridge and river.* W. Camden's "Remaines concerning Britaine," 1636, p. 392 (Sect. "Epitaphs"), where it is ascribed to St Augustine, and accompanied by the following imitation, composed by a "friend" of W. C.,

> Betwixt the stirrop and the ground,
> Mercy I askt, mercy I found.

1559. Miseros prudentia prima reliquit.   Ov. Ep. 4, 12, 47.—*Prudence is the first to leave the unfortunate.* Ill luck has generally to bear the blame of lack of prudence.

1560. Miserum est aliorum incumbere famæ,
Ne collapsa ruant subductis tecta columnis.   Juv. 8, 76.

> Don't support yourself on others;
> If the column falls, where are you?—*Shaw.*

1561. Μισῶ μνήμονα συμπότην, Procille.   Mart. 1, 28.—*I hate a boon companion with a good memory.* One should not always take after-dinner amenities *au pied de la lettre.*

1562. Μισῶ σοφιστὴν ὅστις οὐχ αὑτῷ σοφός.   Eur. Fr. 930.—*I hate the wise man who is not wise in his own affairs.*

1563. Mit der Dummheit kämpfen Götter selbst vergebens.   Schiller, Jungfr. v. Orleans, 3, 6 (Talbot loq.).—*With stupidity the gods themselves battle in vain.*

1564. Mitis depone colla, Sicamber! incende quod adorasti; adora quod incendisti!   Greg. Turon. Hist. Francor., Bk. 2, cap. 31 (Migne, vol. 71, p. 227).—*Meekly bow thy neck, Sicambrian! Burn what thou hast adored* (idols), *and adore what thou hast burnt* (the Cross)! Speech of St Remigius to Clovis, King of the Franks, at his baptism at Reims, 496 A.D.

1565. Mobilium turba Quiritium.   Hor. C. 1, 1, 7.—*A crowd of fickle citizens.* Cp., Mobile (mutatur cum principe) vulgus, Claud. IV. Cons. Hon. 302.—*The fickle mob that ever takes its cue from court.* Hence, viz., from "mobile vulgus," our word *Mob.*

1566. Modeste tamen et circumspecto judicio de tantis viris pronunciandum est, ne, quod plerisque accidit, damnent quæ non intelligunt.   Quint. 10, 1, 26.—*In the case of such eminent men, one should speak with due circumspection, for fear of damning what one does not understand.*

1567. Moi! dis-je, et c'est assez! Corn. Médée, 1, 5.—*Me! I reply,*
and is not that enough?

> Nérine, her confidante, condoles with Medea under the terrible blow
> inflicted by the flight of Jason.
>
> *Nér.* Dans un si grand revers que vous reste-t'-il?
> *Méd.*   Moi:
>   Moi, dis-je, et c'est assez.
>
> This is copied from the corresponding passage in Seneca's play of the
> same name, where the nurse (Nutrix) points out the desperate state of
> the case.
>
> *Nu.* Nihilque superest opibus e tantis tibi?
> *Med.* Medea superest.
> *Nu.* Of all thy great wealth nought remains to thee?
> *Med.* Medea remains!   (Act ii. l. 165).

1568. Mollissima fandi Tempora. Virg. A. 4, 293.—*The most favourable*
opportunity for speaking. An opportune moment for pressing a
request.

1569. Mon âme a son secret, ma vie a son mystère. Félix Arvers,
Sonnet imité de l'italien, Heures Perdues, Paris, 1833, p. 71.—
My soul has its secret, my life its mystery.

1570. Moniti meliora sequamur. Virg. A. 3, 188.—*Being admonished,*
let us pursue a better course.

1571. Monstro quod ipse tibi possis dare: semita certe
Tranquillæ per virtutem, patet unica vitæ.   Juv. 10, 363.

> I but teach
> The blessings man by his own powers may reach.
> The path to peace is virtue.—*Gifford.*

1572. Monstrum horrendum, informe, ingens, cui lumen ademptum.
Virg. A. 3, 658.—*An awful, hideous, huge, sightless monster.*
Description of Polyphemus, the Cyclops, after his one eye had
been put out by Ulysses.

1573. Mon verre n'est pas grand, mais je bois dans mon verre. A. de
Musset, La coupe et les Lèvres (*Dédicace*).—*My glass is not large,*
but I drink from my glass. "A poor thing, but my own."

1574. Moriamur pro rege nostro, Maria Theresia!—*Let us die for our*
King, Maria Theresa!

> Acclamation with which Maria Theresa, with her infant son in her arms
> (aft. Joseph II.), is supposed to have been received by the Hungarian Diet
> at Presburg, 11th Sept. 1741, in the war with Frederick II. Hertslet
> (Treppenwitz der Weltgeschichte, Berlin, 5th ed., p. 280) classes both
> words and scene among his historical myths; the youthful prince not
> having arrived at Presburg till ten days later (Sept. 21), and the actual
> words of the nobles, on the occasion referred to, having been, "*Vitam*
> *nostram et sanguinem consecramus.*"

1575. Moriemur inultæ?
Sed moriamur, ait. Sic, sic juvat ire sub umbras.
                                                    Virg. A. 4, 659.

Death of Dido.

To die, and unrevenged! she cried,
Yet let me die! thus, thus I'll go
Rejoicing to the shades below.—*Conington.*

And id. ibid. 2, 670: Nunquam omnes hodie moriemur inulti—*Not all of us to-day shall perish unavenged,* which Horace (Sat. 2, 8, 34) parodies as follows:

Nos nisi damnose bibimus, moriemur inulti.

Except we drink his cellar dry,
'Tis plain that unavenged we die.—*Ed.*

1576. Mors.—Death.

(i.) Pallida mors æquo pulsat pede pauperum tabernas
Regumque turres.   O beate Sexti,
Vitæ summa brevis spem nos vetat inchoare longam.   Hor. C. 1, 4, 13.

Pale death, impartial, walks his rounds: he knocks at cottage-gate
And palace-portal.   Sextius, child of bliss!
How should a mortal's hopes be long, when short his being's date?
—*Conington.*

(ii.) Sub tua purpurei venient vestigia reges
Deposito luxu, turba cum paupere mixti.
Omnia mors æquat.   Claud. Rapt. Pros. 2, 300.

Kings in thy train shall come, their purple robes
And state put off, mixed with the common herd:
Death levels all.—*Ed.*

(iii.) Le pauvre en sa cabane, où le chaume le couvre
Est sujet à ses lois.
Et la garde qui veille aux barrières du Louvre
N'en défend pas nos rois.   Malherbe, Ode à du Périer.

The poor cannot evade beneath their thatch
The law of earthly things;
Nor can the guard that at the Louvre keeps watch
Save from death's grasp our kings.—*Ed.*

(iv.) Nec forma æternum, aut cuiquam est fortuna perennis:
Longius aut propius, mors sua quemque manet.   Prop. 2, 28 (21), 57.

Beauty must fade; fortune has but its day:
Death, soon or late, claims each one for its prey.—*Ed.*

(v.)   Tibi crescit omne
Et quod occasus videt, et quod ortus.
Parce venturis; tibi, Mors, paramur;
Sis licet segnis, properamus ipsi:
Prima quæ vitam dedit, hora carpsit.   Sen. Herc. Fur. 870.

Thine, Death, is all that lives and grows,
Or in the east, or in the west.
We come, we come! for thee we're drest,
And hasten fast though thou delay;
With life's first hour 'gins life's decay.—*Ed.*

(vi.) Miremur periisse homines? monumenta fatiscunt:
Mors etiam saxis nominibusque venit.   Auson. Epigr. 35, 9.—
Can you wonder that men perish, when even their monuments fall to pieces? Death comes even to marbles, and stone inscriptions.

(vii.) Mors ultima linea rerum est. Hors. Ep. 1, 16, 79.—*Death is the furthest limit of human vicissitude.* (viii.) Mors sola fatetur Quantula sint hominum corpuscula. Juv. 10, 172.—*Death alone proves how puny is the human frame.* Originally said of Alexander the Great. Macaulay quotes the line of Louis XIV., whose stature, reputed tall during his lifetime, was discovered •n the exhumation of his body (in the First Revolution) not to have exceeded 5 ft. 8 in. (*Essay on Mirabeau*). (ix.) Dulce et decorum est pro patria mori. Hor. C. 3, 2, 13.—*It is sweet and honourable to die for one's country.* Cf. O fortunata mors, quæ naturæ debita, pro patria est potissimum reddita! Cic. Phil. 14, 112, 31.—*Happy is the death which, though due to nature, is cheerfully surrendered for the sake of one's country.* (x.) Optima mors parca quæ venit apta die. Prop. 3, 5, 18.—*That death is best which arrives opportunely and soon.* (xi.) Quem di diligunt, Adolescens moritur, dum valet, sentit, sapit. Plaut. Bacch. 4, 7, 18.—*Whom the gods love dies young, while his strength and senses and faculties are in their full vigour.* Cp. Men. Bis Fallens, p. 891, ὃν οἱ θεοὶ φιλοῦσιν ἀποθνήσκει νέος—*Whom the gods love dies young.* Byron says (Childe Harold, 4, 102), "Heaven gives his favourites early death." (xii.) Optanda mors est, sine metu mortis mori. Sen. Troad. 870.—*That death is to be desired which is free from all fear of death.* (xiii.) Mortem optare, malum; timere, pejus. Aus. Sap. (Periander, 3).—*To wish for death is bad: to fear it, worse.*

> (xiv.) Las d'espérer, et de me plaindre
> Des Muses, des Grands, et du Sort,
> C'est icy que j'attends la Mort,
> Sans la désirer, ny la craindre.   F. Maynard.

> Ceasing to hope, or to accuse
> The court, or fortune, or the Muse;
> The call of death I wait for here,
> Without desire and without fear.—*Ed.*

*** These last lines, which will be found in the *Notice* of Prosper Blanchemain's ed. of Maynard's *Philandre* (Genève, Gay, 1867, p. xviii), are said to have been inscribed over Maynard's study door, after a last ineffectual visit to Court during the Regency, 1644. Variants of the second and third lines are given in Barbin's *Recueil des plus belles pièces*, etc., 5 vols., Paris, 1692, (vol. 2, p. 314 a); and in Deslandes' *Réflexions sur les grands hommes qui se sont morts en plaisantant*, Rochefort, 1755, p. 38.

(xv.) Scire mori sors prima viris, sed proxima cogi. Luc. 9, 211.—*To die of one's own choice is man's happiest lot; the next best to be slain.*

> (xvi.) Eripere vitam nemo non homini potest;
> At nemo mortem.   Sen. Phœn. 152.

> Any can rob me of the right to live;
> But none the right to die.—*Ed.*

(xvii.) Morte magis metuenda senectus. Juv. 11, 45.—*Old age is more to be dreaded than death.* (xviii.) Mors misera non est, aditus ad mortem est miser. Ribb. ex Incert. incertor, 109 (i. 307).—*It is not death which is wretched, but the approach to it.* (xix.) τὸ γαρ θανεῖν οὐκ αἰσχρόν, ἀλλ' αἰσχρῶς θανεῖν. Menand. Monost. 504.—*Death is no shame, but shamefully to die.* (xx.) Nihil sic revocat a peccato, quam frequens mortis meditatio. St Aug. Lib. exhort. (*sic*), in Langius, p. 762.—*Nothing preserves a man from sin so much as frequent meditation on death.* (xxi.) Mourir n'est rien, c'est notre dernière heure. Sedaine, Le Déserteur, 2, 2.—*Music by P. A. Monsigny. Drama in three acts, produced at the Comédie Italienne, March 9, 1769 (Alexis sings).—To die is nothing: 'tis but our last hour.*

(xxii.) Heureux l'inconnu, qui s'est bien sceu connaître,
Il ne voit pas de mal à mourir plus qu'à naître:
   Il s'en va comme il est venu.
Mais hélas! que la mort fait une horreur extrême
A qui meurt de tous trop connu,
   Et trop peu connu de soy mesme.
        Jean Hesnault, Œuvres divers, etc., par le
sieur D. H., Paris (Ribou), 1670, 12mo.—*Happy the man who, though
unknown to others, has learnt to know himself well: he thinks no more of
dying than of being born: he departs as he came. But, alas! what a
horror death presents to the man who, though too well known to the world,
is but little known to himself!* (xxiii.) Mortem aliquid ultra est? Vita, si
cupias mori. Sen. Agam. 996.—Electra loq.: *Is there anything after death?*
Ægistheus. *Yes, life, if you desire to die.* (xxiv.) Acerba semper et
immatura mors eorum, qui immortale aliquid parant. Plin. Ep. 5, 5.—
*The deaths of those men who have some immortal work in hand, always
seems cruelly premature.*

1577. Mortales inimicitias, sempiternas amicitias. Cic. Rab. Post. 12,
32.—*Let our enmities be short-lived, our friendships eternal.*

1578. Mortalia facta peribunt,
  Nedum sermonum stet honos et gratia vivax.   Hor. A. P. 68.

    Man's works must perish; how should words evade
    The general doom, and flourish undecayed?—*Conington.*

1579. Mortalium rerum misera beatitudo. Boeth. de Cons. 2, 4.—*The
miserable blessedness attending human affairs.*

1580. Mortua quin etiam jungebat corpora vivis,
  Componens manibusque manus, atque oribus ora,
  Tormenti genus.   Virg. A. 8, 485.

      He chained the living to the dead;
      Hand joined to hand, and face to face,
      In noisome, pestilent embrace.—*Conington.*

    Often applied by Keble, so Card. Newman relates, to the position of the
Church of England, locked in the deadly embrace of an Erastian State.
Fifty Years at East Brent, etc., ed. L. E. Denison, Lond., 1902, p. 337.

1581. Mortui non mordent. Chil. p. 473 ("Maledicentia").—*Dead men
do not bite.* Tr. of a saying of Theodotus of Chios, reported by
Plutarch (Pomp. 77, fin.; Vitæ, p. 787), νέκρους οὐ δάκνειν.

1582. Mourir pour la patrie,
  C'est le sort le plus beau, le plus digne d'envie.

    Dumas (père) and Aug. Maquet, "Chevalier de Maison
Rouge" (1847), Act 5, fin. Music by Alph. Varney.—*To die
for one's country is the grandest and most enviable lot of all.*
Refrain of the "Chorus of the Girondins," borrowed (with
change of *mourons* to *mourir*) from the *Roland à Roncevaux*
(words and music) of Rouget de Lisle, author of the
"Marseillaise."

1583. Mulier cupido quod dicit amanti,
  In vento et rapida scribere oportet aqua.

    Cat. 70, 3.—*What a woman says to her lover, ought to be
written on the winds, or on water.* Fleeting vows and professions.

1584. Mulier profecto nata est ex ipsa mora.   Plaut. Mil, 4, 7, 9.—
Woman certainly is the offspring of tardiness itself.

1585. Mulier quum sola cogitat male cogitat.   Syr. 335.—*A woman
who thinks alone, thinks of mischief.*

1586. Mulier recte olet, ubi nihil olet.   Plaut. Most. 1, 3, 116.—*A woman
smells sweetest when she smells of nothing.*

1587. Multæ terricolis linguæ, cœlestibus una, *or,* Πολλαὶ μὲν θνητοῖς
γλῶτται, μία δ' ἀθανάτοισιν.   Henry F. Cary.—*The inhabitants
of earth have many languages, those of heaven have but one.*
Motto written for the "Polyglot Series" of the Scriptures of
H. Bagster & Sons.

1588. Multa fero ut placeam genus irritabile vatum.   Hor. Ep. 2, 2, 102.

> Much I endure indeed (perhaps you know it),
> To please the irritable *genus* poet.—*Ed.*

1589. Multa ferunt anni venientes commoda secum;
Multa recedentes adimunt.   Hor. A. P. 175.

> Years, as they come, bring blessings in their train:
> Years, as they go, take blessings back again.—*Conington.*

1590. Multa petentibus
Desunt multa.   Bene est cui Deus obtulit
Parca, quod satis est, manu.   Hor. C. 3, 16, 42.

> Who much require will always want.
> 'Tis best if, just what life demands,
> Heav'n furnish us with sparing hands.—*Ed.*

1591. Multa quidem scripsi: sed quæ vitiosa putavi
Emendaturis ignibus ipse dedi.   Ov. T. 4, 10, 61.

> *Literary Corrections.*
> I've written much; but what I thought to blame
> I threw, correctively, into the flame.

1592. Multa renascentur quæ jam cecidere, cadentque
Quæ nunc sunt in honore vocabula, si volet usus,
Quem penes arbitrium est, et jus, et norma loquendi.
                        Hor. A. P. 70.

> Yes, words long faded may again revive;
> And words may fade now blooming and alive,
> If usage wills it so, to whom belongs
> The rule and law, the government of tongues.—*Conington.*

1593. Multi Committunt eadem diverso crimina fato,
Ille crucem sceleris pretium tulit, hic diadema.   Juv. 13, 103.

> Men the same crimes commit with varying end;
> And some a scaffold, some a throne ascend.—*Ed.*

1594. Multi, inquam, sunt, Lucili, qui non donant, sed projiciunt; non
voco ego liberalem, pecuniæ suæ iratum.   Sen. Ep. 120, 9.—
*There are many who do not give, but throw away; I don't call a
man liberal who is angry with his money.*

1595. Multis ille bonis flebilis occidit;
Nulli flebilior quam tibi, Virgili.   Hor. C. 1, 24, 9.

> By many a good man wept, Quintilius dies;
> By none than you, my Virgil, trulier wept.—*Conington.*

1596. Multos experimur ingratos, plures facimus.   Sen. Ben. 1, 1, init.
—*We find many ungrateful; we make more.*

1597. Multos in summa pericula misit
Venturi timor ipse mali.   Fortissimus ille est
Qui promtus metuenda pati, si cominus instent,
Et differre potest.   Lucan. 7, 104.

> *True Courage.*
> Many's the mortal whom the very dread
> Of coming ill has into danger sped.
> But bravest he who, prompt to meet his fate,
> Can face the shock, or can with patience wait.—*Ed.*

1598. Multum non multa, *or*, Non multa sed multum.—*Much, not many things.*

> Prov. quoted by Plin. Ep. 7, 9, init., "Aiunt enim multum legendum esse, non multa"—*'Tis said we ought to read much* (intently), *rather than many things.*   Multa magis quam multorum lectione formanda mens. Quint. 10, 1, 59.—*The mind is better formed by close application to one author than by reading a number of different authors.*   The saying, 'Timeo virum unius libri' (*or*, "Cave hominem unius libri"), *I fear* (or, *beware of*) *the man of one book*, is used either of a student of this kind, or of a man who is for ever posing opponents with the authority of his sole and favourite writer, and is unread in any other work.

1599. Murranum hic, atavos et avorum antiqua sonantem
Nomina, per regesque actum genus omne Latinos.
                              Virg. A. 12, 529.

> Murranus too, whose boastful tongue
> With high-born sires and grandsires rung,
> And pedigrees of long renown
> Through Latian monarchs handed down.—*Conington.*

N.

1600. Nach Kanossa gehen wir nicht.—*We are not going to Canossa.*
Bismarck in Parliament, May 14, 1872.

> Canossa is a castle now in ruins near Reggio Emilia, where in Jan. 1077, the Emperor Henry IV. did three days' penance, barefoot, bareheaded and in the snow, before Gregory VII. (Hildebrand) would grant him absolution.   The phrase was used at the beginning of the *Kulturkampf* contest with the Papacy (1872), Bismarck implying that the revived German Empire would not surrender so abjectly to the Papal claims as it had eight hundred years before.   In 1885, B. practically swallowed his own words by proposing the Pope as arbiter between Germany and Spain in the matter of the Caroline Is.; and in 1886-87 went still farther on the road to Canossa by repealing the more offensive clauses of the "May Laws," thus in the end leaving the Pope master of the situation.

1601. Nam genus, et proavos, et quæ non fecimus ipsi,
Vix ea nostra voco.   Ov. M. 13, 140.

> For birth and lineage and all such renown,
> Bequeathed, not made, can scarce be called our own.—*Ed.*

1602. Nam jam non domus accipiet te læta, neque uxor
Optuma, nec dulces occurrent oscula nati
Præripere, et tacita pectus dulcedine tangent.   Lucr. 3, 907.

> *A Father's Death.*
>
> No more shall thy family welcome thee home,
> Nor around thee thy wife and sweet little ones come;
> All clamouring joyous to snatch the first kiss,
> Transporting thy bosom with exquisite bliss.—*Ed.*

1603. Nam neque divitibus contingunt gaudia solis,
Nec vixit male qui natus moriensque fefellit.   Hor. Ep. 1, 17, 9.

> Joys do not happen to the rich alone,
> Nor he liv'd ill, that lived and died unknown.—*Ed.*

1604. Nam nunc mores nihil faciunt quod licet, nisi quod lubet.   Plaut.
Trin. 4, 3, 25.—*Society nowadays takes no account of what is
right, but only of what is agreeable.*

1605. Nam quæ inscitia est Advorsum stimulum calces!   Ter. Phorm.
1, 2, 27.—*What folly 'tis to kick against the pricks!*   Cf. Si
stimulos pugnis cædis, manibus plus dolet.   Plaut. Truc. 4, 2, 55.
—*If you fight the goad with your fists, so much the worse for
your knuckles.*   Evil is often only aggravated by useless opposition.

1606. Nam quum magna malæ superest audacia causæ,
Creditur a multis fiducia.   Juv. 13, 109.

> Urge a bad cause with boundless impudence,
> And 'twill be thought by many innocence.—*Ed.*

1607. Nam si violandum est jus, regnandi gratia
Violandum est: aliis rebus pietatem colas.
                                   Cæsar ap. Cic. Off. 3, 21, 82.

> A tr. of Eur. Phœn. 524 (Eteocles loq.):—
>
> εἴπερ γὰρ ἀδικεῖν χρή, τυραννίδος πέρι
> κάλλιστον ἀδικεῖν, τἄλλα δ' εὐσεβεῖν χρεών.
>
> If one must break the law, then for a crown
> The sin had best excuse; but, else, revere the gods.—*Ed.*

The lines were often on Cæsar's lips (so Cicero says) when aiming at the
supreme power.

1608. Nam tua res agitur paries quum proximus ardet:
Et neglecta solent incendia sumere vires.   Hor. Ep. 1, 18, 84.

> No time for sleeping with a fire next door;
> Neglect such things, they only blaze the more.—*Conington.*

1609. Nascentes morimur, finisque ab origine pendet. Manil. Astr. 4, 16.
—*We are born but to die, and our end joins on to the beginning.*

In his metrical version of the "Imitation," Corneille has, in Bk. 2,
cap. 12, l. 1657, "Chaque instant de la vie est un pas vers la mort"; a

line which, about twenty years later (1670), he reproduced in his "heroic comedy" of *Tite et Bérénice*, 5, 1. Voltaire inserted the sentiment in his Fête de Bélébat (1725), "L'instant où nous naissons est un pas vers la mort"; and, finally, Delavigne, in his *Louis XI* (1832), makes Nemours say to S. Francis de Paul (1, 9), "Chaque pas dans la vie est un pas vers la mort." Alex. pp. 377-8.

1610. Natales grate numeras? ignoscis amicis?
Lenior et melior fis accedente senecta?   Hor. Ep. 2, 2, 210.

Signs of Improvement.
D'ye keep your birthdays thankfully? forgive?
Grow gentler, better, every day you live?—*Ed.*

1611. Natio comœda est.   Rides? meliore cachinno
Concutitur: flet, si lacrymas conspexit amici,
Nec dolet.   Igniculum brumæ si tempore poscas,
Accipit endromidem: si dixeris, Æstuo, sudat.
Non sumus ergo pares.   Juv. 3, 100.

Greeks.
The race are actors born.   Smile, and your Greek
Will laugh until the tears run down his cheek.
He'll weep as soon if he observe a friend
In tears; but feels no grief.   For fire you send
In winter, straight his overcoat he gets;
And, if you cry "How hot it is!" he sweats.
We are not therefore equal.—*Ed.*

1612. Natura abhorret vacuum.   Rabelais, 1, 5.—*Nature abhors a vacuum.*

1613. Natura il fece, e poi roppe la stampa.   Ariosto, Orl. Fur. 10, 84.
Nature broke the mould
In which she cast him, after fashioning
Her work.—*Rose.*

Said originally of Zerbino, Duca di Roscia, the handsome son of the K. of Scotland, it has been applied to Raphael and others, as, *e.g.*, by Lord Byron in his *Monody on the Death of Sheridan*, 117:
Sighing that nature formed but one such man,
And broke the die—in moulding Sheridan.

1614. Natura in operationibus suis non facit saltum.   Jacques Tissot, *Discours véritable de la Vie* etc. *du Géant Theutobocus*, Lyon, 1613; reprinted in Ed. Fournier's *Variétés hist. et littéraires*, Paris, 1855-63, vol. 9, p. 247.—*Nature in her operations does not proceed by leaps.*   All is gradual, continuous, progressive.

Tissot is quoting an old and well-established axiom in physics.   "Operatur natura," he says, "quantum et quamdiu potest, sans neant moins faire aucun sault ab extremis ad extrema. Natura enim in operationibus suis, etc.," *ut supra*.   His contemporary, Sir E. Coke, applies it to law: "Natura non facit saltus, ita nec lex." *Coke upon Littleton*, pp. 238b, 239.—*Law, like nature, does not proceed by leaps.*   Leibnitz (Nouv. Essais, ed. E. Bontroux, Paris, 1886, p. 135) says, "C'est une de mes grandes maximes et des plus vérifiées, que la nature ne fait jamais des sauts." Linnæus (Philosoph. Botan., Stockholm, p. 27, Sect. 77) follows suit with "Primum et ultimum hoc in botanicis desideratum est, *Natura non facit saltus.*"

o

1615. Naturalia non sunt turpia; tr. of οὐκ αἰσχρὸν οὐδὲν τῶν ἀναγκαίων βροτοῖς. Eur. Fragm. 863.—*None of man's necessary (natural) actions are shameful.*

1616. Naturam expellas furca, tamen usque recurret. Hor. Ep. 1, 10, 24.

> Drive nature out with might and main,
> She's certain to return again.—*Ed.*

Destouches imitates it in his *Glorieux*, 3, 5:

> Je ne le sais que trop:
> Chassez le naturel, il revient au galop.

La Fontaine, 2, 18 (La Chatte metamorphosée en Femme), also speaking of *le naturel*, concludes thus:

> Jamais vous n'en serez les maîtres.
> Qu'on lui ferme la porte au nez,
> Il reviendra par les fenêtres.

1617. Naviget Anticyram. Hor. S. 2, 3, 166.—*Let him take a trip to Anticyra!* He's mad! to Bedlam with him! Hellebore, supposed to be good for insanity, was found at Anticyra, a town on the Gulf of Corinth.

1618. Ne Æsopum quidem trivit. Chil. 286.—*He has not even thumbed his Æsop yet.* A backward scholar. In Ar. Av. 471 is, ἀμαθὴς γὰρ ἔφυς κοὐ πολυπράγμων, οὐδ' Αἴσωπον πεπάτηκας—*You're stupid by nature, and not inquisitive: you haven't even thumbed your Æsop.*

1619. Νεανίας γὰρ ὅστις ὢν Ἄρη στυγεῖ
κόμη μόνον καὶ σάρκες, ἔργα δ' οὐδαμοῦ.
Ὁρᾷς τὸν εὐτράπεζον, ὡς ἡδὺς βίος,
ὅ τ' ὄλβος ἔξωθέν τίς ἐστι πραγμάτων.
ἀλλ' οὐκ ἔνεστι στέφανος οὐδ' εὐανδρία,
εἰ μή τι καὶ τολμῶσι κινδύνου μέτα.
οἱ γὰρ πόνοι τίκτουσι τὴν εὐανδρίαν,
ἡ δ' εὐλάβεια σκότον ἔχει καθ' Ἑλλάδα,
τὸ διαβιῶναι μόνον ἀεὶ θηρωμένη.   Eur. Fr. 875.

> What is the youth that shuns the tented field
> But curls and pretty cheeks, and nothing more?
> Certes, the luxurious life is sweet enough;
> Bliss, but to stand outside all serious effort!
> But never yet was crown of manlihood
> Won, save with daring and with danger fraught.
> For work's the sire of true manliness,
> While prudence, all Greece through, is reckoned shame,
> Prolonged existence being its only aim.—*Ed.*

1620. Nec benefecit, nec malefecit, sed interfecit. Facetiæ Cantabrig., Lond., 1825, p. 134.—*He did neither good nor ill, but murder.* Punning impromptu "theme" on the question, "Cæsare occiso, an Brutus beneficit, aut maleficit?"—ascribed to Porson, also to Curran.

1621. Nec caput nec pedes. Cic. Fam. 7, 31, 2.—*Neither beginning nor end.* Neither head nor tail. All confusion: good for nothing.

1622. Nec conjugis unquam
Prætendi tædas: aut hæc in fœdera veni. Virg. A. 4, 338.— *I never pretended to be your hasband, nor entered into any such covenant.* Æneas' repudiation of poor Dido's appeal for honourable wedlock.

> In the form "*Non* hæc in fœdera veni," in law and elsewhere, the words are used to disavow alleged non-fulfilment of contracts, and to assert one's freedom from agreements never actually entered into. "In reply to the conditions to which *X.* now wishes to bind me, I can only say, *Non hæc in fœdera veni;* these were no part of the original engagement."

1623. Nec deus intersit nisi dignus vindice nodus. Hor. A. P. 191.— *Don't bring in a god unless the situation requires a champion of the kind.*

> Advice to dramatic authors. Such an introduction was called a *Deus ex machina* ("a god in a machine"), or, in Greek, ἀπὸ μηχανῆς θεὸς (Men. p. 912), *i.e.*, some divinity made to appear in the air by stage machinery, in order to lend help at a critical juncture of the play.

1624. Necesse est cum insanientibus furere, nisi solus relinquaris.— *With the mad you must be mad yourself, unless you would be left alone.*

> Formed from Petr. Sat. 3,—Doctores . . . necesse habent cum insanientibus furere. Nam nisi dixerint quæ adolescentuli probent, ut ait Cicero, "Soli in scholis relinquentur."—*The teachers* (of rhetoric) *think it necessary to be "insane with the insane"; for if they did not say what their pupils approve, they would, as Cicero says, be the only occupants of the class-room left.*

1625. Necesse est multos timeat quem multi timent. Laber. (vol. ii. 361).—*Needs must he fear many whom many fear.* Sen. (de Ira, 2, 11, 3) speaks of the sensational effect the words produced in the theatre in the middle of the Second Civil War, 50 B.C.

1626. Necessitas feriis caret. Pall. 1, 6, 7 (ed. J. C. Schmitt, Biblioth. Teubner, 1898).—*Necessity has no vacations,* or, as we say, "knows no law."

1627. Nec facile invenias multis e millibus unum
Virtutem pretium qui putet esse sui.
Ipse decor, recte facti si præmia desint,
Non movet, et gratis pœnitet esse probum. Ov. Ep. 2, 3, 11.

> To find one in a thousand it is hard
> Who reckons virtue as its own reward:
> E'en honour fails unless it's dearly bought,
> For people grudge to be upright for naught.—*Ed.*

1628. Nec frustra ac sine caussa quid facere dignum Deo est. Cic. Div. 2, 60, 125.—*Purposeless and unmeaning action is unworthy of the idea of God.*

1629. Nec loquor hæc, quia sit major prudentia nobis;
Sed sim, quam medico, notior ipse mihi.   Ov. Ep. 1, 3, 91.—
*I do not say this because I have any great powers of foresight,
but because I know myself better than my doctor does.*

1630. Nec lusisse pudet, sed non incidere ludum.   Hor. Ep. 1, 14, 36.

Wild Oats.

No shame I count it to have had my sport,
The shame were not to cut such follies short.—*Ed.*

1631. Nec meus hic sermo est, sed quæ præcepit Ofella.   Hor. S. 2, 2, 2.
—*These ideas are not mine, but what Ofella told me.*

1632. Nec minor est virtus, quam quærere, parta tueri:
Casus inest illic, hic erit artis opus.   Ov. A. A. 2, 13.

'Tis no small art to keep what you've acquired:
Chance lies in one; for t' other skill's required.—*Ed.*

1633. Nec mora, nec requies.   Virg. G. 3, 110.—*No delay, no rest.*
No intermission allowed: immediate action.

1634. Nec multo opus est nec diu.   Sen. Q. N. 3, Præf. fin.—"*Man
wants but little, nor that little long.*"—Young, *Night Thoughts,*
14, 118.   Cf. Goldsmith's *Hermit,* st. 8 :

Man wants but little here below,
Nor wants that little long.

1635. Nec pietas ulla est velatum sæpe videri
Vortier ad lapidem, atque omneis accedere ad aras.
Lucr. 5, 1197.—*That is not piety, to be often seen bending with
veiled head before the image of the god, and to visit all the altars.*

1636. Nec pluribus impar.—*I suffice for more worlds than one.*   Motto
of Louis XIV., with Sun for emblem.

According to Fournier (*L. D. L.*, p. 315 n.), it was Douvrier, the antiquary
(? herald), who originated (or adapted) the motto and crest in honour of the
Roy Soleil on the occasion of the famous tournament which he gave his wife
and his mother in 1662.   The words had already been adopted more than a
century before by Philip II., who, as King of Spain and the Indies, had a
better right to speak in the character of the sun shining over more realms
than one.

1637. Nec (*or* Ne *or* Non) plus ultra.—*Farther than this you cannot go.*
Thus far and no farther.   Unsurpassed.

Tradition makes this the inscription on the Pillars of Hercules at Calpe
and Abila—either side of Gibraltar Straits—signifying the confines of the
then known world.   Pind. (Ol. 3, fin.) mentions the Pillars and the prohibi-
tion to pass them : τὸ πόρσω δ' ἔστι σοφοῖς ἄβατον κἀσόφοις—*Beyond it is
impassable for fools or wise.*   The discovery of America upset the ancient
dictum, and, under Charles V., Spain proudly inscribed the words, *Plus
ultra,* on her heraldic "pillars" to typify the achievement.   A parallel, in
another sphere, may be instituted in the *Non plus ultra* sonata of Woelff,
which he published in 1807 (Op. 41), as the highest point to which mechani-
cal difficulty could be carried on the pianoforte.   The challenge was taken
up by Dussek in the shape of a *Plus ultra*—the "Retour à Paris" sonata,
Op. 71—which he appropriately dedicated to his rival.

1638. Nec pluteum cædit, nec demorsos sapit ungues.   Pers. 1, 106.—
It does not smack of the desk, or bitten nails.   Said of insipid
poetry, composed without care and labour.

1639. Nec scire fas est omnia.   Hor. C. 4, 4, 22.—*It is not permitted
us to know all things.*

1640. Nec sibi cœnarum quivis temere arroget artem,
Non prius exacta tenui ratione saporum.   Hor. S. 2, 4, 35.

> Let no man fancy he knows how to dine
> Till he has learnt how taste and taste combine.—*Conington.*

Lit. *No one can pretend the art of giving dinners, until he has mastered the
subtle law of flavours.*

1641. Nec, si forte roges, possim tibi dicere quot sint.
Pauperis est numerare pecus.   Ov. M. 13, 823.

> *Polyphemus.*
> Nor can I tell how many more I keep;
> 'Tis only the poor man that counts his sheep.—*Ed.*

1642. Nec tibi quid liceat, sed quid fecisse decebit
Occurrat; mentemque domet respectus honesti.
Claud. IV. Cons. Hon. 267. – *Consider not what you may do
but what you ought, and let your sense of what is right govern
your conduct.*

Cf. Quid deceat vos, non quantum liceat vobis, spectare debetis. Cic. Rab.
Post. 5, 11.—*You ought to consider what is becoming, not what is lawful:*
and, Omnia mihi licent, sed omnia non expediunt. Vulg. Cor. 1, 10, 23.—
All things are lawful to me, but all things are not expedient.

1643. Nec Veneris pharetris macer est, aut lampade fervet:
Inde faces ardent; veniunt a dote sagittæ.   Juv. 6, 138.

> *The Mercenary Lover.*
> Not Venus' quiver makes him lean,
>   Nor Cupid's flambeau scorch:
> It is her money-bags, I ween,
>   Thence come both darts and torch.—*Ed.*

1644 Nec verbum verbo curabis reddere fidus Interpres.—Hor. A. P.
133.—*Even in a faithful translation it is not necessary to give
word for word.*

1645. Nec vero illa parva vis naturæ est rationisque, quod, unum hoc
animal sentit quid sit ordo quid sit quod deceat, in factis
dictisque quis modus.   Cic. Off. 1, 4, 14.—*It is no slight characteristic of the nature of the perceptive faculties of man, that he
alone of all living creatures goes feeling after the discovery of an
order, a law of good taste, a measure for his words and actions.*
(Mr Matthew Arnold, tr. in *Essays in Criticism* (1875), p. 54.)

1646. Nec vidisse semel satis est, juvat usque morari.   Virg. A. 6, 487.
—*Nor are they satisfied to have merely seen him, they were de-
lighted to prolong the interview.*   The ghosts of departed Trojans
crowding round Æneas when he visits the infernal regions.

1647. Ne faut-il que délibérer?
   La cour en conseillers foisonne:
   Est-il besoin d'exécuter?
   L'on ne rencontre plus personne.
                           La Font. 2, 2 (Conseil des Rats).
   Have plans to be discussed? Of course,
      Then counsellors abound.
   Should plans resolved be put in force?
      Then no one's to be found.—*Ed.*

1648. Ne forçons point notre talent,
   Nous ne ferions rien avec grâce.   La Font. (L'Ane et le
   petit Chien), 4, 5.—*Don't force your powers unduly, if you aim
   at a graceful effect.*

1649. Negligere quid de se quisque sentiat, non solum arrogantis est,
   sed omnino dissoluti. Cic. Off. 1, 28, 99.—*To be careless of
   what persons think of you, is not merely a mark of presumption,
   but of an utterly abandoned character.*

1650. Nella chiesa
   Co' santi, ed in taverna co' ghiottoni.   Dante, Inf. 22, 14.—
   In church with saints, and in tavern with gluttons.   Your company
   will correspond with the place.

1651. Nel mezzo del cammin di nostra vita. Dante, Inf. 1, 1.—*"In
   the midway of our mortal life."*—Cary.   Opening words of the
   Divine Comedy, marking its date of composition—the thirty-
   fifth year of the poet's age, 1300 A.D.

1652. Nel militare, il superiore ha sempre ragione, ma specialissi-
   mamente poi quando ha torto.   Paulo Fambri, Il Caporal di
   settimana, 3, 13.—*In the army the superior officer is invariably
   right, more particularly when he is wrong.*

1653. Nemo doctus unquam . . . mutationem consilii inconstantiam
   dixit esse.   Cic. Att. 16, 7, 3.—*No sensible man ever imputed
   inconsistency to another for changing his mind.*

1654. Nemo enim est tam senex, qui se annum non putet posse vivere.
   Cic. Sen. 7, 24.—*No man is so old as not to think he can live one
   year more.*

1655. Nemo læditur nisi a seipso.   Chil. p. 231.—*No man is injured
   save by himself.*   Man is his own worst enemy.
      The axiom is the subject of a treatise addressed by St Chrysostom to
   Olympias, ἔπεμψά σοι ἅπερ ἔγραψα πρώην, ὅτι τὸν ἑαυτὸν οὐκ ἀδικοῦντα οὐδεὶς
   ἕτερος παραβλάψαι δυνήσεται   Ep. ad Olympiad. 4, § 4 (Migne, iii. 595).—*I
   sent you what I wrote yesterday—that no one can harm the man who does
   himself no wrong.*

1656. Nemo malus felix.   Juv. 4, 8.—*No wicked man can be happy.*

1657. Nemo mathematicus genium indemnatus habebit.   Juv. 6, 562.—
   No mathematician is thought a genius until he is condemned.   A
   saying which would apply both to Galileo and to Dr Colenso.

1658. Nemo me impune lacessit.—*No one provokes me with impunity.*
Motto of the Crown of Scotland and of all the Scottish regiments,
and the characteristic epigraph of the Scotch people—" Wha
daur meddle wi' me ?" Over the entrance to Holyrood it is
"lacesset."

1659. Nemo me lacrumis decoret, nec funera fletu
Faxit. Cur ? Volito vivu' per ora virom.
Enn. ap. Cic. Tusc. 1, 15, 34.

Inscription for his own Bust.
Weep not for me, nor mourn when I am gone.
On lips of men I live, and flutter on.—*Ed.*

1660. Nemo mortalium omnibus horis sapit. Plin. 7, 40, 2.—*No man
is wise at all times.*

1661. Nemo propheta acceptus est in patriâ suâ. Vulg. Luc. 4, 24.—
No prophet is accepted in his own country.

1662. Nemo quam bene vivat, sed quamdiu, curat: quum omnibus possit
contingere ut bene vivat, ut diu nulli. Sen. Ep. 22, 13.—*No
one cares how well he may live, but how long: a thing which it is
impossible to count upon, while the other is within every one's reach.*
"Non quamdiu, sed quam bene,"—Motto (formed from above)
of Duke Ernest of Saxe-Coburg, bro. of the Prince Consort.

1663. Nemo solus satis sapit. Plaut. Mil. 3, 3, 12.—*No man is sufficiently wise by himself.* We all stand in need of friendly advice.

1664. Ne musca quidem. Suet. Dom. 3.—*Not even a fly.* Domitian. was
so fond of fly-catching that he could not be said to be "alone,"
if a fly remained alive in the room. (2.) Natus nemo. Plaut.
Most. 2, 1, 55.—*Not a living creature.* Perfect solitude.

1665. Νέους φίλους ποιῶν, λῶστε, τῶν παλαιῶν μὴ ἐπιλανθάνου. Apostol.
12, 1.—*While you are making new friends, my good fellow, don't
forget the old ones.*

1666. Νήπιοι, οὐδὲ ἴσασιν ὅσῳ πλέον ἥμισυ παντός. Hes. Op. et D. 40.—
Fools, they know not how much more the half is than the whole.
Said to his bro. Perses, urging him to settle a dispute amicably
without going to law. Half of the estate would be better than
the whole after the costs of the trial had been deducted.

1667. Ne puero gladium (commiseris), Chil. p. 176; *or,* Μὴ παιδὶ
μάχαιραν. Prov. ap. Stob. 43, 136.—*Don't put a knife into a
child's hand.* Don't entrust the inexperienced with power.
One of my earliest recollections is the explosion of a large loaded horse-
pistol which a maid put into my hands as a suitable plaything, and the
terror of my mother on hearing the report. Erasmus (Chil., *ut supra*) tells
of a Mendicant Friar who preached before Henry VII. on the morals of
princes with considerable freedom, and of whom the king afterwards remarked, Videbatur furiosi manibus commissus gladius—*He was like a
madman with a sword in his hand.*

1668. Nequam illud verbum 'st, Bene volt, nisi qui bene facit. Plaut.
Trin. 2, 4, 38.—*That expression, " Good wishes," is idle without
good deeds.*

1669. Neque enim lex æquior ulla est
Quam necis artifices arte perire sua.   Ov. A. A. 1, 655.

This is the justest law that Heaven imparts,
That murderers should die by their own arts.—*Ed.*

1670. Neque fœmina, amissa pudicitia, alia abnuerit. Tac. A. 4, 3.—
Once a woman has lost her chastity, she will refuse nothing.
Cf. Ego illum periisse duco, cui quidem periit pudor. Plaut. Bacch.
3, 3, 81.—*I count him lost who has lost all sense of shame.*

1671. Neque mala vel bona quæ vulgus putet. Tac. A. 6, 22.—*The
public is no real judge of what is good or bad.*

1672. Neque quies gentium sine armis, neque arma sine stipendiis, neque
stipendia sine tributis haberi queunt. Tac. H. 4, 74.—*Inter-
national peace cannot be maintained without armies; armies must
be paid, and the pay requires taxation.*

1673. Nervos belli pecuniam. Cic. Phil. 5, 2, 5.—*Money makes the
sinews of war.*

Cf. Libanius, orat. 46 (vol. ii. p. 479, Ed. Reiske), τὰ νεῦρα τοῦ πολέμου
—*The sinews of war;* and Rabelais, 1, 46, Les nerfs des batailles sont les
pécunes—*Cash is the sinews of battles.* Diog. Laert. 4, 7, 48, ascribes to
Bion the saying, τὸν πλοῦτον, νεῦρα πραγμάτων—*Money is the sinews of
affairs:* and, *Vectigalia nervos esse reipublicæ*, Cic. Man. 7, 17.

1674. Nescio qua natale solum dulcedine captos
Ducit, et immemores non sinit esse sui.   Ov. Ep. 1, 3, 35.

Home, Sweet Home.
There's a magical charm in the land of our birth,
That entrances beyond every region of earth:
Its spell is upon us where'er we may roam,
And forbids us to dim the sweet image of home.—*Ed.*

1675. Nescire autem quid antea quam natus sis acciderit, id est semper
esse puerum.   Quid enim est ætas hominis, nisi memoria rerum
veterum cum superiorum ætate contexitur? Cic. Or. 34, 120.—
*To be unacquainted with events which took place before our birth
is always to remain a child.   Intelligent existence loses its meaning,
without the aid of history to bring recent events into direct con-
tinuity with the past.*

1676. Nescis tu quam meticulosa res sit ire ad judicem. Plaut. Most.
5, 1, 52.—*You don't know what a frightful thing it is to go to law.*

1677. Nessun maggior dolore
Che ricordarsi del tempo felice
Nella miseria.   Dante, Inf. 5, 121.

(*Francesca da Rimini*) There is no greater woe
Than in the hour of misery to recall
The happy days of yore.—*Ed.*

The words form the motto of Byron's *Corsair*, and are referred to in "Locksley Hall":

> This is truth the poet sings,
> That a sorrow's crown of sorrows is remembering happier things.

Dante took the sentiment from Boethius (De Cons. Phil., 2, Prosa, 4), In omni adversitate fortunæ infelicissimum genus est infortunii fuisse felicem—*Of all reverses of fortune, the unhappiest is that of the man who has once been happy.* Chaucer, of course, copied from "Boece" in his *Troylus and Cressida,* 3, 1625:

> For of fortune's sharpe adversite,
> The worst kind of infortune is this,
> A man that hath been in prosperite,
> And it remember when it passed is.

The following may also be consulted: (i.) Super flumina Babylonis illic sedimus et flevimus, quum recordaremur Sion. Vulg. Ps. 137, 1.—*By the waters of Babylon*, etc.: also, "Jerusalem remembered in the days of her miseries all her pleasant things that she had in the days of old" (Lam. 1, 7, A.V.): and, Duplex enim illos acceperat tædium et gemitus cum memoria præteritorum. Vulg. Sap. 11, 13.—*A double affliction came upon them, and a groaning for the remembrance of the past.* (ii.) Miserum istuc verbum et pessumum 'st, Habuisse, et nihil habere. Plaut. Rud. 5, 2, 34.—*A miserable and hateful expression that—I had, but have not.* (iii.) Nihil est enim tam miserabile quam ex beato miser. Cic. Part. Or. 17, 57.—*Nothing so miserable as the wretched who have once been happy.* (iv.) "Nihil infelicius quam fuisse felicem," says Matt. Paris (Chron., vol. ii. p. 611, Rolls Ser., 1874), recording the jeers of King John's evil counsellors after he had signed Magna Charta: "Fuisti rex, nunc fex: fuisti maximus, nunc minimus. *Nihil infelicius,*" etc. (v.) Il ben passato è la presente noia. Tasso, Aminta, 2, 2.—*Happiness in the past is the sorrow of the present.* (vi.) Jean Bertaut, in his Chanson, "Les cieux inexorables," has (st. 7),

> Félicité passée
> Qui ne peut revenir,
> Tourment de ma pénsée,
> Que n'ai-je en te perdant, perdu le souvenir?

> Past happiness,—days that can ne'er come again!
> (Thou torment of my thoughts)
> When I lost you, ah! why did your memory remain?—*Ed.*

And (vii.) Alfred de Musset exclaims in *Le Saule,*

> Écoute, moribonde! il n'est pire douleur,
> Qu'un souvenir heureux dans les jours de malheur.

> Hear, dying one, hear! there is no greater sadness
> Than in grief to remember the past days of gladness.—*Ed.*

1678. Ne supra crepidam sutor judicaret; quod et ipsum in proverbium venit. Plin. 35, 10, 85.—*"A cobbler should stick to his last"—a saying that has passed into a proverb.*

When a cobbler, not content with pointing out defects in a shoe of Apelles' painting, presumed to criticise the drawing of the leg, the artist checked him with the rebuke here quoted. It is often said of those who offer opinions on subjects with which they are not professionally acquainted. *Supra plantam ascendere* (or *evagari*) is another form of the saying, *see* Val. Max. 8, 12; and Ammian. Marcellinus, 28, 1, 10. The younger Pliny (Ep. 1, 10) says, De pictore, sculptore, fictore, nisi artifex judicare . . . non potest—*None but an artist is qualified to criticise a painter, sculptor or statuary.*

1679. Ne te longis ambagibus ultra
　　　Quam satis est morer.
　　　　　　Hor. Ep. 1, 7, 82.—*To make a long story short.*

1680. Neu regio foret ulla suis animantibus orba,
　　　Astra tenent cæleste solum, formæque deorum. Ov. M. 1, 72.
　　　　Creation nowhere lacks inhabitants:
　　　　Heaven has its stars, and moving shapes of gods.—*Ed.*

1681. Nicht grösseren Vorteil wüsst' ich zu nennen
　　　Als des Feindes Verdienst erkennen. Goethe, Sprichwörtlich, 2,
　　　p. 337.—*I know no greater gain than to recognise an enemy's worth.*

1682. Nichts halb zu thun ist edler Geister Art. Wieland, Oberon, 5,
　　　30, 1.—*To do nothing by halves is the way of noble souls.*

1683. Nichts ist dauernd als der Wechsel. Ludw. Börne, *Rede auf Jean
　　　Paul*, Coll. Works, 1, 313.—*Nothing is permanent except change.*
　　　Taken as motto by Heine for his *Harzreise* (1824). Büchm. p. 240.

1684. Nichts ist höher zu schätzen, als der Wert des Tages. Goethe,
　　　Sprüche in Prosa, Eth. VI., No. 537, p. 115 (Hempel's ed.).—
　　　*Nothing should be valued more highly than the value of a single
　　　day.* Cf. Was aber ist deine Pflicht? Die Forderung des
　　　Tages. Id. ibid.—*What is thy duty? The claims of each day.*

1685. Nichtswürdig ist die Nation, die nicht
　　　Ihr Alles freudig setzt an ihre Ehre. Schiller, Jungfr. v.
　　　Orleans, 1, 5 (Dunois loq.).—*Unworthy is the nation that does not
　　　gladly stake its all for its honour.*

1686. Nihil ad Andromachen. Tert. Pudic. cap. 8, n. 65.—*This has
　　　nothing to do with Andromache.* Beside the question.
　　　　Prov. taken from the ancient stage, in which the pantomime acted the
　　　words delivered by the reciter. If his impersonation was poor or inappro-
　　　priate, it was said to have "nothing to do with" the character represented.
　　　Similar expressions are *Nihil ad Bacchum, nihil ad versum, nihil ad rem*
　　　(*see* Chil. pp. 173-4), all meaning *Not to the point, irrelevant.*

1687. Nihil cum fidibus graculo. Gell. Præf. 19.—*Jackdaws have no
　　　business with a lute.* Ignoramuses have nothing to do with poetry.

1688. Nihil enim legit, quod non excerperet. Dicere etiam solebat,
　　　nullum esse librum tam malum, ut non aliqua parte prodesset.
　　　Plin. Ep. 3, 5, 10.—*He never read a book without making extracts
　　　from it. He also used to say, that no book was so bad but what
　　　some part of it might be of use.* Said of the elder Pliny.

1689. Nihil est ab omni
　　　Parte beatum. Hor. C. 2, 16, 27.—*Unmixed happiness is not to
　　　be found in this world.*

1690. Nihil est, Antipho, Quin male narrando possit depravarier. Ter.
　　　Phorm. 4, 4, 15.—*No tale so good, my Antipho, but can be spoilt
　　　i' the telling.*

1691. Nihil est enim simul et inventum, et perfectum. Cic. Brut. 18, 70.
—*Nothing is ever invented and brought to perfection at once.* This
is also a maxim in English law.

1692. Nihil est furacius illo:
Non fuit Autolyci tam piceata manus. Mart. 8, 59, 3.
> It is the greatest thief the world e'er knew;
> Autolycus had not such hands of glue.—*Ed.*

1693. Nihil est hirsutius illis. Ov. T. 2, 259.—*Nothing can be more
rugged.* Said of the "Annals" of Rome, as a piece of reading.

1694. Nihil est miserum nisi quum putes. Boeth. Cons. 2, 4.—*Nothing
is miserable, if you don't think it so.*

1695. Nihil est quod credere de se
Non possit, quum laudatur dis æqua potestas.
Juv. 4, 70.—*There is nothing that he* (the Emp. Domitian)
*would not believe of himself, when he is flattered as being the
equal of the gods.*

1696. Nihil hic nisi carmina desunt. Virg. E. 8, 67.—*Nothing is wanting here but a song.*

1697. Nihil otiosum . . . in Scripturis divinis. Origen, Comment. in
Ep. ad Romanos, Lib. I. cap. 1, 8.—*Holy Scripture never uses
her words idly, i.e.,* without some special meaning. Said of the
slight difference to be observed in St Paul's "Salutations" to
the various churches, compared with that which he addresses to
the Church of Rome.

1698. Nihil sub sole novum. Vulg. Eccles. 1, 10.—*There is nothing
new under the sun.*

1699. Nihil tam absurde dici potest quod non dicatur ab aliquo philosophorum. Cic. Div. 2, 119.—*There is nothing too absurd for a
philosopher to utter.*

1700. Nihil tam difficile 'st, quin quærendo investigari possiet.
Ter. Heaut. 4, 2, 8.
> Nothing so hard but search will find it out. Herrick, *Seek and Find.*

1701. Nihil tam munitum, quod non expugnari pecunia possit. Cic.
Verr. 1, 2, 4.—*Nothing so strongly fortified but what money can
capture it.*

1702. Nihil turpius est quam grandis natu senex, qui nullum aliud
habet argumentum, quo se probet diu vixisse, præter ætatem.
Sen. Tranq. 3, 7.—*Nothing more despicable than an old man,
who has no other token to produce of his long life, except his
years.*

> On the distinction between advance in years and corresponding moral (or
> intellectual) progress, many authors may be cited. Plaut. Trin. 2, 2, 88,
> says, Non ætate, verum ingenio adipiscitur sapientia—*Wisdom does not
> come with years, but by study.* Cic. Sen. 18, 62, Non cani, non rugæ

repente auctoritatem arripere possunt; sed honeste acta superior ætas fructus capit auctoritatis extremos—*Neither grey hairs nor wrinkles can of themselves command authority: that honour only comes as the crowning fruits of a well-spent life.* S. Ambrose, Ep. 1, 18 (Migne iii. p. 974), writes, Non annorum canities est laudanda, sed morum—*Not whiteness of age, but whiteness of morals, deserves praise:* and, Corona dignitatis senectus, quæ 'in viis justitiæ reperitur. Vulg. Prov. 16, 31.—*Old age is a crown of dignity, when it is found in the ways of justice.*

1703. Nil admirari prope res est una, Numici,
Solaque, quæ possit facere et servare beatum.   Hor. Ep. 1, 6, 1.

> Not to admire, Numicius, is the best—
> The only way to make and keep men blest.—*Conington.*

1704. Nil æquale homini fuit illi.   Hor S. 1, 3, 9.—*There was nothing consistent in that man.* Cf. id. ibid. 18, Nil fuit unquam Sic impar sibi—*"So strange a jumble ne'er was seen before"* (Conington). A mass of inconsistencies and contradictions.

1705. Nil agit exemplum litem quod lite resolvit. Hor. S. 2, 3, 103.—*An instance, which solves one difficulty by raising another, is not to the purpose.*

1706. Nil consuetudine majus. Ov. A. A. 2, 345.—*Nothing greater than habit.*

1707. Nil desperandum Teucro duce et auspice Teucro. Hor. C. 1, 7, 27. —*There is nothing to be despaired of when we are under Teucer's leadership and auspices.*

1708. Nil dictu fœdum visuque hæc limina tangat,
Intra quæ puer est.

> .   .   .   .   .
> Maxima debetur puero reverentia.   Si quid
> Turpe paras, ne tu pueri contemseris annos:
> Sed peccaturo obsistat tibi filius infans.   Juv. 14, 44.

> *The Training of Youth.*
> Let no immodest sights or sounds e'er come
> Within the precincts of a young boy's home!
> The greatest reverence to a child is due;
> And if some shameful course you would pursue,
> Slight not his weakness, and your foul intent
> Let a consideration of his youth prevent.—*Ed.*

1709. Nil ego contulerim jucundo sanus amico. Hor. S. 1, 5, 44.—*While I have my senses, there is nothing in the world I would prefer to an agreeable friend.*

1710. Nil erit ulterius quod nostris moribus addat
Posteritas; eadem cupient facientque minores,
Omne in præcipiti vitium stetit.   Juv. 1, 147.

> Nothing is left, nothing, for future times,
> To add to the full catalogue of crimes.
> Our children needs must feel the same desires,
> And act the same mad follies as their sires:
> Vice has attained its zenith.—*Gifford.*

1711. Nil habet infelix paupertas durius in se,
Quam quod ridiculos homines facit.   Juv. 3, 152.

Unhappy poverty has no sting more cruel
Than that it turns a man to ridicule.—*Ed.*

1712. Nil mortalibus arduum est:
Cælum ipsum petimus stultitia.   Hor. C. 1, 3, 37.

Ballooning.
Nothing for mortal aims too high;
Our madness e'en would scale the sky.—*Ed.*

1713. Nil nisi turpe juvat: curæ est sua cuique voluptas.
Hæc quoque ab alterius grata dolore venit.
Ov. A. A. 1, 749.—*Nothing but what is shameful pleases: each one cares only for his own enjoyment, and if it can be procured at another's expense, it is all the more agreeable.*

1714. Nil non mortale tenemus,
Pectoris exceptis ingeniique bonis.
Ov. T. 3, 7, 43.—*Nothing have we that is not transitory in its enjoyment, excepting only the endowments of the heart and mind.*

1715. Nil oriturum alias, nil ortum tale fatentes.   Hor. Ep. 2, 1, 17.

Augustus Cæsar.
Like whom to mortal eyes
None e'er has risen, and none e'er shall rise.—*Pope.*

1716. Ni l'or ni la grandeur ne nous rendent heureux. La Font. Contes, 5, 9, 1 (Philémon et Baucis).—*Neither wealth nor honours can confer happiness.*

1717. Nil rectum nisi quod placuit sibi ducunt. Hor. Ep. 2, 1, 83.—*They think nothing right except what pleases themselves.*

1718. Nil sine magno
Vita labore dedit mortalibus.
Hor. S. 1, 9, 59.—*Nothing is granted to man in this world without great labour.*

1719. Nil spernat auris, nec tamen credat statim. Phædr. 3, 10, 51.—*The ear should neither despise what it hears, nor yet believe too readily.*

1720. Nil · Unquam · Peccavit · Nisi · Quod · Mortua · Est.   J. Gruter, Inscriptiones, Pag. DCCXCV.—*The only wrong she ever did was to die.*   Touching tribute to his wife, Julia J. F. Prisca, erected by Clodius Hilarus.

1721. Nimia est voluptas, si diu abfueris a domo,
Domum si redieris, si tibi nulla est ægritudo animo obviam.
Plaut. Stich. 4, 1, 18.—*It is too great a happiness, if after being absent from home for a time you find no troubles awaiting your return.*

1722. Nimirum insanus paucis videatur, eo quod
Maxima pars hominum morbo jactatur eodem.   Hor. S. 2, 3, 120.
Few men can see much madness in his whim,
Becau-e the mass of mortals ail like him.—*Conington.*

1723. Nimis uncis Naribus indulges. Pers. 1, 40.—*You sneer too palpably.*

1724. Nimium boni est, cui nil malist.   Enn. Incert. (vol. i. 76).—
He lives too well who has no ill.

1725. Nitimur in vetitum semper, cupimusque negata. Ov. Am. 3, 4, 17.
—*We are always striving after what is forbidden, and coveting
the prohibited.*

> Quicquid servatur, cupimus magis, ipsaque furem
> Cura vocat. Pauci, quod sinit alter, amant.   Ov. Am. 3, 4, 25.

*Whatever is carefully guarded we covet all the more, and the very solicitude
invites a thief: few long for what others leave alone.*   Quod licet ingratum
est: quod non licet acrius urit. Id. Am. 2, 19, 3.—*What, is lawful is
unattractive; what is unlawful excites all the more keenly.*   Permissum fit
vile nefas. Maximianus Etruscus (falsely attrib. to Cornelius Gallus), Eleg.
3, 77 (in Lemaire's Biblioth. Class. Lat., vol. 140, p. 246).—*Permitted sin
loses its value:* and, Vile est quod licet. Petr. 93.—*What is lawful is of
little value.*

1726. Ni un pouce de notre territoire, ni une pierre de nos forteresses.
Jules Favre, *Journal Officiel,* Sept. 7, 1870.—*Not an inch of our
territory, nor a stone of our fortresses.*

> Famous but futile declaration of Favre, as Minister for Foreign Affairs
and V.P. of the Committee of National Defence, addressed after the battle
of Sedan to all the diplomatic representatives of France.   The sentence
began, "Nous ne céderons ni un pouce," etc.   Such a speech, though
essentially French, was not only foolish, but in the circumstances absolutely suicidal, since it made it impossible for Bismarck to come to terms
with him in the interview at Ferrières ten days later. [Alex. pp. 503-4.]

1727. Noblesse oblige.   Duc de Lévis, *Max. et Reflexions,* li., Paris,
1808, p. 13.—*Nobility has its obligations.*

> The idea that M. de Lévis was quoting his own family motto, or that he
composed the sentiment to serve as motto for his house, seems to have
little foundation. (See Fourn. *L.D.L.,* p. 426 and N.)   At the outbreak of
the plague at Carthage (*c.* 257 A.D.), S. Cyprian conjured his flock to brave
the contagion in ministration to the dead and dying.—*Respondere nos decet
natalibus nostris,* he said (Vita Pontii, 9, prefixed to S. Cyprian's Works)—
"We should answer to our birth."   In his *Life of St Cyprian* (p. 245),
Archbishop Benson observes: "His epigrammatic '*Respondere natalibus*'
is a nobler version of *Noblesse oblige,* and no less defies rendering."   The
Grave pondus illum magna nobilitas premit, of No. 858, *supra,* has also, in
its *strict* sense, much the same meaning.

1728. Nodum in scirpo quæris. Prov. (Ter. Andr. 5, 4, 38).—*You are
looking for a knot in a bulrush.*   Seeking difficulties where none
exist.

1729. Noli, obsecro, istum disturbare.   Val. Max. 8, 7, Ext. 7.—*I pray
you, do not disturb it.*

> Gen. quoted as, Noli turbare circulos meos—*Do not disturb my circles.*
Archimedes' expostulation to the Roman soldier, during the siege of

Syracuse, 212 B.C., who surprised him engaged upon some geometrical problem figured on the sand, and not being able to get any other reply, put him to death.

1730. Noli pugnare duobus. Cat. 62, 64.—*Don't fight with two at once.* πρὸς δύο οὐδ' ὁ Ἡρακλῆς λέγεται οἷος τε εἶναι. Plat. Phæd., cap. 38 fin., p. 89; and, Ne Hercules quidem adversus duos. Chil. p. 115.—*Even Hercules is no match for two at once.*

1731. Nomen amicitia est, nomen inane fides. Ov. A. A. 1, 740.— *Friendship, fidelity, are but empty names.*

1732. Nomen atque omen. Plaut. Pers. 4, 4, 73.—*Both name and omen in one.* A good omen in the name.

1733. Non adeo cecidi, quamvis abjectus, ut infra Te quoque sim; inferius quo nihil esse potest.　　Ov. T. 5, 8, 1.

> I have not sunk so low, though great my fall,
> As to reach thee, the lowest depth of all.—*Ed.*

1734. Non amo te, Sabidi, nec possum dicere quare; Hoc tantum possum dicere; non amo te.　　Mart. 1, 33.

> I do not love you, Dr Fell,
> But why I cannot tell,
> But this I know full well,
> I do not love you, Dr Fell.

> Tom Brown, *Works*, Lond., 1760, vol. 4, p. 100.

The task of translating Martial's epigram is said to have been set to T. B., in his undergraduate days at Christ Church, by Dr John Fell (1625-1686), successively Canon and Dean of Christ Church, Chancellor of the University, and Bishop of Oxford. Others think that Brown borrowed from Thos. Forde's *Virtus Rediviva* (1661),

> "I love thee not, Nel! but why I can't tell!"

1735. Non Angli sed angeli. Bed. 2, 1.—*Not Angles but Angels.*

Traditional exclamation of Gregory the Great, then (*c.* 578 A.D.) Abbot of St Andrea, on seeing some fair-haired English captives exposed for sale in the slave-market in Rome.

1736. Non bene conveniunt, nec in una sede morantur Majestas et amor.　　Ov. M. 2, 846.

> Ill-matched are love and majesty, the throne
> Is not love's dwelling-place.—*Ed.*

1737. Non bene junctarum discordia semina rerum.　　Ov. M. 1, 9.—*The jarring seeds of ill-assorted things.*

1738. Non bene olet, qui bene semper olet. Mart. 2, 12, 4.—*That smells not sweet, that always sweetly smells.*

1739. Non, c'est l'eunuque au milieu du sérail, Il n'y fait rien et nuit à qui veut faire.　　A. Piron (Panthéon, Petits Poètes Fr., Paris, 1858, vol. i. 157).

> No, he's the eunuch stationed in the harem;
> No work does he, and hinders those who would.—*Ed.*

*** Epigram on Desfontaines, and applicable to all who can criticise but not create.

1740. Non convivere, nec videre saltem
       Non audire licet: nec Urbe tota
       Quisquam est tam prope, tam proculque nobis.   Mart. 1, 87.

> *An Unsociable Neighbour.*
> He will not live with me, nor can
>   I get a glimpse of him, nor hear:
> All the town through, there's not a man
>   So far from me, and yet so near.

1741. Non cuicunque datum est habere nasum.   Mart. 1, 42, 18.—*It is
       not given to every man to be smart;* lit., "to have a nose."

> "Everyone cannot be witty."—*Shaw.*

1742. Non cuivis homini contingit adire Corinthum.   Hor. Ep. 1, 17, 36.

> You know the proverb, "Corinth town is fair,
>   But 'tis not every man that can get there."—*Conington.*

The prov. "Non cuivis," etc., is quoted of any difficult attainment which
only good fortune or wealth can achieve.   In Gr. it is, οὐ παντὸς ἀνδρός εἰς
Κόρινθον ἔσθ᾽ ὁ πλοῦς.   Strabo, 8, 6, 20 (p. 325); a parody of which is to be
found in Nicolaus (Mein. p. 1177), οὐ παντὸς ἀνδρὸς ἐπὶ τραπεζᾶν ἐσθ᾽ ὁ
πλοῦς—*It is not every parasite that can find his way to a dinner-table.*

1743. Non dee guerra co' morti aver chi vive.   Tasso, Gerus. Liber.
       13, st. 39.— *War with the dead no living man may wage.*

> The following bear on the same subject:
> Nullum cum victis certamen et æthere cassis.   Virg. A. 11, 104.
>
> No war may soldier wage, they say,
>   With vanquished man or senseless clay.—*Conington.*

Hamilcar, in the First Punic War, on the request of a truce for burying
the enemy's dead, said: Μάχεσθαι μὲν τοῖς ζῶσι, διαλελύσθαι δὲ πρὸς τοὺς
τελευτηκότας.   Diod. Sic. 24, 9, §§ 2, 3.—*That he warred with the living, but
was at peace with the dead.*   Charles Quint, on being urged by Alva to
force Luther's tomb at Wittenberg and gibbet the corpse, is said to have
replied, "Nihil mihi ultra cum Luthero . . . neque mihi cum mortuis
bellum." C. Juncker, Vita M. Lutheri, Frankfurt, 1699, p. 219.—*I have
nothing further to do with Luther, nor have I any war with the dead.*   For
the historical merits of the story, see W. Hertslet's "Treppenwitz der
Weltgeschichte," 5th ed., pp. 246-7.   Pope, it may be with this tale in
his mind, is the first to have introduced into English citation the "I war
not with the dead" of his *Iliad* vii. 485, apparently as an expression of the
sentiment, rather than the words, of Agamemnon (Il. 7, 408).

1744. Non eadem est ætas, non mens.   Hor. Ep. 1, 1, 4.— *My age, my
       tastes, no longer are the same.*

1745. Non ego mordaci destrinxi carmine quenquam,
       Nec meus ullius crimina versus habet.
     Candidus a salibus suffusis felle refugi:
       Nulla venenato littera mixta joco est.   Ov. T. 2, 563.

> I never wounded soul with verse of mine,
>   Nor do my works a single charge contain:
> My pen is free of gall, and not a line
>   Breathes poison, tho' conveyed in joking strain.—*Ed.*

Crebillon says (Discours de réception à l'Académie Fr., 1731), "Aucun fiel
n'a jamais empoisonné ma plume"—*My pen was never dipped in gall.*

1746. Non ego nec Teucris Italos parere jubebo.   Virg. A. 12, 189.

> I will not force Italia's band
> To Teucrian rule to bow.—*Conington.*

Æneas, on the eve of battle with Turnus, declares that should victory be his, he would not reduce the enemy to the position of a subject race, but that either should occupy the country in mutual amity. The application of this to the relations of England towards Ireland is obvious, and in this connection the line has had the honour of being thrice quoted in Parliament: first, by Mr Pitt (1799) in his great speech proposing the Union; next, by Mr Isaac Butt in an equally forcible speech against the Union (June 30, 1874); and, lastly, by Mr J. Morley on the (Irish) Financial Relations Committee, March 31, 1897. The line had, and still has, a direct application upon Boer and British relations in the "settlement" that followed the termination of the great three years' war.

1747. Non ego omnino lucrum omne esse utile homini existimo.
Scio ego, multos jam lucrum luculentos homines reddidit;
Est etiam, ubi profecto damnum præstet facere, quam lucrum.

> Plaut. Capt. 2, 2, 75 (Hegio loq.).—*For my part I don't altogether reckon all gains to be to a man's advantage. I know that gain has made many a man rich; and again there are times when it is better to lose than win.*

1748. Non ego sum stultus, ut ante fui. Ov. Am. 3, 11, 32.—*I am no longer the fool I was.* I have learned by experience.

1748A. Non enim si malum est dolor, carere eo malo satis est ad bene vivendum. Hoc dixerit potius Ennius, "Nimium boni est, cui nihil est mali." Cic. Fin. 2, 13, 41.—*Granted that pain is an evil, yet its absence does not necessarily constitute a happy life. Ennius will tell you rather,*

> "He lives too well who has no ill."

1749. Non equidem invideo; miror magis. Virg. E. 1, 11.—*I do not indeed envy you, I am only the rather surprised.*

1750. Non est in medico semper relevetur ut æger;
Interdum docta plus valet arte malum.   Ov. Ep. 1, 3, 17.

> Doctors can't always cure a man that's ill;
> Sickness sometimes defeats all human skill.—*Ed.*

1751. Non est nostri ingenii. Cic. Clu. 1, 4.—*It is not within my powers.*

1751A. Non est paupertas, Nestor, habere nihil. Mart. 11, 32, 8.—*Straitened means and absolute destitution are two very different things.*

1752. Non è ver che sia la morte
Il peggior di tutt' i mali;
È un sollievo de' mortali
Che son stanchi di soffrir.   Metast. Adriano, 3, 6.

> Death is not, as some maintain,
> Far the worst of all our woes;
> It is a relief to those
> Who are wearied out with pain.—*Ed.*

P

In 1886 a public statue was dedicated in Rome to Metastasio on his birth-
day, and the well-known lines were cited on the occasion. The ceremony
took place in floods of rain, in consequence of which some wit of the day
altered the two last lines to—

C'è quest' acqua ne' miei stivali,
Che son stanco di soffrir.—'*Tis this water in my boots, that
I can no longer bear.*

1753. Non fa scienza,
Senza lo ritenere, avere inteso.
Dante, Par. 5, 41.—*To have understood a thing is not know-
ledge: you must remember it.*

1754. Non fumum ex fulgore, sed ex fumo dare lucem. Hor. A. P. 143.
Not smoke from fire his object is to bring,
But fire from smoke, a very different thing.—*Conington.*

Horace compares the heavy productions of the mere verse-writer with the
brilliant results of the true poet: the one is all smoke, the other all fire.

1755. Non hæc sine numine Divum Eveniunt. Virg. A. 2, 777.—*These
things do not occur without the Deity's ordering.* Not mere
accident.

1756. Non hoc ista sibi tempus spectacula poscit. Virg. A. 6, 37.—*The
present moment is not one for such exhibitions as those.*

1757. Non hominis culpa, sed ista loci. Ov. T. 5, 7, 60.—*Not the man's
fault, but that of the place.* Circumstances were too strong for
him.

1758. Non ignara mali miseris succurrere disco.   Virg. A. 1, 630.
Myself not ignorant of woe,
Compassion I have learned to show.—*Conington.*

Cf. Garrick, *Prologue on Quitting the Stage* (1776), "A fellow-feeling makes
us wondrous kind." Guillard, in his opera of *Œdipe à Colone*, 2, 4 (1785),
(Music by Sacchini), makes Theseus say, *J'ai connu le malheur et j'y sais
compatir.* Cardinal Newman, also, speaking of those he had left behind
him in the Anglican Communion, says, "I am now in the position of the
fugitive Queen in the well-known passage, who *Haud ignara mali* herself,
had learned to sympathise with those who were inheritors of her wanderings."—*Letter to Dr Pusey,* p. 6.

1759. Non in dialectica complacuit Deo salvum facere populum suum.
S. Ambrose, de Fide i. 5, sec. 42 (Migne, vol. xvi. p. 537).—*It is
not the will of God to save His people by dialectic.*

Neither individuals nor people are converted by logic. What "saves"
is faith. Newman, applying the qu. to his own case, says, "For myself,
it was not logic that carried me on. It is the concrete being that reasons;
pass a number of years, and I find my mind in a new place: how? the
whole man moves: paper logic is but the record of it."—*Apologia,* etc.
(Lond., 1878, 8vo), p. 169.

1760. Non liquet. Quint. 9, 3, 97.—*It is not evident.* As a legal
formula, it exactly corresp. with the Scotch *Not proven,* and
in this sense is used by Cic. Clu. 28, 76.

1761. Non magna eloquimur, sed vivimus. Min. Felix, cap. 38 (Migne, vol. 3, col. 357).—*We don't talk great things: we live them.*   Cf. οὐκ ἐν λέξεσιν ἀλλ᾽ ἐν πράγμασιν μεγαλοφωνία. Orig. *c. Celsum*, 2, p. 101 (ed. Spencer).—*Deeds, not words, are the best eloquence.*

1762. Non men che saver, dubbiar m'aggrata.   Dante, Inf. 11, 93.— *Doubt, no less than knowledge, has its charm.*

1763. Non minus res hominem quam scutus tegit. S. Turpilius (Ribb. ii. p. 104).—*Money screens a man as securely as a shield.*

1764. Non nobis, Domine, non nobis, sed nomini tuo da gloriam.   Vulg. Ps. cxv. 1.—*Not unto us, O Lord, not unto us, but unto Thy name give the praise.*   Often sung as a grace after meals.

1765. Non nostrum inter vos tantas componere lites.   Virg. E. 3, 108.— *It is no business of mine to settle such disputes between you.*

1766. Non omnia possumus omnes.   Virg. E. 8, 63.—*We cannot all do everything.*

1767. Non possidentem multa vocaveris
 Recte beatum.   Rectius occupat
  Nomen beati, qui Deorum
   Muneribus sapienter uti,
 Duramque callet pauperiem pati,
 Pejusque leto flagitium timet;
  Non ille pro caris amicis
   Aut patria timidus perire.   Hor. C. 4, 9, 45.

The Happy Man.
Say not that happily he lives
 Because of boundless wealth possesst!
 More truly his the name of blest
Who wisely uses what God gives;
Who can bear poverty's hard hand;
 Who reckons sin as worse than death—
 He will not shirk to yield his breath
For loving friends or fatherland.—*Ed.*

1768. Non possum ferre, Quirites, Græcam urbem.   Juv. 3, 60.—*I cannot endure, citizens, a Greekified Rome,* or, as we might say, *a Germanised London.*

1769. Non potes in nugas dicere plura meas
 Ipse ego quam dixi.
  Mart. 13, 2, 4.—*You cannot say harder things of my trifles than I have said myself of them.*   A humble author deprecating criticism.

1770. Non pronuba Juno
 Non Hymenæus adest, non illi Gratia lecto.
 Eumenides tenuere faces de funere raptas:
 Eumenides stravere torum.   Ov. M. 6, 428.

Marriage of Tereus and Procne.

No Juno, patroness of bridal rites,
  Hymen nor Grace their genial presence shed:
But Furies held the torches—funeral lights
  Snatch'd from the pyre—and strewed the marriage bed.—*Ed.*

1771. Non propter vitam faciunt patrimonia quidam,
  Sed vitio cæci propter patrimonia vivunt.   Juv. 12, 50.

Some amass riches, not for what they give:
Blind slaves! 'tis but to hug them that they live.—*Ed.*

1772. Non qui soletur, non qui labentia tarde
  Tempora narrando fallat, amicus adest.   Ov. T. 3, 3, 11.

I have no friend to solace or to baulk
Time's tedious slowness with his cheerful talk.—*Ed.*

1773. Non ragioniam di lor, ma guarda, e passa.   Dante, Inf. 3, 51.

Speak not of them, but look, and pass them by.—*Cary.*

1774. Non recuso laborem. St Martin.—*I do not decline the task.*
  Sulp. Severus, Ep. 3 (Migne, xx. p. 182), gives the Saint's words:
  " Domine, si adhuc populo tuo sum necessarius, non recuso
  laborem: fiat voluntas tua!"—*Lord, if I am still necessary to
  Thy people, I do not decline the task.   Thy will be done!*

1775. Non refert quam multos, sed quam bonos habeas (*sc.* libros).
  Sen. Ep. 45, 1.—*It does not matter how many books you may have,
  but whether they are good or no.*

1776. Non satis est pulcra esse poemata; dulcia sunto,
  Et quocumque volent animum auditoris agunto.   Hor. A. P. 99.

Mere grace is not enough: a play should thrill
The hearer's soul, and move it at its will.—*Conington.*

1777. Non scribit, cujus carmina nemo legit.   Mart. 3, 9, 2.—*He does
  not write, whose verses no man reads.*

1778. Non semper ea sunt, quæ videntur: decipit
  Frons prima multos; rara mens intelligit
  Quod interiore condidit cura angulo.
      Phædr. 4, 1, 16.—*Things are not always what they seem: the
  first appearance deceives many, and few discern the carefully concealed secrets of the heart.*

1779. Non si male nunc et olim Sic erit.   Hor. C. 2, 10, 17.

Nor, if affairs look ill to-day
Shall it be always so.—*Ed.*

1780. Non soles respicere te, quom dicas injuste alteri?   Plaut. Ps. 2, 2,
  18.—*Don't you ever think of yourself when you speak harshly of
  others?*

1781. Non stilla una cavat marmor, neque protinus uno est
  Condita Roma die.   Marcell. Palingenius,
  Zodiacus Vitæ, 12, 460.—*One drop of water will not wear a hole
  in marble, nor was Rome built in a day.*

1782. Non sum qualis eram bonæ
    Sub regno Cinaræ.   Hor. C. 4, 1, 3.—*I am not what I was in
    kind Cinara's day.*   Cf. Non sum quod fueram.   Ov. T. 3, 11,
    25.—*I'm not the man I was.*

1782A. Non sunt longa quibus nihil est quod demere possis:
    Sed tu, Cosconi, disticha longa facis.   Mart. 2, 77, 7.

> *To Cosconius*
> Where you can't spare a line, no epigram's too long:
> But e'en your distiches "drag their slow length along."—*Ed.*

An echo of this is found in Rivarol's well-known answer to some one who
asked his opinion of a distich of his composing.   "C'est bien," said he,
"c'est bien, mais il y a des longueurs," totally unaware that the witty *mot*
had been made seventeen hundred years before.   (*Esprit de Rivarol*, 1808,
p. 161; and Alex. p. 287.)

1783. Non tali auxilio, nec defensoribus istis
    Tempus eget.   Virg. A. 2, 521.—*The times require other aid
    and other defenders than these.*

1784. Non tamen idcirco crimen liber omnis habebit;
    Nil prodest, quod non lædere possit idem.   Ov. T. 2, 265.

> You will not say all books should be accused;
> There's nought so good but it may be abused.—*Ed.*

1785. Non ut edam vivo, sed ut vivam edo.   Quint. 9, 3, 85.—*I don't
    live to eat, but eat to live:* and the "living," or rather the long
    life, depends upon the abstemiousness practised.   As says the
    prov. qu. in Don Quixote, 2, 43:

> Come poco, cena mas,
> Duerme en alto, y viviras.
> Would you live? then, sleep high up;
> Dine on little, on still less sup.

1786. Noris quam elegans formarum spectator siem.   Ter. Eun. 3, 5, 18.
    —*You know what a nice judge of beauty I am.*

1787. Noscenda est mensura sui spectandaque rebus
    In summis minimisque.   Juv. 11, 35.—*A man should know his
    own measure and keep it in view in all affairs, great or small.*

1788. Noscitur a sociis.   Prov.—*A man is known by his company;* or,
    in hexameter verse,

> Noscitur e socio, qui non cognoscitur ex se.
> His friendships show the man, who does not show himself.

"Dis-moi qui tu hantes, et je te dirai qui tu es."   As a Law Maxim, in the
interpretation of written instruments, the phrase signifies that *the meaning
of a word may be ascertained by referring to the meaning of the words
associated with it.*

1789. Nos duo turba sumus.   Ov. M. 1, 355.—*We two are a multitude.*
    Deucalion to Pyrrha, the pair who re-peopled the earth after the
    deluge according to the mythological tradition.   According to
    Lord Coke, it takes *ten* to make a crowd.

1790. Nos hæc novimus esse nihil. Mart. 13, 2, 8.—*We know that these things are of no consequence.* Mere trifles.

1791. Nos numerus sumus et fruges consumere nati,
Sponsi Penelopæ, nebulones, Alcinoique,
In cute curanda plus æquo operata juventus. Hor. Ep. 1, 2, 27.

> *Jeunesse Dorée.*
>
> But what are we? a mere consuming class,
> Just fit for counting roughly in the mass:
> Like to the suitors, or Alcinous' clan,
> Who spread vast pains upon the husk of man.—*Conington.*

Fruges consumere nati is often applied to those spoilt children of Fortune, who come into the world with their bread ready buttered.

1792. Nosse velint omnes, mercedem solvere nemo. Juv. 7, 157.—*All wish to know, but none to pay the price.*

1793. Nostra sine auxilio fugiunt bona. Carpite florem,
Qui nisi carptus erit, turpiter ipse cadet. Ov. A. A. 3, 79.

> Pleasures fly without our helping; cull the blossom of to-day:
> Left upon its stalk, to-morrow of itself 'twill fall away.—*Ed.*

1794. Notandi sunt tibi mores. Hor. A. P. 156.—*Set yourself to study men's manners.*

1795. Notre vie est du vent tissu. Joubert, Pensées, Max., etc., Titre 7, 72.—*Our life is woven wind.*

1796. Notte! funesta, atroce, orribil notte! V. Alfieri, Oreste, 1, init.— *That fatal night, atrocious, horrible!*

1797. Nourri dans le sérail j'en connais les détours. Rac. Bajazet, Act 4, sc. 7 (Acomat loq.).—*Seraglio-bred, I know my way about.* To be "at home," on familiar ground; to "know the ropes."

1798. Nous avons changé tout cela. Mol. Méd. Malgré lui, 2, 6.—*We have changed all that kind of thing.*

> Sganarelle, the pretended physician, declaring that the liver was on the left side, the heart on the right, is asked by Géronte to account for such an inversion of the usual arrangement, to which he replies, " Oui, cela était autrefois ainsi; *mais nous avons changé tout cela, et nous faisons maintenant la médicine d'une méthode toute nouvelle.*"

1799. Nous avons tous assez de force pour supporter les maux d'autrui. La Rochef., § 19, p. 34.—*We all have sufficient strength to support the misfortunes of others.*

1800. Nous dansons sur un volcan. Salvandy, *Paris, ou le Livre des cent-et-un* (Paris, 1832, vol. i. p. 398, 2nd ed.).—*We are dancing on a volcano.*

> Remark of M. de Salvandy, ex-ambassador of France at the court of Ferdinand II., K. of the Two Sicilies, to Louis Philippe, on the occasion of a fête given by the latter on May 31, 1830 at the Palais Royal in honour of his brother-in-law, the Majesty aforesaid. The scene was magnificence itself, and the King attended in person. " Ceci, Monseigneur, est une fête toute napolitaine," observed Salvandy to the host of the evening;

"nous dansons sur un volcan." A month later the volcano exploded, leaving the giver of the gala heir to a forlorn "constitutional" arrangement, to which, even his descendants have failed to succeed. Alex. p. 543; and Fourn. *L.D.L.*, cap. 63.

1801. Nous désirerions peu de choses avec ardeur, si nous connaissions parfaitement ce que nous désirons. La Rochef., § 461, p. 88.— *We should be less eager in our desires, if we were more perfectly acquainted with the object of our wishes.*

1802. Nous l'acceptons le cœur léger. Émile Ollivier, *Journal Officiel*, July 16, 1870.—*We accept* (the responsibility of the war) *with a light heart.* From Ollivier's celebrated speech in the Corps Législatif, July 15, 1870.

1803. Nous n'écoutons d'instincts que ceux qui sont les nôtres, Et ne croyons le mal que quand il est venu.

La Font. 1, 8, fin. (L'hirondelle et les petits oiseaux).

We list to no instincts but what are our own, Nor credit misfortune until it has come.—*Ed.*

1804. Nous ne trouvons guère de gens de bon sens que ceux qui sont de notre avis. La Rochef. Max., § 354, p. 76.—*We seldom find any persons of good sense, except those who are of our way of thinking.*

1805. Nous sommes assemblés par la volonté nationale, nous n'en sortirons que par la force. Mirabeau (Fourn. *L.D.L.*, pp. 372-3).— *We are here by the will of the nation, and we shall not leave except we are driven out by force.* Reply of Mirabeau to the Marquis de Dreux-Brézé, Grand Master of the Ceremonies, when sent by Louis XVI., on June 23, 1789, to dissolve the National Assembly, according to the version given by the Marquis' son, M. Scipion de Dreux-Brézé, in the French House of Peers on March 9, 1833.

It will be seen that in this account the audacious "*Allez dire à votre maître*," still more the "*Esclave! dis à ton maître*," with which the sentence has commonly been made to begin, and the "*la force des baionnettes*" with which it generally concludes, are both of them wanting: and, as the younger Brézé confidently invited correction if he were at fault, we must suppose his version of the famous words to be the true one. At the same time, it is not a little singular that in the *Moniteur's* report of the proceedings (No. of 20th to 24th June 1789, p. 48, col. 1), and in Hugou's (N. J.) *Mémoires Hist. de la Révolution*, etc., Paris, 1790 (vol. ii. p. 88), the "baionnettes" should be mentioned. According to Hugou, who agrees almost *verbatim* with the *Moniteur*, Mirabeau's speech ended as follows: "Je vous déclare que, si l'on vous a chargé de nous faire sortir d'ici, vous devez demander des ordres pour employer la force, car nous ne quitterons nos places que par la puissance de la baionnette"—words which were received with the acclamation of "*Tel est le vœu de l'Assemblée!*" (*V.* also Alex. pp. 41-2; *Tableaux Hist. de la Rév. Française*, Paris (Auber, Éditeur), 1802, fol., vol. i. p. 2; and Chamfort, vol. ii. p. 175.)

1806. Novi ingenium mulierum; Nolunt ubi velis; ubi nolis, cupiunt ultro. Ter. Eun. 4, 7, 42.— *I know women's ways: when you will, they won't; and when you won't, then they will with a vengeance.*

1807. Nox erat, et placidum carpebant fessa soporem
    Corpora per terras, sylvæque et sæva quiêrant
    Æquora: quum medio volvuntur sidera lapsu,
    Quum tacet omnis ager, pecudes, pictæque volucres,
    Quæque lacus late liquidos, quæque aspera dumis
    Rura tenent, somno positæ sub nocte silenti,
    Lenibant curas, et corda oblita laborum.   Virg. A. 4, 522.

> 'Tis night: earth's tired ones taste the balm,
>   The precious balm of sleep,
> And in the forest there is calm,
>   And on the savage deep:
> The stars are in their middle flight:
>   The fields are hushed: each bird or beast
> That dwells beside the silver lake
> Or haunts the tangles of the brake,
>   In placid slumber lies, released
> From trouble by the touch of night.—*Conington.*

1808. Nudo detrahere vestimenta me jubes.   Plaut. As. 1, 1, 79.—*You are bidding me strip a naked man of his clothes.* Asking an impossibility; like our saying, "It's ill pulling the breeks off a Hielandman."

1809. Nugis addere pondus.   Hor. Ep. 1, 19, 42.—*To give consequence to trifles.*

1810. Nulla ætas ad perdiscendum sera est.   S. Ambrose, Ep. 1, 18, (Migne, iii. p. 974).—*It is never too late to learn.*

1811. Nulla cosa per legame musaico armonizzata si può della sua loquela in altra trasmutare sanza rompere tutta sua dolcézza e armonia. Dante, Conv. 1, 7, fin.—*No poetical work can be translated without losing all its sweetness and harmony.* Dante instances Homer and the Psalter as cases in point.

1812. Nulla dies sine linea.   Prov.—*No day without a line.*

> Plin. (35, 10, 36, § 84) relates of Apelles that, Nunquam tam occupatam diem agendi, ut non lineam ducendo exerceret artem: quod ab eo in proverbium venit: *his day was never so full of business, but that he drew a line to keep his art in practice: and from him the saying passed into a proverb.* Anthony Trollope took the words as motto, with ref. to his own trade of writing.

1813. Nulla placere diu, nec vivere carmina possunt,
    Quæ scribuntur aquæ potoribus.   Hor. Ep. 1, 19, 2.

> No poetry can please or hope to live
> That water-drinkers to the public give.—*Ed.*

> οἶνός τοι χαρίεντι πέλει ταχὺς ἵππος ἀοιδῷ,
> ὕδωρ δὲ πίνων οὐδὲν ἂν τέκοι σοφόν.   Cratinus, p. 41.
> The witty bard finds a swift steed in wine,
> While water-drinkers can write nothing fine.—*Ed.*

> Possum nil ego sobrius; bibenti
> Succurrent mihi quindecim poetæ.   Mart. 11, 6, 12.
> Sober, I can write nothing: when I'm drinking
> A fifteen-poet power aids my thinking.—*Ed.*

1814. Nulla recordanti lux est ingrata gravisque,
  Nulla subit cujus non meminisse velit.
  Ampliat ætatis spatium sibi vir bonus: hoc est
  Vivere bis, vita posse priore frui.   Mart. 10, 23, 5.

A Good Life.

No day's remembrance shall the good regret;
Nothing there is he fain would now forget:
He makes his time allotted doubly last,
And lives twice o'er as he recalls the past.—*Ed.*

1815. Nulla reparabilis arte
  Læsa pudicitia est: deperit illa semel.   Ov. H. 5, 103.

Chastity.

When once a woman's virtue's gone,
No art the damage can atone:
'Tis ruined once for all.—*Ed.*

1816. Nulla sancta societas
  Nec fides regni est.   Enn. Trag. Incert. xxxviii. (i. p. 80).
  —*Where the throne's shared, there cannot be good faith.*

  Cf. Nulla fides regni sociis, omnisque potestas
      Impatiens consortis erit.   Luc. 1, 92.

  Trust 'twixt associate kings does not reside:
  No chief will brook a colleague at his side.—*Ed.*

1817. Nulla unquam de vita hominis cunctatio longa est. Juv. 6, 221.
  —*No delay's too long where a man's life is at stake.* Cf. In
  judicando criminosa est celeritas. Syr. 254.—*In trying a man,
  haste is criminal.*

1818. Nulla venustas,
  Nulla in tam magno est corpore mica salis.   Cat. 86, 3.—*There
  is no grace, no grain of wit in all that large body.* A ponderous,
  dull work, or person.

1819. Nulle terre sans seigneur—*No land without its lord;* and, L'argent
  n'a pas de maître—*Money owns no master.* are two old proverbs
  which exactly express between them the difference between real
  property and the impersonal wealth existing in money.

1820. Nulli est homini perpetuum bonum.   Plaut. Curc. 1, 3, 33.—"*No
  blessing lasts for ever.*"—Thornton.

1821. Nulli secundus.—*Second to none.*   Motto of the Coldstream Regt.
  of Foot Guards. Appul. Florida, 1, 9, 32 (ed. Bipont. 1788, p. 120).
  Hippias eloquentia nulli secundus.—*In eloquence Hippias was
  second to none.*   Cæsar (in Plut. Cæs. 11) says, ἐβουλόμην παρὰ
  τούτοις εἶναι πρῶτος, ἢ παρὰ Ῥωμαίοις δεύτερος.—*I would rather be
  the first man here than the second in Rome.* "Better to reign in
  Hell than serve in Heaven," is the avowed sentiment of the
  "lost archangel" in "Paradise Lost," i. 261.

1822. Nullius addictus jurare in verba magistri,
  Quo me cunque rapit tempestas, deferor hospes.
                    Hor. Ep. 1, 1. 14.   Imitated by Pope, Sat. 3, 24:
> Sworn to no master, of no sect am I;
> As drives the storm, at any door I knock,
> And house with Montaigne now, and now with Locke.

1823. Nullius Veneris, sine pondere et arte.   Hor. A. P., 320.—*Devoid
  of charm, or weight, or art.*

1824. Nullum est jam dictum, quod non dictum sit prius.   Ter. Eun.
  Prol. 41.—*Nothing can be said now that has not been said before.*

  Ælius Donatus, commenting upon the qu., ap. Hieron. Commentar. in
  Eccles. i. (Migne, vol. xxiii. 390), says, "Pereant qui ante nos nostra
  dixerunt"—*Bad luck to the fellows who said our good things before us!*
  Goethe (Sprüche) says, "Alles Gescheidte ist schon gedacht worden, man
  muss nur versuchen es noch einmal zu denken"—*Everything that is worth
  thinking has already been thought out; one must only try to think it again.*
  Also,
> Wer kann was Dummes, wer was Kluges denken,
> Das nicht die Vorwelt schon gedacht?   Goethe, Faust, Pt. 2, Act 2.

  Meph. What is there, wise or foolish, one can think,
    That former ages have not thought before ?—*Ed.*

1825. Nullum est sine nomine saxum.   Lucan. 9, 973.—*Not a stone but
  has its history.*   Said of the ruins of Troy.

1826. Nullum magnum ingenium sine mixtura dementiæ fuit.   Sen.
  Tranq. 17, 10.—*No great genius was ever free from some tincture
  of madness.*   Cf. "Omnes ingeniosos melancholicos," Aristotle ap.
  Cic. Tusc. 1, 33, 80.—*All clever men are touched with melancholy.*
  Dryden (Abs. and Achit. 1, 163) says,

> Great wits are sure to madness near allied,
> And thin partitions do their bounds divide.

1827. Nullum numen habes si sit prudentia; nos te,
  Nos facimus, Fortuna, deam cæloque locamus.   Juv. 10, 365.

                    To Fortune.
> No worship hadst thou, Fortune, were we wise;
> We make thee god, and lift thee to the skies.—*Ed.*

1828. Nullum quod tetigit non ornavit.   Dr Johnson.—*He touched
  nothing that he did not adorn.*   Epitaph on Dr Goldsmith in
  Westminster Abbey.   The inscription runs as follows:—

> Olivarii Goldsmith,
> Poetæ, Physici, Historici,
> Qui nullum fere scribendi genus
>   non tetigit,
> Nullum quod tetigit non ornavit,
>   etc. etc.

1829. Nullum simile quatuor pedibus currit.   Prov.—*No simile ever yet
  ran on all fours: or,* Omne simile claudicat (Toute comparaison
  cloche).—*Every simile limps.*   No comparison was ever yet
  absolutely perfect in all its parts.

1830. Nul n'aura de l'esprit, hors nous et nos amis. Mol., Les Fem. Sav.
3, 2, fin. (Armande loq.).—*No one shall be witty save we and our
friends.*

1831. Nul n'est content de sa fortune,
Ni mécontent de son esprit.
> Mme. Deshoulières, Réflexions viii. (Petits Poëtes Franç.
> Panthéon Littér., Paris, 1838, p. 25).—*No one is satisfied with
> his fortune or dissatisfied with his wit.*

1832. Numero deus impare gaudet. Virg. E. 8, 75.—*The god delights
in odd numbers.*

1833. Nunc animis opus, Ænea, nunc pectore firmo. Virg. A. 6, 261

> Now for a heart that scorns dismay,
> Now for a soul prepared!—*Conington.*

1834. Nunc patimur longæ pacis mala. Sævior armis
Luxuria incubuit, victumque ulciscitur orbem.
Nullum crimen abest facinusque libidinis, ex quo
Paupertas Romana perit.   Juv. 6, 292.

> *The Evils of Peace.*
>
> We reap the evils of protracted peace:
> Luxury, more fell than arms, oppresses us,
> And has avenged a subjugated world.
> There lacks no crime, nor villainy of lust,
> Since Rome her pristine poverty forsook.—*Ed.*

1835. Nunquam aliud natura, aliud sapientia dicit. Juv. 14, 321.

> Wisdom and nature, are they not the same?—*Ch. Badham, M.D.*

1836. Nunquam se plus agere, quam nihil quum ageret; nunquam minus
solum esse, quam quum solus esset. Cic. Rep. 1, 17, 27.—He
used to say that, *he never had more to do than when he had
nothing to do, and never was less alone than when alone.*

> Saying of P. Scipio Africanus, quoted by Cato, to whom is also attributed,
> "Nunquam se minus otiosum esse, quam quum otiosus esset," in Cic. Off.
> 3, 1, 1.—*He never had less leisure than when free from official business.*
> Plut., in his *Reg. et Imperatorun Apophthegmata,* Scipio, I. (Didot, p. 237),
> records the same of the same man. ὁπότε σχολάζοι (ἔλεγε) πλείονα πράττειν.
> —*He used to say that leisure only gave him the more to do.*

1837. Nunquam vacat lascivisse districtis: nihilque tam certum est vitia
otii negotio discuti. Sen. Ep. 56, 9.—*Business prevents a man
having the time to go wrong, and nothing is more certain, than
that the vices engendered by leisure can be shaken off by work.*

1838. Nur der Irrtum ist das Leben,
Und das Wissen ist der Tod.   Schiller, Kassandra, stanza 8.
—*Life is only error, and knowledge comes with death.*

1839. Nur der verdient die Gunst der Frauen,
  Der kräftigst sie zu schützen weiss.

Goethe, Faust, Pt. 2, Act 3, Vor dem Palaste.

Faust. He only wins a woman's favour
  Who with strong arm in need can save her.—*Ed.*

1840. Nur der verdient sich Freiheit wie das Leben,
  Der täglich sie erobern muss.

Goethe, Faust, Pt. 2, Act 5, Grosser Vorhof des Palastes.

Faust. Freedom alone he earns, as well as life,
  Who, day by day, must conquer them anew.—*A. Swanwick.*

1841. Nusquam tuta fides.   Virg. A. 4, 373.

No faith on earth, in heaven no trust.—*Conington.*

No one is to be trusted.   Dido upbraiding Æneas for his desertion.

1842. Nympha pudica Deum vidit, et erubuit.   R. Crashaw, Epigram.
  Sacr. Liber, Lond., 1634 (2nd ed., 1670), p. 299.

Aquæ in Vinum Versæ.
The conscious water saw its God, and blush'd.—*R. Crashaw.*

The following "history" of this celebrated line is given for what it is
worth.   Acc. to this account, it is said that Milton, when at St Paul's
School, having to do a verse-theme on the Miracle of Cana, wrote on his
slate a single line—"The conscious water saw its God, and blushed."
Dryden, thirty years later, on being given the same subject at Westminster,
merely transposed Crashaw's Latin, "Vidit, et erubuit, nympha pudica
Deum"; adding a version in English,

The modest water, awed by power Divine,
Beheld its God, and blushed itself to wine.

1843. Ny trop haut, ny trop bas, c'est le souverain style;
  Tel fut celuy d'Homère, et celuy de Virgile.

Ronsard, Œuvr. Choisies, Paris (Moland), n.d., p. 340.

A Luy Mesme.
Not too high, nor too low—is of all styles the best,
As the epics of Homer and Virgil attest.—*Ed.*

O.*

1844. Obscuris vera involvens.   Virg. A. 6, 100.—*Cloaking the truth
  in mystery.*   The response of the Cumæan Sibyl to Æneas.

1845. Obsequium amicos, veritas odium parit.   Ter. And. 1, 1, 41.—
  Obsequiousness makes friends, truth enemies.

1846. Obstupui, steteruntque comæ, et vox faucibus hæsit.

Virg. A. 2, 774.

I stood appalled, my hair erect,
And fear my tongue-tied utterance checked.—*Conington.*

* Including the Greek Ω.

1847. O cæca nocentum
Consilia, O semper timidum scelus!   Stat. Theb. 2, 489.
How blind the counsels of the guilty breast!
How timid always crime!—*Ed.*

1848. Occidit miseros crambe repetita magistros.   Juv. 7, 154.
Like warmed-up cabbage served at each repast,
The repetition kills the wretch at last.—*Gifford.*

Said of recitations which masters had to endure in school.
First they read the essay sitting,
Then recite it standing, lastly
Sing it : sure *this everlasting*
Cabbage is enough to kill him.—*Shaw.*

Reference is made to the prov., δὶς κράμβη θάνατος (*Cabbage twice running*
is death), as qu. *e.g.* by S. Basil. Ep. 187 (Migne, vol. iii. p. 664). The
phrase is something akin to the French *toujours perdrix*, q.v. Wearisome,
"damnable iteration."

1849. Occidit una domus, sed non domus una perire
Digna fuit.   Ov. M. 1, 240.—*One family fell, but it was not*
the only one that deserved the doom.

1850. Occupet extremum scabies! mihi turpe relinqui est.   Hor. A. P.
417.—*The devil take the hindmost! I'm ashamed to be left*
behind.

1851. O certe necessarium Adœ peccatum, quod Christi morte deletum
est! O felix culpa, quæ talem et tantum meruit Redemptorem!
—*O sin of Adam, certainly necessary as procuring its atonement*
by the death of Christ! Blessed transgression, that didst merit
such a Redeemer and so mighty a one! From the Morning Office
for Easter Eve at the Benediction of the Lights.

1852. O Corydon, Corydon, secretum divitis ullum
Esse putas? Servi ut taceant, jumenta loquentur,
Et canis, et postes, et marmora.   Juv. 9, 102.
Poor simple Corydon! do you suppose
Aught is kept secret that a rich man does?
If servants do not tell, the dumb things must,—
The house-dog, or the doors, or marble bust.—*Ed.*

1853. O dass sie ewig grünen bliebe,
Die schöne Zeit der jungen Liebe!
Schiller, Lied von der Glocke, st. 6.
Would it might ever blooming prove,
The happy season of young love!—*Ed.*

1854. O dea certe.   Virg. A. 1, 328.—*A goddess indeed!*

1855. O degli altri poeti onore e lume,
Vagliami 'l lungo studio, e 'l grande amore,
Che m' han fatto cercar lo tuo volume.
Tu se' lo mio maestro e lo mio autore:
Tu se' solo colui da cu' io tolsi
Lo bello stile, che m' ha fatto onore.   Dante, Inf. 1, 82.

Virgil.

Glory and light of all the tuneful train!
May it avail me, that I long with zeal
Have sought thy volume, and with love immense
Have conned it o'er.   My master, author, thou!
From whom alone I have derived the style
Which for its beauty into fame exalts me.—*Cary.*

Macaulay recited the passage as he stood before Dante's monument in Santa Croce (Nov. 1838), and adds, "I was proud to think that I had a right to apostrophise him thus." Trevelyan's *Life and Letters of Lord Macaulay,* London, 1881, pp. 353-4.

1856. O der Einfall war kindisch, aber göttlich schön! Schiller, D. Carlos, 1, 2 (Don. C. loq.).—*Oh, the idea was childish, but divinely beautiful!*

1857. Oderint dum metuant. Accius, Atreus, V.—*Let them hate me, so they fear me.*

> A favourite qu. of Caligula (Suet. Cal. 30), but denounced by Seneca (de Ira, 1, 20, 4) as an abominable sentiment—*dira atque abominanda.* Tiberius (Suet. Tib. 59) changed the line to "Oderint dum probent," Let them hate me, so long as *they support my government.* Enn. Trag. (Ribb. i. 80) says, Quem metuunt oderunt, quem quisque odit periisse expetit.—*Whom men fear they hate, and whom they hate they wish dead.*

1858. Odero, si potero: si non, invitus amabo. Ov. Am. 3, 11, 35.— *I would hate if I could: as it is, I must love against my will.*

1859. Oderunt peccare boni virtutis amore:
Tu nihil admittes in te formidine pœnæ.   Hor. Ep. 1, 16, 52.

> 'Tis love of right that keeps the good from wrong,
> You do no harm because you fear the thong.—*Conington.*

To the first line (above) has been added by a later hand (*see* Orelli's Horace, Turin, 1852, *in l.*), thus making an antithetical couplet,

Oderunt peccare mali formidine pœnæ.

The wicked dare not sin from fear of pain.

1860. Odi et amo.   Quare id faciam, fortasse requiris.
Nescio! sed fieri sentio, et excrucior.   Cat. 85.

> I love and hate: why so, you may inquire:
> I know not: but 'tis so, I am on fire.—*Ed.*

Cf. Regnard's "On aime sans raison et sans raison l'on hait" (Les Folies Amoureuses, 2, 2: Agathe to Albert).—*One loves without reason, and without reason one hates.*

1861. O dii immortales! non intelligunt homines, quam magnum vectigal sit parsimonia!   Cic. Parad. 6, 3, 49.—*Ye immortal gods! If men could only understand what a wonderful revenue lies in thrift!*

1862. Odimus accipitrem qui semper vivit in armis. Ov. A. A. 2, 147. —*I hate the hawk that always lives in arms.* Applied before now to the first Napoleon.

1863. Odi profanum vulgus et arceo. Hor. C. 3, 1, 1.

> I bid the unhallowed crowd avaunt!—*Conington.*

1864. Odi puerulos præcoqui sapientia. Incert. in Ribb., vol. 2, p. 151.
—*I hate precociously clever little boys.*

> Κρέσσονα μὲν ἁλικίας Νόον φέρβεται Γλῶσσάν τε. Pind. Pyth. 5, 146.—*He has a mind and tongue beyond his years.* The prov. says, Ante barbam doces senes.— *You're teaching your elders before your beard is grown:* and, Pers. 4, 4, Scilicet ingenium et rerum prudentia velox Ante pilos venit: dicenda tacendaque calles.—*Evidently your judgment and knowledge of the world has arrived before the hair on your lip: you know when to speak and when to hold your tongue.*

1865. O di quam ineptus! quam se ipse amans sine rivali! Cic. Q. F.
3, 8, 4.—*What perfect absurdity! A man in love with himself, and not a rival to dispute his pretensions!* Said of Pompey.

1866. O Domine Deus speravi in te;
O care mi Iesu, nunc libera me!
In dura catena, in misera pœna
> Desidero te.
Languendo, gemendo et genu flectendo
Adoro, imploro ut liberes me. Mary Stuart, 1586.

> *Fotheringay.*
> O Lord and my God, I have trusted in Thee.
> O Jesu, my lov'd one, now liberate me!
> In durance and chains, and in pitiful pains
> I languish for Thee.
> Now fainting, now sighing, now bending the knee,
> I adore, and implore Thee to liberate me.—*Ferdinand Hoffmann.*

1867. O domus antiqua, heu quam dispari
Dominare domino! Incert. (Ribb. i. 303).—*O ancient house!*
ah! how unworthy is the lord that owns thee now.

1868. O dulces comitum valete cœtus,
Longe quos simul a domo profectos
Diverse variæ viæ reportant. Cat. 46, 9.

> And you, ye band of comrades tried and true,
> Who side by side went forth from home, farewell!
> How far apart the paths shall carry you
> Back to your native shore, ah, who can tell?—*Sir T. Martin.*

1869. O faciles dare summa Deos, eademque tueri
Difficiles. Luc. 1, 510.

> Freely they grant, the blessed gods,
> But grudge the tenure of our goods.—*Ed.*

1870. O formose puer, nimium ne crede colori. Virg. E. 2, 17.—*My pretty boy, trust not too much to your rosy looks!*

1871. O fortunatam natam me consule Romam! Cic. ap. Quint. 9, 4, 41.

> How fortunate a natal day was thine
> In that late consulate, O Rome of mine!—*Gifford.*

Juvenal, who quotes the wretched jingle (10, 122), remarks that Cicero might have laughed at Antony's assassins—*si sic omnia dixisset*—if all that the great orator had said had been in this style.

1872. O fortunatos nimium, sua si bona norint,
    Agricolas; quibus ipsa, procul discordibus armis,
    Fundit humo facilem victum justissima tellus.   Virg. G. 2, 458.

The Country Labourer.
Too happy swains, did ye but know
Your bliss, on whom your fields bestow,
Far from war's din and scenes of blood,
A measure just of kindly food.—*Ed.*

1873. Oh, Bone custos, salve: columen vero familiæ,
    Cui commendavi filium hinc abiens meum.
        Ter. Phor. 2, 1, 56.—*O my good guardian, I salute thee!*
A trusty prop, indeed, of my establishment art thou, into whose
hands I committed my son when I went away.

Said ironically by Demipho to his servant, Geta, for palpably neglecting his trust during the former's absence; and applied by Cardinal Newman to the Anglican Church in regard of her custody of the Eucharist (Letter to Rev. H. J. Coleridge in *Essays, Hist. and Critical*, vol. ii. p. 110. London, 1871).

1874. Oh! c'était le bon temps, j'étais bien malheureuse! Rulhière, Sur le renversement de ma fortune (pub. Paris, 1808, p. 43, with his *Jeux de mains*).—*Oh! what good days those were! I was very unhappy.*

The original saying is Sophie Arnould's, the actress, which Rulhière put into verse:—
Un jour une actrice fameuse
Me contait les fureurs de son premier amant;
Moitié riant, moitié rêveuse,
Elle ajouta ce mot charmant;
"Oh! c'était le bon temps, j'étais bien malheureuse!"

Collin d'Harleville, in his *Souvenirs*, also reproduced the famous saying,—
Nous n'avions pas le sou, et nous étions contens:
Nous étions malheureux: c'était là le bon temps.

We hadn't a penny, and we thought it sublime:
How wretched we were!—oh, it was a good time!

1875. Ohe! Jam satis est.   Hor. S. 1, 5, 12.—*Hold, that is enough!*

1876. Oh! le vraisemblable, le vraisemblable! c'est la mort du vrai en histoire: c'est l'espoir des mauvais historiens, et c'est la terreur des bons.   Fourn. *L. D. L.*, cap. 4.—*Probability! probability! I am weary of the very name—the mortal foe of historical truth, the hope of all bad historians, and the terror of the good.*

1877. O homines ad servitutem paratos. Tac. A. 3, 65.—*Oh, that men should so lay themselves out for slavery!* Common exclamation of Emp. Tiberius on leaving the senate-house. Cf. the "Ich bin es müde über Sklaven zu herrschen" of Fredk. the Great, in Ed. Vehse's *Preussen*, 4, 175.—*I am weary of lording it over slaves.* Acc. to Vehse, the reflection was found recorded in a *Kabinetsordre* of 1785.

1878. Οἵη περ φύλλων γενεὴ, τοιήδε καὶ ἀνδρῶν. Hom. Il. 6, 146.—*As the generation of leaves, so is that of men.*

1879. O imitatores, servum pecus, ut mihi sæpe
Bilem, sæpe jocum vestri movere tumultus? Hor. Ep. 1, 19, 19.

Poetical Plagiarists.
Ye wretched mimics, whose fond heats have been
How oft! the objects of my mirth and spleen!—*Francis.*

1880. Οἴμοι· τί δ'οἴμοι; θνητά τοι πεπόνθαμεν. Eur. Bellerophon, Fr. 22.
—*Alas! but why "Alas"? We have only suffered what befits mortals to bear.*

1881. Οἷον ἡμῶν ἐγένετο τὸ συμπόσιον, . . . ὅσων χαρίτων πλῆρες· ἓν μόνον ἡμῖν ἔλειπε, σύ· τὰ δ' ἄλλα οὔ. Alciphro, 1, 39.—*Our party* (symposium) *was wonderfully pleasant, and quite delightful but for one thing—you were not there. Otherwise it was perfect.* " Ego me in Cumano," Cic. writes to his brother (Q. Fratrem, 2, 12, 1), "præterquam quod sine te, ceterum satis commode oblectabam." —*Except that I had not you with me, I amused myself well enough at Cumanum in other respects:* and Horace (Ep. 1, 10, 50) assures his friend Fuscus, "Excepto quod non simul esses, cœtera lætus."—*Except that you were not with me, I was otherwise happy.*

1882. Οἱ πλεῖστοι κακοί. Bias, in Diog. Laert. 1, 88.—*The greater part of mankind is bad.*

1883. O l'amour d'une Mère! amour que nul n'oublie!
Pain merveilleux, que Dieu partage et multiplie!
Table toujours servie au paternel foyer!
Chacun en a sa part, et tous l'ont tout entier.
V. Hugo, Feuilles d'Automne, Pref.

A Mother's Love.
Love of a mother, love that all embraces!
Miraculous bread that God gives and increases!
Board always spread in the paternal hall,
Where each partakes, and each enjoys it all.—*Ed.*

1884. Olet lucernam. Prov.—*It smells of the lamp.*
Said of literary productions that bear the marks of midnight study. Cf. Et oleum et operam perdidi. Plaut. Pœn. 1, 2, 119.—*I have lost both my time and trouble* (lit., *my oil and my labour*). I have laboured in vain.

1885. O Liberté, que de crimes ou commet en ton nom! Mme. Roland. *V.* Honoré Riouffe's " Mémoires d'un détenu," Sec. ed., p. 66; and "Tableaux Hist. de la Révol. Fr." (Auber Éditeur), 1802, vol. 3—inscription under portrait.—*O Liberty! what crimes are committed in thy name!*

Q

Apostrophe of Mme. Roland on the scaffold, Nov. 8, 1793, close to the colossal statue of Liberty then erected on the Place Louis XV., now Place de la Concorde. This is the traditional form of her last words, though, from more genuine sources (Helen M. Williams, *Letters containing a Sketch of the Politics of France*, Lond., 1795, vol. i. 209), it would appear that the actual words were, "Ah! Liberté, comme on t'a jouée!" or, according to Alger (*Glimpses of the French Revolution*, Lond., 1894, p. 20), "Comme on t'a trompée." During her last moments, la citoyenne Roland asked, calmly and collectedly, for something on which she could record her thoughts; and had the materials (and the time) been provided her, the reflections of that clear, undaunted spirit—at such an hour—might have come down to us as one of the most treasured memorials of the Revolution.

1886. O lieb' so lang du lieben kannst,
       O lieb' so lang du lieben magst;
       Die Stunde kommt, die Stunde naht
       Wo du an Gräbern stehst und klagst.
                              Ferd. Freiligrath, Der Liebe Dauer, init.

> Oh love, while 'tis within thy power,
>   Love, while thy love is strong and deep!
> Ere, all too soon, arrive the hour
>   Thou at the grave shalt stand and weep.—*Ed.*

1887. O matre pulchra filia pulchrior. Hor. C. 1, 16, 1.—*Of lovely mother daughter lovelier still!*

1888. Ὁ μὴ δαρεὶς ἄνθρωπος οὐ παιδεύεται. Men. Mon. 422.—*He that will not be flogged will never be educated.* Motto of Goethe's *Dichtung u. Wahrheit.*

1889. O mihi praeteritos referat si Jupiter annos! Virg. A. 8, 560.—*Oh! if Jove would but give me back my past years!*

1890. Omina sunt aliquid. Ov. Am. 1, 12, 3.—*There is something in omens.*

1891. O miseras hominum menteis! o pectora caeca!
       Qualibus in tenebreis vitae, quanteisque pericleis
       Degitur hocc'aevi quodquomqu'est.   Lucret. 2, 14.

> Blind, wretched man! in what dark paths of strife
> We walk this little journey of our life!—*Creech.*

1892. O miseri quorum gaudia crimen habent! Maximian, Eleg. 1, 180.

> Alas for those whose joys are fraught with guilt!—*Ed.*

1893. Ὄμμα γὰρ δόμων νομίζω δεσπότου παρουσίαν. Æsch. Pers. 169.—
       The master's presence is the eye of the household.

1894. Omne aevum curae: cunctis sua displicet aetas. Auson. Id. 15, 10.
       —*Every age has its cares: each one thinks his own time of life disagreeable.*

1895. Omne animi vitium tanto conspectius in se
       Crimen habet, quanto major qui peccat habetur.   Juv. 8, 140.

> Where guilt's concern'd, the high'r th' offender's station,
> The more it glares in public estimation.—*Ed.*

1896. Omne ignotum pro magnifico. Tac. Agr. 30.—*Everything un-known is supposed to be wonderful.* In the original, Galgacus, the Highland chieftain, is speaking, not without contempt, of Agricola's persuasion that he would find beyond the Grampians the "sovereign" herb which was to cure his son, 84 A.D.

1897. Omne solum forti patria est, ut piscibus æquor. Ov. F. 1, 493.— *The brave make every clime their home, like fish in every sea.*

> ἅπας μὲν ἀὴρ ἀετῷ περάσιμος,
> ἅπασα δὲ χθών ἀνδρὶ γενναίῳ πατρίς.   Eur. Fr. 866.

> Like eagles, who thro' ev'ry sky can roam,
> In every land the noble find their home.—*Ed.*

1898. Omnes, quibus res sunt minus secundæ, magis sunt, nescio quomodo, Suspiciosi: ad contumeliam omnia accipiunt magis ; Propter suam impotentiam se semper credunt negligi.
     Ter. Ad. 4, 3, 14.—*All those whose affairs are not in a pro-sperous condition, are, I don't know why, extremely suspicious: they take almost everything as an affront, and always fancy they are treated with neglect because they are poor.*

1899. Omnes, quum secundæ res sunt maxume, tum maxume Meditari secum oportet, quo pacto advorsum ærumnam ferant; Pericla, damna, exilia; peregre rediens semper cogitet, Aut filii peccatum, aut uxoris mortem, aut morbum filiæ: Communia esse hæc; fieri posse; ut ne quid animo sit novum: Quidquid præter spem eveniat, omne id deputare esse in lucro.
                                   Ter. Phorm. 2, 1, 11.

> *Demiph.* Every man, when things are prosp'ring specially, then specially,
> Should consider in himself how he may bear adversity.
> Home returning after absence, let him, as he goes along,
> Think of dangers, losses, wife dead, daughter ill, or son gone
>   wrong:
> 'Tis the common lot, and no one should be taken by surprise:
> It is so much gain if it be better than he may surmise.—*Ed.*

1900. Omnes sapientes decet conferre et fabulari. Plaut. Rud. 2, 3, 8.— *All wise people ought to consult and confabulate together.*

1901. Omne tulit punctum qui miscuit utile dulci, Lectorem delectando pariterque monendo.   Hor. A. P. 343.

> All votes he gains who can unite
> Profit with pleasure, and delight
> His reader's fancy, all the time
> He gives instruction couched in rhyme.—*Ed.*

1902. Omne vivum ex ovo.—*Every living thing proceeds from an egg.* Celebrated dictum of William Harvey, the discoverer of the circulation of the blood, on the origin of life. See Marshall (A. M.), *Biological Lectures,* p. 161.

> Fumag. (No. 288) points out a passage in Harvey's *Exercitationes de generatione animalium* which gives the point, if not the exact words, of the quotation: "Asserimus . . . omnia *omnino animalia,* etiam vivipara

. . . ex ovo progigni . . . ut et semina plantarum omnium; ideoque non inepte ab Empedocle dicitur, *oviparum genus arboreum.*" Lond., 1651, 4to, p. 2, Ex. 1.

1903. Omne vovemus
Hoc tibi; nec tanto careat mihi nomine charta.
    Tib. 4, 1, 26.—*All this work I dedicate to you, and may my poem not lack the sanction of so distinguished a name.*

1904. Omnia debemur vobis; paullumque morati,
Serius aut citius sedem properamus ad unam.
Tendimus huc omnes: hæc est domus ultima, vosque
Humani generis longissima regna tenetis.   Ov. M. 10, 32.

> *King Death.*
>
> Thine are we all: after a little space,
> Sooner or late, all hasten to one place.
> We all tend hitherwards; 'tis our last home;
> And 'neath thy lasting rule at length we come.—*Ed.*

1905. Omnia fert ætas, animum quoque.   Virg. E. 9, 51.—*Time bears away all things, even the memory.*

1906. Omnia fui et nihil expedit.   Eutropius, 8, 19; and Spart. Severus, 18.—*I have been all things, and it avails me nothing now.*   Last words of the Emp. Septimius Severus at York, where he expired Feb. 4th, 211 A.D.

1907. Omnia Græce!
Quum sit turpe magis nostris nescire Latine.   Juv. 6, 187.

> All must be Greek! Indeed! 'Twere greater wrong
> (One 'd think it) not to know one's mother tongue.—*Ed.*

1908. Omnia inconsulti impetus cœpta initiis valida spatio languescunt.
Tac. H. 3, 58.—*All enterprise entered upon with more zeal than discretion, is apt to be vigorous enough at starting, and languid toward the close.*

1909. Omnia jam fient, fieri quæ posse negabam:
Et nihil est de quo non sit habenda fides.
    Ov. T. 1, 8, 7.—*Everything that I used to think impossible will now take place, and there is nothing that may not be expected.*

1910. Omnia mea mecum porto.   Bias, ap. Cic. Par. 1, 8.—*All my goods I carry with me.*

> Saying of Bias; and also of Simonides (*mecum mea sunt cuncta*), when refusing to encumber himself in his escape from a sinking ship (*see* Phædr. 4, 21, 14).   Seneca (Const. 5, 6) quotes *Omnia mea mecum sunt* of Stilpo, the Epicurean.

1911. Omnia mutantur, nihil interit.   Ov. M. 15, 165.

> *Transmigration.*
>
> Thus all things are but altered, nothing dies.—*Dryden.*

1912. Omnia mutantur, nos et mutamur in illis. Matthias Borbonius, *Delitiæ Poetarum Germanorum*, Collectore A. F. G. G. (Francofurti, 1612), Pars I. p. 685.—*All things change, and we change amongst them.* One of a series of mottoes for various Emperors, this being designed for Lothair I. (795-855).

Among the epigrams of John Owen, the British Martial, we find (8, 58) a couplet, evidently inspired by the line of Borbonius:

Tempora mutantur, nos et mutamur in illis:
Quomodo ? fit semper tempore pejor homo.

Times change, and we change with them too. How so ?
With time men only the more vicious grow.—*Ed.*

1913. Omnia prius experiri, quam armis, sapientem decet. Ter. Eun. 4, 7, 19.—*A wise man will try all methods before having recourse to arms.*

1914. Omnia tuta timens. Virg. A. 4, 298.—*Distrusting all things, even what seemed safe.* Said of poor Dido.

[*She feels each stirring of the air*]
And e'en in safety dreads a snare.—*Conington.*

1915. Omnia vincit amor, et nos cedamus amori. Virg. E. 10, 69.

Love conquers all, and we must yield to love.—*Dryden.*

1916. Omnibus hoc vitium est cantoribus, inter amicos
Ut nunquam inducant animum cantare rogati;
Injussi nunquam desistant. Hor. S. 1, 3, 1.

Drawing-room Singers.
All singers have this fault: if asked to sing
In friendly circle, they can never bring
Themselves to yield consent : yet, if unasked,
They'll sing and sing, till patience' self is tasked.—*Ed.*

1917. Omnibus hostes
Reddite nos populis, civile avertite bellum.
Luc. 2, 52.—*Commit us to hostilities with the whole world, but save us from civil war !*

1918. Omnibus in terris, quæ sunt a Gadibus usque
Auroram et Gangem, pauci dignoscere possunt
Vera bona, atque illis multum diversa, remota
Erroris nebula. Juv. 10, 1.

In every clime, from Ganges distant stream
To Cadiz, gilded by the western beam,
Few, from the clouds of mental error free,
In its true light, or good or evil see.—*Gifford.*

1919. Omnis ars imitatio est naturæ. Sen. Ep. 65, 3.—*All art is an imitation of nature.* Cf. Ars æmula naturæ. Appul. Met. 2, 4. —*Art emulates nature.*

1920. Omnis homo mendax. Vulg. Ps. 115, 2.—*All men are liars.* This is what the Psalmist said "in his haste."

1921. Omnis Minervæ homo. Petr. 43, 8.—*A Jack of all trades.*

1922. Omnium horarum homo. *See* Quint. 6, 3, 110.—*A man ready for every emergency.*

1923. On affaiblit toujours tout ce qu'on exagère. La Harpe, Mélanie, 1, 1 (M. de Faublas loq.).—*Exaggeration invariably weakens the point of everything we have to say.*

1924. On aime à deviner les autres, mais on n'aime pas à être deviné. La Rochef., § 280, p. 68.—*One likes to read others, but one does not like being read oneself.*

1925. On a souvent besoin d'un plus petit que soi. La Font. 2, 11. (Le Lion et le Rat).—*One often needs the help of one smaller than one's self.*

1926. On commence par être dupe,
On finit par être fripon.
　　　　Mme. Deshoulières, Réflexion sur le Jeu (Petits Poètes Français, Panthéon, p. 26).—*One begins by being a dupe, and one ends by being a swindler.* "Generally speaking, play finds a man a cully, and leaves him a knave." J. Puckle († 1724), *The Club*, London, 1900, 12°, p. 35.

1927. On devient cuisinier, mais on naît rotisseur. Brillat-Savarin, Physiologie du Goût, Aphor. xv. (1st ed., Paris, 1826).—*Cooking may be acquired: roasting is a gift of nature.*

1928. On donne des conseils, mais on n'inspire point de conduite. La Rochef., § 400, p. 81.—*We give good advice, but it is not enforced by our own practice.*

1929. On entre, on crie—
Et c'est la vie!
On crie, on sort—
Et c'est la mort!
　　　　Ausone de Chancel, 1836.—*We enter and cry, and such is life! We cry and depart, and such is death!*

　　Thanks to M. Roger Alexandre, we have some further particulars of this remarkable quatrain. It appears that de Chancel wrote it in his sister-in-law's album in 1836 where it slept for twenty-seven years, when the quotation was printed in the *Figaro* of Oct. 29, 1863 over the name of Edmond Texier. It should be noticed that the third line, as de Chancel wrote it, is "On *baille*, on sort." Alex. pp. 535-6.

1930. On est, quand on le veut, le maître de son sort. Ferrier, Adraste (Paris, 1682, p. 60), 5, 5.—*Man is, when he wishes, his destiny's lord.*

1931. On jette enfin de la terre sur la tête, et en voilà pour jamais. Pasc. Pensées, 29, 55.—*A little earth cast upon the head, and so good-bye for ever!* The long farewell to the departed, "until the day dawn and the shadows flee away."

1932. On lui trouve de la bonté, de l'amabilité; mais, en frottant un peu, cela sent le cosaque. Napoleon, said of Alexander I. of Russia, in *Mémoires, Correspondance, etc.. du Général Lafayette*, Paris, 1838, vol. 5, p. 403.—*A kind and amiable man enough; but rub a little more closely, and you become aware of the Cossack within.*

1933. On n'aime plus comme on aimait jadis. Mme. Antoinette Des-houlières, refrain of *Ballade*, (Petits Poètes Fr., Panthéon, p. 24).—*No one loves now as they used to do.*

1934. On n'a point pour la mort de dispense de Rome. Mol. L'Étourdi, 2, 4, (Anselme loq.).—*There is no dispensation at Rome to be had against death.*

1935. On ne donne rien si libéralement que ses conseils. La Rochef., § 110, p. 45.—*There is nothing which men give so freely as their advice.*

1936. On ne loue d'ordinaire que pour être loué. La Rochef., § 146, p. 49. —*Praise is commonly bestowed in the expectation that it will be repaid with interest.*

1937. On ne perd les états que par timidité. Volt. Mahomet, 1, 1.— *'Tis timidity only that throws states away*—a saying which, if not precisely applicable to poor Louis XVI., was literally realised in the case of his pusillanimous successor, Louis Philippe.

1938. On ne peut contenter tout le monde et son père. Prov.—*It is impossible to please all the world and one's father too.*

The saying was borrowed by La Fontaine to point the moral to his fable of the Miller, his Son, and the Ass (3, 1):

Est bien fou de cerveau
Qui prétend contenter tout le monde et son père.

Cf. Leonardo Bruni of Arezzo, detto il "Aretino," *Epistolar. Fam. Libri VIII.*, recensente Laurentio Mehus, Pars Prima, Florentiæ, 1741. "Ita utrisque displiceo; istis, quod non obsequor, illis, quod non sequor. Lib. III. Ep. 3, ad Nicolaum.—*So it ends in my displeasing both sides: the one, because I refuse to comply with them; the other, because I decline to follow them.* In Lib. II. Ep. 16 (ad eundem) he says: "Denique loquantur omnes ut libet: Ego, si michi et tibi uni satisfecero, ceteros omnes cum suis judiciis flocci pendo, eorumque opiniones et oblocutiones vix unius assis existimo."

1939. On ne ramène guère un traître par l'impunité, au lieu que par la punition l'on en rend mille autres sages. Richelieu, *Mercure historique et Politique*, Juillet 1688, pp. 7, 8.—*No man ever yet converted a single traitor by letting him off, whereas punishment will show a thousand others the error of their ways.* Doubtless the Cardinal had Cinq-Mars in his mind.

1940. On n'est jamais servi si bien que par soi-même. Étienne, Brueys et Palaprat, Comédie en un acte (Théâtre Fr., Nov. 28, 1807), sc. 2 (Palaprat loq.).—*One is never so well served as by oneself.* If you want a thing done, do it yourself.

1941. On n'est jamais si heureux, ni si malheureux qu'on se l'imagine. La Rochef., § 49, p. 37.—*One is never so happy or so unhappy as one imagines* (at the moment).

1942. On n'est jamais si riche que quand on déménage.   Prov.—*One never appears so rich as when one is moving house.*   Such a collection of things!

> A memorably witty application of the saying was made by President Hénault *à propos* of the general examen of conscience with which he unburdened himself at the age of fifty (1735), in preparation for a death for which he had seven lustres still to wait.   *En vérité,* he is reported to have said to a friend when all was over, *en vérité, l'on n'est jamais si riche que quand on déménage.*   Nouv. Biographie (Didot); and Quit. p. 294.

1943. On n'est jamais si ridicule par les qualités que l'on a que par celles que l'on affecte d'avoir.   La Rochef., § 134, p. 47.—*We are never rendered so ridiculous by the qualities we possess, as by those which we affect to have.*

1944. On n'est jamais trahi que par ses siens.   Prov.—*One is never betrayed except by one's own friends.*

1945. On ne vit qu'à Paris, et l'on végète ailleurs.   Gresset, Le Méchant, 3, 9 (Valère loq.).—*In Paris only can one be said to live: elsewhere one vegetates.*

1946. On n'imagine pas combien il faut d'esprit pour n'être pas ridicule. Chamf. Max., vol. 2, p. 44.—*No one would imagine the amount of brains it takes to avoid being ridiculous.*

1947. O noctes cœnæque deum! quibus ipse, meique,
Ante larem proprium vescor, vernasque procaces
Pasco libatis dapibus.   Hor. S. 2, 6, 65.

> O nights and suppers, most divine!
> When met together, I and mine
> Round my own hearth have bite and sup;
> What's left my merry slaves eat up.—*Ed.*

1948. Onorate l'altissimo poeta!   Dante, Inf. 4, 80.—*Honour to the illustrious poet!* sc. Virgil.   A few lines farther bring us to more of the great singers of antiquity—Horace, Ovid, and Lucan; the whole group of poets together, headed by Homer (*poeta sovrano*), being summed up in the words:

> Così vidi adunar la bella scuola
> Di quel signor dell' altissimo canto
> Che sovra gli altri, com' aquila, vola.
>
> *Homer.*
>
> So I beheld united the bright school
> Of him the monarch of sublimest song,
> That o'er the others like an eagle soars.—*Cary.*

1949. On pardonne aisément les torts que l'on partage.   H. Bis et J. V. E. Jouy, Opera of Guillaume Tell, Act. 2, sc. 3 (produced Aug. 3, 1829).   Mathilde to Arnold.—*We easily pardon faults which we ourselves share.*

1950. On pardonne tant que l'on aime. La Rochef., § 337, p. 75.—
When one loves, it is easy to forgive.

1951. On peut avoir divers sujets de dégoûts dans la vie; mais on n'a
jamais raison de mépriser la mort. La Rochef., § 528, p. 96.—
*One may have various grounds for disgust with life, but there are
never sufficient reasons for making light of death.*

1952. On peut dire que son esprit brille aux dépens de sa mémoire. Le
Sage, Gil Blas, 3, 11.—*His wit shines at the expense of his
memory.* Second-hand jokes. Cf. R. B. Sheridan (Reply to
Mr Dundas): "The right hon. gentleman is indebted to his
memory for his jests, and to his imagination for his facts."

1953. On peut être plus fin qu'un autre, mais non pas plus fin que tous
les autres. La Rochef., § 416, p. 83.—*One may be sharper than
another man, but one cannot be sharper than all the world.*

1954. On revient toujours
A ses premiers amours. C. G. Étienne, "Joconde, ou les
Coureurs d'Aventures," 3, 1 (Music by Nicolo), Paris, 1814.—
One always returns to one's first love.

In the comic opera, Joconde, suspecting the fidelity of his mistress,
Édile, sets off to make the world's tour with the Count of Martigue, but
soon regrets his decision, admitting that,

On pense, on pense encore,
A celle qu'on adore,
Et l'on revient toujours, etc.

1955. On sait si peu de choses quand on ne sait pas tout. Mrs Bishop's
Memoir of Mrs Augustus Craven, vol. 2, p. 85 (where it is
attributed to Sir Mountstuart E. Grant-Duff).—*One knows so
little, when one does not know all* (or, *all the circumstances*). In
"Corinne" (Bk. 18, chap. 5), Mme. de Stael says, *Tout comprendre rend très-indulgent* ("Understanding everything makes
one very indulgent"), which has become a proverb in the shape
of *Tout comprendre c'est tout pardonner.*

1956. On s'attend à tout, et on n'est jamais préparé à rien. Mme.
Swetchine, Airelles xciv.—*One expects anything, and one is
prepared for nothing.*

1957. On s'éveille, on se lève, on s'habille et l'on sort:
On rentre, on dîne, on soupe, on se couche et l'on dort.
Ant. P. A. de Piis, "L'Harmonie Imitative,"
etc., Chant 1, 143. (Œuvres Choisies, Paris, 1810, vol. 1, p. 8.)

The Art of Compression.

Woke, rose, dress'd myself and then out o' doors stept;
Came home again, dined, supped, to bed, and then slept.—*Ed.*

*** The object of the "Harmonie," it should be added, was to demon-
strate the concise expressiveness of the French language—"tant on peut
énoncer de choses en deux lignes."

1958. On spécule sur tout, jusques sur la famine. Armand Charlemagne, L'Agioteur, sc. 16. Comédie en un acte, Paris (Barba), 8 Brumaire, An 4ᵉ, 1796. (Eugène to Bénard).—*Men speculate on everything, even on famine.*

1959. O nuit désastreuse! O nuit effroyable, où retentit tout à coup comme un éclat de tonnerre cette étonnante nouvelle : Madame se meurt! Madame est morte! Bossuet, *Oraison funèbre* de Henriette-Anne d'Angleterre, Duchesse d'Orléans, daughter of Charles I., at St Denis, August 21, 1670.—*Oh disastrous night! dreadful night! when, like a thunder-clap, resounded these fearful tidings: Her Highness is dying! Her Highness is dead!*

1960. Onus est honos. Incertus Com. (Ribb. 2, 147).—*Office is a burden.*

1961. Onus probandi. Dig. 31, 1, 22.—*The burden of proof.* Obligation to prove (Lew. and S.).

1962. On y met des sénateurs en attendant. Talleyrand, Album Perdu, pp. 96-7.—*Meanwhile we bury senators there.*

> On arriving on one occasion at the capital, it happened that Talleyrand had as companion of his *coupé de voyage* a "distinguished foreigner," who, as they passed the Barrière d'Italie, asked the name of the grand dome (Pantheon) which now began to rise into view. On receiving the desired information, the gentleman exclaimed with effusiveness: "Oh! oh! c'est là que la patrie reconnaissante placera la dépouille mortelle des grands hommes qui l'auront illustrée." "Justement," drily replied the prince; adding, after a pause, "*on y met des sénateurs en attendant.*"

1963. ῞Ωι φίλοι οὐδεὶς φίλος. Arist. ap. Diog. Laert. 5, § 21.—*The man of many friends has none that's true.* As Gray says, *Death of a Favourite Cat:*

> A favourite has no friend.

1964. O plumbeum pugionem! Cic. Fin. 4, 18, 48.—*What a dagger of lead!* What a feeble argument!

1965. ῞Οπου πλείων κόπος, πολὺ κερδός. St Ignatius, Ep. ad Polycarp. 1.—*The greater the pain, the greater the gain.* Said of the sufferings of the martyrs.

1966. ῞Οπου τις ἀλγεῖ, κεῖσε καὶ τὴν χεῖρ' ἔχει. Plut. Mor. p. 621 (de Garrulitate, 22).—*Where the pain is, there goes the hand.* In Lat., Ubi dolor, ibi digitus. Said of one who is always harping on some particular grievance.

1967. ῎Οψει δὲ με περὶ Φιλίππους. Plut. Cæs. 69.—*Thou shalt see me at Philippi.*

> Famous speech of Cæsar's apparition to Brutus (ὁ σός, ὦ Βροῦτε, δαίμων κακός, "Thy evil genius, Brutus"), on the eve of encountering Antony and Octavius on the plains of Philippi, 42 B.C. So, Shakesp. *J. Cæsar*, 4, 3:—
>
> *Brutus.* Speak to me what thou art.
> *Ghost.* Thy evil spirit, Brutus.
> *Brut.* Why com'st thou?
> *Ghost.* To tell thee, thou shalt see me at Philippi.

1968. Optima Graiorum sententia, quippe homini aiunt,
Non nasci esse bonum, natum aut cito morte potiri.

Auson. Id. 15, 49.

Wise Greeks, who said of man's mortality,
Not to be born is best, or soon to die.—*Ed.*

1969. Optima quæque dies miseris mortalibus ævi
Prima fugit; subeunt morbi tristisque senectus,
Et labor, et duræ rapit inclementia mortis.　　Virg. G. 3, 66.

Life's happiest days are first to take their flight,
Poor mortals that we are! Sickness and age,
Labour and sorrow come apace, till Death,
Stern and relentless, snatches us away.—*Ed.*

Delille translates it, "Hélas! nos plus beaux jours s'envolent les
premiers!"

1970. Optimum est aliena insania frui.　Plin. 18, 5.—*It is best to profit
by the folly of others.*

1971. O qualis facies et quali digna tabella!　Juv. 10, 157.—*What a
face for a fine picture!*　May be said either satirically or
seriously.

1972. O quanta species, inquit, cerebrum non habet.　Phædr. 1, 7, 2.—
Pity so fine a face should have no brains!　The Fox and the
Mask.

1973. O quid solutis est beatius curis?
Quum mens onus reponit, ac peregrino
Labore fessi venimus larem ad nostrum,
Desideratoque acquiescimus lecto.
Hoc est, quod unum est pro laboribus tantis.　　Cat. 31, 7.

No Place like Home.

How sweet to cast care to the wind,
And of its burden ease the mind!
And, after wand'ring long, to come
All weary to my own dear home,
And rest my head on my own bed—
This, this alone repays such toil accomplishéd!—*Ed.*

1974. Orandum est ut sit mens sana in corpore sano.　Juv. 10, 356.—
We should pray for a sound mind in a sound body.

1975. Ore rotundo.　Hor. A. P. 323.—*In well-turned phrase.*　Polished
diction: flowing periods.

1976. O Richard! o mon roi, l'univers t'abandonne;
Sur la terre il n'est donc que moi qui s'interesse à ta personne.
Comédie en 3 Actes par Sedaine, musique de Grétry,
1, 2 (Produced Oct. 21, 1784).　Blondel sings,—*O Richard! O
my King! the world abandons thee, and I am the only person
on earth that has thy welfare at heart!*

Such sentiments of devotion to the throne were sure of appreciation
at Court, where Grétry's opera became at once popular, and where
"Blondel's" air received an historical recognition, owing to its being sung

at the memorable dinner given to the officers of the Flanders Regiment at
Versailles, Oct. 3, 1789. The King and Marie Antoinette appeared after
dinner, the band striking up the air of Sedaine's song, while white cockades
were distributed and the tricolour trodden under foot.

1977. Origo et fons belli. Flor. 3, 6.—*The origin and source of the
war.* In common parlance the words are generally transposed
—*fons et origo.*

1978. Ornari res ipsa negat, contenta docere. Manil. Astron. 3, 39.—
*The subject of itself is incompatible with an ornamental style, con-
tent if it is able to instruct.* Educational or scientific treatises.

1979. Ornata hoc ipso, quod ornamenta neglexerant. Cic. Att. 2, 1, 1.
—*Ornate for the very reason that ornament had been neglected.*
Of poems, writings, etc.

1980. O rus, quando ego te adspiciam ? quandoque licebit
Nunc veterum libris, nunc somno et inertibus horis
Ducere sollicitæ jucunda oblivia vitæ ?   Hor. S. 2, 6, 60.

> *Country Pleasures.*
> O my dear homestead in the country ! when
> Shall I behold your pleasant face again ?
> And, studying now, now dozing and at ease,
> Imbibe forgetfulness of all this tease ?—*Conington.*

1981. O sæclum insipiens et inficetum! Cat. 43, 8.—*O the dull witless
age!*

1982. O sancta damnatio! Aug. contra Ep. Parmen. 3, 21 (vol. ix. 46 F).
—*O holy condemnation!*

1983. O sancta simplicitas!—*What divine simplicity!* Exclamation of
John Huss at the stake, July 6, 1415, on seeing an old woman
bringing her fagot to throw on the pile.

Büchm. (p. 509) cites Zincgreff-Weidner's *Apophthegmata,* Amsterdam,
1653 (Pᵗ. 3, p. 383), as the first authority for this tradition, making it a
man peasant. The usual legend represents it as in the text.

1984. Ὡς δ᾽ ἔστι μύθων τῶν Λιβυστικῶν λόγος
πληγέντ᾽ ἀτράκτῳ τοξικῷ τὸν αἰετὸν
εἰπεῖν, ἰδόντα μηχανὴν πτερώματος·
τάδ᾽ οὐχ ὑπ᾽ ἄλλων, ἀλλὰ τοῖς αὐτῶν πτεροῖς
ἁλισκόμεσθα.   Æsch. Fr. 123.

> So in the Lybyan fables it is told
> That once an eagle, stricken with a dart,
> Said, when he saw the fashion of the shaft,
> With our own feathers, not by others' hands,
> Are we now smitten.—*E. H. Plumptre.*

1985. Ὡς ἥκιστα ἢ ὡς ἥδιστα. Plut. Vit. p. 112 (Solon 28). In Lat.,
Aut quam minime, aut quam jucundissime.—*As briefly, or as
pleasantly as possible.* Originally said of the kind of speech
to be used with kings and great personages, it equally applies
to the mode in which bad news should be communicated. *V.*
Chil. 631. (*Procul a Jove,* etc.)

1986. Os hebes est, positæque movent fastidia mensæ,
Et queror, invisi quum venit hora cibi.   Ov. Ep. 1, 10, 7.

The Invalid.
Jaded my appetite, I loathe my food,
And curse each hateful meal in peevish mood.—*Ed.*

1987. O socii, neque enim ignari sumus ante malorum;
O passi graviora, dabit Deus his quoque finem.   Virg. A. 1, 198.

My comrades, for I speak to those
Who are not ignorant of woes,
Worse have ye suffered, and from these
God will in time grant due release.—*Conington.*

1988. Ὡς τεθνηξόμενος τῶν σῶν ἀγαθῶν ἀπόλαυε,
ὡς δὲ βιωσόμενος φείδευ σῶν κτεάνων·
Ἔστι δ' ἀνὴρ σοφὸς οὗτος, ὃς ἄμφω ταῦτα νοήσας,
φειδοῖ καὶ δαπάνῃ μέτρον ἐφηρμόσατο.   Lucian., Anth. Pal. 10, 26.

Vive tanquam victurus, vive tanquam moriturus.
In view of death, thy earthly goods enjoy;
In view of life, economy employ.
He's the wise man who both these rules obeys,
And strikes the mean 'twixt stint and lavishness.—*Ed.*

1989. Ὅστις δ' ὁμιλῶν ἥδεται κακοῖς ἀνήρ,
οὐ πώποτ' ἠρώτησα, γιγνώσκων ὅτι
τοιοῦτός ἐστιν οἷσπερ ἥδεται ξυνών.   Eur. Phœnix, Fr. 7.

Noscitur a Sociis.
Whoso takes pleasure in bad company,
I never questioned; knowing that the man
Must needs be like the folk he likes to mix with.—*Ed.*
Cf. Talis est quisque qualis ejus dilectio. St Aug. Tract. in Ep. Ioann.
2, 14.—*Such is each man as his liking.*

1990. Ὡς τοῖσιν εὖ φρονοῦσι συμμαχεῖ τύχη.   Eur. Pirithous, Fr. 7.—
Fortune fights on the side of the prudent.

1991. Ὅταν τύχῃ τις εὐνοοῦντος οἰκέτου,
οὐκ ἔστιν οὐδὲν κτῆμα κάλλιον βίῳ.
Men. Fr. 98 (p. 989).—*Whoso lights upon a kindly-natured
servant has got the best treasure in the world.* On the other
hand, Hippothoon (in Stobæus, 67, 14) says the same of a
sympathetic wife—ἄριστον ἀνδρὶ κτῆμα συμπαθὴς γυνή.

1992. O tempora, O Mores! Cic. Deiot. 11, 31.—*Alas! for the degen-
eracy of our times, and the low standard of our morals!*

1993. O tenebris tantis tam clarum extollere lumen
Qui primus potuisti, illustrans commoda vitæ.   Lucret. 3, 1.—
*O thou that wert the first to let in daylight on all this darkness,
elucidating those things which are of use to human life!*

The whole passage is addressed to Epicurus, but, according to Macaulay
(*Essays*, London, 1885, p. 892), is more applicable to Lord Bacon.
Illustrans commoda vitæ is the motto of the Royal Institution of Great
Britain.

1994. Otio qui nescit uti, plus negoti habet,
Quam si cuist negotiosus animus in negotio.   Enn. Trag.
Iphigenia, III. (i. p. 44).—*The man who does not know how to
employ his leisure, has more business on his hands than the man
who is busy about his business.*

1995. Otium cum dignitate, *or,* Cum dignitate otium.   Cic. Sest. 45,
98.—*Leisure with dignity.*   Dignified retirement earned by
meritorious service.   "On Cicero's entry into public life, he
had taken for his motto, 'Leisure and Honour' (*Otium cum
dignitate*)."   Boissier's *Cicero and his Friends,* Engl. transl.
p. 224, Lond., 1897.

1996. Οὐκ ἀγαθὸν πολυκοιρανίη· εἷς κοίρανος ἔστω,
Εἷς βασιλεύς.   Hom. Il. 2, 204.

> A multitude of rulers bodes but ill,
> Be one our lord, our king.—*Calverley.*

1997. Οὐκ ἔστιν οὐδὲν χωρὶς ἀνθρώποις θεῶν.
σπουδάζομεν δὲ πόλλ' ὑπ' ἐλπίδων μάτην
πόνους ἔχοντες, οὐδὲν εἰδότες σαφές.   Eur. Thyestes, Fr. 6.

> There's nothing happens to men without God's will.
> Yet we must fash ourselves, led by vain hopes,
> And take great trouble, knowing nothing sure.—*Ed.*

1998. Οὐκοῦν εἰς αὔριον τὰ σπουδαῖα.   Plut. Vit. (Pelop. 10).—*Business
to-morrow!* as Archias remarked, when he put aside the letter
warning him of the conspiracy against his life.

1999. Οὐκ ὠνοῦμαι μυρίων δραχμῶν μεταμέλειαν.   Gell. 1, 8, 6.—*I am
not going to give ten thousand drachmæ (£320) for repentance.*
Demosthenes to the courtesan, Lais.

2000. Οὐ λέγειν τύγ' ἐσσὶ δεινός, ἀλλὰ σιγῆν ἀδύνατος.   Epicharmi Frag.
268. (Frag. Philosoph. Gr., ed. Mullachius, Paris, 1860).—*Though
poor in speech, thou canst not hold thy tongue.*   V. Gell. 1, 15, 15.

2001. Où peut-on être mieux qu'au sein de sa famille?   J. F. Marmontel,
Lucile, sc. 4 (Com. Opera in 1 Act, Music by Grétry, 1769).—
Where can one be better than in the bosom of one's family?   It
goes on,

> Tout est content, le cœur, les yeux,
> Vivons, aimons comme nos aieux!

It was sung by the crowd on the entry of Louis XVI. into Paris,
Thursday, July 16, 1789, two days after the taking of the Bastille.   The
song was also repeated on the following Sept. 7th, when the "Dames
Françaises"—wives of Parisian artists—presented the Nat. Assembly with
offerings of their own jewels and trinkets for the popular cause.   N. J.
Hugou, *Mémoires Hist. de la Révol. Fr.*, vol. iii. p. 312; and Chamfort,
Tableaux Historiques, xxvi. (vol. 3, p. 189).

2002. Οὐθὲν γὰρ, ὡς φάμεν, μάτην ἡ φύσις ποιεῖ.   Arist. Pol. 1, 2, 10
(Didot, p. 483, 42).—*Nature, so we say, does nothing without a
meaning.*

2003. Ouvrez: c'est la fortune de la France! Chateaubriand, *Analyse raisonnée de l'hist. de France*, Paris, 1845, ed. F. Didot, p. 206. —*Open! the fortune of France stands at the door!* Romantic speech put into the mouth of Philip VI. on his retreat from the field of Crécy, Aug. 26, 1346, to the Castle of Broye. The chatelain demanded who knocked so loud at night-time. The king's actual words were, "Ouvrez, ouvrez, chastelain, *c'est l'infortuné roy de France*," Open! open, the unfortunate King of France stands at the door! Froissart, Bk. I. Pt. 1, cap. 292; Fournier, *L.D.L.*, pp. 90-94.

2003A. O wunderschön ist Gottes Erde,
    Und wert darauf vergnügt zu sein;
    Drum will ich, bis ich Asche werde,
    Mich dieser schönen Erde freun.

L. Hölty, Aufmunterung zur Freude.

> How beautiful is God's dear earth!
> How greatly our enjoying worth!
> Troth, will I, till my soul takes flight,
> In this fair earth find my delight.—*Ed.*

P.*

2004. Pactum serva.—*Keep troth.* Inscription on Edward the First's tomb in Westminster Abbey.

2005. Παιδεία ἄρα ἐστὶν ἡ ἔντευξις τῶν ἠθῶν. τοῦτο καὶ Θουκυδίδης ἔοικε λέγειν περὶ ἱστορίας λέγων· ὅτι καὶ ἱστορία φιλοσοφία ἐστὶν ἐκ παραδειγμάτων. Dion. Hal., Ars Rhetorica, 11, 2 (Tauchnitz ed., p. 212).—*Education should be the cultivation of character; just as Thucydides (1, 22) used to say of history, that it was philosophy teaching by examples.*

2006. Παίζω· μεταβολὰς γὰρ πόνων ἀεὶ φιλῶ. Eur. Fr. 986.—*I'm playing; for I always like a change from work.*

2007. Palam muttire plebeio piaculum est. Enn. Teleph. Fr. 2 (Ribb. i. 63).—*It is a parlous thing for a common man to speak his mind openly.* Qu. by Phædrus (3, Epilog. 34) as a maxim that he had often learnt as a boy.

2008. Pallentes radere mores
    Doctus, et ingenuo culpam defigere ludo.   Pers. 5, 15.

The Satirist.

> To banter shady morals is your trade,
> And gibbet faults in polish'd pasquinade.—*Ed.*

* Including the Greek Π (Pi), Φ (Phi), and Ψ (Psi).

2009. Pallor in ore sedet: macies in corpore toto:
Nusquam recta acies: livent rubigine dentes:
Pectora felle virent; lingua est suffusa veneno:
Risus abest; nisi quem visi movere dolores.   Ov. M. 2, 775.

> *Descripcioun of Envie.*
> On Envie's cheek an asshy palenesse sate,
> And pyning honger all her flesh devore:
> Her grudgeful eies wold never looke you strayt,
> And in her mouth her teethe were cankred ore;
> Her breast was greene with gall's malicious store,
> Whyle spyghtfull poison did her tongue suffuse.
> Ne smyle ne gladnesse wonne within her dore,
> Save when the hurt of other folke she vues.—*Ed.*

2010. Palmam qui meruit ferat.   J. Jortin, *Lusus Poetici*, Ed. Tertia,
Lond., 1748, 4°, p. 22, *Ad ventos*, st. 4.—*Let him bear the palm
who has deserved it.*   Motto of the great Nelson and of the
Royal Nav. School.

> The whole stanza runs as follows:
> Et nobis faciles parcite et hostibus.
> Concurrant pariter cum ratibus rates:
> Spectent numina ponti, et
> Palmam qui meruit, ferat.
>
> *To the Winds.*
> On friend and foe breathe soft and calm,
> As ship with ship in battle meets;
> And, while the sea-gods watch the fleets,
> Let him who merits bear the palm.—*Ed.*

2011. Panem et circenses.   Juv. 10, 81.—*Bread and horse* (circus)
racing, the only two objects, according to Juvenal, that really
interested the Roman people.

> Voltaire writes to Mme. Necker, March 1770—"Il ne fallait aux Romains
> que *panem et circenses;* nous avons retranché *panem*, il nous suffit de
> *circenses*, c'est-à-dire de l'opéra-comique." Had Voltaire lived to witness
> the march of the women of Paris to Versailles (Oct. 5, 1789) shouting for
> bread, he would have found a parallel for both parts of the quotation.

2012. Πᾶν πρᾶγμα δύο ἔχει λαβάς, τὴν μὲν φορητὴν, τὴν δὲ ἀφόρητον . . .
καὶ λήψῃ αὐτὸ καθ' ὅ φορητόν ἐστιν.   Epictetus, *Enchirid.* 43.—
*Everything has two handles, that by which it may be borne, and
that by which it cannot.   Do thou seize it by the handle by which
it may be carried.*   There is a right way, and a wrong, of doing
everything.

2013. Πάντα καθαρὰ τοῖς καθαροῖς.   N. T. Tit. i. 15.—*To the pure all
things are pure.*

2014. Παντῶν δὲ μάλιστ' αἰσχύνεο σαυτον.   Aureum Pythagoreorum
Carmen, line 12.   (Mullach's Fragmm. Philosoph. Græcor., vol. i.
p. 192).—*'Fore all things, reverence thyself.*   In his "Colours
of Good and Evil," iii., Bacon has, "Maxime omnium teipsum
reverere" (vol. 2, p. 235).

2015. Parcite paucarum diffundere crimen in omnes,
Spectetur meritis quæque puella suis.   Ov. A. A. 3, 9.—*Do not visit the faults of a few on all: let every girl be considered on her own merits.*

2016. Par droit de conquête et par droit de naissance.   L'Abbé Cassagnes, *Henry le Grand au Roy*, 3rd ed., 1662, p. 20, ver. 5. —*By right of conquest and by right of birth.*

> *Henry IV.* Lorsqu' après cent combats, je posséday la France,
> Et par droit de conquête, et par droit de naissance.

> The 2nd l. was borrowed *verbatim* by Volt. for the opening of his *Henriade*:—
> Je chant ce héros qui régna sur la France,
> *Et par droit de conquête,* etc., etc.

2017. Pares autem cum paribus, vetere proverbio, facillime congregantur.   Cic. Sen. 3, 7.—*Like goes naturally with like, according to the old proverb.*   "Birds of a feather," etc.

2018. Parfois, élus maudits de la fureur suprême,

> .   .   .   .

Ces envoyés du ciel sont apparus au monde,
Comme s'ils venaient de l'enfer.
V. Hugo, *Buonaparte*, Strophe 1, 1822.—*Sometimes these messengers of heaven, the accursed elect of the divine wrath, have appeared on earth as though they came from hell.*

2019. Parigi, o cara, noi lasceremo,
La vita uniti trascorreremo.
F. M. Piave, La Traviata, 3, 6 (Music by Verdi).—*We shall leave Paris, darling, and journey thro' life hand in hand.*

2020. Paris (*or* La couronne) vaut bien une messe.—*Paris (or The crown) is well worth a mass.*

> In 1593 Henry IV. was advancing rapidly towards the throne of France, the chief obstacle remaining in his path being his own Calvinistic tenets, which he finally abandoned by the "leap perilous" of July 23, entering Paris in triumph the following March 22, 1594.   Tradition represents the Huguenot, Sully, as having already urged the King to attend mass as he did himself.   "*Sire, sire,*" he pleaded. "*la couronne vaut bien une messe.*" *See* "Recueil Géneral des *Caquets de l'Acouchée*, etc.. 5e iournée (p. 136), Imprimé au temps de ne plus fe fafcher," 1623, n.p., 8vo.

2021. Par ma foi! il y a plus de quarante ans que je dis de la prose sans que j'en susse rien!   Mol. Bourg. Gentilh 2, 6.—*My word! here have I been talking prose for more than forty years without knowing it!*

> Famous remark of M. Jourdain, when informed by his teacher in philosophy that he habitually conversed in "prose," which has passed into a prov. (*faire de la prose sans le savoir*) for those astonishing "discoveries" of which everyone has long been cognisant except the "discoverer" himself.   Molière's play appeared in 1670-1, and ten years later Mme. de Sévigné begins her letter of June 12, 1680, with. "Comment, ma fille! J'ai donc fait un sermon sans y penser?   J'en suis aussi étonnée que M. le Comte de Soissons, quand *on lui découvrit qu'il faisait de la prose.*"

R

2022. Par negotiis neque supra erat.   Tac. A. 6, 39.—*Equal to, but not above his business.*

> Said of Poppæus Sabinus, who had held in succession several Proconsular appointments in the reign of Tiberius, *nullam ob eximiam virtutem, sed quod par negotiis*, etc., "not on account of any special excellence, but because he was equal to," etc., *ut supra.*

2023. Par nobile fratrum.   Hor. S. 2, 3, 243.—*A fine pair of brothers, forsooth!*

2024. Parole di sera il vento se le mena.   Prov.—*Evening words the wind carries away.*

2025. Par pari referto.   Ter. Eun. 3, 1, 55.—*Give him back tit for tat!*

2026. Pars benefici est quod petitur si belle neges.   Syr. 469.
Pars beneficii est, quod petitur, si cito neges.   Macr. Sat. 2, 7, 11.
—*The next thing to granting a favour is to refuse it graciously, or else to refuse it at once.*

2027. Pars sanitatis, velle sanari.   Sen. Hipp. 249.—*'Tis half the cure to be willing to be cured.*

2028. Partage de Montgommery: tout d'un côté, et rien de l'autre. Prov. (Quit. p. 583).—*A Montgomery division, all on one side, and none on the other.*   An old Norman family whose immense estates descended by custom to the eldest son.

2029. Parthis mendacior.   Hor. Ep. 2, 1, 112.—*More lying than the Parthians.*

> So also *Punica fides*, Sall. J., 108, 3, "The faith of a Carthaginian," *i.e.*, perfidy; and Κρῆτες ἀεὶ ψεῦσται, Callimachus, *Hymn to Jupiter*, 8.—*The Cretans are always liars*, qu. by St Paul, Tit. i. 12.

2030. Parturiunt montes, nascetur ridiculus mus.   Hor. A. P. 139.—*The mountain is in labour, and a ridiculous mouse will be born.* A grand flourish ending in a ridiculous bathos.

> Allusion is made to the Greek proverbial saying, as preserved in Athenæus (xiv. p. 616), Ὤδινεν ὄρος, Ζεὺς δ' ἐφοβεῖτο, τὸ δ' ἔτεκε μῦν.—*The mountain was in travail, Jove was alarmed and—she brought forth a mouse!*   Phædrus (4, 22) renders it,

> > Mons parturibat, gemitus immanes ciens;
> > Eratque in terris maxima expectatio.
> > At ille murem peperit.

> > The mountain groaned in pangs of birth,
> >   Great expectation fill'd the earth,
> >   And lo! a mouse was born!—*Ed.*

2031. Parva leves capiunt animos.   Ov. A. A. 1, 159.—*Small minds are affected by trifles.*

2032. Parva, sed apta mihi, sed nulli obnoxia, sed non Sordida; parta meo sed tamen ære domus.   Ariosto.

> *The Poet's House.*
> Small, but it suits: 'tis mortgaged not to any:
> Clean, and (what's more) bought out of my own money.—*Ed.*

Inscription placed by Ludovico Ariosto over the entrance to his house in the Contrada di Mirasole, Ferrara. Dilapidated and obliterated by time, the lines have not long since been renewed and replaced in their original situation. *V.* Fumag. 203, and authorities there given, and the Coleridge ed. (1899) of Byron's Works, vol. ii. p. 487.

2033. Parva sunt hæc: sed parva ista non contemnendo majores nostri maximam hanc rem fecerunt. Liv. 6, 41.—*These are small matters, it is true: but it was by not despising these small things that our forefathers raised their country to her present great position.*

2034. Parvis componere magna. Virg. E. 1, 24.—*To compare great things with small.*

2035. Parvula (nam exemplo est) magni formica laboris
Ore trahit, quodcunque potest, atque addit acervo,
Quem struit, haud ignara ac non incauta futuri. Hor. S. 1, 1, 33.

> E'en so the ant (for no bad pattern she),
> That tiny type of giant industry,
> Drags grain by grain, and adds it to the sum
> Of her full heap, foreseeing cold to come.—*Conington.*

2036. Parvum parva decent. Hor. Ep. 1, 7, 44.

> Small things become small folks.—*Conington.*

2037. Passato il pericolo, gabbato il santo. Prov.—*The danger being past, the saint is cheated.*

> Oh! combien le péril enrichirait les dieux,
> Si nous nous souvenions des vœux qu'il nous fait faire!
> Mais, le péril passé, l'on ne se souvient guère
> De ce qu'on a promis aux cieux. La Font. Fab. 9, 13.

2038. Passez-moi la rhubarbe, et je vous passerai le séné. Quit. p. 629. —*Pass my rhubarb, and I'll pass your senna.* Mutual concessions of two doctors prescribing opp. remedies for the same sick case.

> In Molière's *L'Am. Méd.*, 2, 4, Tomès is for bleeding, des Fonandrès for the emetic. In the next act, des Fonandrès proposes a compromise. "Qu'il me passe mon émétique pour la malade dont il s'agit, et je lui passerai tout ce qu'il voudra pour le premier malade dont il sera question." The qu. is used in the case of a compromise brought about by mutual concessions. The objection is withdrawn on the one side, on condition of a corresponding yielding of the point on the part of the other. In the sense of "passing" anything at table ("Pass the pepper, pray")—the words have a funny effect in English which is not intended in the original.

2039. Passons au déluge! Rac. Plaid. 3, 3.—*Go on to the deluge!*

> At the conclusion of his speech for the defence, L'Intimé at last says, to the great relief of Dandin the judge, "Je finis." On which Dandin ejaculates,
>
> *Dandin.* Ah!
> *L'Intimé.* Avant la naissance du monde . . .
> *Dandin* (baillant). Avocat, ah! *passons au déluge.*

2040. Πάταξον μὲν, ἄκουσον δέ.   Plut. Vitæ, p. 140 (Themist. 11, 3).—
Strike, but hear ! Themistocles disputing with Eurybiades, the
Spartan admiral, as to the best means of resisting Xerxes'
attack, 480 B.C.

2041. Patellæ dignum operculum.   Hieron. Ep. 7, 5.—*A cover worthy
of the pot.* Like suits like.

2042. Παθήματα μαθήματα.—*Sufferings are lessons.* We learn wisdom
by bitter experience. In Latin the saw runs, "Nocumentum
documentum."—*Harming 's warning.*

> The maxim is apparently derived from Herod. 1, 207 (where Crœsus says
> to Cyrus) τὰ δέ μοι παθ᾽,ματα, ἐόντα ἀχάριτα, μαθήματα γεγόνεε—*My suffer-
> ings, owing to their unpleasant nature, became so many lessons.* Cf. Æsch.
> Agam. 176, τὸν πάθει μάθος θέντα κυρίως ἔχειν—"[Zeus] fixeth fast the law
> that *pain is gain.*" E. H. Plumptre tr.: and Ἔμαθεν ἀφ᾽ ὧν ἔπαθε τὴν
> ὑπακοήν. D. Paul. *ad Hebr.* 5, 8.—*He learnt obedience by the things that He
> suffered.*

2043. Patience et longueur de temps
Font plus que force ni que rage.   La Font. 2, 11 (*Le Lion et le
Rat*).—*Patience and length of time do more than violence and
rage.*

2044. Patres Conscripti took a boat and went to Philippi :
Stormum surgebat, et boatum overturnebat.
Omnes drownderunt, qui swim-away non potuerunt,
Excipe John Periwig, who was tied to the tail of a dead pig.

> School-boys' mock-Latin verse of unknown origin. The variety of the
> third and fourth lines is,
>> Trumpeter unus erat qui coatum scarlet habebat
>> Et magnum periwig, tied about with the tail of a dead pig.
>
> Cf. in Wright and Halliwell's *Reliquiæ Antiquæ*, Lond., 1841, 8ᵛᵒ, vol. 1,
> p. 91.
>> Fratres Carmeli navigant in a bothe apud Eli,
>> Non sunt in cæli, quia . . .
>> Omnes drencherunt, quia sterisman non habuerunt, etc.

2045. Patriæ pietatis imago.   Virg. A. 10, 824.—*The picture of paternal
affection.*

2046. Pauca Catonis
Verba, sed a pleno venientia pectore veri.   Luc. 9, 188.

> Few were the words of Cato, but they came
> Straight from the heart, with earnest truth aflame.—*Ed.*

2047. Pauper enim non est, cui rerum suppetit usus.
Si ventri bene, si lateri est pedibusque tuis, nil
Divitiæ poterunt regales addere majus.   Hor. Ep. 1, 12, 4.

> He is not poor whose means, though small, suffice.
> If stomach, lungs and limbs are in good health,
> You could procure no more with royal wealth.—*Ed.*

2048. Pauper sum, fateor, patior: quod di dant fero.   Plaut. Aul. 1, 2,
10.—*I am poor, I own, but I bear it: I put up with what the
gods send me.*

2049. Paupertas est, non quæ pauca possidet, sed quæ multa non possidet. Sen. Ep. 87, 35. —*Poverty is not the enjoyment of little, but the lack of much.*

The terms Pauper, Paupertas (*Poor, Poverty*), had, in the first century A.D. and before, a distinct meeting, signifying a condition of "poor circumstances," and of "small" (and even "straitened") means, but denoting a respectable class of persons widely remote from the state of "Penuria" and "Egestas." Our own word "poor" has also something of the same distinction. *See* above, No. 1751A.

2050. Paupertas fugitur, totoque arcessitur orbe. Luc. 1, 166.— *Poverty is shunned and arraigned throughout the world.*

"Άπολις, ἄοικος, πατρίδος ἐστερημένος,
πτωχὸς, πλανήτης, βίον ἔχων ἐφήμερον. Eur. Fr. 264.

The Outcast.

City-less, homeless, driven from my ain countrée;
A beggar, and a wanderer, just the creature of a day.—*Ed.*

2051. Paupertatis pudor et fuga. Hor. Ep. 1, 18, 24.—*The shame and dread of poverty.*

2052. Pavor est utrobique molestus. Hor. Ep. 1, 6, 10.—*Either way, there is trouble to be feared.*

2053. Pax majora decet. Peragit tranquilla potestas
Quod violenta nequit, mandataque fortius urget
Imperiosa quies.
Claud. Cons. Mall. 239.—*Great works require peace. Power, employed quietly, effects what violence cannot accomplish: and calmness is all puissant in enforcing commands with success.*

2054. Pax optima rerum
Quas homini novisse datum est: pax una triumphis
Innumeris potior. Sil. 11, 595.

Peace.

Peace, the best blessing known on earth,
Alone, a thousand triumphs is worth!—*Ed.*

2056. Payer en monnaie de singe, *or* en gambades. Prov. Quit. p. 646; and *Tableaux Hist. de la Rév. Fr.* (Auber, Éditeur), 1802, vol. i. p. 207.—*To pay "monkeys' money," or "in capers."*

According to an old edict of St Louis, strolling players escaped the *aubaine* on entering Paris by making their monkeys dance to the crowd. The expression now applies to all or any who satisfy all requirements demanded of them ("pay their footing") by some exhibition of their respective talents—song, speech, sentiment, etc.

2057. Pectus est enim quod dissertos facit. Quint. 10, 7, 15.—*The heart it is that makes men eloquent.* "The heart it is," echoed Neander, more than a millennium afterwards, "that makes the true divine," (*Pectus est quod facit theologum*). "The history of the Church is to be understood only in proportion to the student's *personal experience* of the significance of the life of Christ." *Chambers's Encyclopædia, s.v.* "Neander."

2058. Pedibus timor addidit alas. Virg. A. 8, 224.—*Fear gave wings to his feet.*

2059. Pégase est un cheval qui porte
Les grands hommes à l'Hospital.
   Maynard, Épigramme (*Recueil des plus beaux vers de MM. . . . Maynard,* Paris, 1638, p. 425).—*Pegasus* (the winged horse of the Muses) *is a steed that carries distinguished men to the workhouse.*

2060. Peine forte et dure.—*Strong and severe punishment.*

> Term used in old English law for the practice of "pressing," with heavy weights placed on the chest, prisoners who refused to "plead." Throughout Elizabeth's reign this torture was used, mainly in the case of recusant Catholics: the most memorable instance, because the most atrocious, being that of Margaret Clitheroe, the martyr of York, who was "pressed" to death in 1586, "your hands and feet tied to posts, and a sharp stone under your back"—a refinement of cruelty hardly imaginable in our day. Her crime was that she had sheltered a priest, whose name she would not divulge. So late as 1741, the horrible practice survived, and claimed its last victim. Thirty years later, the barbarity was virtually abolished, and in 1828 the Statute made "standing mute" equivalent to the plea of "Not guilty." When a kind hostess "presses" upon you the seductive muffin, or "presses" you to take "just another cup" of tea, she little thinks where the term came from. (Morris's *Troubles of our Catholic Forefathers,* vol. 3, p. 417.)

2061. Pejor est bello timor ipse belli. Sen. Thyest. 572.—*The fear of war is worse than war itself.*

2062. Pendent opera interrupta, minæque
Murorum ingentes, æquataque machina cælo. Virg. A. 4, 88.

      The Strike.
  The works all slack and aimless lie,
  Grim bastions looming from on high,
  And monster cranes that mate the sky.— *Conington.*

2063. Penitus toto divisos orbe Britannos. Virg. E. 1, 67.—*The Britons, a race entirely cut off from the rest of the world.*

2064. Per angusta ad augusta.—*Thro' Hardship to Honour.* Motto of Margrave Ernest of Brandenburg (†1642), and the password of the "conspirators" in Piave's opera of *Ernani* (Music by Verdi), 3, 3, and 4.

2065. Peras imposuit Jupiter nobis duas;
Propriis repletam vitiis post tergum dedit,
Alienis ante pectus suspendit gravem. Phædr. 4, 10, 1.

     The Mote and the Beam.
  With wallets twain almighty Jove
  Has saddled all mankind:
  Our neighbours' failings hang before,
  Our own faults hang behind.—*Ed.*

2066. Perch' egli incontra che più volte piega
L'opinion corrente in falsa parte,
E poi l'affetto l'intelletto lega. Dante, Par. 13, 118.

Bias in Judging.
Since it befalls that in most instances
Current opinion leans to false; and then
The judgment's warped by inclination.—*Cary* (altered).

2067. Percontatorem fugito, nam garrulus idem est,
Nec retinent patulæ commissa fideliter aures.
Et semel emissum volat irrevocabile verbum.   Hor.Ep.1,18,69.

Chatterboxes.
Avoid a ceaseless questioner: he burns
To tell the next he talks with what he learns.
Wide ears retain no secrets, and you know
You can't get back a word you once let go.—*Conington.*

2068. Per damna, per cædes, ab ipso
Ducit opes animumque ferro.   Hor. C. 4, 4, 59.

Persecution.
Laughs carnage, havoc, all to scorn,
And draws new spirit from the knife.—*Conington.*

2069. Perdidit arma, locum virtutis deseruit, qui
Semper in augenda festinat et obruitur re.   Hor. Ep. 1, 16, 67.

The wretch whose thoughts by gain are all engrossed
Has flung away his sword, betrayed his post.—*Conington.*

2070. Perdis, et in damno gratia nulla tuo.   Ov. A. A. 1, 434.—*You
lose, and get no thanks for it.*

2071. Perditur inter hæc misero lux, non sine votis.   Hor. S. 2, 6, 59.

And so my day between my fingers slips,
While fond regrets keep rising to my lips.—*Conington.*

2072. Pereant amici, dum inimici una intercidant.   Incert. Ribb. i. 299.

Perish our friends, if with them fall our foes!

This line, from some unknown tragic poet, is quoted by Cicero, Deiot. 9,
25, and styled a " monstrous line " (*versus immanis*): and is also referred to
by S. Augustine (c. Faustum, 16), who denounces it as *Illa notissima . . .
et furiosa sententia* ("That most notorious and insane sentiment"). That
the thought was borrowed from the Greeks may be inferred from the
saying of Plutarch (Mor. p. 61; de Adulatore, cap. 4): μηδαμῆ μηδαμῶς
ἐπαινοῦμεν τὸ, Ἐρρέτω φίλος σύν ἐχθρῷ.—*By no manner of means do we
applaud the saying, "Let our friend perish, if our enemy perish with him."*

2073. Pereunt et imputantur.   Mart. 5, 20, 13.—*They* (days, hours,
etc.) *pass by, and are placed to our account.*   Common inscription on clocks and dials.

2074. Perfectum nihil est, aliquid dum restat agendum.   Law Maxim
(gen. quoted in the form, "Nihil perfectum est dum aliquid
restat agendum").—*Nothing is complete, while there remains
something to be done.*

2075. Perfer et obdura: dolor hic tibi proderit olim:
Sæpe tulit lassis succus amarus opem.   Ov. Am. 3, 11, 7.

264 PERFERVIDUM—PERICULUM.

Patience.

Bear and endure: some day your pains will tell.
The bitter draught has oft made sick men well.—*Ed.*

Cf. Perfer et obdura: multo graviora tulisti. Ov. T. 5, 11, 7.—*Bear and endure: you have borne much harder things than this.*

2076. Perfervidum ingenium Scotorum.—*The fiery temper of the Scots.* Buchanan, *Hist. of Scotland* (ed. Ruddiman, p. 321), uses "*præfervida ingenia*" to describe the characteristic impatience of the Scots at Flodden (1513), in quitting an advantageous position on the hill to engage the enemy on lower ground where they met with defeat (Hume-Brown's *Hist. of Scotland*, Camb., 1899, i. 338, and N.).

Talking of the Scots, and thinking of them, and of the praises lavished upon the country by their native poets, it is a little curious, almost startling in its way, as one turns over Ribbeck's pages, suddenly to tumble upon this fragmentary fragment of Pacuvius:

Calidonia altrix terra exuperantum virum,

which may be Englished, "Calidonia, thou nurse of men that excel!" (*or*, "of men that are men!*") Pacuvius flourished about the middle of the second century B.C., when Caledonia was not yet "invented," and when, so far from having attained the rank of a "worse England" of Dr Johnson's day and definition, it was still plunged in the "barbarous" condition described by Mr Hume, and found a healthy (and remunerative) outlet for its energy in depredations upon the "peaceful and effeminate" Briton across the border. The father of Latin tragedy, as Cicero would have him to be. was not (needless to say) speaking of a North Britain which was yet in the making, but of quite another "Calydon," associated in our minds with Deianira and Meleager and Atalanta (Madame Méléagre), and a famous boar, and Mr Swinburne. Still, with Scott's line in one's head, one cannot but be struck by the coincidence—a mere coincidence, certainly, but a curious one.

2077. Periculosæ plenum opus aleæ
Tractas, et incedis per ignes
Suppositos cineri doloso. Hor. C. 2, 1, 6.

To an Historian.

You've got in hand a ticklish task,
A risky game of chance to play:
O'er treacherous ashes lies your way
That underlying fires mask.—*Ed.*

2078. Periculosum est credere et non credere.
.   .   .   .   .   .
Ergo exploranda est veritas multum, prius
Quam stulta prave judicet sententia.
Phædr. 3, 10 (1, 5 and 6).—*It is as dangerous to believe too readily, as to refuse credence altogether . . . therefore, one should carefully examine into the truth of any matter, rather than rashly form a wrong judgment.*

2079. Periculum in mora. Prov.—*Danger in delay.* V. Liv. 38, 25, 13.

2080. Perierunt tempora longi Servitii.   Juv. 3, 124.

 All my long hours of service thrown away.—*Ed.*

 Said of a client who had been long waiting for advancement.

2081. Περὶ ὄνου σκιᾶς [μάχεσθαι]. Ar. Vesp. 191.—[*To fight*] *for an ass's shadow.* To dispute about trifles.

 The passage runs:—

  ΒΔ. Περὶ τοῦ μαχεῖ νῷν δῆτα ;   ΦΙ. Περὶ ὄνου σκιᾶς.

  Bdelucleon. What fight'st thou then for ?
  Philocleon.   For an ass's shade.

 The Latin equivalent is *de asini umbra disceptare;* and cf. Hor. Ep. 1, 18, 15. Alter rixatur de lana sæpe caprina (*One man will fight you for a lock of wool*). *See* also Soph. Fr. 308 (Cedalion), τὰ πάντ' ὄνου σκιά ("All is but an ass's shadow," *i.e.*, mere nothing). Apostolius (Cent. xvii. 69) has preserved the story of a man who hired a donkey for the day, but was withstood by the owner, when in the midday's heat he would have sate down in the beast's shadow for which he had not bargained. He goes on to say that the apologue was employed by Demosthenes to arouse the attention of the judges in a capital case that he was defending. and that he remarked at its conclusion, " You can listen to a tale of an ass's shadow, but when it is a question of life and death, you are too tired to attend."

2082. Périsse l'univers pourvu que je me venge !   Cyrano de Bergerac, *La Mort d Agrippine* (1653), 4, 5. *Tragédie,* etc., Paris, 1654, p. 76 (Agrippine loq.).—*Let the world perish, so I be avenged!*

2083. Périssent les colonies, plutôt qu'un principe !—*Perish our colonies, rather than sacrifice a principle!*

 "Perish India, evacuate Gibraltar," etc. The phrase is the *résumé* of the speech of Dupont de Nemours in the Nat. Assembly, May 13, 1791, on the "colour" question, in the franchise proposed to be accorded to the mixed races of the West Indian colonies of France. "Il vaudrait mieux sacrifier les colonies qu'un principe," exclaimed de Nemours on this vital point of republican "equality," being supported in his policy by Robespierre, who also avouched: "Périssent les colonies, si les colons veulent nous forcer à décréter ce qui convient le plus à leurs intérêts !" (*Moniteur,* May 15, 1791.)

2084. Perjuria ridet amantum Jupiter.   Tib. 3, 6, 49.

 At lovers' perjuries, they say, Jove laughs. *Shakesp.* "Rom. and Jul.," 2, 2.

2085. Per me si va nella città dolente,
  Per me si va nell' eterno dolore,
  Per me si va tra la perduta gente.   Dante, Inf. 3, 1.

      The Gate of Hell.

  Thro' me you go into th' City Dolorous,
  Thro' me you go to everlasting pain,
  Thro' me you go among the lost, lost souls.—*Ed.*

2086. Permitte divis cætera. Hor. C. 1, 9, 9.—*Leave the future to the gods.*

2087. Per omne fas ac nefas. Liv. 6, 14, 10.—*Right or wrong.* In every possible way.

2088. Perpetui fructum donavi nominis: idque
Quo dare nil potui munere majus, habes.   Ov. T. 5, 14, 13.

The Poet to his Wife.
A name that shall for ever shine;
The greatest I could give, is thine.—*Ed.*

2089. Persicos odi, puer, apparatus.   Hor. C. 1, 38, 1.
No Persian cumber, boy, for me.—*Conington.*

2090. Per undas et ignes fluctuat nec mergitur.—*Through water and fire she tosses but is not submerged.*   Motto of the city of Paris, with emblem of ship on ocean.

2091. Per varios casus, per tot discrimina rerum,
Tendimus in Latium: sedes ubi fata quietas
Ostendunt.   Virg. A. 1, 204.

Through chance, through peril lies our way
To Latium, where the fates display
A mansion of abiding stay.—*Conington.*

The Bishop of Manchester (Fraser) cleverly applied the above to those who sought a solution of their religious disquietude in the peace of the "Latin" Church.

2092. Per varios præceps casus rota volvitur ævi. Sil. 6, 121.—*Through chance and change time's wheel rolls swiftly on.*

2093. Petitio principii. Logical term.—*Begging the question.* A fallacy in argument, by which you assume that which has to be proved; one of the premises being the same as the conclusion, or dependent upon it. *E g.,* "It is true, because I saw it in the paper," where it is assumed that the newspaper is correctly informed.

2094. Peu de chose nous console, parce que peu de chose nous afflige. Pasc. Pens. 24, 11.—*Little consoles us, because little afflicts us.*

2095. Peu de gens connaissent la mort; on la souffre non par résolution, mais par la stupidité et par la coutume, et la plupart des hommes meurent parce qu'on meurt. La Rochef. p. 182.—*Few understand death: it is met not with resolution, but with the stupid acquiescence of custom; and most men die only because it is the thing to do.*

2096. Peu de gens savent être vieux. La Rochef. Max., § 445, p. 86.—*Few people know how to be old.*

2097. Peuple d'enfants!—*Nation of children!* Exclamation of P. Ferrari anent the French. (Mrs Bishop's *Life of Mrs Aug. Craven,* vol. ii. p. 126.)

2098. Pharmaca das ægroto : aurum tibi porrigit æger;
Tu morbum curas illius; ille tuum.
Owen (J.), Epigr. 1, 21 (Ad pauperem medicum).

To a Needy Physician.
You give the patient drugs; he hands your fee:
Thus each relieves th' other's necessity.—*Ed.*

2099. Φημὶ πολυχρονίην μελέτην ἔμεναι, φίλε, καὶ δή
Ταύτην ἀνθρώποισι τελευτῶσαν φύσιν εἶναι.
Evenus, 9.—*I say that habit is a very persistent thing, and
at last becomes to men a nature.* Custom is second nature.

2100. Φιλοκαλοῦμεν μετ᾽ εὐτελείας. Thuc. 2, 40, 1 (Pericles loq.).—*We
cultivate our taste for the beautiful without extravagance.*

2100A. Philosophe sans le savoir.—*A philosopher without being aware
of it.* Title of a play of Sedaine (Comédie Française, 1765).

2101. Φοβοῦ (or Τίμα) τὸ γῆρας, οὐ γὰρ ἔρχεται μόνον. Men. Mon. 491.
—*Fear (or respect) old age, for it does not come alone.*

Cf. Senectus ipsa est morbus. Ter. Phorm. 4, 1, 9.—*Old age is a disease
in itself;* and

Σφόδρ᾽ ἐστὶν ἡμῶν ὁ βίος οἴνῳ προσφερής·
ὅταν ᾖ τὸ λοιπὸν μικρόν, ὄξος γίνεται.　　Antiphanes, Incert. 68.

The life of man you may with wine compare:
The last pint in the cask turns vinegar.—*Ed.*

2102. Pia fraus.—*A pious fraud,* either in a good sense, as a *kind
deception,* or with the idea of veiling rascality under the cloak
of religion.

In the story of the transformation into a boy of Telethusa, wife of Lygdus
and mother of Iphis, Ovid says (Met. 9, 710) that, by a " pious fraud," the
deception passed unnoticed (*Impercepta pia mendacia fraude latebant*).

2102A. Piano, pianissimo,
Senza parlar.　　Sterbini, Barbiere d. Seviglia, 1, 1.　Music
by Rossini.—*Quietly, quietly, speak not a word!*

2103. Pictoribus atque poetis
Quidlibet audendi semper fuit æqua potestas.
Scimus, et hanc veniam petimusque damusque vicissim.
Hor. A. P. 9.

Poets and painters (sure you know the plea)
Have always been allowed their fancy free.
I own it: 'tis a fair excuse to plead:
By turns we claim it, and by turns concede.—*Conington.*

2104. Piger scribendi ferre laborem,
Scribendi recte; nam, ut multum, nil moror.　　Hor. S. 1, 4, 12.

Fluent, yet indolent, he would rebel
Against the toil of writing, writing well;
Not writing much, for that I grant you.—*Conington.*

2105. Pingo in æternitatem.—*I paint for posterity.*

On Agatharchus, the scene painter, boasting of his rapidity of execution,
Zeuxis quietly remarked, Ἐγὼ δὲ πολλῷ χρόνῳ. Plut. Vitæ, p. 190 (Pericles
13, 2).—*But I paint for a long time.* In id. Mor. p. 113 (*De Amicorum
Multit.* 5, p. 94 *f*), the rejoinder is reported as: Ὁμολογῶ ἐν πολλῷ χρόνῳ
γράφειν, καὶ γὰρ εἰς πολύν—*I confess I take a long time, but then I paint for
a long time.*

2106. Plato enim mihi unus instar est omnium. Antimachus ap. Cic. Brut. 51, 191.—*To my mind Plato alone is worth them all.*

2107. Plausus tunc arte carebat. Ov. A. A. 1, 113.—*In those days applause was genuine and unaffected.* Said of the games held by Romulus. Cf. id. ibid. 106, "Scena sine arte fuit"—*The stage then was devoid of art.*

2108. Plebs venit, ac virides passim disjecta per herbas.
Potat, et accumbit cum pare quisque sua.   Ov. F. 3, 525.

   Holiday-Making.
   Stretch'd on the grass, the people, far and wide,
   Drink and carouse, each by his sweetheart's side.—*Ed.*

2109. Plerumque stulti risum dum captant levem,
   Gravi destringunt alios contumelia,
   Et sibi nocivum concitant periculum.
      Phædr. 1, 29, 1.—*Fools, generally, in trying to raise a silly laugh, wound others with gross affronts and cause grave danger to themselves.*

2110. Pluma haud interest. Plaut. Most. 2, 1, 60.—*There isn't the odds of a feather.* Not a pin to choose between them.

2111. Plura sunt, Lucili, quæ nos terrent quam quæ premunt; et sæpius opinione quam re laboramus. Sen. Ep. 13, 4.—*We are often more frightened than hurt; and suffer more from imagination than reality.* He repeats the idea in his Thyest. 572, "Pejor est bello timor ipse belli"—*The fear of war (battle) is worse than war itself.* ——

2112. Pluris est oculatus testis unus quam auriti decem.
   Qui audiunt audita dicunt: qui vident, plane sciunt.
      Plaut. Truc. 2, 6, 8.—*One eye-witness is worth ten who speak from hearsay. Hearers can only tell what they heard; those who see, know the fact positively.*

   Cf. ὦτα γὰρ τυγχάνει ἀνθρώποισι ἐόντα ἀπιστότερα ὀφθαλμῶν. Hdt. 1, 8 (Candaules to Gyges).—*Men's ears are mostly less trustworthy than their eyes.*

2113. Plus aloes quam mellis habet. Juv. 6, 181.—*He has in him more aloes than honey.* Descriptive of a writer whose strength lies in sarcasm.

2114. Plus ça change, plus c'est la même chose. Alph. Karr, En Fumant, Paris (Lévy), 1861, p. 54. (*V.* "Esprit d'Alphonse Karr," Paris, 1877, p. 110). — *The more changes there are, the more does it seem to be only the same thing over again.*

   Witty aphorism, suggested by the successive constitutions etc., under which France has lived since the Revolution. Karr was fond of repeating the *mot*, and made it the title of two volumes of his collected political essays in 1875. Like every other "original" remark, the saying had been anticipated—by Shakespeare, *e.g.*, who, in *As You Like It*, 1, 1, has: "*Oliver.* Good monsieur Charles!—what's the new news at the new court? *Charles.* There's no news at the court, sir, but the old news." In the Vaudeville of *Les Auvergnats* of Désaugiers and Gentil, Paris (1812), sc. 2, occurs the line, "Il y a de nouveau que c'est toujours la même chose." Sixty years later the same thought was echoed in the *Fille de Madame Angot* (1, 14), of Clairville, Siraudin and Koning, where Clairette observes that, after all, the Directory, Consulate, and Empire were only the monarchy over again, and therefore concludes that,

C' n'était pas la peine,
Non, pas la peine, assurément,
De changer de gouvernement.

*** *V.* Alex. pp. 80-1 and 234-5; and Fumag. No. 577.

2115. Plus dolet quam necesse est, qui ante dolet quam necesse sit. Sen. Ep. 98, 8.—*He who grieves before he need, grieves more than he need.*

2116. Plus fait douceur que violence. La Font. 6, 3 (*Phébus et Borée,* fin.). —*Gentleness does more than violence.*

2117. Plus je vis d'étrangers, plus j'aimai ma patrie. De Belloy, *Siége de Calais,* 2, 3 (Paris, 1765, p. 28). Harcourt loq.—*The more I saw of foreigners the more I loved my own country.* Generally qu., even by Voltaire to the author himself (Letter of Mar. 31, 1761), as "Plus je vis *l'étranger,*" etc.

2118. Plus ne m'est rien, rien ne m'est plus. —*Everything to me now is nothing.* Motto adopted by Valentine Visconti (daughter of Gian Galeazzo Visconti, Duke of Milan) after the death of her husband Louis de Bourbon, son of Charles V. of France, in 1407.

2119. Plus salis quam sumptus. Nep. Att. 13, 2.—*More taste than expense.* Said of Atticus' house on the Quirinal.

2120. Plus vetustis nam favet
Invidia mordax, quam bonis præsentibus. Phædr. 5, Prol. 8.

For carping envy always spares
Old things, rather than modern wares.—*Ed.*

2121. Poema . . . ita festivum, ita concinnum, ita elegans, nihil ut fieri possit argutius. (ic. Pison. 29, 70.—*A poem so gay, neat and elegant, that nothing could be more brilliant in its way.*

2122. Point d'argent, point de Suisse. Racine, Plaideurs, 1, 1 (Petit-Jean loq.) —*No money, no Swiss.* Intended in the play as a hit at the Swiss Guards. the proverb is used to signify that if you want a thing, you must pay for it. Nothing for nothing.

Quit., p. 657, says that the words were used by Albert de la Pierre to the French Marshal Lautrec during the campaign of 1522 in the Milanese, as representative of the Swiss mercenaries who constituted the Marshal's chief source of defence. Strictly business-like, as is their national character, the Swiss soldiers insisted on prompt payment for their services. It was either *argent ou congé. See* also Fumag. 1209.

2123. Πολλοί τοι ναρθηκοφόροι, Βάκχοι δέ τε παῦροι.   Prov. in Plat.
Phædo, 69 C. cap. 13.—*Many carry the wands* in the Bacchanal
procession, *but few are inspired by the god.* Many officials, few
initiates; many versifiers, few poets; many sciolists, few men
of science, and many called, but few chosen.

2124. Πολὺ κρεῖττόν ἐστιν ἕν καλῶς μεμαθηκέναι,
ἢ πολλὰ φαύλως περιβεβλῆσθαι πράγματα.
                                              Men. Incert. Fr. p. 1033.
> Far better 'tis to have learnt one thing well,
> Than t' aim at many things imperfectly.—*Ed.*

2125. Ponamus nimios gemitus ; flagrantior æquo
Non debet dolor esse viri, nec vulnere major.   Juv. 13, 11.
> Then moderate thy grief; 'tis mean to show
> An anguish disproportioned to the blow.—*Gifford.*

2126. Pone seram, cohibe; sed quis custodiet ipsos
Custodes?   Juv. 6, 347.
> Clap on a lock, keep watch and ward !
> But who the guards themselves shall guard?—*Ed.*

Fumag., *l.c.,* points out the γελοῖον γὰρ τόν γε φύλακα φύλακος δεῖσθαι in
Plat. Rep. 3, 403. – *It would be ridiculous indeed if a watchman needed a
watcher.*

2127. Ποντίων τε κυμάτων
Ἀνήριθμον γέλασμα.
ÆEsch. Prom. 89.—*"Of ocean waves that smile innumerous,"*
Plumptre. Keble (*Christ. Year,* Sec. Sunday after Trinity) speaks
of the " many-twinkling smile of ocean," and Lucretius (5, 1005),
of " ridentibus undis."

2128. Ponto nox incubat atra,
Intonuere poli et crebris micat ignibus æther.   Virg. A. 1, 89.
> *A Storm at Sea.*
> Clouds black as night brood o'er the deep :
> The thunder rolls, the lightnings leap.—*Ed.*

Cf. the description of a storm at sea in Pacuvius, Incert. 45.

2129. Populus me sibilat ; at mihi plaudo
Ipse domi, simul ac nummos contemplor in arca. Hor. S. 1, 1, 66.
> *The Miser.*
> Folks hiss me, said he, but myself I clap
> When I tell o'er my treasures on my lap.—*Conington.*

2130. Porro unum est necessarium.   Vulg. Luc. 10, 42.—*But one thing
is needful.*

2131. Post cœnam stabis, aut passus mille meabis. Coll. Salern. v. 212
(vol. i. p. 451).—*After supper you should either stand, or walk a
mile:* also, Post prandium stabis, post cœnam ambulabis—*After
dinner rest a while, after supper walk a mile*

2132. Post mediam noctem visus quum somnia vera. Hor. S. 1, 10, 33.
—*He appeared to me after midnight, when dreams are true.*

2133. Πότερα θέλεις σοι μαλθακὰ ψευδῆ λέγω,
ἢ σκλήρ' ἀληθῆ; φραζε· σὴ γὰρ ἡ κρίσις.   Eur. Fr. 853.

Truth v. Flattery.

Wouldst thou then have me tell thee smooth-lipped lies,
Or stubborn truths? It is for thee to say.—*Ed.*

2134. Pour être assez bon, il faut l'être trop.   Prov.—*In order to be good enough, one must* (often) *be too good.* It is best to err on the side of benevolence.

2135. Pour moi, menacé du naufrage,
Je dois, en affrontant l'orage,
Penser, vivre et mourir en roi.

" Fédéric " (Fredk. II. of Prussia), Œuvres Complettes, 1790, 8vo, vol. xi. (Corresp. avec Voltaire, vol. ii. Lettre cxv.), pp. 257-8.—*As for me, threatened as I am with shipwreck, I ought to think, live and die as befits a king.* Written three days before the battle of Mersebourg (October 9, 1757), when the fortunes of Prussia were trembling in the balance.

2136. Pour obtenir un bien si grand, si précieux,
J'ay fait la guerre aux Rois, je l'eusse faite aux Dieux.

Isaac Du Ryer, Alcionée, 3, 5 (from *Alcionee*, Tragedie de P. DV Ryer, Paris, MDCXXXX. p. 48).   Alcionée loq.:

To win such a treasure of price, I have even
Taken arms against kings, and I would against Heaven.—*Ed.*

2137. Pour qui ne les craint pas il n'est point de prodiges.   Volt. Semiramis, 2, 7.—*There are no miracles for those who fear them not.*

2138. Ποῦ στῶ.—*Where I may stand.* A base; a standpoint; a footing; a "locus standi"; a "Poû stô."

Phrase traditionally connected with the name of Archimedes (212 B.C.), who said that, given a sufficient fulcrum or standpoint, he could move the earth, Δὸς μοι ποῦ στῶ καὶ κινῶ τὴν γῆν. Pappus Alexandr. Collectio, lib. viii., prop. 10, § xi. (ed. Hultsch, Berlin, 1878). Tzetzes (ed. J. Bekker) reproduces the original Doric of Archimedes' saying, δόμμυ πᾶ βῶ καὶ χαριστίωνι τὰν γᾶν κινάσω πᾶσαν—*Give me a base, and I will move the whole earth with a lever.* The Latin form is, "Da ubi consistam, et terram movebo," and the conditions under which the proposition in question might be actually carried out have been elaborated by Jas. Ferguson, the astronomer. His well-known exclamation, Εὑρηκα (*I have found it!*), is said to have escaped his lips in the bath, on solving the problem proposed to him by King Hiero, viz., the amount of alloy used by the goldsmith in making the golden crown ordered by the king. Overjoyed and quite overpowered by the discovery, Archimedes leapt out of the water and ran out into the street, just as he was, shouting, "*Heureka heureka!*" See Büchmann, pp. 451-2; Ferguson (James), *Astronomy Explained*, etc., London, 1803, chap. 7, p. 83; and Vitruvius Pollio, *De Architectura*, ix. 215 fin. and 216.

2139. Præcepto monitus, sæpe te considera.   Phædr. 3, 8, 1.—*Warned by the lesson, often consider your own case.*

2140. Præcipuum munus annalium reor, ne virtutes sileantur, atque pravis dictis factisque ex posteritate et infamia metus sit.
Tac. A. 3, 65.
History.

This I hold to be the chief office of history, to rescue virtuous actions from oblivion, and to make men fear the infamy which posterity will surely attach to vile words and deeds.

2141. Præmissi, non amissi.   St Cyprian, De Mortalit, c. 15.—*Not lost, but gone before.*   St Cyprian bids us not to sorrow for the faithful departed, Quum sciamus non eos amitti, sed præmitti—*Being assured that they are not lost, but gone before.*   Sen. Ep. 63, 16, fin. has, Quem putamus perisse, præmissus est—*Whom you deem lost, is (only) gone before.*

2142. Præsertim ut nunc sunt mores; adeo res redit;
Si quis quid reddit, magna habenda 'st gratia.
Ter. Phorm. 1, 2, 5 (Davus loq.).—*Especially as times are now.   Things are come to such a pass, that a man must be thanked extremely if he only pay his debts.*

2143. Prætulit arma togæ, sed pacem armatus amavit.
Juvit sumta ducem, juvit dimissa potestas.
Casta domus, luxuque carens, corruptaque nunquam
Fortuna domini: clarum et venerabile nomén.   Luc. 9, 199.

Pompey.
Arms he preferred to peaceful civic dress,
Yet, e'en in arms, was Peace his true mistréss.
Pleas'd was he to resign. or to retain
The helm of power: his household, chaste and plain,
Was ne'er corrupted by its master's fame—
He leaves a proud and venerable name.—*Ed.*

2144. Prendre sur les anciens, c'est pirater au delà de la ligne ; mais piller les modernes, c'est filouter au coin des rues.   Chamfort, Max., vol. ii. p. 85.—*Borrowing from ancient writers is privateering on the high seas; but pilfering modern authors is like picking pockets at the street-corner.*

2145. Prima et maxima peccantium est pœna. peccasse . . . quoniam sceleris in scelere supplicium est.   Sen Ep. 97, 12.—*The first and greatest punishment of sinners, is the sin itself; since the penalty of crime lies in its commission.*   Cf. id. de Ira, 3, 26, 2, Maxima est factæ injuriæ pœna, peccasse.

2146. Primo avulso, non deficit alter Aureus.   Virg. A. 6, 143.
The Golden Bough.
One plucked, another fills its room,
And burgeons with like precious bloom.—*Conington.*

Altered to *Uno* avulso, etc., the line was put up by Carmeline, a well-known Parisian tooth-drawer of the seventeenth century, over his door, to signify that if it were necessary to remove a patient's tooth, another was forthcoming to supply its place. V. *Chevræana* (Urbain Chevreau), Paris, 1697, Pt. 1, p. 142.

2147. Primum Graius homo mortaleis tollere contra
Est oculos ausus, primusque obsistere contra.
Quem neque fama deûm, nec fulmina, nec minitanti
Murmure compressit cælum : sed eo magis acrem
Irritât animi virtutem, effringere ut arta
Naturæ primus portarum claustra cupiret.
Ergo vivida vis animi pervicit, et extra
Processit longe flammantia mœnia mondi :
Atque omne immensum peragravit mente animoque;
Unde refert nobis victor, quid possit oriri,
Quid nequeat : finita potestas denique quoique
Quanam sit ratione, atque alte terminus hærens.
Quare relligio pedibus subjecta, vicissim
Obteritur, nos exæquat victoria cælo.   Lucr. 1, 67.

Epicurus.

A Greek was he who first raised mortal eyes,
And lodged his daring challenge to the skies :
Nor could the thought of gods, or muttered thunder,
Or angry lightning keep th' inquirer under ;
But rather gave his mind a keener zest,
Urging him on in the mysterious quest ;
So that he longed to burst in Nature's portals
That barred the secret from the eyes of mortals.
Thus, the keen vigour of his mind prevailed
And the bright bastions of the world outsailed.
His reason and his soul's intelligence
Swept the whole area of that void immense.
Thence he return'd victorious, to declare
What men might hope for and what cease to fear ;
The law, in short, by which all power that is
Lies within fixed, unvarying boundaries.
Thus crushing superstition 'neath his feet,
Victorious man and gods as equals meet.—*Ed.*

2148. Primus in Indis.—*First in India.*   Motto of the 39th Foot.

2149. Primus in orbe deos fecit timor.   Petr. Fr. 27, from whom it was borrowed *verbatim* by Statius, T. 3, 661.—*It was fear first made the gods.*   Crébillon says, in his Xercès (1749), 1, 1 (Artaban loq.) : " La crainte fit les dieux ; l'audace a fait les rois "—*Fear made the gods ; audacity made kings.*   If it be true that fear made the gods, the question remains, Who made fear?

2150. Principes mortales, rempublicam æternam.   Tac. A. 3, 6.—*Princes are mortal, the republic* (the state) *is eternal.*

2151. Principibus placuisse viris non ultima laus est.   Hor. Ep. 1, 17, 35.—*To have pleased the great is no slight praise.*

2152. Principiis obsta: sero medicina paratur
Quum mala per longas convaluere moras.   Ov. R. A. 91.

> Check the first symptoms: medicine's thrown away
> When sickness has grown stronger by delay.—*Ed.*

2153. Priusquam incipias, consulto; et, ubi consulueris, mature facto
opus est.   Sall. C. 1.—*Before you begin, deliberation is necessary,
but, after counsel taken, speedy execution is required.*

2154. Pro aris et focis.   Cic. N.D., 3, 40, 94.—*For altars and hearths.
For hearth and home.*

> A common saying, meaning the defence of one's nearest and dearest; as
> in Sall. C. 59, 5: Pro patria, pro liberis, pro aris atque focis suis cernere—
> *To fight for country, children, for hearth and home.*   Amongst the Romans,
> the family or household gods (*Penates*) had their altars (*aræ*) in the *im-
> pluvium*, and the tutelar deities of each dwelling (*Lares*) their *niches* round
> the hearth or ingle-nook (*foci*).

2155. Pro captu lectoris habent sua fata libelli.   Terent. Maurus, De
Literis, Syllabis, etc., line 1286.—*The fortune of a book depends
upon the opinion of the reader.*

2156. Proclivi scriptioni præstat ardua.   J. A. Bengel.—*The more difficult the reading, the more likely is it to be the right one.*   See his
Apparatus Criticus ad N. Test., Introd., § 34, p. 69 (Tubingæ,
1763, 4°).

> This canon of criticism, called by Scrivener (Introd. to Criticism of N. T.,
> 1883, p. 493) "Bengel's prime canon," is generally misunderstood and mis-
> applied.   *Proclivis scriptio*, says Dr Abbott, "is not a reading easy to under-
> stand, but one into which the scribe (copvist) would easily fall; and *scriptio
> ardua* is that which would come less naturally to him.   The question is
> not of the interpreter, but of the scribe." (Internat. Crit. Commentary,
> Lond., 1897, p. xlv, *Epp. to the Ephesians and Colossians.*)   Bengel himself
> qu., *à propos*, Lactant. 3, 8 (Migne, p. 370 A), *Bonorum natura in arduo
> posita est; malorum, in præcipiti.*

2157. Procul O! procul este, profani.   Virg. A. 6, 258.

> Hence, ye profane! unhallowed ones, far hence!—*Ed.*

2158. Proh Pudor!   Mart. 10, 68, 6.—*Fie, for shame!*   The ingenious
Mr Hare (A. J. C.), in his *Story of My Life* (vol. ii. p. 69), relates instances of two English families (Greene-Wilkinson and
Geo. Cavendish) each having fortunes left to them, *proh pudor*—
for opening a "pew-door" to an elderly gentleman!

2159. Promessi sposi.—*Affianced lovers.*   Title of the well-known novel
of Alessandro Manzoni (1825-7).

2160. Promettre c'est donner, espérer c'est jouir.   Delille, *Jardins* (1782),
Chant 2.—*Promising is giving, and hoping is realising.*

> To this (A. R. B. Alissan) de Chazet replied, in the time of the "Terror"
> (*v.* Fourn. *L.D.A.*, pp. 156-7):

> Ah! s'il est vrai que l'espérance
> Au sein des plus affreux tourments,
> Soit pour nous une jouissance,
> Nous jouissons depuis longtemps.

2161. Promittas facito: quid enim promittere lædit?
Pollicitis dives quilibet esse potest. Ov. A. A. 1, 443.

> Promise at large! what harm in promises?
> All may be rich in such commodities.—*Ed.*

2162. Pronaque quum spectent animalia cætera terram,
Os homini sublime dedit, cælumque tueri
Jussit, et erectos ad sidera tollere vultus. Ov. M. 1, 84.

> *The Creation of Man.*
> Thus while the brute creation downward bend
> Their sight, and to their earthy mother tend,
> Man looks aloft, and with uplifted eyes
> Beholds his own hereditary skies.—*Dryden.*

2163. Proprium humani ingenii est odisse quem læseris. Tac. Agr. 42.
—*'Tis characteristic of man to hate those he has injured.*

> Cf. Hoc habent pessimum animi fortuna insolentes; quos læserunt, et
> oderunt. Sen. de Ira, 2, 33, 1.—*Fortune's minions have no worse trait than
> this—they hate those whom they have injured.*
>
> Cf. Dryden, *Conquest of Granada,* Pt. 2, A. 1, Sc. 2.
> Forgiveness to the injured does belong,
> For they ne'er pardon who have done the wrong.

2164. Pro quibus ut meritis referatur gratia, jurat
Se fore mancipium tempus in omne tuum. Ov. Ep. 4, 5, 39.

> Thanks for such favours that he may repay,
> Your faithful slave he vows to be for aye.—*Ed.*

2165. Pro re nata. Cic. Att. 7. 14, 3.—*For present circumstances.*

2166. Pro re nitorem, et gloriam pro copia:
Qui habent, meminerint sese unde oriundi sient. Plaut. Aul.
3, 6, 5.—*Smartness for men of means, and parade according to
a man's circumstances. Those who "possess" should remember
their origin.*

2167. Prospera lux oritur, linguisque animisque favete:
Nunc dicenda bono sunt bona verba die. Ov. F. 1, 71.
—*A happy day is dawning, let your words and thoughts be
propitious On so auspicious a day nought but auspicious words
should be spoken.*

2168. Prosperum ac felix scelus Virtus vocatur. Sen. Herc. Fur. 251.
—*Crime when it speeds and prospers, virtue's called:* and id.
Hippol. 598, Honesta quædam scelera successus facit—*Success
makes some crimes quite honourable deeds.*

> Treason doth never prosper, what's the reason?
> Why if it prosper, none dare call it treason.
> —*Sir John Harrington* (†1612), Epigr. **4,** 5.

2169. Pro virtute erat felix temeritas. Sen. Ben. 1, 13.—*He showed
a successful recklessness which passed for valour.* Said of
Alexander the Great.

2170. Provocarem ad Philippum, inquit, sed sobrium.   Val. Max. 6, 2,
Ext. 1.—*I will appeal to Philip, she said, but to Philip sober.*

Appeal of a foreign woman against judgment pronounced by Philip, King
of Macedon, when he was tipsy. The appeal was allowed, and, on the
King's recovering his sobriety, the sentence reversed. Hence the common
saying of *appealing from Philip drunk to Philip sober;* when your opponent,
or judge, is so led away by passion, excitement, or what not, as to be
unable to take a reasonable view of the case.

2171. Proximus ardet Ucalegon.   Virg. A. 2, 311.—*Your neighbour
Ucalegon's house is on fire.*   Danger threatens you.   Applicable
to the rapid spread of war or epidemics.

2172. Proximus a tectis ignis defenditur ægre.   Ov. R. A. 625.—*It is
difficult to keep off a fire when next door is in flames.*

2173. Proximus huic gradus est, bene desperare salutem,
Seque semel vera scire perisse fide.   Ov. Ep. 3, 7, 23.
—*The next best thing is to despair of safety altogether, and to
feel assured that one is ruined for good and all.*

2174. Proximus sum egomet mihi.   Ter. And. 4, 1, 12.—*I am my own
nearest kin.*   Charity begins at home.   Take care of number one.

2175. Ψευδῶν δὲ καιρὸν ἔσθ' ὅπου τιμᾷ θεός.   Æsch. Fr. 273.—"*There is
a time when God doth falsehood prize!*"   Plumptre tr.

2176. Ψυχῇ βίαιον οὐδὲν ἔμμονον μάθημα.   Plat. Rep. 7, 536 E.—*No
forced learning ever lasts.*   An authoritative condemnation of
the art of "cramming."   Shakesp. "Taming of the Shrew," 1, 1,
says:
No profit grows where is no pleasure ta'en,
In brief, sir, study what you most affect.

2177. Ψυχῆς ἰατρεῖον.   Diod. Sic. 1, 49.—*Hospital* (or *surgery*) *for the
mind.*   Inscr. over the Library of Osymandyas, King of Kings,
at Thebes.

In the Latin form, *Nutrimentum spiritus,* it stands over the R. Library
of Berlin, built 1780 by Fredk. the Great; although "Animi medicina" (*or*
"officina") would have been a more correct rendering.   In the sick-room
at Winchester School is written, ψυχῆς νοσούσης εἰσὶν ἰατροὶ λόγοι. Æsch.
Prom. 378.—*Words are physicians of a mind diseased.*   Cp. Menand. Inc.
Fab., Fr. xxiii. (p. 976):
λύπης ἰατρός ἐστιν ἀνθρώποις λόγος·
ψυχῆς γὰρ οὗτος μόνος ἔχει θελκτήρια.

Words are the medicine for human grief;
Nought acts upon the soul with such a charm.—*Ed.*

2178. Pudet et hæc opprobria nobis
Et dici potuisse, et non potuisse refelli.
Ov. M. 1, 758.—*It is disgraceful that such slander could
have been said against us, and should be incapable of refutation.*
To hear an open slander is a curse;
But not to find an answer is a worse.—*Dryden.*

2179. Pulchra accipiat. Tr. of ἡ καλὴ λαβέτω. Lucian, Dial. 9, 5, 1.— *Let the beauty have it* ("For the most fair"), inscribed on the Golden Apple awarded by Paris to Venus, in preference to Juno and Minerva.

2180. Punitis ingeniis, gliscit auctoritas: neque aliud externi Reges, aut qui eadem sævitia usi sunt, nisi dedecus sibi atque illis gloriam peperere. Tac. A. 4, 35.

Liberty of the Press.

The influence exerted by men of genius is only increased by persecution; and all that foreign sovereigns, or such as have adopted their cruel policy, have effected, has been merely to bring obloquy upon themselves, and glory on the author whom they have proscribed.

Q.

2181. Quæ caret ora cruore nostro? Hor. C. 2, 1, 36.—*What shore is not watered with our blood?*

The line seems "made" for some highly-distinguished regiment that had covered itself with glory in all parts of the world, and a proud motto it would be: none prouder. Apparently, however, it has never been adopted in the annals of the British army, and still remains at the disposal of the Corps that shall best deserve it.

2182. Quæ latet inque bonis cessat non cognita rebus,
Apparet virtus arguiturque malis. Ov. T. 4, 3, 79.

In prosp'rous times true worth to hide is wont;
'Tis trouble brings the hero to the front.—*Ed.*

2183. Quæ lucis miseris tam dira cupido? Virg. A. 6, 721.

This direful longing for the light,
Whence comes it, say, and why?—*Conington.*

Originally said of the souls in the nether world who were eagerly awaiting re-incarnation in other forms, the line seems to find an application in the passionate "clinging to life" of those who have been denied everything that makes life worth living.

2184. Quæ peccamus juvenes, luimus senes. Prov. (Chil. p. 481, Malum Conduplicatum).—*We pay in old age the penalty of excesses in youth.*

2185. Quæ prosunt omnibus artes.—*Arts that are of service to all.* Motto of the Surgeons' Company.

2186. Quæque ipse miserrima vidi, Et quorum pars magna fui. Virg. A. 2, 5.—*Scenes of misery which I myself witnessed, and in which I took a principal part.*

2187. Quæ regio in terris nostri non plena laboris? Virg. A. 1, 460.— *Search the world through—where is our work not found?* Appropriate motto of the R. Engineers. Strictly speaking, it means, "What part of the world is not full of our troubles (*or* sad story)?"

2188. Quærere ut absumant, absumta requirere certant;
Atque ipsæ vitiis sunt alimenta vices.

> Ov. F. 1, 213.—*Men struggle to acquire in order to spend,
> and when it is spent they begin the struggle again, the vicissitudes
> themselves serving to feed their passions.*

2189. Quæris Alcidæ parem? Nemo est nisi ipse. Sen. Herc. Fur. 84.
—*Do you seek Alcides' equal? None but himself can be his
match.*

> Cf. Louis Theobald († 1744), *Double Falsehood*, 3, 1. (Lond., 1728, 8º,
> p. 25).
>
> > *Julio.* None but itself can be its parallel.

2190. Quæ sint, quæ fuerint, quæ mox ventura trahantur. Virg. G. 4, 393.
—*What is, what has been, and what shall be in time to come.*
Past, present, and future.

2191. Quæ te dementia cepit? Virg. E. 2, 69.—*What madness has
seized you?*

2192. Quæ venit ex tuto, minus est accepta voluptas. Ov. A. A. 3, 603.
—*Pleasure that is indulged in without risk loses half its attrac-
tion.* Stolen waters are sweet, and bread eaten in secret is
pleasant.

2193. Quæ virtus et quanta, boni, sit vivere parvo. Hor. S. 2, 2, 1.

> What and how great the virtue, friends, to live
> On what the gods with frugal bounty give.—*Francis.*

2194. Qualem commendes etiam atque etiam aspice ; ne mox
Incutiant aliena tibi peccata pudorem. Hor. Ep. 1, 18, 76.

> *Testimonials to Character.*
>
> Look round and round the man you recommend,
> For yours will be the shame should he offend.—*Conington.*

2195. Qualis artifex pereo ! Suet. Nero, 49.—*What an artist is lost in me!*

> Said by Nero shortly before his death while giving directions as to his
> funeral. He then stabbed himself, and, as he lay dying, his actual last
> words, to the Prætorian Guaids who came in to dispatch him, were, *Sero*
> (It is too late), and, with reference to their oath of allegiance, *Hæc est fides?*
> (Is this your fidelity to me ?)

2196. Qualis populea mœrens Philomela sub umbra
Flet noctem, ramoque sedens miserabile carmen
Integrat, et mæstis late loca quæstibus implet. Virg. G. 4, 511.

> *The Nightingale.*
>
> So 'mid the poplar's shade sad Philomel
> All night doth weep, and sitting on the bough
> Her dirge renews, while the surrounding air
> Is vocal with the lovelorn dolorous lay.—*Ed.*

2197. Quam continuis et quantis longa senectus
Plena malis !

> Juv. 10, 190.—*What constant and grievous troubles beset
> old age!*

2198. Quamdiu stabit Colyseus, stabit et Roma; quando cadet Colyseus, cadet Roma; quando cadet Roma, cadet et mundus. Carolus du Fresne du Cange (Ducange), Glossarium ad Scriptores med. et infimæ Latinitatis, Paris, 1678, vol. 1, col. 1049. Quoted by Gibbon (chap. lxxi.).

> While stands the Coliseum, Rome shall stand;
> When falls the Coliseum, Rome shall fall;
> And when Rome falls—the world.—*Byron*, "Ch. Harold," 4, 145.

2199. Quam inique comparatum est! hi qui minus habent
Ut semper aliquid addant divitioribus.
    Ter. Phorm. 1, 1, 7.—*How unjust is fate! that they who have but little should be always adding to the abundance of the rich!*

2200. Quam veterrumu 'st tam homini optumu 'st amicus. Plaut. Truc. 1, 2, 71.—*A man's oldest friend is his best friend.*

2201. Quamvis digressu veteris confusus amici,
    Laudo tamen.   Juv. 3, 1.

> I am loth to lose an old friend,
> But he's wise to go.—*Shaw.*

2202. Quand les vices nous quittent, nous nous flattons de la créance que c'est nous qui les quittons. La Rochef., § 197, p. 55.—*When vices forsake us, we flatter ourselves with the idea that it is we who are forsaking them.*

2203. Quand nous serons à dix, nous ferons une croix. Mol. L'Étourdi, 1, 11 (Mascarille loq.).—*When we get to ten, we will make a cross.* Clearing the ground and simplifying matters as we proceed.

> Prov. and phrase used in any enumeration of things, and particularly in reckoning up anyone's faults or virtues, successes or failures, as does Mascarille in the play, when counting up the several blunders committed by L'Étourdi in the course of the day. The figure 10 would represent the crowning-point, to be marked by a "croix," derived from the simple fact that the number is indicated by a St Andrew's Cross—**X**. *V.* Quitard, p. 275.

2204. Quand on a tout perdu, quand on n'a plus d'espoir,
    La vie est un opprobre, et la mort un devoir.   Volt. Mérope, 2, 7.

Despair.

Mérope. When all is lost, and hope's last gleam has fled,
    Life's a disgrace; our place is with the dead.—*Ed.*

Some jocular person has suggested as an alternative of line 2,

"D'un pan de sa chemise on se fait un mouchoir."

2205. Quand on est jeune, on se soigne pour plaire, et quand on est vieille, on se soigne pour ne pas déplaire. Mme. de Labrosse, (communicated orally).—*When a woman is young she keeps herself neat in order to please, and when she is old, to avoid displeasing.*

2206. Quand on est mort, c'est pour longtemps,
Dit un vieil adage
    Fort sage.   M. A. Désaugiers, Le Délire Bachique, init.

> When one is dead, it is for long;
> Says a sage old adage.—*Ed.*

Molière (Le Dépit Amoureux, 5, 4) makes Mascarille say, "On ne meurt qu'une fois, et c'est pour si longtemps." Voltaire, at forty-seven, in his verses to Mme du Châtelet, sentimentalises thus:

> On meurt deux fois, je le vois bien;
> Cesser d'aimer et d'être aimable,
> C'est une mort insupportable;
> Cesser de vivre, ce n'est rien.

2207. Quand on l'ignore, ce n'est rien;
Quand on le sait, c'est peu de chose.
    La Font. La coupe enchantée, l. 24 (Contes et Nouv.).

> 'Tis nothing, if you're unaware;
> And if you know, it's hardly more.—*Ed.*

2208. Quand on n'a pas ce que l'on aime,
Il faut aimer ce que l'on a.
    Corneille (Thos.), L'Inconnu, Nouv. Prologue (Crispin loq.).
—*When you have not what you love, you must fain love what you have.*   Fourn. (*L.D.A.*, pp. 192-3) observes that Bussy de Rabutin had quoted the lines nearly forty years before in writing to Mme. de Sévigné, May 23, 1667, and their authorship is unknown.

2209. Quandoque bonus dormitat Homerus!
Verum operi longo fas est obrepere somnum.
    Hor. A. P. 359.—*Sometimes good Homer himself even nods: but in so long a work it is allowable if there should be a drowsy interval or so.*

2210. Quandoquidem populus iste vult decipi, decipiatur.   J. A. Thuani (de Thou), Historia, 17, 7, Lond. (Bentley), 1733, fol. p. 587.—
Since this people insists on being deceived, let it be deceived.

Remark of Carlo Caraffa (†1561, when he was put to death by Pius IV.), nephew of Paul IV. (Giov. Pietro Caraffa), on observing the profound reverence with which his entry into Paris as Cardinal Legate was greeted by the populace, 1556 A.D.   Büchm., p. 120, finds the first half of the saying (*Mundus vult decipi*) in the *Paradoxa* of Seb. Franck, 1533, No. 236 (247).

2211. Quando ullum inveniet parem?   Hor. C. 1, 24, 8.—*When shall we look upon his like again?*

2212. Quand quelqu'un vous dit qu'il n'appartient à aucun parti, commencez par être sui qu'il n'est du votre. Mme. Swetchine, vol. 2, Pensée cxxxv.—*When anyone tells you that he belongs to no party, you may be quite sure that he does not belong to yours.*

2213. Quand sur une personne on prétend se régler,
C'est par les beaux côtez qu'il lui faut ressembler.
Mol. Femmes Savantes, 1, 1. Armande loq.:

> If the style of some friend you would fain emulate,
> His good points are the features you should imitate.—*Ed.*

*** For the *Ana* of this couplet, *v.* Fourn. *L.D.A.*, p. 107.

2214. Quand tout le monde a tort, tout le monde a raison. La Chaussée,
Gouvernante (1747), 1, 3. Œuvres, Paris, 1762, vol. 3, p. 84.
(Le Président to his son, Sainville).—*When all the world is
wrong, all the world is right:* meaning that the general con-
sensus of opinion cannot be mistaken in its estimate of facts,
although it may clash with particular theories. The unanimity
is too large to suppose the bias of an interested interpretation.

2215. Quand une fois j'ai pris ma résolution, je vais droit à mon but,
et je renverse tout de ma soutane rouge. Richelieu, ap. Fourn.
L.D.L., p. 256.—*Once I have made up my mind, I go straight to
the point, and sweep everything out of my way with my red
soutane.*

2216. Quand vous m'aurez tué, il ne me faudra que six pieds de
terre. Mathieu Molé. Biographie Universelle (1821), *art.* Molé
(Mathieu), p. 289.— *When you have killed me, I shall need no more
than six feet of ground.* Reply of Molé, President of Parliament
of Paris, when attempt was made to intimidate him by death
during the war of the Fronde.

2217. Quanti est sapere! Ter. Eun. 4, 7, 21.—*What a fine thing it is to
be clever!*

2218. Quanto quisque sibi plura negaverit,
A Dis plura feret. Nil cupientium
Nudus castra peto, et transfuga divitum
Partes linquere gestio. Hor. C. 3, 16, 21.

> He that denies himself shall gain the more
> From bounteous heaven. I strip me of my pride,
> Desert the rich man's standard, and pass o'er
> To bare contentment's side.—*Conington.*

2219. Quare tolle jocos: non est jocus esse malignum;
Nunquam sunt grati qui nocuere sales. Sen. Epigr. 5, 17.

Mauvaise Plaisanterie.

> Then cease your jokes; there lies no joke in spite:
> The wit that wounds can ne'er be in the right.—*Ed.*

2220. Quatuor sunt maxime comprehendendæ veritatis offendicula . . .
videlicet, fragilis et indignæ auctoritatis exemplum, consuetu-
dinis diuturnitas, vulgi sensus imperiti, et propriæ ignorantiæ
occultatio cum ostentatione sapientiæ apparentis. Rog. Bacon,

Opus Majus, 1, 1. — *The chief obstacles in the way of truth* (or *causes of error) are four:* viz., *the plea of an authority that does not deserve the name, long-standing habit, popular prejudice, and an ingrained ignorance that masquerades as so much knowledge.*

2221. Que diable allait-il faire dans cette galère?   Mol., Fourb. de Scapin (1671), 2, 11 (Géronte loq.). — *What the deuce was he doing in that galley?*   Said of any one who mixes himself up in a business in which he is clearly out of place.   Molière took the line from the *Pédant joué* (1654) of Cyrano de Bergerac, 2, 4 — *Que diable aller faire aussi dans la galère d'un Turc?*   V. No. 1189.

2222. Que la Suisse soit libre, et que nos noms périssent!   Lemierre, Guillaume Tell, 1, 1 (Tell to Melchtal). — *Let our names perish, provided Switzerland be free!*

2223. Que la terre est petite, à qui la voit des cieux!   Delille, Dithyrambe sur l'immortalité de l'âme. — *How small earth seems to him who views it from the skies!*

2224. Quel giorno più non vi leggemmo avante.   Dante, Inf. 5, 138. — *That day we read not any further.*   Francesca, speaking of her reading with Paolo the story of Lancelot and Guinevere.

2225. Quelque rare que soit le véritable amour, il l'est encore moins que la véritable amitié.   La Rochef., § 496, p. 91 — *However rare true love may be, it is not so uncommon as true friendship.*   " Rarum genus!" exclaims Cicero, speaking of friends really worthy of our esteem (Am. 79), "et quidem omnia præclara rara" — *A rare kind indeed! but, then, all admirable* (perfect) *things are rare.*

2226. Quelques seigneurs sans importance.   Meilhac and Lud. Halévy, Les Brigands, Operetta (1869), 2, 10. — *Some lords and gentlemen of no importance.*   Gloria-Cassis, introducing himself and suite to the brigand Pietro, (whom he takes for the Baron of Campotasso): — " Moi d'abord, le comte de Gloria-Cassis, grand d'Espagne de onzième classe, chef réel de l'ambassade . . . Pablo précepteur . . . *Quelques seigneurs sans importance.*"

2227. Que messieurs les assassins commencent!   Alph. Karr, Mm. les Assassins, 1885, Pref. — *Let the assassin-gentlemen begin first.*

> Celebrated phrase (of which the author was partic. proud) on the question of the abolition of the death-penalty.   Karr himself (*v. supra*) refers the reader to his *Guêpes* of 1840, where the qu. is not to be found: but *see* Alex. pp. 27-8.

2228. Quem recitas, meus est, O Fidentine, libellus: Sed male quum recitas, incipit esse tuus.   Mart. 1, 39.

> The verse you recite, Fidentinus, is mine: But recited so ill it begins to be thine. — *Ed.*

2229. Quem res plus nimio delectavere secundæ,
Mutatæ quatient.   Hor. Ep. 1, 10, 30.

> Take too much pleasure in good things, you'll feel
> The shock of adverse fortune makes you reel.— *Conington.*

2230. Quem sæpe transit casus aliquando invenit.   Sen. Herc. Fur. 328.
—Who oft escapes mishap is hit at last.

2231. Qu'est-ce que le Tiers État?--Tout.   Qu'a-t-il été jusqu'à
present dans l'ordre politique?—Rien.   Que demande-t-il?—A
être quelque chose. [Abbé Sieyès, Paris], 3ᵉ Edition, 1789.
*—What is the Third Estate?—Everything.   What has it been
hitherto in the political order?—Nothing.   What does it ask?—
To be something.*

> First words of Sieyès' celebrated pamphlet (pub. without name of author
> or place), which more than anything else hastened the inevitable change
> that was to sweep away the old French monarchy.   It was composed in
> 1788, made its appearance in the first days of the New Year, and was
> reprinted two or three times within the month.   Successive editions
> followed, which were circulated and read in every corner of the kingdom.
> Acc. to L. B. de Lauraguais (*Lettres à Mme. . . .*, Paris, 1802, pp. 161-2),
> Chamfort had hit upon a title of his own for the forthcoming brochure, and
> had made Sieyès a present of it.   Here it is—*Qu'est-ce que le Tiers État?—
> Tout.   Qu'a-t-il?—Rien?*   So tickled was he with the conceit, as to predict
> that it would be the only thing about the pamphlet that the public would
> remember.   That the "puritan Abbé" utilised his friend's suggestion is
> evident, although his own cautious modification of it, as quoted, was no
> better, considered as a statement of fact.

2232. Questo secol morto, al quale incombe
Tanta nebbia di tedio.   Leopardi, Canzone ad Angelo
Mai.—*This dead age of ours, that has hanging over it so great a
cloud of weariness.*

2233. Que votre âme et vos mœurs peintes dans vos ouvrages,
N'offrent jamais de vous que de nobles images.   Boil. L'A.P. 4, 91.

> Men's works reflect their character: take care
> That yours a noble heart and soul declare.—*Ed.*

2234. Que vouliez-vous qu'il fît contre trois?—Qu'il mourût!   Corneille,
Horace, 3, 6.

> *Julie.*   One against three—what *could* he do?
> *The elder Horace.*   Why, die!

> Chamfort (Caractères, i. p. 30) pretends that some one, who had seen
> the celebrated pantomimist, Noverre, represent this famous scene in his
> "Ballet" *Les Horaces* (Opera, Paris, 1777), suggested to the versatile artiste
> "de faire danser les *Maximes* de Larochefoucauld."   Casimir Delavigne,
> in his *Comédiens* (1821), 1, 2, reproduces the line to describe the case of a
> patient and his three doctors,—

> *Granville.*   Ils étaient trois docteurs, et pourtant—
> *Pembrock.*   Le pauvre homme!
>   Que vouliez-vous qu'il fît contre trois?
> *Granv.*   Qu'il mourût!

2235. Qui amant, ipsi sibi somnia fingunt.   Virg. E. 8, 108.—*People in love imagine dreams of their own.*

2236. Quia me vestigia terrent
Omnia te adversum spectantia, nulla retrorsum.   Hor. Ep. 1, 1, 74.

> I'm frightened at those footsteps: every track
> Leads to your home, but ne'er a one leads back.—*Conington.*

Reply of the fox to the sick lion who invited him into his den.   From the above has been formed the phrase *Vestigia nulla retrorsum,* "No stepping back again," "Retreat is impossible." Motto of Hampden, and of the Buckinghamshire regiment which he raised in the Great Rebellion.

2237. Qui asinum non potest, stratum cædit.   Prov.   (Petron. 45, 8).— *He who cannot touch the ass, beats the housings.* If you cannot find the real culprit, avenge yourself on the nearest, and generally most unoffending object.

2238. Qui Bavium non odit, amet tua carmina, Mævi;
Atque idem jungat vulpes, et mulgeat hircos.   Virg. E. 3, 90.

> Who hates not Bavius, may love Mævius' notes;
> And let the same yoke wolves, and milk he-goats.—*Ed.*

2239. Qui cavet, ne decipiatur, vix cavet, quum etiam cavet.
Etiam quum cavisse ratus est, sæpe is cautor captus est.   Plaut. Capt. 2, 2, 5 (Hegio loq.).—*He who is on his guard against deception, is scarce wary enough even at his wariest: even when he thinks he's safe, he's not so clever but what he's often caught.*

2240. Quicquid ages igitur, magna spectabere scena.   Ov. Ep. 3, 1, 59. —*Whatever therefore you do, will be displayed upon a large stage.* You will have a fine field for your talents.

2241. Quicquid agunt homines, votum, timor, ira, voluptas,
Gaudia, discursus, nostri est farrago libelli.   Juv. 1, 85.

> All that men do—their wishes, fear, and rage,
> Pleasure, joy, bustle, crowd my motley page.—*Ed.*

(Motto of first forty numbers of the *Tatler*, 1709.)

2242. Quicquid delirant reges, plectuntur Achivi.   Hor. Ep. 1, 2, 14.

> Let kings go mad and blunder as they may,
> The people in the end are sure to pay.—*Conington.*

Cf. Humiles laborant ubi potentes dissident. Phædr. 1, 30, 1.—*Humble folk are in danger when great ones fall out.* A new application was found for the qu., with reference to the power wielded by the Fourth Estate, when the German Emperor, William II., recalled the saying of Bismarck that "The windows which our Press smashes, we shall have to pay for." (V. *Times*, Jan. 23, 1900.) Almost every journal within the Kaiser's dominions was teeming at the time with acrimonious attacks upon the policy of England in S. Africa, and the reproof was intended to put some check upon the reckless malevolence thus displayed.

2243. Quicquid gerimus, fortuna vocatur.   Luc. 5, 292.—*All our exploits are put down to luck.*

2244. Quicquid in his igitur vitii rude carmen habebit,
Emendaturus, si licuisset, erat.
Ov. M. 1, Epigr. 5.—*Whatever faults may be found in this unpolished poem, the author would have corrected had time allowed.*

2245. Quicunque turpi fraude semel innotuit,
Etiamsi verum dicit, amittit fidem.
Phædr. 1, 10, 1.—*The man who has once been caught out in a shameful falsehood is not believed even if he tell the truth.*

From this, by way of Von Nicolay's poem of *Der Lügner*, has been formed the current German distich (*v.* Büchm. p. 415):

Wer einmal lügt, dem glaubt man nicht,
Selbst dann, wenn er die Wahrheit spricht.

Who once has lied, no man believes,
Though he speak truly, nor deceives.—*Ed.*

2246. Qui Curios simulant, et Bacchanalia vivunt. Juv. 2, 3.—*Who affect the principles of the Curii, and live like Bacchanals.* M. Curius Dentatus (Conqueror of Pyrrhus), *e.g.*, was noted for the simplicity of his life.

2247. Quid agis, dulcissime rerum? Hor. S. 1, 9, 4.—*How are you, sweetest of creatures?*

2248. Quid brevi fortes jaculamur ævo
Multa? quid terras alio calentes
Sole mutamus? patriæ quis exsul
Se quoque fugit?   Hor. C. 2, 16, 17.

With life so short, why such vast aims and high?
Why seek new climes, warm'd by another sun?
What exile, tho' his fatherland he fly,
Himself can also shun?—*Ed.*

2249. Quid crastina volveret ætas
Scire nefas homini.   Stat. Theb. 3, 562.

What coming ages may unfold,
To mortal man may not be told.—*Ed.*

2250. Quid datur a Divis felici optatius hora? Cat. 62, 30.—*What better boon can Heaven bestow than the happy nick of time?*

2251. Quid deceat, quid non, obliti. Hor. Ep. 1, 6, 62.—"*Lost to all self-respect, all sense of shame.*"—Conington. So also, on observing the proprieties in composition, Quid deceat, quid non, quo virtus, quo ferat error. Id. A. P. 308.—*Good taste or not; knowledge, or the reverse.*

2252. Quid, de quoque viro, et cui dicas, sæpe caveto. Hor. Ep. 1, 18, 68.

Beware, if there is room
For warning, what you mention, and to whom.—*Conington.*

2253. Quid domini faciant audent quum talia fures? Virg. E. 3, 16.—*What can the masters do, when their own servants take to thieving?*

2254. Quid enim contendat hirondo
      Cycneis?   Lucret. 3, 6.

> For how should swallows with the swan contend?

2255. Quid enim ratione timemus
      Aut cupimus? quid tam dextro pede concipis, ut te
      Conatus non pœniteat votique peracti?   Juv. 10, 4.

> For what, with reason, do we seek or shun?
> What plan, how happily soe'er begun,
> But, finished, we our own success lament,
> And rue the pains so fatally misspent?—*Gifford.*

2256. Quid enim salvis infamia nummis? Juv. 1, 48.—*What matters disgrace provided the money is safe?*

2257. Quid est dulcius otio litterato? Cic. Tusc. 5, 36, 105.—*What is sweeter than literary leisure?*

2258. Quid faciunt pauci contra tot millia fortes? Ov. F. 2, 229.—*What can a few gallant fellows do against so many thousand?*

2260. Quid leges sine moribus Vanæ proficiunt?   Hor. C. 3, 24, 35.

> And what are laws, unless obeyed
> In the same spirit they were made?—*Francis* (altered).

2261. Quid me alta silentia cogis Rumpere? Virg. A. 10, 63.—*Why force me to break this pent-up silence?*

2262. Quid, mea quum pugnat sententia secum?
      Quod petiit, spernit; repetit, quod nuper omisit?
      Æstuat et vitæ disconvenit ordine toto?   Hor. Ep. 1, 1, 97.

> How, if my mind's inconsequent? Rejects
> What late it longed for, what it loath'd affects?
> Shifts every moment, with itself at strife,
> And makes a chaos of an ordered life?—*Conington.*

2263. Quid mentem traxisse polo, quid profuit altum
      Erexisse caput, pecudum si more pererrant?
      Claud. Rapt. Pros. 3, 41.—*What are men the better for deriving a soul from heaven, and for being able to raise their countenance aloft, if they go astray after the manner of brute beasts?*

2264. Quid minuat curas, quid te tibi reddat amicum,
      Quid pure tranquillet, honos, an dulce lucellum,
      An secretum iter et fallentis semita vitæ?
      Hor. Ep. 1, 18, 101.—*(Ascertain) the secret which will relieve your cares, put you on good terms with yourself, and give you real peace of mind? Is it to be found in fame, or pleasant gains? Or in a retired and hidden path of life?*

2265. Quid non miraculo est quum primum in notitiam venit? Quam multa fieri non posse, prius quam sint facta judicantur?

Plin. 7, 1.—*What is there that does not seem wonderful the first time it becomes known? How many things are pronounced impossible until they have been accomplished?*

2266. Quid non mortalia pectora cogis,
   Auri sacra fames ?   Virg. A. 3, 56.

> Fell lust of gold ! abhorred, accurst !
> What will not man to slake such thirst ?—*Conington.*

2267. Quid novi ex Africa ?—*What novelty* (or *news*) *from Africa?*

> Pliny, 8, 16 (17), quotes the " vulgare Græciæ dictum, Semper Africam aliquid novi afferre," (*Africa is always bringing us something new*), evidently referring to the ἀεὶ Λιβύη φέρει τι καινόν, cited in Arist. Hist. Animalium, 8, 28, 7.

2268. Quid numeras annos ? vixi maturior annis.
   Acta senem faciunt ; hæc numeranda tibi.   Ov. Liv. 447.

> Why number years ? His years man oft outstrips.
> 'Tis deeds give age : let these be on your lips.—*Ed.*

2269. Quid obseratis auribus fundis preces ? Hor. Epod. 17, 53.—*Why do you pour your prayers into ears that are sealed against your petition?*

2270. Quid oportet
   Nos facere, a vulgo longe lateque remotos ?   Hor. S. 1, 6, 17.

> Say, how shall we, who differ far and wide
> From the mere vulgar, this great point decide ?—*Francis.*

2271. Quidquid præcipies, esto brevis; ut cito dicta
   Percipiant animi dociles, teneantque fideles.
   Omne supervacuum pleno de pectore manat.   Hor. A. P. 335.

> Whene'er you lecture, be concise : the soul
> Takes in short maxims, and retains them whole ;
> But pour in water when the vessel's filled,
> It simply dribbles over and is spilled.—*Conington.*

2272. Quidquid sub terra est, in apricum proferet ætas. Hor. Ep. 1, 6, 24.—*Time brings to light whate'er the earth conceals.*

2273. Quid quisque vitet, nunquam homini satis
   Cautum est in horas.
      Hor. C. 2, 13, 13.—*Man never takes sufficient precaution to shun the dangers of the hour.*

2274. Quid rides ?   Mutato nomine de te
   Fabula narratur.   Hor. S. 1, 1, 69.

> Wherefore do you laugh ?
> Change but the name, of thee the tale is told.—*Francis.*

2275. Quid Romæ faciam? mentiri nescio: librum
   Si malus est, nequeo laudare et poscere.   Juv. 3, 41.

> What should I do at Rome ? I cannot lie.
> If a book's bad, I'll neither praise, nor buy.—*Ed.*

2276. Quid si nunc cœlum ruat ?   Prov. ap. Ter. Heaut. 4, 3, 41.—*What if the sky were to fall now ?*   Improbabilities.

2277. Quid sit futurum cras fuge quærere, et
Quem sors dierum cunque dabit, lucro
     Appone.   Hor. C. 1, 9, 13.

> Oh ! ask not what the morn will bring,
>   But count as gain each day that chance
> May give you.—*Conington.*

2278. Quid tam difficile quam in plurimorum controversiis dijudicandis, ab omnibus diligi ? Consequeris tamen, ut eos ipsos quos contra statuas, æquos placatosque dimittas: itaque efficis ut, quum gratiæ causâ nihil facias, omnia tamen sint grata quæ facis. Cic. Or. 10, 34.—*What could be more difficult than that the judge who has to decide a multitude of cases should be universally esteemed? You, however, succeed in leaving a sense of justice and satisfaction even with those against whom judgment is given; so that though you do nothing by favour, all that you do is favourably received.* This high encomium, originally addressed to M. T. Brutus, was as happily as deservedly applied to Baron Bramwell on his retirement from the Bench (1881) by L. C. J. Coleridge.

2279. Quid te exempta juvat spinis de pluribus una? Hor. Ep. 2, 2, 212.

> Where is the gain in pulling from the mind
> One thorn, if all the rest remain behind?—*Conington.*

2280. Quid te vana juvant miseræ ludibria chartæ ?
Hoc lege, quod possit dicere vita, Meum est.   Mart. 10, 4, 7.

> Why with such silly trash your mind debase?
> Read what your conscience echoes—Just my case?—*Ed.*

2281. Quid tibi cum pelago ? Terra contenta fuisses. Ov. Am. 3, 8, 49.
— *What business had you with the sea ? You might have been content with the land.*

2282. Quid tibi tantopere est, mortalis, quod nimis ægreis
Luctibus indulges ? quid mortem congemis ac fles ?
Nam gratum fuerit tibi vita anteacta priorque,
Et non omnia, pertusum congesta quasi in vas,
Commoda perfluxere atque ingrata interiere ;
Quur non, ut plenus vitæ conviva, recedis
Æquo animoque capis securam, stulte, quietem ? Lucret. 3, 946.

> Why this deep grief, poor child of mortal breath,
> Why this sad weeping at the thought of death?
> If life has had its joys, and has not all
> Run thro' a sieve, but can some sweets recall ;
> Why dost thou not, like a replenished guest,
> Rise, foolish one, and calmly take thy rest?—*Ed.*

2283. Quid tristes querimoniæ,
Si non supplicio culpa reciditur ?   Hor. C. 3, 24, 33.

What can sad complaints avail
Unless sharp justice kill the taint of sin ?—*Conington.*

2284. Quid verum atque decens curo et rogo et omnis in hoc sum.
Hor. Ep. 1, 1, 11.—*Truth and taste, this is what occupies me,
what I am in search of and wholly absorbed in.*

2285. Quid victor gaudes ?   Hæc te victoria perdet !
Heu quanto regnis nox stetit una tuis !   Ov. F. 2, 811.

The Rape of Lucrece.
Why, conqueror, boast ? this victory all has lost :
How much a single night thy realm has cost !—*Ed.*

2286. Quid voveat dulci matricula majus alumno,
Qui sapere, et fari ut possit quæ sentiat, et cui
Gratia, fama, valetudo contingat abunde,
Et mundus victus, non deficiente crumena ?   Hor. Ep. 1, 4, 8.

What could fond nurse wish more for her sweet pet
Than friends, good looks, and health without a let,
A shrewd clear head, a tongue to speak his mind,
A seemly household, and a purse well lined.—*Conington.*

2287. Qui e nuce nuculeum esse volt frangit nucem.   Plaut. Curc.
1, 1, 55.—*Who would eat the kernel must first break the shell.*
No advantage is to be gained without effort.   Cf. " Il n'y a pas
d'omelette sans casser des œufs."

2288. Qui est-ce qui ne l'aimerait pas ? il est si vicieux. Album Perdu,
p. 97.—*Who can help loving him?   He is so essentially vicious.*
Said of Talleyrand.

2289. Qui est maître de sa soif est maître de sa santé. Prov.—*He who
is master of his thirst, is master of his health.*

2290. Quieta movere magna merces videbatur. Sall. C. 21.—*To upset
the settled order of things, they thought a handsome offer.*   The
bribe held out (with other inducements) by Catiline to the
following of desperadoes, young patrician profligates and gaol-
birds, whom he was rallying round the standard of his conspiracy.
For the reverse, " quieta *non* movere," *see* No. 1514.

2291. Qui facit per alium facit per se.   Law Max.—*He who does an act
through the medium of another party is in law considered as
doing it himself*—Broome, p. 784.   The maxim seems to be an
abbrev. of *Qui facit per alium est perinde ac si faciat per se
ipsum.* Boniface VIII., Liber Sextus Decretalium ("The Sext"),
Lib. V. tit. xx., de Regulis Juris, 72.

2292. Qui finem quæris amoris,
(Cedit amor rebus) res age; tutus eris.
Ov. R. A. 143.—*You seek to bring your love-making to an*

T

end. Then, since love and business don't agree, be occupied and you will be safe.

2293. Qui fingit sacros auro vel marmore vultus,
　　　Non facit ille deos: qui rogat, ille facit.　　Mart. 8, 24, 5.

> He makes no gods who carves in gold or stone;
> The man who worships makes the gods alone.—*Ed.*

2294. Qui fit, Mæcenas, ut nemo, quam sibi sortem
　　　Seu ratio dederit, seu fors objecerit, illa
　　　Contentus vivat; laudet diversa sequentes?　　Hor. S. 1, 1, 1.

> How comes it, say, Mæcenas, if you can
> That none will live like a contented man
> Where chance or choice directs, but each must praise
> The folk who pass through life by other ways?—*Conington.*

2295. Qui genus jactat suum,
　　　Aliena laudat.　　Sen. Herc. Fur. 340.

> Whoso boasteth of his birth,
> Praises but another's worth.—*Ed.*

2296. Qui homo mature quæsivit pecuniam,
　　　Nisi eam mature parcit, mature esurit.
　　　　　Plaut. Curc. 3, 1, 10.—*He who has got wealth betimes, unless he save betimes, will come to want betimes.*

2297. Qui jacet in terra non habet unde cadat.　Alanus de Insulis, Doctrinale Altum, seu Lib. Parabolarum, Daventry (Jac. de Breda), 1492, 8vo, p. 8 (no pagination).—*Who lies upon the ground can fall no lower.*

> This line being quoted—with the variation of *Qui procumbit humi*, for *Qui jacet in terra*—by Charles I. to M. Pomponne de Bellièvre (the French minister), who was for the king's flying, the ambassador replied, "Sire, on peut lui faire tomber la tête." *Opuscules* de M. Louis Du Four de Longuerue, Yverdon, 1784, vol. 2, pp. 260-1.　Cf. Bunyan, Pilgrim's Progress, Pt. 2: "He that is down needs fear no fall;" and Butler, Hudibras, 1, 3, 876: "He that is down can fall no lower."

2298. Qui me commôrit, melius non tangere, clamo,
　　　Flebit, et insignis tota cantabitur urbe.　　Hor. S. 2, 1, 45.

> 　　　　　But should one seek
> To quarrel with me, you shall hear him shriek.
> Don't say I gave no warning: up and down
> He shall be trolled and chorussed thro' the town.—*Conington.*

2299. Qui me délivrera des Grecs et des Romains?　Berchoux, Élégie (1801), Œuvres (Michaud),1829, vol. 4, p. 107.—*Who will deliver me from the Greeks and Romans?*

> Like Mr Blimber's young gentlemen, Berchoux suffered much from "this terrible people, these implacable enemies" of youth, who embittered his early days, and even pursued him in later life in the masterpieces of Racine and Corneille.　A little below he apostrophises the whole "Race d'Agamemnon, qui ne finit jamais!" and either line is capable of more than one humorous application.

2300. Qui medice vivit, misere vivit. Prov.—*He who lives by medical prescription, leads a miserable life.*

2301. Qui mores hominum multorum vidit, et urbes. Hor. A. P. 142.
Ulysses.
Who many towns and men and manners saw.—*Ed.*

2302. Qui n'a pas l'esprit de son âge,
De son âge a tout le malheur.
Volt. Stances à Mme. du Châtelet (1741).
Who lacks the spirit of his age,
Has nought but its unhappiness.—*Ed.*

2303. Qui n'a plus qu'un moment à vivre,
N'a plus rien à dissimuler.
Philippe Quinault, Atys, 1, 6. Tragédie, n. p. (Ballard), 1738, p. 11 (Atys to Sangaride).—*He who has but a moment to live, has no cause for dissembling.*

2304. Qui ne sait dissimuler, ne sait régner. Max. of Louis XI.—*He who does not know how to dissemble, knows not how to reign.*

Speaking of his son and successor, Charles VIII., the king remarked, "Il en saura toujours assez, s'il retient bien cette maxime: *qui ne sait dissimuler*," etc. (Roche et Chasles, Hist. de France, Paris, 1847, vol. 2, p. 30). Richelieu, or the playwright who wrote under his patronage, makes the "king of Bithynia" say, "Savoir dissimuler est le savoir des rois"—*Dissimulation is the art of kings* (Richelieu, *Mirame*, 1, 2, in *Théatre Français*, Lyon, 1780, vol. 4, p. 22).

2305. Qui nil molitur inepte. Hor. A. P. 140.—*One who never turns out foolish work.* Said of Homer.

2306. Qui nil potest sperare, desperet nihil. Sen. Med. 163.—*Who nought can hope, should nought despair.*

2307. Qui nolet fieri desidiosus, amet. Ov. Am. 1, 9, 46.—*If any man wish to escape idleness, let him fall in love.*

2308. Qui non est hodie, cras minus aptus erit. Ov. R. A. 94.—*He who is not ready to-day, will be less ready to-morrow.*

2309. Qui non vetat peccare, quum possit, jubet. Sen. Troad. 295.—*He who does not forbid wrong-doing, when he could do so, enjoins it.*

2310. Quintili Vare, redde legiones. Suet. Aug. 23.—*Quintilius Varus, give me back my legions!*

In the year 9 A.D., Arminius (Hermann), chief of the German tribe of the Cherusci, gave battle to P. Quintilius Varus, the Roman commander, in the Iburg Valley, near Osnabrück. The whole of the imperial forces (15,000) were annihilated, and Varus destroyed himself. When the news reached the court, Augustus was almost beside himself with grief. For months he kept calling to the dead Varus to give him back his lost legions, and the anniversary of the disaster was ever after observed as a day of mourning. A "legion" equalled 5000 men; half a modern "division."

2311. Qui nunc it per iter tenebricosum
Illuc unde negant redire quemquam.   Cat. 3, 11.

> Who now is journeying down that darksome track,
> From whence they say no traveller comes back.—*Ed.*

2312. Qui parcit virgæ odit filium.   Vulg. Prov. xiii. 24.—*He that
spareth his rod, hateth his son.*

2313. Qui peccat ebrius luat sobrius.   Law Max.—*He that is guilty of
an offence when he is drunk, shall pay the penalty thereof when
he is sober.*

2314. Qui peut avec les plus rares talents . . . n'être pas convaincu de
son inutilité, quand il considère qu'il laisse en mourant un
monde où tant de gens se trouvent pour le remplacer? La Bruy.
cap. 2 (Mérite personnel), init.—*Talents, even of the rarest kind,
should not blind a man to the fact of his own insignificance, when
he considers the numbers of men that can supply the vacancy
caused by his death.* Again (id. ibid., *ad fin.*), "Il n'y a guère
d'homme . . . si nécessaire aux siens, qu'il n'ait de quoi se faire
moins regretter." Wisest among the moralist's wise reflections,
and well deserving a place in the thoughts of the self-important!
The world does not own, nor has it room for the "necessary
man": in church or in state, even the most inefficient person
can be replaced.

2315. Qui que tu sois, voici ton maître;
Il l'est, le fut, ou le doit être.

Volt. Poés. Mélées, 41 (Panthéon, vol. 2).

Inscription for a Bust of Cupid.

> See here your master, be you who you may!
> He is, or was, or shall be yours one day.—*Ed.*

2316. Qui recte vivendi prorogat horam,
Rusticus expectat dum defluat amnis; at ille
Labitur et labetur in omne volubilis ævum.   Hor. Ep. 1, 2, 41.

Procrastination.

> He who puts off the time for mending, stands
> A clodpoll by the stream with folded hands,
> Waiting till all the water be gone past;
> But it will run and run while time shall last.—*Conington.*

2317. Qui rit Vendredi, Dimanche pleurera. Racine, Plaideurs, sc. 1
(Monologue du petit Jean).—*He who laughs Friday, will weep
Sunday.*

2318. Quis desiderio sit pudor aut modus
Tam cari capitis?   Hor. C. 1, 24, 1.

> Why blush to let our tears unmeasured fall
> For one so dear?—*Conington.*

2319. Qui se sent galeux se gratte. Prov.—*Whom the cap fits, let him
wear it.*

2320. Quis est enim, qui totum diem jaculans, non aliquando collineet?
Cic. Div. 2, 59, 121.—*Who is there who is shooting all day long*

but will sometimes hit the mark? Of happy guesses, lucky prophecies, etc.

2321. Quis fallere possit amantem? Virg. A. 4, 296.—*Who could deceive a lover?*

2321A. Quis furor est census corpore ferre suo! Ov. A. A. 3, 172.—*What madness to carry all one's income on one's back!* Extravagant dress.

2322. Qui sibi semitam non sapiunt, alteri monstrant viam.
Quibu' divitias pollicentur, ab eis dracumam ipsi petunt.
De his divitiis sibi deducant dracumam, reddant cætera.

Enn. Telamo, Rib. 1, 61.—*They don't know the way themselves, and pretend to show it to others. They promise wealth to those they are glad enough to get a shilling from. I say, let them take the shilling out of this promised wealth, and hand over the balance!* On astrologers, fortune-tellers, quacks, impostors, etc.

2323. Quisnam igitur liber? Sapiens qui sibi imperiosus;
Quem neque pauperies neque mors neque vincula terrent;
Responsare cupidinibus, contemnere honores
Fortis, et in seipso totus teres atque rotundus. Hor. S. 2, 7, 83.

> Who then is free? The sage who self restrains;
> Who fears nor poverty, nor death, nor chains;
> Who curbs desire, honours can despise,
> And, free from crotchets, on himself relies.—*Ed.*

2324. Quis nescit, primam esse historiæ legem, ne quid falsi dicere audeat? deinde ne quid veri non audeat? ne qua suspicio gratiæ sit in scribendo? ne qua simultatis? Cic. de Or. 2, 15, 62. —*The first duty of a historian is not to dare to say anything that is false; the second, to suppress nothing that is true: and to guard at once against all suspicions either of partiality or of resentment.*

2325. Quisque suos patimur Manes: exinde per amplum
Mittimur Elysium, et pauci læta arva tenemus. Virg. A. 6, 743.

> *Purgatory.*
> Each for himself, we all sustain
> The durance of our ghostly pain;
> Then to Elysium we repair,
> The few, and breathe the blissful air.—*Conington.*

2326. Quis, quid, ubi, quibus auxiliis, cur, quomodo, quando?—*Who, what, where, by what means, why, how, when?* A doggerel *memoria technica* containing all the possible parts into which any subject may be divided for analysis.

2327. Quisquis amat dictis absentem rodere vitam,
Hanc mensam indignam noverit esse sibi.

St August. Vita, vol. x. p. 183 C.

> He that is wont to slander absent men,
> Shall never at this table sit again.—*Dr Neale.*

Possidius, Bp. of Calama, his disciple and biographer, says (in above reference) that St Augustine had these lines inscribed on the common board at which he entertained guests and visitors, and that he refused to remain at table with them if they infringed the rule.

2328. Quis scit an adjiciant hodiernæ crastina summæ
Tempora Di superi?   Hor. C. 4, 7, 17.—*Who knows if God will add a morrow to the total of to-day?*

2329 Quis tulerit Gracchos de seditione querentes?   Juv. 2, 24.

Who'd bear to hear the Gracchi chide sedition?

"The Gracchi" are, of course, the two famous brothers, Tib. Sempronius (b. 168 B.C.) and Caius Sempronius (b. 159 B.C.), both tribunes, and both far-sighted reformers and defenders of the rights of the people. They rank among the most illustrious statesmen that Rome produced, and can well afford the foolish calumny of the satirist. The line applies to those who are found loudly denouncing any line of action for which they are themselves chiefly notorious,—"Satan rebuking sin."

2330. Qui stupet in titulis et imaginibus. Hor. S. 1, 6, 17.—The "people," *whom a title or a coronet strikes dumb.* It is said that an Englishman "dearly loves a lord," and it would seem that the foible was just as prevalent in the Rome of the first century as it is in the London of to-day.

2331. Qui tacet consentire videtur.   Law Max. in Corpus Canon. Jur. (Liber Sextus Decretal., lib. 5, tit. 12, reg. 43).—*Silence gives consent* In Euripides (Iph. in Aul. 1142), Clytemnestra says, αὐτὸ δὲ σιγᾶν ὁμολογοῦντός ἐστί σοῦ—*Your silence is a sign that you consent.*

2332. Qui terret plus ipse timet: sors ista tyrannis
Convenit.   Claud IV. Cons. Hon. 290.

Who causes fear, himself shall suffer worse:
Such ever is the tyrant's fitting curse.—*Ed.*

2333. Qui timide rogat, Docet negare.   Sen. Hipp. 593.—*He who asks timidly, courts a refusal.* Claims urged with confidence are the most likely to be successful.

2334. Qui trop embrasse, mal étreint.   Prov.—*Who grasps too much, will hold but ill.* A man allowed to take as many sovereigns out of a bag as he could hold, would probably grasp more than he could grip.   He who attempts too much, as a rule fails.

Quitard (p. 362) speaks of a statue erected to Buffon with the epigraph, *Naturam amplectitur omnem,* "he embraces the whole of nature"; to which a wit added, *Qui trop embrasse mal étreint,* and the inscription was accordingly altered.

2335. Qui utuntur vino vetere, sapientes puto,
Et qui libenter veteres spectant fabulas.   Plaut. Cas. Prol. 5.

Old Wine, old Books, old Friends.
Those who like their wine *old*, I call them wise,
And so are they who like old comedies.—*Ed.*

2336. Qui vit sans folie, n'est pas si sage qu'il le croit. La Rochef., § 214, p. 57.—*He who never plays the fool sometimes is not as wise as he thinks.* Solemnity and stupidity often go together.

2337. Quocunque aspicio, nihil est nisi mortis imago. Ov. T. 1, 11, 23.

> Turn where I may, look where I will,
> Pictures of death confront me still.—*Ed.*

2338. Quod ab initio non valet in tractu temporis non convalescit. Law Max.—*That which was void from the beginning does not become valid by lapse of time.*

2339. Quodcunque ostendis mihi sic, incredulus odi. Hor. A. P. 188.

> If scenes like these before my eyes be thrust,
> They shock belief and generate disgust.—*Conington.*

2340. Quod est absurdum (or Q.E.A.).—*Which is absurd.* Argument in logic or in mathematics, in which the opposite view is refuted by demonstration of its absurdity, and termed therefore a *Reductio ad absurdum.*

2341. Quod facis, fac citius. Vulg. Joann. cap. 13, 27.—*What thou doest, do quickly.*

2342. Quod medicorum est
Promittunt medici, tractant fabrilia fabri.
Scribimus indocti doctique poemata passim. Hor. Ep. 2, 1, 115.

> Doctors prescribe, who understand the rules,
> And only workmen handle workmen's tools:
> But literate and illiterate, those who can,
> And those who can't, write verses to a man.—*Sir T. Martin.*

2343. Quod non es, simula. Ov. R. A. 497.—*Feign to be that which you are not.*

2344. Quod non vetat lex, hoc vetat fieri pudor. Sen. Troad. 335.—*What though the law allows it, propriety forbids.*

2345. Quod satis est cui contingit nihil amplius optet. Hor. Ep. 1, 2, 46.

> Having got
> What will suffice you, seek no happier lot.—*Conington.*

2346. Quod scripsi, scripsi. Vulg. Joann. 20, 22.—*What I have written, I have written.*

2347. Quod semper, quod ubique, et quod ab omnibus creditum est. Vinc. Lirin., Commonitor, c. 2.—*What has always, everywhere, and by all been believed.*

"In the Catholic Church," says Vincent, "great care must be taken that we hold *Quod semper, quod ubique, et quod ab omnibus creditum est.*" The words may be taken as a general definition of the teaching of Christianity. To require the literal application of this theological axiom to every point of the received Faith, would be to destroy its force. No doctrine, not excepting that of the Holy Trinity itself, could stand such a test. It would imply, rather, the general concurrence of the Church's teaching with what has been implicitly believed or explicitly defined from the beginning; and, negatively, the absence of all conflicting statements the other way. "The Rule of Vincent is not of a mathematical or demonstrative character, but moral, and requires practical judgment and good sense to apply it." Newman (Card.), *Lectures on the Prophetical Office of the Church* (1837), pp. 68-9, ed. 2.

2348. Quod si deficiant vires, audacia certe
    Laus erit; in magnis et voluisse sat est.   Prop. 2, 10, 5.

The Will for the Deed.

> Though you should fail, I'll praise your courage still;
> Enough, in great things, e'en to show the will.—*Ed.*

Est nobis voluisse satis; nec munera parva
Respueris.   Tibullus 4, 1, 7.—*Let the will stand for the deed, and despise not gifts though small.*

Ut desint vires tamen est laudanda voluntas. Ov. Ep. 3, 4, 79.—*Though the power be wanting, yet the will deserves praise.*

Ut jam nil præstes, animi sum factus amici
Debitor, et meritum velle juvare voco.   Ov. Ep. 4, 8, 5.—*Though you cannot give me any assistance, I am still indebted for your friendly disposition, and I consider the willingness to help a merit.*

2349. Quod si in hoc erro, quod animos hominum immortales esse credam, lubenter erro; nec mihi hunc errorem quo delector, dum vivo, extorqueri volo. Cic. Sen. 23, 85.—*But if I am mistaken in my belief of the soul's immortality, I am glad to be mistaken, nor shall anyone rob me of the pleasing delusion as long as I live.*

2350. Quod si mea numina non sunt
    Magna satis, dubitem haud equidem implorare quod usquam est.
    Flectere si nequeo superos Acheronta movebo.   Virg. A. 7, 310.

> If strength like mine be yet too weak,
> I care not whose the aid I seek:
> What choice 'twixt under and above?
> If heaven be firm, the shades shall move.—*Conington.*

"If the gods of Elysium will not help me, I must have recourse to the powers of the lower world." This is the speech of Juno, when she turned to the Furies to stay the onward progress of Æneas. The words have been applied to any appeal from a higher to a lower tribunal—from the Crown to the nation, from the Upper House to the Lower, from Parliament to the people, from ministers to the mob.

2351. Quod sis, esse velis, nihilque malis:
    Summum nec metuas diem, nec optes.   Mart. 10, 47, 12.

> Choose what you are, no other state prefer;
> And your last day neither desire nor fear.—*Ed.*

Cf. Milton, Paradise Lost, 11, 553:

> Nor love thy life, nor hate; but what thou liv'st
> Live well; how long or short permit to heaven.

2352. Quod verum est, meum est. Perseverabo Epicurum tibi ingerere, ut isti qui in verba jurant, nec quid dicatur æstimant sed a quo, sciant quæ optima sunt esse communia. *Sen. Ep.* 12, 10.—*What is true, belongs to me. I shall go on quoting Epicurus to you, in order that those who swear by particular authors, and never consider what is said, but only who says it, may know that all the best maxims are common property.*

2353. Quo fata trahunt retrahuntque, sequamur; Quicquid erit, superanda omnis fortuna ferendo est.

Virg. A. 5, 709.

My chief, let fate cry on or back
'Tis ours to follow, nothing slack:
Whate'er betide, he only cures
The stroke of Fortune who endures.—*Conington.*

2353A. Quo fit ut omnis
Votiva pateat veluti descripta tabella
Vita senis. *Hor. S.* 2, 1, 32.

So here, as in a votive tablet penned,
You see the veteran's life from end to end.—*Conington.*

Said of Lucilius, the satirist, the lines were appropriately chosen by Boswell to figure upon the title-page of his famous biography.

2354. Quoi qu'en dise Aristote et sa docte cabale,
Le tabac est divin, il n'est rien qui n'égale.

Corneille (Thos.), *Festin de Pierre*, 1, 1.

For all Aristotle may state *au contraire,*
Tobacco's divine; nought with it can compare.—*Ed.*

Thomas Corneille's comedy is a versification of the prose of Molière's play of the same name, which opens with (Sganarelle to Guzman), "Quoi que puisse dire Aristote et toute la philosophie, il n'est rien d'égal au tabac."

2355. Quo mihi fortunam, si non conceditur uti? *Hor. Ep.* 1, 5, 12.

Why should the gods have put me at my ease,
If I mayn't use my fortune as I please?—*Conington.*

2356. Qu'on parle mal ou bien du fameux cardinal,
Ma prose ni mes vers n'en diront jamais rien;
Il m'a fait trop de bien pour en dire du mal;
Il m'a fait trop de mal pour en dire du bien. Corneille.

Sur le Cardinal Richelieu.

Of this Cardinal great let men speak as they will,
In verse or in prose I'll not mention his name:
Too much good has he done me, to speak of him ill,
Too much ill, to uphold his good fame.—*Ed.*

Applied by Dr Johnson to Lord Chatham (W. Seward's *Supplemental Anecdotes*, p. 152).

2357. Quo res cunque cadent, unum et commune periclum,
Una salus ambobus erit. *Virg. A.* 2, 709.

Now, whether fortune smiles or lowers,
One risk, one safety shall be ours.—*Conington.*

2358. Quo ruitis generosa domus ? male creditur hosti :
Simplex nobilitas, perfida tela cave!   Ov. F. 2, 225.

> Whither, O high-born house ? 'Tis ill to trust the foe:
> Ye guileless chiefs beware a traitor's blow !—*Ed.*

Addressed to the Fabii who, entrapped in ambuscade by the Veientes,
were exterminated to a man.

2359. Quos Deus vult perdere, prius dementat.—*Whom God would ruin,
he first deprives of reason.*

Spite of its spurious Latinity and purely modern origin, this line has
secured a reputation and respectability not attaching to many finely-
expressed thoughts of the ancients; and even in Boswell's day it had
become one of the sayings "which everyone repeats, but nobody knows
where to find." In a note of Malone (Boswell's *Johnson,* Croker ed., London, 1853, 8vo, p. 718), it is remarked that "perhaps no scrap of Latin
whatever has been more quoted than this": and he adds that it was once
made the subject of a bet amongst "some gentlemen of Cambridge," with
the result that it was discovered at last in the Fragments of Euripides—
"in what edition, I do not recollect." At this point I am able to come to
Mr Malone's assistance. The edition of Euripides in question is "*Cambridge,* 1694, *fol.*," and the editor is Joshua Barnes, Fellow of Emman.
Coll.—"*maxime senior,*" as he expressly states on the title-page—he was
then exactly forty years of age. In his *Index Prior,* under letter D—there
is no Index pagination—will be found the momentous and epoch-making
words—*Deus quos vult perdere, dementat prius;* referring the reader to the
Euripidean *Incerta* on his p. 515, line 436, for the following (which is also
to be found in the Scholium on Sophocles' Antigone, 620):—

> "Οταν δ' ὁ δαίμων ἀνδρὶ πορσύνη κακά,
> τὸν νοῦν ἔβλαψε πρῶτον ᾧ βουλεύεται.

> For those whom God to ruin has designed,
> He fits for fate and first destroys their mind.
>   —*Dryden,* "Hind and Panther," 3, 1094.

Barnes has, however, achieved in this matter a posthumous triumph
which he does not deserve. His extraordinary memory, and his equally
characteristic want of judgment, suggested to his contemporaries the
"Epitaph *à la* Ménage" of, "Joshua Barnes, *Felicis Memoriæ, Judicium
Expectans*" (of happy memory, awaiting judgment), and in this particular
case he had borrowed from James Dupont, who thirty years before had
rendered the same "Euripidean" fragment into *Quem Jupiter vult perdere,
dementat prius.* (*V.* Dupont's Homeri Gnomologia, Camb. 1660, p. 282.)

A cognate saying is preserved in *Oratores Græci,* ed. Reiske, vol. 8,
p. 198, under the title of "Lycurgus contra Leocratem":

> ὅταν γὰρ ὀργὴ δαιμόνων βλάπτῃ τινὰ,
> τοῦτ᾽ αὐτὸ πρῶτον ἐξαφαιρεῖται φρενῶν
> τὸν νοῦν τὸν ἐσθλὸν, εἰς δὲ τὴν χείρω τρέπει
> γνώμην, ἵν᾽ εἰδῇ μηδὲν ὧν ἁμαρτάνει.—*Whenever the wrath of the
gods would injure any, they first take from him his natural sound reason,
and pervert his judgment, so that he is quite unconscious of the errors he
commits.*

Cp. also the "Stultum facit fortuna quem vult perdere" of Syrus (612)
—*The man whom Fortune would ruin, she robs of his wits:* and the
remark of Velleius Paterculus (2, 57), where, commenting on Cæsar's
total disregard of the many presages of his death, he says: Profecto
ineluctabilis fatorum vis, cujuscunque fortunam mutare constituit, consilia
corrumpit—*Certainly, the inevitable force of fate blinds the judgment of those
for whom it has destined a reverse of fortune.*

2360. Quos ego ——. Virg. A. 1, 135.—*Whom I——* (sc. will punish).
Instance of *aposiopesis,* or break in the middle of a speech.

2361. Quo semel est imbuta recens servabit odorem
Testa diu.   Hor. Ep. 1, 2, 69.

> The smell that's first imparted will adhere
> To seasoned jars through many an after year.—*Conington.*

Cp. Moore (*Farewell, but whenever,* etc.):

> You may break, you may shatter the vase, if you will,
> But the scent of the roses will cling to it still.

2362. Quosque ego fraterno dilexi more sodales,
O mihi Thesea pectora juncta fide!
Dum licet, amplectar: nunquam fortasse licebit
Amplius.   In lucro, quæ datur hora, mihi est.   Ov. T. 1, 3, 65.

Parting.

> The comrades I loved with the warmth of a brother—
> Hearts twined in a friendship that never can wane!—
> While there's time, we embrace—there may not be another;
> E'en the moment allowed must be reckoned as gain.—*Ed.*

2363. Quot capitum vivunt, totidem studiorum
Millia.   Hor. S. 2, 1, 27.

> Count all the folks in all the world, you'll find
> A separate fancy for each separate mind.—*Conington.*

2364. Quo teneam vultus mutantem Protea nodo?   Hor. Ep. 1, 1, 90.

> How shall I hold this Proteus in my gripe,
> How fix him down in one enduring type?—*Conington.*

2365. Quot homines, tot sententiæ; suus cuique mos.   Ter. Phorm.
2, 4, 14.—*Many men, many minds; each has his own humour.*
As many opinions as there are persons to give them, and no two
precisely alike.

2366. Quot pæne verba, tot sententiæ sunt; quot sensus, tot victoriæ.
S. Vincent Lirin., Commonitor, 1, 18.—*Almost every word is a
sentence in itself, and every thought amounts to a demonstration.*
Said of Tertullian's writings.

> St Jerome speaks of St Paul's style as, Non verba, sed tonitrua—*Not so
> much "words," as "thunderings."*   (Ep. 48, ad Pammachium, cap. 13.)

2367. Quot servi, tot hostes, in proverbio est.   Festus, De Verborum
Signif. (ed. Müller, p. 261).—*"So many servants, so many
enemies," has passed into a proverb:* and, Totidem hostes nobis
esse quot servos.   Macrobius Sat. 1, 11, 13.

2368. Quousque tandem, Catilina, abutere patientia nostra?   Cic. Cat.
1, 1, 1.—*How long Catiline, pray, will you abuse our patience?*
Opening of Cicero's famous invective against Catiline.

2369. Quumque superba foret Babylon spolianda tropæis,
Bella geri placuit nullos habitura triumphos. Luc. 1, 10 and 12.

The Civil War.

And when proud Babylon might have been despoiled,
  It was resolved, instead, to wage a war
That could not bring such triumphs in its train.—*Ed.*

Lord Macaulay (Essay on *Ranke's History of the Popes*) applies the lines
to the fruitless theological hostilities which the various Protestant sects
chose to wage against each other, in the early history of the Reformation,
instead of uniting their forces against the unswerving front of the Catholic
Church.

2370. Quum relego, scripsisse pudet: quia plurima cerno
Me quoque qui feci judice, digna lini.   Ov. Ep. 1, 5, 15.

When I read what I've written, I'm often abased;
There's so much in my judgment that should be erased.—*Ed.*

2371. Quum Romæ fueris, Romano vivite more.   Prov.—*When at
Rome, do as Rome does.*

On the question of fasting or no on Saturday, St Ambrose replied to
St Augustine: Quando hic sum, non jejuno Sabbato; quando Romæ sum
jejuno Sabbato: et ad quam cunque ecclesiam veneritis, ejus morem ser-
vate, si pati scandalum non vultis, aut facere. St Aug. Ep. 36, cap. 14
(vol. ii. p. 62).—*When I am at Milan, I don't fast Saturdays: when I am
at Rome, I do.   Always observe the rule of the Church where you find yourself, so as neither to take or give offence.*   In Rome, Saturday (Sabbato) is a
fast to-day as in the fifth century, whereas in other parts of the Church
no such rule obtains.

2372. Qu'une nuit paraît longue à la douleur qui veille! Saurin,
Blanche et Guiscard, (Œuvres, Paris, 1783, 2 vols., 8vo),
A. 5, S. 5 (Blanche loq.).—*How long the night that's passed in
wakeful grief!*

R.

2373. Raisonner sur l'amour, c'est perdre la raison.   Boufflers, Le Cœur,
(Œuvres de M. le Chev. de Boufflers, Londres, 1782, p. 56).—*To
reason about love is to lose one's reason.*   Cf. La logique du cœur
est absurde.   Mlle. Lespinasse, Lettres, Paris, 1811, vol. 1, p. 200
(Lettre xlvii., Aug. 27, 1774).—*It is absurd to bring logic to bear
on affairs of the heart.*

2374. Rapiamus, amici, Occasionem de die. Hor. Epod. 13, 3.—*Friends,
let us take advantage of the day,* and enjoy ourselves.

2375. Rara avis in terris, nigroque simillima cygno. Juv. 6, 165.—*A
bird rarely seen on the earth, and very like a black swan.*
Anything extraordinary or unique.   Cf. id. 7, 202. Corvus
albus.—*A white crow.*

2376. Rara temporum felicitate, ubi sentire quæ velis, et quæ sentias dicere licet. Tac. H. 1, 1.—*A period, as rare as it was happy; when it was allowable not only to think as we chose, but to give free utterance to one's thoughts,* viz., the reigns of Nerva and Trajan, 96–117 A.D.

> The character of Trajan's government is testified to by the sentiment, afterwards proverbial, with which each new successor to the throne of the Cæsars was greeted. The wish expressed was that he might be *Felicior Augusto, melior Trajano* (Eutrop. Hist. Rom. 8, 5)—"Happier than Augustus, and better than Trajan."

2377. Rarement à courir le monde,
On devient plus homme de bien.
F. S. Regnier-Desmarais, Le Voyage de Munik, Poésies Françoises, La Haye, 1716, vol. i. p. 216.

> *The Rolling Stone.*
> To be always on the move,
> Rarely makes an honest man.—*Ed.*

> The versatile Abbé Desmarais is describing a jaunt that he took on horseback from Paris to Munich. They had left the Rhine and the Neckar behind them, and now were following the course of the Danube, which, rising in a Protestant country, flows through a Catholic nation, and finally empties itself amongst the Infidels.

> Desja nous avons veu le Danube inconstant,
> Qui tantost Catholique, et tantost Protestant,
> Sert Rome, et Luther de son onde ;
> Et qui comptant après pour rien
> Le Romain, le Luthérien,
> Finit sa course vagabonde,
> Par n'estre pas même Chrestien.
> *Rarement à courir,* etc., etc.

2378. Rari quippe boni ; numero vix sunt totidem quot
Thebarum portæ, vel divitis ostia Nili.   Juv. 13, 26.

> Few are the good : their numbers scarce compile
> As many gates as Thebes, or mouths as Nile.—*Ed.*

2379. Raro sermo illis, et magna libido tacendi.   Juv. 2, 14.

> *Quakers.*
> Seldom they speak and silence much prefer.—*Ed.*

2380. Rarus enim ferme sensus communis in illa
Fortuna.   Juv. 8, 73.

> With such a fortune, it were rare
> If tact and taste were also there.—*Ed.*

2381. Raum für alle hat die Erde.   Schiller, Der Alpenjäger.—*Earth has room for all.*

2382. Raum ist in der kleinsten Hütte
Für ein glücklich liebend Paar.
Schiller, Der Jüngling am Bache, fin.

> The smallest cottage will find room
> For a happy, loving pair.—*Ed.*

2383. Rebus in angustis facile est contemnere vitam;
Fortiter ille facit qui miser esse potest.   Mart. 11, 56, 15.

True Courage.
The coward flies to death his woes to cure:
The brave is he who can his woes endure.—*Ed.*

2384. Recta et vera loquere, sed neque vere neque recte adhuc
Fecisti unquam.
Plaut. Capt. 5, 2, 7 (Hegio to Stalagmus, loq.).—*You speak right and true enough, but you have never acted rightly or truly yet.*

2385. Reculer pour mieux sauter.—*To go back a step in order to take a better leap.*

This is said of any change of tactics, attitude, or position adopted preparatory to taking some decided step.   The phrase is at least as old as the sixteenth century, since we find it in Montaigne (Essais, 1, 38, *ad fin.*), "Ils se sont seulement reculez pour mieux saulter."

2386. Rege beatior.   Hor. C. 3, 9, 4.—*Happier than a king.*   My father's motto.

"Ce bonheur a peut-être existé dans les temps les plus reculés," says Quitard (*à propos* of the prov., "Heureux comme un roi," and not without the thought of the Revolution in his mind), "mais Dieu sait ce qu'il est aujourd'hui.   Il y a peu de malheurs qui ne lui soient préférables." Horace, however, says not "as happy *as* a king," but "happier *than* a king," and therein lies all the difference.   While Lesbia smiled and Lydia loved, both Catullus and Horace could describe themselves, in immortal verse, as the possessors of a felicity transcending that of men or kings or even gods themselves: and it is possible that it may have almost approached the joy of the street-urchin as he shouts in your ear with nerve-shattering force, and in absolute bliss.   *V.* Quitard, p. 454.

2387. Regia, crede mihi, res est succurrere lapsis.   Ov. Ep. 2, 9, 11.—*Believe me, it is a royal deed to succour the fallen.*

2388. Regnare nolo, liber ut non sim mihi.   Phædr. 3, 7, 27.

The Dog and the Wolf.
I would not care to be a king to lose my liberty.—*Ed.*

Cf. Ego semper pluris feci Potioremque habui libertatem multo quam pecuniam.   Næv. *Agitatoria*, Fr. III. (Rib. 2, 7).—*I have always valued and preferred my liberty far beyond money.*

2389. Re infecta.   Cæs. B. G. 7, 17, 5.—*The business being unfinished.*   The object unaccomplished: nothing done.

2390. Reipublicæ forma, laudari facilius quam evenire, vel si evenit, haud diuturna esse potest.   Tac. A. 4, 33.—*To praise a republican form of government is more easy than to establish it, and even if established, it cannot be of long duration.*

2391. Religentem esse oportet, religiosum 'st nefas.   Poet. ap. Gell. 4, 9, 1.—*A man should be devout but not a devotee.*—Religious, without being superstitious.

2392. Rem facias: rem,
Si possis recte, si non quocunque modo rem.   Hor. Ep. 1, 1, 65.
Make money, money, man;
Well, if so be,—if not, which way you can.—*Conington.*

2393. Remis velisque.   Sil. 1, 568.—*With oar and sail, i.e.,* with might
and main; so also, Remis ventisque.   Virg. A. 3, 563—*With
oars and wind.*   Cf. Armis et castris. Cic. Off. 2, 24, 84 (*With
arms and camps*), and Equis virisque, Liv. 5, 37 (*With horse and
foot*), in same sense, *i.e.,* with vigour, tooth and nail.

2394. Rem strenuus auge.   Hor. Ep. 1, 7, 71.—*Do your utmost to get on.*

2395. Requiescat in pace, *or* R.I.P.—*May he rest in peace.*   The prayer
of piety for the departed.

> We pray for the repose of the souls that have gone before us, but it is
> characteristic of the stronger faith of the earlier generation of Christians,
> as shown by the most ancient sepulchral inscriptions, that they recorded
> the repose of the loved ones they had consigned to mother earth, not in
> the optative but indicative mood; not as a matter of speculation, but of
> fact.   Requies*cit* in pace, Requie*vit* in pace, Dor*mit* in pace, Κεῖται ἐν
> εἰρήνῃ, Migra*vit* ad Dominum (*He rests in peace, He sleeps in peace, He reposes
> in peace, He has departed to the Lord); whatever might be the wording,
> there was no hesitation as to the fact that was commemorated. (*V.* Jan
> Grüter's *Inscriptiones Antiquæ,* etc., pp. ml to mlxii).   So wholly had the
> Reformation banished the idea of all such pious duties towards the dead,
> that Sydney Smith in his amusing and semi-profane fashion declared that
> the initials stood for "Respected in the Parish."

2396. Rerum natura, nusquam magis quam in minimis, tota est.—Plin.
11, 2.—*The perfect totality of nature is nowhere more observable
than in its minutest details.*   Fumag. (p. 375) qu. *Maximus in
minimis Deus,* as a derivation from the above.

2396A. Res est magna tacere, Mathon.   Mart. 4, 81, 6.—*Silence is an
admirable thing, Matho.*

2397. Res est sacra miser.   Sen. Epigr. 4, 9.—*A man in misfortune is
a sacred object.*   Written while in exile in Corsica.

2398. Restat iter cœlo: cœlo tentabimus ire;
Da veniam cœpto, Jupiter alte, meo.   Ov. A. A. 2, 37.
Dædalus.
One way remains—by air: by air a way we'll try;
Pardon the bold adventure, Jove most high!—*Ed.*

> When Gambetta left Paris by balloon to join his colleagues at Tours
> during the siege (Oct, 1870), he might have employed the same language.

2399. Res urget me nulla; meo sum pauper in ære.   Hor. Ep. 2, 2, 12.
—*I am not in any way constrained in the matter; though poor
I am out of debt.*   Poor but honest.

2400. Revenons à nos moutons.   La Farce de Maistre Pierre Patelin,
Anon., 15th cent., sc. xix., l. 1291 (*see* the ed. of 1732, 12mo).
—*Let us come back to our sheep.*

> In the farce, a cloth merchant suing his shepherd for stolen mutton
> discovers in the attorney on the other side (Patelin) the man who had

already robbed him of some cloth; upon which, dropping the charge
against the shepherd, he begins accusing the lawyer of his offence; and to
recall him to the point the Justice impatiently interrupts with *Sus, revenons
à nos moutons!* F. Génin's ed. of the text of 1490 (Paris, 1854, p. 110)
makes it "à *ces* moutons"—prob. an error for *ses*. In the *Pâtelin* of
de Brueys et de Palaprat (*Œuvres de Théâtre*, Paris, 1756), A. 3, s. 2, the
magistrate, Bartolin, says to Guillaume the draper, "Laissez-là ce drap et
cet homme, et *revenez à vos moutons*." The phrase is commonly used, after
some digression, to bring back the conversation to the original subject—
pour en revenir à nos moutons. The original is generally traced to Martial's
story (6, 19) of the goats which his next neighbour had appropriated.
Instead of establishing the theft, his counsel, Posthumus, begins a long
harangue on Roman history from Cannæ downwards, until Martial pulls
him up with, *Jam dic, Posthume, de tribus capellis* ("Now, Posthumus,
a word if you please about the three goats"). *See* Quit. p. 545, and
Alex. p. 439.

2401. Rex est qui metuit nihil,
     Rex est qui cupiet nihil ;
     Hoc regnum sibi quisque dat.   Sen. Thyest. 388.

  He is a king that fears not aught,
  He is a king that covets naught:
  A kingdom, that each soul alive
  May to himself at pleasure give.—*Ed.*

2402. Rex non potest peccare.—*The king can do no wrong.*   Whatever
     be amiss in the condition of public affairs is not to be imputed
     to him personally.   (2.) Rex nunquam moritur.—*The king never
     dies.*   In Anglia non est interregnum—*There is no interregnum
     in England.*   "The demise is immediately followed by the
     succession, there is no interval ; the sovereign always exists,
     the person only is changed."—*Lord Lyndhurst.*

2403. Rhipeus justissimus unus
     Qui fuit in Teucris, et servantissimus æqui.   Virg. A. 2, 426.

  [*Then Rhipeus dies:*] No purer son
  Troy ever bred, more jealous none
  Of sacred right.—*Conington.*

2403A. Rideamus γέλωτα Σαρδάνιον.   Cic. Fam. 7, 25.—*Let us laugh
     sardonically.*

2404. Ridentem dicere verum
     Quid vetat?   Ut pueris olim dant crustula blandi
     Doctores elementa velint ut discere prima.   Hor. S. 1, 1, 24.

  Why truth may not be gay I cannot see.
  Just as, we know, judicious teachers coax
  With sugar-plum or cake their little folks
  To learn their alphabet.—*Conington.*

2405. Ride si sapis.   Mart. 2, 41, 1.—*Laugh if you are wise.*   Be merry
     and wise.

2406. Ridiculum acri
     Fortius ac melius magnas plerumque secat res.   Hor. S. 1, 10, 14.

  And pleasantry will often clean cut through
  Hard knots that gravity would scarce undo.—*Conington.*

2407. Rien ne manque à sa gloire, il manquait à la nôtre. Saurin.—
Nothing is wanting to his fame, he was wanting to our own.

> Inscription written beneath the bust of Molière, when, in 1773, a
> hundred years after his death, it was placed in the Academy to which in
> his lifetime he was refused admission.

2408. Rien ne m'est plus, plus ne m'est rien.—*Nothing is left me, and
everything is now as nothing.* Motto chosen by Valentine
Visconti, widow of Louis, Duke of Orleans, the son of
Charles V. of France, 1407. (Mrs C. Bearne, *Pictures of the
Old French Court*, Lond., 1900, p. 249.)

2408A. Rien ne m'est feur que la chose incertaine;
    Obscur, fors ce qui est tout euident;
    Doubte ne fais, fors en chofe certaine;
    Science tiens à soudain accident.
                  F. Villon, *Ballade dv Concovrs de Blois.*

> Nought hold I sure except what's still uncertain,
> Deem nought obscure save the self-evident;
> If I'm in doubt, 'tis on what's sure and certain,
> And am prepared for any accident.—*Ed.*

** Rien n'est certain que l'inattendu. Prov.—*Nothing is certain but the
unexpected.*

2409. Rien n'empêche tant d'être naturel, que l'envie de le paraître.
La Rochef. Max., § 453, p. 87.—*Nothing so much prevents our
being natural, as the desire to seem so.*

2410. Rien ne pèse tant qu'un secret. La Font. 8, 6, 1 (*Les Femmes et
le Secret*).—*Nothing weighs so heavily as a secret.*

2411. Rien n'est beau que le vrai; le vrai seul est aimable. Boil.
Ep. 9, 43.—*Nothing is beautiful but truth; truth alone is
lovely.*

2412. Rien n'est si dangereux qu'un ignorant ami;
    Mieux vaudroit un sage ennemi.
                La Font. 8, 10, fin. (L'Ours et l'Amateur).

> Nothing so dangerous as an ignorant friend:
> A foe of common sense heav'n rather send!—*Ed.*

2413. Rien ne trouble sa fin: c'est le soir d'un beau jour. La Font.
Contes, 5, 9, 14 (Philémon et Baucis).—*Nothing disturbs his last
moments; it is like the evening of a fine day.*

2414. Rien ne vaut poulain s'il ne rompt son lien. Prov.—*A colt is
worth nothing unless he breaks his halter.* "No man is ever good
for much who has not been carried off his feet by enthusiasm
between twenty and thirty."—Froude, Short Studies (*Trac-
tarians*), 4th Series, 1882, p. 175.

2415. Risorgerò nemico ognor più crudo,
Cenere anco sepolto e spirto ignudo.
			Tasso, Ger. Lib., Cant. 9, fin.	Soliman (wounded and a
fugitive) loq.:
> Still will I rise a more inveterate foe
> And, dead, pursue them from the shades below.—*Hoole.*

These lines were whispered in the ear of his counsel, Jules Favre, by
Orsini, when sentence of death was pronounced on him for the *attentat* of
January 14, 1858 (*vide* Nassau Senior's Conversations).

2416. Risu inepto res ineptior nulla est.	Cat. 39, 16.—*Nothing can be
more silly than silly laughter.*

2417. Romæ rus optas, absentem rusticus Urbem
Tollis ad astra levis.			Hor. S. 2, 7, 28.
> Give me the country, is at Rome your cry:
> When there, you laud the city to the sky.—*Ed.*

Cf. id. Ep. 1, 8, 12: Romæ Tibur amem, ventosus, Tibure Romam.
> Wayward, I pine for Tibur when in Rome;
> At Tibur I regret my city home.—*Ed.*

2418. Roma locuta est, causa finita est.—*Rome has spoken, the case is
concluded.*

This is founded upon the following passage from St Augustine (vol. v.
p. 449 F), Serm. 131, 10: *Jam enim de hac causa duo concilia missa sunt
ad sedem Apostolicam. Inde etiam rescripta venerunt; causa finita est;
utinam aliquando error finiatur!* "Already the results of two councils on
this (Pelagian) question have been sent to the Apostolic See, and rescripts
have been returned thence. The case is finished; if only the heresy would
come to an end as well!"

2419. Romani ghiotti, e mal devoti.	Prov.—*The Romans are gluttons,
and not over religious.*

2420. Roma parentem,
Roma patrem patriæ Ciceronem libera dixit.	Juv. 8, 243.
Pater Patriæ.
> Parent and father of the fatherland,
> Was Cicero styled by liberated Rome.—*Ed.*

On the defeat of Catiline in 63 B.C., Cicero was hailed as "Father of his
country," in the general relief felt at the suppression of the conspiracy,
and he was hardly the man to forget the public distinction thus conferred
(*v.* Pro Sestio, 57).	Lucan (9, 601) also salutes Cato Uticensis as "Ecce
parens verus patriæ!" (*Behold the true parent of his country!*), in his
admiration of the single-handed opponent of Cæsar's advance to power.
Romulus was the first so dubbed (Ov. F. 2, 127), and under the Cæsars the
title denoted the paternal "clemency" of the sovereign (Sen. Clem. 1, 14, 2).

2421. Romulus et Liber pater et cum Castore Pollux
Post ingentia facta deorum in templa recepti.
			Hor. Ep. 2, 1, 5. – *Romulus and Bacchus, Castor and Pollux,
were received into the temples of the gods after the performance of
noble deeds.*

No such prowess or accomplishments seem nowadays demanded of
candidates for public honours, peerages, and decorations, which are merely
assigned as the appendages of wealth, or the rewards of party.

2422. Roy ne puys, Prince (*or* Duc) ne daygne, Rohan suys.   Motto of
the house of Rohan.—*King I cannot be, Prince* (or *Duke*) *I would
not be, Rohan I remain.*

A proud motto indeed, and thoroughly characteristic of the ancient
Breton family of which it is the boast—one of the dozen or half-dozen
noble and non-regnant houses of the highest rank that Europe has
to show. Descended from the old dukes of Brittany, the Rohans were
related to every royal line in Christendom, and a lady of that lineage is
said to have responded to the proposals of a King of France with, "Je suis
trop pauvre pour être votre femme, et de trop bonne maison pour être
votre maîtresse." By Louis XIV. the de Rohans, in virtue of their
ancient descent, were granted the rank of "princes étrangers," and treated
with all the respect and dignity befitting their origin. Henri, the *grand
duc de Rohan*, the leader of the Huguenots and devoted follower of Henri
Quatre, is the most celebrated member of the family, and the Cardinal
(Louis Réné Edouard) of unhappy Diamond Necklace fame, the most
notorious. Banished from France by the Revolution, the Rohans are
still represented by the Rohan-Guémenée-Rocheforts, now domiciled (and
naturalised) in Austria—that refuge of more than one lost cause. Sainte-
Beuve, *Causeries du Lundi*, vol. 12, 247-94.

2423. Ruhe ist die erste Bürgerpflicht.   Graf von der Schulenberg-
Kehnert (*v.* Büchm. p. 524).—*Tranquillity is the citizen's first
duty.*   Part of a general order posted in the public places of
Berlin three days after the battle of Jena (Oct. 14, 1806), which,
for the time, practically obliterated the Prussian kingdom.

2424. Rura mihi et rigui placeant in vallibus amnes,
Flumina amem sylvasque inglorius.   Virg. G. 2, 485.

> Let field and grove, let babbling brook and stream,
> Be my delightful tho' inglorious theme.—*Ed.*

2425. Rusticus es, Corydon.   Virg. E. 2, 56.—*You are but a rustic,
Corydon.*   You are very simple, green.

S.

2426. Sache qu'on ne prend jamais le roi, pas même aux échecs.   Dreux
de Radier, Tablettes Historiques, vol. 1, p. 148 (Fourn. *L.D.L.*,
p. 67).—*Know that the king is never taken, not even at chess.*

Anecdote of Louis VI. at the battle of Brenneville, 1119 A.D.   An
English horseman had seized the king's reins, exclaiming, "the king is
taken," whereupon Louis is supposed to have made the *mot* given above.

2427. Sæpe Faunorum voces exauditæ, sæpe visæ formæ deorum.
Cic. N. D., 2, 2, 6.—*Often have been clearly heard the voices of
the sylvan deities, and god-like shapes are often seen.*

Applicable to the spirit of nature pervading beautiful scenery with its
manifold life.   Here and there by fountain or grove one imagines glimpses
of the fabled gods.

2428. Sæpe mihi dubiam traxit sententia mentem,
Curarent superi terras, an nullus inesset
Rector, et incerto fluerent mortalia casu.   Claud. Rufin. 1, I.

The Agnostic.

Oft has the thought perplexed my wondering mind,
If the gods minded earth ; or if the world
Were left to drift, with no one at the helm.—*Ed.*

2429. Sæpe premente deo fert deus alter opem. Ov. T. 1, 2, 4.—*When*
we are assailed by one deity, another often comes to our assistance.

2430. Sæpe rogare soles qualis sim, Prisce, futurus,
Si fiam locuples simque repente potens.
Quemquam posse putas mores narrare futuros ?
Dic mihi, si fias tu leo, qualis eris ?   Mart. 12, 93.

Foolish Questions.

Priscus, you often ask what sort of man
I'd be, if rich and suddenly grown great.
Forecast such possibilities who can?
Were you a lion, what would be your state?—*Ed.*

Addison takes the last line for his paper (*Spectator* 13) on Nicolini's
combat with the lion at H.M. Theatre in 1710; the part of lion being
acted successively by a tailor, a candle-snuffer, and an amateur.

2431. Sæpe stilum vertas, iterum quæ digna legi sint
Scripturus ; neque te ut miretur turba labores,
Contentus paucis lectoribus.   Hor. S. 1, 10, 72.

Oh yes ! believe me, you must draw your pen
Not once or twice, but o'er and o'er again
Through what you've written, if you would entice
The man that reads you once to read you twice,
Not making popular applause your cue,
But looking to fit audience, although few.—*Conington.*

2432. Sæpe summa ingenia in occulto latent. Plaut. Capt. 1, 2, 62.—
The most brilliant talents often lie concealed in obscurity.

2433. Sæpe tacens vocem verbaque vultus habet. Ov. A. A. 1, 574.—
Often a silent countenance conveys words and meaning of its own.

2434. Salus populi suprema lex esto. Law Max. ap Cic. Leg. 3, 3, 8.—
The public welfare is the highest law. One of the laws of the
XII. Tables.

2435. Salva conscientia. Sen. Ep. 117, 1.—*With a safe conscience.*
(2.) Salva fide. Cic. Off. 3, 10, 44.—*Without breaking one's word.*
(3.) Salvis auspiciis. Cic. Prov. Cons. 19, 45.—*With safe auspices.*
(4.) Salvo jure nostræ veteris amicitiæ. Cic. Fam. 13, 77, 1.—
Without damage to the claims of our old friendship. (5.) Salvo
ordine. Stat. S. 5, 1, 181.—*Saving our order.* (6.) Salvo poetæ
sensu. Quint. 1, 9, 2.—*Preserving the poet's meaning.* (7.) Salvo
pudore. Ov. Ep. 1, 2, 66.—*With a due regard to decency.*

2436. Salve, o casta e pia dimora! Achille de Lauzières (tr. from the French of J. Barbier and M. Carré). Faust, Opera, Music by Gounod, Act 3, sc. 4. (Faust before Marguerite's house).— *Hail! thou chaste and pious abode!*

2437. Sanctius his animal, mentisque capacius altæ
Deerat adhuc, et quod dominari in cætera posset:
Natus homo est.   Ov. M. 1, 76.

> A creature of a more exalted kind
> Was wanting yet, and then was man designed;
> Conscious of thought, of more capacious breast
> For empire formed, and fit to rule the rest.—*Dryden.*

2438. Sanctus haberi, Justitiæque tenax factis dictisque mereris?
Agnosco procerem.   Juv. 8, 24.

> Dare to be just,
> Firm to your word, and faithful to your trust:
> These praises hear, at least deserve to hear,
> I grant your claim, and recognise the peer.—*Gifford.*

2439. Sans peur et sans reproche.— *Without fear and without reproach.*

> Pierre du Terrail, Chevalier Bayard of the Château Bayard near Grenoble (1476-1524), the pearl of French chivalry, earned even in his lifetime the glorious and immortal title of the "Chevalier sans peur, etc.," by which he has since been distinguished. In 1525, the year following his death, appeared "La tresioyeuse plaisante et recreative hystoire . . . du bon chevalier *sans paour et sans reprouche*, le gentil seigneur de Bayart," to be seen in the Bibliothèque Nationale. *V.* Büchm. p. 472.

2440. Sans phrase.— *Without phrases.* Without circumlocution or equivocation, simply, expeditiously.

> The words have become notorious in connection with the famous *La mort sans phrase*, attributed to Sieyès on the occasion of voting the sentence on Louis XVI. The *Moniteur* of the day (Jan. 20, 1793) records his vote thus: "*Syeyes* (*sic*). La Mort."; *i.e.*, the Abbé confined the wording of his vote to these two words, without adding the justifying reasons given by some (but not many) of the other members of the Convention. *V.* No. 1159.

2441. Satis diu hoc jam saxum volvo. Prov. (Ter. Eun. 5, 9, 55).—*I have now been rolling this stone sufficiently long.* Figure borrowed from the story of Sisyphus.

2442. Satis diu vel naturæ vixi, vel gloriæ. Cic. Marcell. 8, 25.—*I have lived long enough to satisfy the claims both of nature and military glory.* Uttered by C. J. Cæsar at fifty-four, not two years before his assassination.

2443. Satis superque est. Plaut. Amph. 1, 1, 14.—*Enough, and more than enough.* Said of anything which is carried to an unnecessary length.

2444. Satis superque me benignitas tua Ditavit. Hor. Epod. 1, 31.— *Your bounty has enriched me enough, and more than enough.* Written by the poet to his patron, Mæcenas.

2445. Saucius ejurat pugnam gladiator, et idem
      Immemor antiqui vulneris arma capit.
          Ov. Ep. 1, 5, 37.—*The wounded gladiator forswears fighting,*
      and yet forgetting his old wound he takes up arms again.

2446. Sa veuve inconsolable continue son commerce. Les Enfants de
      la Bonnetière, in L'Artiste, vol. i. p. 272 (1832). Alex. p. 528.—
      His inconsolable widow keeps on the business.

> Charlet, the designer of the lithograph from which the quotation is taken,
> vouches that the inscription was copied from the tomb of a certain "P.
> Gonnet, marchand bonnetier, of No. 17, Rue Maubuée, Paris, who deceased
> June 1, 1822," and that Veuve Gonnet took the opportunity to advertise the
> public that the shop was still willing to take orders. I know one parallel
> in English, but whether it is older or more recent than the Gonnet case I
> cannot say. The sepulchral inscription in question is as follows:—

> Beneath this stone, in hopes of Zion,
> Is laid the Landlord of the *Lion.*

> — • —

> Resigned unto the heavenly will,
> His widow keeps the business still.

2447. Scheint die Sonne noch so schön,
      Einmal muss sie untergehen.
              Ferd. Raimund, Der Bauer als Millionär, 2, 6.
      (Büchm. p. 244).

> Shine the sun never so bright,
> At last he sinketh out of sight.—*Ed.*

2448. Scilicet expectas, ut tradat mater honestos
      Atque alios mores, quam quos habet?
              Juv. 6, 239.—*Can you expect that a mother will inculcate on*
      her children any better principles than she practises herself?

2449. Scimus, et hanc veniam petimusque damusque vicissim.
                                              Hor. A. P. 11.
      I own it : 'tis a fair excuse to plead ;
      By turns we claim it, and by turns concede.—*Conington.*

> *Damus petimusque vicissim* is the M. of British Guiana, and its peculiar
> appropriateness was evidenced in the Venezuelan difficulty of 1895-6, and
> in the final award of the Arbitration Tribunal of Oct. 3, 1899.

2450. Scire tuum nihil est, nisi te scire hoc sciat alter. Per. 1, 27.—
      Your knowledge is of no account unless others know that you
      know.

2451. Scribendi recte sapere est et principium et fons.   Hor. A. P. 309.
      Of writing well be sure the secret lies
      In wisdom : therefore study to be wise.—*Conington.*

2452. Scribendo dicimus diligentius, dicendo scribimus facilius.—*The*
      habit of writing enables us to speak with greater accuracy; and
      that of speaking to write with greater facility. This is formed
      from "Ut scribendo dicamus diligentius, dicendo scribamus
      facilius" (Quint. 10, 7, 29).

2453. Scribentem juvat ipse favor, minuitque laborem,
Cumque suo crescens pectore fervet opus.   Ov. Ep. 3, 9, 21.

Favour assists and cheers the author's art,
And, as it grows, his work comes from the heart.—*Ed.*

2454. Scribimus, et scriptos absumimus igne libellos ;
Exitus est studii parva favilla mei.   Ov. T. 5, 12, 61.

I write, and throw into the flame what's writ ;
A little ash is all that comes of it.—*Ed.*

2455. Scriptorum chorus omnis amat nemus et fugit urbem,
Rite cliens Bacchi somno gaudentis et umbra.   Hor. Ep. 2, 2, 77.

Bards fly from town and haunt the wood and glade :
Bacchus, their chief, likes sleeping in the shade.—*Conington.*

2456. Scriptura rerum, de quibus loquitur, definitiones non tradit, ut
nec etiam natura.   Spinoza, Tract. Theol. Pol. 7, 13.—*Scripture,
any more than Nature, lays down no definition of the things of
which it speaks.*

2457. Se a ciascun l'interno affanno
Si leggesse in fronte scritto,
Quanti mai che invidia fanno
Ci farebbero pietà !

Metastasio, Giuseppe Riconosciuto, Pt. I.—*If the secret
troubles of every one were written on his forehead for all to read,
how many who now excite envy, would excite our pity !*

2458. Secreta hæc murmura vulgi.   Juv. 10, 89.—*These sullen murmur-
ings of the people.*

2459. Securus judicat orbis terrarum.   St Aug. contra Epist. Parmen.
iii. 24 (vol. ix. 48 C).—*The verdict of the world is conclusive.*

Respecting the Donatist schism in N. Africa of the fifth century, the
world (says St Augustine) is of opinion that their separation cannot be
defended on its own grounds, much less when referred to the principle of
unity which is of the Church's essence. Its judgment is too wide to admit
of partiality, and too unanimous to allow of doubt. The decision is
absolute. The passage owes its celebrity to Newman's employment of it,
and the weight that it had in undermining his faith in the Anglican position will be remembered by all who have read his *Apologia.* Its immediate
effect upon himself was to "pulverise the *Via Media* into atoms," since it
meant that "the deliberate judgment in which the whole Church rests and
acquiesces is an infallible prescription, and a final sentence, against such
portions of it as protest and secede" (J. H. Newman, *Apologia pro vita
sua,* Lond., 1878, 8vo, p. 117). The maxim, "L'universale non s'inganna"
(*The world at large is never taken in*), is but another form of the same
truth, to which may be added the pertinent reflection of Quitard
(pp. 597-8): "Il est rare, en effet, que le jugement de tous ne soit pas la
révélation du vrai, et l'instinct du bien. Mais il ne faut pas confondre la
voix du peuple avec les bruits populaires."

2460. Sed Cæsar in omnia præceps
Nil actum credens, si quid superesset agendum,
Instat atrox.   Lucan. 2, 656.

But Cæsar in headlong career,
Counting nought done, if aught whate'er
Remained undone, drives fiercely on.—*Ed.*

2461. Sed de me ut sileam.   Ov. Ep. 1, 2, 145.—*But, not to speak of myself.*

2462. Sed difficulter continetur spiritus,
Integritatis qui sinceræ conscius
A noxiorum premitur insolentiis.

   Phædr. 3, Epil. 29.—*The spirit of conscious integrity is with difficulty restrained, when offended by the insolent attacks of guilty men.*

2463. Sedet æternumque sedebit Infelix Theseus.   Virg. A. 6, 617.—*There sits the unhappy Theseus, and will ever sit.*   Imprisoned in the lower world for his attempt to rescue Proserpine, Theseus remained until rescued by Hercules.

2464. Sed fugit, interea, fugit irreparabile tempus,
Singula dum capti circumvectamur amore.   Virg. G. 3, 284.

Sight-seeing.

But time, perforce, slips by as we go through
In detail every thing that charms the view.—*Ed.*

2465. Sed fulgente trahit constrictos gloria curru
Non minus ignotos generosis.   Hor. S. 1, 6, 23.

But glory like a conqueror drags behind
Her glittering car the souls of all mankind:
Nor less the lowly than the noble feels
The onward roll of those victorious wheels.—*Conington.*

2466. Seditione dolis scelere atque libidine et ira,
Iliacos intra muros peccatur, et extra.   Hor. Ep. 1, 2, 15.

Strife, treachery, crime, lust, rage—'tis error all;
One mass of faults within, without the wall.—*Conington.*

2467. Sed nec mihi dicere promtum, Nec facere est illi.   Ov. M. 13, 10.
—*As little skill have I in speech, as he in action.*   Ajax' reply, when contending with Ulysses for the arms of Achilles.   "I have no small talk, and Peel has no manners," said another Ajax, when called upon to form the second administration of the young Queen in 1841.

2468. Sed nisi peccassem, quid tu concedere posses?
Materiam veniæ sors tibi nostra dedit.   Ov. T. 2, 31.

But what could you forgive, had I not erred?
The grounds for pardon my misdeeds conferred.—*Ed.*

2469. Sed non in Cæsare tantum
Nomen erat, nec fama ducis: sed nescia virtus
Stare loco: solusque pudor non vincere bello.   Luc. 1, 143.

> But more there was in Cæsar's fame
> Than titled leadership and name:
> His was the keen, unsated breast
> That never knew repose or rest;
> His only shame, in battle fray,
> To fight and not to gain the day.—*Ed.*

2470. Sed nunc non erat his locus.   Hor. A. P. 19.

All in their way good things, but not just now.—*Conington.*

2471. Sed quid poetas? Opifices post mortem nobilitari volunt. Quid enim Phidias sui similem speciem inclusit in clypeo Minervæ, quum inscribere non liceret? Quid? Nostri Philosophi nonne in his ipsis libris, quos scribunt de contemnenda gloria, sua nomina inscribunt? Cic. Tusc. 1, 15, 34.—*But not poets only; artists also wish to be rendered famous after death. Else, how is it that Phidias, when he was not allowed to write his name on the sculpture, included a portrait of himself among the figures of Minerva's shield? I might say the same of our philosophers. Have they not, even in the very works in which they preach contempt for human glory, inscribed their own names upon the title-page?*

It will be remembered that Sir J. Reynolds inscribed his name upon the hem of Mrs Siddon's robe, in his portrait of her as the Tragic Muse. The letters are now barely legible.

2472. Sed tamen amoto quæramus seria ludo.   Hor. S. 1, 1, 27.—*But, joking apart, let us devote ourselves to more serious matters.*

2473. Sed te, mihi crede, memento
Nunc in pellicula, cerdo, tenere tua.   Mart. 3, 16, 5.

> *Stick to your Last.*
> But, trust me, good cobbler, and pray recollect
> Henceforward to stick to your last.—*Ed.*

2474. Sed tu Ingenio verbis concipe plura meis.   Ov. R. A. 360.—*You must please to understand more than is expressed by my words.* The reader is to read between the lines.

2475. Sed vatem egregium cui non sit publica vena,
Qui nihil expositum soleat deducere, nec qui
Communi feriat carmen triviale moneta,
Hunc qualem nequeo monstrare, et sentio tantum,
Anxietate carens animus facit.   Juv. 7, 53.

> *The Ideal Poet.*
> The perfect poet, of no vulgar vein,
> Who will produce no trite and hackneyed strain,
> Nor mint you trivial verse of common ore,
> He—whom I cannot paint but feel the more—
> Must have a mind by hardship undistressed,
> And by no sad anxieties opprest.—*Ed.*

2476. Segnius irritant animos demissa per aurem,
Quam quæ sunt oculis subjecta fidelibus, et quæ
Ipse sibi tradit spectator.   Hor. A. P. 180.

> A thing when heard, remember, strikes less keen
> On the spectator's mind than when 'tis seen.—*Conington.*

> Cf. Sen. Ep. 6, 5, Homines amplius oculis quam auribus credunt—*Men
> believe what they see far more than what they hear.*

2477. Seigneur, tant de prudence entraîne trop de soin :
Je ne sais point prévoir les malheurs de si loin.
                              Rac. Andromaque, 1, 2.

> *Pyrrhus.* Such prudence, sir, entaileth too much care :
> I can't foresee disaster quite so far.—*Ed.*

2478. Sei im Besitze, und du wohnst im Recht.   Schiller, Wallensteins
Tod, 1, 4.—*Be in possession and you are in the right.*

2479. Semen est sanguis Christianorum.   Tert. Apol. 50, ad fin.—*The
blood of Christians is seed.*

> Don't think, says Tertullian (addressing the pagan persecutors of his
> day), that persecution will have any effect in diminishing the number of
> Christians. *Plures efficimur quoties metimur a vobis, semen est s. C.*, "The
> more you mow us down, the more we grow. The blood of the martyrs is
> the harvest-seed of the Church."

2480. Semper avarus eget : certum voto pete finem :
Invidus alterius macrescit rebus opimis.
Invidia Siculi non invenere tyranni
Majus tormentum.   Hor. Ep. 1, 2, 56.

> The miser's always needy : draw a line
> Within whose bound your wishes to confine.
> His neighbour's fatness makes the envious lean :
> No tyrant e'er devised a pang so keen.—*Conington.*

2481. Semper eadem.—*Always the same.*   Motto of Queen Elizabeth.

> Thou sun, shine on her joyously ! Ye breezes, waft her wide !
> Our glorious *Semper eadem !* the banner of our pride !—*Macaulay* (Armada).

> For the motto of her predecessor, our first queen-regnant, see "Veritas"
> below. Mary the Second seems to have been contented with her husband's
> *Je maintiendray*, but *Semper eadem* figured upon her hearse in the Abbey,
> along with *Dieu et mon droit* and other texts. Anne, on the other hand,
> returned to Elizabeth's motto, and on her accession expressly ordered that
> it should always accompany the blazon of the royal arms. It is too late
> now, but it cannot but be a matter of regret that the famous epigraph
> of Elizabeth was not also adopted and borne by a greater queen-regnant
> than them all. It would not have cancelled the existing mottoes of the
> Crown, as neither did it in those other reigns, beside that the very wording
> of the phrase implies the absence of all change : a personal, rather than an
> official "touch," that linked our female sovereigns in a golden chain. At
> no period of her prolonged reign, in youth, or middle life, or extreme age,
> would the revival of the *Semper eadem* have been premature, and lateness
> would but have made it more impressive. It would always have had its
> meaning, sometimes a very deep one, and often its own felicitous applica-
> tion : in the hour of her great sorrow, for example ; or fifteen years later (with

even greater significance), when to the old style of our sovereigns was added the title of "Empress," that sounded at first strangely in English ears. How fitly, again, might the motto have been adopted to grace and signalise the year of Jubilee! What trains of thought it would have stirred! What added feelings of loyalty it would have kindled! An expression of something greater than sentiment, the symbol of confidence and strength; which, in those dark moments of distress that must come at times to every country, would have steadied the pulses of the nation, and with its watchword of unchanging steadfastness have braced the nerve to meet the event with courage.

2482. Semper ego auditor tantum, nunquamne repono? Juv. 1, 1.

> Shall I ever listen only,
> And make no retaliation.—*Shaw.*

2483. Semper enim falsis a vero petitur veritas. Sen. Q. N. lib. 4, Præf. med.—*Falsehood always attacks truth in the guise of truth.*

2484. Semper eris pauper, si pauper es, Æmiliane;
Dantur opes nulli nunc nisi divitibus.   Mart. 5, 81.

> If poor, Emilian, you'll be poor always;
> Wealth is but given to rich men nowadays.—*Ed.*

2485. Semper honos, nomenque tuum, laudesque manebunt. Virg. A. 1, 609.

> Always shall live your honour, name, and praise.—*Conington.*

2486. Semper tu scito: flamma fumo est proxuma:
Fumo comburi nihil potest, flamma potest.
    Plaut. Curc. 1, 1, 53.—*Where there is smoke there is fire: smoke can't burn, but fire can.* Avoid not only sin, but its occasions.

2487. Sempre al pensier tornavano
Gl' irrevocati dì.   Manzoni, Adelchi, Act 4.

> Ever in thought returned to me
> The days that are no more.—*Ed.*

2488. Senilis stultitia, quæ deliratio appellari solet, senum levium est, non omnium. Cic. Sen. 11, 36.—*That foolishness of old age, which is called dotage, is the fruit of a frivolous life, and is not universal.*

> Senex delirans. Ter. Ad. 4, 7, 43.—*A doting old man.* (2.) Senile illud facinus. App. Met. 4, p. 148, 9.—*That wicked old thing.* Said of an old woman.

2489. Se non è vero, è ben trovato.   Prov.—*If it is not true, it is a happy invention.*

> Source unknown: apparently a common saying in the 16th cent. Fumag. (No. 1364) quotes the *Marmi* of Antonio Franc. Doni (1st ed., 1552) for *Se non è vero, egli è stato un bel trovato* (Florence ed., 1863, p. 76). In his *Gli eroici furori* (Paris, 1585, Pt. 2, Dialog. 3), Giordano Bruno has *Se non è vero, è molto ben trovato* (Opere di G. Bruno, pub. Ad. Wagner, Leipzig, 1830, vol. 1, p. 415); and a little later we get the prov. in French, "*Si cela n'est vray, il est bien trouvé*," in Estienne Pasquier's (1547-1616) *Recherches de la France*, lib. viii. 43 A.   (Paris, 1665, p. 719.)

2490. S'entendre comme larrons en foire.　Prov.—*To come to an understanding* (act in concert) *like thieves at a fair.*

2491. Septem convivium, novem convitium.　Prov.—*Seven's a banquet,
nine's a brawl.*

2492. Septem urbs alta jugis, toti quæ præsidet orbi.　Prop. 3, 11, 57.
The city built on seven hills, that governs all the world.—*Ed.*

2493. Sequitur fortunam, ut semper, et odit
Damnatos.　　Juv. 10, 73.
[The mob] *follows, as ever, the lead of fortune, and hates the
fallen.*　Said of the fall of Sejanus, 31 A.D.

2494. Sequiturque patrem non passibus æquis.　Virg. A. 2, 724.—*He
follows his father with unequal steps.*　Said of Iulus trying to
keep pace with his father Æneas.

Applicable to the son of any distinguished man who "follows in his
father's steps," but not with as great a "stride" of progress and power:
e.g., Richard Cromwell, Louis Racine, the younger Kean, etc.

2495. Sera parsimonia in fundo est.　Prov. (Sen. Ep. 1, 5).—*It is too late
to save when all is spent* (lit., "at the bottom of the purse").
Cf. δειλὴ δ'ἐνὶ πυθμένι φειδώ.　Hes. 367.—*It's poor savings when
you come to the bottom of the cup.*

2496. Seria quum possim, quod delectantia malim
Scribere, tu causa es, lector.　　Mart. 5, 16, 1.
Reader, it is for you this pleasing strain,
When I might write in a more serious vein.—*Ed.*

2497. Serit arbores quæ sæclo prosint alteri.　Cæcil. Statius, Syne-
phebi, Fr. II. (ii. 80).—*He is planting trees which will benefit a
future age.*　"He that plants pears, plants for his heirs."

2498. Sero.—*Too late.*　Among prov. sayings illustrative of typically
procrastinatory action may be quoted the following :—

(1.) Sero sapiunt Phryges. Fest. p. 343, ed. Müll.—*The Trojans are wise
when it is too late.*　In the tenth year of the Trojan war they begin to
think of the advisability of restoring Helen.　(2.) Sero clypeum post vulnera
sumo. Ov. T. 1, 3, 35.—*Too late to take the shield now that I'm wounded.*

(3.) Sero respicitur tellus, ubi fune soluto,
Currit in immensum panda carina salum.　Ov. Am. 2, 11, 23.

It is too late to look back to the land,
With moorings loosed, and keel slipped from the strand.—*Ed.*

(4.) Serum auxilium post prælium. Liv. 3, 5.—*Aid comes too late after the
fight is over.*　Cf. the (identical) μετὰ τὸν πόλεμον ἡ συμμαχία of Diogenes
Cynicus in Diog. Laert. 6, 50; and μετὰ τὸν πόλεμον ἥκειν (see Chil.
p. 637), *to arrive after the battle*, as Grouchy did after Waterloo.　(5.) Post
festum venire (κατόπιν ἑορτῆς ἥκομεν. Plat. Gorg. 447A)—*To come after the
feast.*　(6.) Post mortem medicina (*or* medicus)—*After death the doctor.*

2499. Sero molunt deorum molæ.　Chil. p. 728 (*Ultio*).—*The mills of
the gods grind slowly.*　Retribution, though delayed, always

overtakes the wicked. This truth is enforced by many authors, *e.g.*:

(1.) ὀψὲ θεῶν ἀλέουσι μύλοι, ἀλέουσι δὲ λεπτά. Sextus Empiricus, *Adversus Grammaticos*, 1, 13, § 287, (J. A. Fabricius, Lipsiæ, 1842, vol. 2, p. 112).—"*The mills of God grind slowly, but they grind exceeding small.*"—Longfellow. (2.) Sera tamen tacitis poena venit pedibus. Tib. 1, 9, 4.—*Though late, with silent steps punition comes.*

(3.) Raro antecedentem scelestum
Deseruit pede poena claudo.   Hor. C. 3, 2, 31.

Though vengeance halt, she seldom leaves
The wretch whose flying steps she hounds.—*Conington.*

(4.) Lento enim gradu ad vindictam sui divina procedit ira: tarditatemque supplicii gravitate compensat. Val. Max. 1, Ext. 3, fin.—*The divine wrath moves with slow steps in the path of retribution, and makes up for slowness by the severity of the punishment inflicted.*

2500. Servetur ad imum
Qualis ab incepto processerit, et sibi constet.   Hor. A. P. 126.

Literary Composition.
See it be wrought on one consistent plan,
And end the same creation it began.—*Conington.*

2501. Seul roi de qui le pauvre ait gardé la mémoire.   P. Ph. Gudin de la Brenellerie.

The only king remembered of the poor.

Said of Henry IV. with reference to his celebrated *poule au pot.* The line occurs in a piece which de la Brenellerie sent to the Academy in competition for the Poetry prize of 1779, and was pronounced a fitting inscription for the statue of Henry the Great. Under date August of that year, Grimm refers to the usual meeting of the Academy on St Louis' Day (July 25), to read over the papers sent in by the candidates for the *Prix*, and adds: "Il ne faut pas oublier un très-beau vers qui se trouve dans une des pièces qui ont concouru, et que l'Académie a cru devoir citer comme un vers digne de servir d'inscription à la statue de Henri IV. Ce beau vers est de M. Gudin, auteur de la tragédie de *Coriolan*," etc. Grimm's (F. M.) *Correspondance*, Paris, 1830, vol. 10, p. 208; Fourn. *L.D.A.*, pp. 227-8; and Larousse, *Dict. Univ.*, *s.v.* GUDIN.

2502. Severæ Musa tragœdiæ.   Hor. C. 2, 1, 9.—*The stern muse of tragedy* (Melpomene).

2503. Sex horis dormire sat est juvenique senique:
Septem vix pigro; nulli concedimus octo. Coll. Sal., vol. i. l. 129.

Six hours' sleep's enough for old and young:
Slugs scarce taken seven ; and eight we grant to none.—*Ed.*

Cf. Six hours to sleep, in law's grave study six :
Four spend in prayer, the rest on nature fix.
—*Quoted by Sir E. Coke.*

2504. Si bene commemini causæ sunt quinque bibendi :
Hospitis adventus, præsens sitis, atque futura,
Et vini bonitas, et quælibet altera causa.
Père Sirmond, ap. Menagiana, Amsterdam, 1693, p. 139.

> If on my theme I rightly think
> There are five reasons why men drink:
> Good wine; a friend; because I'm dry;
> Or lest I should be by and by:
> Or any other reason why.—*Dean Aldrich*, 1710.

2505. Sibi quisque ruri metit.   Prov. (Plaut. Most. 3, 2, 112).—*Every man reaps his own field.*   Every one consults his own interests.

2506. Sic agitur censura et sic exempla parantur,
    Quum vindex alios quod monet ipse facit.   Ov. F. 6, 647.

> Censors are just, and good examples teach,
> When worthy censors practise what they preach.—*Ed.*

2507. Siccis omnia nam dura deus proposuit; neque
    Mordaces aliter diffugiunt solicitudines.   Hor. C. 1, 18, 3.

> Life is all one path of troubles
> To the water-drinker's soul:
> Carking cares will fly like bubbles
> If you drown them in the bowl.—*Ed.*

2508. Si c'est un crime de l'aimer,
    On n'en doit justement blasmer
    Que les beautez qui sont en elle;
    La faute en est aux dieux
    Qui la firent si belle,
    Et non pas à mes yeux.
        Jean de Lingendes, Recueil des plus belles pièces des poètes fr. (1692), vol. 3, p. 36ᴀ.

> If it be a crime to love her,
> 'Seems to me the only sinner
> Is the loveliness that's in her;
> You must blame the gods above her
> Who such beauty did devise,
> And not my poor foolish eyes.—*Ed.*

*** Gresset in *Le Méchant* (2, 7) parodies Lingendes with " La faute en est aux dieux qui la firent si *bête*."

2509. Sic noctem patera, sic ducam carmine, donec
    Injiciat radios in mea vina dies.   Prop. 4, 6, 85.

> *The Convivial Toper.*
> With songs and toasts I'll pass the night away,
> Till on my wine-glass morning sheds its ray. —*Ed.*

2510. Si consilium vis,
    Permittes ipsis expendere numinibus quid
    Conveniat nobis, rebusque sit utile nostris.
    Nam pro jucundis aptissima quæque dabunt Di.
    Carior est illis homo quam sibi.   Juv. 10, 346.

> If you take my advice, you will allow
> The gods themselves their blessings to bestow,
> Such as they deem are most appropriate
> And serviceable to our several state.
> They'll give what's fit, 'stead of some fancied whim:
> Man loves himself not half as they love him.—*Ed.*

2511. Sic qui pauperiem veritus, potiore metallis
Libertate caret, dominum vehet improbus, atque
Serviet æternum, quia parvo nesciet uti.   Hor. Ep. 1, 10, 39.

> So he who fearing penury loses hold
> Of independence, better far than gold,
> Will toil, a hopeless drudge, till life is spent
> Because he'll never, never learn content.—*Conington.*

2512. Sic quum transierint mei
Nullo cum strepitu dies,
Plebeius moriar senex.
Illi mors gravis incubat,
Qui notus nimis omnibus,
Ignotus moritur sibi.   Sen. Thyest. 398.

> So when my days, in quiet passed,
> Have reached their span, I'll die at last,
> Both name and fame unsought:
> Who to the world is fully known,
> A stranger to himself alone,
> Finds death a dreadful thought.—*Ed.*

2513. Sic ruit in celebres cultissima fœmina ludos.   Ov. A. A. 1, 97.—
Thus every fashionable lady flocks to the celebrated games: viz.,
the races in the Circus, or at Pompey's theatre.

2514. Sic sedit: sic culta fuit: sic stamina nevit:
Neglectæ collo sic jacuere comæ.   Ov. F. 2, 771.

> *Lucrece.*
> Thus sate she: thus attired: her thread thus spun:
> Thus on her neck her hair lay all undone.—*Ed.*

2515. Sic, sic se habere rem necesse prorsus est:
Ratione vincis, do lubens manus, Plato.
Trans. by Dean Bland (Prov. of Eton Coll.) of Addison's *Cato:*
> It must be so—Plato, thou reasonest well.

2516. Sic transit gloria mundi.—*Thus the glory of this world passeth away.*

> The words are recited in one of the most impressive portions of the ceremonial attending the Pope's coronation.   Proceeding from the Sagristia of St Peter's in his *sedia gestatoria,* the Pope-elect and his procession halt three times on the way—once always before St Peter's statue—and on each occasion a silver reed bearing a lock of tow at its summit is ignited and raised aloft by one of the Masters of the Ceremonies, who, as the tow flares away in its socket, says, *Sancte Pater, sic transit gloria mundi!* It is said that when the customary words were addressed to Sixtus V. (May 1, 1585), he exclaimed, "Our glory shall never pass away, for we have no other glory than to do righteous judgment!"   In the "Imitation" (1, 3, 6) is, O quam cito transit gloria mundi!—*Oh! how quickly the glory of this world passes away!*

2517. Sicut meus est mos
Nescio quid meditans nugarum, totus in illis.   Hor. S. 1, 9, 1.
> Deep in some bagatelle, you know my way.—*Conington.*

2518. Sicut populus, sic sacerdos.   Prov. (Vulg. Os. 4, 9).—*Like people, like priest.*

2519. Sic visum Veneri; cui placet impares
Formas atque animos sub juga ahenea
    Sævo mittere cum joco.   Hor. C. 1, 33, 10.
So Venus wills it: 'neath her brazen yoke,
She loves to couple forms and minds unlike,
    All for a heartless joke.—*Conington.*

2520. Si damnosa senem juvat alea, ludit et hæres.   Juv. 14, 4.—*If the father loves the ruinous dice-box, the heir will play too.*   Force of bad example.

2521. Si Dieu me donne encore de la vie, je ferai qu'il n'y aura point de laboureur en mon royaume qui n'ait moyen d'avoir une poule dans son pot.   Hardouin de Péréfixe, Hist. de Henry le Grand, Paris, 1876, p. 335.—*If God grant me life, I will see that every labouring man in my kingdom shall have his fowl to put in the pot.*

"La poule au pot!" The famous dream and *mot* of the bon Henry! There is no valid reason for questioning the essential veracity of the tradition, spite of the fun that has been poked at it. It will be observed that the original authority for this truly royal sentiment omits the introductory *Je veux* or *je souhais*, with which the saying is usually prefaced, together with other picturesque and circumstantial details, such as the dish making its appearance "on the table," and "at each Sunday's dinner" —garnishings of fancy with which later generations have "dressed" the Bearnais' chicken. Péréfixe's own relation, on the other hand, has about it all the simplicity of fact—"Je ferai que" (*I shall see that*) is king-like spoken; and he adds that the words occurred in conversation with the Duke of Savoy (Charles Emmanuel, 1580-1630) at St Germains, who, in fact, paid a visit to the French king, at St Germains, in 1600. On the accession of Louis XVI. in 1774, the hopes formed of the young and virtuous king found expression in a *Resurrexit*, discovered one morning attached to the pedestal of Henry the Fourth's statue on the Pont Neuf. The incident gave rise to the following epigram:—

    Resurrexit! j'approuve fort ce mot,
    Mais, pour y croire, il faut la poule au pot.

This was succeeded by another, expressing the opinion that the "chicken" must be nearly ready,

    Car depuis deux cent ans qu'on nous l'avait promise
    On n'a pas cessé de la plumer.   Larousse, Fleurs Historiques, p. 502.

2522. Si Dieu n'existait pas, il faudrait l'inventer.   Volt. Ep. 96, 22 (A l'auteur des Trois Imposteurs, 1769).—*If God did not exist, it would be necessary to invent Him.*

The (anonymous) *Traité des trois imposteurs* had come out the year previous, and was pronounced by Voltaire to be "très mauvais ouvrage, plein d'un athéisme grossier." In his own rejoinder, the passage in question concludes thus,

    Si les cieux, dépouillés de son empreinte auguste,
    Pouvaient jamais cesser de le manifester,
    Si Dieu n'existait pas, il faudrait l'inventer.

Tillotson († 1694) had already said, "If God were not a necessary Being of Himself, he might almost seem to be made for the use and benefit of men." (*Sermons*, Lond., 1707-12, vol. 1, p. 696, Serm. 93.)

2523. Sie sollen ihn nicht haben,
Den freien deutschen Rhein.
Nic. Becker, Rheinisch. Jahrbuch, 1841, p. 365; Büchm.
p. 256.—*They never shall possess it, the free, the German Rhine.*

2524. Si foret in terris, rideret Democritus.　Hor. Ep. 2, 1, 194.
O could Democritus return to earth
In truth 'twould wake his wildest peals of mirth.—*Conington.*

2525. Si fore vis sanus, ablue sæpe manus.　Coll. Salern.i.p.449,ver.125.
—*If you would keep in health, wash your hands frequently.*

2526. Si fractus illabatur orbis,
Impavidum ferient ruinæ.　Hor. C. 3, 3, 7.

　　Were earth itself in ruin laid,
　　The wreck would find him undismayed.—*Ed.*

This quality of intrepidity, which Hor. predicates of "the just," might
be applied to one who was the very reverse —the Great Frederick. Applicable to him at any phase of the Seven Years' War, it is particularly
descriptive of his position after the campaign of 1759.

2527. Si fuit errandum, causas habet error honestas　Ov. H. 7, 109.—
If I sinned, the sin has fair excuse. Dido to Æneas. If she
did go astray, she might plead excuse, seeing that the gods had
thrown such a lover in her way.

2528. Signa te, signa; temere me tangis et angis:
Roma tibi subito motibus ibit amor.
Dict. Littéraire, 1768, vol. 2, pp. 228-9.—*Sign, sign thyself*
(with the cross)! *thy rash touch gives me pain: O Rome, thy
love will depart in sudden flight.*

Example of a *Palindrome* verse, *i.e.*, one reading the same either way,
which makes as much sense (or nonsense) as such ingenious conundrums
usually do. It is also to be found in Tabouret's *Bizarrures et Tovches Dv
Seignevr des Accords*, etc., Roven, 1616, p. 84, where it is said, "L'on dit
que le diable, portât Sainct Antibie à Rome sur ses espausles, composa
celuy cy." Much better is the Gk. example, said to be still legible in the
former baptistery of S. Sophia—Νίψον ἀνομήματα, μὴ μόναν ὄψιν—*Wash my
sins, not my face only.* It is repeated in the baptistery of N. D. des
Victoires, Paris, and is inscribed on the fonts of Hadleigh and Worling-
worth, Suffolk. The "*MadamimadaM*"—or the first man's self-introduc-
tion to his wife—is perhaps the best, because the simplest, palindrome in
the English tongue.

2529. Si je recule, tuez-moi; si j'avance, suivez-moi; si je meurs,
vengez-moi! Chambers's Encyclop., *art.* LAROCHEJAQUELIN.—
*If I retreat, kill me; if I go forward, follow me; if I die,
avenge me!*
　　Charge delivered to his soldiers by Henri, Comte de Larochejaquelin, on
being called to the command of the Vendean Royalists in the spring of
1793. After inflicting a series of crushing defeats upon the enemy, and
having driven them beyond the Loire, he was at length out-numbered by
the powers of darkness, and fell fighting at Nouaillé, March 4, 1794. He
was not yet two-and-twenty. Rarely, indeed, has such military talent,
such fortitude and fidelity, such noble courage, combined with the most

X

perfect modesty and gentleness, been found united in one so young! His brothers were called Leonidas, Bayard, and Philip Sidney—but they died long before.

2530. Si je savais un mot plus cochon que *cochon*, je le choisirais. Sardou, Rabagas, 2, 5 (Vuillard loq.).—*If I knew a term more swinish than "swine," I would employ it.*

2531. Si jeunesse savait! si vieillesse pouvait! H. Estienne, Les Prémices, Epigr. 191.—*If youth only knew! if age only could!* Quitard (p. 481) cites *à propos* the prov., supposed to be as old as the twelfth cent.,

> Si jeune savait et vieux pouvait,
> Jamais disette n'y aurait.

> If young knew, and old could,
> Dearth in country never would.

2532. Si l'amour porte des ailes,
N'est-ce pas pour voltiger?
  Beaum. Mar. de Figaro, 4, 10. (Basile sings).—*If Cupid has wings, is it not that he may flutter hither and thither?* An apology for the inconstancy of Love.

2533. Si la pauvreté est la mère des crimes, le défaut d'esprit en est le père. La Bruy. chap xi. (De l'homme), vol. 2, p. 27.—*If poverty is the mother of crime, a shallow brain is the father of it.*

2534. Silent enim leges inter arma. Cic. Mil. 4, 10.—*The laws are silent in time of war.* Martial law prevails. Cf. Leges bello siluere coactæ. Luc 1, 277.—*Owing to the war, the laws have been in abeyance.*

2535. S'il fait beau, prends ton manteau; s'il pleut, prends-le si tu veux. Prov.—*If it's fine, take your cloak; if it rains, you can please yourself.*

> Ingrediare viam cælo licet usque sereno,
> Ad subitas nunquam scortea desit aquas.   Mart. 14, 130.

> However fine it be when you go out,
> In case of showers take your overcoat.—*Ed.*

2536. S'il n'en reste qu'un, je serai celui-là. V. Hugo, Les Châtiments, livre vii. poésie 17. (*Ultima verba*).—*If one only be left, I shall be that one.*

Writing a year after the *coup d'état* of 1851, and just at the moment of the assumption of the rôle of Emperor by "Napoléon le petit," Hugo from his exile in Jersey renews his vows of fidelity to the republican cause, unshaken by the desertions of some and the indifference of others. The piece concludes—

> Si l'on est plus de mille, eh bien, j'en suis! Si même
> Ils ne sont plus que cent, je brave encore Sylla;
> S'il en demeure dix, je serai le dixième.
> *Et s'il n'en reste qu'un, je serai celui-là!*

More than two hundred years before, in 1625, Henry, the great Duke of Rohan, had told his Huguenot co-religionists of Montauban: "Je vous prie de croire que je ne vous abandonnerai point, quoi qu'il arrive. Quand il n'y aurait que deux personnes de la Religion, *je serai un des deux.*" Sainte-Beuve, Le Duc de Rohan, Causeries du Lundi, vol. 12, p. 265.

2537. S'il pleut à la Madeleine,
    On voit pourrir noix et chataignes.

> If it rain on St Magdalene's day,
>   Walnuts and chestnuts will rot away.

On the other hand, rain on this day (July 22) is sometimes said to be "St M. Magdalen washing her handkerchief to go to St James' Fair" (July 25). *Folk Lore Journal,* qu. by R. Inwards, "Weather Lore," Lond., 1893, p. 32.

> Also,   S'il pleut le jour de S. Médard
>   Il pleuvra quarante jours plus tard.
>
>   If it rain the day of St Medard (June 8),
>   'Twill rain for forty afterward.
>
> And,   S'il pleut le jour de S. Gervais et S. Protais
>   Il pleuvra quarante jours après.—*If it rain on SS. Gervasius and Protasius' day* (June 19), *it will rain for forty days afterwards.*
>
>   Quand il pleut à la Saint Calais,
>   Il pleut quarante jours après.—*When it rains on St Calais' day* (July 1), *'twill rain for forty afterwards.*

2538. S'il y a beaucoup d'art à savoir parler à propos, il n'y en a pas moins à savoir se taire. La Rochef. Max., De la Conversation, p. 147.—*If there is great art in knowing how to speak to the purpose, there is not less in knowing when to be silent.*

> ῍Η λέγε τι σιγῆς κρεῖσσον, ἢ σιγὴν ἔχε. Eur. Fr. 864.—*Either say something better than silence, or hold your tongue.*

2539. Si metuis, si prava cupis, si duceris ira,
    Servitii patiere jugum; tolerabis iniquas
Interius leges.   Tunc omnia jure tenebis
Quum poteris rex esse sui.   Claud. IV. Cons. Hon. 259.

> *Qui facit peccatum, servus est peccati.*
> Give way t' impure desires, to anger, fear—
> And you're a slave; compell'd the yoke to bear,
> And bow before that inner lord's commands.
> Depose him, and the future's in your hands.—*Ed.*

2540. Simia simia est, etiamsi aurea gestet insignia.   Chil. p. 255, tr. of πίθηκος ὁ πίθηκος, κἂν χρύσεα ἔχῃ σύμβολα.   Prov. ap. Lucian. Adv. Indoct. 4.—*An ape is an ape for all he wear golden trappings.*

2541. Si mihi pergit quæ volt dicere; ea quæ non volt audiet.   Ter. And. 5, 4, 17.—*If he persists in saying to me what he likes, he shall hear things he will not like.*

2542. Similem habent labiæ lactucam comedente asino carduos.   Incert. in Rib. ii. p. 152.—*Like lips, like lettuce, as the ass said when he ate the thistles.*   Like has met its like. St Jerome, writing to Chromatium (Ep. 1, 7), says that the only time M. L. Crassus was ever known to laugh was over this line.

2543. Similia similibus curantur.   Samuel Hahnemann, Organon der
Heilkunst (1810).—*Like diseases are cured by like remedies.*
The homœopathic *raison d'être.*

2544. Si monumentum requiris, circumspice.—*If you seek his monument,
look around you.*

> Inscription on Sir C. Wren, on the north door (inside) of S. Paul's Cathedral.
> Applicable to any great man whose best monument consists in the beneficial
> results which he has produced.   It has been cruelly suggested as an appro-
> priate epitaph for certain "successful" country practitioners, as they lie
> in the churchyard surrounded by their former patients.

2545. Simplex munditiis.   Hor. C. 1, 5, 5.—*So trim, so simple.*—Conington.
Plain in thy neatness.—Francis.   Neat but not gaudy.

2546. Si mutabile pectus
Est tibi, consiliis, non curribus, utere nostris,
Dum potes, et solidis etiamnum sedibus adstas.   Ov. M. 2, 145.

> *Phœbus to Phaethon.*
> To change your mind if yet you choose,
> My counsel, not my chariot, use
> While yet you may, and solid ground
> 'Neath your aspiring feet be found.—*Ed.*

2547. Si natura negat, facit indignatio versum.   Juv. 1, 79.

> *The Satirist.*
> Though Nature grudge poetic fire,
> Just indignation will inspire.—*Ed.*

2548. Sincerum est nisi vas, quodcunque infundis acescit.
Hor. Ep. 1, 2, 54.

> Whate'er you pour
> Into an unclean vessel will turn sour.—*Ed.*

** The author's mind must itself be clean and wholesome, or it will foul
all that it takes in and all that it puts out.

2549. Sine Cerere et Libero friget Venus.   Ter. Eun. 4, 5, 6 (Chremes
loq.).—*Without Ceres* (food) *and Liber* (wine) *Venus* (love) *starves.*

> Love in a hut, with water and a crust
> Is—Lord forgive us—cinders, ashes, dust.—*Keats,* Lamia, Pt. 2.

> Cf. Eurip. Bacch. 773.   Οἴνου δὲ μηκέτ' ὄντος, οὐκ ἔστιν Κύπρις—*Where
> wine is wanting, Venus never comes.*

2550. Sine doctrina vita est quasi mortis imago.   Dion. Cato, 3, 1.—
Life without learning becomes a picture of death.   Qu. by Mol.
Bourg. Gentilhomme, 2, 6.   Cf. Sen. Ep. 82, 2, Otium sine literis
mors est, et hominis vivi sepultura—*An unlettered leisure is
death and burial while still alive.*

2551. Sine me vocari pessimum, ut dives vocer !
An dives omnes quærimus, nemo an bonus.
Non quare et unde, quid habeas tantum rogant.   Sen. Ep. 115, 14.

> Call me the worst names, so you call me rich !
> One's money, not one's morals, all would know;
> Nor how, or where one came by 't, but "How much."—*Ed.*

Tr. of first three lines of a fragment of the *Bellerophon* of Euripides, beginning, Ἔα με κερδαίνοντα κεκλῆσθαι κακόν. Seneca adds that on its production the audience were so incensed at the sentiment as to hiss the actor off the stage, until Euripides begged them to suspend their judgment until the finale. *V.* Eur. Bellerophon, Fr. 5, Dindorf.

2552. Sine rivali teque et tua solus amares.   Hor. A. P. 444.

> You live, untroubled by advice
> Sole tenant of your own fool's paradise.—*Conington.*

Cf. Cic. Tusc. 5, 22, 63: In hoc enim genere nescio quo pacto magis quam in aliis suum cuique pulcrum est: adhuc neminem cognovi poetam, qui sibi non optimus videretur.—*I don't know why, but in this class more than in any other, every man's own goose is a swan. I never yet knew a poet that did not think himself the best writer of his day.*

2553. Singula de nobis anni prædantur euntes;
Eripuere jocos, Venerem, convivia, ludum:
Tendunt extorquere poemata.   Hor. Ep. 2, 2, 55.

> Years as they roll cut all our pleasures short;
> Our pleasant mirth, our loves, our wine, our sport,
> And then they stretch their power, and wrest at last
> Even the gift of singing of the past.—*Anth. Trollope.*

2554. Si noles sanus, curres hydropicus.   Hor. Ep. 1, 2, 34.—*If you won't (take exercise) when in health, you'll be running fast enough when the dropsy has got hold of you.*

2555. Si non errasset, fecerat illa minus.   Mart. 1, 22, 8.—*Had she not erred, her achievements* (or *history*) *had been less.* Said of the hand which M. Scævola thrust into the flames, after his fruitless attempt to assassinate Lars Porsena, 509 B.C.

2556. Si nos servaremus in necessariis unitatem, in non necessariis libertatem, in utrisque charitatem, optimo certe loco essent res nostræ. Rupertus Meldenius, Parænesis Votiva pro pace Ecclesiæ ad Theologos Augustanæ Confessionis, 1617, p. 39 (Bodl. Library). —*If we would only observe unity on necessary points, liberty on non-necessary ones, and charity in both, our prospects would certainly be in the best possible condition.*

Often qu. as *In necessariis unitas, in dubiis libertas, in omnibus caritas.* Nothing is known of the author, and the place and date of publication are conjectural. Büchm. places the latter between 1621 and 1625. By 1628 it had already passed into a prov. *See* Fr. Lücke's "Über das Alter, etc., des kirchlichen Friedenspruches *In Necessariis*," etc., Göttingen, 1850, p. 46; Dr Schaff's *St Augustine, Melanchthon, Neander*, pp. 89-90; and Büchm. pp. 438-9.

2557. Si nous n'avions point de défauts, nous ne prendrions pas tant de plaisir à en remarquer dans les autres.   La Rochef., § 31, p. 35. —*If we had not ourselves so many faults, we should not take so much pleasure in remarking on those of others.*

2558. Sint licet assumpti juvenes ad pontificatum,
Petri annos potuit nemo videre tamen.
                                   Guilielmus Burius, Brevis Romanor.
Pontificum Notitia, Mechlin, 1675, p. 259.

> Though many Popes of youthful age have reigned,
> None to the years of Peter have attained.—*Ed.*

This distich of Burio's represents an unquestionable truth. Pius the Ninth, elected *ætatis suæ* fifty-four, and Leo XIII., in his sixty-ninth year, have alone exceeded the traditional "twenty-five years" of the Prince of the Apostles; since Benedict XIII., although he survived his election by thirty years, was deposed by the Council of Constance (1415) in the twenty-first of his pontificate. On the other hand, juvenile elections have not been attended by long reigns. Alexander I., chosen at twenty (109 A.D.), reigned 10 *y.* 7 *m.* John XI., made Pope at twenty-five (931 A.D.), reigned 4 *y.* 10 *m.* John the Twelfth, the "Boy Pope," elected at the unusually early age of sixteen,—who, by the way, personally invested our St Dunstan with the Pallium,—reigned only 7 *y.* 9 *m.*, being a mere youth when he died; and Gregory V., who ascended the throne at twenty-four, occupied St Peter's chair less than three years, 996-999 A.D. The formula, "Non videbis annos Petri" (*Thou shalt not see the years of Peter*), supposed to be addressed to each successive Pope at his coronation, is a myth, and so is the tapping the forehead of each defunct Pope with a silver (or ivory) mallet by the Card. Camerlengo in certification of his decease. On the death of Leo XIII. the legend was once more circulated, and was authoritatively denied.

2559. Sint Mæcenates, non deerunt, Flacce, Marones.
    Virgiliumque tibi vel tua rura dabunt.

       Mart. 8, 56, 5.—*Let there only be Mæcenases, and Maroes will not be wanting; even your own fields will produce a Virgil.* Given the patron and the poet will be forthcoming. Of a similar kind is the sentiment in Adam de La Halle's "Roi de Sicile" (Œuvr. Compl., ed. Coussemaker, Paris, 1872, p. 284),

> Mais s'encore fust Charles en Franche le roial,
> Encore trouvast-on Rolant et Parcheval.

> If in France to-day were Charles the royal,
> He'd find again his Roland and Percival.

2560. Sint ut sunt, aut non sint.—*Let them be as they are, or not at all.*

    Reply supposed to have been made by Ricci, General of the Jesuits, when required by Clement XIV. (Ganganelli) to reform the Society's constitutions. In reality, the words were spoken by Clement XIII. (Rezzonico), when, in answer to Card. de Rochechouart's petition on behalf of France for some modification of the rules of the Order (1761), he said, "Qu'ils soient ce qu'ils sont, on qu'ils ne soient plus." Crétineau-Joly, *Clement XIV. et les Jésuites,* Paris, 1848, p. 381 n.; and Fumag. No. 901.

2561. Si numeres anno soles et nubila toto,
    Invenies nitidum sæpius isse diem.   Ov. T. 5, 8, 31.

> If you count cloud and sunshine through the year,
> You'll find the total less of foul than fair.—*Ed.*

2562. Si on les chasse de leurs palais, ils se retireront dans la cabane du pauvre qu'ils ont nourri. Si on leur ôte leur croix d'or, ils prendront une croix de bois: c'est une croix de bois qui a sauvé la terre! De Montlosier (Mémoires du Comte de M.), Biblioth. des Mém. rélatifs à l'hist. de France, 18ᵉ siècle, Nouv. Série, ed. Lescure, vol. 36, p. 82, Paris, 1881.—*If the bishops are driven from their palaces, they will retire to the hovels of the poor whom they have fed. If you take their gold crosses, they will find one of wood. It was a wooden cross that saved the world!* Speech in the Nat. Assembly (1790) protesting against the proposed confiscation of Church property.

2563. Si parva licet componere magnis.   Virg. G. 4, 176.—*To compare small things with great.*

2564. Si personne n'y va, c'est qu'on n'y voit personne.   C. Delavigne, École des vieillards, 2, 1 (Mme. Sinclair loq.).—*If no one goes there, 'tis because there's no one there to be seen.* Of places of resort of former days which have now fallen out of fashion.

2565. Si possem, sanior essem,
 Sed trahit invitam nova vis; aliudque cupido,
 Mens aliud suadet: video meliora proboque;
 Deteriora sequor.   Ov. M. 7, 18.

> I would be saner if I could,
> But a strange force impels me 'gainst my will.
> This passion urges, judgment that: I see
> The better way and I approve, and yet
> I follow what is worse.—*Ed.*

> Cf. Volt., Brutus, 4, 3, Je chéris la vertu, mais j'embrasse le crime—*I cherish virtue, but make choice of crime.*

2566. Si qua recordanti benefacta priora voluptas
 Est homini, quum se cogitat esse pium,
 Nec sanctam violasse fidem, nec fœdere in ullo
 Divom ad fallendos numine abusum homines;
 Multa parata manent in longa ætate, Catulle,
 Ex hoc ingrato gaudio amore tibi.   Cat. 76, 1.

> If a man loves to muse on days of yore,
> And think that he was generous, true and kind;
> Never broke faith, ne'er promised, vowed and swore,
> Only to screen the ruin he designed—
> Then you've, Catullus, joys enough in store
> To blot this misplaced passion from your mind.—*Ed.*

2567. Si qua voles apte nubere, nube pari.   Ov. H. 9, 32.—*If you wish to marry suitably, marry your equal.*

2568. Si quid aliud est in philosophia boni, hoc est, quod stemma non inspicit: omnes, si ad primam originem revocentur, a diis sunt. Sen. Ep. 44, 1.—*If there be one good thing in philosophy it is this, that it takes no account of birth: all men, if you trace them back far enough, sprang from the gods.*

2569. Si quid novisti rectius istis,
 Candidus imperti; si non, his utere mecum.   Hor. Ep. 1, 6, 67.

> If you can mend these precepts, do:
> If not, what serves for me may serve for you.—*Conington.*

2570. Si quid per jocum Dixi, nolito in serium convortere.   Plaut. Pœn. 5, 5, 41.—*If I have said anything in joke, don't take it all seriously (literally).*

2571. Sire, Henri IV. avait reconquis son peuple; ici c'est le peuple qui a reconquis son roi. Chamf. Tables Hist. (vol. 3, p. 141).— *Sire, Henri IV. reconquered his people; in this case it is the people who have reconquered their king.*

> Speech of Bailly, first Mayor of Paris, to Louis XVI. on his arrival at the Hôtel de Ville, July 17, 1789, three days after the taking of the Bastille. Hugou says that the words were spoken at the Barrière de la Conférence, accompanied by the presentation of the city's keys (vol. 3, p. 312).

2572. Si sol splendescat Maria purificante,
Major erit glacies post festum quam fuit ante.

> If Candlemas day (Feb. 2) be fair and bright,
> Winter will have another flight.

> On the other hand,

> If Candlemas day bring clouds and rain,
> Winter is gone and won't come again.

> A North American tradition has it that on Feb. 2 the bear comes out to see his shadow at noon: if he doesn't see it, he remains out; if he sees it, he returns to his den for six weeks longer (R. Inwards, *Weather Lore*, Lond., 1893, p. 16).

2573. Si tacuisses, philosophus mansisses.—*If you had held your tongue, you would have passed for a philosopher.* Formed from the "Intellexeram si tacuisses" of Boeth. Cons. 2, 7.

> An absurd story that Boethius tells, of the total discomfiture of a self-styled "philosopher" by a man in the company who started with the proposition that philosophy would bear any amount of contumely in silence. This was admitted; whereupon the other discharged a volley of abuse which only ended from end of breath. When he had finished, his victim asked whether he might be considered a philosopher now, (*Jam tandem intelligisne me esse philosophum?*)—"I should have believed it," rejoined the man, "if you had not opened your mouth" (*intellexeram si tacuisses*).

2574. Sit bona librorum et provisæ frugis in annum
Copia, neu fluitem dubiæ spe pendulus horæ. Hor. Ep. 1, 18, 109.

> Let me have books and stores for one year hence,
> Nor make my life one flutter of suspense.—*Conington.*

2575. Si tibi deficiant medici, medici tibi fiant
Hæc tria; mens læta, requies, moderata diæta.
Coll. Salern. i. p. 445.

> If doctors fail, here's my prescription—try it,
> These three—good spirits, rest, and moderate diet.—*Ed.*

2576. Sit mihi quod nunc est: etiam minus; et mihi vivam
Quod superest ævi, si quid superesse volunt di.
Hor. Ep. 1, 18, 107.

> O may I yet possess
> The goods I have, or, if Heaven pleases, less!
> Let the few years that fate may grant me still
> Be all my own, not held at other's will.—*Conington.*

2577. Sit piger ad pœnas princeps, ad præmia velox. Ov. Ep. 1, 2, 123.

> Kings should be slow to punish, swift to praise.—*Ed.*

2578. Sit tibi terra levis (*abbrev.* S.T.T.L.)   Mart. 9, 30. 11.—*May earth lie light upon thee.*   Common funeral inscription.

> Ovid, in the same spirit, prays for the repose of Tibullus (Am. 3, 9, 67),
>
>> Ossa quieta precor tuta requiescite in urna,
>> Et sit humus cineri non onerosa tuo.
>
>> Inurned in peace, may thy bones rest, I pray;
>> And on thy ashes earth no burden lay.
>
> Κούφα σοι χθὼν ἐπάνωθε πέσοι (*Lightly fall the earth upon thee!*) petitions the Chorus in the *Alcestis* of Euripides (l. 462) over the dead body of the heroine, untimely rapt away.

2579. Sit tua cura sequi: me duce tutus eris.   Ov. A. A. 2, 58.—*You have only to follow: under my guidance you will be safe.*

2580. Si vous voulez savoir le prix de l'argent, essayez d'en emprunter.   Prov. (Quit. p. 70).—*If you would know the price of money, try to borrow some.*

2581. Σκηνὴ πᾶς ὁ βίος καὶ παίγνιον.   Anth. Pal. 10, 72.—*All life's a stage and comedy.*

> Ὁ κόσμος σκηνὴ, ὁ βίος πάροδος· ἦλθες, εἶδες, ἀπῆλθες (Mundus scena, vita transitus; venisti, vidisti, abisti).   M. Apostol., Cent. xii. 58.—*The world's a stage, and life the passage across it.   You come on, look around you, and you go off.*   (2.) Quomodo fabula, sic vita; non quam diu sed quam bene acta sit refert.   Sen. Ep. 77, 17.—*Life is like a play: and its excellence, not its length, is the important thing.*   (3.) Hic humanæ vitæ mimus, qui nobis partes quæ male agamus, assignat.   Id. ibid. 80, 7.—*This comedy of human life, which distributes parts to us that we render ill enough.*   (4.) Fere totus mundus exercet histrioniam.   Petr. Fr. 10.—*Nearly all the world acts the player's part.*   (5.) Augustus Cæsar, on his deathbed, is said to have asked his friends if he had acted his part in life's comedy fairly well, and added, with a line from the Greek comics, Εἰ δὲ πᾶν ἔχει καλῶς, τῷ παιγνίῳ Δότε κρότον, καὶ πάντες ὑμεῖς μετὰ χαρᾶς κτυπήσατε (*If you approve, please clap the piece, and all bring down the house with glad applause*).   Suet. Aug. 99, and Frag. Comicorum Anon., ccclxi., Mein. p. 1251.   (6. Rabelais is credited with the "last words" of *Tire le rideau, la farce est jouée,* v. No. 1179.   (7.) Dieu est le poëte, les hommes ne sont que les acteurs.   Ces grandes pièces qui se jouent sur la terre ont été composées dans le ciel. Jean Balzac, Socrate Chrétien, Paris. 1657, p. 101.— *God is the poet, men are but the actors: the great pieces that are played on earth have been already composed above.*

> (8.) Ce monde-ci n'est qu'une œuvre comique,
>> Où chacun fait ses rôles différents.   J. B. Rousseau, Epigr. 1, 14.
>
> This world is but a comedy,
>> Where each one plays the part allotted him.

2582. Σκιᾶς ὄναρ ἄνθρωποι.   Pind. Pyth. 8, 95.—*A shadow's dream are men.*

2583. Socci et cothurni musicam.   Aus. Epist. 10, 38.—*Comedy and tragedy.*

2584. Sogno d'infermi, e fola di romanzi.   Petrarch, Trionfo d'Amore, Cap. 4, 66.—*A sick man's dream, a fable of romance.*   Description of human life.   Nonentities, unrealities, *res vanissimæ.*

330 SOLAMEN—SOLVITUR.

2585. Solamen miseris socios habuisse malorum. M. Neander, Ethice vetus et sapiens veterum Latinorum, etc., Lipsiæ, 1590, p. 411. —*It is a comfort to the wretched to have companions in misfortune.*

> The Rev. Ed. Marshall, who supplies (*N. and Q.*. 6th ser., i. 132) the reference for the qu., also gives the variant of "*doloris*" (for "*malorum*"), which is found in Winterton's *Poetæ Minores Græci*, Cantab., 1652; and of "*miserum*" (for "*miseris*"), as it stands in M. O. W. Schonheim's *Proverbia Illustr. et Applicata*, etc., Lips., 1728, p. 227. Cf. Sen. Cons. Marc. 12, 5: Malevoli solatii genus est turba miserorum—*A crowd of fellow-sufferers is a miserable kind of comfort;* and ἡ ἰσομοιρία τῶν κακῶν ἔχουσά τινα ὅμως τὸ μετὰ πολλῶν κούφισιν. Thuc. 7, 75.—*Partnership in suffering has, to a certain extent, the alleviation of being borne in company.*

2586. Sola salus servire Deo, sunt cætera fraudes.—*Salvation is alone found in the service of God, other ways are deceitful.* Inscription over a fireplace in the old palace of the Dukes of Lancaster, at Enfield, Middlesex.

2587. Solem quis dicere falsum Audeat? Virg. G. 1, 463.—*Who will dare call the sun a deceiver?* Applied by Théophile Gautier to photography; in which connection cf. also, Quis solem fallere possit? Ov. A. A. 2, 573.—*Who can deceive the sun?*

2588. Solis nosse Deos et cæli numina vobis,
Aut solis nescire datum.   Lucan. 1, 452.

> *The Druids.*
>
> You have the monopoly of "the Truth," it seems;
> Or else are singular in its ignorance.—*Ed.*

2589. Solitudinem faciunt, pacem appellant. Tac. Agr. 30.—*They make a solitude, and call it peace.*

2590. Sollicitant alii remis freta cæca; ruuntque
In ferrum: penetrant aulas, et limina regum.   Virg. G. 2, 503.

> Some to the seas, and some to camps resort,
> And some with impudence invade the court.—*Dryden.*

2591. Solve senescentem mature sanus equum, ne
Peccet ad extremum ridendus, et ilia ducat.   Hor. Ep. 1, 1, 8.

> Give rest in time to that old horse, for fear
> At last he founder 'mid the general jeer.—*Conington.*

2592. Solvitur ambulando.—*The difficulty is solved by walking.*

> Said of the "*Achilles and Tortoise*" puzzle, in which, though (according to mathematics) A. is never able to pass T. in the race, the apparent impossibility is solved by allowing the two competitors to make the trial. The phrase is thus used of any fallacy which can be disproved by putting the matter to a practical test. Πρὸς τὸν εἰπόντα, ὅτι κίνησις οὐκ ἔστιν, ἀναστὰς περιεπάτει. Diogenes, in Diog. Laert. 6, 2, 39.—*In answer to one who said that there was no such thing as motion, he got up and walked.*

2593. Solvuntur risu tabulæ. *See* Hor. S. 2, 1, 86.

> O, then a laugh will cut the matter short:
> The case breaks down.—*Conington.*

Solvuntur risu tabulæ is said of any question which only succeeds in raising general amusement, and may thus be said to be "laughed out of court."

2594. Songez que du haut de ces monuments quarante siècles vous contemplent.—*Soldiers! reflect that from the summit of these monuments forty centuries are looking at you!* Legend of a medal representing Napoleon addressing his troops before the battle of the Pyramids, July 21, 1798. (Delaroche's *Trésor Numismatique,* and J. H. Rose, *Life of Napoleon,* Lond., 1902, vol. 1, p. 234.)

2595. Son image est partout, excepté dans ma poche. Alex. p. 255.— *His picture is everywhere, except in my pocket.*

A quotation that, in one form or another, constitutes the litany of the penniless all the world over. M. Roger Alexandre, to whose entertaining *Musée de la Conversation* this Dictionary is indebted for many humorous citations from the French, speaks of the line being traditionally ascribed to Dorvigny, and forming the last of an impromptu "quatrain" (of five lines) on the King's name—Louis XVI. It appears, however, from the *Improvisateur français* of Sallentin, that the acrostic is of much earlier date, and comes down to us, like much else, from the reign of Louis le Grand.

> L ouis est un héros sans peur et sans reproche.
> O n désire le voir. Aussitôt qu'on l'approche,
> U n sentiment d'amour enflamme tous les cœurs.
> I l ne trouve chez nous que des adorateurs.
> S on image est partout, excepté dans ma poche.

2596. Σοφὴν δὲ μισῶ· μὴ γὰρ ἔν γ' ἐμοῖς δόμοις
Εἴη φρονοῦσα πλεῖον ἢ γυναῖκα χρή.
> Eurip. Hipp. 640.—*I hate a clever woman. I would have no woman in my house that knows more than a woman should.*

2597. Sors tua mortalis; non est mortale quod optas.
Plus etiam quam quod superis contingere fas sit,
Nescius affectas. Ov. M. 2, 56.

> Thou art but man; and that thou covetest,
> Unknowing, nor man nor gods may hope t' attain.—*Ed.*

Speech of Apollo to Phaethon, on the petition of the latter for permission to guide the chariot of the sun.

2598. Sortes Virgili, *or* Virgilianæ. Lampr. Alex. Sever. 14, 5.— *Virgilian oracles,* or *chances.*

Divination of one's fortune ascertained by the words first lit upon at the opening of some book (Virgil or other) selected for the purpose. The Gospels were also frequently used in the same way. The Emp. Alex. Severus (193-211 A.D.) is said to have read his future fortunes in the words, *Tu regere imperio,* etc. (*q.v.*), and Gordian (238 A.D.) to have learnt the briefness of his reign from the *Ostendent terris hunc tantum fata* of Æneid 6, 870. Rabelais and his fellow monk, Pierre Lamy, chanced on the line, *Heu fuge crudeles terras, fuge litus avarum* (A. 3, 44), and forthwith fled from the convent of Fontenay le Comte (1523). Charles I. is reported to have lighted at the Bodleian Library upon the passage describing the decapitated body of King Priam,

> Jacet ingens litore trancus,
> Avulsumque humeris caput.   Virg. A. 2, 557.

> Now on the shore behold him dead,
> A nameless trunk, a trunkless head;

while Falkland, at the same time, opened the Æneid at the untimely death of Pallas told in the tenth Book.

2599. Sortilegis egeant dubii, semperque futuris
Casibus ancipites: me non oracula certum,
Sed mors certa facit: pavido fortique cadendum est.
Lucan. 9, 581.

> Let those oppressed with constant doubts and fears
> About their fate, consult the soothsayers:
> To me no seer save death th' assurance gave;
> All men must fall, the coward and the brave.—*Ed.*

2600. So schaff' ich am sausenden Webstuhl der Zeit,
Und wirke der Gottheit lebendiges Kleid.
Goethe, Faust, P^t. I., *Night.*

> *Spirit of the Earth to Faust.*
> I sit at the whirring loom of time,
> And weave the endless garment of God.—*Ed.*

2601. Soumis avec respect à sa volonté sainte,
Je crains Dieu, cher Abner, et n'ai d'autre crainte.   Rac. Ath. 1, 1.

> *Joad.* Humbly accepting what His will decides,
> I fear God, Abner, and fear nought besides.—*Ed.*

2602. Souvent la peur d'un mal nous conduit dans un pire.   Boil. L'A. P. 1, 64.—*Fear of one evil often lands us in a worse.*

2603. Soyez plutôt maçon, si c'est votre talent.   Boil. L'A. P. 4, 26. —*Rather be a bricklayer, if your talent lies that way*, than waste time in attempting things for which you have no gift.

2604. Soyons amis, Cinna.   Corn. Cinna, 5, 3.—*Let's be friends, Cinna!* Augustus to Cinna, who had been detected in a conspiracy against the Emperor's life, and whom, on the advice of his consort, Livia, he unconditionally pardoned and restored to friendship.   See the story in Seneca (De Clementia, 1, 9).

2605. Σπάρτην ἔλαχες· κείνην κόσμει,   Eurip. Telephus, Fr. 9.
τὰς δὲ Μυκήνας ἡμεῖς ἰδίᾳ.

> Your lot is Sparta, let her be your care;
> But Mycenæ is my own affair.—*Ed.*

The importance of this qu. chiefly consists in the popular misapprehension of its meaning. Erasmus (Chil. p. 638), possibly repeating an existing version, tr. it, *Spartam nactus es, hanc exorna*, and although he admits other meanings, it is in this form that the saying is generally known, and understood as a command to "adorn" one's country, office, or lot in life, whatever it may be. In this sense Ed. Burke cites the words in his *Reflections on the Rev. in France*, and his most recent editor, Mr E. J. Payne (Clarendon Press Ed., p. 185 n.), points out *in l.* the mistake both in interpretation and application. The line, he says, "is apparently the speech of Agamemnon to Menelaus: *see* Cic. Att. 1, 20, and 4, 6, 2; and Plut. περὶ τῆς εὐθυμίας, cap. 13 (472E). The passage is mistr. by Erasmus, and the wrong meaning kept up in Burke's allusion. Κοσμεῖν means to rule, and not to improve or decorate." On the other hand, Lew. and S. (*s.v.* "Sparta"), while equally rejecting the notion of "adorning," transl. the words, "Sparta is your country, *make the most of it.*"

2606. Spectatum admissi risum teneatis amici? Hor. A. P. 5.— *Being admitted to the sight, could you, my friends, restrain your laughter?* Was there ever anything so preposterous?

2607. Spectatum veniunt, veniunt spectentur ut ipsæ. Ov. A. A. 1, 99.—*The ladies come to see, and to be seen.*

> Chaucer, *Wyf of Bath*, Prol., l. 6134, has
> And for to see, and eke for to seye.

2608. Spem gregis. Virg. E. 1, 15.—*The hope of the flock.* The flower of the family.

2609. Spem pretio non emo. Ter. Ad. 2, 2, 11.—*I do not wish to purchase mere hopes.* I do not barter gold for fallacious expectations.

2610. Speravimus ista Dum fortuna fuit. Virg. A. 10, 42.

> Such hopes I had while Heaven was kind.—*Dryden.*

2611. Spernere mundum, spernere te ipsum, spernere te sperni.— *Despise the world, despise yourself, despise being despised.* Maxim of S. Philip Neri, and the acme of self-effacement and self-depreciation.

2612. Sperne voluptates; nocet empta dolore voluptas. Hor. Ep. 1, 2, 55.

> Make light of pleasure: pleasure bought with pain
> Yields little profit, and much more of bane.—*Conington.*

2613. Spirat tragicum satis, et feliciter audet. Hor. Ep. 2, 1, 166. —*It breathes the tragic vein well enough, and is happy in its attempts.* Said of the Roman drama.

2614. Spiritus quidem promptus est, caro vero infirma. Vulg. Marc. 14, 38.—*The spirit indeed is willing, but the flesh is weak.*

2615. Spirto gentil, ne' sogni miei,
Brillasti un dì, ma ti perdei.

> F. Janetti, La Favorita (Opera), Music by Donizetti, 4, 3 (Fernando sings).— *Sweet spirit, thou shinedst once in my dreams, but I have lost thee!* Transl. from the French of Royer and Waez.

2616. Splendida vitia.—*Splendid vices.* Said of the virtues of the heathen.

> The phrase has been traced, failing earlier examples, to Peter Martyr's (Vermigli) *Loci Communes,* cl. iii. cap. xii. sect. 7, p. 649, Tigur. 1587 (Lond., 1583), where he says that "however noble may have been the pagan virtues of the past, they were, in the sight of God, only so much splendid sin" (tamen coram Deo nihil aliud erant nisi *gloriosa et splendida peccata*). Leibnitz, writing a hundred years later, declares himself opposed to those "qui ont cru faire beaucoup d'honneur à notre Religion, en disant que les vertus des Payens n'étoient que *splendida peccata* —des vices éclatans." (*Essai de Théodicée,* 1710, § 259.) *See* also Rev. E. Marshall in *Notes and Queries,* Nov. 1891, p. 397.

2617. Splendide mendax. Hor. C. 3, 11, 35.—*Gloriously false.* "That splendid falsehood."—*Conington.* Hypermnestra, alone of the daughters of Danaus, preserved the life of her husband, Lynceus, when ordered by her father to slay him. A tradition of the "Schools" asserts that the qu. was once translated "lying in state."

2618. Sponte sua numeros carmen veniebat ad aptos;
Et quod tentabam dicere, versus erat. Ov. T. 4, 10, 25.

> *The Poet's Childhood.*
> The words to numbers moved spontaneously,
> And what I stammered out was poetry.—*Ed.*

*** Comp. Pope (Prol. to *Satires,* 127), "I lisped in numbers," etc.

2619. Stabat mater dolorosa
Juxta crucem lacrymosa
Qua pendebat Filius.

> Giacopone da Todi (Jacobus de Benedictis),
13th cent., disciple of St Francis.

> At the cross her station keeping
> Stood the mournful mother weeping,
> Where He hung, the dying Lord.—*Dr Irons.*

2620. Stare putes, adeo procedunt tempora tarde. Ov. T. 5, 10, 5.
— *The time goes so slowly that you would think it stood still.* Ovid in exile.

2621. State contenti. umana gente, al *quia.* Dante, Purg. 3, 37.— *Rest contented, mortals, with the "fact"* of the unsearchable things of God, without seeking the How and the Why.

2622. Stat magni nominis umbra. Lucan. 1, 135.

> *Pompey.*
> He stands, the shadow of a mighty name.—*Ed.*

> Just prior to his death, a photograph was taken at Cannes of Lord Brougham in a group with other friends, in which the principal figure was hardly more than a "blurr"; and the accident was seized upon by a biographer to typify the general "ineffectualness" of career that left the famous Whig chancellor but a *magni nominis umbra* after all—without, and not within, the assemblage of the great ones of the earth.

2623. Stat sua cuique dies; breve et irreparabile tempus
Omnibus est vitæ; sed famam extendere factis,
Hoc virtutis opus.   Virg. A. 10, 467.

> Each has his destined time: a span
> Is all the heritage of man:
> 'Tis virtue's part by deeds of praise
> To lengthen fame through after days.—*Conington.*

2624. Stemmata quid faciunt? quid prodest, Pontice, longo
Sanguine censeri? pictosque ostendere vultus
Majorum?

Tota licet veteres exornent undique ceræ
Atria, nobilitas sola est atque unica virtus.

Juv. 8, 1-3, and 19-20.

'Tis only Noble to be Good.

> What serve your pedigrees, your noble birth
> And family busts, as proofs of personal worth?
> Though rows of ancestors your galleries dress,
> Virtue's the one true patent of noblesse.—*Ed.*

** 'Twas not the ancestors or the pedigrees that were at fault, the satirist maintains, so much as their degenerate representatives, who debauched themselves under the very noses of their honoured progenitors. With the moral of the quotation may be compared the saying of Euripides (Ægeus, Fr. 11),

> ἦ που κρεῖσσον τῆς εὐγενίας
> τὸ καλῶς πράσσειν—*A good life is far better than high birth;* and Voltaire's Mahomet (1, 4),

> Les mortels sont égaux: ce n'est point la naissance,
> C'est la seule vertu qui fait leur différence.

> We men are all equal: it is not high birth,
> But virtue alone is the standard of worth.—*Ed.*

2625. Sternitur infelix alieno vulnere, cælumque
Adspicit et dulces moriens reminiscitur Argos.   Virg. A. 10, 781.

Antor's Death.

> Now, prostrate by an unmeant wound,
> In death he welters on the ground,
> And gazing on Italian skies
> Of his loved Argos dreams, and dies.—*Conington.*

2626. Stet quicunque volet potens
Aulæ culmine lubrico.
Me dulcis saturet quies:
  Obscuro positus loco,
  Leni perfruar otio.   Sen. Thyest. 391.

> Anxious for power, let him who will
>   Climb to the palace' slippery heights:
> But rather let me take my fill
>   Of sweet retirement's delights;
> And, buried in my humble nest,
> Enjoy the fruits of ease and rest.—*Ed.*

2627. Stilus optimus et præstantissimus dicendi effector ac magister. Cic. de Or. 1, 33, 150.—*Writing is the best and most efficacious help and master in the art of speaking.*

2628. Strabonem Appellat pætum pater. Hor. S. 1, 3, 44.—*A father will speak of his squinting son, as having a slight cast in the eye.* Every man's own geese are swans.

2629. Strenua nos exercet inertia; navibus atque
Quadrigis petimus bene vivere; quod petis hic est,
Est Ulubris, animus si non te deficit æquus.   Hor. Ep. 1, 11, 28.

> Anxious through seas and land to search for rest
> Is but laborious idleness at best;—*Francis.*
> No: what you seek at Ulubræ you'll find,
> If to the quest you bring a balanced mind.—*Conington.*

2630. Studiis florentem ignobilis oti. Virg. G. 4, 564.—*Indulging in the studies of inglorious leisure.*

> Affecting studies of less noisy praise.—*Dryden.*

Said of the author's composition of his Georgics. The poet intimates that while Cæsar was pursuing his high destiny in arms, he (Virgil) was passing his time at Naples, in the pleasing but inglorious pursuit of his own peculiar studies.

2631. Studium discendi voluntate, quæ cogi non potest, constat. Quint. 1, 3, 8.—*The pursuit of learning is one that must be followed willingly or not at all.*

2632. Stulta est clementia, quum tot ubique
Vatibus occurras, perituræ parcere chartæ.   Juv. 1, 17.

> Since I'm ever meeting poets,
> It's sheer nonsense to grudge paper,
> For they'll spoil it if I do not.—*Shaw.*

2633. Stulte, quid o frustra votis puerilibus optas,
Quæ non ulla tulit, fertque feretque dies?
      Ov. T. 3, 8, 11.—*Fool, why do you vainly wish with childish desire for things which time has never produced, nor does, nor ever will bring about?*

2634. Stultissimum in luctu capillum sibi evellere, quasi calvitio mæror levaretur. Bion ap. Cic. Tusc. 3, 26, 62.—*It is worse than foolish to tear one's hair in grief, as if sorrow could be relieved by baldness.* Witty remark of Bion on the rage of Agamemnon.

2635. Stulti stolidi fatui fungi bardi blenni buccones. Plaut. Bacch. 5, 1, 2.—*Fools, stupids, dolts, simpletons, nincompoops, addlepates, fatheads!*

2636. Stultitiam patiuntur opes. Hor. Ep. 1, 18, 29.—*Riches can afford to be foolish.*

2637. Stultorum incurata pudor malus ulcera celat. Hor. Ep. 1, 16, 24.

> O, 'tis a false, false shame that would conceal
> From doctors' eyes the sores it cannot heal.—*Conington.*

2638. Stultum me fateor, liceat concedere veris,
Atque etiam insanum.   Hor. S. 2, 3, 305.

> I own I'm foolish (let the truth be told),
> Nay, even mad.—*Ed.*

2639. Sua cuique deus fit dira cupido. Virg. A. 9, 185.—*Each man's fierce passion becomes his god.*

> Passion surging past control
> Plays the god to each one's soul.—*Conington.*

2640. Suam quoique sponsam, mihi meam: suum quoique amorem, mihi meum. Atilius, ex incert. I. (Ribb. 2, 37).

> Each man his wife, but give me mine:
> Each man his love, but mine for me.—*Ed.*

> A line of M. Atilius the dramatist, *poeta durissimus* (a most rugged poet) as Cicero calls him (Att. 14, 20, 3).

2641. Suave, mari magno turbantibus æquora venteis,
E terra magnum alterius spectare laborem;
Non quia vexari quemquam est jocunda voluptas,
Sed, quibus ipse maleis careas, quia cernere suave est.
Per campos instructa, tua sine parte pericli,
Suave etiam belli certamina magna tueri.   Lucret. 2, 1.

> *Suave mari magno.*
> Sweet, from the land, to watch some labouring sail
> Lashed by the fury of the sea and gale:
> Not that there's pleasure in another's harm;
> In your own safety 'tis that lies the charm.
> Sweet, too, secure from danger in the fray,
> To view the battle's terrible array.—*Ed.*

2642. Suaviter in modo, fortiter in re.—*Gentle in manner, vigorous in performance.*

> Claudio Aquaviva, fifth General of the Jesuits (1581-1615), says in "Industriæ ad curandos animæ morbos" (Roma, 1606), cap. 2, 4: Nec difficile erit videre, quomodo efficacia cum suavitate conjungi debeat, ut et *fortes in fine consequendo, et suaves in modo et ratione assequendi simus* ("Vigorous in attaining our end, and gentle in the means and way thereto"); with which may be compared the Scripture (Vulg. Sap. 8, 1): Attingit ergo a fine usque ad finem *fortiter*, et disponit omnia *suaviter*—*Wisdom reacheth from end to end mightily, and ordereth all things sweetly.* A correspondent of the *Intermédiaire des Chercheurs* (No. 481, 1888) points out a phrase of Himerius the Sophist—Oratio, 7, 15 (Dübner's Ed., in Didot) —which exactly corresponds with the Jesuit maxim: πρᾶος τοὺς λόγους, ὀξὺς τὰ πράγματα—*Mild in speech, sharp in action.*

2643. Sublime, familier, solide, enjoué, tendre,
Aisé, profond, naïf et fin.
Digne de l'univers: l'univers pour l'entendre
Aime à redevenir Latin.

> Houdart de La Motte, La Puissance des Vers (Œuvres, Paris, 1754, vol. i. p. 118).

Y

Horace.

Sublime yet familiar, real, gay, full of feeling,
　Easy, deep, artless, shrewd is his vein.
World-poet! to hear thee the nations are willing
　To become Latin-speaking again.—*Ed.*

Petron. 118, 5, speaks of *Horatii curiosa felicitas,* Horace's "singular felicity" of expression; Quint. (10, 1, 96) of his "felicitous audacity in choice of words" (*verbis felicissime audax*); and Johnson (Boswell, Croker's ed., p. 617) says, "The lyrical part of Horace can never be perfectly translated."

2644. Subtilis veterum judex et callidus audis.　Hor. S. 2, 7, 101.—*You are considered a fine and knowing judge of the old masters.　A clever connoisseur of ancient works of art.*

2645. Sufficit diei malitia sua.　Vulg. Matt. 6, 34.—*Sufficient unto the day is the evil thereof.*

2646. Sumite materiam vestris, qui scribitis, æquam
　　Viribus, et versate diu quid ferre recusent,
　　Quid valeant humeri.　Cui lecta potenter erit res,
　Nec facundia deseret hunc, nec lucidus ordo.　　　Hor. A. P. 38.

　　　Good authors, take a brother bard's advice:
　　　Ponder your subject o'er not once or twice,
　　　And oft and oft consider if the weight
　　　You hope to lift be, or be not too great.
　　　Let but our theme be equal to our powers,
　　　Choice language, clear arrangement, both are ours.—*Conington.*

2647. Summa igitur et perfecta gloria constat ex tribus his, si diligit multitudo; si fidem habet; si cum admiratione quadam honore dignos putat.　Cic. Off. 2, 9, 31.—*The ideal of human glory is based upon these three points: a people's love, their confidence, and a feeling of admiration founded upon a sense of worth.*

2648. Summa petit livor: perflant altissima venti.　　　Ov. R. A. 369.

　　　Envy aims high: great summits feel the wind.—*Ed.*

2649. Summum crede nefas animam præferre pudori,
　　Et propter vitam vivendi perdere causas.　　　Juv. 8, 83.

　　　Think it a crime to purchase breath with shame,
　　　And for the sake of life to lose life's aim.—*Ed.*

2650. Summum jus summa injuria.　Law Max. ap. Cic. Off. 1, 10, 33.—*The extremity of the law is the extremity of injustice.*

　　　Cic. quotes it as *Jam tritum sermone proverbium*—"A trite and proverbial expression" It had already done duty in Ter. Heaut. 4, 5, 48: Dicunt, jus summum sæpe summa malitia est—*Extreme right (law) is often extreme wrong.*　Cf. Col. 1, 7, 2: Summum jus antiqui summam putabant crucem—*Our ancestors used to call extreme law extreme punishment* (lit., *an extreme cross*).

2651. Sumque argumenti conditor ipse mei.　Ov. T. 5, 1, 10.—*I am myself the subject of my own poems.*

2652. Sunt aliquid Manes: letum non omnia finit,
Luridaque evictos effugit umbra rogos.   Prop. 4, 7, 1.

To Cynthia's Shade.

There is an after life: death ends not all:
Nor can the grave th' æthereal soul enthrall.—*Ed.*

2653. Sunt bona, sunt quædam mediocria, sunt mala plura
Quæ legis hic: aliter non fit, Avite, liber.   Mart. 1, 17.

There's good, there's middling, and there's more to blame
In my poor book: but all books are the same.—*Ed.*

2654. Sunt delicta tamen quibus ignovisse velimus.   Hor. A. P. 347.

Some faults may claim forgiveness.—*Conington.*

2655. Sunt lachrymæ rerum, et mentem mortalia tangunt.
Virg. A. 1, 462.

Our history has its tears, and human hearts
Are touched by scenes of human suffering.—*Ed.*

The line was quoted by C. J. Fox (Jan. 1806) as Pitt lay a-dying, in
deprecation of any censure being made at that moment in Parliament upon
the policy of his great rival. (Macaulay, *art.* on W. PITT, in *Encyclop.
Brit.*)

2656. Sunt nisi præmissi quos periisse putas. J. Weavers' Ancient Fun.
Monuments, Lond., 1631.   Motto of Frontisp.—*Those whom you
think dead are only gone before.*

2657. Sunt superis sua jura. Ov. M. 9, 499.—*Even the gods themselves
are bound by law.*

2658. Sunt tamen inter se communia sacra poetis,
Diversum quamvis quisque sequamur iter.   Ov. Ep. 2, 10, 17.

Poet with poet a common art combines,
Though each strikes out his own respective lines.—*Ed.*

2659. Superat quoniam fortuna, sequamur,
Quoque vocat vertamus iter.   Virg. A. 5, 22.

Since fate constrains, let us obey
And follow where it leads the way.—*Ed.*

2660. Super et Garamantas et Indos Proferet imperium. Virg. A. 6, 795.

O'er Ind and Garamant extreme
Shall stretch his boundless reign.—*Conington.*

Said of the Empire of Augustus Cæsar, and applicable to England's
Indian possessions.

2661. Superstitionem . in qua inest timor inanis deorum . religionem,
quæ deorum cultu pio continetur. Cic. N.D. 1, 42, 117.—*Superstition, which is an ignorant fear of God; Religion, which
consists in His loving worship.*

2662. Supremum vale. Ov. M. 10, 62.—*A last farewell.*

> Cf. Virg. A. 11, 97:
>> Salve æternum mihi, maxime Palla,
>> Æternumque vale.
>> Hail mighty firstling of the dead,
>> Hail and farewell for aye!—*Conington.*
> And, In perpetuum, frater, ave atque vale.   Cat. 101, 10.—*For ever,*
> *brother, hail and farewell!*   Catullus at his brother's tomb.

2663. Surgunt indocti et cælum rapiunt.   S. Aug. Conf. 8, 8.—*The*
unlearned arise and take heaven by force.   Said of S. Anthony
(the Illiterate), the solitary of the Egyptian desert and the
father of Monachism, born in the middle of the 3rd century.

2664. Sursum corda.—*Lift up your hearts!*   Versicle in the Preface to
the Mass, with Response " Habemus ad Dominum "—*We lift*
them up unto the Lord.   Cf. Levemus corda nostra cum manibus
ad Dominum in cælos.   Vulg. Lam. 3, 41.—*Let us lift up our*
hearts with our hands to God in the heavens.   See No. 1220.

2665. Surtout pas de zèle.—*Above all things, no zeal!*   Favourite
maxim of Talleyrand.

> Sainte-Beuve (Critiques et Portraits, 1841, vol. 3, p. 324) quotes a
> certain diplomat who in early life had been strictly cautioned by Talley-
> rand : *N'ayez pas de zèle!* as an essential rule of conduct.   Mme. de Rémusat
> (Mémoires, Paris, 1880, vol. 3, p. 174) states that on resigning the portfolio
> of Foreign Affairs in 1815, Talleyrand commended the *personnel* of the
> Office to his successor, Champagny, in these words : "Vous les trouverez
> fidèles, habiles, exacts, mais, grâce à mes soins, nullement zélés"—*You*
> *will find them faithful, able, exact, and, thanks to my training, the reverse of*
> *zealous.*   Büchm. p. 489, and Alex. p. 547.

2666. Sur un mince cristal l'hiver conduit leurs pas,
         Le précipice est sous la glace;
     Telle est de vos plaisirs la légère surface :
         Glissez, mortels, n'appuyez pas.
         Pierre Chas. Roy.   Composed for a design of Winter by
Lancret, engraved by Larmessin.

> *Skating.*
> O'er thinnest crystal winter guides their flight,
>   While underneath the gulphing waters lie;
> A type of pleasure, perilous and slight—
>   Touch it but lightly and pass quickly by.—*Ed.*
> Roy, the author of the quatrain, in spite of the vituperations of Voltaire,
> was at the least an average sample of the epigrammatic elegance of the
> day, and the print in question seems to have enjoyed so much vogue that
> we find Mrs Piozzi at Brighthelmstone (? 1776) engaging her friends in
> competitive renderings of Roy's descriptive lines.   Although no "skaiter,"
> Johnson, not, perhaps, without recollection of certain "sliding in Christ-
> church meadows," contributed two *impromptu* versions, one of which runs:
>> O'er ice the rapid skaiter flies,
>>   With sport above and death below;
>> When mischief lurks in gay disguise,
>>   Thus lightly touch and lightly go.

Piozzi, *Anecdotes* (4th ed., Lond., 1786), p. 142; Johnson, *Works*, Lond., 1818, vol. i. p. 121. Voltaire says (somewhere): Pour jouir de la vie, il faut glisser sur beaucoup—*To enjoy life, we must touch much of it lightly.*

2667. Sus Minervam. Prov. Cic. Ac. 1, 5, 18.—*A pig teaching Minerva.*

Sus Minervam (*sc.* docet) in proverbio est, ubi quis id docet alterum, cujus ipse inscius est. Festus de Verb. signif. p. 310, ed. C. O. Müller, Lipsiæ, 1839.—*"A sow teaching Minerva" has passed into a proverb for any one who attempts to instruct another upon a subject of which he himself is ignorant.*

2668. Suspectum semper invisumque dominantibus, qui proximus destinaretur. Tac. H. 1, 21.—*The reigning prince always suspects and hates his heir.*

2669. Suspendens omnia naso. Hor. S. 2, 8, 64.—*Turning up one's nose at everything.* Sneering at, ridiculing everything.

2670. Suum cuique decus posteritas rependit. Tac. A. 4, 35.—*Posterity grants every one his due honour.* Thus Lord Bacon left his character to be judged by after generations.

T.*

2671. Τὰ ἀρχαῖα ἔθη κρατείτω. Concil. Nicæn. Canon. VI., in L'Abbe's "Concilia" (Florence, 1759), vol. ii. p. 669.—*Let the ancient customs prevail:* as who should say, "State super vias . . . et interrogate de semitis antiquis quæ sit via bona," etc. Jerem. 6, 16.—*Stand ye on the ways, and ask for the old paths.*

This is the beginning of the famous Sixth Canon of the Council of Nice (325 A.D.), which regulated the several jurisdictions of the Patriarchates of Alexandria and of Antioch (the second and third of the greater sees of the Church) after the analogy of that of Rome, which the Council did not presume to define, it being inherent in St Peter's See.

2672. Tabesne cadavera solvat
An rogus haud refert.
Luc. 7, 809.—*It matters little whether the body be destroyed by corruption or the flames.*

2673. Tabula ex naufragio. Cic. Att. 4, 18, 3.—*A plank in a shipwreck.* The last means of escape.

2674. Tabula rasa.—*A clean tablet,* one from which the writing has been erased. A blank sheet of paper. A clean slate.

The mind, when unable to collect itself or remember any given circumstance, is termed metaphorically a *tabula rasa* in post-classical Latin, just as we say "a blank." Among the Greeks the figure was common. Aristotle compares the mind to a "tablet on which nothing has been written," ὥσπερ ἐν γραμματείῳ ᾧ μηθὲν ὑπάρχει ἐντελεχείᾳ γεγραμμένον (*De Anima*, 3, 4, 11); and Plut. (Placita Philosophorum, 4, 11) speaks of the soul at birth, ὥσπερ χάρτης ἐνεργῶν εἰς ἀπογραφήν, as "so much paper ready for writing on."

* And the Greek Θ (Th).

2675. Tacent, satis laudant. Ter. Eun. 3, 2, 23.—*They are silent, which is sufficient praise.*

2676. Tacitum vivit sub pectore vulnus. Virg. A. 4, 67.—*The secret wound still rankles in her heart.*

2677. Tadeln können zwar die Thoren,
Aber klüger handeln nicht.
Aug. Friedr. Ernst Langbein, Die neue Eva.—*Fools can certainly find fault, but they cannot act more wisely themselves.* Often quoted in the second line as "*Aber besser machen nicht.*"

2678. Tages Arbeit, Abends Gäste!
Saure Wochen, frohe Feste!
Sei dein künftig Zauberwort!
Goethe, Der Schatzgräber (1798).
Work by day, at evening guests,
Weeks of toil, and happy feasts,
Be thy future's augury!—*Ed.*

2679. Talent, goût, esprit, bon sens, choses différentes, non incompatibles. Entre le bon sens et le bon goût il y a la différence de la cause à son effet. Entre esprit et talent il y a la proportion du tout à sa partie. La Bruy. Car. cap. xii. (Des Jugements), vol. ii. p. 80.—*Talent, taste, wit, good sense, are very different things, but by no means incompatible. Between good sense and good taste, there is all the difference between cause and effect; while wit and talent stand in the relation of a whole to its part.*

2680. Tale tuum carmen nobis, divine poeta,
Quale sopor fessis. Virg. E. 5, 45.
Sweet are thy strains, singer inspired,
As sleep to men with labour tired.—*Ed.*
Sometimes used ironically in speaking of poets and preachers whose compositions have the effect of a narcotic.

2681. Talis est quisque, qualis ejus dilectio. Aug. in Ep. Joh. Cap. 2, Tract. 2, vol. 3, Pt. 2, p. 614 E.—*Every man is what his likings make him.*

2682. Tam diu discendum est, quamdiu nescias, et, si proverbio credimus, quamdiu vivas. Sen. Ep. 76, 2.—*We have to go on learning, as long as we are ignorant, and if the proverb is to be believed, as long as life lasts.* Cf. Γηράσκω δ' αἰεὶ πολλὰ διδασκόμενος. Solon, Fr. 18 [10].—*As I grow old I am always learning more and more.*

2683. Tamen ad mores natura recurrit
Damnatos, fixa et mutari nescia. Nam quis
Peccandi finem posuit sibi? quando recepit
Ejectum semel attrita de fronte ruborem?
Quisnam hominum est quem tu contentum videris uno
Flagitio? Juv. 13, 239.

Fixa et mutari nescia.

Back to its curséd ways will nature range,
Fixed and incapable of actual change.
For who says to himself, "Thus far I'll go
In sinning, but no farther?"   Can the brow
Regain the power of blushing when it's gone?
Who is content with one offence alone?—*Ed.*

2684. Tamen hoc tolerabile, si non Et furere incipias. Juv. 6, 614.—
*However, this would be bearable if you did not begin to rave
into the bargain.*

2685. T'amo, Francesca, t'amo,
E disperato è l'amor mio.
Silvio Pellico, Francesca da Rimini, 3, 2.—*I love thee,
Francesca, I love thee, and my love is in despair!*

2686. Tam sæpe nostrum decipi Fabullinum
Miraris, Aule? Semper homo bonus tiro est.   Mart. 12, 51.

What wonder if Fabullus should have been
So oft deceived? A good man's always green.—*Ed.*

2687. Tanquam in speculo.   Cic. Pis. 29, 71.—*As in a mirror.*

2688. Tantæ molis erat Romanæ condere gentem.   Virg. A. 1, 33.

So vast the labour to create
The fabric of the Roman state.—*Conington.*

2689. Tantæne animis cœlestibus iræ.   Virg. A. 1, 11.

Can heavenly natures nourish hate,
So fierce, so blindly passionate?—*Conington.*

Cf. Tant de fiel entre-t-il dans l'âme des dévots? Boil. Lutrin, Chant 1, 12.
—*Can so much gall* (spite) *find place in godly souls?*

2690. Tanta est quærendi cura decoris.
Tot premit ordinibus, tot adhuc compagibus altum
Ædificat caput.   Andromachen a fronte videbis;
Post minor est: credas aliam.   Juv. 6, 501.

Head-dresses.

No pains are deemed too great in fashion's cause.
With tier on tier the lofty structure's reared,
So that the lady who in front appeared
A second Andromache—if you view the dame
Behind, she's stunted, and scarce seems the same.—*Ed.*

2691. Tanti non es, ais? Sapis Luperce.   Mart. 1, 118, 18.

The Author trying to Sell his Book.

"Four and sixpence! He's not worth it."
Right you are again, Lupercus.—*Shaw.*

2692. Tanto cardine rerum.   Virg. A. 1, 672.—*At such a juncture.*   A
critical moment.

2693. Tanto major famæ sitis est, quam
Virtutis.   Quis enim virtutem amplectitur ipsam,
Præmia si tollas?   Juv. 10, 140.

> So much the greater is the thirst for fame
> Than virtue.   Who will virtue's self embrace,
> If she can give no salary or place?—*Ed.*

2694. Tanto nomini nullum par elogium.—*No eulogium could do justice
to so great a name.*   Inscription composed by Dr Ferroni for
Spinazzi's monument of Nicholas Macchiavelli, erected in 1787
in the church of Santa Croce, Florence.   Fumag. 182.

2695. Tantum religio potuit suadere malorum!   Lucret. 1, 102.

> *The Sacrifice of Iphigenia.*
> Alas that wickedness so great
> Could in religion's name be perpetrate!—*Ed.*

2696. Tantum series juncturaque pollet,
Tantum de medio sumptis accedit honoris.   Hor. A. P. 242.

> So much may order and arrangement do
> To make the cheap seem choice, the threadbare new.—*Conington.*

2697. Tantus amor laudum, tantæ est victoria curæ.   Virg. G. 3, 112.
—*Such is the love of praise, so great the eagerness for victory.*

2698. Τὰ πλεῖστα θνητοῖς τῶν κακῶν αὐθαίρετα.   Eur. Fr. 840.—*Most of
our troubles are of our own seeking.*

2699. Tarda sit illa dies, et nostro serior ævo.   Ov. M. 15, 868.—*Far
may that day be yet, and after our time!*   Wish expressed by
the poet for the prolongation of the life of Augustus.

2700. Tarda solet magnis rebus inesse fides.   Ov. H. 17, 130.—*Confidence is slow in reposing itself in undertakings of any
magnitude.*

2701. Tarde, quæ credita lædunt, Credimus.   Ov. H. 2, 9.—*We're slow
to believe things which, if believed, must wound us.*

2702. Tecum prius ergo vòluta
Hæc animo ante tubas.   Galeatum sero duelli
Pœnitet.   Juv. 1, 168.

> Think then on this before the bugles play;
> Once on the field, too late to shirk the fray.—*Ed.*

> Cf. Gladiatorem in arena capere consilium.   Prov. in Sen. Ep. 22, 1.—
> *The gladiator is making his plans after having entered the arena.*   Taking
> counsel too late.

2703. Τῇδε Σάων ὁ Δίκωνος Ἀκάνθιος ἱερὸν ὕπνον
κοιμᾶται· θνάσκειν μὴ λέγε τοὺς ἀγαθούς.
                              Callimachus, Anth. Pal. vii. 451, (i. 326).

> Here Dicon's Saon, th' Acanthian, doth lie
> In deepest sleep.   Say not that good men die.—*Ed.*

2704. Tel brille au second rang, qui s'éclipse au premier. Volt.
Henriade (1723), Chant I. 31.—*Some will shine in the second
rank who are lost in the first.*

2705. Telephus et Peleus, quum pauper et exul, uterque
Projicit ampullas et sesquipedalia verba. Hor. A. P. 96.

> Peleus or Telephus, suppose him poor
> Or driven to exile, talks in tropes no more;
> His yard-long words desert him.—*Conington.*

2706. Tel excelle à rimer qui juge sottement. Boil. L'Art P. Chant. 4,
82.—*Some can rhyme very well who reason foolishly enough.*

2707. Telle jadis Carthage
Vit sur ses murs détruits Marius malheureux,
Et ces deux grands débris se consolaient entre eux.
                    Delille, Jardins, Chant IV.

> Thus, Carthage once
> Saw on her crumbling walls poor Marius:
> The two great ruins comforting each other.—*Ed.*

Chamfort makes the passage the subject of one of his happiest anecdotes.
"On disputait chez Madame de Luxembourg," he says, "sur ce vers de
l'abbé Delille,

> Et ces deux grands débris se consolaient entre eux.

"On annonce le bailly de Breteuil et madame de La Reinière. 'Le vers
est bon,' dit la maréchale." (Œuvres choisies, i. 43.)

2708. Tel maître, tel valet. Prov. (Quit. p. 679).—*Like master, like man.*
Qualis dominus, talis est servus. Petron. Sat. 58.—*As is the
master, so is the servant.*

> Such mistress, such Nan;
> Such master, such man.—Thos. Tusser, *April's Abstract.*

2709. Telumque imbelle sine ictu. Virg. A. 2, 544.

> A feeble dart, no blood that drew.—*Conington.*

May be applied to any feeble or pointless argument.

2710. Tel vous semble applaudir, qui vous raille et vous joue;
Aimez qu'on vous conseille, et non pas qu'on vous loue.
Boil. L'A. P. Ch. 1, 192.—*Such an one seems to applaud,
while he is really making game of you: prefer those who advise
you to those who praise.*

2711. Tempora labuntur, tacitisque senescimus annis:
Et fugiunt fræno non remorante dies. Ov. F. 6, 771.

> Time slips away, and noiselessly with years we older grow,
> And days rush on without a rein to check or curb their flow.—*Ed.*

Inscribed (incorrectly) on an ivory *portarium* in the B. Museum.

2712. Temporis ars medicina fere est; data tempore prosunt,
Et data non apto tempore vina nocent. Ov. R. A. 131.

> Medicine must have its hours: a glass of port
> Does good at proper times; but else, does hurt.—*Ed.*

2713. Temporis illius colui fovuique poetas,
Quotque aderant vates rebar adesse deos.   Ov. T. 4, 10, 41.

Ovid's Youth.

I loved, revered the poets of that day;
Each bard a perfect god seemed in his way.—*Ed.*

2714. Tempus edax rerum, tuque invidiosa vetustas,
Omnia destruitis, vitiataque dentibus ævi
Paullatim lenta consumitis omnia morte.   Ov. M. 15, 234.

Tempus Edax.

Devouring time and envious age,
All falls to ruin 'neath your rage!
All, by degrees, ye wear away
With gnawing tooth and slow decay.—*Ed.*

2715. Τὴν δὲ μάλιστα γαμεῖν, ἥτις σέθεν ἔγγυθι ναίει.   Hes. Op. 698.
—*Above all, choose a wife from your own neighbourhood.*

2716. Tenerorum lusor amorum.   Ov. T. 3, 3, 73.—*The singer of tender
loves.*   His own epitaph.

2717. Teneros animos aliena opprobria sæpe
Absterrent vitiis.   Hor. S. 1, 4, 128.

A neighbour's scandal many a time
Has kept young minds from running into crime.—*Conington.*

2718. Tenet insanabile multos Scribendi cacoethes.   Juv. 7, 51.—*The
incurable itch for scribbling infects many.*

Cacoethes = any *bad habit*, a passion, itch : as *c. carpendi.* love of fault-
finding; *c. loquendi*, an itching to be always speaking, etc.

2719. Tenez; voilà (dit-elle) à chacun une écaille.
Des sottises d'autrui nous vivons au Palais;
Messieurs, l'huître était bonne.' Adieu! vivez en paix.
Boil. Ep. 2, à M. L'Abbé des Roches.

The Lawyers and the Oyster.

Then take (says Justice), take ye each a shell:
We thrive at Westminster on fools like you:
'Twas a fat oyster—live in peace—Adieu!—*Pope.*

2720. Tenia una cara como una bendicion.   Cervantes, Don Quijote, 1,
2, 4.—*He had a face like a benediction.*

2721. Τὴν κατὰ σαυτὸν ἔλα. (sc. βέμβικα).   Epigr. of Callimachus in
Diog. Laert. 1, 4, 80.—*Whip your own* (top): *i.e.*, Marry in
your own rank of life.

2722. Τὴν μὲν ζωγραφίαν ποίησιν σιωπῶσαν, τὴν δὲ ποίησιν ζωγραφίαν
λαλοῦσαν προσαγορεύει.   Simonid. in Plut. Mor. p. 424 (de Gloria
Athen. 3).   Simonides calls "*Painting silent poetry, and poetry
a picture speaking.*"   So in Latin, Poëma loquens pictura, pictura
tacitum poëma debet esse.   Auct. Her. 4, 28, 39.—*A poem should
be a picture speaking, and a picture a silent poem.*

2723. Tentanda via est qua me quoque possim
Tollere humo, victorque virum volitare per ora.   Virg. G. 3, 8.

The Poet's Ambition.

I'll lift my head and get my verses heard,
And fly from mouth to mouth a household word.—*Ed.*

2724. Tertius e cœlo cecidit Cato.   Juv. 2, 40.—*A third Cato has fallen from heaven.*

Two Catos only—the Censor, and the opponent of Cæsar—are famous in history, both celebrated for their rigid stoicism; hence, Juvenal ironically gives the name of a "*third* Cato" to the effeminate monster he is satirising. Cf. "Sapientum octavus." Hor. S. 2, 3, 296.—*An eighth wise man, i.e.,* in addition to the famous "Seven" of Greece. Sappho is the "Tenth" Muse, Plat. Ep. 20.

2725. Testimonium animæ naturaliter Christianæ.   Tert. Apol. 17.—*Evidence of a soul naturally Christian.* The belief in a Supreme Being entertained by the heathen is a testimony to the truth of Christianity.

2726. Tetigisti acu.   Plaut. Rud. 5, 2, 19.—*You have touched it with the needle.* You have hit the nail on the head.

2727. Tetrum ante omnia vultum.   Juv. 10, 191.—*A countenance hideous beyond all conception.* Motto of Steele's *Spectator* 17 on the Ugly Club.

2728. Θέλω, θέλω μανῆναι.   Anacreontea, 8 [31], Bergk. vol. iii. p. 302.—*I will, I will be mad!*

Refrain of a song (*To himself drunk,* Εἰς ἑαυτὸν μεμεθυσμένον),

"Αφες με, τοὺς θεούς σοι,
πιεῖν πιεῖν ἀμυστί·
θέλω θέλω μανῆναι.—*By all thy gods, I pray thee, let me drink deep at one draught! I will, I will be mad!* Horace imitates the sentiment (C. 2, 7, 26): Non ego sanius Bacchabor Edonis: recepto Dulce mihi furere est amico—*I'll revel as madly as any Bacchanal: 'tis sweet to play the fool when friends come home again.*

2729. Θύε ταῖς χάρισι.   Diog. Laert. 4, 6.—*Sacrifice to the Graces!* Xenocrates, the disciple of Plato, was of so forbidding a cast of countenance, that his master would say to him,—Ξενόκρατες, θύε ταῖς χάρισι. More than two thousand years later, a Plato of a different type wrote, " I must from time to time remind you, of what you cannot attend to too much, *Sacrifice to the Graces.*" Lord Chesterfield's *Letters to his Son,* Lond., 1774, vol. 1, Letter cxii.

2730. Tibi summum rerum judicium dii dedere; nobis obsequi gloria relicta est.   Tac. A. 6, 8.—*To you the gods have given the supreme ordering of affairs; to us is left the glory of obeying your commands.* Addressed to the aged debauchee Tiberius by M. Terentius, when exculpating himself from collusion with the conspiracy of Sejanus (31 A.D.).

2731. Timeo Danaos et dona ferentes.   Virg. A. 2, 49.

> Whate'er it be, a Greek I fear,
> Though presents in his hand he bear.—*Conington.*

2732. Τὸ δ'εὖ νικάτω.   Æsch. Ag. 121.—*May the right prevail!*

2733. Τὸ γαμεῖν, ἐάν τις τὴν ἀλήθειαν σκοπῇ,
κακὸν μὲν ἐστιν, ἀλλ' ἀναγκαῖον κακόν.   Menand. Inc. Fab. Fr. 105.

> Marriage, to tell the truth, must be pronounced
> An evil, though a necessary one.—*Ed.*

The Latin equivalent is, Malum est mulier, sed necessarium malum, Chil. p. 52 (*A wife is an evil, but a necessary one*), and it may be observed that Alexander Severus speaks of his own lords of the Treasury in the same terms. Lampridius, Alex. Sev. 46.

2734. Τοῖς τοι δικαίοις χὠ βραχὺς νικᾷ μέγαν.   Soph. O. C. 880.—*In a just cause, e'en weakness wins the day.*

2735. Tolle moras; semper nocuit differre paratis. Luc. 1, 281.—*An end to delays! It has always been hurtful to postpone when you are ready to act.*

2736. Tolle periclum,
Jam vaga prosiliet frænis natura remotis.   Hor. S. 2, 7, 74.

> But take away the danger, in a trice
> Nature unbridled plunges into vice.—*Conington.*

2737. Tollite barbarum Morem.   Hor. C. 1, 27, 2.—*Away with such a barbarous custom!*

2738. Tollite jampridem victricia, tollite signa!
Viribus utendum est quas fecimus.   Arma tenenti
Omnia dat qui justa negat.   Luc. 1, 347.

> *The Rubicon.*
>
> Your long-victorious standards raise aloft!
> Put forth your strength! Though just demands have failed,
> The arm'd opponent will get all he asks.—*Ed.*

The words are put by the poet into Cæsar's mouth on his memorable decision (49 B.C.) to march straight on the capital and oust Pompey from power: but they also have an application for another momentous decision in history, the consequences of which brought about a struggle, far bloodier and more prolonged than any that fell within the limits of the Second Civil War. They apply to Majuba, and they express its significance, and its sting: although the awful harvesting of that fatuous sowing was left for after years to demonstrate. *Arma tenenti omnia dat qui justa negat*, says Lucan, speaking of Cæsar's rejected proposals of disarmament; and, says Mr Morley of the "peace" of March 1881, "the galling argument was that government had given to men with arms in their hands what we refused to their prayers." (*See* Mr Morley's "Life of Gladstone," vol. iii. chapter 3.)

2739. Τόλμα ἀεὶ, κἄν τι τρηχὺ νέμωσι θεοί.   Eur. Telephus, Fr. 16.—*How stiff soe'er the task assigned, dare on!*

2740. Τῶν εὐτυχούντων πάντες εἰσὶ συγγενεῖς. Men. Monost. 510.—*Every-one is kinsman to the fortunate.*

2741. Τὸ νικᾶν αὐτὸν αὑτὸν πασῶν νικῶν πρώτη τε καὶ ἀρίστη.   Plato, Leges, 1, 626 E.—*Self-conquest is the first and finest of all victories.*

2742. Tonto, sin saber Latin, nunca es gran tonto.   Prov.—*A fool, except he know Latin, is never a great fool.*

2743. Tota teguntur
Pergama dumetis: etiam periere ruinæ.   Luc. 9, 968.

The straggling wild-thorn covers all the ground
Where once was Troy; its very ruins are gone.—*Ed.*

The last words are often quoted of the rapid disappearance of old buildings, monuments, societies, or associations of former years.

2744. Τὸ τεχνίον πᾶσα γαῖα τρέφει.   Suet. Ner. 40.—*Every country supports art.*   Reply of Nero when the astrologers predicted his destitution.   *V.* No. 2195.   With γε and ἀνατρέφει, the words will make a *versus senarius*—τὸ τεχνίον γε πᾶσα κ.τ.λ.

2745. Τὸ τε διανίστασθαι νύκτωρ· τοῦτο γὰρ καὶ πρὸς ὑγίειαν, καὶ οἰκονομίαν, καὶ φιλοσοφίαν χρήσιμον.   Arist. Œc. 1, 6, 6.—*It is well to rise before day, because it conduces to health, wealth, and wisdom.* "Early to bed," etc.

2746. Toto cælo.—*By the whole heavens width.*   Said of any marked difference.   To disagree by whole diameters.

Nunquamne tibi, Prætextate, venit in mentem toto, ut aiunt, cælo errasse Virgilium?   Macr. Sat. 3, 12, 10.—*Do you ever remember that saying about Virgil's being a "whole heaven" wrong?*   Tota erras via.   Ter. Eun. 2, 2, 14.—*You're on the wrong track all the way.*

2747. Toto principatu suo hostis generis humani.   Plin. 7, 8, 6, § 46.—*Throughout his reign, he* (Nero) *showed himself the enemy of the human race.*

2748. Toujours en vedette.   Frederick the Great, Exposé du gouvernement Prussien, fin.—*Always on outpost duty.*   In the unsettled condition of the frontier during the Seven Years' War, the King insisted on the government of the country remaining under the direct control of the Crown, which must be "always on guard" against surprise of the enemy.

2749. Toujours perdrix.—*Always partridges.*   Said of anything which occurs in wearisome repetition.

The phrase is ascribed to Henry IV.   It appears that on being rebuked for his gallantries by his confessor, the king revenged himself on his spiritual father by giving him nothing but partridges for dinner for several days in succession.   When the priest complained, Henry remarked that need of *variety* was evidently as much felt by the confessor as the penitent. Büchmann, p. 475, refers to a *Curiosa Relacion poetica, En Coplas Castellanas del verdadero aspecto del mundo, etc.* (printed by Vallés, Barcelona, 1837), in which occurs:

Como dice el adagio,
Que cansa de comer perdices.—*As the adage goes, one gets tired of eating partridges.*   I have also heard that a continuous diet of pigeons will produce a fever.

2750. Tous les discours sont des sottises,
      Partant d'un homme sans éclat;
      Ce seraient paroles exquises
      Si c'était un grand qui parlât.   Mol. Amph. 2, 1.

> All sayings are mere fooleries,
> If floated by some obscure wit:
> But the remark's profound and wise,
> Should some great man have uttered it.—*Ed.*

2751. Tous les événements sont enchainés dans le meilleur des mondes
      possibles. Volt. Candide, ou l'Optimisme, 1759, fin. (Dr Pang-
      loss to Candide).—*Every occurrence has its links of causation in
      the best of all possible worlds.*

> So far reaching in its application is this principle that, as his teacher
> points out, Candide's enjoyment of the confitures which he was devouring
> at the moment, might be remotely, yet correctly, traced to the "grands
> coups de pied dans le derrière" that he had received in former days in a
> certain country house of his acquaintance. Undisturbed by the cumulative
> arguments of the doctor, Candide philosophically remarks at the conclusion,
> "*Cela est bien, mais il faut cultiver son jardin.*" Reduced to the required
> epigrammatic shape, the qu. is generally given as, "Tout est pour le
> mieux dans le meilleur des mondes possibles"—*Everything is for the best
> in the best of all possible worlds.* The optimist doctrines of Leibnitz here
> ridiculed by Voltaire are best enunciated in his "Essai sur la Théodicée"
> (1710), where (1, 8) he says of the universe, "Nisi inter omnes possibiles
> mundos optimus esset, Deus nullum produxisset."

2752. Tous les genres sont bons, hors le genre ennuyeux. Volt.
      L'Enfant Prod. Préface.—*All kinds* (of books, writers, etc.) *are
      good except the kind that bores you.*

2753. Tous les méchants sont buveurs d'eau;
      C'est bien prouvé par le déluge.
                        L. P. Comte de Ségur, Chanson morale,
      (*Romans et Chansons* par M. L. Cte. de S. de l'Académie Fr.,
      Paris, 1820, pp. 95-6).

> All bad men are water-drinkers,
> And the deluge is the proof.

> *⁎⁎* Ségur instances the history of Noah and of the Flood as a Scriptural
> warning against teetotalism.

2754. Tout bien ou rien. Prov.—*Either well or nothing.* Either do
      the thing well or not at all.

2755. Tout chemin mène à Rome. Prov.—*All roads lead to Rome.*
      Tous chemins vont à Rome. La Font. Fables, 12, 28 (*Le Juge,*
      etc.). In Italian, *Tutte le strade conducono a Roma.* So long as
      the end is attained, the means may be considered immaterial.

2756. Tout citoyen est roi sous un roi citoyen. Favart (C. S.), Les
      Trois Sultanes, 2, 3 (1761).—*Every citizen is a king under a
      citizen king.*

> Curious that this should have been written under Louis XV. instead of
> Louis Philippe! Although at the time of the play, the *corvée, e.g.,* was

as much a matter of daily occurrence as the tides, Roxelane cheerfully declares,

> Point d'esclaves chez nous : on ne respire en France
> Que les plaisirs, *la liberté*, et l'aisance.
> Tout citoyen est roi sous un roi citoyen.

2757. Tout doit tendre au bon sens : mais pour y parvenir, Le chemin est glissant et pénible à tenir.   Boil. L'A. P. 1, 45.

> Before you good sense as your aim ever keep,
> Though the path that leads thither be slipp'ry and steep.—*Ed.*

Cf. *Id. ibid.* Cant. 3, 413 :

> Au dépens du bon sens gardez de plaisanter.—*Take care not to sacrifice good sense in your desire to be funny.*

2758. Toute femme varie.   Francis I.—*Every woman is fickle.* (*V.* 1232.)

> Brantôme (*Vie des Dames Gallantes*, Disc. IV.) says that he remembers, in the royal apartments at Chambord, being shown by a valet de chambre of the late King these words written in large characters, "au costé de la fenestre"—which his guide assured him were in Francis' hand.   Hugo, in *Le Roi s'amuse*, 4, 2, represents Francis entering Saltabadil's tavern, singing—

> Souvent femme varie,
> Bien fol est qui s'y fie !
> Une femme souvent
> N'est qu'une plume au vent.

2759. Toutes les fois que je donne une place vacante, je fais cent mécontents, et un ingrat.   Volt. Siècle de Louis XIV. (Panthéon Littér. vol. 4, cap. 26, p. 196).—*Every time I give away a vacant place, I make a hundred persons discontented, and one ungrateful.*

2759A. Τοῦτ' ἔστι τὸ ζῆν, οὐκ ἑαυτῷ ζῆν μόνον.   Men. Incert. Fr. 257, p. 1012.—*Real life means living not for self alone.*

2760. Tout est perdu fors l'honneur.   Francis I.—*All is lost save our honour.*

> This celebrated saying is found in slightly different shape in the original letter written by Francis I. to his mother, Louisa of Savoy, after the battle of Pavia, Feb. 24, 1525, "Madame, pour vous faire scavoir comment se porte le ressort de mon infortune, de toutes choses ne m'est demouré que l'honneur et la vie qui est saulve . . . j'ay prié qu'on me laissast pour écrire ces lettres," etc. *Journal d'un bourgeois de Paris*, p. 137 (Collection Dupuy, vol. DCCXLII.), pub. in Dulaure's *Histoire de Paris*, 1837, vol. 3, p. 209.—*Madame, I have begged to be allowed to write this letter, to inform you what hope I have of recovering from my present misfortune, in which all that remains is my honour, and my life which is safe*, etc.   *See* Champollion, Captivité de François I. (Documents inédits, pp. 129-30).   Cf. Ov. 4, 16, 49, Omnia perdidimus, tantummodo vita relicta est—*I have lost everything; only life is left.*

2761. Tout faiseur de journaux doit tribut au malin.   La Font. Lettre à M. Simon de Troyes, Feb. 1686.—*Every journalist owes toll to the evil one.*

> The Letter refers to the contemporary ventures in literary journalism— the first of their kind—of Bayle (*Nouvelles de la République des lettres*, started 1684), and Le Clerc (*Bibliothèque Universelle*, beginning in 1686).

2762. Tout flatteur vit au dépens de celui qui l'écoute.   La Font. 1, 2 (Corbeau et Renard).—*Every flatterer lives at the expense of those who listen to him.*

2763. Tout le monde se plaint de sa mémoire, et personne ne se plaint de son jugement.   La Rochef. Max., § 89, p. 42.—*Every one complains of his memory, but none of his judgment.*

2764. Tout notre mal vient de ne pouvoir être seuls.   La Bruy. chap xi. (De l'homme), vol. 2, p. 47.—*All our ills come from not being able to be alone.*

2765. Tout passe, tout casse, tout lasse.   "Quelques six milles proverbes" par le P. Charles Cahier, S. J., 1856, p. 97.—*Everything passes, everything perishes, everything palls.*   This is the correct order of words in this oft-repeated saying.

2766. Tout soldat français porte dans sa giberne le bâton de maréchal de France.—*Every French soldier carries a field-marshal's baton in his knapsack.*   Attributed to Napoleon.

   As usual, the epigram of tradition cannot be verified by documentary chapter and verse.   A couple of approximate authorities are, however, producible—(1) Louis XVIII.'s speech to the St Cyr students (Aug. 8, 1819), after their execution of a military evolution in the quadrangle of St Cloud: "Rappelez-vous bien qu'il n'est aucun de vous, qui n'ait dans sa giberne le bâton de maréchal du duc de Reggio; c'est à vous à l'en faire sortir." *Moniteur Univ.*, Aug. 10, 1819.—*Remember that there is not one of you that may not have in his knapsack the field-marshal's bâton of the Duke of Reggio* (Oudinot): *it is for you to produce it.*   (2) Nous avons tous un brevet de maréchal de France dans notre giberne.   E. Blaze, *La vie militaire sous l'Empire*, Paris, 1837, vol. i. pp. 5 and 394.— *We all of us have a field-marshal's patent in our knapsack.*   Alex., p. 300; and Büchm., pp. 490-1.

2767. Tout vient à point à qui sait attendre.   Prov.—*Everything comes to him who knows how to wait for it.*   Quitard (p. 81) quotes Bossuet to the same effect.   "La science des occasions et des temps est la principale partie des affaires.   Précipiter ses affaires, c'est le propre de la faiblesse."

2768. Traduttori, traditori.   Prov.—*Translators, traitors.*

2769. Trahit ipse furoris
   Impetus, et visum est lenti quæsisse nocentem.   Lucan. 2, 109.
      Rage drags them on, and 'twere sheer waste of time
      To investigate the nature of the crime.—*Ed.*
   Peculiarly applicable to the proceedings of the Revolutionary Tribunal of '93 and its agents.

2770. Trahit sua quemque voluptas.   Virg. E. 2, 65.—*Each follows his own peculiar pleasure.*   Cf. Lucr. 2, 258, Progredimur quo ducit quemque voluptas.

2771. Trasumanar significar per verba
   Non si poría.
      Dante, Par. 1, 70.— *Words could not tell the superhuman change*, sc. in the realms of Paradise.

2772. Tre cose belle in questo mondo: prete parato, cavaliere armato, e donna ornata. Prov.—*Three things are beautiful in this world: a priest in his vestments, a knight in armour, and a woman in her jewels.*

2773. Tre donne e un papero fanno un mercato. Prov.—*Three women and a goose make a market.*

2774. Tremblez! vous êtes immortels!

Delille, L'Immortalité de l'âme.

Tremble, ye tyrants, for ye cannot die!—*Ed.*

2775. Tres faciunt collegium.—*Three make a college;* a Quorum, Committee, Corporation. Formed from the "Tres facere existimat collegium" (Digest. 87, de Verb. Significatione, 50, 16), attributed to Neratius Priscus, Consul and Jurisconsult, 100 A.D.

2776. Tria juncta in uno.—*Three joined in one.* Motto of the Order of the Bath.

An order of knighthood originating with Henry IV. in 1399, revived by George I. as a military order in 1725, and extended to civilians by Statute of 1847. The modern motto, with badge of emblematic Rose, Shamrock and Thistle, denotes the union of the three kingdoms.

2777. Tribus Anticyris caput insanabile. Hor. A. P. 300.—*A head not three Anticyræ could cure.*

There were two Anticyræ, both famous for their hellebore, the ancient specific for madness; one in Phocis on the Gulf of Corinth, referred to by Ovid (Ep. 4, 3, 54), and the other on the Sinus Maliacus, now Gulf of Zeitorim, S. of Thessaly, mentioned in Hor. S. 2, 3, 83, and Gell. 17, 15. Horace, therefore, describes a man so insane that it would take *three* Anticyræ, did they exist, to cure him of his disease. *See* No. 1617.

2778. Tristis eris, si solus eris. Ov. R. A. 583.—*You will be sad if you live alone.*

2779. Trois degrez d'élévation du Pole renversent toute la Jurisprudence. Un Méridien décide de la vérité, ou peu d'années de possession. Les loix fondementales changent. Le droit a ses époches. Plaisante justice qu'une rivière ou une montagne borne! Vérité au-deçà des Pyrrénées, erreur au-delà. Pasc. Pens. 25, 5.—*Three degrees of polar elevation upset the whole of jurisprudence. Truth (or its opposite) is decided by a meridian, or by a few years' occupation: fundamental laws are changed, and equity becomes a matter of epochs. A funny sort of justice, indeed, that depends upon the boundaries of nature! Truth on one side of the Pyrenees; error on the other!*

2780. Tros Tyriusve mihi nullo discrimine agetur. Virg. A. 1, 574.—*Whether Trojan or Tyrian, it shall make no difference in my treatment of them.* I shall act impartially towards all.

z

2781. Truditur dies die,
Novæque pergunt interire lunæ.   Hor. C. 2, 18, 15.
> Day presses on the heels of day,
> And moons increase to their decay.—*Francis.*

2782. Tu dors, Brutus, et Rome est dans les fers !
Volt. Mort de César, 2, 2.
> What! Brutus, dost thou sleep, and Rome in chains?—*Ed.*

2783. Tui me miseret, mei piget.   Enn. ap. Cic. Div. 1, 31, 66.—*I am sorry for you, vexed with myself.*

2784. Tum denique homines nostra intelligimus bona,
Quum, quæ in potestate habuimus, ea amisimus.   Plaut. Capt. 1, 2, 39.—*We begin to value our blessings when we have lost them.* Cf. *Much Ado about N.*, 4, 1, "What we have we prize not to the worth, Whiles we enjoy it; but," etc.

2785. Tu mihi curarum requies, tu nocte vel atra
Lumen, et in solis tu mihi turba locis.   Tib. 4, 13, 11.
> My rest from care, my star in darkest night,
> My company when alone, constant delight.—*Ed.*

These lines, which the poet addressed to his mistress, were very felicitously inscribed by a Chartreux around the walls of his study.

2786. Tum meæ (si quid loquar audiendum)
Vocis accedet bona pars.
Hor. C. 4, 2, 45.—*Then, if I can say anything worth listening to, I will heartily add the tribute of my voice.*

2787. Tunc autem consummata est infelicitas, ubi turpia non solum delectant, sed etiam placent : et desinit esse remedio locus, ubi quæ fuerant vitia, mores sunt. Sen. Ep. 39, fin.—*Then is the lowest stage of degradation reached, when abominable practices produce not merely pleasure but satisfaction; and all hope of remedy vanishes when vice itself has become habitual.*

2788. Tu ne cede malis, sed contra audentior ito
Quam tua te fortuna sinet.   Virg. A. 6, 95.
> Yet still despond not, but proceed
> Along the path where fate may lead.—*Conington.*

2789. Tu ne quæsieris (scire nefas), quem mihi, quem tibi
Finem di dederint, Leuconoe.
Hor. C. 1, 11, 1.—*Enquire not, Leuconoe (for 'tis forbidden), what end the gods have appointed either for thee or for me.*

2790. Tunica propior pallio est. Plaut. Trin. 5, 2, 30.—*My tunic is nearer to me than my cloak.* Charity begins at home.

In other tongues we have kindred proverbs: Das Hemd ist mir näher als der Rock. Büchm. p. 366.—*My shirt is nearer to me than my coat.* La chemise est plus proche que le pourpoint.—*My shirt is nearer to me than my doublet.* La peau est plus proche que la chemise. Quit. p. 218.—*My skin is nearer than my shirt;* and in Greek, ἀπωτέρω ἢ γόνυ κνήμα. Theocr. 16, 18.—*My calf is further than my knee.*

2791. Tu nihil invita dices faciesve Minerva. Hor. A. P. 385.—*Beware of attempting anything* (in literary composition) *for which nature has not gifted you—i.e.*, against the grain. Nihil decet invita, ut aiunt, Minerva, id est, adversante et repugnante natura. Cic. Off. 1, 31, 110.—*Nothing that we write in the teeth of Minerva, as they say*, i.e., *against our natural capacities, will do us credit.* Boileau, in imitation, begins his *L'Art Poétique* with

> C'est en vain qu' au Parnasse un téméraire auteur
> Pense de l'art des vers attaindre la hauteur.
>
> .   .   .   .   .   .
> Si son astre en naissant ne l'a formé poëte.

2792. Tu pol si sapis, Quod scis nescis. Ter. Eun. 4, 4, 54.—*You, hark ye, if you are wise, will not know what you do know.* You must affect ignorance.

2793. Tu proverai sì come sa di sale
Lo pane altrui, e com' è duro calle
Lo scender e'l salir per l'altrui scale.   Dante, Par. Cant. 17, 58.

> *Cacciaguida prophecies Dante's exile.*
> Thou shalt prove
> How salt the savour is of other's bread:
> How hard the passage, to descend and climb
> By other's stairs.—*Cary.*

"Condemned to learn by experience that no food is so bitter as the bread of dependence, and no ascent so painful as the staircase of a patron."— Macaulay, *Essay on Dante*, Jan. 1824 (Misc. Writings and Speeches).

2794. Tu, quamcunque Deus tibi fortunaverit horam,
Grata sume manu ; neu dulcia differ in annum,
Ut quocunque loco fueris, vixisse libenter
Te dicas.   Hor. Ep. 1, 11, 22.

> Seize then each happy hour the gods dispense,
> Nor fix enjoyment for a twelvemonth hence ;
> So you may testify with truth, where'er
> You're quartered, 'tis a pleasure to be there.—*Conington.*

2795. Tuque, O! dubiis ne defice rebus. Virg. A. 6, 196.—*And oh! desert me not in this troublous affair!*

2796. Tu quoque, Brute !—*Thou also, Brutus!* Sometimes quoted as *Et tu, Brute!*

> Exclamation of Julius Cæsar on recognising M. Junius Brutus amongst his murderers. Suet. (C. J. Cæsar, 82) says that the actual words were, καὶ σὺ εἶ ἐκείνων, καὶ σὺ τέκνον;—*And art thou one of them? What! thou, my son?*

2797. Turba gravis paci, placidæque inimica quieti. Mart. de Spect. 4, 1. —*A crowd that disturbs one's peace, and is the enemy of calm quiet.* Said of informers, spies, etc.

2798. Turba Remi sequitur fortunam, ut semper, et odit Damnatos. Juv. 10, 73.—*The Roman crowd follows, as ever, the lead of fortune, and hates the fallen.* Said of the fall of Sejanus, 31 A.D.

2799. Tu regere imperio populos, Romane, memento:
Hæ tibi erunt artes, pacisque imponere morem,
Parcere subjectis, et debellare superbos.   Virg. A. 6, 852.

Rome.

Remember, Roman, thy high destiny,
To hold the world 'neath thine imperial sway;
Be these thy arts—the terms of peace to give,
To crush the proud, and bid the prostrate live.—*Ed.*

The whole passage, written at the brilliant dawning of the world-wide
empire of the Cæsars (19 B.C.), is as follows:—

Excudent alii spirantia mollius æra;
Credo equidem, vivos ducent de marmore vultus;
Orabunt causas melius, cœlique meatus
Describent radio, et surgentia sidera dicent;
Tu regere imperio populos, etc., *ut supra.*

Though Greece in bronze or marble deftlier make
The forms that seem to breathe, the looks that speak;
Plead causes better; chart the starry skies,
Describe their courses, tell when planets rise—
Yet, Roman, thine's the nobler destiny,
To hold the world 'neath thine imperial sway, etc.—*Ed.*

2800. Turne, quod optanti Divum promittere nemo
Auderet, volvenda dies en! attulit ultro.   Virg. A. 9, 6.

Turnus, what never God would dare
To promise to his suppliant's prayer,
Lo here, the lapse of time has brought
E'en to your hands, unasked, unsought.—*Conington.*

2801. Turpe est difficiles habere nugas,
Et stultus labor est ineptiarum.   Mart. 2, 86, 9.

To me it is a labour that provokes,
To toil at wit, and make a task of jokes.—*Ed.*

2802. Turpissimam aiebat Fabius imperatori excusationem esse, *Non
putavi:* ego turpissimam homini puto.   Omnia puta, exspecta:
etiam in bonis moribus aliquid existet asperius.   Sen. de Ira, 2, 31.
—*Fabius used to say that a commander could not make a more
disgraceful excuse than to plead "I never expected it." It is in
truth a most shameful reason for any one to urge. Imagine
everything, expect everything: even when things are going on well,
some reverse may occur.*

2803. Turpius ejicitur quam non admittitur hospes. Ov. T. 5, 6, 13.—
*It is more disgraceful to turn a guest out of doors, than not
to admit him.*

2804. Tuta scelera esse possunt; secura non possunt. Sen. Ep. 97, 11.
—*Crimes may be well guarded, but they cannot be secure against
disclosure.*

2805. Tutti siam macchiati d'una pece. Petrarch, Trionfo d'Amore, 3, 99.—*We are all tarred with the same brush.*

2806. Tu vero felix, Agricola, non vitæ tantum claritate, sed etiam opportunitate mortis. Tac. Agr. 45.—*Happy wert thou, Agricola, not only in a life of distinction, but in the appropriate hour of thy death.*

2807. Tyran, descends du trône, et fais place à ton maître. Corn. Héraclius, 1, 2 (Pulchérie loq.).—*Tyrant, come down from the throne, and make room for your master!* A favourite line with the friends of the exiled Bourbons during the First Empire.

U.

2808. Ubi amor condimentum inerit, cuivis placiturum credo. Plaut. Cas. 2, 3, 5.—*Where love is the seasoning, I imagine the dish will please any one's taste.*

2809. Ubicunque ars ostentatur, veritas abesse videatur. Quint. 9, 3, 102.—*Wherever art makes itself felt, truth seems to be wanting.* Tasso (Gerusalemmc Liber., 16, 9) says, L'arte che tutto fa, nulla si scopre—*The art that creates the whole thing, nowhere reveals itself.* Compressed into the form of an adage, the idea is concisely stated in the Latin, Ars est celare artem—*Art consists in its concealment.*

2810. Ulterius ne tende odiis. Virg. A. 12, 938.—*Let your enmity no farther go.* Appeal made by Turnus to Æneas to spare the life of a fallen foe. (2.) Ulterius tentare veto. Virg. A. 12, 806. —*I forbid all further attempts.* I prohibit your proceeding further.

2811. Ultima ratio regum.—*The final argument of kings,* viz., cannon.

> Inscription on cannon of Louis XIV. (1650), and adopted in the form *Ultima ratio regis* for the same purpose by Prussia since Frederick the Great's time, 1742. In his comedy of *En esta vida todo es verdad y todo mentira* (Jorn. II^da, esc. xxiii.) published before 1644, Calderon speaks of powder and shot as "Ultima razon de Reyes." Büchm. pp. 316-7, and Fumag. No. 605.

2812. Ultima semper Expectanda dies homini ; dicique beatus
Ante obitum nemo supremaque funera debet.   Ov. M. 3, 135.

> The approach of your last day always attend,
> And call none happy till his death and end.—*Ed.*

> Ante mortem ne laudes hominem quemquam. Vulg. Ecclus. 11, 30.— *Praise not any man before his death.* Πρὶν δ' ἂν τελευτήσῃ ἐπισχέειν, μηδὲ καλέειν κω ὄλβιον ἀλλ' εὐτυχέα. Hdt. 1, 32.—*Call no man happy till you know the nature of his death; he is at best but fortunate.* Solon to Crœsus in the discussion on human happiness. Referring to this passage, Juvenal

358 UM—UN DÎNER.

(10, 274) speaks of Crœsus, "quem vox justi facunda Solonis Respicere ad longæ jussit spatia ultima vitæ"—*Whom Solon rightly referred to the closing scenes of a long life*—before pronouncing on his final felicity or not. Prof. Mayor, in his edition of Juvenal *in l.*, remarks: "This maxim is very frequently cited (in the Classics), especially in Tragedy, of which it is the keynote." For example, compare Sophocles, Œdipus Tyrannus, 1528-30, where the chorus comments on the hero's history with:

ὥστε θνητὸν ὄντ' ἐκείνην τὴν τελευταίαν ἰδεῖν
ἡμέραν ἐπισκοποῦντα μηδέν' ὀλβίζειν, πρὶν ἂν
τέρμα τοῦ βίου περάσῃ μηδὲν ἀλγεινὸν παθών.

Thus keeping that last final day in view,
We must call no man happy till he has crossed
Life's farthest bound without a taste of woe.—*Ed.*

*** Further instances may be consulted in Æsch. Agam. 928 ; Eur. Andromache, 100-2, and Troad. 509; and Arist. Nic. Eth. 1, 10. George Herbert, in his *Jacula Prudentum*, says: "Praise day at night, and life at end."

2813. Um Gut's zu thun, braucht's keiner Ueberlegung ;
Der Zweifel ist 's, der Gutes böse macht.
Bedenke nicht! gewähre wie du's fühlst.
Goethe, Iphigenia, 5, 3 fin. (Iphigenia loq.).—*To do good, requires no consideration: 'tis doubt that turns good to evil. Don't reflect, act as you feel.*

2814. Una dies aperit, conficit una dies. Auson. Id. 14, 40.
The Rose.
One day sees it bloom, and one day sees it die.—*Ed.*

2815. Una furtiva lagrima
Negli occhi suoi spuntò.
Felice Romani, in Donizetti's Op. of L'Elisire d'Amore, 2, 8.
—*A secret tear welled in her eyes.*

2816. Una salus victis nullam sperare salutem. Virg. A. 2, 354.
No safety can the vanquish'd find
Till hope of safety be resigned.—*Conington.*

2817. Unde nil majus generatur ipso,
Nec viget quicquam simile, aut secundum. Hor. C. 1, 12, 17.
No mightier birth may He beget,
No like, no second has He known.—*Conington.*

2818. Unde tibi frontem libertatemque parentis,
Quum facias pejora senex ? Juv. 14, 56.
Like Father, like Son.
When you do worse yourself, can you expect
Your son should hold your grey hairs in respect?—*Ed.*

2819. Un dîner réchauffé ne valut jamais rien. Boil. Le Lutrin, ch. 1, v. 104.—*A warmed-up dinner was never good for anything yet.* Serve up your own ideas rather than a hash made up of other writers' thoughts.

2820. Un dîner sans façon est une perfidie. Berchoux, La Gastronomie, Chant 2, fin.—*To ask a man to take pot-luck is an act of perfidy.* A line or two above he says—

> Si parfois on vous prie
> A dîner sans façon et sans cérémonie,
> Refusez promptement.

2821. Und wenn der Mensch in seiner Qual verstummt, Gab mir ein Gott zu sagen, wie ich leide. Goethe, Tasso, 5, 5, fin.

> While most men's agony merely leaves them dumb,
> God gave me (*the poet*) a voice to express my sufferings.—*Ed.*

2822. Und wenn ich dich lieb habe, was geht 's dich an? Goethe, Wilh. Meisters Lehrjahre, 4, 9 (Philine loq.).—*And if I love you, what matters it to you?* Unselfish love is not conditioned upon reciprocity.

> For the history of this "odd" (*wunderlich*) saying, *see* his "Wahrheit und Dichtung" (3, 14, *ad fin.*).

2823. Une bonne pensée de quelque endroit qu'elle parte, vaudra toujours mieux qu'une sottise de son crû, n'en déplaise à ceux qui se vantent de trouver tout chez eux, et de tenir rien de personne. Fr. de la Mothe le Vayer, Œuvres, 1669, Paris, vol. 9, p. 341.—*A good sentiment, no matter who may be its author, will always be worth a foolish saying of one's own, with all deference to those who pride themselves on finding all they require from their own resources, without being indebted to any one else.*

2824. Une femme qui n'a pas été jolie n'a pas été jeune. Mme. Swetchine, Airelles cxxv.—*A woman who has not been pretty has never been young.*

2825. Une froideur ou une incivilité qui vient de ceux qui sont audessus de nous nous les fait haïr, mais un salut ou un sourire nous les réconcilie. La Bruy. Car. chap. ix., Des Grands (vol. i. p. 170).—*A coldness or an incivility shown towards us by a superior, makes us hate him; and yet a salute or a smile is quite enough to reconcile us.*

2826. Une nation frivole qui rit sottement et qui croit rire gaiement, de tout ce qui n'est pas dans ses mœurs, ou plutôt dans ses modes. Volt. Lettre à M. de Marsais, Oct. 12, 1755.—*A frivolous people who laugh foolishly while they think they laugh wittily, at everything that is not agreeable to their ideas, or rather to their fashions.* Said by Voltaire of his own countrymen, the French.

2827. Un frère est un ami donné par la nature. Baudouin (L'aîné), Demetrius, 5, 2 (1785).—*A brother is a friend given us by nature:* with which comp. "Cum his (propinquis) amicitiam natura ipsa peperit." Cic. Am. 5, 19.—*With relatives nature herself creates for us friends.*

> According to Fournier (*L.D.A.*, pp. 351-8), this line (with two more) was with Baudouin's consent made a present of to Gabriel Legouvé for

insertion in his *Mort d'Abel* (3, 3), where, singularly enough, the words are put into the mouth of Cain! Parody has turned the saying into "Un père est un banquier donné par la nature."—*A father is a banker that nature supplies us with.*

2828. Un grand destin commence, un grand destin s'achève,
L'Empire est prêt à choir, et la France s'élève. Corn. Attila, 1, 2.

> A glorious hour is at hand with destin'd triumph bright,
> The Empire's tottering, and France arises in her might.—*Ed.*

Valamir speaks. This would have been a happy quotation at the Restoration, or on the fall of the Second Empire.

2829. Un homme d'esprit serait souvent bien embarrassé sans la compagnie des sots. La Rochef., § 140, p. 48.—*A wit would often be much at a loss if it were not for the company of fools.* His wit requires a foil to set it off, and a butt to aim at.

2830. Uno scherzo di natura,
Un uom senza architettura.

Guadagnoli, Il cadetto militare.—*A freak of nature, a man without any architecture about him.* Said of any singularly hideous or misshapen person.

2831. Un peu d'Encens bruslé rajuste bien des choses. Cyrano de Bergerac, Agrippine (Paris, 1654), 2, 4. Sejanus loq.—*A little incense burnt sets many things straight.* A little flattery skilfully and opportunely applied works wonders.

> Quit., *s.v.* "Encens," speaks of a certain Pope, who, on being compared to the Deity Himself by a monk who was present, remarked: "*C'est un peu fort, mais ça fait toujours plaisir*" (It's a little strong, but pleasant all the same).

2832. Un prince est le premier serviteur et le premier magistrat de l'État. Frederick II., Mémoires de Brandebourg (Œuvres, ed. Preuss., vol. 1, p. 123).—*A prince is the first servant and the first magistrate of the State.* See Büchm. pp. 520-1, who records no less than six different places in which Frederick enunciated this maxim, and each time in the French, and not the German language.

> In 1717 (Mar. 25) Massillon, preaching before Louis XV., reminded the nine-year-old King: "Ce n'est pas le souverain, c'est la loi, Sire, qui doit régner sur les peuples. Vous n'en êtes que le ministre et le premier dépositaire."—*It is not the sovereign, but the law, that should be supreme over nations. You are only the law's minister, and its chief trustee.* Suet. (Tib. 29) makes Tiberius openly declare in senate, that "a good and serviceable prince ought to be the servant both of the senate and of the whole body of citizens" (*bonum et salutarem principem . . . senatui servire debere, et universis civibus*).

2833. Unser Gefühl für Natur gleicht der Empfindung des Kranken für die Gesundheit. Schiller, Naive und sentimentalische Dichtung.—*Our feeling for nature resembles that of the sick for health.*

2834. Un sot qui a un moment d'esprit étonne et scandalise, comme des chevaux de fiacre au galop. Chamf. Max. et Pensées, vol. ii. p. 17.—*When a fool once in a way says something clever, one is astonished and shocked, like seeing a cab-horse at full gallop.*

2835. Un sot trouve toujours un plus sot qui l'admire. Boil. L'A. P. 1 (last line).—*Every fool finds a bigger fool than himself to admire him.*

2836. Un Tiens vaut, ce dit-on, mieux que deux Tu l'auras,
L'un est sur, l'autre ne l'est pas.
La Font. 5, 3 (Petit Poisson et Pêcheur).—*A bird in the hand, they say, is worth two in the bush: one is sure and the other is not.*

2837. Unum Scilicet egregii mortalem altique silenti. Hor. S. 2, 6, 57.
—*A person of most uncommon and profound taciturnity.*

2838. Unus homo nobis cunctando restituit rem,
Non ponebat enim rumores ante salutem.
Enn. ap. Cic. Off. 1, 24, 84.—*One Roman by delaying saved the State, for he put the country's welfare before his own reputation.*

Quintus Fabius Max. Cunctator († 203 B.C.), Dictator, and Commander of the Roman forces after the defeat at Lake Thrasymene (221 B.C.). He is celebrated for the masterly inactivity that gained for him the name of the "Delayer" (Cunctator), shown in declining direct engagements, and in confining his attack to a guerilla warfare on the heights, intercepting stragglers and convoys and harassing the enemy while awaiting reinforcements from Rome.

2839. Unus ille dies mihi immortalitatis instar fuit. Cic. Pis. 22, 52.—*That day alone was to me like a foretaste of immortality,* viz., the day of his return from banishment and the reception he met with at Rome.

2840. Unus Pellæo juveni non sufficit orbis:
Æstuat infelix angusto limite mundi. Juv. 10, 168.
Alexander.
One world sufficed not Pella's youth, he'd rage
Against a universe's narrow cage.—*Ed.*

2841. Urbem quam dicunt Romam, Meliboee, putavi
Stultus ego huic nostræ similem. Virg. E. 1, 20.
The city, Meliboeus, they call Rome
I fondly thought was like our town at home.—*Ed.*

2842. Urbes constituit ætas: hora dissolvit. Momento fit cinis; diu silva. Sen. Q. N. 3, 27, 3.—*It takes an age to build a city, but an hour can bring it to nothing. A forest is long in growing, but a moment reduces it to ashes.*

2843. **Urbi et Orbi.**—*To the City and to the World.* Papal rescripts are promulgated by being proclaimed at or near the Roman Chancery, and also affixed to the gates of the Vatican, thus securing the double *publicatio Urbi et Orbi.* (Addis & Arnold, Catholic Dict., *s.v.* " Promulgation.")

2844. **Urit enim fulgore suo, qui prægravat artes**
    Infra se positas : exstinctus amabitur idem.   **Hor. Ep. 2, 1, 13.**

> He that excels the talent of his days
> Is apt to scorch his rivals with the blaze :
> And yet they'll sing his praises when he's gone.—*Ed.*

2845. **Urticæ proxima sæpe rosa est.**   Ov. R. A. 46.

> Oft is the nettle near the rose.—*Ed.*

2846. **Ὕς διὰ ῥόδων.** Crates. Γείτ. 6.—"*A bull in a china-shop.*" Lit. " A pig in a rose-garden " : not, however, to be confused with the particular pig which, because it *would* " come into the garden," was therefore called " Maud."

2847. **Usque adeone mori miserum est ?** Virg. 12, 646.—*Is it so hard a thing to die ?*

2848. **Usque adeo nulli sincera voluptas,**
    Sollicitique aliquid lætis intervenit.   Ov. M. 7, 453.

> *Surgit amari aliquid.*
> Man ne'er may count on pure untroubled joy,
> Some grief steps in his pleasure to alloy.—*Ed.*

2849. **Utendum est ætate ; cito pede labitur ætas :**
    Nec bona tam sequitur, quam bona prima fuit.   Ov. A. A. 3, 65.

> Employ your youth : its footsteps hurry fast ;
> Pleasures to come don't equal pleasures past.—*Ed.*

2850. **Ut illum di perdant primus qui horas repperit,**
    Quique adeo primus statuit hic solarium !
    Qui mihi comminuit misero articulatim diem.
    Nam unum me puero venter erat solarium,
    Multo omnium istorum optimum et verissumum :
    Ubivis monebat esse, nisi quom nil erat ;
    Nunc etiam quom est, non estur, nisi soli lubet.
    Itaque adeo jam oppletum oppidum 'st solariis
    Major pars populi jam aridi reptant fame.

> Aquilius, Bœtia, Rib. 2, 38 (Parasite loq.).—*Now may the gods confound the man who invented clocks and first set up a dial in this place, breaking up the day, to my sorrow, into so many pieces ! Why, when I was a lad, my belly was my dial, by far the best and truest of them all : it bade you eat when you would, save when the cupboard was bare. Nowadays, even if the meat be there, you mustn't touch it except as the sun pleases. In short, the town's so choke-full of the machines that more than half the folk are crawling along, mere atomies of hunger.*

2851. Utinam his potius nugis tota ille dedisset
Tempora sævitiæ.   Juv. 4, 150.

> Would that on trifles such as these he'd spent
> His cruel, cruel reign!—*Ed.*

Said of Domitian, who could turn from the occupation of murdering his subjects to the question of cooking a turbot—the theme of the poet's Fourth Satire.

2852. Ut jugulent homines, surgunt de nocte latrones. Hor. Ep. 1, 2, 32.

> Rogues rise o' nights men's lives and gold to take.—*Sir T. Martin.*

2853. Ut nemo in sese tentat descendere, nemo!
Sed præcedenti spectatur mantica tergo.   Pers. 4, 23.

> None, none descends into himself to find
> The secret imperfections of his mind;—*Dryden.*
> But does not fail to scrutinise the pack
> Of faults his neighbour carries on his back.—*Ed.*

2854. Ut nervis alienis mobile lignum.   Hor. S. 2, 7, 82.

> Just like a puppet that requires
> Some one behind to pull the wires.—*Ed.*

2855. Ut pictura, poesis: erit quæ, si propius stes,
Te capiat magis, et quædam, si longius abstes:
Hæc amat obscurum: volet hæc sub luce videri,
Judicis argutum quæ non formidat acumen:
Hæc placuit semel: hæc decies repetita placebit. Hor. A. P. 361.

> Poems are like a painting: some close by,
> Some at a distance, most delight the eye:
> This loves the shade, that needs a stronger light
> And challenges the critic's piercing sight:
> That gives us pleasure for a single view,
> And this, ten times repeated, still is new.—*Francis.*

2856. Ut puto, deus fio. Suet. Vesp. 23.—*I suppose, I am changing into a god.* Dying jest of the Emperor Vespasian, with reference to the "divine honours," and title of *divus* bestowed upon the Cæsars after death, and sometimes before it.

2857. Utque alios industria, ita hunc ignavia ad famam protulerat.
Tac. A. 16, 18.—*While some owe their advancement to their industry, he had attained celebrity by his innate indolence.*
Said of C. Petronius, a friend of Nero, and victim of Tigellinus, Nero's favourite.

2858. *Ut* quent laxis *R*esonare fibris
*Mi*ra gestorum *F*amuli tuorum,
  *Sol*ve polluti *La*bii reatum
    *S*ancte *I*ohannes.

Paulus Diaconus, Sandys' *Hist. of Class. Scholarship* (1903), p. 612.—*That thy servants may be able to sing thy marvellous acts to the loosened strings, absolve them, St John, from the guilt of polluted lips.*

Mediæval Sapphic verse of a hymn to St John the Baptist, in which the names of the notes in the musical gamut may be traced in the syllables italicised above, *Ut* (*Do*), *Re*, *Mi*, etc.; the *Si*, or seventh note, being formed out of the initials of the two last words of the stanza. The verse, as long ago as the 11th century, was used by Guido of Arezzo in teaching singing, the structure of the melody exhibiting, at the beginning of each phrase, a gradual ascent of six successive tones, and thereby helping to fix the sounds of these tones in the memory. The melody, with its literal notation indicated over the words, runs as follows:—

C DF	DED	DDCD	EE
Ut queant	laxis	resonare	fibris
EFGE	DECD	FGA	GFEDD
mira	gestorum	famuli	tuorum
GAGFE	FGD	AGA	FGAA
solve	polluti	labii	reatum
	GFED	GED	
	Sancte	Iohannes	

"The invention of this system (diastematic notation) is commonly ascribed to Guy of Arezzo, but a study of the MSS. proves that the method, which had been forming for two centuries before his time, is the work of the theorists and copyists of those ages. What Guy did was to perfect the system by fixing the clefs and the number of the lines," *i.e.*, the four lines of the staff. *Gregorian Music*, etc., by the Benedictines of Stanbrook, 1897, p. 22. *See* also Kiesewetter, R. G., *Guido von Arrezzo, Sein Leben und Werken*, Leipsic, 1840; Notes and Queries, vol. xii. p. 432; Orelli's *Horace* (1852), vol. ii. p. 926; and Dümmler, *Poetæ Lat. Aevi Car.*, *App. Carminum Dub.* i. 83.

2859. Ut quis ex longinquo revenerat, miracula narrabant. Tac. A. 2, 24.
—*Like all who come back from distant parts, they had wonderful things to tell.*

Cf. Matthias Claudius "Urians Reise um die Welt."
Wenn jemand eine Reise thut,
So kann er was verzählen.

Travellers' Tales.
When anyone a journey takes,
He has some yarns to spin.—*Ed.*

2860. Ut quod alîs cibus est, alieis fuat acre venenum. Lucr. 4, 639.—
So that what is one man's meat, is other men's poison.

2861. Ut ridentibus arrident, ita flentibus adflent
Humani vultus: si vis me flere, dolendum est
Primum ipsi tibi, tunc tua me infortunia lædent.
Hor. A. P. 101.

Smiles are contagious: so are tears; to see
Another sobbing, brings a sob from me.
No, no, good Peleus; set the example, pray,
And weep yourself, then weep perhaps I may.—*Conington.*

Cf. Churchill, *Rosciad*, 861:
But spite of all the criticising elves,
Those who would make us feel, must feel themselves.

2862. Utrumque enim vitium est, et omnibus credere, et nulli. Sen.
Ep. 3, 4.—*It is equally a mistake to trust all, and none.* Cf.
Πίστεις γάρ τοι ὁμῶς καὶ ἀπιστίαι ὤλεσαν ἄνδρας. Hes. Op. 370.
—*Trust and distrust alike have proved men's ruin.*

2863. Ut sæpe summa ingenia in occulto latent! Plaut. Capt. 1, 2, 62.
—*How often is the greatest genius buried in obscurity!*
Full many a flower is born to blush unseen.—*Gray*, "Elegy," st. 14.

2864. Ut sementem feceris, ita metes. Prov. ap. Cic. de Or. 2, 65, 261.—
As you have sown, so shall you reap. As you have made your
bed, so must you lie.

2865. Ut sylvæ foliis pronos mutantur in annos;
Prima cadunt; ita verborum vetus interit ætas,
Et juvenum ritu florent modo nata vigentque.
Debemur morti nos nostraque.   Hor. A. P. 60.

> As woodland leaves change with the changing year,
>   And those that opened first the first decay,
> So is 't with words: the old ones disappear,
>   And those coined later live and have their day.
> Both we and all that's ours must bow to death.—*Ed.*

2866. Uxorem, Postume, ducis?
Dic, qua Tisiphone, quibus exagitare colubris?   Juv. 6, 28.

> What! Posthumus, take a wife? What Fury, drest
> With snakes for hair, has your poor brain possest?—*Ed.*

2867. Uxorem quare locupletem ducere nolim,
Quæritis? uxori nubere nolo meæ.   Mart. 8, 12, 1.

> You ask why I don't marry a rich wife;
> I'd rather not be henpecked all my life.—*Ed.*

Lit., *I'd rather not be my wife's wife.* Cf. Anacr. 86: κεῖνος οὐκ ἔγημεν,
ἀλλ' ἐγήματο—*He did not marry, but was* (very much) *married.* The grey
mare the better horse.

V.

2868. Væ victis! Liv. 5, 48, 9.—*So much the worse for* (or *Woe to*) *the
conquered!*
Exclamation of Brennus, chief of the Senonian Gauls (390 B.C.), on
throwing his sword into the balance as a make-weight, when settling the
price of peace with Rome. It is copied by Saurin (Œuvres, 2 vols., Paris,
1783), Spartacus 3, 3, where Messala says to Spartacus: *La loi de l'univers,
c'est malheur aux vaincus!* ("Woe to the conquered is the law of the
world!").

2869. Valeant mendacia vatum. Ov. F. 6, 253.—*Away with the lies of
poets!*

2870. Vana contemnere. Liv. 9, 17, 9.—*Despising vain fears.* Said of
Alexander the Great, and quoted by the *Times* (Feb. 16, 1891)
of Gen. Sherman, as gifted with "that invaluable quality of

military insight which Livy ascribes to Alexander in the historic words, *Bene ausus vana contemnere.*"

2871. Vana sine viribus ira. Liv. 1, 10, 4.—*Anger, without force to back it, is mere vanity.*

2872. Vanitas vanitatum, et omnia vanitas. Vulg. Eccles. 1, 2.— *Vanity of vanities, all is vanity.*

2873. Vederti, udirti, e non amarti . . . umana
Cosa non è.
> Silv. Pellico, Francesca da Rimini, 1, 5.—*To see thee, hear thee, and not love thee, is not in mortal's power.* The misshapen Lanciotto, Francesca's husband, speaks thus of his brother and rival, Paolo.

2874. Vedi Napoli, e poi mori. Prov.—*See Naples and then die.* The Italian " wag " of to-day says that the prov. means, that you should see Naples first, " and then " Mori, a picturesque village between Riva and Roveredo, in N. Italy.

2875. Vehemens in utramque partem, Menedeme, es nimis,
Aut largitate nimia, aut parsimonia.
> Ter. Heaut. 3, 1, 31.—*You run into extremes both ways, Menedemus; either too lavish, or else too niggardly.*

> Cf. Hor. S. 1, 1, 103:
>> Non ego, avarum
>> Quum veto te fieri, vappam jubeo ac nebulonem.
>
>> *Est modus in rebus.*
>> In bidding you your miser's ways forsake,
>> I don't mean, Be a vaurien or a rake.—*Ed.*

2876. Vellem nescire literas! Suet. Ner. 10.—*I wish I had never learnt to (read or) write!* Exclamation of Nero on signing his first death-warrant.

2877. Velocius ac citius nos
Corrumpunt vitiorum exempla domestica, magnis
Quum subeunt animos auctoribus.   Juv. 14, 31.
>> A parent's bad example seen at home
>> Corrupts most quickly: such suggestions come
>> Under the sanction of authority.—*Ed.*

2878. Velocius quam asparagi coquantur. Suet. Aug. 87.—*Quicker than you can cook asparagus.* A phrase of Augustus Cæsar.

2879. Velut ægri somnia, vanæ
Fingentur species, ut nec pes, nec caput uni
Reddatur formæ.
> Hor. A. P. 7.—*Like sick men's dreams, when shadowy images appear, and neither head nor feet fit their respective forms.* Said of a badly composed work, without connection, and with a confusion of images.

2880. Venerabile impostura. Parini, L'Impostura, 1.—*Venerable imposture.* Fumag. No. 1367.

2881. Venia sit dicto. Plin. Ep. 5, 6.—*Pardon the expression* (or *remark*).

2882. Veni, Creator Spiritus,
Mentes tuorum visita, etc.
        Attrib. to Charlemagne, but found in earlier MSS., and probably composed by Gregory the Great (Addis & Arnold's Cath. Dictionary, *s.v.* "Hymns").—*Come, Creator Spirit, and visit thine elect souls, etc.* Sung on the Day of Pentecost.

It was this hymn that the sixteen Carmelite nuns of Compiègne sang on their knees at the foot of the guillotine at the Barrière du Trône (now Place de la Nation), July 17, 1794. The first to die was Marie Jeanne Meunier, a novice, who mounted the bloody stairs with a light step, and for the *Veni Creator* substituted the *Laudate* (Ps. cxvi.), which was immediately taken up by the rest of the community, as one by one they went to receive their crown. At last the prioress, Madeleine Lidoine, who had asked to be executed the last, was left singing alone, until her voice was also silenced by the fatal knife, and all was still. The only crime that Fouquier Tinville could charge them with was their "obstinate clinging to the ancient faith." *The Carmelites of Compiègne*, by Mme. de Courson, Lond., 1902, pp. 17-21; and J. G. Alger, *Glimpses of the F. Revolution*, Lond., 1894, p. 245 *seqq.*

2883. Venient annis sæcula seris,
Quibus Oceanus vincula rerum
Laxet, et ingens pateat tellus,
Tiphysque novos detegat orbes ;
Nec sit terris ultima Thule.   Sen. Med. 375.

> *Discovery of America Foretold.*
> The time will come in later years
> When Ocean shall unlock his bars,
> And a vast continent appear:
> Another Tiphys point the helm
> Towards a new-discovered realm ;
> Nor any longer Thule's isle
> Be the last spot of earthly soil.—*Ed.*

2884. Venit summa dies et ineluctabile tempus
Dardaniæ. Fuimus Troes ; fuit Ilium, et ingens
Gloria Teucrorum.   Virg. A. 2, 324.

> *The Fall of Troy.*
> 'Tis come, the inevitable hour,
> The supreme day of Dardan power;
> Our history's ended : Troy's no more,
> And all her mighty glory o'er.—*Ed.*

2885. Veni, vidi, vici. Suet. Cæs. 37 ; and ἦλθον, εἶδον, ἐνίκησα. Plut. Cæs. 50.—*I came, I saw, I conquered.* Inscription on the banners of the triumph of Caius Julius Cæsar, after his victory over Pharnaces, son of Mithridates, near Zela, in Pontus, Aug. 2, 47 B.C. *See also* Sen. Suasoriæ, 2, 22; and No. 89.

2886. Ventum ad supremum est. Virg. A. 12, 803.—*We have reached the end.* The last moment. A desperate crisis.

2887. Ventum seminabunt et turbinem metent. Vulg. Os. 8, 7.—*They shall sow the wind and they shall reap the whirlwind.* No. 2864.

2888. Verba dat omnis amor. Ov. R. A. 95.—*Love* (or *a Lover*) *always deceives.*

2889. Verba facit emortuo. Plaut. Pœn. 4, 2, 18.—*He is talking to a dead man.* Waste of breath.

2890. Verba nitent phaleris, at nullas verba medullas
Intus habent.
> Palingenius (Pier Angelo Manzolli), Zodiacus Vitæ, 6, 35.
—*The words make a fine show, but they have no pith in them.* Ornate, but feeble poetry. Fine phrases: empty compliments.

> Boil., in *L'Art Poétique* (Chant. 3, 139), has—
>> Tous ces pompeux amas d'expressions frivoles
>> Sont d'un déclamateur amoureux de paroles.
>> All that this pomp of empty phrase affords
>> Is the display of one who loves fine words.—*Ed.*

2891. Verbaque provisam rem non invita sequentur. Hor. A. P. 311. —*When you have well thought out your subject, words will come spontaneously.*

2892. Verbosa ac grandis epistola venit a Capreis. Juv. 10, 71.—*A lengthy and momentous letter has arrived from Capri,* viz., Tiberius' villa there. An important letter from the palace, from headquarters, etc. This was the famous despatch of Oct. 18, 31 A.D., conveying Sejanus' death-signal.

2893. Verbum non amplius addam. Hor. S. 1, 1, 121.—*I will not add another word.*

2894. Ver erat æternum, placidique tepentibus auris
Mulcebant Zephyri natos sine semine flores.   Ov. M. 1, 107.
> *The Golden Age.*
> 'Twas one long spring: winds from the south-west blown
> Gently caressed the flowers no hand had sown.—*Ed.*

2895. VERITAS.—*Truth.*

> (1.) Veritatem laborare nimio sæpe, ut aiunt, exstingui nunquam. Liv. 22, 39.—*As the saying is, Truth may be blamed, but never shamed.* It may often be attacked, but never killed. (2.) Simplex ratio veritatis. Cic. de Or. 1, 53, 229.—*Truth's methods are very simple.* (3.) Veritas temporis filia.—*Truth is the daughter of time.* Motto of Queen Mary I., taken from the saying of a forgotten Greek poet quoted by Gellius (12, 11, 7) as, "Veritatem temporis filiam esse dixit." (4.) Il n'est point de secrets que le temps ne révèle. Rac. Britann. 4, 4.—*There are no secrets that time brings not to light.* (5.) Aime la vérité, mais pardonne à l'erreur. Volt. Troisième Discours sur l'homme.—*Love truth, but pardon* (deal gently with) *error.* (6.) Veritatis cultores, fraudis inimici. Cic. Off. 1, 30, 109.—*Worshippers of truth, foes of falsehood.* Motto of the journal called *Truth.* (7.) In omni re vincit imitationem veritas. Cic. de Or. 3, 57, 215.—*In everything truth surpasses its counterfeit.*

2896. Vérité envers le monde, Humilité envers Dieu, Dignité envers
soi-même.—*Truth towards the world, Humility towards God,
Reverence towards oneself.* G. Sand's motto. (A. J. C. Hare's
Biog. Sketches, 1895.)

2897. Vernunft und Wissenschaft,
Des Menschen allerhöchste Kraft !
Goethe, Faust I., Studirzimmer (Mephist. loq.).—*Reason
and knowledge, the highest strength of man!*

2898. Versus inopes rerum nugæque canoræ. Hor. A. P. 322.—*Verses
devoid of thought, melodious trifles.*

2899. Vertere seria ludo. Hor. A. P. 226.—*To turn serious matters
into jest.*

2900. Vestibulum ante ipsum primisque in faucibus Orci
Luctus et ultrices posuere cubilia Curæ ;
Pallentesque habitant Morbi, tristisque Senectus,
Et Metus, et malesuada Fames, ac turpis Egestas,
Terribiles visu formæ ; Letumque, Labosque ;
Tum consanguineus Leti Sopor ; et mala mentis
Gaudia ; mortiferumque adverso in limine Bellum.
Virg. A. 6, 273.

The Gates of Hades.

At Orcus' portals hold their lair
Wild Sorrow and avenging Care ;
And pale Diseases cluster there,
And pleasureless Decay ;
Foul Penury, and Fears that kill
And Hunger, counsellor of ill,
A ghastly presence they :
Suffering and Death the threshold keep,
And with them Death's blood-brother Sleep :
Ill joys with their seducing spells
And deadly War are at the door.—*Conington.*

2901. Vetat enim dominans ille in nobis deus iniussu hinc nos suo
demigrare. Cic. Tusc. 1, 30, 74.—*The God that dwells within us
forbids us to depart hence without His leave.* Suicide. Plato
had already said as much (in Phædo, 62B), ἔν τινι φρουρᾷ ἐσμεν
ἄνθρωποι, καὶ οὐ δεῖ δὴ ἑαυτὸν ἐκ ταύτης λύειν οὐδ' ἀποδι-
δράσκειν—*We men are in a kind of prison, and no one has the
right to open the door and run away by himself.*

2902. Vetera extollimus, recentium incuriosi. Tac. A. 2, 88.—*We extol
old things, regardless of the productions of our own time.*

2903. Vetus autem illud Catonis admodum scitum est, qui mirari se
aiebat, quod non rideret haruspex, haruspicem quum vidisset.
Cic. Div. 2, 24, 51.—*That old remark of Cato's is very well
known, when he said he used to wonder how two augurs could look
one another in the face without laughing.*

2 A

2904. **Via media.**—*A middle way.* Any middle course between two extremes.

> The name is given, in particular, to the High Anglican doctrine of the Caroline divines, revived by the Tractarians (1833-43), and thought to be at once the *middle and true course* between pure Protestantism and "the errors of Rome."

2905. **Viamque insiste domandi,**
Dum faciles animi juvenum, dum mobilis ætas.   Virg. G. 3, 164.

> Pursue a course of training, while young hearts
> Can be impressed, and you can mould their parts.—*Ed.*

2906. **Vicisti Galilæe!** (Νενίκηκας Γαλιλαῖε.)   Theod., Hist. Eccl. 3, 20 (Migne, Series Græca, vol. 82, p. 943).—*Thou hast conquered, O Galilæan!* Dying words of Julian the Apostate, addressed to the Christ he had denied, June 26, 363 A.D.

> A tradition devoid of historical foundation. Ammianus Marcellinus, who was present, does not mention the incident (xxv. 3), nor does the sophist Libanius, another contemporary (Libanius, Orat. Parental. capp. 136-140). Theodoret (390-457) is the first to circulate the story fifty years later, alleging that Julian accompanied the apostrophe with the hideously dramatic action of casting drops of his blood to heaven as he spoke. The words have also been applied to the moral victory of Galileo Galilei over the orthodox prejudices of his age. *V.* Flammarion's *Popular Astronomy*, London, 1894, p. 423, and No. 2285.

2907. **Victoria Pyrrhica.**—*A Pyrrhic victory*, in which the conqueror comes off worse than the conquered.

> Pyrrhus, King of Epirus, in his Tarentine campaign against Rome (280 B.C.), defeated the enemy at Ascoli with such severe losses to his own side, that, according to Plutarch (*Pyrrhus*, cap. 21), he is reported to have said, Ἂν ἔτι μίαν μάχην Ρωμαίους νικήσωμεν, ἀπολούμεθα παντελῶς— *If we win one more battle like this against the Romans, we shall be utterly done for.* Such an equivocal success is also called Καδμείη νίκη (Hdt. 1, 166), or Cadmæa victoria, with allusion to the internecine strife of the Sparti, the armed men who sprang from the dragon's teeth sown by Cadmus. (*V.* Plato, Leges, 641C.)
> For the converse—defeats which amount to victories—see Marshal Duke de Villars' letter to Louis XIV. after the retreat of the French from Malplaquet, 1709.—"Si Dieu nous fait la grâce de perdre encore une bataille pareille, Votre Majesté peut compter que ses ennemis sont détruits"—*If God give us the grace to lose another battle of the same kind, your Majesty may count upon the entire destruction of your enemies.* (Roche et Chasles, Hist. de France, Paris, 1843, vol. 2, p. 320.)

2908. **Videant consules ne quid respublica detrimenti capiat.** Cæs. B. C. 1, 5, 3 (*or* Dent magistratus operam ne quid, etc.).—*Let the consuls* (or *magistrates*) *take care that the republic suffer no damage.* Well-known formula by which unlimited power was entrusted to the consuls, or dictator, in a time of national emergency.

2909. **Vilius argentum est auro, virtutibus aurum.**
O cives, cives, quærenda pecunia primum est,
Virtus post nummos.   Hor. Ep. 1, 1, 52.

Gold counts for more than silver, all men hold:
Why doubt that virtue counts for more than gold?
Seek money first, good friends, and virtue next.—*Conington.*

2910. Vincere scis, Hannibal; victoria uti nescis. Liv. 22, 51.—*You know how to win a victory, Hannibal, but you don't know how to profit by it.*

> Speech of Maharbal, General of Cavalry, after the battle of Cannæ (216 B.C.). If they pushed on at once, he himself leading the way with his horse, he engaged that in five days' time Hannibal should "banquet in the Capitol." The distance is over 200 miles, and would have taken ten days at least.

2911. Vindictam mandasse sat est: plus nominis horror,
   Quam tuus ensis, aget: minuit præsentia famam.
         Claud. B. Gild. 384.—*It is sufficient to have commanded punishment: the dread of your name will do more than the sharpness of your sword. Your presence would weaken your prestige. V.* Nos. 458, 1468.

2912. Violenta nemo imperia continuit diu:
   Moderata durant.   Sen. Troad. 259.

> No one has governed long by violence:
> The firm but gentle rule it is that lasts.—*Ed.*

2913. Vi ravviso, o luoghi ameni,
   In cui lieti, in cui sereni
   Si tranquillo i dì passai
   Della prima gioventù, etc.
         Felice Romani, in Bellini's opera of *La Sonnambula*, 1, 6. (Rodolfo loq.).—*I revisit ye, O pleasant scenes, where I spent in peace the happy and serene days of early youth!*

2914. Vir bonus est quis ?
   Qui consulta patrum, qui leges juraque servat.
                         Hor. Ep. 1, 16, 40.

> Whom call we good ? The man who keeps intact
> Each law, each right, each statute and each act.—*Conington.*

2915. Vires acquirit eundo. Virg. A. 4, 175.—*It gathers force as it progresses.* Said of Report, Rumour, or Scandal.

2916. Virginibus puerisque canto.   Hor. C. 3, 1, 4.—*I sing to boys and girls.* I write what may be put into the hands of young people. Harb., p. 303, cites a parallel in Ovid (T. 2, 370): Solet hic pueris virginibusque legi—*He (Menander) is the common reading for both boys and girls.*

2917. Virtus est medium vitiorum, et utrinque reductum.
                         Hor. Ep. 1, 18, 9.

> Between these faults 'tis virtue's place to stand
> At distance from the extreme on either hand.—*Conington.*

2918. Virtus est vitium fugere, et sapientia prima
    Stultitia caruisse.   Hor. Ep. 1, 1, 41.

> To fly from vice is virtue: to be free
> From foolishness is wisdom's first degree.—*Conington.*

2919. Virtus, repulsæ nescia sordidæ,
    Intaminatis fulget honoribus:
      Nec sumit aut ponit secures
        Arbitrio popularis auræ.   Hor. C. 3, 2, 17.

> True virtue never knows defeat:
>   Her robes she keeps unsullied still,
> Nor takes, nor quits, her curule seat
>   To please a people's veering will.—*Conington.*

2920. Virtute ambire oportet, non favitoribus.
    Sat habet favitorum semper, qui recte facit.
                          Plaut. Am. Prol. 78.
          The Actor.

> We seek your votes by merit, not by claqueurs:
> An honest actor's always sure of backers.—*Ed.*

2921. Virtute duce, comite fortuna.   Cic. Fam. 10, 3, 2.—*With virtue
for leader, and fortune for companion.*

2922. Virtutem doctrina paret, naturane donet?   Hor. Ep. 1, 18, 100.

> Is virtue raised by culture, or self-sown?—*Conington.*

A common problem amongst philosophers.

2923. Virtutem incolumen odimus,
    Sublatam ex oculis quærimus, invidi.   Hor. C. 3, 24, 31.

> Though living virtue we despise,
> We follow her when dead with envious eyes.—*Francis.*

2924. Virtutem videant, intabescantque relicta.   Pers. 3, 38.

> In all her charms set Virtue in their eye,
> And let them see their loss, despair, and die.—*Gifford.*

So Milton, Par. Lost, iv. 846:

>   Abash'd the devil stood,
> And felt how awful goodness is, and saw
> Virtue in her shape how lovely.

2924A. Virtute pares, necessitate, quæ ultimum ac maximum telum est,
    superiores estis. Liv. 4, 28.—*In valour you are equal; in
    desperation, the last and greatest arm of all, you are superior.*

Vectius Messius, the Volscian general, in the war with Rome, 428 B.C., addressing his troops before battle. From this passage is probably formed the saying, *Ingens telum necessitas* ("Necessity is a mighty weapon"). Bacon (*Colours of Good and Evil*, iv.) writes, "Necessity . . . hath many times an advantage, because it awaketh the powers of the mind and strengtheneth endeavour: *Cæteris pares, necessitate certe superiores estis.*"

2925. Virtutis enim laus omnis in actione consistit. Cic. Off. 1, 6, 19.—
The glory of virtue consists entirely in action.

2925A. Virtutis veræ custos rigidusque satelles. Hor. Ep. 1, 1, 17.—
Dame Virtue's henchman and most trusty guard. Said of himself, when, after the battle of Philippi and at the lowest ebb of
his fortunes, he obtained employment in the civil department
of the State.

2926. Virtutum viva imago. Sen. Tranq. 15, 5.—*A living embodiment
of the virtues.* Said of Cato Uticensis.

2927. Vis comica.—*Comic powers.* Talent for comedy.

> A phrase formed, by a misposition of commas, out of lines of Caius
> Julius Cæsar (Suet., *Terentii Vita*) on the writings of Terence. He says:
>
> Lenibus atque utinam scriptis adjuncta foret vis,
> Comica ut æquato virtus polleret honore
> Cum Græcis.—*I wish that his* (Terence's) *smoothly-flowing lines
> had such force, as to make his comic talents take equal rank with the Greek
> dramatists.* Cæsar is far from denying Terence a *comica virtus*, but only
> considers it as falling short of his Greek models.

2928. Vis recte vivere? Quis non?
Si virtus hoc una potest dare ; fortis omissis
Hoc age deliciis. Virtutem verba putas, et
Lucum ligna. Hor. Ep. 1, 6, 29.

> You wish to live aright (and who does not?)
> If virtue holds the secret, don't defer;
> Be off with pleasure, and be on with her.
> But no: you think all morals sophist's tricks,
> Bring virtue down to words, a grove to sticks.—*Conington.*

2929. Vitæ est avidus, quisquis non vult
Mundo secum pereunte mori. Sen. Thyest. 882.

> Too greedy he of life, who still would live
> When all the world around is perishing.—*Ed.*

2930. Vitæ post-scenia. Lucret. 4, 1182.—*The back scenes* (or, Behind
the scenes) *of life.*

2931. Vitam quæ faciunt beatiorem,
Jucundissime Martialis, hæc sunt:
Res non parta labore, sed relicta:
Non ingratus ager: focus perennis:
Lis nunquam: toga rara: mens quieta:
Vires ingenuæ: salubre corpus:
Prudens simplicitas: pares amici:
Convictus facilis: sine arte mensæ:
Nox non ebria, sed soluta curis. Mart. 10, 47, 1.

The Elements of Happiness.
The things that make life happiest,
Martial my own, in these consist.
An income left (not earned by toil),
A cheerful hearth, a grateful soil;
No law, and work all but resigned,
And perfect quietness of mind:
A frame that natural health attends,
With frugal tastes, congenial friends,
A wholesome diet, artless fare,
Nights free from revelry, or care.—*Ed.*

2932. Vitanda est improba Siren
    Desidia: aut, quicquid vita meliore parasti,
    Ponendum æquo animo.   Hor. S. 2, 3, 14.

    Then stop your ears to sloth's enchanting voice,
    Or give up your best hopes: there lies your choice.—*Conington.*

2933. Vita sine proposito vaga est. Sen. Ep. 95, 46.—*A life without an aim is a sadly desultory one.*

2934. Vitiosum est ubique, quod nimium est. Sen. Tranq. 9, 6.—*Excess (redundancy) in everything is a fault.*

2935. Vivamus, mea Lesbia, atque amemus;
    Rumoresque senum severiorum
    Omnes unius æstimemus assis.
    Soles occidere et redire possunt;
    Nobis, quum semel occidit brevis lux,
    Nox est perpetua una dormienda.   Cat. 5, 1.

To Lesbia.
Live we and love we, Lesbia dear;
And not a penny-piece we'll care
Though scolding elders prate amain.
Suns may set and rise again,
But we, when vanished this brief light,
Must sleep in one unending night.—*Ed.*

2936. Vive la Nation! L'Abbé Sieyès.—*Long live the Nation!* Declared by Sieyès to have been first uttered by himself, and to have much astonished those who heard him.

    Other important historical particulars seem to have been communicated to the few *intimes* who were admitted to the impenetrable seclusion of the Abbé's last years. Thus, it would appear that the designation of "Assemblée Nationale" (June 1789) originated with himself; and that it was the confiscation, in lieu of redemption, of the ecclesiastical tithe of Aug. 11, 1789, which drew from him the caustic rejoinder: "Ils veulent être libres, et ils ne savent pas être justes!" (*They would be free, and yet cannot be just.*) On the other hand, Sieyès disowned the saying commonly attributed to him (after the 18th Brumaire) respecting Bonaparte: "Nous avons un maître; il peut tout, il sait tout, et il veut tout." (*We have a master; he can do everything, he knows everything, and he wills everything.*) Mignet (F.), *Notice hist. sur M. de Sieyès* (Institut de France, Pièces diverses, vol. for 1836): Sainte Beuve, *Causeries du Lundi*, vol. v. pp. 214-5; Hugou, *Mémoires de la Révolution*, iv. pp. 192-207. *V.* No. 1159.

2937. Vivendum recte est, quum propter plurima, tum his
Præcipue causis, ut linguas mancipiorum
Contemnas, nam lingua mali pars pessima servi.   Juv. 9, 118.

> Keep right for many reasons; specially
> For this—that servants' tongues you may defy.
> The tongue of a bad servant's his worst part.—*Ed.*

2938. Vivent les gueux!—*Long live the beggars!*

> Cry dating from the Spanish Netherlands in Nov. 1565, when a number
> of malcontent nobles, under Count Louis of Nassau and Henry de Brede-
> rode, banded themselves together to resist the introduction of the Inquisition
> under Philip II.   On approaching the Regent, Margaret of Parma, with a
> petition to this effect, they were tauntingly alluded to by one of her
> courtiers as *Les gueux*, which they adopted forthwith as the title of their
> association.   The struggle, thus inaugurated, ended some eighty years after
> in the independence of the Dutch Republic.   The words are repeated now
> without any political allusion.

2939. Vivere est cogitare. Cic. Tusc. 5, 38, 111.—*The essence of life is
thinking.*   To live is to think.

> Joubert says (somewhere), Vivre, c'est penser et sentir son âme—*Living
> means thinking, and being conscious of one's soul.*   *V.* No. 618.

2940. Vivere, Lucili, militare est.   Sen. Ep. 96, 3.—*To live, Lucilius,
is to fight.*

> Cf. Volt. Mahomet, 2, 4, Ma vie est un combat—(Mahomet loq.) *My
> life is a warfare* (words adopted by Beaumarchais for his motto); Vulg.
> Iob. 7, 1, Militia est vita hominis super terram—*Man's life on earth is
> a warfare*; and Goethe, Westöstlich. Divan (1819),

> Dieser ist ein Mensch gewesen,
> Und das heisst ein Kämpfer sein.

> Here lies one who was a man,
> And that means to be a fighter.

2941. Vivere si recte nescis, decede peritis.   Hor. Ep. 2, 2, 213.

> If live you cannot as befits a man,
> Make room, at least, you may for those who can.—*Conington.*

2942. Vive sine invidia, mollesque inglorius annos
Exige, amicitias et tibi junge pares.   Ov. T. 3, 4, 43.

> Live without envy, tranquil and obscure:
> Choose friends from equals, only such endure.—*Ed.*

2943. Vive, valeque.   Hor. S. 2, 5, 110.—*Adieu, good-bye.*   Good-bye,
God bless you!

2944. Vivite felices, quibus est fortuna peracta
Jam sua.   Nos alia ex aliis in fata vocamur.   Virg. A. 3, 493.

> Live and be blest! 'tis sweet to feel
> Fate's book is closed and under seal.
> For us, alas! that volume stern
> Has many another page to turn.—*Conington.*

2945. Vivitur exiguo melius: natura beatis
Omnibus esse dedit, si quis cognoverit uti.   Claud. Ruf. 1, 215.

> Small means are best: nature puts happiness
> In each man's way, could he the secret guess.—*Ed.*

2946. Vivitur parvo bene, cui paternum
Splendet in mensa tenui salinum,
Nec leves somnos timor, aut cupido
Sordidus, aufert.   Hor. C. 2, 16, 13.

> More happy he, whose modest board
>   His father's well-worn silver brightens:
> No fear, no lust for sordid hoard,
>   His light sleep frightens.—*Conington.*

2947. Vivo et regno, simul ista reliqui
Quæ vos ad cœlum effertis rumore secundo.   Hor. Ep. 1, 10, 8.

> *Country* v. *Town.*

> I breathe, and am a king, when once I'm free
> From things you rave about in ecstasy.—*Ed.*

2948. Vix a te videor posse tenere manus.   Ov. Am. 1, 4, 10.—*I can
scarcely keep my hands off you!* as Sydney Smith said to the
lady in red velvet, whose gown reminded him so vividly of his
pulpit cushion.

2949. Vix duo tresve mihi de tot superestis amici;
Cætera Fortunæ, non mea, turba fuit.   Ov. T. 1, 5, 33.

> Two or three friends are all that now remain;
> The rest were never mine, but Fortune's train.—*Ed.*

2950. Vix equidem credo, sed et insultare jacenti
Te mihi, nec verbis parcere, fama refert.   Ov. Ep. 4, 3, 27.

> I scarce can credit it, yet fame affirms
> You flout my downfall in unmeasured terms.—*Ed.*

2951. Vixere fortes ante Agamemnona
Multi: sed omnes illacrymabiles
Urgentur ignotique longa
Nocte, carent quia vate sacro.   Hor. C. 4, 9, 25.

> Before Atrides men were brave,
>   But ah! oblivion, dark and long,
> Has locked them in a tearless grave,
>   For lack of consecrating song.—*Conington.*

Cf. Ov. Ep. 4, 8, 47:

> Carmine fit vivax virtus: expersque sepulcri
> Notitiam seræ posteritatis habet.

> Song makes great deeds immortal, cheats the tomb,
> And hands down fame to ages yet to come.—*Ed.*

2952. Vocalis Nymphe, quæ nec reticere loquenti,
Nec prior ipsa loqui didicit, resonabilis Echo. Ov. M. 3, 357.

Echo.

Responsive Echo! vocal Nymph, that ne'er
Can learn to hold her tongue when others speak,
And yet will never first the silence break.—*Ed.*

2953. Vogue la galère!—*Come what may!* (Lit. *Let the galley sail!*)

In Rabelais (i. 3) the saying appears as "Vogue la galée," so that it must
be as old as the 16th century; and Des Marets and Rathery, in their
edition of Gargantua (1857, vol. 1, p. 19n.), cite an old rondeau, beginning,

Y avoit trois filles, toutes trois d'un grand,
Disoient l'une à l'autre; Je n'ay point d'amant.
Et hé! hé!
Vogue la galée!
Donnez-luy du vent!

2954. Voilà bien du bruit pour une omelette! Volt. Lettre à Thieriot,
Dec. 24, 1758.—*What a row all about an omelette!*

Voltaire is alluding here to the story told of Des Barreaux at some inn,
where, though it happened to be a day of abstinence, he had ordered an
omelette *au lard.* Just as he was about to sit down to meat, a sudden
thunderclap shook the house from top to bottom, upon which the poet hastily
seized the forbidden food, and threw it out of window with the above
exclamation. During the year (1758) the *De l'esprit* of Claude A. Helvétius,
the encyclopædist, had made its appearance and created much sensation.
In it Helvétius had followed the doctrines of Locke, with the result that
the book was condemned by the Sorbonne, and ordered by the Parliament
of Paris to be publicly burnt. What a fuss about nothing! is Voltaire's
feeling on the subject. Quel fracas pour le livre de M. Helvétius! *Voilà
bien du bruit pour une omelette!* Quelle pitié! etc.

2955. Voluptarium venenum. Sen. Ep. 95, 25.—*A voluptuous poison.*
Said of mushrooms.

2956. Voluptates commendat rarior usus. Juv. 11, 208.—*Pleasure com-
mends itself by sparing use.*

2957. Vom sichern Port lässt sichs gemächlich rathen. Schiller,
W. Tell, 1, 1 (Ruodi).—"*Safe in the port, 'tis easy to advise*"
—Sir T. Martin.

2958. Vor dem Tod erschrickst du? Du wünchest unsterblich zu leben?
Leb' im Ganzen! Wenn du lange dahin bist, es bleibt.
Schiller, Unsterblichkeit.

Art thou afraid of death? Would'st thou be really immortal?
Live in the whole! when thou hast passed away, it remains.—*Ed.*

Cf. the reply of Frederick the Great to his guards, on their complaining
of what they thought exposure to unnecessary danger: "Wollt ihr immer
leben?" (*Would you live for ever?*")

2959. Vos exemplaria Græca
Nocturna versate manu, versate diurna. Hor. A. P. 268.

My friends, make Greece your model when you write,
And turn her volumes over day and night.—*Conington.*

2960. Vos sapere et solos aio bene vivere, quorum
Conspicitur nitidis fundata pecunia villis.   Hor. Ep. 1, 15, 45.

Why Pay Rent?

You only are the wise and lucky fellows,
Who see your money in your tidy villas!—*Ed.*

Here's an advertisement for suburban building societies!

2961. Vos valete et plaudite. Ter. Heaut. 5, 5, 23.—*Adieu, and give us
your applause.* The usual *finale* of the Latin comedy, and the
traditional last words of Augustus; but see No. 2581.

2962. Vous aurez toujours des voisins. Quit. p. 666.—*You will always
have neighbours.*

Remark of a peasant to Louis XIV. while watching the work of enlarging
the park at Versailles. The king asked the man his thoughts: "Je pense,
sire, que vous avez beau agrandir votre parc, *vous aurez toujours des voisins.*"
(*I think, Sire, that, extend your park as you please, you'll always have some
neighbours.*) J. B. Rousseau (Bk. 3, Ode 7) puts the incident into verse:

Pardonnez; je songeais que de votre héritage
Vous avez beau vouloir élargir les confins:
Quand vous l'agrandiriez trente fois davantage,
Vous aurez toujours des voisins.

While you enlarge the bounds of your estate,
I thought how vain was all this labour;
For, should you make it thirty times as great,
You'll always have some neighbour.—*Ed.*

But the story is as old as Apuleius (Met. 9, p. 235, 11), where one of the
three brothers whom the rich tyrant put to death in order to seize their
land, says with his last breath: "Scias, licet privato suis possessionibus
paupere, fines usque et usque proterminaveris, habiturum te tamen vicinum
aliquem."—*What though you rob the poor of his land in order to keep extending your boundaries, know that you will always have some neighbour.*

2963. Vous avez fait trois fautes d'orthographe. V. Hugo, Marion de
Lorme, 5, 2.—*You have made three mistakes in the spelling.*

In the play, Saverny, after examining his own death-warrant, which he
has to initial, observes certain misspellings in the writing, which he
proceeds to correct before handing back the document to the clerk of the
court. The incident and remark are borrowed from a similar episode in
the life of Favras.

Sav. Le récit de ma mort signé de ma paraphe!

(*Signs, and re-examines the paper.*)

Monsieur, vous avez fait trois fautes d'orthographe.

2964. Vous êtes Empereur, seigneur, et vous pleurez? Rac. Bérénice
(1740), 4, 5 (Bérénice to Titus).—*You are Emperor, sire, and
you weep?*

In these words a reminiscent allusion has been detected to the affecting
farewell (1659) between the young Louis XIV. and his beloved Maria Mancini,
Mazarin's niece, whom the Cardinal with genuine disinterest temporarily
"exiled" to Brouage, in order to leave no obstacle in the way of a pacifica-
tion with Spain, which should include a match with the Infanta Maria

Theresa. At the sight of her royal lover's tears, Mdlle. de Mancini exclaimed, *Vous pleurez et vous êtes le maître!* ("You weeping, and you the
master!") Mme. de Motteville, in Collection Petitot, 2e Série, vol. 40,
p. 11. Fourn. *L.D.L.*, pp. 269-274.

2965. Vous êtes orfèvre, Monsieur Josse! Molière, L'Amour Médecin,
1, 1 (Sganarelle loq.).—*You are a jeweller, Mr Josse!*

   Josse advises Sganarelle to buy a *parure* of diamonds and rubies as a cure
for his daughter's melancholy. Hence the latter's reply, which has ever
since passed into a proverbial rejoinder, where any one has an obvious
interest in the advice offered.

2966. Vous l'avez voulu, vous l'avez voulu, George Dandin, vous l'avez
voulu! Mol., G. Dandin, 1, 9.—*You wished it, you wished it,
George Dandin, you wished it!* It is all your own doing, you
have brought it on yourself.

2967. Vous me forcez, seigneur . . . d'être plus grand que vous. P. L.
de Belloy, Siége de Calais, 5, 2.—*You force me, my lord, to be
greater than you.* Eustache de Saint Pierre, the Mayor of
Calais, to Edward III. at the famous siege of 1347.

2968. Vous parlez devant un homme à qui tout Naples est connu.
Mol. L'Av. 5, 5 (Anselme loq.).—*You are speaking in the presence
of one to whom all Naples is well known.* Said of those who
undertake to instruct a man who is a complete master of the
subject.

2969. Vous vous écartez de la question.—*You are wandering from the
point.*

   A saying that belongs to the French Revolution period. In Feb. (22)
1787, Calonne, the then Minister of Finance, obtained a convocation of the
"Notables," before whom he laid various measures of retrenchment and
reform, including an equal distribution of the taxes. The noblesse, who
were more accustomed to tax than to be taxed, scouted the proposition, and
the minister fell; but not before the situation had been sketched in one of
the wittiest political caricatures ever put on paper. The original is among
the "dessins inédits" of the Bibliothèque Nationale, but has been reproduced more than once, and may be seen in Georges Veyrat's *La Caricature
à travers les Siècles*, Paris, 1895, pp. 35-6. In the drawing, Calonne is
represented as a "monkey-cook," standing at the buffet of the *Cour Royale*,
and asking a troop of barn-door fowls that he had assembled before him,
the pertinent question, "A quelle sauce elles veulent être mangées"
(*What sauce they wished to be eaten with*)? A turkey, speaking for the
others, indignantly rejoins, "Mais nous ne voulons être mangés!" (*But we
don't wish to be eaten*) to which the monkey replies, "Vous sortez de la
question" (*You wander from the point*). *V.* Carlyle, Hist. of the F.
Revolution, vol. 1, Bk. iii., chap. iii. The idea was borrowed and repeated
in Philipon's *La Caricature*, No. 165, Jan. 2, 1833.

2969A. Vox clamantis in deserto. Vulg. Es. 40, 3.—*The voice of one
crying in the wilderness.*

2970. Vox cycnea. Cic. de Or. 3, 2, 6.—*The swan-song.* Last utterance,
speech, or composition of orator or poet.

   Referring to the last speech of L. Licinius Crassus in the Senate
against the democratic policy of the Consul Philip (Sept. 13, 95 B.C.),

Cicero (*in l.*) describes it as "that perfect swan-song, in voice and words" (*illa tanquam cycnea vox et oratio*); going on to say how its echoes were still sounding in their ears, and how, after his death, men would even come down to the House only to view the place where he had then stood. *V.* id. Tusc. 1, 30, 73; and

> Dulcia defecta modulatur carmina lingua,
> Cantator cycnus funeris ipse sui.   Mart. 13, 77.

> Chanting sweet melodies with failing breath,
> The swan is his own chorister at death.—*Ed.*

In Gk., Æsch. (Agam. 1444) makes Clytemnæstra say of Cassandra, that

> κύκνου δίκην
> Τὸν ὕστατον μέλψασα θανάσιμον γόον.

> Swan-like, she chanted her last dying plaint.

See the passage in Plato (Phædo, 85 B), saying that the swans, as sacred to Apollo, at their death "sing the joys of the life to come" (τὰ ἐν "Αιδου ἀγαθὰ ᾄδουσι); the τὸ κύκνειον ᾄσας ἀποθανεῖν of Chrysippus, ap. Athenæum, 616 B; and Lucian, Timon, cap. 47, ᾄσαντά με κ.τ.λ.

2971. Vox populi, vox Dei.   Alcuin (see below).—*The voice of the people is the voice of God.*

Büchmann (pp. 324-5) instances a passage in Alcuin's *Capitulare admonitionis ad Carolum*, § ix. (Baluzio, Miscell., vol. 1, p. 376, Paris, 1678), where it is said, "Nec audiendi qui solent dicere, *Vox populi, vox Dei*, quum tumultuositas vulgi semper insaniæ proxima sit"—*They are not to be listened to who say, "Voice of people, voice of God," since popular uproar is always akin to insanity.*   The saying is, therefore, earlier than the eighth century.   William Malmesbury (De gestis pontificum Anglor., lib. 1, 14) quotes it with reference to the election of Archbishop Odo, 992 A.D., as "illud proverbium, *Vox populi*," etc.   A similar sentiment occurs in Hesiod (Op. 761):

> φήμη δ'οὔτις πάμπαν ἀπόλλυται, ἥν τινα πολλοὶ
> λαοὶ φημίξουσι· θεὸς νύ τις ἐστὶ καὶ αὐτή.—*The saying that's voiced by many people never wholly dies, since it is itself divine.*

2972. Vox tantum atque ossa supersunt.
Vox manet.   Ov. M. 3, 398.

> *Echo Pining for Narcissus.*

> Her voice, and eke her bones are all that's left.
> Her voice, I say, remains.—*Ed.*

2973. Vulgare amici nomen, sed rara est fides.   Phædr. 3, 9, 1.—*Nothing is more common than the name of friend, nothing more rare than fidelity* (true friendship).   La Fontaine (4, 17, "Parole de Socrate") renders it,—

> Rien n'est plus commun que ce nom,
> Rien n'est plus rare que la chose.

> *Friends.*

> There's nought so common as the name,
> And nothing rarer than the thing.—*Ed.*

2974. Vulgus ex veritate pauca, ex opinione multa æstimat.   Cic. Rosc. Com. 10. 29.—*The common people judge of most things by report, few things by the real facts.*   Cf. Illa vox vulgaris, Audivi. Cic. Planc. 23, 57.—*That common saying, "I heard so and so."*

W.

2975. Wage du zu irren und zu träumen:
Hoher Sinn liegt oft in kind'schem Spiel.
Schiller, Thekla, fin.—*Dare to err and to dream; a deep meaning often lies in childish play.*

2976. Wär' der Gedank' nicht so verwünscht gescheidt,
Man wär' versucht, ihn herzlich dumm zu nennen.
Schiller, Piccolom, 2, 7.—*Were not the thought so cursedly sensible, one were tempted to call it thoroughly stupid.*

2977. Warte nur, balde
Ruhest du auch!   Goethe, Über allen Gipfeln.

> Only wait! soon, soon
> Thou too shalt rest!

2978. Was du ererbt von deinen Vätern hast,
Erwirb' es, um es zu besitzen.   Goethe, Faust, Nacht.

> *Faust.* What from thy fathers thou inheritedst
> Earn for thyself, to make it truly thine.—*Ed.*

2979. Was frag' ich viel nach Geld und Gut,
Wenn ich zufrieden bin?   Joh. M. Miller, Zufriedenheit.

> What care I much for gold and goods,
> So I contented be?—*Ed.*

2980. Was Gott thut, das ist wohlgethan. Sam. Rodigast.—*What God does, is done well.* First line of hymn. Büchm. p. 136.

2981. Was Hänschen nicht lernt, lernt Hans nimmer. Prov.—*What young John does not learn, old John never will.*

2982. Was ist der langen Rede kurzer Sinn? Schiller, Picc. 1, 2.—*What's the short meaning of this long harangue?* Questenberg to Butler.

2983. Was ist der Mensch? Halb Tier, halb Engel. Joachim L. Evers, Vierhundert Lieder, 1797, No. 369.—*What is man? Half beast, half angel.* Büchm. p. 139.

2984. Was Jeder thun soll, thut Keiner. Prov.—*What is every one's business is no one's business.*

2985. Wasser thuts freilich nicht. M. Luther, Kleiner Katechismus (1529), Art. IV. (on Baptism).—*Water, of course, cannot do it.*

> The question of the catechist is, "How can water do such great things?" (Forgiveness of sins, etc.). (*A.*) "Water, of course, cannot do it, but the Word of God, which is in and with the water," etc. Like many passages with us in the Book of Common Prayer, the words have become proverbial in Germany, and are capable of more than one application.

2986. Was uns Alle bändigt, das Gemeine. Goethe, Epiloge zu Schillers
Glocke (1806), str. 4.—*That which enslaves us all, vulgarity.*

> Und hinter ihm in wesenlosem Scheine,
> Lag, was uns Alle bändigt, das Gemeine.
> In shadowy outline far behind him lay,
> That which enslaves us all—vulgarity.—*Ed.*

Tribute on Schiller's death.   The beautifully-proud assumption of
inferiority implied in the "uns Alle"—as though Goethe were but one
of the *profanum vulgus*—will not be lost on the reader.

2987. Was vom Herzen kommt, das geht zum Herzen.   Prov.—*What
comes straight from the heart, goes straight to the heart.*

2988. Was von mir, ein Esel spricht,
Das acht' ich nicht.
   Gleim, Fabeln (Berlin, 1756), p. 9, Fab. 4 ("Der Löwe u.
der Fuchs").—*What an ass may say of me, that I do not heed.*

2989. Welch Glück geliebt zu werden:
Und lieben, Götter, welch ein Glück!
   Goethe, Wilkom. und Abschied.—*What happiness is it to
be loved! and to love—ye gods, what bliss!*

2990. Wem Gott will rechte Gunst erweisen,
Den schickt er in die weite Welt.
   J. Freiherr v. Eichendorff, Der frohe Wandersmann.

> Whom God would a true service render,
> He sends in the wide world to wander.—*Ed.*

2991. Wenn der Leib in Staub zerfallen,
Lebt der grosse Name noch.   Schiller, Siegesfest, 9th st.

> Though the body turn to dust,
> Still the glorious name lives on.—*Ed.*

2992. Wenn dich die Lästerzunge sticht,
So lass dir dies zum Troste sagen:
Die schlechtsten Früchte sind es nicht,
Woran die Wespen nagen.
   G. A. Bürger, Trost. (Götting. Musenalmanach, 1787, p. 7).

> *Calumny.*
> If calumny wound thee, to solace thee, say,
> 'Tis not always the worst fruit on which the wasps prey.—*Ed.*

2993. Wenn die Rose selbst sich schmückt,
Schmückt sie auch den Garten.
   Friedr. Rückert, Gedichte, Buch. vi., Reihe 1: "Welt und Ich."

> When the rose herself adorns,
> She adorns the garden too.—*Ed.*

2994. Wenn mancher Mann wüsste,
Was mancher Mann wär',
Tät' Mancher Mann manchem Mann
Manchmal mehr Ehr'.
   V. Grieshaber's *Alt deutsche Predigten*, 2, 8.

If many a man knew
What many men were,
Then many to many
Would show more honour.—*Ed.*

Cf. Büchmann's *Geflügelte Worte*, 12th ed., p. 54.

2995. Wenn Menschen auseinandergehn,
So sagen sie—auf Wiedersehn!
Ja Wiederseh'n!

Ed. von Feuchtersleben, Nach altdeutscher Weise,
fin. — *When men part from one another, they say, " Let's meet
again, yes, once again!"*

2996. Wer andern eine Grube gräbt, fällt selbst hinein. Prov.— *Who
digs a pit for others, falls into it himself.* Cf. Vulg. Prov. 26,
27, Qui fodit foveam, incidet in eam.

2997. Wer den Dichter will verstehen,
Muss in Dichters Lande gehen.

Goethe, Motto of " Noten etc. zu besserem Verständniss des
W.-O. Divans."

Who the poet would understand,
Must explore the poet's land.—*Ed.*

2998. Wer einmal lügt, dem glaubt man nicht,
Selbst dann, wenn er die Wahrheit spricht.

See von Nicolay's "Lügner."

Who once has lied, will none believe,
Though he speak truly, nor deceive.—*Ed.*

2999. Wer nicht liebt Wein, Weib und Gesang,
Der bleibt ein Narr sein Leben lang;
Sagt Doktor Martin Luther.   Joh. H. Voss.

Who loves not woman, wine, and song,
Remains a fool his whole life long;
Saith doctor Martin Luther.—*Ed.*

According to Büchm. (pp. 125-7)—whom see for further history of the
lines—they first appeared in the *Wandsbecker Bothen* of 1775 (No. 75),
under the title of "Devise an einen Poeten," and were inserted two years
later in Voss's Musenalmanach (Hamburg), p. 107, with the heading of
"Gesundheit" and the signature of "Dr M. Luther."

3000. Wer nichts thut, irrt nicht; und wer nicht irrt, bessert sich nicht.
Paul Winkler, "Guten Gedanken Drei Tausend," Görlitz, 1685.
—*Who does nothing, makes no mistakes; and who makes no mis-
takes, never makes any progress.*

Es giebt Menschen die gar nicht irren, weil sie sich nichts Vernünftiges
vorsetzen. Goethe, Reflexionen u. Maximen, Sect. iii.—*Some men make
no mistakes, for the simple reason that they never set about anything in
earnest.* (2.) Chi non fa, non falla. Prov.—*He who does nothing, makes no
mistakes.* It may also mean, "When in doubt, don't act." (3.) Oh dame!
écoutez donc! les gens qui ne veulent rien faire de rien n'avancent rien, et
sont bons à rien. Beaum. Mariage de Figaro, 2, 2 (Figaro to Suzanne).—
*Listen to me, then! Those who venture nothing gain nothing, and are good
for nothing. See* No. 1026.

3001. Wer niemals einen Rausch gehabt,
      Der ist ein schlechter Mann.
                    Joachim Perinet, Das Neu-Sonntags Kind.

> Who never had a good carouse,
> Can't be an honest man.

*** A Vaudeville of 1793, with music by Wenzel Müller. The second
line is generally quoted as "Der ist kein braver Mann."

3002. Wer nie sein Brod mit Thränen ass,
      Wer nie die kummervollen Nächte
      Auf seinem Bette weinend sass,
      Der kennt Euch nicht, Ihr himmlischen Mächte.
            Goethe, Wilh. Meister's Lehrjahren, 2, 13 (The Harper's
      Song).

> Who never ate with tears his bread,
>   Nor, through the sorrow-laden hours
> Of night, sat weeping on his bed,
>   He knows ye not, ye heavenly powers!—*Ed.*

Speaking of these lines in his *Reflexionen und Maximen*, Goethe remarks, "Books have their experiences, which cannot be taken from
them"; and mentions that the book containing them came into the hands
of the beautiful and heroic Louise of Prussia, Queen of Frederick
William III., and were of comfort to her during the dark hours of her
country's downfall and Napoleon's temporary ascendency.

3003. Wer seinen Kindern giebt das Brot,
      Und leidet nachmals selber Not,
      Den soll man schlagen mit der Keule tot.
                    Rüdiger v. Hünchhover (1290), Der Schlägel.

> Who gives his children all his bread,
> And comes himself to grievous need,
> Shall with the club be smitten dead.—*Ed.*

Büchm. (whom see, p. 119, for the fable connected with these lines) says
that they are to be found affixed to many town-gates in N. Germany, side
by side with a massive club for emblem.

3004. Wer über gewisse Dinge den Verstand nicht verliert, der hat
      keinen zu verlieren. Lessing, Emilia Galotti, 4, 7.—*He who does
      not lose his reason on certain subjects, has none to lose.* Cf. No. 2414.

3005. Wie die Alten sungen, so zwitschern auch die Jungen.   Prov.—
      As the elders sing, so will the young ones twitter. Like father,
      like son.

3006. Wie gewonnen, so zerronnen.   Prov.—*As it is gained, so is it
      spent.*   Light come, light go.

3007. Willst du die Andern versteh'n, blick' in dein eigenes Herz.
      Schiller, Votivtafeln.—*Look into your own heart, if you would
      understand others.*

3008. Willst du immer weiter schweifen?
Sieh', das Gute liegt so nah!
Lerne nur das Glück ergreifen:
Denn das Glück ist immer da.　　Goethe, Erinnerung.

> Why keep always wand'ring farther,
> With such blessings lying near?
> Seize the lucky moment, rather;
> For the chance is always here.—*Ed.*

3009. Wo alles liebt, kann Carl allein nicht hassen.　Schiller,
D. Carlos, 1, 1.—*Where all men love* (sc. the young queen,
Isabelle of Valois), *Charles can't alone feel hate.*

3010. Wo der liebe Gott eine Kirche baut, da baut der Teufel eine
Kapelle.　Prov.—*Where God builds a church, there the devil
builds a chapel.*

> Wherever God erects a house of prayer,
> The devil always builds a chapel there;
> And 'twill be found, upon examination,
> The latter has the largest congregation.
> —Defoe, *True-born Englishman*, Pt. I., 1. 1.

3011. Wo man singet, lass dich ruhig nieder,
Ohne Furcht, was man im Lande glaubt;
Wo man singet, wird kein Mensch beraubt;
Bösewichter haben keine Lieder.

　　　　　　Joh. G. Seume, Die Gesänge, 1. 1.

> Wherever men sing you can well settle down,
> Without heed to what creed they belong:
> Where there's singing, you'll never be robbed of your own,
> For bad men have never a song.—*Ed.*

Generally quoted as—

> Wo man sing't, da lass dich ruhig nieder,
> Böse Menschen haben keine Lieder.

3012. Wo viel Licht ist, ist starker Schatten.　Goethe, Götz von
Berlichingen, Act 1.—*Fuller the light, the shadows stronger fall.*

Z.

3013. Ζηλωτὸς ὅστις εὐτύχησεν ἐς τέκνα.　Eur. Or. 542.—*He is to be
envied who has prospered with his children.*

3014. Ζώη μοῦ, σᾶς ἀγαπῶ.—Byron's Maid of Athens. "It means,"
adds the author in a note, " '*My life, I love you!*' which sounds
very prettily in all languages, and is as much in fashion in
Greece at this day as, Juvenal tells us, the two first words were
among the Roman ladies, whose erotic expressions were all
Hellenized."

2 B

3015. Ζῶμεν γὰρ οὐχ ὡς θέλομεν, ἀλλ' ὡς δυνάμεθα. Menand., Andria, 13.
(Meineke, p. 877).—*We live not as we would but as we can.*

> Cæcilius Statius (Ribb. vol. 2, p. 75) reproduces the saying in his *Plocium*,
> frag. xi., Vivas ut possis, quando nec quis ut velis—*Live as you can, since
> you can't live as you would:* and Terence in Andria (4, 5, 10), Ut quimus,
> aiunt; quando ut volumus non licet—*As they say, one must do as one
> can, when one can't do as one would.*

3016. Zu viel kann man wohl trinken,
    Doch trinkt man nie genug.
        Lessing, Lieder, 1, 6.—*One can easily drink too much, but*
enough (the exact quantity) *never.*

3017. Zwar weiss ich viel, doch möcht' ich Alles weissen.   Goethe,
    Faust, Pt. I., Night (Wagner to Faust).—*True, I know much,*
yet I would all things know.

3018. Zwischen Sinnenglück und Seelenfrieden
    Bleibt dem Menschen nur die bange Wahl;
Auf der Stirn des hohen Uraniden
    Leuchtet ihr vermählter Strahl.
          Schiller, Das Ideal u. das Leben, st. 1.

> With man, the choice,
> Timid and anxious, hesitates between
> The senses' pleasure and the soul's content;
> While on celestial brows, aloft, serene,
> The beams of both are blent.—*Bulwer Lytton.*

ADESPOTA.*

3019. Absente auxilio perquirimus undique frustra,
Sed nobis ingens indicis auxilium est.

Use of an Index.
Without a key we search and search in vain,
But a good index is a monstrous gain.—*Ed.*

3020. Ah quam dulce est meminisse! *Ah! how pleasant it is to re-member! V.* Nos. 514, 815, 868, 891.

3021. Ars est celare artem.—*The perfection of art lies in its concealment. V.* No. 2809.

Ovid has, Si latet ars prodest (A. A. 2, 313)—*If the art is hidden, it succeeds;* and (M. 10, 252), Ars adeo latet arte sua—*So artfully is the sculptor's art concealed:* said of Pygmalion's "living" statue of Galatea.

3022. Audax ad omnia fœmina, quæ vel amat vel odit.—*A woman will dare anything, when she loves or hates. V.* No. 190.

3023. Bonis nocet quisquis pepercerit malis.—*Who spares the guilty, harms the good. V.* Nos. 714, 1939.

3024. Breve gaudium.—*A short-lived joy.*

Such are most earthly pleasures: even of Messrs Tupman and Snodgrass' escapade with the runaway horse, it is said that "the heat was a short one." *Pickwick,* chap. v.

3025. Cela doit être beau, car je n'y comprends rien.—*That ought to be fine, for I don't understand a word of it. V.* Nos. 333, 1175.

Said of any obscure, involved statement, designed to impress the public with the extreme cleverness and erudition of the speaker or writer. Quint. (8, 2, 18) mentions some teacher in philosophy of Livy's time, who trained his pupils to purposely "darken" their language with a view to this effect. "Unde illa scilicet egregia laudatio; *Tanto melior: ne ego quidem intellexi"*—hence that truly remarkable compliment—*Bravo! excellent! Why, I didn't even understand you myself!*

3026. Ce n'est pas être bien aisé que de rire. St Evremond (?)—*Laughter is not a sign of being at one's ease. V.* Nos. 844, 2416.

---

* For the following unverified quotations, which the compiler has failed to trace to their legitimate authors, see the paragraph on the subject in the Preface.

3027. Ce qui est moins que moi m'éteint et m'assomme; ce qui est à côté de moi m'ennuie et me fatigue; il n'y a ce qui est au dessus de moi qui me soutienne, et m'arrache à moi-même.— *What is beneath me crushes and wearies me to death; what is on a level with me bores me and fatigues; it is only what is above me that can support and lift me out of myself.*

3028. Ce qu'on fait maintenant, on le dit; et la cause en est bien excusable : on fait si peu de chose.—*If anything is done nowadays, you are sure to hear of it, and it's only natural: so little is done at all.*

3029. C'est l'imagination qui gouverne le genre humain.—*Men are governed by their imagination.* Attrib. to Napoleon.

3030. C'est plus qu'un crime, c'est une faute.—*It is worse than a crime; it is a blunder.*

> Supposed to have been spoken of the assassination of the Duke d'Enghien by Bonaparte in the ditch at Vincennes, March 20th, 1804. The *mot* is so good that it has been claimed by, or at least ascribed to, many—to Talleyrand, to Fouché, to Boulay; but whether ever said, and on what occasion, remains unknown. Sainte Beuve, in his *M. de Talleyrand* (1869), observes in connection with the subject that, "Ces mots historiques voyagent jusqu' à ce qu'ils aient trouvé, pour les endosser, le nom auquel il conviennent le mieux," and the remark applies to various other vagrant and unaffiliated *dictons* of the sort. Considered merely as a "saying," it is excellent, and might be applied in a hundred ways, from the execution of Charles I., of which indeed the words might be very appropriately spoken, down to the last *faux pas* perpetrated in a London drawing-room. (*See* Fourn. *L.D.L.*, pp. 439-40; and Alex. pp. 120-1.)

3031. Corruptio optimi pessima.—*The corruption of the best becomes the worst.* Qu. in Feltham's *Resolves*, art. "Of Women" (1628).

> For sweetest things turn sourest by their deeds;
> Lilies that fester, smell far worse than weeds.—Shakesp. *Sonn.* 94.

> Probably derived from Arist. (Nic. Ethics, 8, 10, 1-2), where, speaking of various forms of government, he says that a Tyranny, being a παρέκβασις (*perversion*) or φθορά (*corruption*) of the best form, *i.e.*, the monarchical, must necessarily be the worst of all (κάκιστον δὲ τὸ ἐναντίον τῷ βελτίστῳ— *that which is contrary to the best is the worst*). Aquinas, borrowing directly from Aristotle, says, Præterea, sicut regnum est optimum regimen, ita tyrannis est *pessima corruptio regiminis.* Summa Theol., Prima Sec., Quæst. cv. art. 1, 5 (Migne, vol. 2, p. 859).—*Since a monarchy is the best form of government, so a tyranny is the worst corruption of government.*

3032. Coutume, opinion, reines de notre sort,
Vous réglez des mortels et la vie, et la mort.—*Custom, opinion, arbiters of our fate, ye rule both the lives and deaths of mankind.* V. No. 357.

3033. Croyez-moi, l'erreur aussi a son mérite.—*Believe me, error has also its merits.*

3034. Dans l'amour, il y a toujours un qui baise, et l'autre qui tend la joue.—*In love, there is always one who kisses, and another who offers the cheek* (to be kissed).

3035. Dans l'art d'intéresser consiste l'art d'écrire.—*The art of writing consists in the art of interesting the reader.* *V.* Nos. 1776, 1901.

3036. Defuncti ne injuria afficiantur.—*The dead should not be evil spoken of.* *V.* No. 462.

3037. Déjà!—*What, already!*

> Rejoinder supposed to have been made at the bedside of the Abbé Terray (1778), Finance Minister of Louis XV., on the sick man complaining that he was suffering "the torments of the damned." Lebrun turns the incident into an epigram (*Réponse de Bouvard à un Prélat*), which concludes with—
>
> Mort Dieu! Bouvard, dit le prélat, je souffre
> Comme un damné—*Quoi, déjà, monseigneur?*
>
> "'Sdeath!" muttered the prelate; "I suffer, Bouvard,
> The pains of the damned." "What, *already,* my lord?"
>
> It is also related of others, and in particular of Louis Philippe at the deathbed of Talleyrand (1838). *See* Fourn. *L.D.L.*, pp. 442-3.

3038. De l'absolu pouvoir vous ignorez l'ivresse,
Et du lâche flatteur la voix enchantresse.

> Of power you know not the intoxication,
> Nor the flattering magic of base adulation.—*Ed.*

3039. De male quæsitis vix gaudet tertius hæres,
Nec habet eventus sordida præda bonos.

> *Light come, light go.*
> Goods, ill got, seldom to a third heir descend,
> Nor shameful gains come to a prosp'rous end.—*Ed.*
>
> A mediæval epigram, probably prompted by the seizure of church property. Cf. Nos. 1476 and 3138.

3040. De omnibus rebus, et quibusdam aliis.—*About everything in the world, and some other matters beside.* A voluminous treatise. *See* No. 855. Sometimes qu. as *De omni re scibili* ("on every knowable subject").

> Giovanni Pico, Count of Mirandola (1463-1494), the wonder of his time and the last of the Schoolmen, published at Rome, when only *ætatis suæ* 23, nine hundred theses on every imaginable topic (drawn from Latin, Greek, Hebrew, and Arabic writers), and challenged all the scholars of Europe to dispute the propositions. The eleventh of the theses bore the title of *Ad omnis scibilis investigationem et intellectionem* ("On the examination and understanding of all that may be known").

3041. De par le roy, défense à Dieu
De faire des miracles en ce lieu.

> 'Tis forbidden to God, by his Majesty's grace,
> To work any miracles in this place.—*Ed.*
>
> The death, in 1727, of François de Paris, Jansenist deacon, was for some time afterwards followed by such extraordinary scenes at his tomb on account of the "miracles" said to have been performed there,—"pilgrims" from Flanders and Germany vying with the "Convulsionaries" of the place in their hideous Corybantine ecstasies,—that the king in 1732 closed the churchyard as the best means of stopping the scandal. Some one, soon after, penned and affixed to the cemetery gates of St Médard, where his grave lay, the above quotation.

3042. Era un papagallo istrutto:
Lo sapea mal, ma sapea un po' di tutto.

> A well-trained parrot, he could talk and sing:
> He knew it wrong, but he knew everything.—*Ed.*

This seems to be borrowed from the mock-heroic *Margites*, generally printed with the Homeric *fragmenta* at the end of the Odyssey—*see* Bothe's (F. H.) *Homeri Carmina*, Lipsiæ, 1835 (Odyssey, vol. 2, p. 369). In the passage in question, the principal character is some vapouring fellow, of whom it is said that πόλλ' ἠπίστατο ἔργα, κακῶς δ' ἠπίστατο πάντα—*Many arts he knew, and he knew them all ill.*

3043. Es lag ihm nichts an der brutalen letzten Consequenz seiner Ansichten.—*He never cared for the last brutal consequences of his views.* Said of Bismarck.

3044. Fais ce que dois, advienne que pourra.—*Do your duty, come what may. V. No. 770.*

3045. Festinare nocet, nocet et cunctatio sæpe;
Tempore quæque suo qui facit, ille sapit.

> Hurry is bad, and oft as bad, delay;
> Each thing at its own time is wisdom's way.—*Ed.*

*** *V.* Nos. 439, 456, 793, 2735.

3046. Finis coronat opus.—*The end crowns the work. V.* No. 373.

3047. Fit scelus indulgens per nubila sæcula virtus.—*In danger's hour* (a national crisis) *leniency is crime.*

> It was sufficient to bring Louis XVI. to the scaffold. In a time of great emergency a weak and irresolute government, not certain of the popular mind, and (what is much more) not knowing its own, may place the lives and fortunes of citizens in extreme peril. No policy is so cruel as that which lives by temporising and concession. A fine and far-reaching line and sentiment: but who wrote it? *V.* Nos. 362, 366, 714, 1939.

3048. Græcum est, non potest legi.—*It is Greek, it cannot be read.*

> The origin of the Boar's head served every Christmas at Queen's College, Oxon., is traced to a remote period, when a scholar of the College, encountering a wild boar in Bagley Wood, thrust the volume of Aristotle which he was reading into the savage brute's jaws, crying out, "Græcum est non potest intelligi!" and so both choked his assailant and saved his own life.

3049. GRAM loquitur; DIA verba docet; RHET verba colorat;
MUS canit; AR numerat; GEO ponderat; AST colit astra.

> *Grammar teaches correct speech; Logic, the proper use of words, and Rhetoric ornaments them; Music sings, Arithmetic reckons; Geometry measures; Astronomy deals with the heavens.*

A *Memoria Technica* of mediæval origin, giving, in the first line, the *Trivium* of the ordinary student, and, in the second, the *Quadrivium* (for the more advanced) of the remaining four of the seven Liberal Arts.

> Cf. the seven points of knightly education, contained in the following:
> Probitates hæ sunt: equitare, natare, sagittare,
> Cestibus certare, aucupare, scacis ludere, versificare.—*The honourable arts are these: to ride, swim, shoot, box, hawk, play at chess, and write verses.*

3050. Heureux les peuples dont l'histoire est ennuyeux.—*Happy are the people whose history is tedious.*

3051. Hic liber est in quo quærit sua dogmata quisque ;
Invenit et pariter dogmata quisque sua.

The Bible.

Here all men seek the doctrines to their minds;
And each one here his special doctrine finds.—*Ed.*

3052. Hinc venti dociles resono se carcere solvunt,
Et cantum accepta pro libertate rependunt.

On an Organ.

Forth from the sounding-board the winds go free
And with a tune repay their liberty.—*Ed.*

3053. Il fut historien, pour rester orateur.—*He turned historian in order to remain orator.*

Supposed to have been said of Livy in reference to the political speeches which, as he could not deliver them himself, he put into the mouths of personages of Roman history. Unable to get a seat in Parliament, Mr Anthony Trollope uttered his political sentiments in his novels (see his Autobiography and *Phineas Finn*).

3054. Il n'appartient qu'à ceux qui n'espèrent jamais être cités, de ne citer personne.—*It is the business of those only who never hope to have their own writings quoted, to refuse to quote others.* Cf. No. 2823.

3055. Il paraît qu'on n'apprend pas à mourir en tuant les autres.—*It does not appear that killing other people teaches one how to die.*

3056. Il y en a peu qui gagnent à être approfondis.—*Few men rise in our estimation on a closer examination.*

3057. Inter Græcos Græcissimus, inter Latinos Latinissimus.—*In Greek he is the most thorough Grecian, and in Latin the most perfect Roman.* Said of a consummate classical scholar.

3058. Jasper fert myrrhum, thus Melchior. Balthazar aurum.
Hæc quicum secum portet tria nomina regum,
Solvitur a morbo, Domini pietate, caduco.

The Three Kings of Cologne.

Jasper brings myrrh, and Melchior incense brings,
And gold Balthazar to the King of Kings:
Whoso the names of these three monarchs bears
Is safe, through grace, of Epilepsy's fears.—*Ed.*

Mediæval Latin verse. The names of the three Magi borne by anyone, or worn as an amulet, were anciently believed to act as a preservative against the falling sickness.

3059. Je ne suis pas la rose mais j'ai vécu près d'elle.—*I am not the rose, but I have lived near her.*

In one of his songs the Persian poet, Sadi, represents a lump of clay accounting for the perfume still clinging to it, by the fact of its having lain among some fallen petals at a rose-tree's foot.

3060. L'art, c'est être absolument soi-même.—*Art consists in the faithful reflection of the artist's personality.*

3061. La ville est le séjour de profanes humains, les dieux habitent la campagne.—*Town is the dwelling-place of profane mortals, the gods inhabit rural retreats.* Cf. No. 574.

3062. Le bonheur de l'homme en cette vie ne consiste pas à être sans passions, il consiste à en être le maître.—*The happiness of man in this world does not consist in being devoid of passions, but in being able to master them.* Cf. Nos. 490, 2323, 2539.

3063. Le conseil manque à l'âme,
Et le guide au chemin.

> The soul is 'reft of counsel,
> And the path without a guide.—*Ed.*

Cf. No. 62.

3064. Le courage est souvent un effet de la peur.—*Courage is often the effect of fear.* Cf. Nos. 180, 1597.

3065. Le divorce est le sacrement de l'adultère.—*Divorce is the sacrament of adultery.*

3066. Legatus est vir bonus peregré missus ad mentiendum reipublicæ causa.—*An ambassador is an honest man sent to lie abroad for the good of his country.* Said to have been written by Sir H. Wotton in the album of his friend Fleckamore at Augsburg, while on his way to Venice in 1606.

3067. Le général qui n'a jamais fait de fautes, a peu fait la guerre.—*The general who has never made a mistake, has seen little of war.* Attrib. to Napoleon. Cf. Nos. 226, 3000, 3096.

3068. Le monde est le livre des femmes.—*The world is the book of women.*

3069. L'ennui du beau, amène le goût du singulier.—*A surfeit of the beautiful leads to a taste for singularity.* Cf. Nos. 1333, 1334.

3070. Le présent est gros de l'avenir. Leibnitz (?)—*The present moment is big with the events of the future.* Applicable to any time threatening a disruption of the peace of Europe, or to the eve of any political crisis.

3071. Les amis, ces parents que l'on se fait soi-même.—*Friends, those relations that one makes for one's self.* Delille, *Pitié*, has—

> Le sort fait les parents, le choix fait les amis.

> 'Tis Fate gives us kindred, and choice gives us friends.—*Ed.*

Cf. the Greek Νόμιζ' ἀδελφοὺς τοὺς ἀληθινοὺς φίλους.—*Count your true friends as so many brothers.* Cf. No. 1372.

3071a. Les Angloys s'amusent moult tristement.—*The English take their pleasures sadly.*

No apology is offered for this fine old crusted saying, or for the sham Norman-French in which it is worded. In any list of ownerless quotations it well deserves a place. It is traditionally ascribed to Froissart, and Froissart, when consulted, disclaims the parentage. It is to be hoped that some day the real author may be discovered: meanwhile, a suggested solution of the conundrum will be found in No. 121.

3072. Les femmes peuvent tout, parcequ'elles gouvernent les personnes qui gouvernent tout.—*Women can effect everything, because they govern those who govern everything.* "The hand that rocks the cradle rules the world."

Cf. Plutarch, Vita Catonis Maj., c. 8 (4): "We Romans govern the world, but we are governed by our wives;" and *Notes and Queries* (Oct. 29, 1898).

3073. Les grandes passions sont rares, comme les chefs-d'œuvre.—*Great passions* (affections) *are as rare as masterpieces in art.*

3074. Les temps ne sont pas difficiles: ils sont impossibles.—*The times are not difficult, they are impossible.*

The saying is ascribed to Montlosier, and, if really due to his initiation, may possibly belong to the accession of Charles X. and the reactionary (clerical) policy which followed. Cf. No. 1479.

3075. Le style c'est l'homme.—*The style shows the man.*

Celebrated aphorism, supposed to have been enunciated by Buffon in his no less celebrated *Discours de Réception* on admission to the French Academy, August 25, 1753. It is one of those numerous cases where one has to record not what the speaker said, so much as what he ought to have said, and the precise form of the phrase is still undetermined. The quotation merely represents the tradition of the vulgar, rejected by the critics in favour either of *Le style est de l'homme même*, of the *Nouvelle Biographie Générale* (Didot), *s.v.* "Buffon"; or of *Le style est l'homme même* of Richard's edition of Buffon (Paris, 1842), vol. i. p. 10. The unfortunate circumstance militating against the authenticity of the famous axiom in any shape, is its absence in the official report of the *Discours* in the *Recueil des Harangues prononcées par MM. de l'Académie Fr.* (1764, vol. 6, p. 176, second ed.). The passage in question, with the interpolated words in italic, is as follows:—

"Ces choses (les connoissances, les faits et les découvertes) sont hors de l'homme, [*le style est l'homme même*] le style ne peut donc ni s'enlever, ni se transporter, ni s'altérer: s'il est élevé, noble, sublime, l'auteur sera également admiré dans tous les temps."

Mr Roger Alexandre (*Musée de la Conversation*, p. 497) appears to vouch for an existing impression (*plaquette*) of Buffon's "Address," printed in the same year (1753), in which the saying is given in the form *Le style est l'homme même;* but for this solitary witness to the contrary—which I have been unable to verify—I should have concluded that the phrase was never said at all, and with reason: (1) from its absence in the official publication above mentioned; (2) from its absence in the *Correspondance* of (J. M. von) Grimm, who, writing within a week of the event (Sept. 1, 1753), reports the salient points of the "Discourse" almost *verbatim*, and yet nowhere makes an allusion to the celebrated *mot.* Besides, it is hardly imaginable that Buffon, with the extraordinary care that he habitually bestowed upon his published works in the way of accuracy, polish, and effect—his *Époques de la Nature* was copied and re-copied eleven times before being handed to the printer—would have allowed the official report of his famous "Discourse" to have appeared in print *minus* the great saying which made its fortune, had he ever said it. Larousse, in his *Dictionnaire Universelle* (*s.v.* STYLE), accounts for the quotation as a necessary "deduction" from the passage in question, and I wholly agree with him. The sentence, as usually quoted, was never said at all.

3076. Les voleurs vous crient,
      La bourse ou la vie!
   Les médecins vous prennent
      La bourse et la vie.

> The highwayman cries,
> Your purse or your lives!
> The doctor, far worse,
> Takes your life *and* your purse.—*Ed.*

3077. L'imagination est la folle du logis.—*The imagination is the madwoman of the house.* The unreasoning part of our mental equipment.

> Voltaire considered the saying so good that he entered it in his *Dictionnaire Philosophique* under the Art. APPARITION, and named the author: "*Défions-nous des écarts de l'imagination que Malebranche appelait la folle du logis;*" but no one has found it in Malebranche yet. Montaigne and Montesquieu have been equally ransacked for the *mot*, and with as little résult. St Theresa, in her *Château de l'âme* (IVᵉ Demeure, cap. I.), dwells on "la différence qu'il y a entre l'entendement et l'imagination": but, although the saying is also attributed to her, it has not been discovered in her writings.

3078. L'imagination galope, le jugement ne va que le pas.—*The imagination gallops, the judgment merely walks.* The former is impatient for the issue, which the latter patiently awaits.

3079. Man darf nur sterben um gelobt zu werden.   Prov.—*Man has only to die to be praised.*   Cf. No. 2844.

3080. M. l'ambassadeur, j'ai toujours été le maître chez moi, quelquefois chez les autres; ne m'en faites pas souvenir. Louis XIV. to Lord Stair.—*Mr Ambassador, I have always been master in my own affairs, and sometimes in those of other people. I beg your Lordship not to remind me of these things.*

> Rejoinder, supposed to have been provoked by the reflection made by the second Earl Stair (ambassador at the French court) upon the Mardyck Canal works, then (1714) proceeding, as an infraction of existing treaties between the two countries.

3081. Morbus signa cibus blasphemia dogma fuere
      Causæ cur Dominum turba secuta fuit.   St Albert?

> Sickness, food, miracles, blasphemy, the word,
> Are reasons five why crowds pursued our Lord.—*Ed.*

3082. Nemo impetrare potest a Papa bullam nunquam moriendi.—*There is no dispensation to be obtained from the Pope against death.*   Cf. No. 1934.   Ascribed to Thomas à Kempis.

3083. Non aliena putes homini quæ obtingere possunt:
Sors hodierna mihi, cras erit illa tibi.

> To mortals' common fate thy mind resign;
> My lot to-day, to-morrow may be thine.

Ascribed, both Latin and English, to Lady Jane Grey. Cf. Nos. 925
and 926.

3084. Nur die Konflikte nicht zu tragisch nehmen.—*Don't see a tragedy
in every conflict.* Attributed to Bismarck.

3085. Omne Epigramma sit instar apis, sit aculeus illi,
Sint sua mella, sit et corporis exigui.

> Bees and epigrams should, if they are not to fail,
> Have honey, small frames, and a sting in the tail.—*Ed.*

This "Epigram on the Epigram," as it is usually called, is currently
ascribed to Martial by those who have not taken the trouble to verify it in
Martial's works. It is rendered by the author of "Alice in Wonderland":

> Three things must epigrams, like bees, possess:
> Their sting, their honey, and their littleness.—*C. L. Dodgson.*

3086. On est mère, ou on ne l'est pas.—*Either one is a mother, or one is
not.* It must be either one thing, or the other. Cf. No. 988.

3087. Où vas-tu, petit nain?—Je vais faire la guerre.
Et à qui, petit nain?—Aux maîtres de la terre.
Que veux-tu leur ôter?—L'impure vanité.
Quelles armes as-tu?—La pure vérité.
Le monde te haïra!—Contre lui je secoue
Sa terre, son néant, sa poussière et sa boue.

The Author to his Book.

> Where away, little imp? I am off to the fight,
> And with whom, little imp? With the world's men of might.
> What would you take from them? Their foul vanity?
> What arms do you carry? The pure verity.
> The world will detest you! In its face I will flirt
> Its earthiness, emptiness, dustiness, dirt!—*Ed.*

3088. Parum erraturus et pauca facturus.—*As little likely to make a
mistake as to make anything else* (give any real assistance).

Said to have been Sir Gregory Casalis' opinion of Pope Paul III. (as given
in a letter to Henry VIII.) on the prospects of his furthering the King's
business in the divorce. *See* No. 3000.

3089. Perimus licitis.—*We perish by lawful* (but not expedient) *indul-
gences.* Cf. Nos. 1253, 1642, 2344.

3090. Plus je vois les hommes, plus j'admire les chiens.—*The more I see
of men, the more I admire dogs.* Charlet, the painter, says
somewhere, "Ce qu'il y a de meilleur dans l'homme, c'est le
chien."—*The best point in man's character is the dog.*

3091. Plus on approche des grands hommes, plus on trouve qu'ils sont
hommes. Rarement ils sont grands vis-à-vis de leurs valets-de-

chambre.—*The nearer one approaches to great persons, the more
one sees that they are but men. Rarely are they great in the eyes
of their valets.* Heine says, somewhere, " No author is a man of
genius to his publisher." *See* No. 1021.

3092. Poeta nascitur, non fit.—*A man is born a poet, not made one.*
Another form is: Nascimur poetæ, fimus oratores.—*We are born
poets, we are made orators.*

3093. Pour tromper un rival l'artifice est permis:
On peut tout employer contre ses ennemis.

> To outwit a rival use all artifice:
> All means are permitted against enemies.—*Ed.*

Ascribed to Richelieu's comedy of the *Thuileries* by Fournier (*L.D.A.*,
p. 263), but the lines still remain unverified. Cf. No. 579.

3094. Pro patria est, dum ludere videmur.—*We seem to play, but 'tis
for the country's good.*

3095. Quand on ne trouve pas son repos en soi-même, il est inutile de
le chercher ailleurs.—*When we do not possess the source of repose
in ourselves, it is in vain to look for it elsewhere.* Cf. No. 1531.

3096. Quand un homme se vante de n'avoir point fait de fautes à la
guerre, il me persuade qu'il ne l'a pas faite longtemps.—*When a
man boasts of never having made mistakes in war, he convinces
me that his military experiences are of the briefest.* St Evremond
attributes the saying to Turenne. *See* Nos. 3000, 3067.

3097. Quanta dignitas, tantula libertas.—*The greater the official dignity,
the less the personal freedom.* Cf. No. 1960.

3098. Quanto é bella giovinezza,
Che si fugge tuttavia!
Chi vuol esser lieto. sia,
Di doman non c'é certezza.

> How beautiful a thing is youth,
> Ever fleeting, ever flying!
> Be gay! who would be gay; for, sooth,
> On the morn there's no relying.—*Ed.*

*** Cf. Nos. 161, 486, 600, 794, 1521, 1969.

3099. Quid levius pluma? Flumen. Quid flumine? Ventus.
Quid vento? Mulier. Quid muliere? Nihil.

> *La donna é mobile.*

> Than down what's lighter?—Water. Lighter still?
> Air. Than air?—Woman. Than a woman?—Nil.—*Ed.*

*** Cf. Nos. 1232, 1583, 2758.

3099A. Quod non fecerunt barbari, fecerunt Barberini.—*The Barberini
have done even worse than the Barbarians.* Pasquinade on
Urban VIII.'s (Barberini) conversion into cannon (1635) of the
bronze fittings of the Pantheon, which had descended intact
from 27 B.C.

3100. Relata refero.—*I tell the tale as told to me.*

3101. Sans les femmes le commencement de notre vie serait privé de secours, le milieu de plaisirs, et la fin de consolation.—*Without woman, the beginning of life would be destitute of succour, the middle of pleasure, and the end of consolation.* Cf. No. 627.

3102. Si vis amari, ama.—*Love, if you would be loved.*

3103. Soyons doux, si nous voulons être regrettés. La hauteur du génie et les qualités supérieures ne sont pleurées que des anges. —*Be gentle, if you wish to be regretted. Genius and talent have none but the angels to lament their loss.* See No. 270.

3104. Spes bona dat vires, animum quoque spes bona firmat: Vivere spe vidi qui moriturus erat.

Hope.

> Good hope both strength and confidence will give:
> I've known through hope the dying to revive.—*Ed.*

See Nos. 45, 1289.

3104A. Stat crux dum volvitur orbis.—*The cross stands while the earth revolves.* Has this any allusion to the Southern Cross?

3105. Summæ opes, inopia cupiditatum.—*Absence of desire is the greatest riches.* Cf. Nos. 299, 1146.

> In 299 (*q.v.*) Hector, the valet, reads to his master "from Seneca" a passage which much resembles the quot., although the nearest parallel to be found in Seneca himself is the sentence qu. in No. 1146. On the other hand, the words may be a transl. of the saying of Socrates (ap. Stob. Florileg., 17, 31), Ἐρωτηθεὶς πῶς ἂν γένοιτό τις πλούσιος; Εἰ τῶν ἐπιθυμιῶν, ἔφη, εἴη πένης.—*Asked, How a man could become rich? By being poor, said he, in his desires.*

3106. Sunt pueri pueri; pueri puerilia tractant.—*Boys are boys, and boys do boyish things.*

> An equivalent, and perhaps translation, of our own common saying, "Boys will be boys."

3107. Tres medicus facies habet: unam, quando rogatur, Angelicam: mox est, quum juvat ille, Deus.
Post ubi curato poscit sua munera morbo,
Horridus apparet terribilisque Satan.

Doctor and Patient.

> Three shapes a doctor wears. At first we hail
> The angel; then the god, if he prevail.
> Last, when, the cure complete, he asks his fee,
> A hideous demon he appears to be.—*Ed.*

3108. Turpe mori post te solo non posse dolore.—*'Tis shameful not to die of grief alone, now thou art gone.* Clarendon (Hist. of the Rebellion, Bk. VII., Oxford, 1703, vol. ii. p. 270) quotes the line on the lamented death of Falkland in his thirty-fourth year, killed at Newbury fight, Sept. 20, 1643.

3109. Ubi bene, nemo melius; ubi male, nemo pejus.—*Where he is good, no man better; where he is bad, no man worse.* Said (?) of Origen's style.

3110. Ubi lapsus? quid feci?—*Show me my fault! What have I done?* The plea of injured innocence. No. 1332.

In any category of the world's "masterless" *mots*, this quot. deserves to take a front seat, and not without reason. In the first place, it forms the motto of one of the oldest—if not actually the oldest—surviving houses of England's ancient noblesse, in the days before such institutions as Parliamentary "peerages" had swamped the old *gentilhommerie* of feudal times. It is, in short, the device of the Earls of Devon, adopted by the existing (Powderham) branch, on the loss of the Earldom of Devonshire by the attainder and execution of Edward Courtenay, 2nd Earl of Devon in 1539, under that saintliest of English sovereigns, Henry the Eighth. Reference, moreover, is made to the quotation by Gibbon, of whom it has been said that to be mentioned by the historian of the *Decline and Fall of the Roman Empire*, is equivalent to having one's name written on St Peter's dome. In his sixty-first chapter, Gibbon has a note on the Courtenays, which traces their illustrious and princely fortunes from the age of the Crusades to their domicile in France, and thence to their final settlement in this country. The extinction of the elder branch of the family, and the revival of the ancestral dignities in a younger line, is also included in the historian's remarks, who adds, *àpropos* of the quotation, that "the Courtenays still retain the plaintive motto, which asserts the innocence, and deplores the fall, of their ancient house."

Finally, the words have had the honour of being made the subject of a personal application by Cardinal Newman in his *Apologia*. After the publication of the famous "Tract 90" (1841), the author retired to Littlemore, whither he was pursued both by the press, and by the emissaries of a prying Protestantism in *propria persona*. The impertinence of the persecution was intolerable: even a wounded brute should be allowed to creep into his hole and die. "I asked" (he adds), "I asked in the words of a great motto, *Ubi lapsus? quid feci?*" (*Apologia*, etc., 1864, p. 289). Gibbon speaks of the passage as "adopted" by the Courtenays, as if it might belong to some classic original, although its authorship has never yet been discovered. In form, the words might be a portion of a hexameter verse; or might possibly occur in some ancient Latin *fabula*. Who will explain the riddle?

3111. Un livre est un ami qui ne trompe jamais.—*A book is a friend that never plays you false.* V. Nos. 874, 1185, 2177.

According to Jardère (*Ex-libris Ana*, Paris, 1895, pp. 70-2), the line was chosen by Réné Chas. Guilbert (Pixérécourt) as motto for his book-plate. Macaulay says (Essay on *Bacon*). "With the dead there is no rivalry. In the dead there is no change. Plato is never sullen. Cervantes is never petulant. Demosthenes never comes unseasonably. Dante never stays too long," etc.

Jean Grolier (1479-1565), bibliophile and statesman under three of the Valois princes, is not more famous for the artistic bindings of his library than for the *Io. Grolierii et amicorum* (the property of J. Grolier and his friends) which, with real altruism, he had stamped on the covers of each of his volumes. On the other hand, those who want an excuse for not letting a volume go out of the house will find it in the couplet that Theodore Leclercq had inscribed over his shelves:

Tel est le sort facheux de tout livre prêté :
Souvent il est perdu, toujours il est gâté.

*—Such is the miserable lot of every book one lends, it is often lost, and always
damaged. "V.* Fumagalli, Nos. 15-18."

3112. Un seul endroit y mène, et de ce seul endroit
Droite et raide est la côte, et le sentier étroit.

(? Chapelin, or Chapelain).

The Pyramids.

There's but one way there, and that one way hath
A stiff, steep ascent, and a narrow path.—*Ed.*

3113. Veuve d'un peuple-roi, mais reine encore du monde.   (?) Gilbert.

Rome.

An Empire's widow, queen still of the world.—*Ed.*

3114. Vingt siècles descendus dans l'éternelle nuit
Y sont sans mouvement, sans lumière et sans bruit.

The Pyramids.

Twice times ten centuries sunk in endless night
Lie there unmoved, silent, and without light.—*Ed.*

The passage is borrowed from Pierre le Moyne's (1602-71) Saint Lovys,
bk. 5, p. 145 (Paris, 1658, 12°), "Ces siècles . . . en cette obscure nuit,
Y sont sans mouvement, sans lumière, et sans bruit." *V.* No. 2594.

3115. Vivit post funera virtus.—*Virtue survives death.   V.* No. 152.

Motto of the Earls of Shannon (Boyle). In *Notes and Queries* (vol. vi.
79 and 245, and vol. x. 362), Mr R. Pierpoint refers us to Mathias Borbonius,
Dictum Tiberii—one of a series of mottoes for various emperors—where the
words are given in reverse order :

Excole virtutem ; virtus post funera vivit,
Solaque post mortem nos superesse facit.

Cultivate virtue ; after death she lives,
And by his virtues only man survives.

John Owen (*more suo*) perverts the saying to, Vivit enim vitium post
funera, non modo virtus.—*Vice, and not virtue only, survives death.*
The motto, with phœnix for crest, is said to have been inscribed (1527)
by Dr Caius on the tomb, in old St Paul's, of Thomas Linacre (1480-1524),
founder of the Royal College of Physicians.

3116. Vox, et præterea nihil.—*A voice and nothing more.*

Thought to have been said of Echo, or of the Nightingale. *See* Nos.
2196, 2952, 2974. Plutarch, in his Apophthegm, Lacon. Incert. xiii.,
has a story of one who, τίλας τις ἀηδόνα, καὶ βραχεῖαν πάνυ σάρκα εὑρὼν, εἶπε,
Φωνὰ τύ τις ἐσσὶ, καὶ οὐδὲν ἄλλο.—*A man, after plucking a nightingale and
finding little flesh on it, remarked, "Thou art voice, and nought else."* It
is probable that the quotation is merely the Latin translation of Plutarch's
anecdote.

3117. Zerbrich den Kopf dir nicht so sehr :
Zerbrich den Willen—das ist mehr.

Cudgel thy brains, pray, not so sore ;
Cudgel thy will, for that's much more.—*Ed.*

*** Cf. Nos. 490, 818, 2323.

ADDENDA.

3118. Abundant dulcibus vitiis. Quint. 10, 1, 129.—*They abound in delightful faults.* Said of Seneca's works, and applicable to those whose very errors are charming. Cf. No. 2288.

3119. Ἀλλὰ τὰ μὲν προτετύχθαι ἐάσομεν, ἀχνυμενοί περ. Hom. Il. 18, 112. —*"But pass we that, though still my heart be sore."* Lord Derby. Let byegones be byegones.

3120. Aperto vivere voto. Pers. 2, 7.—*Living with every wish declared:* *i.e.,* not professing high aims and aspirations, and concealing the real and shameful desires of the heart within.

3121. A tout seigneur tout honneur. Prov.—*To every lord his proper honour.* To every one his due.

3122. Beneficia eo usque læta sunt, dum videntur exsolvi posse; ubi multum antevenere, pro gratia odium redditur. Tac. A. 4, 18, 3. —*Favours are welcome, so long as it appears possible to requite them; but when they pass all bounds of a return, they are repaid with hatred instead of gratitude.*

3123. Berretta in mano non fece mai danno. Prov.—*Cap in hand never yet did a man harm.* Politeness is never thrown away.

3124. Bon avocat, mauvais voisin. Prov.—*A good lawyer makes a bad neighbour.*

3125. C'est avoir fait un grand pas dans la finesse, que de faire penser de soi, que l'on n'est que médiocrement fin. La Bruy. chap. viii. (La Cour), vol. i. p. 163.—*It is a decided step forwards in the art of finesse to let it be thought that one is only moderately acute.*

3126. Croyez-moi, la prière est un cri d'espérance. A. de Musset, L'Espoir en Dieu.—*Believe me, prayer is a cry of hope.*

3127. Cucullus non facit monachum. Prov.—*The cowl doesn't make the monk.* Professional costume doesn't constitute the professional.

3128. Et in Arcadia ego!—*I, too, have been in Arcadia!* Recollections of youthful pleasure, and the happiness of golden, gone-away days.

The words were written by Bart. Schidone (1570-1615) on his picture, formerly in the Sciarra-Colonna palace (Rome), representing two young shepherds contemplating a skull which they have in their hands. Nic. Poussin (1594-1665) reproduced the words in his celebrated pastoral land-scape in the Louvre, where a couple of youths and a maiden are reading them inscribed upon a tomb. The idea in both is the same—the contrast between youth and age, flower and decay, life and death. Schiller begins his "Resignation" with "Auch ich war in Arkadien geboren," and Delille in his "Jardins" (Str. 3, 139) imitates the sentiment with "Et moi aussi, je fus pasteur dans l'Arcadie." *See* Büchmann, pp. 436-7.

3129. Facile ærumnam ferre possum si inde abest injuria :
    Etiam injuriam, nisi contra constat contumelia.
        Cæcil. Statius, Fallacia, iv. (*Ribbeck*).—*I can well bear hardship, if it is to save me from injury; and injury even, if I have not to face insult.*

3130. Il passa par la gloire, il passa par le crime,
    Et n'est arrivé qu'au malheur.
        V. Hugo, Ode sur Buonaparte(1822), 4th strophe.—*He passed through glory, and then through crime, only to end in disaster.*

3131. Infandum, regina, jubes renovare dolorem   Virg. A. 2, 3.
        Too cruel, lady, is the pain
        You bid me thus revive again.—*Conington.*

   ** Æneas beginning, at Dido's request, his story of the fall of Troy, and his subsequent wanderings.

3132. Ἰοστέφανοι Ἀθᾶναι. Pind. Fr. 76 (46).—*Athens, city of the violet crown.* Title perh. derived both from her native violet (ἴον), and from Ἴων, mythic K. of Attica.

       A maiden crown'd with a fourfold glory,
       Violet and olive-leaf, purple and hoary,
       Athens, a praise without end !—A. C. Swinburne, *Erectheus.*

3133. La hauteur des maisons
    Empêch' de voir la ville.—*I can't see the town for the height of the houses.*

    Fournier (*L.D.A.*, p. 3) cites this from some old "Poitevin" country song, without giving further particulars. In May 1798 came out the Vaudeville of "Le Chaudronnier de Saint Flour," by Armand Gouffé and Henriquez, in which (scene 3) the tinker-hero, Léonard, complains that Paris is a greatly over-rated city, and that
       Ici la hauteur des maisons
       M'empêche de bien voir la ville.
    See Alex. p. 536, and Büchm. p. 151, and Note.

3133A. L'homme est un apprenti, la douleur est son maître ;
    Et nul ne se connaît, tant qu'il n'a pas souffert.
        A. de Musset, Nuit d'Octobre.—*Man is an apprentice, sorrow is his master; and none knows himself until he has suffered.*

3134. Nec te, tua plurima, Panthu,
    Labentem pietas nec Apollinis infula texit.   Virg. A. 2, 529.
       Nor pious deed, nor Phœbus' wreath
       Could save thee, Panthus, from thy death.—*Conington.*

    Panthus was priest of Apollo in the citadel of Troy—in a sense, therefore, *sacerdos* and *vates* in one; and the lines were most happily applied by Mr Gladstone in Parliament, during the Disestablishment (Ireland) debate of 1869, to the Archbishop-poet, Trench, and to the sweeping ecclesiastical changes which even regard for his holy office or his poetic gifts was unable to avert.

                                2 c

3135. Neque enim concludere versum
  Dixeris esse satis : neque, si quis scribat, uti nos,
  Sermoni propiora, putes hunc esse poetam.　　Hor. S. 1, 4, 40.

> 'Tis not enough to turn out lines complete
> Each with its proper quantum of ten feet;
> Colloquial verse a man may write like me,
> But (trust an author) 'tis not poetry.—*Conington.*

3136. Nihil vacuum, neque sine signo apud Deum. Irenæus, iv. 21.—
  Nothing is said idly, or without significance, when God speaks.
  On O. T. types and prophecies.　　Cf. No. 1697.

3137. Nulli jactantius mœrent, quam qui maxime lætantur.　Tac. A.
  2, 77, 6.—*None so demonstrative in their grief as those who most*
  rejoice at the event.　Cf. No. 887.

3138. Ὁ δ' ὄλβος ἄδικος καὶ μετὰ σκαιῶν ξυνὼν,
  ἐξέπτατ' οἴκων, σμικρὸν ἀνθήσας χρόνον.　　Eur. El. 943.

> Ill-gotten wealth, i' the hands of clumsy folk,
> After a short-lived flourish, flies away.—*Ed.*

  *** Cf. Nos. 1476, 3039.

3139. Peccavi. Ter. Ad. 2, 4, 12.—*I have sinned.*

> When in Feb. 1843, Sir Chas. Napier defeated the Ameers of Scinde in
> the battles of Meeanee and Hyderabad, and annexed their territories, it is
> said, on what authority I know not, that he communicated the fact to
> Government in the one word "Peccavi"—*I have Scinde.* "Se non è
> vero," etc.

3140. Si autem de veritate scandalum sumitur, utilius permittitur nasci
  scandalum, quam veritas relinquatur. S. Gregorius M., Hom. vii.
  § 5.—*Should the truth be cause of scandal, better that scandal*
  arise than that truth should be departed from.

3141. Tolerabile est semel anno insanire.　Aug. de Civitate Dei, 6, 10.—
  It is allowable to go mad once a year.　St Augustine is quoting
  a lost passage in Seneca on the annual festivities of the Egyptian
  Osiris.　*V.* Nos. 1556, 2336, 2728.

3142. Tota jacet Babylon; destruxit tecta Lutherus,
  Calvinus muros, et fundamenta Socinus.
  All Babylon (the Catholic Church) *is in ruins.　Luther*
  destroyed the roof, Calvin the walls, and Socinus the foundations.

> "The (Catholic) system bears a character of integrity and indivisibility
> upon it, both at first view and on inspection.　Hence such sayings as the
> *Tota jacet Babylon* of the distich.　Luther did but a part of the work,
> Calvin another portion, Socinus finished it.　To take up with Luther, and
> to reject Calvin and Socinus, would be, according to that epigram, like
> living in a house without a roof to it" (Newman, *Essay on Development,*
> etc., sec. ed., 1846, p. 137).

INDEX IV.—GREEK QUOTATIONS INDEX.

Ἅπασα δὲ χθών ἀνδρὶ γενναίῳ πατρίς, 1897.
Ἅπας μὲν ἀὴρ ἀετῷ περάσιμος, 1897.
Ἄπολις, ἄοικος, πατρίδος ἐστερημένος, 2050.
Ἀπὸ μηχανῆς θεὸς, 1623.
Ἀπωτέρω ἢ γόνυ κνήμα, 2790.
Ἀρετὴ δε, κἄν θάνῃ τις, οὐκ ἀπόλλυται, 152.
Ἄριστον ἀνδρὶ κτῆμα συμπαθὴς γυνή, 1991.
Ἄριστον μὲν ὕδωρ, 155.
Ἀρχαῖα ἔθη (τὰ) κρατείτω, 2671.
Ἀρχὴ ἄνδρα δεικνύει, 1470.
Ἀρχὴ γὰρ λέγεται μὲν ἥμισυ παντὸς, 551.
Ἀρχὴ δὲ τοι ἥμισυ παντὸς, 551.
Ἄσβεστος γέλως, 160.
Ἀσφαλὴς γὰρ ἐστ' ἀμείνων ἢ θρασὺς στρατηλάτης, 793.
Αὐτὸ δὲ σιγᾶν ὁμολογοῦντος ἐστί σοῦ, 2331.
Αὐτὸς ἔφα, 1138.
Αὐτός τι νῦν δρᾷ, χοὔτω δαίμονας κάλει, 66.
Ἄφες με, τοὺς θεούς σοι, πιεῖν πιεῖν ἀμυστί, 2728.
Βαρεῖαν ἐχθροῖς, καὶ φίλοισιν εὐμενῆ, 222.
Βασιλεὺς τοῦ συμποσίου, 149.
Βέλτιόν ἐστιν ἅπαξ ἀποθανεῖν, ἢ ἀεὶ προσδοκᾶν, 219.
Βίος (ὁ) βραχὺς, ἡ δὲ τέχνη μακρὴ, 157.
Βουλαὶ δ' ἔχουσι τῶν γεραιτέρων κράτος, 664.
Γαμεῖν ὁ μέλλων εἰς μετάνοιαν ἔρχεται, 839.
Γάμος γὰρ ἀνθρώποισιν εὐκταῖον κακόν, 840.
Γελοῖον τόν γε φύλακα φύλακος δεῖσθαι, 2126.
Γέλως ἄκαιρος ἐν βροτοῖς δεινὸν κακόν, 844.
Γέλωτα Σαρδάνιον, 2403Α.
Γῆν ὁρῶ, 845.
Γηράσκω δ' αἰεὶ πολλὰ διδασκόμενος, 2682.
Γλαῦκ' εἰς Ἀθήνας, 1109.
Γλυκὺ δ' ἀπείροισι πόλεμος κ.τ.λ., 849.
Γνοῖεν δ', ὡς δὴ δηρὸν ἐγὼ πολέμοιο πέπαυμαι, 850.
Γνῶθι σεαυτόν, 609.
Γυναικὶ κόσμος ὁ τρόπος, οὐ τὰ χρυσία, 863.
Γυναικὸς οὐδὲν ἂν μεῖζον κακὸν κακῆς ἀνὴρ κτήσαιτ' ἄν, 864.
Γυναικὸς οὐδὲν χρῆμ' ἀνὴρ ληΐζεται κ.τ.λ., 864.
Δάκρυ' ἀδάκρυα, 417.
Δεδογμένον τὸ πρᾶγμ'· ἀνερρίφθω κύβος, 74.
Δειλὴ δ' ἐνὶ πυθμένι φειδώ, 2495.

Δὶς ἐξαμαρτεῖν ταὐτὸν οὐκ ἀνδρὸς σοφοῦ, 226.
Δὶς ἢ τρὶς τὰ καλά, 562.
Δὶς κράμβη θάνατος, 1848.
Δόμμυ πᾶ βῶ, καὶ χαριστίωνι τὰν γᾶν κινάσω πᾶσαν, 2138.
Δόσις ὀλίγη τε, φίλη τε, 588.
Δὸς μοι ποῦ στῶ καὶ κινῶ τὴν γῆν, 2138.
Δός τι, καί τι λάμβανε, 1491.
Δότε κρότον, καὶ πάντες ὑμεῖς μετὰ χαρᾶς κτυπήσατε, 2581.
Ἔα με κερδαίνοντα κεκλῆσθαι κακόν, 2551.
Ἐβουλόμην παρὰ τούτοις εἶναι πρῶτος, ἢ παρὰ Ῥωμαίοις κ.τ.λ., 1821.
Ἐγρηγορότος ἐνύπνιον, 1374.
Ἐγὼ δὲ πολλῷ χρόνῳ, 2105.
Εἰ γάρ κεν καὶ σμικρὸν ἐπὶ σμικρῷ καταθεῖο κ.τ.λ., 628.
Εἰ δὲ πᾶν ἔχει καλῶς, τῷ παιγνίῳ δότε κρότον, 2581.
Εἴθ', ὦ λῷστε, σὺ τοιοῦτος ὢν φίλος ἡμῖν γένοιο, 640.
Εἰκόνας εἶναι τῆς ἑκάστου ψυχῆς τοὺς λόγους, 629.
Εἴπερ γὰρ ἀδικεῖν χρή, τυραννίδος πέρι κάλλιστον ἀδικεῖν, 1607.
Εἰς αὔριον τὰ σπουδαῖα, 1998.
Εἷς κοίρανος ἔστω, εἷς βασιλεύς, 1996.
Εἷς οἰωνὸς ἄριστος, ἀμύνεσθαι περὶ πάτρης, 639.
Ἑλοῦ βίον ἄριστον, ἡδὺν δὲ αὐτὸν ἡ συνήθεια ποιήσει, 642.
Ἐλπίδες ἐν ζωοῖσιν· ἀνέλπιστοι δὲ θανόντες, 45.
Ἐλπὶς καὶ σὺ τύχη, μέγα χαίρετε· τὸν λιμέν' εὗρον, 643.
Ἔμαθεν ἀφ' ὧν ἔπαθε τὴν ὑπακοήν, 2042.
Ἐμοῦ θανόντος γαῖα μιχθήτω πυρί, 142.
Ἐν δὲ φάει καὶ ὄλεσσον, 648.
Ἓν μόνον ἡμῖν ἔλειπε, σύ, 1881.
Ἐν μύρτου κλαδὶ τὸ ξίφος φορήσω, 653.
Ἐν νυκτὶ βουλή τοῖς σοφοῖσι γίνεται, 1096.
Ἐν παντὶ πράγει δ' ἔσθ' ὁμιλίας κακῆς κάκιον οὐδέν, 371.
Ἔν τινι φρουρᾷ ἐσμεν ἄνθρωποι κ.τ.λ., 2901.
Ἐν τῷ φρονεῖν γὰρ μηδὲν ἥδιστος βίος, 655.
Ἐξ ὄνυχος λέοντα γράφειν, 737.
Ἐπ' ἀμφότερα νῦν ἄτ' ἐπίκληρος οὖσα δή μέλλει καθευδήσειν, 1055.
Ἔπεα πτερόεντα, 660.
Ἔργα νέων, βουλαὶ δὲ μέσων, εὐχαὶ δε γερόντων, 664.
Ἐρημία μεγάλη 'στιν ἡ μεγάλη πόλις, 1458.
Ἐρρέτω φίλος σίν ἐχθρῷ, 2072.
Ἐρωτηθεὶς τί ἐστιν ἐλπίς; Ἐγρηγορότος, εἶπεν, ἐνύπνιον, 1374.
Ἔσθ' ὁμιλίας κακῆς κάκιον οὐδέν, 371.

Ἔστι δ᾽ ἀνὴρ σοφὸς οὗτος, ὃς ἄμφω ταῦτα νοήσας κ.τ.λ., 1988.

Ἐς τοῦτον ὁρέων, πῖνέ τε καὶ τέρπευ κ.τ.λ., 1521.

Ἔσχατον τὸν τῆς δόξης χιτῶνα ἐν τ. θανάτῳ αὐτῷ ἀποδυόμεθα, 703.

Ἑταῖρος (ὁ), ἕτερος ἐγώ, 94.

Ἕτεροι αὐτοί, 94.

Εὕρηκα, 2138.

Εὐτυχία πολύφιλος, 584.

Ἐχθρὸς γάρ μοι κεῖνος ὁμῶς Ἀΐδαο πύλῃσιν κ.τ.λ., 613.

Ἐχθρῶν ἄδωρα δῶρα κοὐκ ὀνήσιμα, 612.

Ζεῖ χύτρα, ζῇ φιλία, 792.

Ζηλωτὸς ὅστις εὐτύχησεν ἐς τέκνα, 3013.

Ζωγραφία (ἡ), ποίησις σιωπῶσα, 2722.

Ζώη μοῦ, σᾶς ἀγαπῶ, 3013.

Ζῶμεν γὰρ οὐχ ὡς θέλομεν, ἀλλ᾽ ὡς δυνάμεθα, 3015.

Ζῷον ἄπτερον (πολιτικόν) κ.τ.λ., 135, 136.

Ἡ γλῶσσ᾽ ὀμώμοχ᾽, ἡ δὲ φρὴν ἀνώμοτος, 617.

Ἡ δὲ κακὴ βουλὴ τῷ βουλεύσαντι κακίστη, 1480.

Ἡδύ τοι σωθέντα μεμνῆσθαι πόνων, 815.

Ἡ ἐν τῇ φάτνῃ κύων, 247 (6.).

Ἡ καλὴ λαβέτω, 2179.

Ἢ λέγε τι σιγῆς κρεῖσσον, ἢ σιγὴν ἔχε, 2538.

Ἦλθον, εἶδον, ἐνίκησα, 2885.

Ἡμεῖς τοι πατέρων μέγ᾽ ἀμείνονες εὐχόμεθ᾽ εἶναι, 646.

Ἢ πῖθι, ἢ ἄπιθι, 192.

Ἦ που κρεῖσσον τῆς εὐγενίας τὸ καλῶς πράσσειν, 2624.

Ἢ τὰν, ἢ ἐπὶ τᾶς, 697.

Θέλω, θέλω μανῆναι, 2728.

Θεῶν ἐν γούνασι κεῖται, 87.

Θνάσκειν μὴ λέγε τοὺς ἀγαθούς, 2703.

Θύε ταῖς Χάρισι, 2729.

Ἰδοὺ ἡ Ῥόδος, ἰδοὺ καὶ τὸ πήδημα, 903.

Ἰοστέφανοι Ἀθᾶναι, 3132.

Ἰσομοιρία (ἡ) τῶν κακῶν ἔχει τινα ὅμως τὸ μετὰ πολλῶν κούφισιν, 2585.

Ἱστορία (ἡ) φιλοσοφία ἐστὶν ἐκ παραδειγμάτων, 2005.

Ἰχθῦς εἰς Ἑλλήσποντον, 1109.

Καδμείη νίκη, 2907.

Καθάπερ λαμπάδα τὸν βίον παραδιδοῦσι ἄλλοις ἐξ ἄλλων, 711.

Καὶ βρέφος διδάσκεται λέγειν ἀκούειν θ᾽ κ.τ.λ., 1208.

Καιροῖο λαβώμεθα, ὃν προσιόντα ἔστιν ἑλεῖν, ζητεῖν δὲ κ.τ.λ., 413.

Καιρὸν γνῶθι, 1209.

Μηδὲ δίκην δικάσῃς πρὶν ἀμφοῖν μῦθον ἀκούσῃς, 184.

Μηδεὶς ἀγεωμέτρητος εἰσίτω, 1503.

Μηδὲν ἄγαν, 961.

Μηδέν᾽ ὀλβίζειν πρὶν ἂν τέρμα τοῦ βίου περάσῃ, 2812.

Μὴ εἶναι βασιλικὴν ἀτραπὸν ἐπὶ γεωμετρίαν, 1509.

Μὴ κάκα κερδαίνειν· κακὰ κέρδεα ἶσ᾽ ἄτῃσιν, 1513.

Μὴ κίνει Καμαρίναν, 1514.

Μὴ παιδὶ μάχαιραν, 1667.

Μία χελιδὼν ἔαρ οὐ ποιεῖ, 1542.

Μία ψυχὴ δύο σώμασιν ἐνοικοῦσα, 498.

Μισῶ μνήμονα συμπότην, 1561.

Μισῶ σοφιστὴν ὅστις οὐχ αὑτῷ σοφός, 1562.

Μόνου γὰρ αὐτοῦ κ. θεὸς στερίσκεται ἀγένητα ποιεῖν κ.τ.λ., 769.

Μωμήσεταί τις μᾶλλον ἢ μιμήσεται, 1131.

Νεανίας γὰρ ὅστις ὢν Ἄρη στυγεῖ, κόμη μόνον κ. σάρκες κ.τ.λ., 1619.

Νέκρους οὐ δάκνειν, 1581.

Νενίκηκας Γαλιλαῖε, 2906.

Νέοις μὲν ἔργα, βουλὰς δὲ γεραιτέροις, 664.

Νέους φίλους ποιῶν, τῶν παλαιῶν μὴ ἐπιλανθάνου, 1665.

Νεῦρα (Τὰ) τοῦ πολέμου (πραγμάτων), 1673.

Νήπιοι, οὐδὲ ἴσασιν ὅσῳ πλέον ἥμισυ παντός, 1666.

Νήπιος ὃς τά γ᾽ ἕτοιμα λιπὼν, ἀνέτοιμα διώκει, 283.

Νίψον ἀνομήματα, μὴ μόναν ὄψιν, 2528.

Νόμιζ᾽ ἀδελφοὺς τοὺς ἀληθινοὺς φίλους, 3071.

Ξενόκρατες, θύε ταῖς Χάρισι, 2729.

Ὁ βίος βραχὺς, ἡ δὲ τέχνη μακρὴ, 157.

Ὁ δ᾽ ὄλβος ἄδικος, καὶ μετὰ σκαιῶν ξυνὼν, ἐξέπτατ οἴκων, 3138.

Οἱ γὰρ πόνοι τίκτουσι τὴν εὐανδρίαν, 1619.

Οἵη περ φύλλων γενεὴ, τοιήδε καὶ ἀνδρῶν, 1878.

Οἶκος φίλος, οἶκος ἄριστος, 581.

Οἴμοι· τί δ οἴμοι; θνητά τοι πεπόνθαμεν, 1880.

Οἶνός τοι χαρίεντι πέλει ταχὺς ἵππος ἀοιδῷ, 1813.

Οἶνος, ὦ φίλε παῖ, λέγεται καὶ ἀλάθεα, 1129.

Οἴνου δὲ μηκέτ᾽ ὄντος, οὐκ ἔστιν Κύπρις, 2549.

Ὁ κόσμος σκηνὴ, ὁ βίος πάροδος κ.τ.λ., 2581.

Οἱ πλεῖστοι κακοί, 1882.

Ὁ μὴ δαρεὶς ἄνθρωπος οὐ παιδεύεται, 1888.

Ὄμμα γὰρ δόμων νομίζω δεσπότου παρουσίαν, 1893.

Ὃν οἱ θεοὶ φιλοῦσιν ἀποθνήσκει νέος, 1576 (xi.).

Ὀξὺς τὰ πράγματα, 2642.

Ὁπότε σχολάζοι (ἔλεγε) πλείονα πράττειν, 1836.

Ὅπου πλείων κόπος, πολὺ κερδός, 1965.

Ὅπου τις ἀλγεῖ, κεῖσε καὶ τὴν χεῖρ᾽ ἔχει, 1966.

Ὀργὴ φιλοῦντος σμικρὸν ἰσχύει χρόνον, 99.

Ὁ σός, ὦ Βροῦτε, δαίμων κακός, 1967.

Ὅστις δ᾽ ὁμιλῶν ἥδεται κακοῖς ἀνὴρ κ.τ.λ., 1989.

Ὃς χ᾽ ἕτερον μὲν κεύθῃ ἐνὶ φρέσιν, ἄλλο δὲ εἴπῃ, 613.

Ὅταν γὰρ ὀργὴ δαιμόνων βλάπτῃ τινὰ κ.τ.λ., 2359.

Ὅταν δ᾽ ὁ δαίμων ἀνδρὶ πορσύνῃ κακά, τὸν νοῦν ἔβλαψε, 2359.

Ὅταν τύχῃ τις εὐνοοῦντος οἰκέτου κ.τ.λ., 1991.

Ὁ τ᾽ ἐχθρὸς ἡμῖν ἐς τοσόνδ᾽ ἐχθαρτέος κ.τ.λ., 1152.

Οὐδ᾽ Αἴσωπον πεπάτηκας, 1618.

Οὐ γὰρ δοκεῖν ἄριστος, ἀλλ᾽ εἶναι θέλει, 675.

Οὐδὲν γίνεται ἐκ τοῦ μὴ ὄντος, 464.

Οὐδὲν ἐμοί χ᾽ ὑμῖν· παίζετε τοὺς μέτ᾽ ἐμέ, 643.

Οὐδὲν μελεῖ μοι, τἀμὰ γὰρ καλῶς ἔχει, 142.

Οὐθὲν γὰρ, ὡς φάμεν, μάτην ἡ φύσις ποιεῖ, 2002.

Οὐκ ἀγαθὸν πολυκοιρανίη· εἷς κοίρανος ἔστω, εἷς βασιλεύς, 1996.

Οὐκ αἰσχρὸν οὐδὲν τῶν ἀναγκαίων βροτοῖς, 1615.

Οὐκ ἂν γένοιτο χρηστὸς ἐκ κακοῦ πατρός, 1212.

Οὐκ ἐν λέξεσιν, ἀλλ᾽ ἐν πράγμασι μεγαλοφωνία, 1761.

Οὐκ ἔστιν οὐδὲν κτῆμα κάλλιον βίῳ, 1991.

Οὐκ ἔστιν οὐδὲν χωρὶς ἀνθρώποις θεῶν, 1997.

Οὐκοῦν εἰς αὔριον τὰ σπουδαῖα, 1998.

Οὐκ ὠνοῦμαι μυρίων δραχμῶν μεταμέλειαν, 1999.

Οὐ λέγειν τύγ᾽ ἐσσὶ δεινός, ἀλλὰ σιγῆν ἀδύνατος, 2000.

Οὐ μόνον ἡ ἀρχὴ τὸν ἄνδρα δείκνυσι, ἀλλὰ κ. ἀρχὴν ἀνήρ, 1470.

Οὐ παντὸς ἀνδρὸς εἰς Κόρινθον ἐσθ᾽ ὁ πλοῦς, 1742.

Οὐ παντὸς ἀνδρὸς ἐπὶ τράπεζάν ἐσθ᾽ ὁ πλοῦς, 1742.

Οὐ τοῖς ἀθύμοις ἡ τύχη συλλαμβάνει, 182.

Οὔ τοι σύμφορόν ἐστι γυνὴ νέα ἀνδρὶ γέροντι, 302.

Οὐ τὸν τρόπον ἀλλὰ τὸν τόπον μετήλλαξεν, 238.

Ὀψὲ θεῶν ἀλέουσι μύλοι, ἀλέουσι δὲ λεπτά, 2499.

Ὄψει δὲ με περὶ Φιλίππους, 1967.

Παθήματα, μαθήματα, 2042.

Παῖδας εὖ παιδεύετε, 1208.

Παιδεία ἄρα ἐστὶν ἡ ἔντευξις τῶν ἠθῶν κ.τ.λ., 2005.

Παίζω· μεταβολὰς γὰρ πόνων ἀεὶ φιλῶ, 2006.

Παῖς τῆς τύχης, 824.

Παλαιὸς αἶνος, ἔργα μὲν νεωτέρων κ.τ.λ., 664.

2 D

Πᾶν πρᾶγμα δύο ἔχει λαβὰς, 2012.
Πάντα καθαρὰ τοῖς καθαροῖς, 2013.
Πάντων μέσ᾽ ἄριστα, 961.
Πάντων δὲ μάλιστ᾽ αἰσχύνεο σαυτόν, 2014.
Πάταξον μὲν, ἄκουσον δέ, 2040.
Πατρὶς γάρ ἐστι πᾶσ᾽ ἵν᾽ ἂν πράττῃ τις εὖ, 826.
Περὶ ὄνου σκιᾶς μάχεσθαι, 2081.
Πίθηκος ὁ πίθηκος, κἂν χρύσεα ἔχῃ σύμβολα, 2540.
Πῖνέ τε καὶ τέρπευ, ἔσεαι γὰρ ἀποθανὼν τοιοῦτος, 1521.
Πλέον ἥμισυ παντὸς, 1666.
Πλοῦτος, νεῦρα πραγμάτων, 1673.
Ποίησις, ζωγραφία λαλοῦσα, 2722.
Πολλαὶ μὲν θνητοῖς γλῶτται, μία δ᾽ ἀθανάτοισιν, 1587.
Πολλὰ μεταξὺ πέλει κύλικος, καὶ χείλεος ἄκρου, 1124.
Πόλλ᾽ ἠπίστατο ἔργα, κακῶς δ᾽ ἠπίστατο πάντα, 3042.
Πόλλ᾽ οἶδ᾽ ἀλώπηξ, ἀλλ᾽ ἐχῖνος ἓν μέγα, 158.
Πολλοί τοι ναρθηκοφόροι, Βάκχοι δέ τε παῦροι, 2123.
Πόλυ κρεῖττον ἓν καλῶς μεμαθηκέναι, ἢ πολλὰ φαύλως, 2124.
Ποντίων τε κυμάτων ἀνήριθμον γέλασμα, 2127.
Πότερα θέλεις σοι μαλθακὰ ψευδῆ λεγῶ, ἢ σκλήρ᾽ ἀληθῆ; 2133.
Ποῦ στῶ, 2138.
Πρᾶος τοὺς λόγους, ὀξὺς τὰ πράγματα, 2642.
Πρὸς δύο, οὐδ᾽ ὁ Ἡρακλῆς λέγεται οἷός τε εἶναι, 1730.
Πρὸς Κρῆτα κρητίζειν, 389.
Πρὸς ὑγίειαν, καὶ οἰκονομίαν, καὶ φιλοσοφίαν χρήσιμον, 2745.
Πρὸς τὸν εἰπόντα, ὅτι κίνησις οὐκ ἔστιν, ἀναστὰς περιεπάτει, 2592.
Πτωχὸς, πλανήτης, βίον ἔχων ἐφήμερον, 2050.
Σήματα λυγρά, 1429.
Σκηνὴ πᾶς ὁ βίος καὶ παίγνιον, 2581.
Σκιᾶς ὄναρ ἄνθρωποι, 2582.
Σμικρὸν φροντίσαντες Σωκράτους, τῆς δὲ ἀληθείας πολὺ μᾶλλον, 108.
Σοφὴν δὲ μισῶ, 2596.
Σπάρτην ἔλαχες, κείνην κόσμει, 2605.
Σπεῦδε βραδέως, 793.
Σύντομος ἡ πονηρία, βραδεῖα ἡ ἀρετή, 344.
Σφόδρ᾽ ἐστὶν ἡμῶν ὁ βίος οἴνῳ προσφερής κ.τ.λ., 2101.
Σχολῇ ταχύς, 793.
Τὰ ἀρχαῖα ἔθη κρατείτω, 2671.
Τὰ δέ μοι παθήματα, ἐόντα ἀχάριτα, μαθήματα γεγόνε, 2042.
Τάδ᾽ οὐχ ὑπ᾽ ἄλλων, ἀλλὰ τοῖς αὐτῶν πτεροῖς ἁλισκόμεσθα, 1984.

Τὰ ἐλάχιστα ληπτέον τῶν κακῶν, 1552.

Τὰ νεῦρα τῶν πραγμάτων, 1673.

Τὰ ὀνόματα, παραπετάσματα τῶν διανοημάτων, 1268.

Τὰ πάντ᾽ ὄνου σκιά, 2081.

Τὰ πλεῖστα θνητοῖς τῶν κακῶν αὐθαίρετα, 2698.

Τὰ σῦκα σῦκα, τὴν σκάφην σκάφην λέγων, 797.

Ταῦτα θεῶν ἐν γούνασι κεῖται, 87.

Τῇδε Σάων ὁ Δίκωνος Ἀκάνθιος ἱερὸν ὕπνον κοιμᾶται, 2703.

Τὴν δὲ μάλιστα γαμεῖν, ἥτις σέθεν ἔγγυθι ναίει, 2715.

Τὴν κατὰ σαυτὸν ἔλα, 2721.

Τὴν μὲν ζωγραφίαν ποίησιν σιωπῶσαν προσαγορεύει, 2722.

Τίμα τὸ γῆρας, οὐ γὰρ ἔρχεται μόνον, 2101.

Τὸ γαμεῖν, κακὸν μὲν ἐστιν, ἀλλ᾽ ἀναγκαῖον κακόν, 2733.

Τὸ γὰρ αὐτὸ νοεῖν ἐστί τε καὶ εἶναι, 618.

Τὸ γὰρ θανεῖν οὐκ αἰσχρόν, ἀλλ᾽ αἰσχρῶς θανεῖν, 1576 (xix.).

Τὸ δ᾽ εὖ νικάτω, 2732.

Τὸ διαβῶναι μόνον ἀεὶ θηρωμένη, 1619.

Τὸ ἑαυτὸν γνῶναι, 609.

Τὸ εἰθισμένον ὥσπερ πεφυκὸς γίγνεται, 358.

Τοιοῦτος ἐστὶν οἷσπερ ἥδεται ξυνών, 1989.

Τοῖς ὀνόμασι παραπετάσμασι χρῶνται τῶν διανοημάτων, 1268.

Τοῖς τοι δικαίοις χὠ βραχὺς νικᾷ μέγαν, 2734.

Τόλμα ἀεί, κἄν τι τρηχὺ νέμωσι θεοί, 2739.

Τὸν ἑαυτὸν οὐκ ἀδικοῦντα οὐδεὶς ἕτερος παραβλάψαι δύναται, 1655.

Τὸ νικᾶν αὐτὸν αὐτὸν πασῶν νικῶν πρώτη τε καὶ ἀρίστη, 2741.

Τὸν πάθει μάθος θέντα κυρίως ἔχειν, 2042.

Τὸν τεθνηκότα μὴ κακολογεῖν, 462.

Τὸ πόρσω δ᾽ ἔστι σοφοῖς ἄβατον κἀσόφοις, 1637.

Τό τε διανίστασθαι νύκτωρ· τοῦτο γὰρ καὶ πρὸς ὑγίειαν κ.τ.λ., 2745.

Τὸ τεχνίον πᾶσα γαῖα τρέφει, 2744.

Τοῦτ᾽ ἔστι τὸ ζῆν, οὐκ ἑαυτῷ ζῆν μόνον, 2759Α.

Τοῦτο μὲν καὶ τυφλῷ δῆλον, 141.

Τούτῳ νίκα, 1087.

Τῷ γὰρ καλῶς πράσσοντι πᾶσα γῆ πατρίς, 826.

Τῷ γὰρ πονοῦντι χὠ θεὸς συλλαμβάνει, 66.

Τῶν εὐτυχούντων πάντες εἰσὶ συγγενεῖς, 2740.

Ὕδωρ δὲ πίνων οὐδὲν ἂν τέκοι σοφόν, 1813.

Ὑπείροχον ἔμμεναι ἄλλων, 67.

Ὗς διὰ ῥόδων, 2846.

Φείδεο σῶν κτεάνων, 1988.